CW00969444

To: Isobel & Donald

John Smith

Best wishes

Mark H Stuart

June 2005

JOHN SMITH

A LIFE

MARK STUART

POLITICO'S

10 9 8 7 6 5 4 3 2 1

First published in 2005 by
Politico's Publishing
an imprint of Methuen Publishing Ltd
11–12 Buckingham Gate
London SW1E 6LB
www.methuen.co.uk/politicos

Copyright © 2005 by Mark Stuart

ISBN 1 84275 126 3

Methuen Publishing Limited Reg. No. 3543167

A CIP catalogue record for this book is available from
the British Library

Printed and bound in Great Britain
by St. Edmundsbury Press, Bury St. Edmunds, Suffolk

For Emma, Lewis, Jack & Harry

Contents

Preface

IN JUNE 2002, I visited Edinburgh to see Douglas Hurd, the subject of my first biography, *The Public Servant* (Mainstream: Edinburgh, 1998). I was invited to attend Hurd's lecture to the John Smith Memorial Trust, a worthy organisation that runs a highly successful fellowship programme for young professional people from the newly born democracies, notably in the former Soviet Union. Over dinner afterwards, I happened to sit beside Elizabeth Smith who casually remarked that she hoped that a proper biography would be written of her late husband. I am sure that Elizabeth Smith made the remark without giving it further thought, but I knew then I had a subject for my next project. Subsequently, Elizabeth graciously gave it her blessing.

In the first few months, I was greatly assisted by Andy McSmith's excellent biography, *John Smith. Playing the Long Game* (Verso: London, 1993). When Smith died, the book was re-issued in paperback as *John Smith. A Life, 1938–1994* (Mandarin: London, 1994). In the same year, Gordon Brown and James Naughtie's *Life and Soul of the Party* (Mainstream: Edinburgh, 1994) made a useful first attempt to survey Smith's political career in the immediate aftermath of his death, with Elizabeth Smith providing an insightful introduction. Elizabeth and Bill Campbell of Mainstream did a tremendous job in a short space of time in gathering together various bits and pieces written by John Smith. Two other books, *Reclaiming the Ground* (London: Spire, 1993) and *John Smith. An Appreciation* (Hodder & Stoughton, 1994), both edited by Chris Bryant, focused on Smith's Christian Socialist beliefs and his commitment to social justice. Much later, Brian Brivati edited *Guiding Light* (Politico's: London, 2000), a commendable anthology of Smith's speeches. But, overall, Smith did not commit many of his thoughts to paper. Most things that Smith wrote down were scribbled hastily on scraps of paper, and then discarded, as he moved impatiently on to the next target. Fresh documents needed to be hunted down for this biography.

They emerged from a wide variety of sources. Menzies Campbell, a contemporary of Smith's at Glasgow University, let me consult the Luthuli

Campaign file, which demonstrated Smith's commitment to the anti-apartheid cause at university. Newspapers kept by Glasgow University Archive Services and the Glasgow University Library – the *Glasgow University Magazine* and the *Glasgow University Guardian* respectively – gave me valuable insights into Smith's days as a debater in the Glasgow Union. Thomas Harris, Smith's principal private secretary at Trade from 1978–9, read out diary entries relating to the period from May to July 1979 as Smith experienced the painful transition from Government into Opposition. David Ward, Smith's long-time policy adviser, granted me full access to his substantial set of papers relating to John Smith's period as shadow Chancellor and as leader of the opposition. Murray Elder, John's chief of staff, let me look through two boxes relating to John Smith's period as leader of the opposition, which show that relations between Smith and John Major were not as cosy as the former Prime Minister would have us believe. The journalist and biographer Michael Crick lent me his files, especially those relating to Smith's long association with Dunoon Grammar School, and the controversy surrounding Monklands District Council. Alan Haworth, Secretary of the Parliamentary Labour Party, gave diary readings from John's 'Munro Diary', an account of his trips up more than 100 Scottish mountains above 3,000 feet. Haworth also allowed me to consult the Parliamentary Labour Party Minutes from 27 April 1992 until 20 October 1994, revealing how the battle over the Maastricht Treaty dominated parliamentary politics for at least half of Smith's 22 months as Labour leader. Neil Kinnock's papers, housed at the Churchill College Archives in Cambridge, proved to be an invaluable source. Not only did I find speeches and campaign documents relating to John Smith, I also found many files relating to key aspects of Labour's policy review in the late 1980s, and briefing papers hinting at the kind of advice that John Smith as Shadow Chancellor was receiving from academic economists at the time. Neil Kinnock's personal notes of his last NEC meetings as Labour leader also survive, as he tries in vain to secure a swift leadership election and an early reform of one member, one vote. His grip on power is slipping away, as Charles Clarke, his loyal chief of staff urges him – in previously unseen briefing papers – to pursue further and faster reform of the Party before stepping down as leader. Gavin Laird let me see one of his treasured handwritten notes from John Smith relating to one member, one vote, while Elizabeth Thomas, a former colleague of Michael Foot, kept half-a-dozen pieces of correspondence from both Elizabeth and John Smith, dating from the 1970s right through until John Smith's death. Kenneth and Elizabeth Munro, friends of the Smith family, let me read through a vast store of newspapers cuttings relating to the deaths of John

Smith and Donald Dewar, and had kept a videotape of Smith's funeral. Ann Barrett, John Smith's secretary, permitted me to look through her personal papers, mainly relating to the aftermath of Smith's death. Collectively, these documents constitute 'the Smith papers'.

Nevertheless, a large proportion of the research material for this biography came from oral evidence with over 60 close friends and colleagues of John Smith, ranging from interviews with John's sister, Mary McCulloch, to long chats with contemporaries at Glasgow University, the Scottish Bar, as well as civil servants from Smith's days in Government (1974–9), members of Smith's Treasury team as Shadow Chancellor, and extended discussions with at least half of the members of Smith's Private Office as Labour leader. Where possible, I tried to find documentary evidence to back up oral evidence. However, in many cases, this was simply not possible. Readers should beware that at times they may be reading just one unsubstantiated opinion, or two diametrically opposing recollections of the same event. In the former case, I have usually stated the individual's views, and in the latter instance, I have tended to reproduce the competing accounts side by side, sometimes offering a view. Mostly, I have left it up to the reader to decide. Some areas of policy and personnel after John Smith's death (see chapter 25) are so controversial that it is impossible to come to a definitive view. Indeed, it would be fair to say that everything, down to the last dot and comma, is disputed after Smith's death, making it nearly impossible to write an objective account.

Regrettably, I share only four of John Smith's characteristics: I am a Scot, I too had a Scottish country education (at Cultercullen Primary School, and then at Ellon Academy, a comprehensive school), I too am old-fashioned in outlook, and I also share Smith's pro-European beliefs. My biography of Smith needs to be seen through the prism of these four aspects of my character.

Over a decade on from his death, people still rightly shed tears when they recall the life of Rt Hon. John Smith QC MP. Many Labour Party people feel especially warm towards him. Everyone has a John Smith story. But there are many people in the Labour movement who seek to canonise John Smith. It's partly to do with where he is buried. Resting peacefully on Iona, Scotland's most holy isle, can only accentuate the association of ideas between Smith and near-sainthood. Thank goodness Smith was a Presbyterian, or sainthood would have been conferred already! I jest, but the point is clear enough. Smith is one of Labour's lost leaders, and the Labour Party tends to revere those leading lights that have been prematurely taken away from it. People rightly want to hold on to the memory of Smith, as an example of what a good, Socialist Labour Government would have been like had he lived to be Prime

Minister. That is their right. But it would not be right if anyone sought to close down discussion of anything that does not fit an idealised image of John Smith.

Commentators have speculated endlessly since Smith's death on what might have happened if Smith had lived to be Prime Minister. Circumstances change. The world moves on. Smith did not live to face the tough policy choices in the last few years of a Parliament that every political party faces when on the verge of Government. Nor did he have to endure as Prime Minister the perennial charges of betrayal that have characterised left-wing opposition to every previous Labour Government.

At the other extreme, recent Labour history has belonged exclusively to the modernisers. When Tony Blair succeeded John Smith, it was quite understandable that the new leader should want to start afresh, casting aside much of Labour's supposed historical baggage. But some of his supporters have gone too far in making 1994 'Year Zero': at its worst, everything before 1994 is considered irrelevant. Meanwhile, biographers of Tony Blair, Gordon Brown and Peter Mandelson have gone a step further by giving these three figures, as well as people like Philip Gould and Alastair Campbell, starring roles during Smith's period as leader, often long before they were key players. My view is that it would be more historically accurate to forget about what happened subsequently, and instead to look at the actual influence of people at the time. In that light, why not highlight the importance of Margaret Beckett, Frank Dobson, Robin Cook, John Prescott, or even less well known figures like Murray Elder, Michael Montague and Larry Whitty, during the leadership of John Smith?

There is no disputing that John Smith was a good man, of great character, and worthy of remembrance. As a result of writing this biography I have come to admire him greatly. However, his historical reputation is currently trapped between two extreme interpretations: as an opponent of wholesale reform, and therefore seen as largely irrelevant by arch-modernisers who seek to airbrush him out of history; and almost as a saintly figure by his adorers, one or two of whom use Smith's name to propound their supposedly ideologically pure version of democratic socialism. At times, treasured myths about John Smith are not allowed to be challenged. At times, it has felt like carrying a precious vase. On one occasion, in my naïvety, I dropped the vase. But neither extreme version of Smith will do. Writing in *New Century* in the summer of 1994, shortly after Smith's death, the late Ben Pimlott got it right when he remarked:

> Smith did have a gut sense of the party in which he had been reared. He

knew where he stood on the basic objective of Labour politics: tipping the balance in favour of the badly off . . . [Smith had] a solid, unshakeable confidence about who the Labour Party was designed to help. Those who want to be true to John Smith's memory, without myth-making or canonisation, should hold on to that convention.

This biography seeks to give John Smith back his own wee corner in Labour's recent history, nothing more, nothing less. It is a significant wee corner, particularly given Smith's achievement in introducing one member, one vote. More broadly, it also seeks to reconnect New Labour with its past, remembering lost figures dating from Smith's period as leader, of equal or greater importance than Gordon Brown or Tony Blair. Past Labour Governments haven't been very successful. But even if one accepts that previous Labour Governments were disastrously bad, isn't it a dangerous orthodoxy to reject your Party's roots? Too many of the leading architects of New Labour have sought to ditch the Party's past, but if the Labour Party is to survive much beyond the next election, it needs to reconnect with the concept of seeing the Party as having a proud history as part of the wider Labour movement.

Mark Stuart
December 2004

Acknowledgements

THE LIST OF PEOPLE I need to thank is legion, and this summary will not do proper justice. To those who were willing to be interviewed, either by telephone or face to face, sometimes at great length, I accord my heartfelt thanks. I would especially like to thank the following: Hilary Armstrong, Ann Barrett, John Battle, Leo Beckett, Margaret Beckett, Tony Benn, Paul Boateng, Gordon Borrie, Menzies Campbell, Tom Clarke, Yvette Cooper, Michael Crick, Meghnad Desai, Frank Dobson, John Eatwell, Murray Elder, Michael Foot, Derek Foster, John Garlick, Brian Gill, Jimmy Gordon, Mary Goudie, Ross Harper, Thomas Harris, Simon Haskel, Roy Hattersley, Alan Haworth, Denis Healey, Norman Hogg, Derry Irvine, Annie and Alex Kelly, Ian Kirkwood, Gavin Laird, Helen Liddell, John McCluskey, Neil MacCormick, Mary McCulloch, Pat McFadden, Donald Mackay, Ranald MacLean, Emma Maclennan, Dick Mabon, Bruce Millan, Elizabeth Munro, Kenneth Munro, Michael Quinlan, Meta Ramsay, Malcolm Rifkind, Dirk Robertson, Donald Robertson, George Robertson, Bill Rodgers, Chris Smith, Elizabeth Smith, Elizabeth Thomas, David Ward, Larry Whitty, Stuart Scott Whyte and Ruth Wishart. Many thanks to all those who were interviewed, but preferred not to be mentioned by name.

Letters and e-mails from the following provided valuable insights: Dan Corry, Peter Fraser, David Gardner, Andrew Graham, David Hare, Ludovic Kennedy, Neil Kinnock, Meg Russell, Rev. Norman J. Shanks, Sarah Smith, Jack Straw and David Walker. Special mention must also be made of the late James Callaghan, the late Paul Foot and the late Robin Gray, who sent very helpful correspondence.

Thanks are due to Bill Campbell of Mainstream Publishing, for his co-operation in letting me quote selectively from Gordon Brown and James Naughtie, *Life and Soul of the Party* (Mainstream: Edinburgh, 1994), and to Philip Norton (University of Hull) for letting me draw extensively on his valuable data relating to Labour dissent in the 1970s, and for his helpful advice and expertise throughout the project.

On a practical level, I would like to express gratitude to Ann Barrett, Janet and Frank Dobson, Brian Gorman, John Osborne, David Ward and Emma

Maclennan, Kenneth and Elizabeth Munro, and Mr and Mrs Stafford for their kind hospitality during my various trips the length and breadth of the United Kingdom. Philip Cowley at the University of Nottingham and Matthew Bailey at the University of Hull provided a constant stream of articles and welcome advice, while David Denver (Lancaster University) successfully hunted down a reference relating to Robert Burns. Gerry Reilly kindly lent me a copy of a book related to debating at Glasgow University, while Paul Krishnamurty and Roger MacGinty were always on hand to listen not only to my ideas, but also to my many gripes and moans.

In terms of archives and libraries, many thanks are due to: Allen Packwood and his staff for being so helpful during my two visits to consult the Kinnock Collection at Churchill College Archives in Cambridge; to David Weston, Keeper of Special Collections at Glasgow University Library for letting me consult and quote from the *Glasgow University Guardian*; and Glasgow University Archive Services for allowing me to look through back issues of the *Glasgow University Magazine* (GUM). The staff at the National Library of Scotland also deserve a special mention for calling up copies of the *Airdrie and Coatbridge Advertiser*, *Daily Record*, *The Herald*, and *The Scotsman* so efficiently. I also found useful sources in the British Library, the LSE Library, and the Brynmor Jones Library at the University of Hull.

Thanks are also due to a number of individuals for letting me consult at length various papers relating to the life of John Smith: Ann Barrett, Menzies Campbell, Michael Crick, Murray Elder, Thomas Harris, Alan Haworth, Neil Kinnock, Gavin Laird, Elizabeth Munro, Kenneth Munro, Elizabeth Thomas and David Ward.

I would also like to thank those people who gave their kind permission to allow me to quote from documents written by them within various personal papers: Chris Allsopp, Tony Blair, Charles Clarke, Dan Corry, Frank Dobson, John Eatwell, Delyth Evans, Philip Gould, Andrew Graham, David Hare, David Hill, Neil Kinnock, Marista Leishman, Cliff Michelmore, John Patten, Jeff Rooker, Shirley Sheppard and Chris Smith.

I am especially indebted to John Schwartz, formerly at Politico's, but now at IPPR for being so enthusiastic about my project. Sean Magee and Emma Musgrave safely guided the biography to publication with consummate skill.

Apologies are due to my parents, both still staunch Tories, for raising a son who wrote a book about the Labour Party. You mustn't blame yourselves; you tried your best. Finally, I am forever indebted to my wife, Julie Miller, for her free-at-point-of-use editorial skills. Julie, you are quite simply the best. Responsibility for any remaining mistakes rests solely with the author.

Prologue:
11 MAY 1994

LABOUR WAS RIDING high in the opinion polls. John Smith had just led his party to victory in the local elections.[1] An ICM poll for *The Guardian* that morning[2] showed Labour on 44 per cent, with the Conservatives and the Liberal Democrats way back on 26 per cent each. In April 1994, when Gallup asked, 'Do you think Mr Smith is or is not proving a good leader of the Opposition?', 49 per cent of voters thought he was a good leader, while 31 per cent disagreed. More pertinently, when asked a similar question about John Major, 74 per cent of voters expressed their dissatisfaction with his performance. And when asked in the same month who would make the best Prime Minister, 32 per cent chose Smith, 21 per cent Paddy Ashdown, and only 15 per cent selected John Major.[3]

Smith told reporters after the May local elections: 'This rejection of the Conservative Government comes deep from the heart of the British people; it is a very, very strong message they're getting.'[4] By the weekend of 7–8 May, Smith had just embarked on Labour's European election campaign, and it was widely anticipated that the Conservatives would receive another drubbing at the polls.

The Conservatives were in complete disarray. The Euro-sceptics had spent eighteen months giving the Major Government late nights in their ultimately unsuccessful attempt to derail the Maastricht Treaty.[5] Voters dislike parties as divided as they now perceived the Tories to be. After Britain fell out of the Exchange Rate Mechanism (ERM) of the European Monetary System (EMS) on 'Black Wednesday', 16 September 1992, the Conservatives lost their historic lead over Labour on economic competence. They never got it back. By early 1994, Smith could sense that the Tories were finished, and he was tremendously excited by the prospect of returning to government after such a long gap. As James Naughtie puts it: 'Smith was usually beaming as he went about his business.'[6] On one night in January, an exuberant Smith met Tony Benn in the lobby, and claimed that at a dinner of American correspondents that evening, one of them had said to him, 'You are the luckiest man in world politics because the government are in such a mess.'[7] Before Easter, John's close friend Jimmy Gordon telephoned to announce that he'd just bought a house on their favourite island of Iona. John was never to see it.[8]

The main cloud – and it was a big one – on Smith's horizon was the persistent niggling from Labour's modernisers that he hadn't sufficiently transformed the Labour Party to guarantee victory at the general election. On 30 April 1994, Alastair Campbell had been particularly critical of Smith's leadership in an article for *The Spectator*.[9] On 3 May, at one of their regular chats – and what would be their last meeting together – Neil Kinnock had suggested that Smith should flesh out some new themes over the summer in five or six lectures with a view to bringing forward some fresh policies at the 1994 conference in the autumn.[10]

But according to Margaret Beckett, Smith was 'in fine fettle and in high spirits'[11] on the night of 11 May. The occasion was a £500-a head European gala fundraising dinner at the Park Lane Hotel, London. Guests sat down to a mediocre meal of asparagus mousse, lamb in herbs, and a lemon dessert. An auction was held, during which a set of Orwell first editions was bought by John Prescott for £3,500.[12] Celebrity guests also included the British actors Jeremy Irons, Alan Rickman, Neil Pearson (star of *Between the Lines*), and the author Ruth Rendell.[13]

Characteristically, Smith spoke from notes, rather than from a prepared text. He talked expansively on several of his favourite themes, including the importance of building a genuine partnership between government and industry. The speech was sharp and witty: at one point Smith described John Major as 'the Captain Mainwaring of British politics'.

Above all, John Smith's speech reflected the optimism of a political leader confident of victory at the next general election:

> I believe that everything is moving our way. We must never be complacent and must never take anything for granted but I believe the signs are set fairer for the Labour Party than they have been for a very long time.
>
> Thank you all very much for coming here tonight and helping us perhaps partly to achieve that objective. We will do our best to reward your faith in us but please give us the opportunity to serve our country. That is all we ask.[14]

When Smith sat down, Margaret Beckett congratulated him on his final sentence, and was told that it was off the cuff.[15] His party was on the verge of government, and to those gathered there that evening, he appeared to be at the peak of his powers. Larry Whitty, the general secretary of the Labour Party, recalls that Smith was in great form at the top table.[16]

After the speeches, Smith mused with Michel Rocard, guest of honour, about Rocard running France, Rudolf Scharping running Germany, and Smith as Prime Minister of Great Britain: all three men seeking the dual objectives of economic efficiency and social justice.[17] Smith went upstairs with Rocard for a glass of champagne, but also for a serious discussion. Labour and the Parti Socialiste were widely expected to emerge as the two largest parties in the European Parliament. Smith thrashed out with Rocard which of their parties' nominees would get the post of leader of the Parliament, and which would become leader of the Socialist Group.[18]

Chris Smith, John's Environmental Protection spokesperson and hill-walking companion, recalls that John was 'beaming, and hale and hearty'. As Chris said his goodbyes, John was introduced to Chris's partner for the first time. John was still hobbling around after his accident coming down a Munro, and he asked Chris's partner, 'Are you into Munros as well?'[19]

As so often, Smith stayed into the small hours chatting away . . .

One
A COUNTRY
EDUCATION

ACCORDING TO SMITH family lore, and backed up by evidence from the cemetery in Tarbert,[1] John Smith's ancestors hailed from the now derelict community of Allt Beithe (pronounced 'Awlt Bay'), situated on the shores of Loch Fyne in the County of Argyll. John Leitch, probably a farmer or fisherman, seems to have married Catherine Carmichael some time during the second decade of the nineteenth century. Their seventh surviving son, Archibald, was born in 1843. Two years later, it appears that Archibald's parents died during a cholera epidemic that swept the entire village. There is some dispute, however, over how many of the Leitch children actually survived the cholera outbreak, but two facts are fairly certain: that Archibald, aged two, survived, and that Allt Beithe was put to the torch by the locals in an effort to purge the area of disease. The settlement has remained derelict ever since.

Archibald Leitch became a carpenter in Tarbert, establishing a boatyard with the aid of his first two sons, Dugald and Callum. He eventually died in 1930, having fathered two more sons, Donald (who went to university, but died aged only 40) and Archie, as well as three daughters – Catherine, Isabel and Ann. The last of these daughters, Ann, married John Smith, a fisherman (whose ancestry is even more difficult to trace with any accuracy, given the surname is so common), and together they had five children. Ann and John Smith's second son, Archibald Leitch Smith, named after his grandfather, attended Dunoon Grammar School, before studying English and history at Glasgow University, where he joined the Labour Club, encountering the likes of the great John MacCormick, who would later help found the Scottish National Party (SNP).[2]

On graduating from Glasgow, Archie trained as a teacher, taking up his first teaching post at Portnahaven on the island of Islay, where he married Sarah Cameron Scott. The Scotts were originally from Dumfries and Galloway, but Robert Scott, Sarah's father, had moved north to Bonawe, a small place northeast of Oban, to work as a quarryman. Robert died before World War Two, and his widow Mary moved to Dalmally, a small village situated at the northern end of Loch Awe in the County of Argyll. There she ran a boarding house called 'Baddarroch', and it was here, in his grandmother's house, that John Smith, the future Labour leader, was born on 13 September 1938. This was in spite of the fact that his mother and father lived on Islay. Perhaps wishing to have her mother Mary at her side during the birth of her first child, Sarah Smith travelled to the mainland to Dalmally.[3] At the time, it was widely considered safer for expectant mothers to give birth on the mainland.[4] John's sister Mary was born in 1942, and Annie followed in 1946.[5]

John remembered nothing of Islay. When he was only two his father took up an appointment as headmaster of a small primary school in the coastal village of Ardrishaig, set on the shores of Loch Gilp, an inlet of Loch Fyne, not far from the small town of Lochgilphead. Ardrishaig forms the eastern terminus of the Crinan Canal, dug from 1793 until 1801, and engineered by John Rennie. The canal was the major reason for the sudden growth of Ardrishaig, creating a convenient shortcut across the Kintyre peninsula out to sea for boats of all kinds. Inevitably, boat repair yards sprang up at the edge of the village. John Smith fondly recalled the 'puffers', little flat-bottomed boats that plied their way between the islands delivering essential supplies. As children, John and Mary would take their bikes on to the puffers, alight further up the canal, and return via the tow path: 'We weren't supposed to go. Father didn't know.'[6] In days gone by, over 100 skiffs had fished for the plentiful herring, which was often smoked into Loch Fyne kippers. Fishing stocks had dwindled by John Smith's day, contributing to the slow economic decline of the village. John's sister Mary recalls: 'The fish had gone; it was the memory of the fish.'[7] For a time, other industries, mainly the Glengilp Distillery on the south bank of the canal, provided employment, but by 1937 it too was closed. Nowadays, forestry, fish farming, hydroelectricity and an oil depot maintain employment in the village.

Though a relatively small place, Ardrishaig has produced two figures worthy of mention, besides a mere leader of the Labour Party.[8] James Chalmers, a Church of Scotland missionary, met an unfortunate end, consumed by cannibals in New Guinea in 1901. Chalmers's good works are commemorated on a memorial opposite the entrance to the former Royal Hotel (now renamed the Grey Gull Inn) in the village. Further down the seafront a less obtrusive cairn now commemorates John Smith's association with the village. Ardrishaig's third famous son, Neil Dewar, played football for Scotland against Germany in front of Adolf Hitler. The war impinged even on idyllic Ardrishaig. As a very small boy, John Smith would have mixed with the evacuee children from Clydeside, and watched the comings and goings of the sailors from the public bars on the waterfront, given shore leave from the warships, and less obviously from the mysterious submarines moored further out to sea.[9]

The children of the village frequented a sweetie shop – Tibby's – owned by Mrs McVicar. With rationing in force, Mary recalls: 'John and I ate ours all in one go. Annie was good at saving hers.'[10] Ellen Muir, a contemporary, later recalled John inside Jessie McVicar's shop, aged eleven or twelve, always going on about politics.[11] But boys will be boys. The tale is told that, as young boys, John and his friends had stolen a prize rum 'clootie' dumpling from the local show, and were caught sticky-fingered washing down the last morsels with tea brewed in a bucket over a campfire in the disused lemonade factory in Ardrishaig.[12] There was always a touch of undimmed energy and devilment about John Smith, far removed from his later image as a staid bank manager. The childhood naughtiness may also derive from the fact that, because their father was the schoolmaster, John and Mary had to establish early on with the other children that they could still be lots of fun, although Annie, perhaps because she was a lot younger, was fairly quiet.[13]

The cultural life of Ardrishaig reached its peak on Gala Day, always the first Saturday in August, when day-trippers came across on the steamer ferry from Glasgow. John and Mary liked entering the decorated bike competition. At Halloween, the children would dress up in costumes – one year, Mary came as 'Miss Pears' from the Pears soap advert – for a line-up in the village hall, which also held Sunday School parties at Christmas.[14]

The Smith family generally holidayed locally in Dalmally, or more adventurously arranged house exchanges through a teachers' magazine. There was also the family dinghy, the *Mary Joanne*.[15] Occasionally, the children were treated to a film in the village hall, courtesy of a travelling movie man. But the main focus all year round was the local kirk, situated down by the entrance to the Crinan Canal. Archibald Smith became an elder in the kirk and, like most villagers, he and his family observed the Sabbath strictly. Presbyterianism was still strongly rooted in the local community: even in John's youth, the Protestant bands still crossed over to Belfast for the annual Twelfth of July festivities, commemorating the Battle of the Boyne in 1690.[16]

Politically, the Argyll area was Conservative with a large 'C', never failing to return a Conservative member until the surprise win of the SNP's Iain MacCormick (a contemporary of Smith's at Glasgow University) in February 1974. Even then, the SNP's tenure of the seat was relatively short-lived. By 1979, John MacKay,[17] another contemporary of Smith's at Glasgow, won back

Argyll for the Conservatives, held on in 1983 (when the seat became Argyll and Bute) before losing out to the Liberal candidate, Ray Michie, in 1987. Mrs Michie retired from the House of Commons in 2001,[18] and her successor, Alan Reid, retains the seat for the Liberal Democrats, although the main challengers are now Labour. But in Archibald Smith's time, Labour voters were thin on the ground. The only hint of radicalism in Ardrishaig came during World War Two when Argyll County Council wanted to close the school and send the children to Lochgilphead. The parents organised a 'strike', keeping their children at home, and the council reversed its decision. Perhaps radicalism is the wrong word for the village's defiance. Rather, it demonstrates the village's strong sense of community.

John's father, Archie, was a quiet man, with a more pronounced burr in his voice than his son. He was nonetheless a man of definite views: 'Our father was a very typical Scottish schoolmaster. He was definitely the boss, always the one in charge.' Although he expected his children to work hard at their schooling, he was not strict to the point of stifling his children. On the contrary:

> There was always a lively discussion around the table at tea-time, especially around religion . . . You practised religion; it was not imposed . . . He [father] would always throw things out for discussion. We were always given a platform to think for ourselves, rather than being told what to do.[19]

Annie agrees: 'We were given the freedom to think what we wanted, but not to do what we wanted.'[20] For instance, Archie was 'totally supportive' of Mary (and indeed Annie) going to Glasgow School of Art, and loved to discuss, challenge, and listen to Mary's views about her chosen vocation. Sarah Smith had attended Edinburgh Art School, where she'd gained a degree in fashion design, and worked in Jenner's briefly before giving it all up when she married Archie, so the idea of art school may have met with more than average sympathy.[21]

Sarah was an outgoing person but, unlike her husband, she shied away from getting up to talk or give a public speech. Years later, when John died, Mary was asked by Jane Franchi, who was commentating on the funeral for the BBC, what qualities John took from his mother and father. Mary replied, 'father's deep thinking, and from mother, an ability to be at ease with everyone'.[22] On reflection, Mary still thinks this was the right thing to say because John's father was 'a real intellect, but not a man who found it easy to mix with people but our mother was, so in a way John had the best of both worlds'.[23]

The headmaster and his family lived in a schoolhouse attached to the school or, in this case, the 'wee' school, because Ardrishaig Primary School was divided into a wee school for the younger boys, and a larger school, situated across the road, for the older ones. When John reached the age of ten or eleven,[24] he crossed the road to be taught by his father, who by this stage had earned the nickname 'Hairy' Smith.[25] Later, the schoolhouse was enlarged, giving the Smith family a large living room at the back of one of the old classrooms. Wherever the Smiths lived, they always kept a beautiful garden. Mary adds: 'Mum may have complained about the damp in the house, but it was a great upbringing, a great childhood.'[26] (Both the wee school and the big school are now private residences.)

One activity which John enjoyed from an early age was Gaelic singing. Neither his mother nor even his grandmother was a fluent Gaelic speaker. Mary points out: 'Mother didn't really have the Gaelic. Grandmother knew a little, and when we went to Dalmally, she came out with various phrases.'[27] For the rest of his life, John felt he *should* be able to speak Gaelic, but never quite managed it. After John's funeral in 1994, Bill Jacobs, the *Edinburgh Evening News*'s Westminster correspondent, discussed with Donald Dewar his tribute to Smith. Dewar let slip that he had once discovered *Teach Yourself Gaelic* tapes in John's car. Dewar commented: 'John told me he felt that as a Scot he ought to learn Gaelic. And I told him, John, don't be such a fool. It's completely unnecessary.'[28]

A local man, Willie Galbraith, taught the Smith children the Gaelic words to songs. Contrary to popular belief, John won his silver medal at a local area Mod, Mod Chinntire (Kintyre),[29] but definitely not at the National Mod.[30] It was with a great sense of pride that Smith attended the opening ceremony of the 101st National Mod – in the heart of his Monklands East constituency – when the town of Airdrie played host to the Mod in 1993 (see chapter 23).[31]

Smith would still occasionally break into song, late into the night, after having a few drinks with his Labour colleagues. This tendency led Donald Dewar to comment at Smith's funeral that: 'He could start a party in an empty room – and often did – filling it with good cheer, Gaelic songs and argument.'[32] At the funeral, Jimmy Gordon also recalled Smith regaling friends with Sunday School songs from his childhood, complete with the appropriate mimes and gestures, including:

> Seek them out, get them gone,
> All the little rabbits in the field of corn.
> Envy, jealousy, malice and pride,
> They must never in my heart abide.[33]

Other favourite tunes were 'Morag of Dunvegan',[34] and 'Cailinn mo Runsa', which is the Gaelic for 'Darling My Own'.[35] But when Smith appeared on *Desert Island Discs* in May 1991 with Sue Lawley, he chose 'The Road to the

Isles', sung by Father Sidney McEwan, whom he described as 'a marvellous man' and 'also a very beautiful singer'.[36] Despite his Presbyterian upbringing, as a young boy, John befriended McEwan, the Catholic priest at Lochgilphead, and John ended up taking care of McEwan's boat.

On leaving his father's primary school, John attended the junior secondary in Lochgilphead, about two miles away. There, he started debating and wrote for the school magazine.[37] However, Lochgilphead taught only first to third years. Aged fourteen, John had to go on to a senior secondary school if he wanted to progress further academically.

John followed his father by attending Dunoon Grammar School. Founded by the Covenanters – strong Presbyterians led by the Marquis of Argyll – at the beginning of the Civil War in 1641, and firmly in the state sector, Dunoon Grammar's grand outward appearance suggested something closer to an English fee-paying school. Once the site of a bishop's palace, the school was one of the main focal points of the town, with its mock-Gothic tower, heavy stone buttresses and fine mixture of Victorian and Edwardian buildings. Inside, the school was 'all high ceilings, science labs with stained oak-topped benches, inset enamel sinks and brass Bunsen burners'.[38] The town itself would have seemed like a buzzing metropolis to John, compared with Ardrishaig: the arrival and departure of the steamships at the pier would have been familiar enough, but not the rows of boarding houses or the permanent cinema.

Pupils at Dunoon were set according to ability in English and mathematics. The brighter pupils did Latin, while the more mechanically-minded were taught woodwork and metalwork. This system does not seem to have led to social divisions between clever and non-clever children. In those days, there was not the same expectation that a large proportion of pupils would go on to university, although the system seems to have encouraged a healthy number to do so.

One former pupil, Donald Robertson, recalls that the fact that so many children, like John Smith, came to Dunoon from the Inner Hebridean islands and Western Argyll added a distinct Gaelic flavour to the school.[39] The Highland children from outlying areas were often referred to as the 'teuchters'. The distance between Ardrishaig and Dunoon, situated on the end of the Cowal Peninsula, compelled the teuchters to live away from their parents in term-time, taking up lodgings in Dunoon, and returning home only during the school holidays, when John would catch a steamer bound for the Kyles of Bute, and slowly onward to the mouth of the Crinan Canal.

During term-time, John Smith stayed with Mrs Irene McGilp, whose husband announced the arrival and departure of the ferries at Dunoon pier.[40]

Smith later described her as a 'lovely lady who looked after us, and was in a sense our mother'.[41] Another former lodger describes Smith's landlady as having 'ample bosoms' and being 'one of the great scone-makers of Argyll'.[42] Liberated from their strict parental homes, George Robertson recalls that the teuchters could be quite a handful. John Smith was very much 'a free spirit'.[43]

On Smith's arrival at Dunoon, aged fourteen, he met Robert McLaughlan, one year ahead. Bob's first question was, 'Are you a Socialist?' They became firm friends. Soon, McLaughlan recruited Smith to the local Labour Party, where he delighted older members by singing songs. Indeed, McLaughlan recalls John's first singing performance in school, a classroom solo, 'Scots Wha Hae', sung 'in a thin piping voice from a round face'.[44] Briefly, John took up the trumpet:

> It was a silver one, and it defeated him in more ways than one for he put a dent in it to his mortification as well as its owner's. I was always able to chide him about an inability to blow his own trumpet. In fact, however, there was no false modesty about him. He had enormous self-confidence and determination, even when very young. He was always persistent in every cause he espoused.[45]

John and Bob were inseparable. They even started smoking at the same time, John's sense of panache demanding that they smoke only Sobranie Black Russian. Pocket money being short, they had to buy just a few at a time. On one occasion, they showed off their gold-tipped douts at an Argyll Labour Party event in Oban, engendering much laughter among their comrades. On John's death, Bob recalled John's enormous energy as a child: 'I remember how we cycled over most of Cowal nearly half a century ago. I was all right on the flat bit but no good on the hills. He would easily go up them then race down, flash past and return to push me up. That was quite typical of him too.'[46]

Bob McLaughlan had helped to fill John's head with discussion of political matters, building on what John had already discussed with his father at an early age. On John's return from Dunoon during school holidays, Mary recalls 'endless amounts of discussion' between John and his father: 'I remember being sent to bed, and I could still hear them talking.'[47]

Eventually, McLaughlan became chairman of the Labour Club at Glasgow University, and emerged as a brilliant academic, gaining a first-class honours degree, and winning the coveted Snell Scholarship to Balliol College, Oxford.[48] In 1965, McLaughlan returned to Glasgow University, working as a lecturer in its Modern History department from 1965–80. For more than 20 years he was a contributor, then journalist, on the *Glasgow Herald*, until his retirement in 1997. Though Bob's politics changed – he became a strong advocate of the philosophy of Adam Smith – he and John remained firm friends. Bob died in July 1999, aged only 64.[49]

Like his father, John's nickname at school was 'Hairy' because even at that stage he was beginning to show slight signs of losing his hair. Despite being at Dunoon for only his fourth, fifth and sixth years, Smith had left his mark on the place by the time George Robertson arrived three years later.[50] Needless to say, John emerged as dux. Mary recalls: 'I used to think I was good at Latin at Lochgilphead, and then I was told that John got such and such a mark.' Given that it wasn't easy to follow her brother, she chose not to: 'I discovered I didn't have to go to Dunoon, so I went to Oban High instead.' John's youngest sister Annie also went to Oban. It's not clear whether Smith ever knew the true reason why his sisters went to Oban. In later life, he had claimed that it was because Oban High had opened a hostel for girls: 'My parents thought it was nicer to send them to a hostel instead of digs.'[51] In fact, Mary stayed in digs, not a hostel.[52]

However, the Smith family's strong association with the town of Dunoon would be strengthened when Archibald Smith moved there to take up a headmaster's appointment at Dunoon Primary School in 1964. At that time, about 40 per cent of Archie's pupils were Americans, as in 1961 Britain had allowed the United States to establish a base for the new Polaris submarines at Holy Loch, just along the coast. As shadow chancellor (by which stage Labour's defence policy had changed sufficiently to allow him to say it), Smith said he disapproved of the peace marches outside Holy Loch, indicated he'd never been a member of the Campaign for Nuclear Disarmament (CND), and revealed that he 'didn't have any objections to Polaris'.[53]

During his time at Dunoon, Smith also played a leading part in the school's debating society, along with Bob McLaughlan. Mr William Murray, head of English, took an enthusiastic interest in training young debaters, who travelled to other schools to compete in various debating competitions. Other debating stars to emerge from Dunoon include the aforementioned John MacKay, Brian Wilson, Minister of State in various government departments under Blair, ending with Trade and Industry in June 2003, and George Robertson, Secretary of State for Defence from 1997–9. But while John Smith became a successful sergeant in the Army Cadet Corps at Dunoon, Robertson, the future Secretary-General of NATO, had a miserable time as a young cadet.[54] Later in life, Smith recalled that his 'Stewart platoon' had won the prize for drilling in the year that he was sergeant, but he had then taken the distinctly 'un-sergeantly' step of taking the whole platoon into the town to buy each of them an ice cream.[55]

Smith also kept up his interest in Gaelic, participating in Dunoon Grammar's Gaelic choir. A key figure in this regard was Neil Maclean, the science master. In 1921, Maclean won the Gold Medal at the National Mod in Glasgow. (His wife, Jennie Currie, was also a gold medallist at the Inverness Mod of 1923.) Maclean went on to become one of the most popular Gaelic singers of his time, and convened the Dunoon Mod in 1950.[56]

According to Elizabeth Smith (and unlike Elizabeth) in later life John was not 'a home buddy'. The family home remained in Edinburgh, and John made a point of going home most weekends to be with his family, but he never seemed unsettled by the constant travelling and series of rented rooms and flats in London. Elizabeth recalls: 'John could make himself at home, make his nest, wherever he was.'[57] This trait is quite unusual, especially since it carried on into John's middle age. Perhaps that enforced spell living away from home in Dunoon at a relatively early age had left him with that sense that home didn't need to be a specific place. Smith later denied feeling homesick setting off to school on his own every day, and claims to have enjoyed the independence and the freedom that living away from home provided.[58] His sister Mary agrees, arguing that once you got over missing your parents, whether in Dunoon or Oban, living away from home from a relatively early age soon helped develop qualities such as self-reliance, and an ability to deal with people.[59]

On 8 November 1991, John Smith, George Robertson, Brian Wilson and Ray Michie, the local MP, were among the guests who gathered in the Queen's Hall to celebrate Dunoon Grammar's 350th anniversary. That night, Archie Roy, Professor of Astronomy at Glasgow University, and also a science fiction author, had been asked to speak for ten minutes. He droned on for 40. Worse still was the fact that he launched into a tirade against Tory education policy on an occasion which was supposed to be non-political, and in front of a highly political audience composed of figures from all the four main Scottish parties. Joseph Rhodes, the Rector, put his head in his hands as the speaker went on and on. Some people even walked out. George Robertson whispered in his ear that 'the 7th cavalry would come to the rescue'. He was referring, of course to John Smith.

The then shadow chancellor read the situation correctly, making a great speech, winning the audience round by saying what the previous speaker should have said, about how Dunoon was the most wonderful school in the world because we went to it, and recalling the nicknames of former teachers. He recalled his maths teacher, Archie Wyllie – nicknamed 'Bobo' – saying, 'Smith, do you think you will pass Higher Maths?', and the future shadow chancellor replied confidently, 'Of course, sir', before Wyllie replied: 'Don't make me laugh, Smith.' When Smith finally got his Higher Maths, he sped along to Wyllie's office, smugly told his maths teacher the news, but Wyllie just looked at his pupil without blinking, and said, 'That is the final proof, Smith, that standards have dropped so far that even you could gain a pass.'[60] It wouldn't be the last time that Smith excelled at turning round a surly, anxious audience and, within minutes, having them right in the palm of his hand.[61]

Having a father who worked as a headmaster in an Ardrishaig schoolhouse (and one who taught him briefly) helped to instil in John Smith the importance of getting an education and 'sticking in' with his studies. He came from a background where an education was valued above all else. Years later, as Labour leader, Smith recalled: 'The person who had education was the one to be admired and I think that is still my view.'[62] But that education would be administered through comprehensive, rather than private schooling. His great friend Jimmy Gordon recalls that John was 'incredibly idealistic, almost naïve about education', having benefited from 'a Scottish country education', adding: 'It would be nice if we could all get that kind of education. The reality of some city centre or peripheral estate schools is very different.'[63] Kenneth Munro, a long-time friend, recalls that John used to gently tease Elizabeth, Derry Irvine, Kenneth and Meta Ramsay for going to Hutchesons' Grammar in Glasgow, even though the fees in those days were very modest.[64]

In only his second speech as a Labour back bench MP, Smith would later recall his pride in the fact that he had been taught in a comprehensive school: 'I received the whole of my secondary education in the County of Argyll, where fee-paying schools were never heard of, never demanded and are never likely to be asked for by the people who live there.'[65] Indeed, the centrepiece of Smith's aforementioned speech to the 350th anniversary of Dunoon Grammar in 1991 was in praise of Scottish comprehensive education, and is worth quoting at length:

> I believe that Dunoon Grammar School is the embodiment of what I think is the best education that it is possible to obtain in the Western world and that is an education in a Scottish county school. We were comprehensive before the word was invented. We were coeducational before they noticed the difference. And nobody ever thought there was any question but that everybody went to THE SCHOOL.
>
> It didn't matter who you were, where you came from, what your income was – whatever. You all went to the school and got treated the same. You got a splendid education . . . That was the strength and I hope still is the strength of the tradition of the democratic intellect in Scottish education.

And I think we are not unusual in Europe in having that. We are unusual in the United Kingdom in having that.

One of the curiosities south of the border is that whenever they get their hands on education they seek to create divisions of some kind within it. Their natural instinct is to have two types of education – one of which is to segregate according to their educational abilities or else segregate according to income.[66]

Smith's belief in comprehensive education and his instinctive dislike of what he saw as the divisive social effects of public schools stayed with him all his life, and unlike so many so-called Socialist politicians, Smith practised what he preached. He later prided himself in the fact that all three of his daughters were educated in the state sector, at Boroughmuir, even though they lived in Edinburgh, surrounded by fee-paying schools that tended to be the first choice of the city's professional middle class (a curious status-based decision, because the capital city still has many good comprehensive schools), Edinburgh being the major exception to the dominance of the comprehensive system in Scotland. As a family friend explains, it was 'not up for negotiation' that John's children would be educated in the state sector.[67] Neil MacCormick, who also had three daughters, and who also educated them in the state sector, recalls John being asked what he would have done had Boroughmuir been a poor school. Smith replied: 'I'd move house!'[68]

John also wanted his children to be brought up in their native Scotland. He once commented: 'I felt that the children should know where they came from, especially in the world of politics.' It was sad, he thought, for the children of diplomats to have no sense of where they came from. He added: 'I wanted mine to feel that, at least, whatever they did afterwards, if they went to the ends of the earth, they knew where they sprang from, what they were all about.'[69] That meant being proud to be Scottish and having a Scottish accent. There is a fine line to be drawn between being proud to be Scottish and thinking one is superior, especially in relation to the English. Scotland is seen as a better place in which to live. Smith also admitted: 'We didn't want them [the Smith daughters] to live in London because it is such a rootless place.'[70] At other times it manifests itself in a more egalitarian view of the world. This was especially true in the 1987–92 Parliament when Scotland's 50 Labour MPs constituted a fifth of the parliamentary Labour Party, and a tension started to emerge between two views of society, one very southern, metropolitan and trendy (very 'SDP'), the other northern, provincial and old-fashioned.

In Smith's case, his pride in being Scottish might have come across sometimes as a sense of superiority, but it wasn't his fault that he had, unusually for most politicians, such an idyllic and happy childhood, and that he came across as somebody who was so sure of the person he wanted to be. Menzies Campbell, a contemporary of Smith's at Glasgow University (see chapter 2) once made the sage comment that Smith had 'all the virtues of a Scottish Presbyterian and none of the vices'.[71]

In a phrase that Tony Blair might have come up with, John Smith developed a strong radicalism, but in a rural setting. As James Naughtie brilliantly puts it, his father, a Labour Party member, taught him to be egalitarian in outlook, but 'the New Statesman would arrive by boat'.[72] Smith often claimed he was brought up on the Bible and Kingsley Martin's New Statesman.[73] In his obituary of Smith in the Mirror in May 1994, Gordon Brown recalled: 'like so many Socialists before him his politics were shaped more by Kirk and community than by ideological theories'.[74] Smith wasn't precisely 'a son of the manse', but he was very much of that ilk. Brown's upbringing, though literally as a son of the manse, was more urban than Smith's, and as a result the former was more attracted (at least initially) by the radical Scots like James Maxton, one of the 'Red Clydesiders'.[75]

There is little doubt that the impact of being brought up in a small village stayed with John Smith for the rest of his life. For instance, Kenneth Munro recalls that John liked the Scots language and was interested in Gaelic, but by contrast, he disliked the urban demotic. Essentially, John remained, as Kenneth puts it, 'an upright, respectable country boy'.[76] John's fundamental beliefs in common human decency and duty to others, in a sense of community and the relative unimportance of material wealth never really changed. Jimmy Gordon recalls: 'John had this core set of inner beliefs that he essentially learned at the kitchen table from his parents, and if he ran into anything that opposed these beliefs, he opposed them. His views were therefore very country Scottish.'[77]

Two
A STUDENT POLITICIAN

I N THE AUTUMN of 1956, John Smith entered Glasgow University. In the next few years, he would meet up with Alexander or 'Derry' Irvine and Donald Dewar. All three were sons of the professional middle classes, but only Smith had been to a comprehensive school: Dewar had been a day-pupil at the fee-paying Glasgow Academy (where he hadn't fitted in), while Irvine had attended Hutchesons' Boys' Grammar School. Dewar was the eldest of the three, having taken four attempts to pass the requisite Higher Latin to gain entry to Glasgow University.[1] However, Dewar was probably the most politically minded, having been steeped in the ways of the Scottish Labour Party, even during his Glasgow Academy days. The story is told that in May 1955 he pinned Labour's general election posters inside his coat and flashed them at passers by.[2] Their Scottish University education, starting with a four-year history degree (known in Scotland as an MA), preceded study for their legal exams (the LLB). Thus Smith stayed at university from 1956 until 1963.

As an undergraduate, Smith would have listened to the impressive lectures of Professor Esmond Wright, whose greatest passion was American history.[3] Some of Wright's enthusiasm for this subject must have rubbed off because Smith developed an interest in the American Civil War. But Wright was a far greater influence on Bob McLaughlan, later a history lecturer at Glasgow, than on Smith. The work for the MA was far from punishing. Most arts students had only nine or ten classes per week, leaving plenty of time for the corporate life of the university, something that was actively encouraged.[4]

One hugely important aspect for John Smith and his friends was the Glasgow Union.[5] The Union was then a wholly masculine environment (although women could be signed in as guests), and remained so until 1980.[6] There was also a slight tension in the Union between keen debaters who wanted it to remain essentially their domain to be used mainly, but not exclusively, for debating, and the non-debaters who had long wanted most Fridays to be devoted to dances. But in Smith's day, the debaters were in the ascendancy on the Union's board of management.

The Union debates were held on Fridays, starting at 1.15 pm on the first floor of the Glasgow Union building.[7] In the 'opening period', each of the six political parties (see below) would take it in turns to form 'the Government', putting forward a 'Bill' or motion for debate. The students would carry on debating throughout the 'afternoon period', during which maiden speakers would try their hand, and the crowds tended to drift away.[8] However, debates came to life after dinner, in the 'evening session' (which rarely began on time), when the crowds returned, and the political parties put up their best speakers. Question Time, which was fixed during John Smith's period at 10 pm, was generally a rowdy affair, during which the parties performed 'stunts': dressing up in costumes and delivering occasionally amusing, but more often merely smutty scripted routines. Later in the evening, the House might be treated to one or two alumni speakers, many of whom returned year after year, long after they had graduated. The last session, during which the leaders of the main parties summed up, was known as the 'closing round'. Debates sometimes went on until 3 am or 4 am, and students divided on the motion into 'aye' and 'no' lobbies, just as in the House of Commons. Later still, the debaters took part in the post-debate party as dawn approached. The parliamentary feel was enhanced by the fact that a Speaker (always the President of the Union) presided over debates. The Speaker could get flummoxed when debaters raised spurious points of order with ulterior motives in mind. One former Glasgow debater, Dick Mabon, recalls that: 'You could get away with murder when raising points of order with the Speaker because he had to take it.'[9]

After debates, clerks and assistant clerks also wrote up 'crits' of every debater. These crits were only about three lines long, but could be quite cutting. Speakers were given up to five stars for their performances. Glasgow University's monthly magazine, known as *GUM*, covered the activities of the six main parties, and reviewed the principal speakers.[10] Even when debaters were good, reviewers usually picked holes in their performances. But Smith shone.

Six political clubs provided speakers and motions under the aegis of a Debates Committee containing representatives of each of these clubs. As John Smith put it in a rare article for *GUM* in March 1960, the Glasgow system was 'an extremely intelligent way of organising debates – the clubs provide the speakers, a large part of the audience, and the all-important element of continuity'.[11]

The Tory Club had been founded in 1837 to promote the Rectorial candidature of Robert Peel,[12] and was therefore originally known as the Peel

Club. By the 1950s, the Tory Club was by far the largest of the political clubs, numbering consistently around 500 members, roughly twice that of the Labour Club. In the 1950s, Glasgow's middle class still voted Conservative, or more accurately, Conservative and Unionist. The Tories also dominated the 1950s in terms of debating, winning the Union Debating Trophy eight times, seven of these consecutively.[13] In Smith's time, the Tory Club included two future politicians of note. Teddy Taylor was a respected debater in the Glasgow Union: 'This speaker's wit and force captured the attention of anyone interested in fine debating.'[14] Less well remembered is Anna McCurley, who won Renfrew West and Inverclyde for the Conservatives in 1983 from Dickson Mabon (who had defected to the SDP in 1981) before losing out to Labour in 1987.[15]

After a period of slump, the Liberal Club had revived by Smith's time: membership in 1961–2 had recovered to around 300, second only to the Tories, and the Liberals tended to finish a respectable third in the annual Debates Trophy.[16] One of the most prominent figures on the Liberal side was Menzies Campbell. He was three years younger than Smith, and became President of the Glasgow Union in 1964–5. Campbell had a distinguished athletic career as a student, competing in the Tokyo Olympics in 1964, and holding the United Kingdom record for the 100 metres from 1967 until 1974. He followed Smith to the Scottish Bar in 1968, and became a QC in 1982. In later life, Campbell won North East Fife for the SDP/Liberal Alliance (gaining the seat from the Tories) in 1987, and has held it ever since for the Liberal Democrats. From 1989 onwards, he has either been the party's Defence or Foreign Affairs spokesperson. Throughout Paddy Ashdown's leadership (1988–99), Campbell was always a keen supporter of closer co-operation with Labour. Late at night, in this era, John Smith used to upbraid Menzies for not being in the Labour Party.[17]

Campbell remembers John Smith as 'a massively untidy' student, with an occasional haplessness about him. One night, Smith had hired a dinner jacket from Dormie, the famous Glasgow outfitters, for a special function. After the party, Smith ran down Gibson Street in Glasgow, and spun around a lamppost, but his momentum carried him too far causing him to hit a litter basket, tearing the seat of his trousers. Menzies recalls: 'He cursed for ages about the 30 shillings he had to repay the hire company.' Despite the efforts of Elizabeth to smarten up his image, Smith remained scruffy.[18] On one occasion, Smith was standing in the Strangers' Gallery in the House of Commons, sporting another very large rent in the seat of his trousers. To anyone who commented, he shouted back: 'If you look closely, you'll see the split in the Cabinet!'[19]

In the years between 1958 and 1963, the MacCormick family more or less ran the Glasgow Union Scottish Nationalist Association (GUSNA) at the university. John MacCormick had founded the SNP at both national and student level whilst an undergraduate at the Glasgow Union in 1927, and was a contemporary of John Smith's father, Archibald Smith.[20] Archibald was disappointed when John MacCormick split from the Labour Party at the University to form GUSNA. However, the two men retained a mutual respect for one another.[21] John MacCormick later became Rector of Glasgow (1950–3) during one of the high points of Scottish Nationalist sentiment at the University.[22] In 1950, Scottish Nationalist students were among those suspected of stealing the Stone of Destiny from Westminster Abbey. Special Branch officers from London, suspecting that the Stone might be hidden at the university, even put the Union under surveillance, only to succumb to student pranksters carrying large square parcels under their arms.[23]

However, during the 1950s support for the Nationalists ebbed at the university, mirroring the position in the country, as the Nationalists lost momentum after the signing of the Scottish Covenant, calling for Home Rule in 1949. Nevertheless, by the end of the decade, John MacCormick's sons Iain and Neil had done much to revive the vitality of GUSNA: in 1962, its membership stood at around 160.

Neil recalls John's mischievous side. Late one night, John was with a crowd of people walking down Gibson Street. He spotted a road-sweeper's brush lying by the side of the street, whereupon he started singing and dancing with the brush. A policeman spotted him, and called him to order.

POLICEMAN: OK, what's your name?
SMITH: John Smith.
POLICEMAN: Aye, right. And I'm William Shakespeare. Can we start again?[24]

The Labour Club, founded in the late 1940s, was the only political club to have a more egalitarian sounding 'Chairman' at its head, rather than the grander title of 'President'. The Club's membership was consistently third behind the Tories and the Liberals, and fell slightly from 325 in 1961 to around 250 in 1962, owing to a concerted recruitment drive from the Independent Socialists.[25] However, by 1959–60, the Labour Club managed to bring to a halt a seven-year Tory winning run in the annual Union Debates Trophy. The Tories wrested back the prize the following year, but Labour again triumphed in 1961–2, with Donald Dewar at last emerging as an excellent and witty speaker, earning him a share of the Individual Speaker's Prize with the Tory, Malcolm Mackenzie.[26] According to Neil MacCormick, Smith's opening speech of the last debate of the year (on 23 February, with Labour in government trying to nationalise all urban land, imposing a 50 per cent Capital Gains Tax, abolish all NHS charges and nationalise the drug industry) was 'first class', demonstrating 'his usual smooth politics and keen debating'.[27]

As well as the big four parties – the Conservatives, GUSNA, the Liberals and the Labour Club – the Bevanites and other left-wingers sometimes, but not always, chose to scorn the Labour Club to join the Independent Socialists (formerly known as the Socialist Club). When the Labour Club re-established at Glasgow in the late 1940s, the Socialists changed their name to 'Socialist Unity' to distinguish themselves from Labour. In the mid-1950s, the Club had finished in the runner-up position in the Union Debates Tournament, and had a fine trio of debaters in the shape of Archie Neil, David Goldberg (a small, wiry Jewish boxer) and Henry Prais, but overall its membership was small. In short, as Dick Mabon puts it, Socialist Unity was 'good on talent, short on manpower'.[28] By the early 1960s, the Club had fallen dramatically down the Union debating pecking order.[29] The cause of the decline was undoubtedly the Soviet Union's suppression of the Hungarian uprising in 1956, which resulted in many members drifting away, and in another change of name for the Club from Socialist Unity to the 'Independent Socialists'.

The Distributists (nearly always referred to as 'The Distribs') had a largely Catholic membership. Although a Protestant divinity student, John Welsh, had founded the Distributionists in December 1929, it never went out of its way to attract non-Catholics into its membership, which varied between 70 and around 100. The Distributionists were strongly anti-Communist, and led the way in organising Glasgow students' opposition to the Soviet response to the Hungarian uprising of 1956.[30] Ross Harper, a Conservative, caricatures the Distributists' main policy thus: everyone should be entitled to three acres and a cow.[31] Erstwhile President Jimmy Gordon more accurately states that the Distributists were against state and private monopolies, favouring the establishment of small movements and co-operatives that would share profits and ownership.[32] Many of the Club's ideas were based on Hilaire Belloc's *The Servile State*, which railed against the individual being trampled upon by big business and the state, and G. K. Chesterton's *The Restoration of Property*. The Club supported the concept of self-help, and for that reason opposed the idea of a nationally organised welfare state.

The mid–1950s probably represented the peak of the Distributist Club's influence in debating, particularly in the shape of Jimmy Gordon (Hon. Secretary, 1954; President, 1956) and Bill McLaughlin (President in 1954, and not to be confused with Bob McLaughlan, Smith's friend and Labour Club member). By Smith's time, it was often said that the Distributists were 'not the power which they once were',[33] but Jimmy Gordon still dominated university politics on the Union Board, serving as President of the Union in 1958–9, while his friend John Smith was an ordinary Board member.

Being Chairman of the Labour Club entitled Smith to be 'Prime Minister' and 'Leader of the Opposition', depending upon whether it was the Labour Club's turn to be 'in Government' in the debates. On Friday, 16 October 1959, for example, Labour were 'in Government' for the first Union debate, and moved seemingly unrelated motions: (1) insisting upon parity of representation for blacks in Central African legislatures, as well as the immediate freeing of all political prisoners held under emergency regulations, and (2) opposing the admission of General Franco's Spain to the membership of NATO. According to the comments in *GUM*, Smith's reply to the debate was very accomplished: '[Smith] made one of his finest speeches in leading his Government to their eventual 91–37 victory in the division lobbies. His calm, reasoned approach to problems which the Bill raised won him the House right from the beginning of his speech. It was a fine and mettlesome effort.'[34]

The second Union debate of the year was known as the Secretary's Debate. On 6 November 1959, GUSNA, whose turn it was to be 'in Government' put forward the motion: 'Believing the problems of the United Kingdom can only be rectified by the principle of Nationalism, Her Majesty's Government will set in train the self-government of Scotland and Wales, and the union of Northern Ireland and Eire.'[35]

The Nationalists tended to bore the other political clubs by always putting forward a motion on Scottish independence, but on this occasion the inclusion of Ireland in the proposal enlivened the debate, albeit for all the wrong reasons:

> Once again, the House was treated – subjected might be a more accurate word – to that weird zoological spectacle – the Glasgow Irishman emerging from its shell. Bogus Orangemen on one side; phoney Fenians on the other – and, in the middle of it all, an unhappy band of Scottish Nationalists talking relevantly, often eloquently, and always ineffectually, about Scotland, to a House that just was not interested.[36]

By all accounts, it was a poor debate, and had 'one of the most vulgar Question Times on record'. Without prompting, Menzies Campbell recalls this debate accurately, to the exact month, and even remembers John wearing a green shirt with a white collar. More importantly, Menzies is convinced that John made a speech in favour of home rule for Scotland.[37] That is no doubt the case, but it does not mean that as a back bench Labour MP Smith took the same view. Smith followed the Scottish Labour Party line, which was hostile to devolution, until that position became untenable with the rise of the SNP in the late 1960s and early 1970s (see chapter 6).

Back in November 1959, one reviewer, while impressed by Smith's debating skills, took objection to his expression of supposedly Orange sympathies: 'The best speech came from John Smith, who marred an otherwise fine contribution by lapsing astonishingly (in the circumstances) though hardly predictably (to those who know him) into religious bigotry of the most expendable variety.'[38] We don't know exactly what Smith said, and few debaters that evening seem to have covered themselves in glory. Some Scottish Nationalists made 'Sieg Heil' salutes on the motion being carried at 12.35 am, while others sang a variety of sectarian songs.

In the close-knit world of debaters and their cliques, nicknames and reputations for the most minor of misdemeanours tended to stick to their targets. Smith's 'Orange' speech seems to have suffered this fate, for by the end of 1959, Gordon Hunter, past President of the Liberal Club (1958–9) and future President of the Union (1961–2), claimed in a review of the leading debaters at the end of 1959 that John Smith 'doesn't give a damn for anyone or anything. Red when serious, orange when not, his speeches gain force from rapidity of delivery and absence of thought.'[39] And a year later, Teddy Davidson, a Conservative, described Smith as 'so orange he could almost be a Tory'.[40] Privately, three non-Tory contemporaries admit that John did a hilarious impression of an Orangeman's walk, complete with imaginary flute: John's squat build, and his exaggerated swagger apparently added much to the party turn, something he carried on doing in later life, but, as in earlier life, only in jest. But any talk of John being some sort of bigoted Orangeman is absolute nonsense. Nor was John ever biased toward any individual on the grounds of their religion.

It is now difficult to recapture the relative innocence of Catholic and Protestant students entering the arena of the Glasgow Union debating chamber for the first time in the late 1950s. In those days, a decade prior to the Ulster Troubles, it was still possible to sing Orange or rebel songs, for that matter, without causing offence. The words of 'The Auld Orange Flute' and 'Kelly, the Boy from Killan', were actually printed in the official student songbook distributed to first-year students. Songs were sung by everyone, regardless of their religious background. Protestants and Catholics became friends. Witness the enduring friendship of Jimmy Gordon and John Smith. Jimmy recalls that John obtained a record of Orange songs in Argyll, and added songs like 'Dolly's Brae' to the rather worn repertoire of 'The Sash' and

'Derry's Walls' on the one side and 'A Nation Once Again' and 'Kevin Barry' on the other.[41]

Smith also had a life-long regard for the Church of Scotland and enjoyed debating religious matters seriously, and to a high degree. For instance, in the summer term of 1960, debaters argued over the motion, 'This House regrets the Reformation'. Neil MacCormick recalls John arguing late into the night on such weighty ecumenical matters as Papal infallibility. Both the MacCormicks' parents and Donald Dewar's parents were very tolerant of students, so that many of these late night discussions (on many other topics other than religion) took place either in the MacCormick household, or in the Dewars' basement flat.[42]

The third debate of the Union calendar was known as the Inter-'Varsities Debate, in which 'delegates' from other universities were invited to take part. Inter-'Varsities usually took place on a Friday night, and could go on until four in the morning. The political club that had won the Debates Trophy the previous year had the honour of forming the Government, or rather, it nearly always chose to form the Government because Inter-'Varsities night was the most prestigious Union debate in the debating calendar. In November 1959, the Conservative 'Government', echoing Harold Macmillan's often misquoted remark, proposed that: 'This House believes that Britain will go on having it good.' Some 700 people attended the debate, with the debaters dressed in dinner jackets and evening gowns, but by the evening session, the audience, plied with too much drink, had descended into rowdyism.[43] In such an atmosphere, it was difficult to make a good speaking contribution, and this one ended with 'two pretty stock speeches from John Smith and Graham Watt.[44] Not very thrilling. Those who sighed for excitement just had to wait for the party.'[45]

John Smith seems to have left a better impression on the debate reviewer after the Union-Dialectic Parliamentary Debate on 15 January 1960. The Independent Socialists formed the Government, and put forward a motion refusing to co-operate in the supply of nuclear weapons to Germany, calling on the United States and France to make no further nuclear tests, and demanding that Britain destroy its stocks of nuclear weapons and cease their manufacture. While Donald Dewar's speech was 'like the first pint from the barrel – all froth and precious little substance', Smith 'made a clever and well-balanced speech'. Nevertheless, the motion was carried, 'and the chaos that had been threatening for an hour now broke out in its traditional form, the post-Debate party'.[46]

During this academic year (1959–60), Smith moved up the debating hierarchy, competing with Peter Richmond, a Conservative, as the second-string Glasgow Union team in *The Scotsman* debating trophy, another of the inter-university debating contests, reserved for Scottish universities only.

The following year, in November 1960, John Smith and Donald Dewar took part in the Scottish round of the *Observer* Mace debating tournament.[47] But on this occasion, Mr Lionel Daiches, QC, chairman of the judges, chose to leave the debating hall, not once, but twice, missing the entirety of one of the St Andrews' speeches, and the beginning of Donald Dewar's. Despite assured performances from Smith and Dewar, Edinburgh were placed first, a team which comprised David Harcus[48] and Russell Johnston, later Liberal MP for Inverness, Nairn and Lochaber from 1964–97.[49]

In January 1961, John Smith and Donald Dewar combined forces again, this time scraping through the heats of *The Scotsman* debating trophy. Counteracting the Glasgow team's home venue, they were drawn first: a fairly significant disadvantage, since opening the debate is often regarded as the toughest debating task of all, especially if the motion is cast in vague terms. So it proved on this occasion. Dewar proposed the motion: 'That this House regrets the rule of the ad-man.' According to Teddy Davidson, the *GUM* reviewer, 'we have heard Dewar speak better, but it is doubtful if anyone could have done better than he did.' Smith seconded the motion in a speech that earned him a special mention from the judges as the outstanding individual speaker of the evening, but the worthy winners that evening was the team from Queen's College, Dundee. Nevertheless, Teddy Davidson confidently predicted that Glasgow stood a real chance of winning the final: 'On the whole we should not be too disappointed at the result, and if Dewar and Smith are drawn to speak at a more favourable stage of the debate in the final in Aberdeen they may well bring back the trophy to what most of us consider its rightful home.'[50]

Davidson's prediction proved accurate. A month later, Smith and Dewar triumphed in *The Scotsman* final, held in the Marischal College in Aberdeen. They opposed the motion: 'That this House will not fight for democracy' (a much easier motion to attack than to defend), defeating two teams from Queen's College, Dundee, and the aforementioned team from Edinburgh University. The following morning, a picture appeared in *The Scotsman* of Smith and Dewar receiving *The Scotsman* trophy from Mr G. Fraser Cowley, an assistant editor of the paper, and the chairman of the judges.[51]

John Smith's debating strengths lay not in being flamboyant, but in building up a well-argued factual case. Dewar had, after much effort, become a reasonably accomplished debater, combining a mastery of detail with a biting wit (although the shorthand typists in the House of Commons later

struggled to keep up with his staccato delivery and rapidity of speech). Jimmy
Gordon recalls that John's debating style combined rational argument and
passionate conviction. Donald spoke more quickly in clipped tones, but his
speeches were wittier, more intellectual, combined with a tremendous grasp of
the English language.[52] Ross Harper also recalls that Donald was quicker than
Smith in terms of words per minute, but that John was 'more like a full back,
bright and able to respond, more measured in style'.[53]

From an early stage, John Smith proved adept at making devastating
interventions, a talent which would later become his trademark in House of
Commons debates. Malcolm Mackenzie recalls trying and failing to get the
better of Smith in a Union debate: 'I started by saying, "As many economists
have proved." He immediately shouted: "Name one of them." Of course, I
couldn't and my whole argument collapsed around me.'[54]

Dick Mabon noticed that Smith had 'a maturity about him that his years
didn't justify'.[55] Menzies Campbell agrees that John was 'a grown up', and feels
that his maturity may have been due to the freedom and independence from
his parents that he gained from an early age at Dunoon Grammar.[56] John was
never flippant in debates – he always argued for real. There is no record of
John ever taking part in the amusing stunts of Question Time, like Donald
Dewar, who dressed up in all kinds of costumes.

Perhaps an indication John's increased confidence and pre-eminence
within the Glasgow debating fraternity was shown when the debaters treated
the about-to-retire Principal, Sir Hector Hetherington, to a cross-section of
their talents in February 1961. Kenneth Munro recalls: 'Thinking back,
everything [at Glasgow] was marked by a debate.'[57] John MacKay,[58] writing as
'The Slasher' in *GUM*, was fulsome in his praise for Smith's performance:

> John Smith started the procession [of Union speakers] – and showed us
> once again how far he stands above his fellows in the art of debate. His
> speech, delivered without notes, had the complete attention of the House.
> He destroyed the opposition, justified the Government, and showed his
> audience what debating really means.[59]

Smith rounded off the debating year in March 1961 by winning the Union's
Individual Speaker's Prize, jointly with James McMeekin. However, such is
the tradition of cutting crits at Glasgow that Teddy Davidson, reviewing the
year's debating, could not resist taking the shine off their joint triumph: 'In
many ways, this has been a disappointing year, not least of all for those of us
who hoped to see some top-class debating from John Smith and Jim
McMeekin, neither of whom this year spoke to the standard expected of them,
but in spite of this they dominated debating.'[60]

In the same month, Smith was elected as Convener of Debates, succeeding Gordon Hunter. His first major task was to organise a 'summer' debate on 28 April 1961 to mark the formal retirement of Sir Hector Hetherington.[61] By special request of Sir Hector, the debaters, with the exception of one or two professors, were almost entirely students, and no outside celebrities debated the motion: 'That this House considers a belief in democracy is a submission to vulgarity.'[62]

Apart from debating, Smith played football regularly. Donald MacCormick later recalled that Smith became 'a master of Nobby Stiles-like tackles'.[63] On 4 April 1961, Smith took part in a match between the Union Board, calling themselves 'Union Board Unathletic' and a scratch team from the six political clubs, known as 'Political Clubs Disunited'. Union Board Unathletic took the lead after only five minutes, and quickly went two ahead, thanks to Smith who crashed home a Jimmy Gordon pass. The Political Clubs Disunited goalie, Fergus Nicholson (Independent Socialist), then saved confidently a clever attempt by Smith to steer the ball home with his posterior. 'A real piece of cheek, this,' commented Jim McMeekin, the match reviewer. Jimmy Gordon then added a third, and the Board ended the half 4–0 in front. A fifth goal was added in the second half, and for the last 20 minutes, the Board team eased off, allowing the Disunited team to score a consolation goal that looked suspiciously offside, but the referee, Ken Munro, refused to consult the linesman on the perfectly legitimate grounds that there was no linesman. The game ended: Political Club Disunited 1: Union Board Unathletic 5. Apparently, Donald MacCormick was outstanding in defence, while Smith demonstrated 'unexpected skill on the left foot',[64] another unprovoked reference to his supposed Orange leanings.[65]

John also enjoyed visiting his sister Mary, who was then studying for her degree at the Glasgow School of Art. (Their younger sister Annie did the same course a few years later and, like Mary, became an artist.) Mary had a room in a typical student flat in Park Quadrant, and remembers holding a party there which John and Donald Dewar attended. 'They'd got word that Mum had sent up food, including sausage rolls. They came mainly for that, but John liked our art friends because we were a wee bit different.' In his second year, John briefly enrolled in a life-drawing class at the Glasgow School of Art, but he didn't prove very good when it came to drawing nude figures. Mary recalls an irate John coming back from the art class, complaining that the teacher had told him he'd drawn too big a head, leaving no room for the feet: 'I told him [the teacher] he should have given me a bigger piece of paper!'[66]

John Smith settled down to exam work in the six-week term after Easter, when few debates took place. Smith was always very generous with friends who wanted to borrow his books. On one occasion, Kenneth Munro called at John's digs to borrow his copy of Tony Crosland's *The Future of Socialism.* Landlady Mrs MacDonald from Stornaway answered the door: 'Would you like a boiled egg?' John's first question to Kenneth was, 'Did she offer you a boiled egg?'[67]

Smith continued debating virtually until the end of his time at Glasgow. In December 1961, the Glasgow Union first team[68] of Gordon Hunter and John Smith won the Scottish heat of the *Observer* Mace National Debating Competition, held at the Queen Margaret Union, debating a motion which postulated the close proximity of George Orwell's *1984.* According to the reviewer: 'Smith was as effortlessly persuasive as ever, while Hunter combined humour and fire in a speech which won him mention as the best individual speaker of the evening.'[69]

In the early spring of 1962, Smith and Hunter won the coveted *Observer* Mace. Glasgow University quickly acquired a reputation in the mid-1950s as the best debating University in Britain.[70] After a slight lull for two or three years, debating at Glasgow returned to the top drawer from about 1960–4. Thereafter, dominance has never quite returned for a sustained period.

Jimmy Gordon feels that the secret of Glasgow's success lay in the fact that its Union debates tended to follow a political format. A Government would be theoretically formed in every debate, and debaters would have to figure out what to do when they were in power or in opposition, rather than what Jimmy Gordon sees as the 'effete' style at Oxford where students debated motions such as: 'This House would rather . . .'[71] Dick Mabon agrees that Glasgow's debating strength lay in the fact that it was 'not dialectic', but rather 'overwhelmingly political'. As Mabon puts it, 'At Oxford, you could join any Club, but at Glasgow you joined a Club and stuck it out; nobody would dare to belong to two political parties.'[72]

Certainly, Glasgow debaters gained invaluable experience of competition-style debating throughout the academic year, as one student observer put it at the time, by exploiting 'the almost unlimited opportunities for experiment by trial and error'[73] when discussing all sort of political issues. Kenneth Munro views it as 'a tremendous training' for parliamentary politics in later life.[74]

However, for John Smith, who was far more politically-minded than Jimmy Gordon, the weakness of the Glasgow system lay in the fact the political clubs were better at training debaters than promoting what he called 'a meaningful discourse of political issues'. Smith felt that political positions were stated and not examined, with the old slogans 'trotted out'. When Smith expressed such views in a rare article in *GUM* in March 1960,[75] he provoked a fairly hostile response a month later from fellow debaters, James McMeekin (Conservative) and Gordon Hunter (Liberal), who argued that Glasgow's national debating success was not gained at the expense of a low average debating standard. They objected to Smith's 'inference that better politics will necessarily mean better debates'.[76] Smith, however, responded by accusing Mr McMeekin and Mr Hunter of being 'extraordinarily sensitive about any criticism of Union debating', arguing:

> I am glad that Mr Hunter and Mr McMeekin concede the need for greater intellectual activity within political clubs. I cannot understand why they should be so coy about raising the level of politics within Union debates. Of course, better politics does not necessarily mean better debating. Union debates must be more than a series of intellectual theses – as if this was a serious danger. I cannot understand why better politics should mean worse debating. We should attempt to make Union debates a forum for political ideas as well as entertainment. The division between politics and debating, which Mr Hunter and Mr McMeekin seem anxious to make, exists in the other Unions which they disparage. The great strength of Glasgow has been the alliance between politics and debating. It is rather pointless to train people to speak when they have nothing to say.[77]

John Smith, along with an impressive number of his Glasgow contemporaries, was essentially a student politician, schooled in the Union's debating tradition, equipping him with strong debating skills that would be deployed to great effect in his later political career in the House of Commons. Indeed, politicians as diverse as Malcolm Rifkind and Derry Irvine are on record agreeing that, although John subsequently became a fine practitioner of the law, his debating skills were fully developed in the Glasgow Union long before he ever opened a law book, or went to the law courts in Parliament House in Edinburgh.[78]

Three
YOUNG GAITSKELLITE

IN THE LATE 1950s and the early 1960s, the Glasgow University Labour Club played a disproportionately important role in the workings of the Scottish Labour Party. The two organisations were closely integrated, and to a much greater extent than their Conservative and Unionist counterparts. Labour students were regularly deployed to canvass in local and general elections, and the party ran a weekend school at Aberfoyle with the Young Socialists[1] by way of political education.

The Labour Club at Glasgow was the main point of entry for young professionals to enter adult politics. One Tory student correctly identified the benefits that accrued from what he termed 'the largest and best organised body of young Labour opinion in the country':

> In recent years, it [the Labour Club] has demonstrated, in a way that no other club has, the tremendous advantages which a political training in the University can give to anyone venturing into more adult politics ... It is not too much to hope that the next decade will see several ex-club members reach Westminster.[2]

The key Labour Party figure at the time was Willy Marshall, the general secretary of the Scottish Labour Party, who was enormously encouraging of Glasgow students. Marshall spotted Smith's debating talents, and the party paid him to go out canvassing. In the summer of 1956, Jimmy Gordon first met John Smith in a Labour Party members' house on Waldemar Road, where both were enrolling new members.[3] By March 1958, Smith was talking part in the Kelvingrove by-election.[4] A friend in the University Labour Club recalls canvassing for Mary McAllister, the Labour candidate: 'John was full of beans, and went round the constituency on top of a bus, holding a megaphone, chanting, "Wash yer faces, and come out and vote!"'[5] The slogan must have done some good, because Labour gained the seat from the Conservatives on a swing of 8.6 per cent, although McAllister relinquished it a year later in the general election of 1959.[6]

So impressed was Willy Marshall that he wanted to blood Smith in an unwinnable seat at the 1959 election, but Smith later claimed that he looked up the relevant Act of Parliament and discovered he was too young. In fact, Smith was just unlucky: two days after celebrating his 21st birthday on 13 September 1959, qualifying him to stand as a candidate, Harold Macmillan announced the date of the general election for 8 October 1959. There wasn't time to put Smith into a seat at such a late stage.

But such was John Smith's enthusiasm for politics that he and Donald Dewar famously hitched a lift on a fish lorry in order to attend a Fabian Society weekend school in Guildford. Dewar recalled hitchhiking 'in suits, carrying suitcases by the side of the A74 . . . we must have been a totally ridiculous spectacle.'[7]

In 1961, aged only 23, John Smith was selected as Labour's candidate in the East Fife by-election,[8] partly thanks to Willy Marshall, but also with the patronage of John Muir, Labour's organiser in the locality. East Fife, the largest of the Kingdom's four seats, mostly comprised pretty coastal villages and large tracts of farmland – in other words, sticky territory for Labour. However, there were one or two pockets of Labour support, including Leven and Kennoway, the latter a large mining village.

The by-election was caused by the death of Sir James Henderson-Stewart, who had held the seat for 28 years, building up a massive majority of over 15,000.[9] Sir John Gilmour, a local farmer, emerged as the new candidate. The son of a former Secretary of State for Scotland of the same name,[10] Gilmour had been chairman of Sir James's local Liberal Unionist Association. Despite the party's name, the Liberal Unionists had broken away from the Liberals in the 1930s, and were allied with the Conservatives in Scotland, most of whom stood, confusingly, as Unionists. Gilmour chose to stand under the Unionist label, as he had done when he had unsuccessfully contested Clackmannan and East Stirlingshire at the 1945 general election. However, Gilmour faced a tougher task in maintaining his majority than his predecessor because the Liberals chose to put up a candidate for the first time in eleven years, in addition to Labour. Even so, as one journalist commented at the time, had Sir John Gilmour not been returned it would have been 'the biggest surprise since the ancient and royal burgh of Auchtermuchty went bankrupt [1818]'.[11] Such a remark was perhaps an exaggeration because Herbert Asquith had held the seat for over 30 years at the end of the nineteenth century, and the beginning of the twentieth century.[12]

Figures from the centre and right of the Labour Party came along to support John Smith in his by-election campaign, including Dick Mabon[13] and Denis Healey, then a leading member of Hugh Gaitskell's shadow Cabinet, as shadow spokesman for the Commonwealth and the Colonies.[14] Meanwhile, Hugh Gaitskell sent the traditional message of support to Smith.[15]

Notably, John's sister Mary and a number of her school friends journeyed to East Fife to help John's campaign. 'It was an absolute hoot, especially going up to the wealthy houses. We were very polite.'[16] However, Mary got into big trouble from her father for campaigning on a Sunday, the Sabbath. Worse still, a report appeared in the *Glasgow Herald* mentioning Mary's visit.[17] Despite a temporary falling out with her father, Mary never regretted helping out her brother in the campaign.[18]

A large contingent from the Labour Club also descended on Fife to canvass in support of their former chairman. Jimmy Gordon, then a Distributist, was especially valuable because he owned a car. Kenneth Munro recalls a weekend spent with Jimmy in a posh caravan borrowed from a friend. (Kenneth had caught the political bug, and stood unsuccessfully as the Labour candidate for West Aberdeenshire at the 1964 election, finishing a distant third.)[19] During the campaign, Jimmy Gordon met a few Labour MPs (including Willie Hamilton, then the member for Fife West), and was impressed, so much so that he joined the Labour Party, and stood as the Labour candidate for East Renfrewshire at the 1964 general election, then the third safest Tory seat in Scotland.[20] Smith's campaign proved equally hard going in what was then a very traditional Tory area.

At one point, the Liberal candidate, Donald Leach, a London-born physicist, though with a Dundonian wife,[21] accused the Labour Party of degenerating into a second Conservative Party. At a press conference in Cupar, Leach commented that it was remarkable how Smith could write his election address without mentioning nationalisation.[22] Two days later, Smith retaliated by condemning the Liberals as 'a political circus – not a political party'. The Liberals, he claimed appealed to people who were disgruntled with the Tories, but too snobbish to vote Labour. The Labour Party wanted to change society; the Liberals merely wanted to paint it a different colour.[23] Without doubt, Leach ran the liveliest campaign of the three parties. Many of his rallies began with a rendition of 'Donald, whaur's yer troosers?', and one weekend, he organised a car cavalcade, accompanying by a piper, through many of the villages in the constituency, much to the disdain of Sir John Gilmour, very much a traditionalist, who likened the weekend cavalcade to a 'circus advertisement'.[24]

John Smith, as the youngest candidate, made a special appeal in his election address to the young people in the constituency, arguing that 'youth should have a chance'.[25] A *Glasgow Herald* journalist vividly describes Smith's valiant efforts in the final week of the campaign: 'He has as little as two and at most 70 electors at his meetings. He bustles about the division from 7 am to late at night, hardening the pockets of support in Leven and Kennoway . . . and going for the Government policy with everything but the 50-megaton bomb.'[26] Smith's campaign received an unexpected boost in its last few days when the government announced a substantial pit closure programme, involving sixteen Scottish collieries. At the last minute, Smith's helpers busily turned out leaflets that read: 'Pits closing – polls opening.'[27]

There was also a BBC television debate on Monday, 6 November involving the three candidates. The show's format suffered from not having any of the East Fife constituents present for the debate. Instead, their voices came out of a tape recorder. Deprived of good old-fashioned village hall heckling, the debate fell flat. One reviewer singled out Smith for praise, describing him as having 'a shining morning face of one who had not long emerged from his chrysalis of Glasgow University, but was not a bit worse for that'.[28] By the eve of polling, Smith had made a real impact in the constituency. According to *The Scotsman*: 'Labour are, indeed, likely to hold their own with the finest young candidate they have had in Scotland for many years . . . He is 23 and his political acumen, allied to the candour and appearance of his youth, has created a real impression here, even in opposing camps.'[29]

When the results of the East Fife by-election were announced at the County Hall, Cupar in the early hours of 9 November 1961, Sir John Gilmour polled nearly 16,000, way ahead of Smith on 9,000, but Smith pushed Donald Leach into third place, if only by a slender margin of 96 votes.[30] Smith, after congratulating Sir John, claimed that the result was 'quite a victory against the trend of recent elections'.[31]

John had stood no chance of winning the by-election, but East Fife had been a good shop window for him. Instead of standing and losing, ditching East Fife, and searching for a more promising Labour seat, John announced from a very early stage that he was staying on for the 1964 general election. Jimmy Gordon believes that from an early stage in his political career, Smith demonstrated 'a basic sense of loyalty and duty, and a sense of the right thing to do'.[32] Although Smith was short-listed for the Glasgow Rutherglen by-election, he later admitted that he was only there to make up the numbers,[33] and he lost out to his friend and Glasgow councillor, Gregor MacKenzie.[34]

Around this time, John received a letter from Norman Hogg, then Secretary of the South Aberdeen Labour Party, inviting him to put his name forward to become the Labour candidate. John replied that he had already committed himself to East Fife for the 1964 general election. Apart from a desire not to

break his word, Hogg recalls that John's other reason for turning down
Aberdeen South was that he wanted to complete his law studies: 'Unlike
Donald Dewar, John always had a well-ordered approach to his professional
life.'[35] As soon as Smith turned down the seat, Donald Dewar gained the
nomination, contesting the 1964 general election, and unseating Lady
Tweedsmuir in the Labour landslide of 1966. Thus there was a period when
Donald Dewar was inside the House of Commons, while John struggled to be
selected for a seat. By 1970, the positions would be reversed: Donald lost
Aberdeen South, and Smith became the MP for Lanarkshire North. Dewar
had a long search for a seat, not returning to Parliament until 1978.[36]

Derry Irvine recalls that after the East Fife by-election, John was received
as 'a conquering hero'[37] at Glasgow University, even though he had finished
a distant second to the Tory candidate. Shortly after the by-election, John was
back debating, this time speaking against a Conservative 'Government'
motion endorsing the pay pause, opposing coal subsidies and refusing
housing subsidies 'except for slum clearance'. As Philip Noel-Baker, the
Labour MP for South Derby[38] looked on admiringly, a reviewer of the Inter-
'Varsities debate commented: 'John Smith held the House with his customary
fluency and sound argument, and proved that East Fife had sent back a more
statesmanlike Convener of Debates.'[39] Reviewing the same debate, Donald
Dewar noted: 'The new Smith, looking a little smooth like a cat after a
dooking and with [Dick] Mabon hands-in-pocket pose, was nasty in the
nicest possible way.' As early as February 1962 Smith is described by one
reviewer as 'that consummate politician . . . whose style incorporates all that
is best in the Glasgow tradition, and provides a model for every top-notcher
to emulate'.[40]

Both John Smith and Donald Dewar greatly increased their public profiles as
a result of the active part they had played in the campaign to elect Albert
Luthuli,[41] ex-Chief of the Abase-Makolweni of the Grantville Mission Reserve
in South Africa as Rector of Glasgow University.[42] Indeed, at Smith's funeral,
Donald Dewar paid tribute to 'John working his guts out' to elect Luthuli 'at a
time when the horror of apartheid was not a universal student cause'. Luthuli's
victory was poignant and symbolic: he could not take up his appointment
from behind prison bars.[43] In 1960, the Verwoerd government had banned the
ANC, provoking demonstrations, one-day strikes and bus boycotts. Luthuli's
role in organising these protests resulted both in his detention, and in his
winning the Nobel Peace Prize in 1961.

But in recalling Luthuli's successful election as Rector, it is often forgotten that there were false starts along the way. Many students at Glasgow University took several years to be roused out of apathy over apartheid. Three years earlier, the Labour Club, together with GUSNA and the Liberals, had combined forces in a campaign to elect the Rev. Michael Scott, another anti-apartheid activist, but Scott finished a poor third behind Lord Hailsham, the Conservative candidate, and Billy Butlin, MBE, owner of the famous Butlin's holiday camps. Smith hardly covered himself in glory as Joint Chairman of Scott's campaign, alongside the Liberal, Gordon Hunter. One University observer noted in October 1959: 'Smith does nothing about half the campaign's work, and Hunter does nothing about the other half. Look for Smith's hand writ large in the campaign's less reflective aspects: for he is a man of action even when he doesn't know what he is doing.'[44]

To be fair to Smith, it didn't help that the Rev. Michael Scott was not as charismatic a candidate as Luthuli, and was something of a maverick, having been a communist in the 1930s. Nor did some members of the campaign team's want to press an anti-nuclear, as well as an anti-apartheid message. Neil MacCormick recalls that Smith and his Labour Club colleagues were 'expedient CNDers' for the duration of that campaign.[45] Scott's campaign also lacked the necessary funding, and, after the initial launch of The Scottsman pamphlet, replete with the unimaginative slogan 'Michael Scott – the serious candidate', on 18 May 1959, the campaign soon petered out. By contrast, the Hailsham and Butlin campaigns waged an expensive pamphlet war. Hailsham's campaign publications included pungent cartoons and poetic parodies of Smith and Dewar drawn by Ian Jamieson, a gifted student artist of the time, including 'Chuck it, Smith' and 'Dewar's Lament'.[46] The result, announced on 26 October 1959 – Hailsham 1,428, Butlin 1,182 and Scott 493 – made grim reading in the Scott camp.

In the same month, Smith had stepped down from the Union Board's assistant secretaryship to spend more time as chairman of the Labour Club, and to concentrate on his history finals.[47] The tactic paid off, and he gained a good second-class honours degree. It was common for students not to complete their terms in certain student posts. Nevertheless, Smith had completed his earlier term as Present Student Member of the Union Board in March 1959, declining Jimmy Gordon's suggestion that he become Convener of Debates in the subsequent year, a post which he took up two years later in March 1961,[48] after a year as President of the Dialectic Society.

For all his subsequent vigour over the Luthuli campaign, Smith developed a reputation from an early stage of his political career as a man who did not greatly involve himself in the detailed organisation of anything. He would turn

up to events, speak with passion about injustice, but he never liked committees and was most definitely not a political organiser in the mould of
Jimmy Gordon or Donald Dewar. Rather, Smith's great strength lay in his
ability to mobilise and motivate his political contemporaries.

Kenneth Munro met John Smith the day he matriculated in October 1959,
when John was chairman of the Labour Club. As a general rule, the Chief
Whip was in charge of recruiting new students at the Freshers' Fair, but John
Smith had dropped by, and persuaded Ken to join the Labour Club.[49] Munro
went on to become chairman of the Labour Club in 1962–3.

Meta Ramsay had come up to Glasgow University in 1955. Her first
impression of John Smith was that he was 'an aggressive wee debater from the
Highlands'. However, she was indebted to him one summer vacation when
she received a telephone call from a union representative, objecting to the
Student Representative Council (of which she was president) sending out
students to work during an industrial dispute. Ramsay was horrified, and
removed the relevant job adverts from the notice board. However, the
employment convener, a Conservative, complained, claiming that the SRC
was supposed to be apolitical and that its president was behaving in a political
manner, and put down a motion. Meta Ramsay chose to make it a motion of
confidence, allowing her to argue her case from the floor of Council. As Meta
sat in the Council rooms, all dressed in her ceremonial robes, in marched John
Smith with a small army of students, who had been dragged out of the beer bar
to provide moral support to Meta, stamping their feet in agreement at the
appropriate times, and providing lobby fodder when it came to a vote. Ramsay
was never in danger of losing the vote, but she appreciated the gesture, and
likens it to 'the US cavalry coming in'.[50]

Quintin Hailsham's Rectorial victory in 1959, and Rab Butler's three years
earlier, reflected the high tide of Conservative dominance both at the
university and in Scotland more generally.[51] At the 1955 general election, the
Conservatives, together with their allies the Liberal Unionists, the National
Liberals and the Liberal-Conservatives, held more seats in Scotland than the
Labour Party.[52] However, the traditional link between Unionism and the
Conservative Party was beginning to break down even in the mid-1950s.

At university-level politics, the other political clubs began to resent the idea
of the Glasgow Rectorship becoming, as one student put it, 'a sinecure post for
semi-successful Tory politicians or the Rector's gown a sort of consolation
prize for not getting the key to No. 10'.[53] At Rab Butler's installation as Rector
in March 1958, several hundred students engaged in a riot at St Andrew's Hall.
Rarely can an event have been so variously reported. While most accounts

agree that missiles, in the form of tomatoes and bags of flour, were thrown, *The Times* and the *Express* claimed that Butler had been hit by a huge cabbage, *The Scotsman* claimed a turnip had been hurled, while, according to the *News Chronicle*, one student had part-filled a large chemical bottle with urine, and had attempted to sprinkle it over Butler from the balcony before being caught by an attendant. The Butler Rectorial Riot was even reported in Italy by the *Gazetta del Populo* in Turin, albeit inaccurately: 'At the English [!] University of Glasgow the installation of Mr R. A. Butler produced an unusual display of excitement.'[54] Dick Mabon recalls that Butler 'behaved like a gentleman', never for one moment contemplating retaliation, despite being covered in flour and draped in toilet paper.[55]

While Glasgow students could not be roused out of their apathy about apartheid in 1959 (nor indeed a year later, when a boycott of South African goods flopped), at least all the campaign teams on that occasion had condemned apartheid. Kenneth Munro, the Luthuli campaign committee chairman, believes that the horrific events at Sharpeville[56] concentrated minds.[57] Alongside Munro on the campaign committee were Donald Dewar, John Smith, Alan Alexander (then the Labour Club's whip secretary), and Menzies Campbell and David Miller from the Liberals. The Independent Socialists also offered their support, as did the International Club,[58] but it proved a difficult task to maintain discipline in such a broad alliance of the political clubs. Early on, an attempt had been made to persuade Stirling Moss to stand, but he pulled out, and Luthuli came into the frame quite late on.[59]

It is ironic that in 1962, after six years of largely absentee Tory Rectors, the Luthuli campaigners asked their fellow students to elect someone who would never be able to attend. Of course, the crucial difference was that while Butler and Hailsham could visit Glasgow as and when they wished, Luthuli's detention denied him the choice. Kenneth Munro describes the process of trying to keep in touch with Luthuli in South Africa as 'fraught'.[60]

The case against Luthuli's election was that while he was a good man, Glasgow would be making an empty moral gesture, allowing the Rectorship to fall into another three years of neglect. The Luthuli campaign countered thus:

> . . . the students of this university cannot declare an indifference to problems which are seen in an extreme, but by no means unique form in Africa. Racial toleration and a belief in the right of all men to a place in society are ideas worthy of support in Notting Hill or Glasgow as in Natal or Durban . . . The election of Luthuli will make it clear where this University stands. It will be a positive gesture gaining coverage throughout

the world. In South Africa, a country still traditionally sensitive to British opinion, it will be a sensation.[61]

In reality, as Kenneth Munro recalls, the notion of the working Rector had not yet really taken off at Glasgow.[62] Moreover, the likes of Menzies Campbell and Donald Dewar were pretty hard-bitten professional student politicians by this stage, perfectly capable of running Glasgow University's affairs without the presence of a Rector. As Menzies Campbell recalls, it was 'symbolic, a statement about our abhorrence of apartheid; it wasn't about a new refectory'.[63]

One of the things that the Luthuli campaign committee lacked initially, in contrast to the other campaigns, was the financial wherewithal to fund publications and publicity. Kenneth Munro therefore wrote a begging letter to trade unions, Liberal and Labour MPs and peers, Church of Scotland ministers, and well-known celebrities.[64] The best response came from around a dozen trade union branches, mostly, but by no means all, based in Scotland: for example, the Amalgamated Society of Woodworkers (West of Scotland District) sent the princely sum of £10. Of those who replied, only the Scottish area branch of the NUM refused to send money, arguing it had no powers to do so.[65] Seven Church of Scotland ministers sent money and messages of support. It seems they were targeted by the campaign committee because of the Kirk's well-known role in the anti-apartheid cause.[66] A number of high profile Labour MPs also sent money, leading Menzies Campbell to claim fairly accurately that the donation list 'reads like a list of the Left in the early 1960s':[67] Barbara Castle sent a cheque for £1, and apologised that it wasn't more; Harold Wilson enclosed 'a small contribution' (amount unknown), as did Anthony Wedgwood Benn, who commented, 'What a wonderful idea to nominate Lutuli.' Ten other Labour MPs sent contributions, as did a similar number of Liberal and Labour peers, including Bertrand Russell, who sent the following message of support:

> There are few men who are worthy of honours. Certainly, men of power are rarely among these. Those who deserve our recognition are men who serve selflessly and often at great personal sacrifice for their fellow men. There can be no doubt that Chief Albert Lutuli is one of these people, and there are not many who can compare with him in his claim to distinction in the service of mankind.[68]

Luthuli's cause also received celebrity endorsement when Vanessa Redgrave sent the sum of £2, later penning a letter of congratulation to the campaign committee.[69] However, not everyone in the public eye was so forthcoming.

Cliff Michelmore, later of *Holiday* programme fame, but trying to remain impartial as the presenter of the *Tonight* current affairs programme,[70] wrote back: 'As one of my personal friends [presumably Lord Rosebery] is a nominee for your rectorial, I think it would be very unwise of me to support one of his rivals. In any case, I must admit that I am not very interested who becomes Rector of Glasgow University.'[71]

Nor was Lord Reith, the famous former Director-General of the BBC, overly impressed. In Reith's absence, his private secretary, Miss Barbara Hickman commented that 'he [Reith] fundamentally disagrees with the importation, into rectorial elections of people who know little or nothing about the mise-en-scene.'[72] Meanwhile Jeremy Thorpe MP declined to send any money, but agreed that his name could be used as one of those supporting Luthuli.[73]

The Luthuli campaign really began to catch fire when one of its organisers produced a black and gold ribbon badge.[74] But the ultimate success of the Luthuli campaign was due to the fact that the Conservatives had put up two rival candidates. Imperialist-minded Tories and Liberals, who could not stomach the idea of supporting Edward Heath's candidacy (nor that of an African Nationalist), put up the 6th Earl of Rosebery, then President of the National Liberal Party and Chairman of the Scottish Tourist Board.[75] Heath's campaign focused on their candidate's youth, modernity and modest background, which they contrasted with Rosebery's old age, stuffiness and privileged birth.

The Rosebery committee had oodles of money, enough to rent a campaign headquarters from an end of lease premises at 132 Byres Road. One night, the Rosebery team were having a party when Donald Dewar appeared with around 30 Luthuli supporters gathered from the Union spirits bar. Dewar and co. threw stink bombs at the Rosebery headquarters, but were beaten back into an ignominious retreat. Inevitably, the police[76] arrived, and there occurred a 'characteristic altercation between the policeman and Mr. Dewar'.[77] There is no indication in the *Glasgow University Guardian* reports whether or not John Smith was involved.

However, either on that night, or on some other night, John Smith and Donald Dewar, with the aid of Charles MacKay, a Liberal who had just defected from the Rosebery camp with a set of keys for 132 Byres Road, somehow acquired a large quantity of whisky and gin. By remarkable coincidence, on 20 September 1962, the Rosebery campaign had purchased a large quantity of liquor from Grants of St James's, a London-based firm of 'Importers and Bonders of Wines, Spirits and Cigars', including £20.9s.6d. worth of

Gordon's Gin, £10.3s.5d. of Smirnoff Vodka White, and a staggering £28.18s. of Cognac Planquette. The original invoice totalling £117.13s.5d. was used in the Luthuli campaign literature as evidence of the Rosebery camp's 'graft-spree'.[78]

It is alleged that in the early hours of one morning, John Smith telephoned Donald Dewar to say that he had acquired a set of keys to 132 Byres Road.[79] At the time, Elizabeth and Kenneth Munro, recently married, lived in a 'single end'[80] in Govan. Out of the blue, John Smith and Donald Dewar knocked on their door in the early hours, and announced: 'We've got a taxi, can we bring in some things?' They had acquired several cases of whisky and gin, but because the flat was so small, they couldn't think where to put it. John looked under the Munros' bed. John exclaimed to Elizabeth Munro, 'I've never seen so many shoes in my life!' The shoes were moved somewhere else to make room for the alcohol, which, according to Kenneth Munro, remained stuffed under the bed until the Luthuli celebration party two or three weeks later.[81] However, another source claims that the proceeds from the sale of some of the mysteriously acquired whisky were used to fund the campaign.[82] Over 40 years after the event, it is still not possible to prove conclusively whether the alcohol deposited in the Munros' flat was pinched from the Rosebery headquarters and, if so, who precisely stole it. However, one can speculate as to whether John Smith and Donald Dewar would have been admitted to the Faculty of Advocates and the Law Society respectively had they been prosecuted for any criminal offence.

Meanwhile, GUSNA had fielded a candidate of their own. Dr Robert McIntyre, a consultant chest physician, who had briefly held Motherwell for the SNP after winning a by-election (in the absence of the major parties) during World War Two, but had been unsuccessful at subsequent general elections. At the time of the Rectorial campaign, McIntryre was President of the SNP, but because of that, he lacked the necessary cross-party appeal.

On 21 October 1962, Albert Luthuli was elected as Rector, with Robert McIntyre finishing in a respectable second place. The day of the election provoked a response typical of Glasgow University in that era. A car packed with Luthuli supporters was blasting out messages on a loud-hailer when Rosebery supporters chased after the car, covering it in flour. By lunchtime, a crowd of around 2,000 students had gathered, some joining in, but by this stage the police had again been called, and they soon huckled[83] several rioters into the police vans. Some 32 students were detained at Her Majesty's pleasure by the local gaolers, kept in custody on the Monday night, and charged with breach of the peace and being 'part of a riotous and disorderly crowd' at a specially convened sitting of Glasgow Sheriff Court on the Tuesday afternoon.[84] Donald Dewar had been in the thick of the fight, as usual, but had not been arrested, though he did get caught out. Earlier that morning, Donald had rung up the secretary in the law office, where he was doing his apprenticeship, claiming he had 'flu. That ploy worked well until the partners in Donald's law firm turned on their television sets that evening, and saw their apprentice in the thick of the fight, leading the charge against the Rosebery supporters. Donald was duly eviscerated by each of the partners in turn.[85]

As time went on, the initial euphoria generated by Luthuli's election began to dissipate. People began to ask why Luthuli hadn't replied to any of the letters after he became Rector,[86] and whether the election of an absentee Rector had, after all, been an empty gesture: 'Perhaps we were all swayed too easily by the eloquent and persuasive speeches and publications of his sponsors: perhaps we succumbed to the wave of emotionalism which was aroused with such professional expertise.'[87]

On the other hand, perhaps the South African government withheld Luthuli's letters. Moreover, what the anti-apartheid cause needed more than anything was patience in what became a long struggle, and most Glasgow students knew that to give up on their absentee Rector would be to lend a boost to the apartheid regime.

As a Tory student at Glasgow admitted in the early 1960s, the Labour Club was 'by the general standards of the Left . . . a right-wing organisation'.[88] Dick Mabon prefers to say: 'We were categorised as right-wing, but really we were anti-Communist.'[89] At any rate, most members, including John Smith, were keen Gaitskellites. Smith actively participated in the Gaitskellite Campaign for Democratic Socialism (CDS). In February 1960, fifteen prospective parliamentary candidates, including Dick Taverne, Bill Rodgers, Shirley Williams, Ivor Richard and Gordon Borrie, wrote a letter in support of Gaitskell, whom they felt was becoming isolated among his own MPs. This sentiment in support of Gaitskell led a few months later to the formation of CDS. In October 1960, CDS produced a manifesto, and a by-product was *Counterblast*, a pamphlet supporting the concept of the Western nuclear deterrent.[90] *Counterblast* was signed initially by students at Cambridge, but its influence spread more widely, such that Smith became a signatory, certainly by the autumn of 1961.[91]

Donald MacCormick, Labour Club chairman, 1960–1, who became a journalist and presenter of *Newsnight*, later recalled: 'In those days, we were all rabid Gaitskellites, if that is not a contradiction in terms.'[92] Other views, however, were tolerated. On 20 October 1961, Jennie Lee, widow of Aneurin Bevan, spoke at a reception in the Debating Hall of the Union, opposing Britain's entry into the Common Market, advocating nationalisation and a free health service.[93] The Labour Club can be accused of not presenting a united Labour line on the major issues of the day, including Clause IV and the nuclear deterrent. The Club was disunited, but it displayed a marked reluctance to discuss its reasons for this disunity for fear of highlighting those internal divisions. When asked about this desire for cosmetic unity, Donald Dewar, the Labour Chairman, 1961–2 replied that 'in his opinion, if the Club had to choose between being a forum for the dissension of the Labour Party and a platform for the representation of general Labour ideas in the University, he would prefer it to fill the latter role'.[94]

However, in April 1962, one anonymous debates correspondent for the *Glasgow University Guardian* produced a harsher judgement:

> For the past few years the Club leaders have been more Gaitskellite than Gaitskell. Successive right-wingers, John Smith [1959–60], Donald MacCormick [1960–1] and Donald Dewar [1961–2] have bridled their left wing too severely and too successfully. What is surprising is that a revolt has not occurred before.[95]

Hugh Gaitskell, the then leader of the opposition, famously visited Glasgow on May Day 1962. Most people in Glasgow preferred Aneurin Bevan's brand of radical socialism, or that espoused by Glasgow-born Independent Labour Party figures such as James Maxton and John Wheatley. It did not help either that Gaitskell was widely regarded as a Hampstead intellectual, and that his speeches, though as well tailored as the cut of his suits, did not engage in histrionics.

To claim that it turned out to be a fairly eventful Sunday would be something of an understatement. Gaitskell had been invited by the Glasgow Labour Party to attend the Labour movement's annual May Day parade from George Square to Queen's Park. Unfortunately, the Glasgow Trades Council and the Co-operative Party sought to use the march to protest against Macmillan's decision to buy Polaris nuclear missiles from the United States, whereas Gaitskell had come to speak on the subject of unemployment.[96] And so it was that the multilateralist Gaitskell and his wife Dora had to walk at the head of a large body of Labour activists that included CND supporters, communists and an assortment of other left-wing activists that Gaitskell openly despised. The feeling was apparently mutual, judging by the '[H]ugh' signs daubed in white paint along the line of route. Smith's role, along with a group of other loyal Gaitskellite students, including Donald Dewar, was to form a protective cordon around the Labour leader and his wife, but they could do little to prevent the noisy protest when he addressed the crowd from an old bandstand in Queen's Park. Dewar, writing under the pseudonym 'Problemn' in *GUM*, gave a strongly Gaitskellite version of the riot that followed:[97]

> 'Cheer up boys, there's going to be a battle'. And there was: on May Day at the Queen's Park bandstand . . . A pointless rout as bad-mannered as it was politically inept, which will leave a memory and a scar . . . a yelling mass of hysterical men and women, screaming ill-concerted hate and waving their banners . . . And as they pressed and milled around the stockade that was the platform the CND placards rose and fell like Zulu assegais of last century, as the hysterical shouts of their war-dance rose to the sky. And through it all the reporter from the *Daily Worker* ate sandwiches at the press table and smirked . . . Then the police came and it was all over; nothing to do but go and boo the official party as it left . . . Through it all, Gaitskell – hardly a heroic figure in brown suit – grew in stature to the uncommitted and became a hero to his friends. He put his case with dignity and courage in conditions which gave these terms meaning. He got a standing ovation, and deserved it.[98]

However, Dewar neglects to mention that Gaitskell called on the crowd to ignore the CND protesters, dismissing them as 'peanuts'. Acutely embarrassing for Smith was the fact that many of the loudest protests came from activists inside his own Woodside Labour Party (Smith was a member of both the Glasgow University Labour Club and the Woodside Constituency Labour Party). Later, there were calls for the Woodside Labour Party to be disbanded, but fortunately for the activists, including the late Paul Foot, nephew of Michael Foot, the Glasgow Labour Party let the CLP off with a reprimand.[99]

It seems that on the evening of the Queen's Park riot,[100] Gaitskell misjudged the formality of the occasion by turning up in a red tie and a lounge suit only to see everyone else decked out in evening dress and university gowns.[101] He was lined up to speak third, immediately after Smith. But first a Liberal student, David Miller, gave a modest speech in which he said that he felt like 'the curate before the archbishop'. Smith showed no such modesty, and delivered a very politically mature speech extolling the virtues of self-discipline and unity if Labour were to fulfil its main function of regaining power.'[102] Smith's performance hugely impressed Gaitskell, so much so that according to Tom Clarke, attending the dinner as a Young Socialist, Gaitskell opened his speech by saying, 'I was conceited enough to think I was the archbishop.'[103] The following day, Gaitskell attended an informal tea meeting in Hamilton, during which he remarked to Tom Clarke: 'I heard a young student called John Smith in Glasgow last night, and I am sure he's a future leader of the Labour Party.'[104]

The content of Smith's speech that night demonstrated that he shared Gaitskell's belief in the pragmatic pursuit of power. As Brian Brivati rightly points out in his fine biography of Gaitskell, Smith as Labour leader 'shared some of the same ideological instincts, particularly that part of Gaitskell's ideology summed up as "the pursuit of power to put principles into practice"'.[105]

Neil MacCormick agrees with this analysis, arguing that from a very early stage in his political life, Smith's philosophy was that good ideas were no good unless you first gained power. And in order to achieve political power one required a cohesive political party to achieve 'a voluntary cohesiveness'. Such views seem to have come, once again, from John's father, who had first watched the Scottish Nationalist split (both at university and national level) in the late 1920s, and then saw the Labour Party break apart with the formation of the National Government in 1931. Especially in the early 1930s, either you were a Labour Party loyalist (having steered clear of Ramsay MacDonald's National Government), or you weren't. John was therefore 'a party man, but not a party hack'.[106]

One early episode in Smith's political career seems to suggest that he, along with Donald Dewar, sometimes took his student activism a bit too far.[107] The Queen's Park riot had shown that the aforementioned Woodside Labour Party, indeed the whole Glasgow Labour Party was split between Gaitskellite right-wingers and Bevanite left-wingers. Unfortunately, before tempers had been allowed to cool from the Queen's Park riot, Woodside's Conservative MP, William Grant, resigned to become Lord Justice Clerk, provoking a by-election on 22 November 1962 in a constituency that was eminently winnable: at the 1959 general election, the Tory majority over Labour had been only 2,084.[108]

An unhappy mixture of trade union delegates (generally, but not always right-wingers) and constituency party members (predominantly left-wingers) fought it out to see whether 'their' man would be selected at a special meeting of the General Management Committee, at which the short-listed candidates would speak. It is worth pointing out that in the early 1960s the concept of one member, one vote (OMOV) that so came to dominate Smith's short period as Labour leader (see chapter 22) had no bearing on the selection of parliamentary candidates. Rather, the big unions had an in-built advantage because any of the many local union branches in Glasgow could send virtually any number of delegates to the special meeting.

However, on this occasion, the left-wing constituency activists were particularly well organised, quickly coalescing around Neil Carmichael, a local councillor. Members of Carmichael's campaign team included Janey Buchan, later Glasgow's European Member of Parliament from 1979 until June 1994; her late husband Norman Buchan, Labour MP for West Renfrewshire from 1964–83, and then for the redrawn seat of Paisley South from 1983 until his death in 1990; the aforementioned Paul Foot; Maria Fyfe, who became Labour MP for Glasgow Maryhill in 1987, serving until her retirement in 2001; and Jean McCrindle, a leading supporter of the Miners' Strike in 1984–5.[109]

Meanwhile, the Glasgow trade unions were split between Jimmy White, the Transport and General Workers' Union (TGWU) candidate, and Arthur Houston, who had the backing of Alex Donnet, Scottish General Secretary of the General and Municipal Workers (NUGMW). Donnet very much agreed with Willy Marshall's view of promoting leading lights in the Glasgow University Labour Club, of which Houston, aged 38, was by far the most senior. Houston was something of a rough diamond, having served in the Royal Navy during World War Two, and then worked his way through college to gain entry to university. He was no smooth intellectual, but rather an instinctive believer in vigorous debate, had an equally vigorous approach to life, and as Labour Club chairman inculcated the younger students into the merits of active participation in the Labour Party. Houston graduated from Glasgow in 1959, and had stood unsuccessfully as the Labour candidate in that year for the ultra-safe Conservative seat of Renfrewshire East.[110]

The late Paul Foot recalled that many General and Municipal Workers' Union 'delegates' were rallied at a high tea, funded by the union, just before the special conference to which they were ferried by bus.[111] John Smith's involvement in the Woodside selection battle centres on his entitlement to vote at the selection conference and his role in ferrying a large number of pro-Houston delegates (some of whom had highly dubious credentials)in his car to the special conference. According to Janey Buchan, Smith voted as a delegate from a defunct branch of the NUGMW – one supposedly comprised of women cleaners employed in a local bus depot, but which had not existed for two years. She clearly recalls confronting Smith after the meeting: 'He was very shamefaced.' Bob McLaughlan, John's great friend, by this stage a member of the NUGMW's Scottish Office, claims that Smith had only stood in for someone at the last minute because they were ill. But even if this were true, the rules did not entitle Smith to stand in for someone else.[112]

Regardless of the antics of Smith and his fellow law students, Neil Carmichael emerged victorious, and won the seat by 1,368 votes. He went on to represent Woodside until 1974, and the redrawn seat of Glasgow Kelvingrove, until his constituency disappeared in the boundary changes of 1983.[113] Janey Buchan and Paul Foot remained indignant about the Woodside episode for years. Indeed, shortly after Smith's appointment to the Cabinet as Trade Secretary in December 1978, Foot wrote a piece in his column in the *New Statesman*, outlining Smith's Woodside misdemeanours.[114] The episode remained a source of acute embarrassment for Smith, and whenever he was interviewed about it, he remained evasive.

Although neither Smith nor Dewar exactly emerged with their reputations enhanced, Woodside merely reflected a reality then and now in Scottish politics – the great polarisation between left and right in the Labour movement, especially within the city of Glasgow. Both sides were slugging it out, doing their utmost to maximise their own number of delegates. And such behaviour was (and is) entirely typical of young, over-enthusiastic student politicians. As the late Paul Foot recalled: 'John and Donald Dewar were ardent representatives of the Labour Right in those years, and we in the very Left YS [Young Socialists] were hotly opposed to them. But I always had a high regard for both of them, and liked them.'[115]

One of Smith's holiday jobs as a student has passed into folklore. His first job had been fairly dull, working in the motor taxation department in Ardrishaig, but in a later summer as a law student, Smith (brazenly claiming that living in Ardrishaig meant that he knew all about boats) managed to get a job with J. & J. Hamilton, owners of a small fleet of West Coast puffers, the little coal-fired boats that carried freight around the Firth of Clyde. At an earlier age, John had signed on as an unpaid deckhand aboard the fishing smack *Harmony* but, having failed to tell his parents where he'd gone off to, received a good hiding from his father via the use of his father's tawse, the leather strap then used in most Scottish schools to administer corporal punishment.[116]

The young law student became a cook and general dogsbody, mostly referred to as 'the boy', on *The Invercloy*. No one is quite sure how many of the tales Smith told of that summer are apocryphal. However, it seems that as cook, Smith was expected to stick to just the two traditional ways of Scottish cooking: everything had to be either fried or boiled to within an inch of its existence. Sensitive about preserving the boy's innocence, the skipper of the boat initially put up a sign: 'Don't call the cook a ******.' But, during a choppy passage across the Minch, Smith threw up in one bucket, while peeling potatoes in another. Afterwards, the skipper changed the notice to: 'Don't call the ****** a cook.'[117] On another occasion, John was despatched ashore in bright sunshine to telephone the owners that the boat had been unavoidably detained by thick fog.[118] The nostalgia and humour associated with the days of the West Coast puffers were captured in a well-loved book, *The Tales of Para Handy*, written by Neil Munro, which was later made into an equally popular, but very Scottish, television series of the same name. Former members of the Cabinet are asked to leave a book in the House of Commons library when they leave office, and on Labour's defeat in 1979, Smith left Neil Munro's book.[119] For the rest of his life, Smith retained a love of the sea.

His experiences with the puffers gave Smith, if his Ardrishaig childhood hadn't already done so, 'a unique – and quite magnificent – introduction to the Western Isles and the start of a life-long attachment to them'. In later life, he became very sentimental about this group of disparate islands. For a man who later became renowned for his speaking performances in the House of Commons, Smith was normally very prosaic when it came to committing his thoughts to paper. The following description is therefore almost lyrical by Smith's normal standards: 'Heaven, for me, is walking on the springy machair at the edge of a white Hebridean beach watching the summer sun sparkle on the ultramarine sea.'[120]

Whether his children liked it or not, year after year the Smith family eschewed the warmth of the Mediterranean (although in later years, the Smiths went on a number of trips to France), holidaying instead on the Inner Hebridean islands of Mull or nearby Iona, and paid visits to the nearby islands of Islay, Jura, Tiree and Coll. John's children eventually came to love these holidays, as his eldest daughter Sarah later revealed:

> Perhaps my father's most important legacy to us as a family comes from his love of the Highlands and the Western Isles. He resisted our pleas for holidays in France or Spain, and I am glad now that he did. Our family holidays were in the West Highlands and we too came to be enchanted by their beauty and peace.[121]

Smith drew so much pleasure from these holidays that he admitted that they occupied 'a special place in my life, almost in what I might pompously call my philosophy of existence'. Maybe Smith was a 'home buddy' after all (see chapter 1). Had his mother not gone to the mainland to give birth, Smith would have been born in Islay. He regarded himself as 'almost a Hebridean';[122] it was just that he could only return 'home' to the Hebrides on holiday.

Smith's favourite island was Iona, which he described as 'the almost perfect miniature of the Inner Hebrides'.[123] This tiny island saw the birth of Christianity in Scotland when the Irish monks led by St Columba first landed in AD 653. Despite the tourists who flock in the summer to see the ancient abbey, now fully restored, it is still a place of special peace and spirituality. The Rev. Douglas Alexander[124] recalls that Smith returned to Iona again and again, not only to rest, but 'to know recreation as literally re-creation'.[125] Smith would worship unobtrusively in the restored abbey, and clamber to the top of Dùn I, the only hill on the island, wishing there were Munros to climb. Sarah Smith recalls the Smith girls' love of wild flowers on Iona – 'we were very girly girls' – and she and her two sisters would go down to the island's many beaches to poke about for hours in the rockpools or gather shells. When the weather was too inclement to venture outside, John would stick numbers on the keys of a piano so that the girls could pick out a favourite tune.[126]

The great love of John's life was his wife. John doesn't seem to have been involved in a serious relationship until he met Elizabeth Bennett at a Glasgow University Union dance in the autumn of 1962. Indeed, Jimmy Gordon recalls: 'I only remember John and Elizabeth.'[127] By this stage, Smith had just gained his MA in history, and had begun studying for his law degree. Meanwhile, Elizabeth was in her final year studying for a degree in modern languages. Before she knew John personally, she had heard of him as the man who had stood at such a young age in the East Fife by-election a year earlier.[128] She describes herself at that stage as being 'non-political though leftish'.[129] Two contemporaries disagree with that sentiment, arguing that Elizabeth was 'quite a Tory'.[130] Elizabeth was never a Tory. Their view of Elizabeth's politics has more to do with her respectable, bourgeois background, and the fact that she was always immaculately turned out, even in her undergraduate days. Jimmy Gordon also dismisses the idea of Elizabeth as a Tory as 'nonsense'.[131] Elizabeth came from a middle-class family in Glasgow, where her father, Frederick Bennett, worked for the Eagle Star insurance company. Although Frederick did not go to university (Elizabeth becoming the first member of her family to do so), she recalls her father as 'a self-improvement person', always anxious to gain the requisite insurance exam certificates.[132]

Elizabeth was born in Ayr, where the Bennetts lived until Elizabeth was aged six, when the family moved briefly to Dundee for two years, before settling permanently in Glasgow. Elizabeth has very vivid and happy memories of childhood family holidays spent in Arbroath, then a thriving fishing community. There, Grandma Bennett, an unmarried aunt and a great uncle (a widower) shared a large house by the sea. Elizabeth was educated at Hutchesons' Girls' Grammar School, one of the fee-paying schools in Glasgow. Tragedy struck the Bennett family, however, when Elizabeth's father died when she was only seventeen, and sitting her sixth year studies exams.

The extended family stepped in to help out. Elizabeth remembers: 'We didn't really cope.' Elizabeth's mother, also Elizabeth, came from a generation unable and unwilling to share her bereavement with others.[133]

Elizabeth Shanks was a genteel woman, who never worked, hailing from the Dennistoun area of Glasgow. She was not politically minded, but both her uncle and her grandfather had been active in Scottish politics. Robert Shanks had served as a Liberal councillor in Glasgow before World War One, but lost his seat, having become a conscientious objector. Robert then devoted the rest of his short life – he died in 1921 – to a study circle that attempted to apply Christian teachings to national and international problems.

Elizabeth's grandfather, William Shanks, also drew much of his radicalism from Christian teaching, but William became attracted to the cause of Scottish home rule before the Great War, joining the League of Young Scots. Famously, this radical group opposed King Edward VII being crowned Edward the Seventh of Scotland and England because no Edward had hitherto been sovereign of both nations. Under cover of darkness, the Young Scots had chiselled off the 'VI' part of 'Edward VII' on the newly installed red pillar-boxes in Glasgow. William Shanks briefly joined the Liberal cause during World War One, but he eventually reverted back to the Scottish Nationalist cause when the SNP was founded in 1928.[134] Much later on, William Shanks' son, another Robert Shanks, became an active member of the Liberal Party (and its successor, the Liberal Democrats) in the Borders.[135]

After graduating from Glasgow, Elizabeth moved to London to work for the Great Britain–USSR Association, an organisation funded by the Foreign Office. The Association was an official channel of contact for professional Russian people. Elizabeth's job did not amount to anything grand: as an administrative assistant, she worked in a small office. She did not even travel to Russia (though she had as a student), but she met many Russians who came to Britain. These included members of the Bolshoi Ballet and Valentina Tereshkova, the first woman astronaut,[136] and was able to utilise her knowledge of Russian.[137] Elizabeth also met Sir Fitzroy Maclean, the famous diplomat and war hero in Tito's Yugoslavia.[138] Meanwhile, John completed his legal training in Glasgow, and the couple kept in touch by means of cheap late-night flights – '10 pm departure, only two pounds ten shillings, between Glasgow and London'.[139] However, John took the view that Elizabeth should get a 'proper job' to help finance Smith's big professional move from being a Glasgow solicitor to an Edinburgh advocate. So, on Elizabeth's return to Glasgow, she enrolled for teacher training at Jordanhill College, and subsequently taught for a short time at Glasgow High School for Girls.

Elizabeth and John had a long courtship, lasting nearly five years. In 1966, John famously sold his car to buy Elizabeth an engagement ring. In much later life, when quizzed more closely by a journalist, Smith joked: 'It was a terrible car.'[140] John had told Elizabeth from the outset that he wanted to become an MP. Now, proposing to Elizabeth, John reminded her that he was offering an unglamorous life with many rough times along the way. But Elizabeth accepted not only John's proposal of marriage, but also the political life that would go with it. At the 1964 general election, John had stood for a second time as the Labour candidate for East Fife, and Elizabeth, though unfamiliar with political campaigning, enthusiastically joined in and became a quick learner. Most of all, she was struck by John's self-confidence. This was not arrogance on John's part: it was just a certainty about the kind of person he was. Elizabeth recalls it came from a belief in his professional abilities and his sheer love of the Labour Party. Even in the early days, John believed passionately in social justice, and in the idea of a society where people helped one another out. This contrasted with his emotional life, where he was very balanced and equable, experiencing very few highs and lows.[141]

It is fitting that John's widow, Elizabeth, chose as the title of her peerage in 1995 the hill – Gilmorehill – upon which Glasgow University stands, not only as a graduate in her own right, but as a mark of the influence that her husband had on the university, and the influence it had on him. It was some compensation for the fact that Smith had not been alive to accept the conferment of the honorary degree of Doctor of Laws in June 1994, just one month after he died.[143] In 1951, the university erected a gate to mark its quincentenary (1451–1951), situated to one side of the main entrance. Fifty years after that, Donald Dewar and John Smith had the honour of their names being added in gold lettering to the gate, alongside the other famous Glasgow graduates such as James Watt and Adam Smith.[143]

At Glasgow, Smith had been integrated from an early age into the workings of the Scottish Labour Party via the strong links that then existed between the Labour Club and the national party. He essentially carried on the same habits and he enjoyed the same lifestyle as he had done at university – staying up late and socialising, yet imbued with a strong sense of purpose and self-discipline, always driving forward.

Four

ADVOCATE IN EDINBURGH

W HEN SMITH STARTED his law degree, he became an apprentice at
Joseph Mellick's, a very small firm of Glasgow solicitors. Mellick
was not a sole practitioner, but very nearly. He also worked as a
lecturer in law evidence at Glasgow University, and John greatly admired and
respected him.[1] Mellick came from a Jewish background, and one part of his
business was to revise the deeds and wills of Jewish clients who had come from
Central Europe and wanted to take up Scottish names. One of John's regular
tasks would be to make a note of the client's original name, the new name, and
his or her occupation. For some reason, John took great delight in later years
in recalling the last will and testament of one Anatoly Goransky who'd
changed his name to Angus Gordon, but still listed his occupation as 'ritual
slaughterer'.[2]

The workload as a law student became, at least on paper, a lot more
demanding than as a history undergraduate because students had to combine
classes for their degree with their apprenticeship at their law firm. Classes took
place early in the morning, and then after work in the evenings. In between, the
apprentices earned perhaps only £250–£300 a year, working between 10 am and
4 pm, Monday to Friday. (John's main motivation in working for Mellick may
have been that he was offered £50 a year more than some of the other law firms.)[3]
Menzies Campbell recalls it as 'a funny life, doing academic classes in the
morning and the evening, and dealing with a small debt court summons in
between. It was supposed to be a marriage of practice and theory.'[4] Ross Harper
claims that the secret of coping with the increased workload as a law student was
either to get a relaxed law firm or not to go to classes or both. Donald Dewar
became notorious for not turning up at his law firm. In one of Dewar's
obituaries, Ross Harper recalled one occasion when Donald couldn't be found
until someone opened a strong room, and caught him reading the *Daily Record*.
Derry Irvine took exception to Harper's version of events: Dewar, he claimed,
had been reading the *Glasgow Herald*.[5] For most classes, attendance was only a
moral imperative, but Menzies Campbell recalls a compulsory accountancy
class where a register was taken. John Smith, Donald Dewar, Teddy Davidson

and Menzies would sit on the back row, and were completely hopeless at the subject. Donald removed the register, to protect those who had not turned up to the class, provoking an inquisition for a couple of weeks.[6]

Professor David Walker, Regius Professor of Scots Law at Glasgow, was, according to a fellow law student of John's, 'a most remote and forbidding figure', someone who set exacting standards in examinations and, it appears, had little rapport with students. Certainly, John was one student who did not always see eye to eye with Walker. One contemporary comments: 'Walker could see from the student newspapers that John was an active politician, and did not view him as a committed law student.'[7] Walker is long retired, but his general impression of Smith has not changed in the intervening 40 years:

> It was that he was an intending politician and was not interested in law as a study for its own interest. Indeed he absented himself a good deal from my and other classes when he was a fighting a by-election (I don't remember where) but being able he either got a note of the lectures from someone else or studied the topics from the books and passed the necessary exams. He was not, in my estimation, at all a distinguished student of law.[8]

Yet compared with some of his contemporaries, John was a reasonably conscientious law student. Menzies Campbell believes that John was always 'thoroughly professional' in the sense that he never handed in an essay late and never failed an exam. John was nothing like as conscientious as Derry Irvine, who became 'a phenomenon' in the academic sphere, but whereas 'Derry was determined to be the best, John was determined never to fail'.[9]

It was clear both to his lecturers and his student contemporaries that Smith was a student politician rather than a committed lawyer. Brian Gill claims: 'John wanted to train as an advocate, but as a prelude to a career in politics, not as a career lawyer.'[10] Menzies Campbell agrees: 'Politics was always the long-term intent. The law was there to give a greater flexibility in politics.'[11]

After leaving university with his LLB, Smith worked for Donaldson and Alexander, a Glasgow-based firm of solicitors, and after two years was offered a partnership. However, Smith chose to enter the Scottish Bar as an advocate. The move was in some ways risky, not only because of the need to pay the hefty sum of £500, but also because a trainee had to take a year out to work with an advocate, known as 'devilling'.[12] Anyone hoping to become an advocate, or to be 'admitted to the Faculty of Advocates' as it was known, had to endure an immediate loss of income because a trainee, or 'devil', had to show that he or she had been out of the practice of the law, and not earned anything from it in the previous twelve months.[13]

Finding fresh sources of income therefore became Smith's main priority. By betting on the outcome of individual constituency results at the 1966 general election, Smith netted himself a tidy sum.[14] Much later, he explained:

> It was a double bet. We discovered what I thought was an error by the bookmakers. They were giving evens in Conservative seats with a majority of 5,000 [in Scotland], but we thought there was no way Sir Fitzroy Maclean was ever going to lose Bute and North Ayrshire. So we put some money on that. Then, I didn't like the notion of betting on Conservatives, so we got 2:1 against John Mackintosh winning Berwick and East Lothian. And we put the two together, and did very well.[15]

Other more reliable means had to be found to make ends meet during Smith's year of devilling. He worked as a part-time lecturer, teaching law for surveyors at the College of Building in Glasgow.[16] Jimmy Gordon also put some teaching work John's way. Gordon had graduated with honours in classics and, lacking the private means to go into the law, had spent his spare time working both in television and in adult education to supplement his day job as a classics teacher. In neither field did he forget his university pals. He invited both John Smith and Donald Dewar to appear on Scottish Television's *Broadly Speaking*, a panel discussion programme in the early 1960s. As a result of Jimmy's help, John also led courses in public speaking at the Adult Education Service at Glasgow University, usually two hours in the evening, earning him around two guineas a time.[17]

Smith's other major source of income for the year came from working as a night lawyer for the *Daily Record* and the *Sunday Mail*. The job required him to examine every edition of the newspaper before it went to press, checking that the journalists had not libelled anyone. Typically, he'd spend two to two-and-a-half hours perusing all the articles that were intended for publication. While the first edition was being printed, he'd join some of the journalists in the Alhambra bar, and then have the newspaper brought to him hot off the press at eight o'clock for a final look over, before catching the nine o'clock train home to Edinburgh.[18]

John carried on doing this work even after he qualified as an advocate, taking on the Saturday shift for a few years, earning him eight guineas (better than the six guineas on offer for Monday to Thursday shifts on the *Record*) for looking through the pages of the *Sunday Mail*. Working as a night lawyer checking copy was a not uncommon source of income for young advocates and was also a useful way of making contacts.[19] Menzies Campbell, who was admitted to the Faculty of Advocates a year after Smith, in November 1968, and who followed him on the *Sunday Mail*, says that John would also have got to know Sandy Webster, then the editor of the *Sunday Mail*. Webster tolerated the maverick Labour MP Willie Hamilton[20] as a regular columnist. Menzies recalls that Hamilton's articles were 'not just defamatory, they were sometimes incendiary'. Any passages that might incur a contempt of court were removed.[21]

More risk attached to the Bar than becoming a solicitor, but there was the potential for more financial gain. There was also greater prestige attached to being an advocate, partly due to the fact that in the 1960s (though not nowadays) solicitors had no right of audience in the Court of Session, with advocates enjoying a closed shop on divorce and High Court cases.[22] Ross Harper recalls having a conversation with Smith during which they discussed the summit of their ambitions: Smith said he wanted to become Secretary of State for Scotland, and Harper wanted to become a Sheriff at Perth, because of the fishing possibilities on the Tay. Both sides set their ambitions too low in their very early days.[23]

Smith's 'devilmaster' in his year's training was Ian Kirkwood, now Lord Kirkwood QC, a Scottish High Court judge. In theory, the devil had a free run of the devilmaster's papers. In practice, however, Kirkwood, then a junior counsel, would ask the devil to draft writs for use in the Court of Session. These writs are summons or petitions, fairly tight legal documents, setting out the case being made against someone in the courts by the prosecution, or alternatively, 'the Defences', the response to writs. The counsel would tend to hand the matter over to the devil and tell him to get on with it.[24] Smith's task was to provide a straightforward averment of the facts of the case and the legal remedy being sought. When Smith returned with a draft, Kirkwood would go over it with John pointing out why he was amending certain parts of the draft.[25] Lord McCluskey believes that such drafting 'sharpens the mind. It makes you ask: what are the relevant facts of the case? And are they logical with the legal remedy being sought?'[26] Lord Kirkwood remembers that 'John took to it like a duck to water.'[27]

The devilmaster would also ask the devil to write 'opinions' on cases relating to everything from divorce, to claims for legal damages and defamation. 'The Opinion' is the legal position on a case that a counsel is asked to set out. The devil would be required to research extensively into the law books, draft an opinion, and the devilmaster would revise it. It was demanding work: the opinions had to be turned around quickly; and Lord Kirkwood was widely known as one of the most meticulous pleaders in Scotland. He ensured that every comma was in place, and that references were properly set out in the style required in the *Law Reports*.[28]

According to Brian Gill, who is now Scotland's Lord Justice Clerk, John would also have learned three other important skills while devilling: an acute sensitivity to the propriety and integrity of the law; aspects of the law which could not be taught at university but which had to be observed to be learned; and the basic skills of advocacy gleaned while watching his devilmaster perform as an advocate.[29]

It became apparent to Kirkwood from an early stage that Smith not only had a flair for the law, but also that he was a first-class public speaker. He also recalls commenting at the time to a close friend (a Scottish Conservative and Unionist MP) that politically, John was 'really going places'. John didn't mind in the slightest that his boss was a Conservative candidate.[30] Indeed, when Kirkwood invited the Smiths to dinner in the Conservative Club, John was 'absolutely delighted'. Kirkwood recalls that John had that ability to mix socially with everyone, and had absolutely no problems fitting into relatively closed world of the Bar, despite being from the West of Scotland.[31] In any case, the Bar had always had a smattering of advocates from the West and other parts of Scotland: Donald Robertson, from Argyll, became an advocate in 1960; Robin McEwan, from Paisley, later became a High Court judge; Ranald MacLean, who entered the Bar in 1964, was born in Aberdeen and brought up in Inverness, and also became a High Court judge; Brian Gill joined the Bar the same year as John in 1967; and Menzies Campbell, as we have already seen, followed a year later. Campbell recalls that the people from the West tended to be less socially well connected than their Edinburgh counterparts, and were 'a little spiky' as a result.[32]

The Scottish Bar may have seemed a closed world, but once inside, it was an intimate and friendly place to work. In those days, the Bar numbered never more than 120. Advocates called each other by their first names. Nowadays, the Bar numbers over 450. The shelves of leather cases holding the briefing papers now occupy the greater part of the ground floor corridor space in Parliament House in Edinburgh. The old intimacies are not quite what they once were. But in Smith's time, the prosecuting counsel would often invite his defence counsel for dinner, cocktail parties took place nearly every Friday night, and advocates would regularly attend Bar dinners, held in the Laigh Hall of Parliament House, the Reading Room of the Advocates' Library, or in a large private room of one of the city's major hotels.[33] John McCluskey remembers that there was very much 'a collegiate atmosphere among the Faculty of Advocates'.[34]

Smith also liked the characters within the Bar, including Sir Nicholas Fairbairn QC, the Tory MP for Perth and Kinross, a man of great eccentricity but, like Smith, not grey, not dull, a man happiest just being himself. John also loved Lord Stott, a Labour Lord Advocate and another great eccentric, so much so that he hosted a drinks party at his Edinburgh home in late 1984 to mark Stott's retirement from the Bench. Many advocates and their wives attended John and Elizabeth's wedding on 5 July 1967. The service took place at Glasgow University's chapel, and the reception was held at the Royal Stewart Hotel, on the corner of Jamaica Street and Broomielaw, now part of Strathclyde University. Annie, John's younger sister, was Elizabeth's brides-maid, and Jimmy Gordon was John's best man.

One notable family member missing from the wedding was John's sister Mary, who by this time had married Jack McCulloch and emigrated to Canada. Mary recalls: 'I remember Elizabeth saying subsequently, "You just took off to Canada and left us."' Jack had accepted a job with the Associated Electrical Industry in Canada, and neither Jack nor Mary initially expected to stay there for good. However, they eventually settled in Kelowna in the Okanagan Valley in British Columbia, where Mary worked in the fine arts department of a small college. She established a printmaking department, teaching etching and lithography, had her own studio, and in later life exhibited her work internationally. However, back in Scotland, John was always 'completely puzzled' that his sister had chosen to emigrate from his beloved Scotland for good: '"You are planning to come back, aren't you?", he would say.' But Mary had found her piece of Argyll in British Columba: a house overlooking Okanagan Lake, not unlike the Ardrishaig schoolhouse that used to look out on to Loch Fyne.[35]

Five months after John and Elizabeth were married, he was called to the Bar, taking part in a ceremony where he was sworn in, wearing his wig and gown, by a Court of Session judge, known by the grand title of Senator of the College of Justice in Scotland. At this crucial point in Smith's legal career, John McCluskey, nine years Smith's senior, became an important mentor. McCluskey had first met John Smith in a draughty schoolroom in Hamilton when they both failed to get selected as the Labour candidate for the Hamilton by-election (see chapter 5). McCluskey doesn't really see himself as taking Smith 'under his wing'. It was more that he had met Smith socially through Donald Dewar, then Labour MP for Aberdeen South, who came down to Edinburgh quite a lot. McCluskey was very much seen as 'a Labour lawyer', being groomed eventually for one of the law officer posts in a future Labour government, but in 1967 he was an advocate depute, a position that occasion-ally entitled him to take on an assistant in a difficult case for a modest fee. Smith, among others, became the recipient of this 'tiny degree of patronage'.[36]

As a junior, Smith could be called upon to examine some of the witnesses in the courtroom. At this stage in his Bar career, a junior would normally only be given straightforward witnesses, like the ambulance driver arriving to deal with an injured person, or the first person to arrive on the scene of a murder. Advocate deputes would also travel around Scotland where judges sat on circuit in places such as Inverness, Aberdeen, Dundee, Glasgow and Jedburgh. Assistants to advocate deputes might get £10 a day, plus travelling expenses.

An advocate is essentially self-employed, and usually has no hand in the selection of a client.[37] Rather, he or she has to wait to receive instructions from solicitors to act on behalf of clients. Smith would have relied a great deal in his early days on work from Glasgow solicitors – contacts that he would have established while working for Donaldson and Alexander.[38] But his hands were tied because of the archaic system of clerks, now abolished.[39] The clerks played a key role because they would approach a junior counsel on behalf of a client, and were very powerful because only four clerks handled around 100 advocates in 'stables',[40] each clerk having around 25 advocates on his books. Moreover, clerks also collected the fees. Payment, when it came, was always in guineas. A friend recalls that there was 'always a cash flow problem for young advocates.'[41] Often months would go by before clients paid up, and sometimes advocates were never paid at all. One firm of solicitors famously boasted about being able to fund its annual office party out of the interest accumulated from holding on to advocates' fees. Fortunately, Elizabeth's steady wage from teaching kept the Smiths' creditors at bay.[42]

A wise junior advocate would accept a Motion Roll from a clerk every time it was offered to him. A Motion Roll was a hearing on behalf of a client, usually at very short notice. Most junior advocates, despite being cash-strapped, had the sense not to demand a fee (those who did so, tended to fall by the wayside). The priority at this stage for Smith was to get into court at every available opportunity so that he could get himself known by his performances in court.[43] But Smith did not gain a huge amount of experience of conducting cases in front of a jury because civil cases involving juries were diminishing by his time. Rather, a major source of a junior advocate's income lay in dealing with claims for damages or personal injury, including road accidents, medical negligence and industrial accidents, as well as divorce cases.

Ranald MacLean recalls: 'Divorce cases were the crust we got to live off, our bread and butter.'[44] All undefended divorce cases were heard on Thursdays, Fridays, and on a Saturday morning in the Court of Session in Edinburgh in front of three to four judges, each of whom presided over perhaps eight to as many as ten cases each per Saturday morning. The vast majority of divorce cases went undefended, meaning the work was normally straightforward, but provided Smith with 'good experience on his feet in a real live court in front of a real-life judge'.[45]

In divorce cases where adultery needed to be proved, sometimes advocates would apply to the judge for an 'open commission', so that witnesses could give their evidence on oath away from court. Very often, the judge would only agree to a 'closed commission', which involved sending out a questionnaire for the witnesses to fill in. On one occasion, Donald Robertson applied for an open commission in a case involving two sergeants based in Germany with no real expectation that the judge would agree to it. To Robertson's amazement, the judge accepted the need for an open commission. The surprise then shifted to John Smith, who was in the courtroom queuing up for a Motion Roll. Having been very recently admitted as an advocate, Smith was not exactly inundated with work. Out of the blue, the judge, a bit of a wag, solemnly asked Smith if he could possibly spare the time to go to Germany as commissioner to take down the witnesses' statements. Robertson recalls: 'John could hardly believe his luck!'[46] John also dealt with defended cases on his own. A solicitor friend, also from the West of Scotland, who instructed John to represent clients, remembers him saying gleefully, after a success in a contest in court, 'That was a good wee win!'[47]

After Saturday morning divorce court work, some of the advocates and their friends would repair to the nearby Deacon Brodie's Tavern, only a few hundred yards away from Smith's flat, just off the Canongate.[48] Jimmy Gordon sometimes met up with John in the pub, and recalls that John Smith and John McCluskey often shared stories of what the accused had said – in terms of bad language deployed – when charged, or when suspects were rumbled. John told the story of one suspect who appeared unduly relaxed while the police ransacked his flat. He sat on the settee reading his *Daily Record*, until one police officer told him to stand up. At this request, the suspect said: 'Youse have hit the effing jackpot!'[49]

In later life, Smith used to delight in telling friends and fellow Labour MPs funny stories about his early legal career, such as the time a defendant escaped as the jury were giving their verdict. Apparently, Smith had commented: 'If only he [the defendant] had waited a bit longer, he'd have heard himself being found not guilty.'[50] Early on in Smith's career, when he was still a solicitor, two youths had stolen a car, and had headed west from Edinburgh, before being spotted by the police. They'd abandoned the car, absconded, and then been apprehended, and taken to Barlinnie, where Smith interviewed them:

SMITH: Where were you going?

YOUTH: Falkirk.

SMITH: Could you not have got a bus?

YOUTH: The bus service oot there is an absolute disgrace![51]

Sometimes the solicitors that Smith encountered were just as amusing a source of stories as the defendants. Another favourite Smith anecdote, later recalled by Simon Hoggart, involved one solicitor, a large man who had fought on General Franco's side in the Spanish Civil War. Smith had been brought in to defend a thoroughly unpleasant hooligan, and the gruff solicitor introduced John to the youth as follows: 'I have managed to obtain, at considerable expense, the services of one of the most eminent advocates at the Scottish Bar, a junior who is undoubtedly destined for high office. So sit in the corner, you wee c***, and listen to what he says.'[52]

Jimmy Gordon recalls that John was 'great company, you were never bored, and we had good laughs together. I will always remember his belly laughs rather than his elegant repartee.'[53] Kenneth Munro agrees: 'Sometimes you were in danger of dying with laughter. He was the best raconteur I ever met!'[54] However, Jimmy and Kenneth are at slight variance over whether John's humour was vulgar. Jimmy denies that was the case: 'It was more primary school, lavatory humour.'[55] Kenneth, on the other hand admits that John was 'exceedingly bawdy when necessary for the story'.[56]

Smith had also kept in regular touch with his other great friend, Derry Irvine. He prefers to see John's humour in a slightly different sort of light:

> John drew an enormous amount of pleasure and entertainment from the eccentric behaviour of ordinary people. Whether the people John encountered had been arrogant, pompous or vulgar, he saw the humorous side of life, and was a complete fund of real-life stories. They weren't jokes as such, in the sense of being fabrications, but real-life stories that he regarded as funny. John had this colossal talent for telling these stories, and whacking his knee when he came to the punch-line.[57]

Derry Irvine had left Glasgow in June 1962, and by the end of September that year became a student at Cambridge. Derry missed Glasgow and liked to go up to visit John, and John reciprocated, going out on drinking sessions with him. Smith became renowned for his drinking stamina, but he was never a match for Derry, who could drink until the early hours of the morning, and still get up reasonably bright-eyed the following day. James Naughtie accurately sums them up as 'a pair of gossiping, hard-drinking cronies with a happy lawyerly cynicism about politics mingled with an old-fashioned Labour loyalty'.[58]

There were inevitable strains between Donald Dewar and Derry Irvine
when Donald's wife, Alison, left Donald to live with Derry in 1973. Alison
married Derry the following year. Alison and Derry subsequently had two
sons. Derry Irvine strenuously denies the idea that he and Donald shared a
mutual hostility. The media, he claims have generated the idea that they were
'at daggers drawn' which is 'false'.[59] Everyone else interviewed for this
biography disagrees with Derry's analysis. It was said that Derry and Donald
did not speak at length until John Smith's funeral at Iona in May 1994,[60] but
relations between the two men subsequently thawed.

In the Labour government formed in 1997, Dewar, as Scottish Secretary and
about-to-be First Minister of Scotland, worked closely with Irvine, the Lord
Chancellor and chairman of the Cabinet Committee (DSWR – Devolution to
Scotland, Wales and the Regions) charged with shaping John Smith's
'unfinished business'.[61] Lord Irvine recalls that Donald and he not only shared
an equally strong commitment to the principle of devolution, but that Donald
was in and out of Derry's room discussing all aspects of the legislation in a co-
operative manner.[62] Undoubtedly, Donald and Derry's professionalism
kicked in when they were forced to work together as Cabinet colleagues, but
that doesn't mean they had repaired any of the damage from the past.

John Smith, the man in the middle, carried on his friendships separately
with Derry and Donald. Derry recalls that John was 'enormously grown up'
about what had happened. He took the mature view that these things
happened and that he wasn't going to stop his friendship with either of his
close friends, adding that 'John and I were like brothers' and describes their
friendship as 'an unbroken continuity' from 1959 right up until the day John
died.[63]

Five
THAT VITAL SPARK

P ROBABLY THE HARDEST and highest hurdle in becoming an MP
is convincing the selection committee. In safe seats, Labour and
Conservative 'gatekeepers'[1] control handings-out of seats that virtually
guarantee a political career for as long as a candidate wants it. After standing
unsuccessfully for a second time in East Fife in the 1964 general election, Smith
was turned down for seat after seat. He wasn't even a Labour candidate for the
1966 general election. By then he'd chosen to make a success of qualifying as
an advocate before turning his thoughts back to getting selected.[2] In the race
for the Labour nomination for the Hamilton by-election in the autumn of
1967, Smith and his friend John McCluskey lost out to Alex Wilson, a former
miner. This setback was to prove a blessing in disguise: on 2 November 1967,
Wilson lost the seat to the SNP's Winnie Ewing on a huge swing. Had Smith
been selected, it is unlikely that even he could have held the seat for Labour,
and being remembered as the man who lost Hamilton to the SNP might have
killed his political career.

Jimmy Gordon believes it is 'ludicrous really', that someone of Smith's
obvious ability had struggled to get into Parliament. He feels that it had
something to do with the fact that Smith had been such a well-known
Gaitskellite at university, and had actively campaigned against CND.[3] John
McCluskey recalls that 'seats were not allocated on the basis of middle-class
values, such as education or eloquence, or even of talent'.[4] Smith did the hard
work of visiting societies affiliated to the Labour Party and addressing union
meetings, but in those days high quality Labour candidates often found
themselves victims of behind-the-scenes union deals. During 1967, it appears
that Smith seriously contemplated abandoning his political ambitions for a
career in the law.

But Smith's luck turned. He learned that Margaret Herbison (more
commonly known as 'Peggy'), Labour MP for Lanarkshire North, intended to
retire from the House of Commons at the 1970 general election, having held
the seat for Labour since 1945.[5] Smith first heard of her intention from Dick
Stewart, her party agent and full-time constituency secretary. Stewart had

worked down the Lanarkshire pits before serious injury had forced him into an alternative career. He served on the old Lanarkshire County Council before being elected as the first Convener of Strathclyde Regional Council. As such, he strove to ensure that everything ran properly, and was renowned for his total incorruptibility at a time when parts of Labour's organisation – especially in Dundee and Glasgow – were riddled with corruption. Despite his physical ailments and diminutive stature, Stewart was not afraid of grabbing large Labour councillors by the lapels, pinning them against the wall, and telling them to 'effing' support council measures. He became known for his extremely colourful vocabulary when dealing with incompetence or deception. Such language became known as 'Harthill Latin'.[6] Such was his impact that when he finally stood down as Convener of Strathclyde Regional Council, the era that followed was referred to as 'post-Stewart'.

Even with Stewart's backing, the selection battle in North Lanarkshire was very close. Delegates gathered at the YMCA halls in Bothwell Street, Glasgow on an exceptionally cold January afternoon as the candidates sat together in a nearby waiting room. Willy Marshall gathered all the candidates together to inform them that the train from Shotts had been delayed due to snow, and would not arrive for at least an hour. He asked all the candidates whether they would be willing to wait until the train arrived. Tom Clarke,[7] very much the local candidate from Coatbridge, knew that most of the miners arriving from Shotts would support Smith (or rather Dick Stewart), but he didn't want to win in circumstances in which the party was split, so he agreed. Clarke led on the first two ballots, after which Provost David Smith of Dalkeith was eliminated, leaving Smith versus Clarke: Smith just edged the third ballot by nine votes,[8] much to the chagrin of Clarke. The trainload of miners from Shotts had been enough to swing the result in Smith's favour.[9] According to Andy McSmith, years later, both men could recite precisely by how much they had either won or lost that dramatic final vote.[10]

The morning after Smith's victorious selection battle, he returned to work on a High Court case, to discover that Ross Harper, who was working alongside him, had by an amazing coincidence been selected the previous night as the Conservative candidate to fight the Hamilton by-election at the 1970 general election.[11]

Dick Stewart became a huge influence on Smith's political life, serving as his constituency agent right up until the name Lanarkshire North disappeared in the 1983 Boundary Commission changes, when the constituency became known as Monklands East. In October 1992 when, as leader of the opposition, Smith gave the inaugural Richard Stewart Memorial Lecture at Glasgow

University, he praised Stewart's political talents and revealed that, 'I learned from him the crucial distinction between popularity and respect and how, whilst one may be pursued, the other has to be earned.'[12]

In June 1970, Smith comfortably held on in North Lanarkshire, albeit with a reduced majority,[13] reflecting the national swing. He had successfully entered Parliament, aged 31. The General and Municipal Workers' Union (GMWU) had refused to put Smith on their list, despite the efforts of Smith's ally, Alex Donnet. Later, the GMWU merged with the Boilermakers to become the GMBATU, and eventually the union shortened its title to the GMB, meaning that Smith became a member of the GMB after all, but only by virtue of the fact that he had been a boilermaker.[14] Martin Dempsey, later a Monklands district councillor, recalled the day that Smith was nominated to the Boilermakers: 'I took him to the old Trade Council – The Carlton. John was wearing a collar and tie. Some of us had never *seen* a guy with a collar and tie. But within ten minutes, he was part of them.'[15]

On 10 November 1970, Smith chose a Second Reading debate on the Family Supplements Bill to make his maiden speech. He began conventionally enough by paying tribute to his predecessor, Peggy Herbison. However, after only a couple of minutes on his feet, Smith introduced a note of controversy by attacking the fact that the Bill before the House would only distribute £7 million to the working poor, when the Conservatives had promised £30 million before the general election. £7 million, he remarked, was only £1 million more than the peak year for the Speenhamland system of poor relief way back in 1818. 'That is a statistic that the Secretary of State should bear in mind when he considers how generous he is to the present-day poor.'[16]

In short, the Bill was 'a niggardly attempt to solve a gigantic problem' and more 'a piece of window-dressing on the part of the Conservative Government than a real and lasting attempt to solve the problems of poverty'.[17]

Quite unusually for a back bench MP in those days, Smith made another speech the very next day during the Second Reading of the Education (Scotland) Bill in which he attacked the social effects caused by fee-paying schools in Scotland. He accused the Conservatives of lacking any practical knowledge of the Scottish education system, with the notable exception of his old Glasgow Union contemporary, Teddy Taylor,[18] the Conservative MP for Glasgow Cathcart:

> But then in this respect, as in so many others, he [Taylor] is just a gillie among the lairds. He is the one whom they can use as the popular exhibit

whenever they are accused of social prejudice. That is a role which I think
the hon. Member for Cathcart will serve for a long time in the Conservative
Party.[19]

Smith argued that because Scottish Tories did not send their children to
comprehensive schools, they had 'no proprietary stake' in such a system. He
mocked Conservative claims that Edinburgh's fee-paying schools contributed
to a good social mix, and suggested that Tory MPs should take themselves to
working-class areas of Edinburgh where they would see that there was no
social mix. Smith opposed the fee-paying system, not because of Socialist
dogma, but because it led to social injustice: 'We feel that it is wrong that,
because a small section of the community are able to use their social influence
and their money, they are able to aggrandise themselves and their children an
unduly high proportion of these scarce social resources.'[20]

   Good state schools depended on having bright pupils at their head, but they
were often deprived of their best pupils, leading to a demoralising effect on the
teachers and the children left behind in the state sector. Professional people in
Edinburgh had developed the mindset that if they did not send their children
to a fee-paying school, then somehow they were depriving their children.
Smith concluded by arguing that Scottish fee-paying schools were 'a class
symbol' and while they remained so 'we shall not get an educational system
which gives us social justice and a sense of equality.'[21]

   On 28 October 1971, Smith was one of 69 Labour MPs to defy a three-line
Labour whip to vote in favour of the principle of Britain's entry into the
Common Market, after a mammoth six-day debate in the House of
Commons.[22] John Smith explained his reasons for supporting membership of
the EEC in an earlier debate on the White Paper[23] on 26 July 1971:

> I am willing to give up some national sovereignty to gain a sovereignty
> which will be able to do something about controlling the international
> companies of the future . . . as a democratic socialist I believe that the
> fundamental of democratic socialism is that economic forces must
> somehow be brought under popular control and be fashioned towards
> social and political ends which the people determine. If we do not enter
> Europe we shall not be in a position to control them and achieve those
> economic, social and political ends which we on this side hold among our
> main political objectives.[24]

Dick Mabon, a leading pro-European rebel, describes the actions of the 69 as
'courageous – they put themselves on the line'.[25] Smith was proud to have
been one of the 69, and referred to it often in later life. But while he remained
consistent in his support for the European Community throughout his career,

in terms of his political development, although he was one of the 69, he did not become *part* of the 69, or rather, he never became identified with the Jenkinsites, that elite grouping on the Labour right. Bruce Millan recollects: 'John never fitted into that circle.'[26] Nor between 1970–4 did he join pro-European groups within the Labour Party, unlike many others.[27] Bill Rodgers agrees.[28] If anything, Smith's favourite leading politician of the time was Tony Crosland. In the early 1970s, Derry Irvine recalls having the occasional ham and eggs with John and Tony in the canteen in the House of Commons.[29] Yet although Smith liked Crosland, and knew him personally, that did not make him a Croslandite in the sense of being an acolyte or an active participant.

John Smith's other great *cause célèbre* as a back bencher was his long-running opposition to museum charging, and the adverse impact he perceived such a measure would have upon bequests to Scottish galleries. During the Third Reading debate on the Museum and Galleries Admission Charges Bill in October 1972, Smith argued that it was wrong for the government to vary conditions of trust deeds which stipulated that art collections be exhibited free to the public.[30] A year later, he pointed to the 'madness' of 'taking money from people at a door, imposing a deterrent effect upon their entering their galleries, and then taking 45 per cent of what is collected to pay those who collect it'.[31] Museum charging wasn't the sexiest political topic, but it showed Smith's sense of civic pride, some would say his high-mindedness. For him, it was an issue with no moral ambiguity – it was simply 'silly', 'petty and wrong'.[32]

However, Smith abruptly ended his short phase as an independently minded MP, and became a conventional loyalist, parking himself very much in the centre of the party. When asked to define Smith's politics at this stage, Bill [Lord] Rodgers replied: 'Very Scottish'.[33]

For a very short period after Smith became an MP in 1970, Elizabeth acted as John's personal assistant, doing constituency work. It proved disastrous. John was 'totally shambolic' in the way he ran his office. Elizabeth recalls:

> John didn't want to understand filing . . . He was always writing on the backs of envelopes . . . you got the blame if you tidied up his desk or moved anything . . . You'd done him a disservice. He was unreasonable. He would get angry, shout at you . . . At least his moods changed quickly. He never bore a grudge.[34]

Elizabeth and John were close enough to realise very early on that the experiment would not work, and was best abandoned. Nor was their experience atypical: when a couple with an equal relationship take on the role of 'boss' and 'secretary', especially when the office is in the marital home, it rarely works well.

As a back bencher, Smith carried on doing legal work. He gravitated more towards criminal work, partly because it was easier to prepare for than other areas of the law, partly because it was quite well paid, but mostly because criminal cases tended to be available at short notice, and normally lasted three to four days.[35] Ross Harper and Murphy supplied most of Smith's criminal work. Other advocates on their books included Menzies Campbell, Malcolm Rifkind, Nicholas Fairbairn and Michael Ancram. Harper made a special point of holding back vacation work for Smith, and when a young apprentice complained, Harper replied: 'You go down to his next hearing, and you'll find you're listening to the next Prime Minister.'[36]

It was a busy life, but necessary to augment John's meagre salary as an MP, and to support his young family. On 22 November 1968, John and Elizabeth had celebrated the birth of their first daughter, Sarah. Jane followed on 28 July 1971, and less then two years later, Elizabeth gave birth to their third daughter Catherine on 4 May 1973. Unfortunately, Catherine was born with a tumour on her left leg. Elizabeth became worried that the nurses hadn't brought her baby to her. The doctor took Smith aside, and told him about baby Catherine's condition. The baby was whisked to the operating theatre, and several anxious months followed before Catherine was given the all clear. Smith recalled her pulling through as 'my lucky break in life and I ask no more'.[37] Or as he put it to his friend, Kenneth Munro, 'When you've been down in the dark valley, it's marvellous to see the sunny uplands again.'[38]

As a result of working in criminal cases, John McCluskey recalls that Smith developed an excellent ear for false notes in the evidence, and could exploit the fact that the jury had to find the defendant guilty 'beyond reasonable doubt'. He believes that such an ability to convince an audience of one's case was 'an excellent training for parliamentary life'.[39] Lord Kirkwood agrees that Smith's style of 'persuasive oratory in convincing an audience of the rightness of one's case was perfect for politics'.[40] Smith later said that the best course in politics, as in advocacy, was to 'take people close to the decision, but let them make it for themselves',[41] a tactic he would deploy to devastating effect against many Tory ministers, including Leon Brittan, Nigel Lawson and John Major.

Ranald MacLean faced John Smith in the courtroom on a number of occasions in the period from 1972–4, when MacLean was an advocate depute. He discovered that John set high professional standards, and was not above reproving others whom he felt did not always meet his own standards: 'John could be unguarded. He wouldn't withhold his views. I was once reproved by him for mentioning [to the jury] that the victim in a case was the son of a policeman. John pointed out that the case had nothing to do with the father of the victim's occupation. I remember thinking, he's quite right.'[42]

In October 1969, just before Smith became an MP, he had acted as junior counsel to Nicky Fairbairn in the Paddy Meehan trial, which became a notorious miscarriage of justice. Meehan was falsely convicted of a violent murder and robbery in the town of Ayr. In July 1969, two men had broken into the house of Abraham and Rachel Ross, with the intention of robbing from the Rosses' safe. Rachel Ross later died of her injuries. By coincidence, the judge in the Meehan trial was Lord Grant, the Lord Justice Clerk who had resigned as a Conservative MP way back in 1962 to take up his judicial appointment, provoking the Woodside by-election that had so embarrassed John Smith (see chapter 3). Lord Grant was later criticised for making several apparently biased interventions during the trial, and one-sided directions to the jury in his summing up.[43]

It would take a further seven years of appeals to successive Lord Advocates and Secretaries of State for Scotland before Paddy Meehan was finally released, then given a Royal Pardon, despite frequent confessions from one of the guilty men, Ian Waddell.[44] While Nicky Fairbairn was instrumental in persuading Ludovic Kennedy to look into the Meehan case, doubts have been cast by people like Fairbairn on whether John Smith did as much as he could have done to help secure Meehan's release. In Andy McSmith's biography of Smith, Fairbairn is quoted as saying: 'He [Smith] preferred not to get involved in the Paddy Meehan case because it was extremely controversial. He chose to stand well back and keep clean.'[45] McSmith admits that John Smith wrote a private letter to the Secretary of State for Scotland expressing his concern that a miscarriage of justice might have taken place. However, McSmith is mildly critical of John Smith, pointing out that he did not take part in any public campaigns, and was 'too protective of his political reputation to want to link it in any way with a hardened criminal'.[46]

Such a conclusion is apparently strengthened by the preface of Ludovic Kennedy's book on Meehan. Smith is notably absent from those Kennedy acknowledges as helping him.[47] And yet, Smith lent his original case notes to Kennedy. We know this because on the night of the day John Smith died, 12 May 1994, Ludovic Kennedy appeared, by coincidence, on a special *Question Time* in Edinburgh (see chapter 24). As well as paying a short tribute, Kennedy said so.[48] Although Kennedy no longer remembers reading Smith's case notes, he admits he must have done. The reality was that John Smith's contributions during the original Meehan trial were, as Ludovic Kennedy admits, 'minimal': 'Had he made some important point in either examination or cross-examination, I would certainly have included it [in my book].'[49] The fact that

Kennedy does not thank Smith for his help in the preface of the Meehan book is due to the fact that his notes were of no use to Kennedy.[50]

One of John's relaxations, if that is the correct word, was to play tennis with John McCluskey most Tuesday and Thursday mornings in the Lords and Commons Tennis Club in Vincent Square. John Smith had first started playing tennis in the late 1960s while holidaying in France and Galloway with the McCluskeys. Smith took to playing with McCluskey on a weekly basis in Edinburgh. McCluskey recalls:

> John tried to knock the skin off the ball every time with this forehand. If he stood even the slightest chance of hitting the ball at 150 miles an hour, John would have a go at it; no ball was so irretrievable that he wouldn't run for it. It wasn't in John's nature to play a gentle deuce game; it had to be win, win, win. It was always a dour battle.[51]

Hugh MacPherson, a contemporary of Smith's from Glasgow University days[52] and later a journalist with *Tribune*, has a similar recollection of the future Labour leader as 'a figure who thundered round a tennis court to great effect using a fleet pair of feet and ferocious forehand – there being no time in a busy life to acquire a backhand'.[53] Donald MacCormick also recalls Smith's 'haymaking, all-or-nothing forehand drive'.[54]

Smith and McCluskey were both coached at Craiglockhart Tennis Club in Edinburgh by a Polish ex-Davis Cup player. After he had watched a Smith versus McCluskey game, McCluskey asked: 'What did you think of the tennis?' The Pole replied: 'That wasn't tennis; that was war!' Sometimes Smith and McCluskey would combine forces in doubles matches with two Italians, which Smith would turn into epic battles between Scotland and Italy.[55] When Kenneth Munro asked Smith if he'd like to play tennis, Smith replied: 'I've had lessons – I'd beat you!'[56] The late Bob McLaughlan also recalled that Smith 'liked the competition of debate and indeed he was a great competitor'. He cites an occasion long before Mrs Thatcher became leader, when John had commented that she was destined for much greater things. When Bob asked John why, the latter replied: 'Her car is often in the car park before mine.'[57]

When Labour returned to power as a minority government in February 1974, Harold Wilson offered Smith the post of Solicitor-General for Scotland. Joe Haines claims that the government omitted the post of Solicitor-General from the initial list of appointments because Wilson could not think of any bright Scottish Labour lawyers who were in Parliament. When Haines admitted this to the Lobby, half a dozen journalists shouted out Smith's name.[58] At first sight, it seemed an ideal appointment, especially given Smith's considerable legal experience. John McCluskey describes himself as 'the obvious candidate', having been considered as a law officer in the previous Wilson administration, 1966–70. However, he acknowledges that Smith had a more substantial claim to the post by virtue of the fact that he was an MP.[59] Smith discussed the possible career implications of taking the Solicitor-Generalship with Willie Ross, Secretary of State for Scotland from 1966–70, and by February 1974 newly reinstalled in his old post, as well as Lord (John) Wheatley, Labour's Lord Advocate under Clement Attlee.[60]

Smith refused Wilson's offer, reasoning that he might become stuck in a life of Scottish legal affairs, hampering his political advancement.[61] Derry Irvine recalls that: 'John passionately did not want to take the conventional route of a lawyer in politics, and had the sense not to take the job.' Derry had therefore advised him not to touch it, and to aim higher.[62]

Turning down a Prime Minister's offer of promotion is not always a wise thing to do, especially as a young back bencher. However, Bruce Millan, the Minister of State for Scotland, approached John on behalf of Willie Ross, the Secretary of State for Scotland, to ask if he wanted to become Ross's parliamentary private secetary. Millan recalls that John didn't particularly want to become what John described as a parliamentary bag-carrier, but Millan told him that it would be an opportunity to see how government worked, and that he would also gain experience of the Scottish Office. In any case, Willie Ross was so much his own man that Millan assured Smith he wouldn't have much to do, so Smith accepted.[63] In doing so, Smith turned down Roy Hattersley.[64] Hattersley had first learned of John Smith in 1967, while working as Peggy Herbison's parliamentary private secretary, and recalls her telling him that her successor was going to be 'a young Scottish advocate', a phrase with which he was unfamiliar, and 'could I take him under my wing'.[65]

After Labour's second narrow victory of 1974, this time in October, Derry Irvine recalls John returning gleefully from a meeting with Harold Wilson, recounting how the Prime Minister had said how wise Smith had been not to take the solicitor-generalship a few months earlier,[66] although Smith never knew if 'he was having me on'.[67] No wonder Smith was gleeful – he'd just been offered, and accepted, the post of Parliamentary Under-Secretary of State at the Department of Energy, succeeding Gavin Strang, the Labour MP for Edinburgh East since 1970, who moved on to a post at Agriculture. The Ministry of Energy, headed by Eric Varley, was Whitehall's newest creation, having been established in the dying days of Edward Heath's Conservative government, partly in response to the OPEC oil price hike in the previous year.

As Parliamentary Under-Secretary at Energy, Smith played the lead role in piloting the Petroleum and Submarine Pipe-lines Bill through the House of Commons, which brought into being the British National Oil Corporation (BNOC). The Heath government had had a miserable experience with British Petroleum (BP), following the OPEC oil hikes of 1973–4. When Heath, acting on behalf of the government as the major holder of shares in BP, had tried to curb the oil prices rises, BP had instead responded as a commercial company, largely ignoring the government's wishes. The incoming Labour government therefore established BNOC, which essentially brought into state hands the oil reserves then held by British Gas.

At this point, John Smith came to the attention of Labour's most prominent right-winger. Denis Healey, the Chancellor of the Exchequer, recalls that 'oil was always a great problem for the Labour Party'. Healey got on well with Smith, perhaps because they were similar types of person: 'very pragmatic' and 'not ideological'. At any rate, Healey found Smith 'totally reliable'.[68] John Smith also worked closely with Bruce Millan, who was Minister of State for Scotland responsible for the Scottish Economic Planning Department.[69]

On 10 June 1975, Harold Wilson reshuffled his Cabinet, demoting Tony Benn to the Department of Energy and promoting Eric Varley from Energy to Benn's old job at the Department of Trade. Although the Cabinet had been given permission to campaign on both sides of the EEC referendum, Benn had been so vocal in his opposition to the Common Market on economic grounds, and had for several years been promoting radical left-wing solutions for British industry, that employers were distinctly uneasy about him continuing to head up the Department of Trade.

Smith and Benn hailed from opposite ends of the Labour Party, but it says a great deal for both men's characters that they didn't allow their political differences to get in the way of a good working relationship. In the first few weeks of working together, Smith reminded Benn of 'a managing director speaking to a sales conference', but his view of Smith quickly changed when he got to know him better.[70] Derry Irvine recalls how John developed a great admiration for Benn's skills as a Cabinet minister, in the professional sense of how well Benn managed his department. Benn even overcame the fact that he was teetotal while Smith was not. After visiting Benn's house, Smith commented to Irvine: 'All Benn drinks is tea in these great big mugs, but he realises that other people's requirements are different. It's absolutely great; when he gives you whisky, it comes in a tea mug.'[71]

Against the Tide, Benn's published diaries covering the period from 1973–6, make only six references to Smith, but two of them mention regular Tuesday office lunches that Benn held in the department for ministers, their aides, and some of the civil servants and advisers.[72] Benn now refers to these regular Tuesday lunches as 'my Cabinet', and it was something he held in every department he led.[73]

Tony Benn did not get on with everyone with whom he worked. He describes Tommy Balogh, his Minister of State at Energy, as 'an explosive Hungarian economist'. Balogh, along with another Hungarian, Nicky Kaldor, earned the nicknames 'Buddha' (Kaldor) for being slightly on the large side, and 'Pest' (Balogh), supposedly for being intolerable as a colleague.[74] Benn remembers that Balogh was one of those people who had to have powerful people around him and always felt he 'had to be an Adviser with a capital "A"'. He would ring Benn nearly every morning from his bath, calling on his boss to sack someone or another.[75] In later life, Smith loved to recall an incident during his first few weeks as a junior minister when the Saudi oil minister, Sheikh Yamani, visited the Department of Energy's offices. Balogh was so excited that he careered through the revolving doors just as Yamani came into the building, leaving Smith alone in the reception hall to be greeted by the sheikh, who assumed he was Balogh.[76]

It seems to have been at Benn's insistence that Smith gained promotion within the Department of Energy to Minister of State level, aged only 37 when Lord Balogh retired in December 1975. When interviewed for Andy McSmith's biography, Benn did not recall being responsible for Smith's promotion,[77] although now he claims to have 'got him [Smith] promoted'. Nor is there is any diary evidence to support Benn's claim; he merely records: 'At 9 pm I went to see Harold Wilson. All he wanted to tell me was that he was going to take away Tommy Balogh as my Minister of State and that he would promote John Smith to that post.'[78] But the point that matters is that Smith always *thought* Benn was responsible for his promotion to Minister of State, and thereafter felt he owed Benn a debt of gratitude.

Smith also got on well with Bernard Ingham, then the Energy Department's information officer. Ingham had started life as a Labour councillor in Bradford, and eventually ended up as Mrs Thatcher's press secretary. According to Andy McSmith, Ingham was having great difficulty getting on with Tony Benn, and went to Smith to ask him what to do. Smith suggested that Ingham have a row with Benn because he knew his boss didn't like rows. After they'd had a big row, the air was cleared and Benn got on better with Ingham.[79] Benn recalls that 'he [Ingham] got very angry with me . . . he was like a kettle: when he got annoyed, he started overheating and his lid rattled.'[80]

Overall, Benn was generous in delegating responsibility to Smith: apparently the Secretary of State's instructions were: 'Only come to me when you have anything genuinely interesting or politically damaging.'[81] Smith commented later that Benn was 'in his teacher and leader phase – he was very good at delegating and these were very heady days'.[82] Benn recalls that when he joined the department, he left most of the ongoing passage of the Petroleum and Submarine Pipe-lines Bill to Smith, because he 'brilliantly handled it'.[83]

Benn recollects: 'Public ownership was accepted by everyone in the Party then. It was not a left-wing idea.' However, Benn admits that issue of the *extent* of democracy in the nationalised industries had always proved controversial. The Morrisonian model of nationalisation had been 'top-down and bureaucratic', and had not involved common ownership, in other words industrial democracy (worker control of industry) or control through municipal or co-operative Socialist models.[84] Eighteen years later, when Smith, as leader of the opposition, spoke out against nationalisation, his old boss Tony Benn sent him 'a marvellous quotation' from Smith's winding up speech to the Second Reading of the British Petroleum and Submarine Pipe-lines Bill on 30 April 1975:

> We have had many criticisms from Conservative Members, based principally on their ideological opposition to the extension of public enterprise in any form. One of the things that strikes me as curious about this House is that when the Labour Party brings forward proposals for public enterprise it is regarded as doing that in the cause of ideology, and so it is – [Interruption.] We bring forward proposals for public enterprise because we are Socialists. The Conservative Party opposes our proposals root and branch because it is the Conservative Party and believes in private ownership and control, but somehow that is not regarded as ideology of any sort.[85]

Smith's former boss accompanied the quotation with a little note: 'Dear John, In memory of our happy time together.' Benn added in his diary: 'I think that may just slightly alert him to the danger of this silly attack he has made on nationalisation.'[86]

Like Benn, Smith retained an interest in and a kind of nostalgia for his own 'happy time' at the Department of Energy. Long into the 1980s, Smith kept a map of all the British oil fields in his House of Commons office.[87] But he also became extremely angry that the Thatcher government had wasted the opportunities provided by North Sea oil. In Smith's eyes, this once-in-a-lifetime windfall had been squandered on keeping over three million people on the dole. It became a recurring theme, constantly making an appearance in Smith's speeches during the 1980s and 1990s. Even as late as his last parliamentary report to the Labour party conference in September 1993, Smith still referred to those Conservative years 'in which the extraordinary bounty of North Sea Oil offered us an unprecedented opportunity' and yet 'instead of seizing that opportunity, it has been thrown away'.[88]

Unlike so many Labour politicians of today, Smith was never ashamed of Labour's past achievements in government. He was especially proud of the fact that Labour's economic growth figures were higher than the Tories', despite North Sea oil. For instance, Harold Wilson's government achieved an average growth rate of 2.7 per cent per annum, Wilson and Callaghan combined (1974–9) ended up with a 2 per cent growth rate per annum, whereas between 1979–91, the Tories could only manage 1.75 per cent.[89] Smith would remain a believer in certain strategic industries remaining in state control because such undertakings required long-term planning, but not in wholesale national-isation like Tony Benn, and he became convinced that governments should not intervene in the workings of the economy willy-nilly.[90]

Six
DEVOLUTION – UNFINISHED
BUSINESS

A LTHOUGH THE LABOUR Party has always had a committed band of pro-
devolutionists within its ranks, the devolution plans of the early 1970s
were a response to devolutionist and nationalist pressures in Scotland,
and to a lesser extent in Wales, not a policy dreamt up by far-sighted Labour
politicians at Westminster. As one civil servant from the 1970s puts it: 'It
[devolution] was a top-level political judgement intended to keep the
nationalists at bay and the Government in power, not primarily ideological
but practical.'[1] Or, as Philip Ziegler claims, it summed up much of the
philosophy of Harold Wilson: 'Give a part to preserve the whole, make a
concession to avoid having to make a bigger one.'[2] But as far as John Smith was
concerned, much of the groundwork for devolution had already been laid long
before he took over responsibility for the issue in April 1976.

Winnie Ewing's dramatic Hamilton by-election victory for the Scottish
National Party (SNP) in November 1967 had moved Harold Wilson to act,
against the advice of Willie Ross, the Secretary of State for Scotland, who was
hostile to devolution. Even the Conservatives were not immune to the calls for
devolution in this period, as Edward Heath's 'Declaration of Perth' at the
Scottish Conservative and Unionist Association conference in May 1968
demonstrated. Thereafter, Sir Alec Douglas Home's Scottish Constitutional
Committee was charged with investigating the merits of establishing a
devolved assembly.

Never a politician to be outdone by the Tories (and always seeing the issue
in tactical rather than principled terms), Harold Wilson established a Royal
Commission on the Constitution in April 1969 (then known as the Crowther
Commission). Just before the June 1970 election, Alec Home's committee
published its report – *Scotland's Government* – recommending a directly
elected Scottish Convention of 125 members, but the election of a
Conservative government failed to further the cause of devolution.

In the meantime, the Royal Commission established by Wilson, now
chaired by Lord Kilbrandon (following the death of Crowther), after much

hesitation, published its pro-devolution majority report in October 1973.[3] At this point, the Scottish Council of the Labour Party published a report – *Scotland and the UK* – rejecting Kilbrandon's findings. However, the SNP's star, which had waned at the 1970 election, re-emerged in November 1973 as the SNP's Margo MacDonald won another famous by-election victory in the supposedly safe seat of Glasgow Govan. At the February 1974 general election, a minority Labour government was returned, but the SNP won seven seats (though it lost Govan), and polled 21.9 per cent of the vote.

Very little advance thinking had been done in government circles of the consequences of devolution, and many of the issues had not been properly thought through. Some government ministers did not appear to realise that an Assembly in Scotland meant more than a mere talking shop; it involved establishing a Scottish government.[4] To correct this, the Wilson government established the Constitution Unit operating from within the Cabinet Office. The Constitution Unit had a dual function. Not only did it provide the usual Cabinet secretariat, it also engaged in the substantive planning and co-ordination of the Government's devolution plans. In terms of personnel, John Garlick was brought in as a Second Permanent Secretary, and supported by three Under-Secretaries: Michael Quinlan, Stuart Scott Whyte and Gordon Gammie.

Although Harold Wilson was heavily involved in the Ministerial Committee on Devolution,[5] members of the Constitution Unit conducted most of the detailed work via an official committee. Sub-groups of the official committee dealt with various related topics. Michael Quinlan, brought in from a background at the Ministry of Defence,[6] dealt mainly with constitutional matters, the administrative and political structures, Home Office, health and education matters.

Stuart Scott Whyte had considerable experience of Whitehall and of devolution issues,[7] and within the Unit handled finance, industry, economics and agriculture.[8] Gordon Gammie, a Scot with English legal training, was placed at the head of a legal section, which was thought highly necessary, given the enormous legal complexity that would be encountered. In all, the Constitution Unit numbered only twelve to fifteen people.[9]

Ted Short (now Lord Glenamara), Lord President of the Council and Leader of the House of Commons, was at the top of the ministerial tree. Short was clearly in favour of devolution, seeing it as his chance to mark out a place for himself in history. But his title, Lord President of the Council, was in reality just that – a title. The Privy Council Office wasn't (and isn't) a government department: the Cabinet Office, through the Constitution Unit, provided the civil service back-up to Ted Short, and to Gerry Fowler, his Minister of State. By January 1976, Fowler had been replaced by Lord Crowther-Hunt, a dissenting voice on the Kilbrandon Commission.

In June 1974, the Labour government published a Consultative Paper, *Devolution within the UK: Some Alternatives for Discussion*, outlining several options for reform. At first, the Scottish Executive of the Labour Party famously refused to have anything to do with the proposals. History does not record who scheduled the Executive's meeting for 22 June, the night Scotland played Yugoslavia in the 1974 World Cup. Around two-thirds of the Executive members got their priorities right, and skived off to watch the game on television, while the depleted Scottish Executive voted narrowly by a margin of 6:5 in favour of the proposition that 'constitutional tinkering does not make a meaningful contribution to achieving socialist goals'.[10] In July 1974, Labour's NEC ditched its anti-devolutionist stance. A month later, the Scottish Labour Party endorsed the idea of elected assemblies for Scotland and Wales, at a special conference in Glasgow in Dalintober Street, the location of Glasgow's Co-operative Hall. The Dalintober Street episode is not one fondly remembered either by pro or anti-devolutionists. As Andrew Marr rightly points out, 'it was a victory for fix and fear, not a triumph of principle'.[11] Alex Donnet's NUGMW union changed its mind and supported the NEC, arguing that the overriding priority was to return a Labour government to Parliament with a majority.[12]

The controversial decision at Dalintober Street to support 'a directly elected assembly with legislative powers within the context of the political and economic unity of the United Kingdom'[13] cleared the way for the publication of a government White Paper in September.[14] However, the October 1974 election intervened, and the SNP polled 30.4 per cent of the Scottish vote, winning eleven seats, their highest ever total, earning themselves the nickname of the 'Scottish football team'. Harold Wilson now had a tiny overall majority of 3.

Members of the Constitution Unit started out with misgivings about the whole devolution enterprise. The 'slippery slope' argument was raised frequently: the fear that conceding an Assembly would eventually lead to a demand among Scots for full-scale independence. Devolution also raised the danger of appeasing neither hostile Unionists nor hostile supporters of independence. On 10 May 1976, Smith predicted that: 'We shall no doubt be opposed by blinkered unionists and blinkered separatists, but I believe that in the parliamentary debate, we shall beat both.'[15]

Privately, some of the civil servants were sceptical. Early on, John Garlick presented a formal paper to Wilson and Short along the lines of, 'Are you quite sure that you wish to proceed?' The ministers said they did, and thereafter the Constitution Unit performed its task to the best of its abilities.

But the civil servants found charting a way forward, as one official recalls, 'much stickier going than they'd originally thought', much to the frustration of Ted Short.[16] Their initial remit had been to devolve as much power as was consistent with the constitutional and economic unity of the United Kingdom – in other words, limited devolution within a unified state. In the case of Scotland a distinction has to be made between functions where legislative power would be conferred and others where only existing executive powers were to be devolved. As a result of the restricted nature of devolution, they had to engage in a tremendous amount of laborious work analysing the exact functions of government in different fields, and the precise demarcation between devolved matters and those remaining at Westminster.[17]

Establishing devolution within a state that was neither a simple unitary nor a federal system created anomalies relating to representation at Westminster. In particular, Tam Dalyell, MP for West Lothian since 1962 expounded his now famous 'West Lothian Question': if Labour introduced a devolved Assembly in Scotland, what right did Scottish MPs have to vote on English matters when English MPs would have no right to vote on those matters that had been devolved to Scotland? What is not sufficiently understood to this day is that ministers were fully aware of the potential problems in this area. As early as June 1974, the issue had been raised in the government's consultative proposals.[18]

Whitehall collectively thought that the devolution idea was a bad one, especially the Treasury.[19] Sir John Garlick recalls: 'Lots of my permanent secretary colleagues were reluctant to give up their departments' responsibilities.'[20] Running parallel with the devolution proposals was a programme for greater decentralisation by handing more powers to the Scottish Office. But far from this being seen in Whitehall as softening up the Scottish Office, or as a halfway house for the likely transfer of all its powers to a devolved Assembly, Whitehall saw it as a deliberate use of UK legislation to defuse the demand for devolution. The intention was to give something to Scotland, and to stop there, as an alternative to devolution, not as a stepping-stone towards it.[21]

Harold Wilson also faced a sceptical, sometimes hostile, Cabinet. Denis Healey recalls being 'not very keen on devolution' and argued against it in Cabinet and at special Cabinet 'think-ins' or 'away days' held on the subject in 1975. He eventually took the view that 'holding a referendum was the right way to go about it'.[22] Bruce Millan also remembers that certain members of the

Cabinet were 'not enthusiastic, not helpful'.[23] Wilson, however, was nearly always one step ahead of his Cabinet opponents, as was shown in the lead-up to one of these think-ins held at Chequers in April 1975. Before the Cabinet malcontents could make any move against devolution, a leak appeared in the newspapers the day before the Chequers gathering claiming that the government intended to jettison the Devolution Bill. Wilson immediately issued a flat denial. The heavyweights were therefore stymied, while the civil servants saw it as 'a typical piece of Haroldry', the suspicion being that he had himself engineered the leak to provide a basis for re-entrenching the commitment.[24]

The Constitution Unit spent the summer of 1975 devising a White Paper, with Michael Quinlan co-ordinating.[25] In November 1975, the result of his (and others') labours was *Our Changing Democracy*,[26] which firmed up the June 1974 Green Paper. *Our Changing Democracy* proposed a 142-member legislative Assembly for Scotland and a much smaller executive Assembly for Wales, but because of the objections of the Scottish and Welsh party executives and the coolness of Willie Ross, neither assembly would have any economic role or tax-varying powers.[27] It was widely said by nationalists at the time that Willie Ross, as Secretary of State for Scotland, would have 'the powers over the Kingdom of Scotland of the Secretary of State for India and the Viceroy combined'.[28] In January 1976, the devolution enthusiast, Jim Sillars,[29] broke away from the Labour Party in protest to launch the short-lived Scottish Labour Party (SLP), but only one other Labour MP followed him.[30]

In April 1976, Wilson unexpectedly retired as Prime Minister. Six candidates, James Callaghan, Michael Foot, Roy Jenkins, Tony Benn, Denis Healey and Tony Crosland, put their hats in the ring in the subsequent Labour leadership contest, but eventually the field was whittled down to two – James Callaghan and Michael Foot. Smith was much more on the Croslandite, Gaitskellite, even Jenkinsite wing of the Party, but from the very beginning he gave his strong backing to the Callaghan team, probably reckoning that Callaghan was almost bound to win.[31] He was right: Callaghan overcame Foot by 176 votes to 137.[32]

Callaghan's inheritance was that his party was left with no parliamentary majority (thanks to by-election losses). Callaghan replaced Willie Ross with Bruce Millan as Secretary of State for Scotland, and made the pro-devolution Michael Foot Leader of the House of Commons at the expense of Ted Short. Foot remembers that Callaghan was 'not that enthusiastic' about devolution, but he realised 'the survival of the Government depended on the success with which we put through that measure'.[33]

Callaghan made John Smith Minister of State at the Privy Council Office, but in effect he was the minister in charge of the government's devolution legislation. Tony Benn, sad to lose his colleague at the Department of Energy, recalls: 'You could see the guy was on his way up.'[34] The late Lord Callaghan recalls his reasoning: 'I moved him to become a Minister of State because of his lawyer like mind and his Scottish background, which added a dimension to Michael Foot's political understanding and approach to the issue of devolution.'[35]

Although Michael Foot had seniority over Smith, the latter handled the main load of piloting the Bill through the House of Commons, working closely with Bruce Millan and John Morris, the Secretary of State for Wales. In their early portrait of Michael Foot, Simon Hoggart and David Leigh rightly point out that the Leader of the House 'troubled himself hardly at all with the fine print of devolution; this was left to his capable deputy, John Smith.'[36] Lord Callaghan agrees,[37] while Bruce Millan is more blunt in his recollection: 'John did most of the donkey work.'[38] Michael would express exasperation about what to do next, but John would say you need to do this, this and this. Murray Elder recalls: 'John really sorted it all out for Michael.'[39] Smith later admitted as much: 'Michael was a pretty broad-brush chap. One of the nicest men I ever met.'[40]

At this point, Foot was not personally acquainted with Smith, but they quickly became 'intimate friends', and held meetings almost every day in the House of Commons to discuss the progress of the legislation. Foot's special adviser, Elizabeth Thomas, recalls it as 'a happy office' and she had 'tremendous respect' for John's intellect and ability and affection for him as a person.[41]

Foot was an enthusiastic supporter of devolution. Indeed, he would have preferred to call the proposals 'Home Rule', as Keir Hardie had done, but the rest of the Cabinet had been 'afraid' of using that phrase.[42] Foot claims that Smith was also committed to the legislation and was firmly of the view that a change of governmental system would be more democratic for both Scotland and Wales.[43] The late Lord Callaghan agrees that both 'he [Smith] and Foot were keen advocates of devolution'.[44] Despite these claims, it is well known that Smith started out as a sceptic on the merits of devolution.

Neil MacCormick recalls that at Glasgow University John had been 'deeply sceptical' about devolution, supporting the traditional Labour argument that devolution – or independence for that matter – would not address the central issue of the redistribution of wealth. He recalls discussing the issue of devolution at length with John in the period 1974–5: 'John really had to convince himself about the advisability and workability of devolution as an intellectually serious and defensible proposition which could and would work, compatible with his belief about the exercise of power.'[45] For example, in November 1973, Smith expressed doubts in *The Scotsman* about key aspects of the Kilbrandon Report, opposing the reduction in Scotland's representation at Westminster from 71 to 57, and the introduction of the Single Transferable Vote (STV). While Kilbrandon argued that such a voting system would avoid single-party control of the Assembly for long periods, Smith saw it as 'clear discrimination against the Labour Party, designed to thwart the Party of the power granted to it by the voters'. The abolition of the post of Secretary of State for Scotland, with a seat in Cabinet, would be 'a disaster':

> It would be monstrous to have Scottish interests in these affairs represented in the power centre of the United Kingdom by, say, the Minister for Consumer Affairs when he was able to fit in his new duties into gaps in his own departmental work. It would inevitably go to the least important member of the Cabinet, the sweeper-up of miscellaneous odds and sods.[46]

He also cast doubt on the effectiveness of a Scottish Assembly that did not exercise control over financial, trade and industrial policy: 'I doubt if a voice without power would be heard and I am even more suspicious of representation which does not carry responsibility.'[47] Then, in May 1974, in his *Daily Record* column, Smith stated that Kilbrandon devolution price tag was 'too high a price to pay'.[48]

By 19 August 1974, Smith was claiming at the aforementioned Dalintober Street special conference that those who were pressing for devolution without a significant loss of the office of the Secretary of State for Scotland, and a reduction in the number of MPs at Westminster, were being dishonest.[49] One could not have a devolved assembly without wrecking the whole structure of local government. Nevertheless, Smith went along with the NEC-backed motion.[50] Dick Mabon reckons that Smith did so because: 'You had to make up your mind then.'[51] Those were the views of an independent back bencher, but what about when Smith became a minister?

Neil MacCormick's clear recollection is that Smith saw devolution as a 'workable idea' before he went to work for Michael Foot.[52] From 1975–6, MacCormick sat on the Houghton Committee, examining the funding of political parties.[53] He remembers one day arriving in London and being offered a lift in Smith's ministerial car, along with Tam Dalyell. During the trip, Dalyell raised an early variant of the West Lothian Question. While MacCormick supported devolution as a viable intermediate solution on the road to independence, Smith argued in favour of devolution, and not just as a minister defending the government position.[54]

MacCormick argues that Smith had a 'very Highland side', shown by his taste in arts, theatre and poetry, and feels that his 'Highlandness' made him acutely aware of the need to concede enough devolution to preserve the Gaelic culture as part of a unitary settlement with the rest of the United Kingdom. Smith added that he did not wish Scotland to be reduced to the cultural position of the Etruscans, who had disappeared from history save for markings on pottery.[55] Union with England had never involved a cultural merger – under the Treaty of Union in 1707, Scotland retained its own Kirk, its separate legal and education systems – but rather a political collaboration.[56]

Norman Hogg, a forthright sceptic on devolution, rightly argues that John Smith, unlike Donald Dewar, who was only ever really interested in Scottish affairs, always saw the bigger United Kingdom picture when considering devolution.[57] Lord Mackay of Drumadoon concurs: 'John was one of those Scottish politicians like Alistair Darling and George Robertson that you couldn't have imagined fitting into the Scottish Parliament set-up.'[58] After John's death, Menzies Campbell put it most eloquently:

> One could easily see David Steel or Donald Dewar sitting in the Royal High School building.[59] It was more difficult to envisage John confining his talents to Edinburgh. This is not a criticism of them or indeed of him. Merely a recognition that he saw devolved government in Scotland, not as an end in itself, but as a means by which the better government of the United Kingdom might be achieved.[60]

Ten years after Smith's death, Campbell put it more bluntly: 'John was always a fish looking for a bigger pond.'[61] Nonetheless, Sir Michael Quinlan recalls that Smith 'took an energetic hold of it and subsequently became a firm believer in devolution as a matter of personal conviction, and as something that was in the interest of the United Kingdom, not just of Scotland'.[62] Such a sentiment would be borne out in Smith's opening speech on the Scotland and Wales Bill when he emphasised the government's 'unshakable conviction in the maintenance of the Union', declaring that he could think of 'no more spectacular folly' than 'to sunder the Union'.[63]

During most of 1976, the Constitution Unit worked on the conversion of what was necessarily a very broad White Paper into detailed instructions for parliamentary counsel, whose task it was to convert these into a Bill. As it turned out, the approach adopted by the draftsman, involving detailed definition of the areas for legislative devolution and specification of every existing power intended to be devolved for executive action, provided endless opportunities for parliamentary obstruction.[64]

Sitting at meetings of the informal Steering Committee (comprising Smith, Foot, the two territorial Secretaries of State, Bruce Millan (Scotland) and John Morris (Wales), plus John Garlick and two to three of his under-secretaries), which had the task of charting the course of the legislation (and which met at least weekly in Foot's office), Michael Quinlan found Smith 'a delight to work with, quick on the uptake, accessible'. He was also 'a figure of substance who carried political weight' and 'commanded the confidence of the others'.[65] John Garlick also describes Smith as 'hardworking, conscientious, and a good lawyer, and unlike many lawyers he could see the wood as well as the trees'.[66] Stuart Scott Whyte agrees:

> Smith worked very much in the manner of an advocate – his personal training and his personal temperament went well together. When the Government suffered periodic defeats, it was 'water off a duck's back' . . . like a professional advocate who had just lost a case at the Court of Session, operating with a degree of detachment, always looking ahead, never back. Although he was a conscientious member of the Labour Party and the Government, he remained pragmatic, and never allowed himself to get carried away.[67]

Smith's advocate's training also meant that he needed the minimum of briefing during the passage of the Bill.[68] He learned to redefine the legislation as he went along, and on terms that his back benchers were prepared to accept. Bruce Millan concurs that Smith handled the 'technical side' of the bills particularly well.[69]

Lord McCluskey, who dealt with much of the devolution legislation in the House of Lords alongside Lord Kirkhill, the Minister of State at the Scottish Office, also sees Smith's handling of the devolution legislation as 'a work of advocacy' in the sense that a good advocate detaches himself or herself from the cause. Taking a passionate stand on an issue of principle isn't always what wins a criminal case, or indeed a vote in the House of Commons, especially in circumstances where the government has a small or non-existent majority. 'One does not have to believe that the defendant with twenty previous convictions is innocent of his twenty-first offence to mount a defence for his or her twenty-first case.' It also greatly helped Smith that he had spent his legal career arguing from both the prosecution and the defence point of view, sometimes from one week to the next, enabling him to see both sides of an argument, and therefore identifying weaknesses in his opponents' case. Finally, Smith brought a fresh mind to the job. None of the opponents on the Labour back benches could claim of Smith, 'We've heard it all before.' He could argue, quite legitimately, that slightly more than a year after Kilbrandon had reported he had become persuaded of the rational arguments in its favour.[70]

By August 1976, the Government had responded to previous criticisms that the devolution legislation was too timid by issuing a supplementary statement,[71] giving slightly more powers than originally envisaged to the Assembly. Bruce Millan describes the process of negotiating the outstanding issues within the relevant Cabinet committee as 'a fraught exercise'.[72] Eventually, the Scotland and Wales Bill was published in November 1976.

Many of the arguments over the devolution legislation were inevitably economic, principally concerning whether the Assembly would have a taxing function, and whether it would be responsible for overseeing grants and subsidies to industry. The tax-raising function was the most controversial. Officials produced a White Paper on taxation in July 1977 — *Financing the Devolved Services*[73] — suggesting various schemes based on separate Scottish tax receipts. A plan to impose a requisition on the rating system met with a negative response from ministers early on. But a power to apply a small supplementary Inland Revenue surcharge for Scotland through income tax was actively considered. The main problem was that the method of collection of income tax was more difficult in 1977 than it is now. In the 1970s, income tax was collected from the location of the employer, not the location of the employee. A great number of English-based companies with branches in Scotland would therefore have had to undertake the onerous task of identifying their Scottish employees for tax purposes.[74]

After detailed analysis, the surcharge idea was rejected. Ministers did not envisage that it would feature as an issue in the 1979 referendum campaign. Actually, it was successfully portrayed by the No camp as a restriction on the powers of the Assembly.[75] The tax issue came back to haunt Labour in the late 1990s, after John Smith's death, when the Tories ran with a 'Tartan Tax' campaign, and Blair controversially opted for a two-question referendum, the second being on whether Scotland would have a tax-varying power (see chapter 25).

During the autumn of 1976, John Smith and Michael Quinlan visited various parts of federal Canada — it was thought that Scotland could learn lessons from their experience of autonomy. But when Quinlan and Smith asked an eminent Canadian civil servant, after discussion of various detailed issues, whether he had any general advice to offer from the Canadian experience, his reply was 'Like perhaps "Don't?"' (Back home, the advice contributed to the Constitution Unit from the Northern Ireland Office, with its own experience of devolution, was usually sceptical.)[76] During talks with

Peter Lougheed, Premier of Alberta, Smith happened to mention that his sister Mary worked at a fine arts college in Kelowna, British Columbia. Within hours, he was on a jet to pay a brief visit. Mary showed her brother around Kelowna, where, while having a drink in the Legion Hall, he encountered two ex-pat Scottish miners, who had voted for John at the East Fife by-election way back in 1961. Mary recalls: 'John was absolutely thrilled, and that was another reason that I never regretted campaigning for John back in 1961.' (See chapter 3.) John stayed up nearly all night chatting, before flying on to Vancover, and then back in time for the Labour Party conference in Blackpool.[77]

Back home, the Callaghan government now had to contend with a more vigorous opposition to devolution from the Conservative side. Margaret Thatcher, a self-confessed English nationalist, had ousted Edward Heath as leader of the Conservatives in February 1975, and 22 months later, she executed one of those big U-turns that she later eschewed by opposing the Second Reading of the Scotland and Wales Bill. However, like Labour, the Conservatives were also divided, and Thatcher's decision provoked both Alick Buchanan-Smith, shadow Secretary of State for Scotland, and Malcolm Rifkind, then a junior Scottish Office spokesperson, to resign from the Tory front bench.[78]

On the Labour side, Leo Abse[79] and Neil Kinnock, Labour MP for the ultra-safe seat for Bedwelty since 1970, forced Foot and Smith into conceding the idea of post-legislative referendums on devolution. In other words, once the Bill had passed into law, the people of Scotland and Wales would have to vote on the merits of the legislation in a referendum.[80] Kinnock had put down a Commons Early Day Motion, calling for a referendum, which attracted 76 Labour signatures.[81] Initially, Foot was reluctant to concede to Kinnock's demand, but Smith persuaded him that there was no chance of getting the Bill through without making this concession.[82] Leo Abse put down the relevant reasoned amendment demanding a referendum[83] during the four-day debate on the Bill's Second Reading, which, very unusually, the government accepted. As a result, the Scotland and Wales Bill received its Second Reading on 16 December by 292 votes to 247, a comfortable margin of 45. Christopher Harvie points out that of Scotland's 71 MPs, 55 voted for it, and only seven against, and six of them were Tories.[84] More worrying for the Government was that not only had 29 Conservatives abstained, so had 31 Labour MPs.[85] Anti-devolutionist Labour and Conservative MPs clearly did not regard the Second Reading vote as the end of the matter.

After the Second Reading vote, Smith and his civil service colleagues in the Constitution Unit realised that getting the combined Bill through the floor of the House of Commons would prove heavy going. Smith urged that the government should use the momentum of the Second Reading victory to go straight ahead with a guillotine.[86] However, Michael Foot, possessing such a great record as a champion of the rights of back benchers, who had so often expressed outrage at the use of government guillotines to curb those rights, understandably found it difficult to agree to such a course of action. So Smith was forced to press ahead with the committee stage of the Bill without a guillotine.[87]

On 13 January 1977, when the committee stage of the Bill commenced, some 350 amendments were tabled, the most important of which was put down by Professor John P. Mackintosh, a keen supporter of devolution on the Labour side,[88] who attempted to introduce a proportional representation (PR) voting system for the Scottish Assembly, but this was heavily defeated.[89]

By 2 February, Smith had staggered to only Clause 3, with some 112 clauses still waiting to be discussed. Thirteen days later, the only amendment that had been agreed was that Orkney and Shetland should both have one Assembly member each.[90] As Michael Quinlan recalls: 'By that stage, there was no possibility of getting the Bill through without a guillotine. We had clearly become bogged down, and Michael Foot had no option but to agree to it.'[91]

On 22 February 1977, Foot attempted to introduce a guillotine motion, as he had done with five other bills that session, but although the government gained the support of the SNP and Plaid Cymru (both parties wanted the Bill to succeed), eleven of the thirteen Liberals, 274 Conservatives and 22 Labour MPs combined to defeat the government by 312 votes to 283, a majority against the government of 29. A further 21 Labour MPs abstained from voting.[92] On this occasion, Smith spoke poorly at the dispatch box, and for years afterwards MPs recalled him slumped back in his seat looking dejected. No wonder, since he had suggested a guillotine to Michael Foot much earlier. The next day, however, he received a kind note from Francis Pym, his opposite number, telling him not to worry: such low points happened to all politicians in their time in the House of Commons.[93] Michael Foot reflects that the collapse of the joint Bill was 'a very sad defeat'.[94] The Government went through the motions for a few days, but everyone knew that the Bill was a stricken horse. Enoch Powell likened the atmosphere to the period between a person's death and the funeral, when the body is still in the house: people tiptoed past the room as a mark of respect for the dead 'for indeed, this is a dead Bill and everyone knows that it is dead'.[95]

Foot recalls that the government could not have dropped the devolution legislation altogether, even if they had wanted to, because 'the compelling force was to keep a majority in the House of Commons'.[96] Nor had the nationalist threat gone away.[97] Hope for the minority Labour government rested on the fact that the Liberals still supported the broad principle of devolution for Scotland and Wales. The temporary solution to Labour's negative majority was a short-lived Lib-Lab pact agreed with David Steel, the new leader of the Liberal Party, and signed on 24 March 1977. The government then re-introduced devolution legislation in the 1977–8 session of Parliament, but this time as two separate bills, the Scotland Bill and the Wales Bill.

The Scotland Bill received its Second Reading on 14 November 1977, passing by a comfortable margin of 307 votes to 263.[98] However, when the Bill moved to its committee stage (which took place, as with most constitutional bills, in the House of Commons chamber), almost immediately Smith met greater opposition from his own back benchers. Clause 1, as finally agreed by ministers after much internal debate,[99] stated that the provisions of the Bill 'do not affect the unity of the United Kingdom'. Francis Pym, the opposition spokesperson on House of Commons Affairs and Devolution, felt that the legislation impaired the unity of the United Kingdom, and moved an opposition amendment to make it clear that 'nothing in these provisions shall be construed as impairing or in any way affecting the unity of the United Kingdom'. Smith pointed out that the legislation was neither federalist nor separatist, but affirmed the continuity of the United Kingdom and the unabated and undivided sovereignty of Parliament. Smith believed[100] it was wrong to drag the courts into determining whether anything in the Bill impaired the unity of the United Kingdom.[101] Although the Tory amendment was defeated, the government lost the subsequent motion that 'The Clause stand part of the Bill'.[102] Clause 1 had fallen and the government made no attempt to restore it.[103] The defeat did not augur well for the rest of the Bill.

Later that same evening, John Mackintosh tried for a second time to secure a proportional system for the elections to the Scottish Assembly. Under the terms of the Lib-Lab pact, the government granted a free vote on their own side, but Smith's front bench advice involved airing many of the traditional arguments against PR.[104] The debate ran over two days, government ministers were whipped against the amendment, and it failed by a wide margin.[105] While most people can agree that the failure to include a system of PR in the devolution bill (as Kilbrandon had recommended) was a mistake, John Smith's stance merely reflected the realities of Scottish Labour politics at the time. As Smith bluntly put it in a private discussion with David Steel: 'There was no point in discussing the intellectual or political merits of the case: the Scottish Executive of the Labour Party would not have it, and that was that.'[106]

By 10 January 1978, the government had struggled to Clause 42 of the Bill, concerning the Scottish Consolidated Fund, in other words the annual block grant that Scotland received from Westminster. Both supporters and opponents of devolution from the two main parties argued that if Scotland were to have an Assembly, it would be half-baked without having revenue-raising powers of its own. They feared that in the absence of a tax-varying power, the Assembly might simply demand more and more money from London. As Smith argued later on in the Bill's passage, the government had never ruled out introducing a supplementary tax power, but the prevailing structure of PAYE made it difficult to devise an efficient system of devolved taxation: 'Indeed, our present structure could hardly make the task more difficult.'[107] The amendment attempting to introduce such a power was heavily defeated.[108] As this issue came to attract more and more popular attention, Smith, with his first-hand knowledge of Scottish popular opinion, came to favour the provision of a revenue-raising power but failed to convince his colleagues of the case for this.[109]

Smith found himself arguing against many amendments to the Scotland Bill that in fact would be incorporated into the successful Scotland Act two decades later. He opposed the idea of the 'reserved powers' model, the concept used in the Government of Ireland Act 1920 that the Bill should list all powers to be reserved at Westminster, the assumption being that all other powers not listed would be devolved to the Assembly. Smith argued that the government wanted to focus on the positive aspect of devolved powers, rather than looking at the question negatively, and that this approach would lead to greater clarity about what the Scottish Executive and Assembly could and could not do.[110] Once again, the government view prevailed.[111]

Another controversial issue concerned whether the power over abortion should be devolved to the Assembly. In 1978, the government's view that abortion should be a devolved matter narrowly prevailed by a margin of 179 votes to 162,[112] although the issue provoked a rebellion by some 63 Labour back benchers.[113] (The Lords favoured keeping the power at Westminster, and ultimately prevailed.) By contrast, in 1998, the Labour government granted a free vote, but favoured keeping the abortion power at Westminster, fearing that Scottish MPs would vote to tighten the law in Scotland, provoking cross-border traffic in abortions. Smith was in a difficult position as he consistently opposed abortion (see chapter 9). On this occasion, Harry Ewing, the Under-Secretary of State for Scotland, replied for the government, but Smith joined fellow ministers in the division lobbies to oppose the idea of abortion being a United Kingdom matter.

In 1978, as in 1997–8 the Labour governments held the same view that the referendum should involve only those resident in Scotland, and should not be conducted across the United Kingdom as a whole. During the debate on the issue, on 25 January 1978, Smith argued that since the referendum only directly affected people resident in Scotland, it was only right that they and they alone should vote on the Bill's merits. Also, what would happen if there was one vote in England and a different result in Scotland?[114] An attempt by Willie Hamilton, the maverick Labour MP, to introduce a UK-wide referendum on Scottish devolution failed by a wide margin,[115] as did a similar Tory attempt two decades later in June 1997.[116]

Although many northern English Labour MPs opposed devolution, two of the most persistent opponents to the Bill were Welsh and Scottish: the aforementioned Neil Kinnock and Robin Cook.[117] Both men then held the traditional Socialist view that the interests of the working class could only be bettered through wealth redistribution and a welfare state directed centrally from Westminster. Ties of class, rather than nationality, bound the Welsh and Scots to the British state. As Kinnock put it during the Third Reading debate on the Wales Bill on 9 May 1978, he was elected 'to represent working-class people irrespective of their nationality', describing himself as a centrist to the marrow of his bones.[118] At the time, Robin Cook was equally emphatic, commenting that he wanted to 'kill the issue'.[119]

Bruce Millan remembers that Smith spent a great deal of time trying to reassure either indifferent or hostile back benchers about the content of the Bill. Such emollience did not prove easy for someone who 'didn't suffer fools gladly'.[120] Michael Foot recalls that Norman Buchan, the Labour MP for West Renfrewshire, was 'suspicious of John Smith', saying 'he's not on the left of the Party'. Buchan was a left-winger hailing from Smith's Glasgow Union days, who feared that the Scottish nationalists were engaged in fascist propaganda, and believed that the Labour Party should not be encouraging them.[121] Meanwhile, figures on the right of the party did not like the way that Foot was negotiating with the minority parties. Dick Mabon recalls joining a delegation of Labour MPs, which included Brian Walden, to complain to Foot about this matter.[122]

On 25 January 1978, the Labour rebels famously conspired against the government when they put forward an amendment, in the name of George Cunningham, Labour MP for Islington and Finsbury, but a Scot, insisting that 40 per cent of the possible electorate, not merely 40 per cent of those who voted in the referendum, would have to support the proposals for them to pass into law, otherwise a draft order would be brought before Parliament repealing the Act. Smith argued in vain that such a set percentage figure had not been imposed during the EEC referendum of 1975, and that therefore the rules of the referendum should not be changed. The opponents of the Bill wanted people who did not vote to be counted on the No side.[123] The 'Cunningham Amendment' or the '40 per cent rule' was carried by 168 votes to 142.[124] Robin Cook had preferred a 30 per cent rule, but was one of 37 Labour MPs who voted for Cunningham's amendment.[125]

That night, Walter Harrison, Labour's Deputy Chief Whip, ironically with no great personal affinity for devolution, used every parliamentary device and manoeuvre at his and the government's disposal in order to try to win the vote. Harrison, along with two of his fellow whips, Jock Stallard and Jack Dormand, and two SNP MPs[126] refused to come out of the lobby, thus delaying the vote. Sir Myer Galpern, the Deputy Chairman of Ways and Means, asked the Serjeant at Arms to investigate, and eventually the vote was allowed to take place. The incident caused a great deal of synthetic outrage, and ironically all the opprobrium fell at the feet of one of the greatest parliamentarians of all, Michael Foot, a painful experience for a man so wedded to the parliamentary ideal. And yet, Bruce Millan reflects that when everyone repaired to Foot's office after the shabby manoeuvre, Michael Foot did not get angry. Rather, he behaved in 'a saintly manner', merely asking colleagues how best to deal with the controversy.[127] Foot later apologised unreservedly to the House.[128]

Surveying the impact of the Cunningham amendment in 1980, the constitutional expert Vernon Bogdanor was probably right to claim that it 'has some claim to be the most significant back bench initiative in British politics since the war for it played a crucial part in securing the repeal of the Scotland Act, depriving the Scots of an Assembly for which a majority had voted'.[129] The Cunningham amendment created great bitterness both during the referendum campaign and in the recriminations afterwards because it only placed a 40 per cent rule on the Yes side, not on the No side, implying that those voters who abstained on the referendum favoured the status quo.[130] They may have done. During the referendum campaign, an abstention was widely seen as 'half a no vote'. It is worth at least raising the possibility (nay heresy) that the government might have lost the referendum vote altogether (in numerical terms) had there been no Cunningham amendment.

Only minutes after the 40 per cent rule had been carried, the government was defeated again. This time, Jo Grimond, the former Liberal leader and MP for Orkney and Shetland, successfully moved an amendment insisting that if a majority of Orcadians and/or Shetlanders voted no in the referendum, then the Act would not apply in the area or areas that had voted no, and that a commission would be established to investigate the future government of the area. This time, some 50 Labour MPs voted against the Government, inflicting a decisive defeat of 204 votes to 118.[131]

Unfortunately for Smith, the four defeats that the Government suffered during the Bill's committee stage in the House of Commons represented a mere warm-up act on the part of the Labour rebels. On 14 February 1978, at the beginning of the report stage, Tam Dalyell successfully moved an amendment that insisted that if Parliament was dissolved before the referendum was held, then the referendum would be delayed for at least three months. Dalyell feared that the government might dissolve Parliament and hold a referendum and an election on the same day. Referendums, he believed, should be held on separate days from general elections, otherwise the country might move towards a plebiscitary democracy.[132] Despite a categorical assurance from Smith that the government did not wish to see these two matters become tangled,[133] Dalyell's amendment was carried by 242 votes to 223, with 25 Labour MPs voting against the government.[134]

The next day (15 February), Dennis Canavan, Labour MP for West Stirlingshire and a keen supporter of devolution, moved an amendment to delete the Cunningham amendment from the Bill. In a rare foray into debates on the Scotland Bill, Michael Foot spoke in favour of the amendment.[135] However, the government was defeated by 298 votes to 243, with 51 Labour MPs voting against the government.[136] Afterwards, Smith unsuccessfully moved an amendment to reduce the 40 per cent rule to a 'one in three' requirement.[137] By 22 February, the Bill had staggered to its Third Reading.[138]

As Smith waited for the House of Lords to deliberate the various clauses of the Scotland Bill, he enjoyed the diversion of the Glasgow Garscadden by-election campaign in April 1978, in which his old university pal, Donald Dewar, was standing for Labour. Dewar won comfortably, polling 45.4 per cent of the vote, with the SNP trailing in second on 32.9 per cent.[139] A month later, on 31 May, further evidence that the SNP's surge had been halted in its tracks came when George Robertson, like Smith, a former pupil at Dunoon Grammar, held the Hamilton by-election, although the SNP's Margo MacDonald polled 33.4 per cent.[140] Smith helped out Robertson on the very first Saturday of campaigning, and came down from North Lanarkshire regularly thereafter.[141]

Just after 4 pm on Thursday, 6 July 1978, at the start of the Lords amendment stage, John Smith had just given way to Tam Dalyell on a point of order, when three bags of horse manure were hurled from the public gallery: one bag got Smith on the shoulder, while another covered poor Dalyell from the waist upwards. The two culprits were protesting about conditions in Northern Ireland's Long Kesh Prison.[142] Initially, the House bravely tried to carry on its business, but eventually the Speaker, George Thomas, was forced to suspend the sitting of the House.[143] Just at that moment, one of the clerks leant across, and commented to Smith: 'A close encounter of the turd kind.'[144]

During the Scotland Bill's committee stage in the House of Lords (which lasted some thirteen days), peers, while not exactly hurling manure at the government front benches, nevertheless turned up their noses at many aspects of the government's devolution plans, inflicting twelve defeats. For instance, their lordships had voted in favour of Lord Kilbrandon's amendment introducing the Additional Member System for elections to the Assembly.[145] In order to satisfy the Liberals, when the issue came back to the Commons on 6 July 1978, Smith had agreed with David Steel not to make the anti-PR speech he had given at committee stage (a promise to which Smith stuck),[146] and Michael Cocks, the Chief Whip, also said he'd encourage more Labour supporters of proportional representation into the lobbies, but again, the Lords amendment was defeated by 363 votes to 155.[147]

The House of Lords also voted in favour the idea of a Speaker's conference to re-examine the number of Scottish Westminster MPs after a successful referendum,[148] as well as striking out Jo Grimond's plans for separate representation for Orkney and Shetland,[149] but the government was subsequently able to reverse this defeat in the Commons. They also voted for a new clause that would have given the Scottish Assembly the power to apply to the Secretary of State for Scotland to raise taxes, but any measures would be subject to the approval of both Houses of Parliament.[150] In addition, peers had voted to withdraw from the Assembly responsibility for abortion,[151] forestry (by only one vote),[152] the pay and conditions of doctors and dentists,[153] aerodromes,[154] and the British Waterways Board,[155] which was the only major nationalised industry that the government intended to devolve. Earl Ferrers, speaking on behalf of the Conservatives, used an example from Smith's own backyard to point out the anomalies arising from such a measure: Ardrishaig harbour at the mouth of the Crinan Canal would not be devolved, but the Crinan Canal would be.[156]

The report stage in the Lords during June 1978 witnessed a further eighteen defeats. Peers supported the idea of Assembly committees reflecting the party balance in the new legislature.[157] They also successfully inserted a new clause as a means of addressing the West Lothian Question. Post-devolution, if the Westminster government secured a majority in the House of Commons for a piece of English-only legislation on Third Reading only with the assistance of Scottish MPs, a two-week cooling-off period would ensue. The provision was a very weak one, because after the cooling-off period, another Third Reading vote could be held, and the votes of Scottish members could count towards the final result.[158] When the issue came back to the Commons on 17 July, the Tories moved an amendment to the Lords amendment inserting 'Second Reading' instead of 'Third Reading' to the above provisions. Smith was totally opposed to the amendment both in principle and in practice: in principle because it introduced the concept of 'in-and-out voting'; and in practice because the cooling-off period would not ultimately prevent Scottish members from voting on those matters in a Bill that concerned England.[159] The government won the vote on the Tory amendment by a majority of 6,[160] but it only just scraped home after a tied vote on the original Lords amendment when the Deputy Speaker, acting in accordance with the rules of the House, voted for the motion rejecting the amendment.[161] Unfortunately for Smith and the government, the Lords took up the idea of the Tory amendment so that it returned yet again to the Commons on 26 July,[162] and this time the government was defeated by a margin of only 1.[163] The same evening, the government was defeated attempting to overturn the Lords' preference for forestry matters remaining at Westminster.[164]

Smith had to engage in the usual last minute bargaining with the House of Lords in order to secure the Bill's passage: he accepted the two major Lords defeats on the West Lothian Question and forestry and made no attempt to reverse the abortion vote, having lost for a second time in the House of Commons.[165] In return, the Lords did not seek to reverse Commons votes removing the tax-varying power, and restoring British Waterways and aerodromes to the Assembly, along with several other minor matters.[166] These concessions proved amenable to the Lords, and on 31 July 1978, the Scotland Bill finally achieved Royal Assent.

As part of the Scottish devolution referendum campaign in February 1979, Smith took part in a televised Oxford Union debate. Smith debated alongside Emlyn Hooson, later a Liberal Democrat peer. On the other side of the table, he faced Leon (now Lord) Brittan, his future adversary in the Westland debates (see chapter 10) and Leo Abse, the anti-devolutionist MP. Given Smith's great debating skills acquired at the Glasgow Union, he should have been the star performer of the evening, but Abse recalls that he was not used to the frivolity and 'high mannered nonsense' of the Oxford undergraduates, and his own earnest and intense speech was 'a disaster'. According to Abse, it was several months before Smith spoke to him about the Oxford debacle.[167]

When the Scottish devolution referendum took place on 1 March 1979, the Cunningham amendment proved to be an insurmountable obstacle: while 32.9 per cent of the electorate voted yes, 30.8 per cent voted no, and 36.3 per cent did not vote.[168] Had the 40 per cent rule not been passed, then devolution would have come to Scotland by a margin of 51.6 per cent to 48.4 per cent. Several years later, in 1991, John wrote a handwritten letter of condolence to Donald Mackay on the death of his father, the Rev. Donald Mackay, who had been the minister of Greenbank parish church in South Edinburgh and a keen supporter of devolution. In his letter John recalled passing the Greenbank manse, on the morning after the referendum result had become known. He encountered the Rev. Donald Mackay working in his garden. The two men had shared with each other their feelings of annoyance at the outcome of the referendum, during which the minister had observed that, as a good Christian, all he could do was to accept the result and dig his garden furiously.[169] That was John's way too. One had to accept the democratic result, and move on. Nevertheless, John was livid with those who had opposed devolution. A tribal sense of loyalty to the Labour Party meant everything him. As Menzies Campbell recalls: 'If you were in his camp, he would defend you to his last round, but those who transgressed were given a piece of his mind.'[170]

There is little doubt that the devolution experiment in 1979 failed to satisfy those most in favour of devolution. Issues about the lack of a tax-raising power, the failure to incorporate a system of proportional representation, the government's apparent timidity in relation to reducing Scotland's representation at Westminster and the role of the Secretary of State for Scotland all rankled for years afterwards, and all re-emerged in 1997–8. John Smith has been roundly criticised for the plan that he devised. In the first place, the criticism is unfair because he had little to do with the framing of the initial legislation. But the Scotland Act represented an unsatisfactory middle course between keen devolutionists (in the Labour Party, but more especially the Liberals), and the formidable ranks of sceptics in Cabinet, Whitehall, on the Labour back benches and in the Scottish Labour Executive. But that is not to suggest that Smith did not steer the passage of the legislation deftly through the House of Commons. It was just that, as David Steel later pointed out: 'The basic fault throughout was putting Labour Party considerations first and effective devolution second.'[171] Several years later, Smith argued that the devolution legislation 'corresponded with the political circumstances of the time. There is no use being in politics and trying to remain a purist.'[172] He did well with the cards he had been dealt.

Both at the Department of Energy and the Privy Council Office, Smith had proved that he could work well with his left-wing bosses, Tony Benn and Michael Foot. By putting his head down, Smith never became a controversial figure like Neil Kinnock or Robin Cook, both of whom started their political careers as rebellious back benchers. Rather, Smith had successfully placed himself firmly in the middle of the Labour Party, becoming a conventional loyalist, acceptable to both wings, while at the same time demonstrating his undoubted competence in Parliament. It is ironic that Smith made his reputation on an essentially flawed piece of legislation, but his adept handling of a poisoned chalice made him an obvious choice for entry into Cabinet.[173]

Seven
TRADING PLACES

DURING THE SUMMER of 1978, Smith attended events at the Edinburgh
Festival, including a visit to the Festival Fringe where, upon hearing an
accordionist playing an old Gaelic tune, he got up on to the stage and
sang a duet, much to the surprise of a rapt audience. *The Guardian* got a hold
of the story, claiming that Smith had begun his impromptu performance in a
discreet manner, but 'became inflamed by the power of Scottish nationalism'.
Hardly. But the positive audience reaction to Smith's turn led the reporter to
comment: 'With a few more MPs like him we could well have a "Palais" of
Westminster.'[1]

Ironically, Smith was at another social event, a friend's wedding, when
James Callaghan made his famous 'Waiting at the Church' TUC conference
speech on 5 September 1978.[2] John McCluskey, also attending, remembers him
and Smith nipping out of the reception to watch the television coverage of
Callaghan's speech, and 'John watching, horror struck' as Callaghan ruled out
an autumn election.[3]

On 1 November 1978, the date of the Scottish devolution referendum was
announced for 1 March 1979. Only ten days after that announcement Smith
was promoted to Trade Secretary, making him the youngest member of James
Callaghan's Cabinet at the age of 40, some ten weeks younger than David
Owen. As one reviewer had predicted, handling devolution had been 'an
escalator rather than a treadmill for Mr Smith'.[4]

Smith was promoted on Michael Foot's recommendation, although as Foot
recalls 'everyone else understood how good he was'.[5] The late Lord
Callaghan's recollection reinforces Foot's version of events:

> I discussed with Michael Foot the future of John Smith when he did so well
> in performing his task of piloting legislation on devolution through the
> House of Commons . . . I was always impressed by John Smith's work and
> thought of him as a possible future leader of the Labour Party, and it was
> for that reason that he was promoted.[6]

The immediate reason for Smith's promotion to Cabinet was Edmund Dell's[7]
acceptance of a post with a private firm, necessitating his resignation from the

Board of Trade. Smith therefore joined the Cabinet at very short notice, and inherited Dell's private office.[8]

According to Elizabeth Smith, it was later a 'matter of great pride' to John that he had served for six months as the youngest minister in James Callaghan's Cabinet.[9] But at the time, Elizabeth was filled with a mixture of excitement and uncertainty at what lay ahead, as this letter to Elizabeth Thomas, Michael Foot's former special adviser at the Privy Council office, reveals:

> Dear Elizabeth,
>   How kind of you to write to me about John's appointment to the Cabinet. What an exciting and bewildering time it is for me. As a wife I am overjoyed at John's success and I know he will cope magnificently with anything he is required to do. But as a mother I feel a bit nervous about the changes it will make to our lives. I can't help feeling a little threatened by the army of civil servants and all these red boxes which keep arriving. But John cares as deeply as I do about our privacy and family life, and gradually we will work out a system which suits us best.
>   After a time, I expect it will all become ordinary, but at the moment we are still walking six inches above the ground and enjoying every minute of it.[10]

Smith later recalled the fact that he had taken something of a risk, sacrificing his family life for a Cabinet career in London: 'I was always here at weekends but Elizabeth brought the children up single-handed. There was a bad moment when Sarah was about four and we fell out and she said, "You go away back to London." I didn't like that.'[11]

Just as Archibald Smith had demonstrated the importance of education to his son, so John Smith wanted to make sure that his own daughters fulfilled their potential. John wasn't a pushy parent: he didn't demand that they follow his career path. He treated his children as equals. But Sarah Smith, his eldest daughter, recalls that her father 'wouldn't tolerate poor exam performance when the problem was lack of effort or dedication – something he simply couldn't understand' and 'pointed out what advantages we had, and how inexcusable it would be to waste them or even take them for granted'.[12] Smith later admitted, 'We pushed them very hard to go to university . . . I was very conscious of saying "do what you like, but a decision not to go to university is a fateful one."'[13] On the day of Sarah's graduation from Glasgow University, John even escorted her into a lecture hall 'just to make sure I'd seen the inside of one before I left for good'.[14] Later, Catherine emulated her father by studying law at Glasgow University, and Jane studied for a B.Sc. at the Scottish College of Textiles in Galashiels.[15] John died just three weeks before Jane took her finals.

Among family and friends, opinion is divided as to which of John's three daughters is most like him in physical appearance, but there is something about Catherine's bubbly personality that is the image of her father. All three daughters share their father's basic honesty, his confidence, and just as John had learned the value of lively discussion through his father, so he passed that desire to challenge and to argue on to his children.

Family friends recall that John could be quite a strict parent. Nor was he necessarily always sympathetic. Roy Hattersley recalls an occasion when John was a Cabinet minister, and he'd invited a number of guests to his Edinburgh home for a dinner. At one point, Catherine, then aged around six, fell and grazed her knee, but because of the hectic preparations, her superficial scratches went largely ignored:

> Halfway through the evening she was found to be missing. But before the night was ended she was brought home by her grandmother to whose house she had cycled for 'some sympathy'. She spent the rest of the evening sitting at the table between her father and another member of the Labour Cabinet.[16]

John was leader of the opposition when Sarah got a job with the BBC. He didn't live to see Sarah realise her full potential as a television news journalist with Channel Four. She is often to be seen reading the news summary on the nation's best terrestrial news programme, *Channel 4 News*, and has taken turns as the programme's Washington correspondent. Meanwhile, Jane, after a stint working for Bloomberg, a financial services company, now works for Napier University in Edinburgh. On 12 June 2004, Jane married Malcolm Robertson, son of George Robertson, Secretary-General of NATO, at a ceremony on Islay. After a successful debating career at Glasgow, Catherine now pursues her legal career in Oban.

Overall, though it bored those hacks always anxious for gossip, John was a devoted family man and, especially in later life, was besotted with his three daughters. Smith rarely wrote things down, except on scraps of paper and the backs of envelopes, but in one of only a few scraps that survived, constituting 'the Smith papers', Smith made a few notes entitled 'On Being a Father', in which he recalled that of all the responsibilities that he had undertaken in life, fatherhood was the most vital and yet the most fulfilling role of his life: 'I have three daughters now growing from teenagers into adulthood, and it is a big job to make sure that they realise their full potential.'[17]

Just before John entered the Cabinet, the Smith family moved from their home in Edinburgh to a larger Victorian house in the Morningside area, only a few hundred yards away. Among their near neighbours was Sir John

Falconer, a lawyer, and whose son, Charlie Falconer, is now Lord Chancellor. In John's early days as a Cabinet minister, he hosted a champagne and strawberries reception (followed by a dinner) for friends and members of the press in his garden at Morningside. John's sister Mary McCulloch, her husband Jack, and their two children happened to be over from Canada, and were able to attend the occasion. Mary recalls Neil MacCormick piping around the garden, and John enjoying the fact that she had asked a famous BBC reporter: 'And what do you do?'[18]

Donald Mackay, a fellow advocate, also remembers John enjoying the adulation of his colleagues at a Bar dinner to mark his promotion to Cabinet.[19] Jimmy Gordon reminds us that for a brief spell John became quite a high profile figure in the way that a young American senator might be portrayed, and he quite enjoyed the publicity and the media attention.[20] Indeed, Smith became the subject of a short film profile on BBC2's *The Week at Westminster*. John Sergeant, later the BBC's and then ITN's political editor, teamed up with David Wickham, the talented film-maker, to produce these profiles. Smith co-operated, coming out of a lift and walking down a corridor, while Wickham followed behind with a camera on a trolley. Wickham would insist on the best possible light for his filming, meaning that a messenger delivering Smith's red boxes to his Edinburgh home had to wait around for an hour until the light was right at the front of the house.[21] Thomas Harris, Smith's principal private secretary, remembers little about the actual programme, but recalls the camera crew following Smith around for a week: 'I kept looking like a butler standing behind John.'[22]

Smith's promotion to Cabinet was even noticed back in his native Argyll, whence a letter arrived from Forsyth Hamilton:

> Dear John,
>   Now that you are in the Board of Trade, you will be able to help me because my boat collided with Ardrishaig Pier, and then a puffer came in and took the rudder right off and we need a Board of Trade enquiry right away.
>   Please answer by return.
>   Yours,
>   Forsyth Hamilton

A puzzled civil servant asked, 'Secretary of State, will I refer this to the Marine Division?'[23] Smith handled the matter himself.

Despite the adulation and attention, Smith knew he wouldn't serve for long in the Cabinet before a general election was called. The life was beginning to ebb away from the Labour government. Smith's primary role was to keep that government in existence for as long as possible. A civil servant working at the Board of Trade at the time sensed that Smith was 'defter in the politics of the late 1970s than Edmund Dell'. Smith was 'more visible, had greater style and presence, and was more political'.[24] Apparently, when Smith asked a senior civil servant why the weekly meeting of the PLP had not been penned in his diary for Thursday, the official enquired: 'What is the PLP, minister?' Smith's alarm grew still further when he discovered that the Trade Secretary's telephone line to the House of Commons had been out of order for two years.[25] Such deficiencies were quickly put right. Thomas Harris recalls that Callaghan deployed Smith's parliamentary skills to good effect: 'Smith would sit down with MPs from the minority parties with a bottle of Scotch, trying to keep them on board.'[26]

Smith even helped out Michael Foot, still Leader of the House. Foot expressed concern to Smith over how best to secure Labour's manifesto commitment to establish a new Public Lending Right (PLR) – a payment to the author in respect of every borrowing of his or her book from a public library – centrally funded by the general taxpayer. Under the old system, authors only received a one-off royalty payment from the original purchase when the library purchased the book. Technically, the Bill was handled by Shirley Williams, Secretary of State for Education and Science and Paymaster General. As an author himself, Foot was especially anxious to get the legislation through, but his efforts were being hampered by elements on the Tory side and on his own back benches, who feared (as did many librarians) that PLR might result in libraries having to charge the general public to borrow books. In the 1976–7 session, Foot's first attempt to introduce PLR legislation had failed due to persistent filibustering.[27]

John Smith's immediate reaction to Michael's predicament was to ask: 'Who do you want me to speak to? Who's against you?' Then he went directly into the House of Commons tearoom, seeking out the rebel back benchers, and asked them why they objected to the Bill, and what sort of deal he could strike with them to get them to change their minds. This, Murray Elder believes, was 'pure John'.[28]

Smith wound up for the government on the Second Reading debate of the Public Lending Right Bill on Friday, 10 November 1978. In the chamber, Smith put his case for PLR on the grounds of basic fairness:

> We believe it to be an act of simple justice that some recompense out of public funds be made to authors whose works are fundamental to the whole public library system. Without the authors there would not be a large and magnificent public library system such as we are privileged to enjoy.[29]

The Public Lending Right Bill received its Royal Assent in March 1979,[30] one of few legislative achievements of that last session of the Labour government.

Smith undoubtedly excelled as a fixer and a motivator of recalcitrant Labour back benchers in the House of Commons, but because his skills were so much in demand he was never able to detach himself for long enough from the House of Commons to focus entirely on his departmental agenda, or to chart the future direction of policy. Nevertheless, the civil servants liked the fact that Smith possessed the necessary political weight to deliver the goods for his department in Cabinet (a feature noted by civil servants even when Smith served at the Privy Council office). In some respects, the profile and effectiveness of senior ministers are as important as their policy input. The secretary of state has to do the deals, securing support from Cabinet colleagues. It helped the civil servants working under John to be given a clear political 'yes' or 'no' to policy ideas, and Smith's sharp and lively political intelligence, together with his ample reserves of common sense, more often than not helped to achieve that.

Notwithstanding these strengths, almost all the departmental work at Trade was entirely new to Smith: 'He was very conscious of his lack of familiarity with the content of the department, particularly his lack of knowledge of economics,' recalls Thomas Harris. The department's chief economist was brought in to give Smith private tuition in economics for an hour-and-a-half at a time.[31]

John Smith's two parliamentary under-secretaries of state, Stanley Clinton-Davis and Michael Meacher, had been at the Board of Trade for some time, since 1974 and 1976 respectively. Officials regarded Clinton-Davis as a very safe pair of hands, and John Smith agreed: 'John thought the world of him,' comments Thomas Harris.[32] Kenneth Munro remembers that 'John had his moments of incipient pomposity, but mostly he could spot it in others.' When Clinton-Davis lost his seat to 1983 parliamentary boundary redistribution, he eventually became a European Commissioner. Munro, then deputy head of the London office of the European Commission, met Smith one day at the Reform Club. 'How's Stanley?' enquired John. 'Has he gone all Euro-pompous yet?'[33]

Smith looked for loyalty in others, and had a strong contempt for disloyalty.[34] In this regard, Smith's owlish eyebrows were often raised at the innovative ideas expounded by Michael Meacher against the advice of No. 10, particularly through his membership of the Labour co-ordinating committee, which included such left-wingers as Tony Benn and Audrey Wise.[35] One official, who had moved from working in Sir Leo Pliatzky's office to Meacher's office, mentioned his/her change of position to Smith at the top office Christmas party in 1978. Smith is said to have replied: 'Out of the frying pan and into the fire.'[36] Thomas Harris goes much further, describing Meacher as 'a constant thorn in John Smith's side. Smith was forever summoning Meacher into his office to rebuke him for coming up with his own policies, when he should remain loyal to the government.'[37] Indeed, Meacher's naughty schoolboy behaviour (and that of the other left-wingers) became worse as the government drew ever closer to its sell-by date.[38]

Because of the Government's non-existent majority (and therefore the need to be present in the House of Commons for close votes), Smith had little time to travel abroad, as his ministerial job would normally have demanded. Thomas Harris can only recall accompanying Smith (together with Neville Gaffin, John's press secretary, and John Chalmers of the boilermakers) on one major trip, to Singapore, Malaysia and Thailand in January 1979.[39] (In fact, Smith also visited Czechoslovakia in March 1979, but a trip to Egypt had to be cancelled in April because of the calling of the general election.)[40] In Singapore, Smith had a fascinating discussion with Lee Kuan Yew (Harry Lee), as he recalled a visit of the mainland Chinese at the height of the Cold War. Lee's Chinese guests expressed their astonishment at the economic progress his country had made. Lee told Smith: 'We, the descendants of the coolies, showed the mandarins how to run the economy.' Later, Smith flew to Kuala Lumpur where he encountered an 'extremely prickly' Dr Mahathir Mohamed, but he enjoyed being wined and dined at the Guthrie Plantation in Port Dickson, where he spent a pleasant weekend. A photograph of Smith survives, showing him hacking into a rubber tree.

Back at home in the House of Commons, Smith mainly dealt with legislation inherited from Edmund Dell. Because of the imminent election, controversial measures such as introducing an element of industrial demo-cracy on the boards of British companies,[41] which had raised eyebrows among British industrialists, never saw the statute book.[42] Smith attempted to put through a Companies Bill, regulating the conduct of company directors,[43] and in particular making it a criminal offence to engage in insider share dealing.[44] As Smith put it bluntly during the Bill's Second Reading, 'insider dealing is wrong', self-regulation was not sufficient, and criminal sanctions were there-fore needed.[45] But the controversial part of the Bill remained the industrial democracy clause, which sought to impose a legal duty on company directors to take into account the interests of employees as well as shareholders in framing their decisions.[46] Behind the scenes, Smith mediated between left-wingers who wanted greater employee representation on company boards, and the Confederation of British Industry (CBI), who were hostile to any notions of industrial democracy. However, Tory opposition, led by John Nott, prevented the Companies Bill from getting through the House of Commons before the general election. Eighteen months later, the Tories introduced roughly the same bill – minus the industrial democracy clauses – much to the annoyance of Smith.[47]

Smith had more success steering the pilotage arrangements integral to the Merchant Shipping Bill on to the statute book,[48] which, among other things, attempted to reduce accidents at sea. There had been a number of oil tanker spillages off the Welsh coast, as well as the high profile sinking of the *Amoco Cadiz* in 1978. More broadly, the Bill vastly improved the safety of fishing and merchant shipping, ratifying a number of international agreements,[49] and made the conditions of employment for those who worked at sea the same as for those who worked on land. The legislation also altered the rules of competition for liner conferences, which had up until then followed a distinctly mercantilist pattern. Smith favoured liberalisation at a European level, rather than the United Kingdom going on its own. Kenneth Munro, then at the Department of Transport at the European Commission, believes that Smith's stance on the Merchant Shipping Bill demonstrated both his 'general basic sympathy for a bit of liberalisation, and a keenness to arrive at European solutions'.[50] Reading these debates from the Callaghan period,[51] one is struck by Smith's simple yet highly effective clarity in explaining the implications of often very dull legislation, and his total mastery of detail.

During his short time at Trade, Smith also drew to the wider public's attention the pay and working conditions of black employees of British companies operating under the South African apartheid regime. In September 1977, the EEC's nine member states had signed up to a voluntary code of conduct for companies with interests in South Africa.[52] Paragraph 7 of the new code called upon the governments of the Nine to review annually progress being made by their national companies in implementing the code. Because of the delicate political and trade implications of the issue, Smith had very little scope for personal intervention, but he still managed to put on record in a very long written answer an analysis of how well (or badly) British companies were adhering to the code.[53] Most controversially, in Annex F, Smith published the names of those companies that his government felt were not paying wages at the level set out in the code.[54] When the Conservatives came to power in 1979, John Nott, the new Secretary of State, chose to publish the information provided to him by British companies in its raw form, but not to 'name and shame' in the way that his Labour predecessor had done. As Labour's shadow

Trade spokesperson, an irate Smith raised the issue in a House of Commons debate. For him, it was a simple issue of right versus wrong:

> My main accusation is that the Government have done the absolute minimum that they thought they could get away with under the code . . . I accuse the Government of back-pedalling on an important Community obligation of great value in improving the lot of black workers in South Africa.[55]

In his defence, Nott pointed out that the code was voluntary, and that the measurements in the code did not include fringe benefits such as the provision of training opportunities. However, the Secretary of State argued that he had not followed Smith's course in publishing an interpretation of the companies' performance because some of the information relating to wages and conditions was neither verifiable nor complete. That, he said, amounted to compiling a black list of companies under the cover of parliamentary privilege. Nott did not hold back in his criticisms of Smith:

> I note, like all social democrats, the right hon. gentleman claims to have a much bigger heart and much greater feelings than anyone else. That is quite a common claim by those such as himself who believe that they have a monopoly of feelings about black South Africans. It is an absolutely typical piece of social democracy.[56]

Murray Elder recalls that John was quite proud of getting involved in this way – both in government and opposition – especially since the cause of anti-apartheid had been dear to his heart ever since the Luthuli Rectorial campaign at Glasgow University[57] (see chapter 3).

The late Robin Gray, Smith's principal adviser on trade disputes, reflects that during his service, the Department of Trade had some fine ministers in the shape of Edmund Dell and later, Cecil Parkinson: 'But John was as good as any – and when he spoke people listened.' He also had a sense of humour. Gray remembers one meeting where Smith was supposed to make a statement, but his adviser had lost the speaking note. Instead of berating Gray, all Smith said was, 'You can't win them all.'[58] On another occasion, a civil servant working for Michael Meacher heard the division bell ring, and got the car ready for the minister. However, the Secretary of State, deep in a meeting with trade union leaders and Labour back benchers, didn't hear the division bell because it had been turned off in the meeting room. The civil servant watched as a Secretary of State, his two ministers of State, as well as the Labour back benchers all crammed into one car and sped off to catch the vote. Smith could have stood on his dignity and not seen the funny side, but the sense of humanity in him was entertained by it. This ability to retain 'good humour in difficult circumstances' gave Smith a special appeal to those who worked around him, especially at a time when the country was in an uncertain economic and political state.[59]

Smith had no time for pretence. On one occasion a civil servant tried to patronise a Labour MP at a meeting, and was later shocked to learn that the permanent secretary had been summoned to see Smith and was told in no uncertain terms that the guilty official should never appear in Smith's presence again.[60] Robin Gray also remembers: 'John was a down-to-earth Scot, and did not openly suffer fools gladly, but his innate Scottish courtesy rarely, if ever led him to go over the top, except in private, when he gave his views in no uncertain manner.'[61]

Smith's short spell in Cabinet ended as it had started, frantically trying to keep the minor parties from bringing down the government on the famous vote of confidence on 28 March 1979.[62] The story has been told elsewhere that John Smith, Roy Hattersley and Ann Taylor cut a deal with two wavering Ulster Unionists, John Carson and Harold McCusker, in which the government would have agreed to an inquiry into the price of food in Northern Ireland, but that the other eight Unionists voted against the government. The motion of no confidence was carried by just one vote, and a general election ensued.[63]

Jimmy Gordon and John McCluskey were both sitting in John's office in the House of Commons, watching the result of the vote in the chamber, which Smith sensed would lead to a general election defeat. While Smith was glum, McCluskey, who'd been paid very little as Solicitor-General for Scotland, compared with what he could earn as an advocate out of government, said: 'I can see prosperity staring me in the face.'[64]

At this stage of his career, despite considerable ministerial experience, Smith remained essentially a highly professional advocate, deploying his advocacy skills to great effect in the House of Commons. It would be at least a decade before Smith visibly moved beyond that advocacy stage, transforming himself into 'Mr Prudence' as shadow Chancellor of the Exchequer. The long period in between would represent dark days in Labour's history, from which Smith largely absented himself.

Cast into opposition, Smith carried on in his Trade and Industry portfolio, shadowing John Nott, later famous for his role as Defence Secretary during the Falklands War. Unfortunately, due to time pressures, Thomas Harris, by this stage Nott's principal private secretary, only kept a diary of his experiences working for his new boss for three months, but his short record gives a flavour of John Smith's sudden (and it appears painful) adjustment to opposition.

Harris records speaking with John Smith on 3 May, the day of the election, to make arrangements just in case Labour should win, but comments: 'I haven't seen him [Smith] since Easter.' The following morning, after Labour's defeat, Smith met with Harris to make the necessary administrative arrangements for the handover of power. While Smith and Harris expressed their 'mutual regrets' at parting, the former became very annoyed that Nott had not arranged any transport to ferry him to the Palace.[65]

Only a week after the election (10 May), Smith met up with Harris and Vince Cable,[66] his special adviser. Cable offered to work for Smith on a voluntary basis in opposition. Understandably, in his diary Harris records this meeting as 'a sad occasion', but he also notes that the three had a 'thoughtful' discussion, and that Smith was very interested in the Trade department's goings-on.[67] After Smith left office, Harris recalls that as Labour's opposition spokesperson on Trade, 'John immersed himself in the intricacies of the department – everything from the Multifibre Agreement, to GATT, to Britain's trade links with East Asia, especially Japan'.[68]

On Tuesday, 15 May, Margaret Thatcher spoke in the opening round of the debate on the address – the Queen's Speech. Harris records that while Tony Benn 'ostentatiously sat on the opposition benches, Smith had to sit on the stairs.'[69] Partly because Smith had served for so long as a minister in the 1970s, he took a long time to adjust to the psychology of opposition. Alastair Campbell later recalled: 'Smith used to say, "I don't enjoy Opposition. You don't go into politics to be in Opposition. Where's the sense in that?"'[70] On another occasion, he told a reporter: 'I want power for the satisfaction of using it for a proper purpose, and I'm frustrated in Opposition.'[71] Bruce Millan concurs: 'He was not out for the hard slog [of opposition], with no clear point at the end of it.'[72]

It was a reality check to stand in pouring rain at a railway station as an opposition spokesperson without any back-up, having spent five years being ferried around and having your life organised for you as a government minister. Elizabeth remembers that John was 'immensely frustrated' by opposition. He did not regard it as a fruitful period of his life, but as 'a period of waiting' until Labour returned to government. To Smith, the Labour Party was an organism that would carry on inexorably, and he could best serve it in government.[73]

Two months after the general election, Smith found himself attacking the Conservative government's proposed privatisation of British Airways. On

Friday, 20 July, the government achieved 'complete surprise' with John Nott's announcement that it intended to privatise British Airways – choosing a day normally reserved for private members' business – although Smith was at least tipped off in advance to be present for the statement.[74] Smith expressed his 'shock and dismay' on behalf of 'all those who wish well to one of our important public utilities'.[75]

The following Monday (23 July), Smith performed far better during the Second Reading of the Competition Bill. The Bill strengthened the powers of the Director General of Fair Trading and the Monopolies and Mergers Commission to deal with restrictive practices, but abolished the Price Commission. The opposition were furious that the government had brought forward the Bill just before the summer recess, and Kevin McNamara, then Labour MP for Kingston-upon-Hull Central, attempted to filibuster[76] during business of the House questions earlier in the day. Norman St John Stevas, the Leader of the House, allowed the opposition's antics to continue into the beginning of the Second Reading debate, and Nott was annoyed because he thought he'd gained an agreement from Stevas that this would not be allowed to happen.[77] In the opening debate, Nott spoke for only two minutes, provoking complete uproar from the benches opposite.[78] John Smith condemned Nott's two-minute effort as 'the most contemptuous delivered to the House for many decades'.[79] At 9.43 pm, Nott spoke again. Because the government did not move the business of the House motion at 10 pm (which would have allowed the debate to continue), Nott ensured that he would be the first minister to speak when Parliament resumed discussion of the Bill in the autumn.[80] Tom Harris records in his diary: 'John Smith revelled in the tactics of the situation.'[81]

Eight
BACK TO THE BAR

ELIZABETH SMITH'S RECOLLECTION that, only three days after Labour's 1979 general election defeat, John was back at the Scottish Bar[1] is at first sight a fairly telling indication of where Smith's priorities lay at this stage in his professional life. There is no doubt that Smith wanted to become a Queen's Counsel (QC). Many politicians 'take silk', having not really practised much at the Bar, and are regarded in legal circles as having taken 'artificial silks'. John wanted to take the proper route by building up the necessary body of cases to warrant becoming a QC on merit, which he succeeded in doing in 1983.[2]

However, John Smith was not, as the media portrayed him at the time, an Edinburgh lawyer (he didn't come from Edinburgh for a start), always prone to chucking his political career in favour of the Bar. Nor was he, like his old chum Nicky Fairbairn, someone who played at being both a politician and an advocate. Rather, John was always a full-time politician who dabbled in the law, mainly for financial reasons. Ranald MacLean observes: 'Although John was a good lawyer, the law was always a vehicle, a source of income when Labour was not in power, and he always wanted to keep his hand in. His real object was always to become a leading politician.'[3] Donald Mackay agrees: 'Politics was his first love, but he found the law good fun.'[4] Elizabeth Smith recalls that her husband was fond of saying that 'politics should never be your master', and would encourage budding politicians to get a professional qualification first.[5] Paul Boateng recalls being encouraged by John to go back to the law to become a barrister.[6]

With a young family to support, John Smith's career decision also had a financial basis. MPs' pay in the early 1980s was derisory, and being an MP was still seen as a rich man's game. Ross Harper observes: 'The guy had to live.'[7] The conditions, in terms of secretarial support and allowances, were also perfunctory. Jimmy Gordon remarks: 'MPs today don't know how lucky they are.'[8]

Many Labour MPs shared flats in London to make ends meet. John was no exception, and renewed his acquaintance with Norman Hogg, the former secretary of Aberdeen South Labour Party (see chapter 3) and, by this stage, the newly elected Labour MP for East Dunbartonshire. From 1979 until 1983, Norman and John rented out rooms in Kennington Lane, owned by an elderly lady. Originally from Sussex, she was a graduate of Glasgow University, a lifelong socialist, and an ex-Justice of the Peace in central London. Hogg recalls that breakfasts were great fun with John, because the old lady had an eccentric toaster that sent the toast into orbit, and John took great delight in catching it. Apparently, Smith was a 'terribly untidy' flatmate, rumbling in at all hours, partly due to the fact that as shadow Trade Secretary, he frequently attended dinners held by industrialists.[9]

Hogg recalls that John was always well received by the Soviet Embassy.[10] Despite being communists, the Soviets had a high regard for any British politicians who handled trade issues. On the death of Yuri Andropov in February 1984, Smith, by now shadow Employment Secretary, called at the Soviet Embassy in London with Hogg to pay his respects on behalf of the Labour Party. This was at 10 am, but the Embassy staff gave each of them a large glass of vodka, which they were expected to down in one. Smith then extemporised for ten minutes. To Norman Hogg's dismay, however, the Soviets then wanted him to speak. Labour's Deputy Chief Whip, normally a wine drinker, and not used to the vodka, could only blurt out: 'I don't think there is anything I can add to the words we have just heard from my colleague, John Smith.'[11]

In 1983, Smith and Hogg moved out of their Kennington Lane digs. Smith kindly assisted his elderly landlady in winding up her affairs in London so that she could return to her native Sussex. 'John's act of generosity rendered us homeless,' recalls Hogg. For a year, they rented out rooms in the Caledonian Club, but this proved to be a mistake. Smith would return to the Club late at night from the House of Commons only to be regaled by Scottish contemporaries visiting London for just one night, forgetting that John had to get up early for work the next day. Eventually, Richard Caborn, the Labour MP for Sheffield Central, and later Minister for Sport under Tony Blair, assisted Hogg and Smith in finding more suitable accommodation in the Barbican. Hogg and Smith rented two separate flats on the same floor in the complex. Later, when Smith became leader, he moved to larger premises in the complex, but he kept up his friendship with his old flatmate.[12]

Although most of John's legal work was carried out during the long summer recess, it was not unknown for him to spend a week defending an accused in the High Court in Glasgow. This involved John spending the day in court, flying down to London each evening from Monday to Thursday, to enable him to vote in the House of Commons at 10 pm, and subsequently travelling back up to Glasgow in the overnight sleeper from Euston, in time for the following day in court. Not that John slept the whole way north. Parties regularly took place in the sleeper bar. Those parties frequently lasted until the train reached Crewe. Indeed, it was rumoured that on occasion they continued until the train got as far north as Carstairs, where the sleeper divides to allow the coaches for Edinburgh to be separated from those continuing on to Glasgow.[13] Simon Hoggart, the *Guardian* journalist, also recalled catching a sleeper from Glasgow in 1982, and seeing John Smith's name on the manifest: 'He [Smith] appeared at the cabin door clanking miniatures acquired from a friendly steward who knew him well. Ten minutes later, and a Scottish Nationalist MP arrived, pulling from what was clearly a remarkable back pocket in his trousers, an entire bottle of whisky.'[14]

Probably the most unusual, and certainly the most famous case that Smith was involved in concerned a Phantom shooting down a Jaguar. As part of the RAF training exercises in West Germany, Phantom pilots and their navigators were required to fly sorties during which they would home in on targets. However, instead of the firing button triggering a live missile, for training purposes the RAF used a device involving cameras. A pilot's accuracy (and that of his navigator) was assessed on the basis of how well he had been able to take photographs or 'practice kills' of the target area. However, on 25 May 1982 the aircraft were fitted with live ammunition. RAF regulations required that red masking tape be fitted over the master switch in the cockpit, known as the master armourer's switch, as a visual reminder to pilots that their jets were fitted with live missiles. However, on this occasion the RAF base at Wildenwrath, near Dusseldorf was out of stock of red tape, so when the navigator spotted a Jaguar jet early into a sortie, the pilot pressed the fire button-thinking that he was taking a photograph. Instead, he fired a heat-seeking Sidewinder missile that went up the backside of the Jaguar. Fortunately, the pilot in the Jaguar, Flight Lieutenant Stephen Griggs, from RAF Bruggen, was able to bail out and escaped unhurt, but the £7 million aeroplane crashed into a field and was wrecked.[15] The authorities, having lost an expensive piece of kit, set up a Board of Inquiry investigation, and subsequently brought the pilot and the navigator, both from 92 Squadron, before a court martial hearing on charges of negligence likely to cause loss of life and causing the loss of an aircraft, which both men denied.

John Smith, newly appointed shadow Energy spokesperson, defended the pilot, Flight Lieutenant Roy Lawrence, a Welshman, while Ross Harper defended his navigator, Flight Lieutenant Alistair Inverarity, a Scotsman.

Naturally, the press did not pass up the story of a Phantom shooting down a Jaguar, and the case attracted enormous coverage in the Scottish press. The front-page news in the *Daily Record* ran with the headline: 'Big Two Take on RAF.'[16] In the New Year of 1983, Smith and Harper flew to Germany to interview their clients. For the purposes of the court martial, they were both temporarily given the rank of Group Captain, the same rank as the prosecutor, Christopher Eadie. As part of compiling their defence case, 'Group Captain' Smith and 'Group Captain' Harper visited an RAF base, and had got into the cockpit of a Phantom jet. Getting into the cockpit with dignity and ease required a narrower girth than Smith's.[17]

Menzies Campbell hones in on what made John Smith especially 'good at crime': he realised that every case had a best point, and John's gift lay in identifying that best point.[18] In this instance, Smith built a very strong case around the fact that none of the safety devices and failsafe mechanisms had worked when the pilot made his mistake.[19] It formed the core of his final address to the court martial.[20] The presiding judge later commented that it was 'the best court martial speech he'd ever heard'.[21] After four-and-a-half hours deliberation, the court president, Group Captain Don Oakden, found both pilot and navigator guilty of negligence. Plans for a celebration dinner had to be cancelled.[22] The following day, the two men were sentenced to a severe reprimand, but allowed to fly again.[23] Despite the disappointing outcome, Smith and Harper each returned home with a memento of their famous court martial case: a plaque with a picture of an RAF Phantom jet.[24]

Lower profile cases also demonstrate Smith's qualities as an advocate. Donald Mackay recalls that in the early 1980s he appeared for the prosecution against Smith at a murder trial. The case involved a homosexual student from Glasgow University who had returned to his flat to find his male partner having sex with another man. In a fit of rage, the accused had set about the third party with a kitchen knife, stabbing him several times in the back. John, acting as counsel for the defence, appeared to have a very slim chance of getting the charge reduced to one of culpable homicide (manslaughter). At that time, in murder trials in which one member of a couple had killed the other member, it was widely understood that the defence of provocation was only available if the couple were heterosexual. If they were, the jury was entitled to return a verdict of culpable homicide, rather than murder, if the members of the jury took the view that the killing had been provoked by the deceased's sexual conduct. The defence of provocation was not thought to be applicable in murder cases which involved same-sex couples. Smith, however, sought to persuade the jury to return a verdict of culpable homicide, on the basis that fairness and equity to homosexuals entitled them, as much as heterosexuals, to the benefits of the defence of provocation. Despite the fact that the judge directed the members of the jury that a verdict of culpable homicide was not open to them, even if they took the view that the male accused had been provoked by his male partner's sexual conduct, the jury returned a verdict of guilty on that lesser charge. In his plea in mitigation, Smith bravely reminded the judge that in sentencing the accused he must respect the verdict of the jury, notwithstanding the fact that he might take the view that the jury had disregarded his directions. The judge did just that. Although he lost the case, Mackay acknowledges that Smith had produced 'a well conducted defence' and that John had 'a gift of speaking to juries', such that in this case he had been able to persuade them to ignore the direction of the law.[25]

Donald Mackay also noticed another one of John's professional qualities in a very different case, this time in Edinburgh, involving three bogus workmen, posing as plumbers and roofers, who had conned elderly clients out of large sums of money for very little work. John, acting as counsel for the defence, realised his clients had no real defence, and kept his professional distance, discharging his duty, but nothing more. The three men were duly convicted. Mackay, this time on the winning side, cites this case as evidence that John was 'a man of principle', not just 'a formidable opponent, eloquent and articulate', but also someone who could also be 'trusted to play by the rules of the law, keeping his professional distance from his clients in criminal cases'.[26]

Smith never minded the fact that he took part in high profile murder cases as an advocate – as he put it, 'doing the odd murder'[27] – while at the same time remaining on the Labour front bench. The most notable example came in 1984 when Smith defended one of the accused in what was then Scotland's biggest multiple murder trial at Glasgow High Court – the Ice Cream War case.

The Marchetti brothers had been established vendors of ice cream in the Garthamlock area of Glasgow until members of the Campbell family, acting on behalf of 'Fifti Ices', owned by Tam 'The Licensee' McGraw, a Glasgow gangland boss, moved into the area. Film buffs will be familiar with Bill Forsyth's *Comfort and Joy*, which poked fun at the rivalry and the violence between the ice cream van owners. In the real world, the feud got out of hand.[28]

Andrew 'Fat Boy' Doyle, aged eighteen, had been one of the Marchetti van drivers employed to halt the advance of Thomas or 'T.C.' Campbell into Garthamlock. On 29 February 1984, Doyle came under attack from two men disguised with balaclavas, who allegedly discharged a shotgun into the front windscreen of his ice cream van.[29] Then, on 4 April 1984, a group of men, wearing Celtic hats pulled over their faces, used a sledgehammer and pickaxe shafts to smash up another Doyle van.[30] Twelve days later, an unknown group of men poured petrol over the front door of the Doyle family home in 29 Bankend Street, Ruchazie, in the East End of Glasgow, and struck a match, resulting in the deaths of six members of the Doyle family, including an eighteen-month-old infant.

T.C. Campbell, Joseph Steele, Thomas Gray and Gary Moore were all initially accused of murdering the Doyle family. Two other defendants, Thomas Lafferty and John Campbell, were also accused of attempted murder and assault and robbery, while yet another defendant, George Reid, was accused of assault.[31] The initial indictment list contained sixteen other charges, including acts of intimidation and violence, but many of these lesser charges were dropped on the direction of the judge, Lord Kincraig.[32]

John Smith defended Thomas Lafferty, a 39-year-old unemployed married man, who became a client of the famous Glasgow lawyer, Joseph Beltrami. Lafferty, who had married T.C.'s sister, Agnes, was known as 'The Shadow' for the way he hung around his brother-in-law. Agnes always maintained that she owned an ice cream van in her own right, independent of her brother and her husband.[33] But Thomas Lafferty tended to protect his wife when she went out on the van, and inevitably he ran into ice cream vans driven by Andrew Doyle and others.

In July 1984, Agnes Lafferty was released from Longriggend Remand Institution, along with a Tam McGraw, both having faced charges of conspiracy to build up an ice cream business through threats and intimidation. Thomas Lafferty was also released on remand after his attempted murder charge – in the April 1984 attack on the Marchetti van – was dropped.[34]

Smith's main line of defence on Lafferty's behalf was that he was an alcoholic, engaging in frequent drinking sessions in Glasgow's East End, and therefore, it was argued, incapable of taking part in a shooting. As Lafferty told the courtroom at one point: 'I'm an alcoholic, not a cowboy.'[35] Lafferty also denied assaulting a fifteen-year-old girl, and telling her to move away from an ice cream van: 'I can only think it happened because, being drunk, I bumped into her at the van.'[36] A Crown witness, William Love, claimed that Lafferty had given Love a mask, a club and a jacket for an attack on an ice cream van, together with £30 in return for 'doing a message'. Once again, Lafferty stressed his alcoholism: 'I couldn't give him tuppence. Nobody would trust me with money. They know I'd just drink it.'[37]

There were so many charges in the indictment, and so many people telling competing stories that there was insufficient reliable evidence to secure a safe conviction of the accused on many of the charges. Indeed, four Crown witnesses were later charged with perjury. Worse still, much of the evidence was based on what the police claimed Campbell and Steele had said, known as 'police verbal', rather than bona fide tape-recorded evidence. On the direction of the judge, Lafferty was found not guilty of three charges of inciting others to damage a Marchetti ice cream van, and another charge of conspiracy to assault and rob was also dropped.[38] In the next few days of the trial, several other charges against a number of the defendants were also dropped.[39] T.C. Campbell and John Campbell were both cleared of attempting to murder Andrew Doyle in the attack on the ice cream van.[40]

On 10 October 1984, after nine hours deliberation, the jury returned guilty verdicts on Thomas Campbell and Joseph Steele for murdering the Doyle family. Campbell received a life sentence for murder, with the judge recommending that he serve 20 years, and a further ten for an earlier shotgun attack on Andrew Doyle; Steele was sentenced to life imprisonment, and also six years for conspiracy to attack a van driver and of damaging an ice cream van, convictions which added a further seven years to his sentence. Thomas Gray was convicted of the attempted murder of Andrew Doyle, and was sentenced to fourteen years.

Of the initial accused, only Gary Moore escaped conviction. It took more than an hour for the verdicts to be read out and recorded. Smith's man, Lafferty, was found guilty on a reduced charge of assault, taking part in a shotgun attack to the danger of life, and was sentenced to three years. He was admonished on a charge of breach of the peace, but found guilty on a charge of assaulting a fifteen-year-old girl. George Reid got a total of six years, having been found guilty of a knife assault, and malicious damage to an ice cream van, while John Campbell was sent down for a total of four years for his part in attacking an ice cream, and discharging a firearm in the attack.[41] Despite these convictions, the Ice Cream Wars continued to be waged for several years.

Campbell, Steele and Gray appealed against their convictions in 1985, claiming all along that they had been fitted up by the police, but that appeal was refused. In 1987, Campbell went on hunger strike to protest his innocence, and three years later Joe Steele staged a rooftop protest while on a compassionate home visit. In February 1992, William Love, a prosecution witness, admitted lying in the witness stand. At one point Steele 'superglued' himself to the gates of Buckingham Palace, and escaped from jail on four occasions. Eventually, Steele and Campbell were given leave to appeal, but the case was thrown out in February 1998. Donald Dewar, then Scottish Secretary, refused another appeal in December 1998, arguing there were insufficient grounds to allow it. However, the Scottish Criminal Cases Review Commission (established to investigate potential miscarriages of justice) referred the case back to the Appeal Court in Edinburgh, which sat on 17 February 2004. (In the meantime, both men had been granted interim liberation.) Scotland's Lord Justice Clerk, Lord [Brian] Gill, a contemporary of John Smith's at Glasgow, listened to the appeal alongside Lord [Ranald] MacLean, John's old walking chum, and Lord Macfadyen. On 17 March 2004, the two men had their convictions quashed by the Court of Appeal.[42] Over a decade on from John Smith's death, and two decades on from the original crime,[43] justice is still awaited for the Doyle family.

Nine
THE TORTOISE OF LABOUR
POLITICS, 1979–85

IN THE SHADOW Cabinet elections of June 1979, Smith finished in twelfth place with 88 votes, just ahead of Neil Kinnock, who finished fourteenth, polling 79 votes. Smith later claimed that his short stint as a Labour MP of Cabinet rank had allowed him to sneak into the last available slot in the shadow Cabinet.[1] Subsequently, Smith would be re-elected on to the shadow Cabinet in every year from 1979 until 1992, making him the only Labour figure ever to be elected every year for three full Parliaments. In November 1980, Smith backed Denis Healey in the Labour leadership contest over his old friend Michael Foot.[2] Two other candidates, John Silkin and Peter Shore, were eliminated in the first ballot of Labour MPs, and then Foot defeated Healey narrowly by 139 votes to 129.[3]

But the most traumatic episode of Labour's recent history occurred during March 1981 when thirteen Labour MPs (and one Conservative)[4] joined the breakaway Social Democratic Party (SDP) formed by the 'Gang of Four', comprising Shirley Williams, Roy Jenkins, David Owen and William Rodgers. By the end of 1982, further Labour defections had swelled the number of SDP MPs to 29. In their unrivalled study of the SDP, Ivor Crewe and Anthony King clarify the event's magnitude: 'the largest breakaway from any party for nearly a century'.[5] Michael Foot recalls it as 'a real attempted death blow to the Labour Party', adding, 'If John Smith and one or two others had decided to leave then, the Labour Party would have been bust.'[6] It could indeed have been a great deal worse: only a tenth of Labour MPs defected, and Crewe and King estimate that no more than a quarter of the right of the party deserted.[7]

Smith stayed inside the Labour Party, despite the fact that he had defied the Labour whip and entered the division lobbies in support of Britain's entry into the European Community in October 1971, something all the Gang of Four had done. However, having been one of the 69 Labour rebels in 1971 was not a good predictor of who would defect from Labour to the SDP. Research by Crewe and King shows that of the 22 Labour defectors who served in the 1970 Parliament, eleven voted for European entry, with two others abstaining.[8]

Andy McSmith claims that the difference between right-wing Labour MPs like Giles Radice, George Robertson and John Smith on the one hand, and the Gang of Four on the other, 'had come down to a single, tactical question: whether to stay in the Labour Party, or leave'.[9] McSmith is partly right. Tactics formed only one of the reasons why Smith stayed. Roy Hattersley recalls that he stuck with the Labour Party for three reasons, and he feels that Smith did so for two out of three of those reasons. The reason that applied to Hattersley but not to Smith was ideological: Hattersley still believed in the idea of a socialist government, whereas Smith was 'not ideological'. The second reason (which applied to both of them) was that they were Labour Party men with a tribal instinct that hankered back to an earlier age. Thirdly (and this reason was indeed tactical), both made the sensible calculation that the SDP's temporary popularity was 'a short-term phenomenon' and that the party was going nowhere.[10]

Elizabeth Smith agrees that even in these dark days, 'it simply never occurred to him to leave it, however much those who did might criticise him for not leaving with them'. She reflects that John had a 'deep commitment to the things Labour stands for'. Had Labour simply fallen apart in this period, John would rather have left politics than join another party.[11] Michael Foot also recalls, 'John Smith, you see, wouldn't have dreamt of going'.[12] Jimmy Gordon puts it simply: 'John was visceral about the Labour Party. The Labour Party was an institution that he revered.'[13] Menzies Campbell is even more emphatic: 'John would have fought to the death for his Labour Party membership card.'[14] Smith therefore belonged to that group of loyalists identified by Crewe and King whose 'emotional attachments to the Labour party were simply too strong for them to contemplate leaving'.[15] But as Crewe and King point out, many Labour MPs – including Smith – stayed in the party *despite* believing that its prospects for survival were bleak.[16]

Smith was also sponsored by a trade union, the General and Municipal Workers' Union. Indeed, when Smith had been asked directly why a pro-European like him hadn't joined the SDP, he had replied: 'I am comfortable with the unions. They aren't. That's the big difference.'[17] Again, Crewe and King's analysis shows that defection was more likely if a potential defector did not have these ties of loyalty.[18]

There may also have been a Scottish dimension influencing the decision to defect. Among Scottish Labour MPs, only Robert Maclennan[19] and Dick Mabon joined the SDP, and even Mabon did not leave in the first batch in February and March, waiting until the autumn of 1981. Smith later commented: 'You'll notice very few Scots went.'[20] George Robertson and Donald Dewar, for instance, kept the faith.

So Smith stayed in the Labour Party, despite being chided by two members of the Gang of Four, both former Cabinet colleagues. Bill Rodgers' abiding image of Smith around the time of the SDP split is 'passing me, with his scuffed shoes, looking slightly shamed, shuffling his feet, and looking down'. Rodgers regarded Smith as 'a great disappointment' because he failed to do anything between 1979 and 1981.[21]

Meanwhile, David Owen accused Smith of 'fudging and mudging' in his efforts to hold the Labour Party together. According to Crewe and King, 'Smith replied that Owen would realize sooner or later that fudging and mudging were an essential part of politics.'[22] Five years later, Smith still hadn't forgiven Owen: 'I don't go knocking people, but David Owen isn't a very compelling person. He sees himself as a great oak and won't let any other tree grow in his shadow. There's an arrogance there which I don't find attractive.'[23]

Nor had Smith any time for Roy Jenkins after he left the Labour Party. Smith's secretary Ann Barrett recalls John's expression at finding Jenkins opposite him when John was Guest of Honour at a dinner hosted by the German Ambassador.[24] Smith used to delight in recounting the last line of a speech by 'Woy' Jenkins (complete with impersonation), which emphasised the need to enhance Britain's image as 'a major (w)ranking power in the world'.[25]

Smith subsequently made a point of rubbishing the SDP publicly, despite the fact that his views on key issues were far closer to the party he had refused to join than the one he stayed in. For example, on the fifth anniversary of the SDP, Smith commented on *Newsnight* that 'the SDP is a right-wing alternative to Labour'.[26] John was also 'pretty ruthless' in his advice to his old friend Menzies Campbell about the later rows between David Owen and David Steel. At the 1986 Eastbourne Liberal Party assembly, Steel lost a crucial defence vote by only 652 votes to 625. The vote had a decisive impact on the future of the Alliance; Steel was seen as being 'one down' in his battle with David Owen.[27] Late one night, Menzies Campbell discussed these events with John Smith, mentioning that the vote had only been lost narrowly. John replied: 'Why didn't the Chairman call it the other way?'[28]

Many of the loyal Labour MPs in the centre and on the right of the Labour Party like Smith rallied around the banner of 'Solidarity', a parliamentary faction determined to see off the challenge of the Bennite left.[29] Solidarity came into being after the Wembley conference of January 1981 during which the left altered the party rules in their favour, introducing mandatory reselection for all MPs, and creating an electoral college system for the leadership and deputy leadership contests.[30] Solidarity aimed to combat the

advance of the left in the constituency Labour parties (CLPs) and to protect
centrist and right-of-centre MPs from being deselected.[31] Partly financed by
key Labour-supporting businessmen like Michael Montague (see below),
Solidarity paid the affiliation fees of socialist societies, enabling them to send
delegates to conference to vote on important party matters. Even moderate
Labour MPs like Bruce Millan felt it necessary to organise to prevent control
of the party drifting away from them.[32]

John Smith has been criticised, mainly by allies of Neil Kinnock, for being
insufficiently vigorous in the defence of the Labour Party in its darkest
hours. While Millan, Roy Hattersley, Ann Taylor, Gerald Kaufman, Jack
Cunningham, George Robertson and Donald Dewar took up the baton of the
right, fighting key battles with the left, Smith largely kept his head down, and
went back to his legal career. Roy Hattersley recalls that Smith 'never came to
a Solidarity Committee meeting, but if Solidarity was holding a rally at the
Labour Party Conference, he would turn up and speak'.[33] Mary Goudie, the
secretary of Solidarity from 1981–7, remembers that John became the second
most popular speaker at Solidarity events (behind Roy Hattersley, but just
ahead of Gerald Kaufman), regularly talking at Labour Party rallies (regionally
and nationally), constituency parties, branches, and affiliated organisations
such as the Society of Labour Lawyers and the Fabians.[34] Smith appeared
regularly on *BBC Breakfast News*, *Newsnight* and *Question Time*, becoming a
kind of public face of moderation against the general backdrop of Labour
extremism. He also used his considerable interpersonal skills behind the
scenes with those MPs, especially in Scotland, who were tempted by defection
to the SDP. John was never a great writer. More prolific wordsmiths like Roy
Hattersley and Donald Dewar penned most Solidarity documents. John might
occasionally look over the documents, and offer general legal guidance, but
that was largely it.[35] Even in Parliament, Smith lowered his profile in the early
1980s. Andy McSmith has calculated that Smith made only two speeches in the
House of Commons in 1981 between February and November 1981, and then
did not made another speech for thirteen months until the end of 1982, when
Foot appointed him shadow Energy secretary.[36] As McSmith admits, that did
not include the monthly Trade Questions. Nevertheless, historians trawling
over the documents may be tempted to conclude, like John Rentoul, that
'Smith kept his political profile below sea level during the Bennite
ascendancy'.[37]

But what the documents fail to show is that, although Smith wasn't an
organiser, he excelled at the sort of instinctive wheeler-dealing, the arm-
twisting, threatening and cajoling of colleagues required in the many battles

which were crucial to the position of Solidarity within the parliamentary Labour Party and in the wider Labour movement. Smith admitted to an interviewer shortly before his heart attack that he was 'a bit lazy'.[38] Avoiding creating unnecessary political enemies undoubtedly formed a key part of Smith's political philosophy. But he was never lazy in the sense that in every part of his professional life, he had a sense of urgency and purpose about him, and always conveyed a boundless energy and enthusiasm for the task at hand. The metropolitan political classes did not appreciate the work that John did in Scotland on Fridays and Saturdays.[39] Smith also found that he simply couldn't get elected onto the NEC, where the key battles were being fought between left and right. His first attempt to get elected in 1982 failed miserably when he polled only 36,000 votes (fifteenth place),[40] dropping down to sixteenth place, and garnering only 33,000 votes a year later.[41]

Despite retaining a strong personal affection for Tony Benn, his former boss at the Department of Energy, Smith increasingly despaired at Benn's activities. Colleagues recall Smith shaking his head and saying 'The man's mad'.[42] At one of the Labour conferences in the early 1980s when the hard left of the party effectively took control, Kenneth Munro went with Smith to a conference bar in Blackpool. John looked down at the beer mats, which read: 'John Smith's Bitter'. Smith commented: 'You're bloody right he is!'[43]

The splits between the left and the right of the Labour Party had come to a head in the bitter deputy leadership contest between Denis Healey and Tony Benn in September 1981, which Healey won by less than 1 per cent. Smith had supported Healey's campaign, but acknowledged when interviewed in November 1984 that the electoral consequences of the splits had led to a 'credibility gap' with the electorate because the party 'had spent a good deal of its period in opposition fighting each other'.[44]

Labour in the early 1980s was the subject of extremist infiltration. As Denis Healey recalls: 'We had Trots in the Party.'[45] Smith played a small part in dealing with the Militant Tendency, whom he once described as 'the impossibilists'.[46] Militant was a Troskyite organisation, which successfully infiltrated key committees at CLP and trade union level, exerting an influence on Labour Party politics way beyond its tiny membership. Based on the findings of the Hayward-Hughes Report of 1982, Michael Foot and Jim Mortimer, Labour's general secretary, proposed establishing a register of organisations eligible for affiliation had they applied, with the clear intention of making Militant ineligible under stringent new criteria.[47] In practice, it translated to a policy of expelling around 100 members of the Labour Party.[48]

John Smith became concerned that the Mortimer proposals were so full of legal loopholes that Militant might take legal action to block this expulsion attempt. After the Blackpool Labour Party Conference in the autumn of 1982, he discussed the problem with Derry Irvine.[49] Tony Blair, who had been accepted into Irvine's Chambers in 1977, was called in to assist, but was not introduced to Smith at this stage. Irvine and Blair advised the Labour Party that it might provoke legal action if it pursued Foot and Mortimer's course of action.[50] The register idea was dropped, and only five members of Militant's editorial board were singled out for expulsion. In November 1982, the NEC proposed that Militant should be deemed ineligible for affiliation to the Labour Party.[51] As Blair and Irvine had anticipated, Militant applied for an injunction. In the end, the NEC made a lucky escape on a narrow point of law. Although Mr Justice Nourse ruled that Labour was bound by the principle of natural justice, Militant should have applied a writ blocking the expulsions much earlier when Foot and Mortimer had come up with their original report in June 1982. In Derry Irvine's words, Militant had 'slept on their legal rights'.[52] Nourse's judgment cleared the way for the NEC to proscribe Militant, which they did by eighteen votes to nine in December 1982.[53]

In the mid-1980s, problems with Militant re-emerged, as this time the Labour leadership tried to discipline the local Liverpool Labour Party, and lost the case. After consulting John Smith, Derry Irvine, by this stage a senior QC, only agreed to take on subsequent cases if Labour 'got its tackle in order' by putting the whole matter in the hands of the lawyers, granting Irvine plenipotentiary powers. Neil Kinnock proved to be an excellent client, and Labour generally won disciplinary cases against Militant thereafter.[54]

Meanwhile, in May 1982, before Blair had considered putting in for the Beaconsfield by-election, he consulted Irvine, who then spoke to John Smith.[55] During the by-election, Smith paid a visit to the constituency. Blair finished a predictably poor third. It mattered little. After an unusually short apprenticeship as a parliamentary candidate, Blair entered Parliament a year later as MP for Sedgefield. The first meeting proper between John Smith and Tony Blair didn't occur until around the time of Militant in Liverpool when Blair arrived at the House of Commons for dinner, expecting to discuss deep matters of policy with Smith. Instead, both men apparently drank almost until dawn, allegedly 'emptying every bottle in sight and raiding every drinks cupboard including Denis Healey's'.[56] Murray Elder's clear recollection is that Blair met Smith face to face before Blair entered Parliament to discuss whether Blair should put himself forward for the Beaconsfield by-election.[57] At any rate, after the 1987 general election, Blair and Smith got to know each other much better on a trip to China, during which Chinese officials unwisely challenged Smith to a drinking game, and Blair looked on as Smith taught the inebriated Chinese hosts the words of 'Auld Lang Syne'.[58]

On Irvine's suggestion, Tony Blair also drafted a paper for Smith as shadow Trade and Industry secretary on the legal implications of the privatisation of state-owned industries: 'Tony did a cracking good job and did make an impression on John.'[59] Indeed, Smith had been so impressed that he had circulated the paper to his shadow Cabinet colleagues.[60]

Labour's 1983 general election manifesto – *New Hope for Britain* – which Gerald Kaufman memorably described as 'the longest suicide note in history', contained many policies that were anathema to Smith, including unilateral nuclear disarmament, and withdrawal from the European Economic Community.

For the duration of the 1983 election campaign, Smith, still the party's Energy spokesperson, concentrated on the issue of high unemployment. On 23 May, he appeared in the first of two party political broadcasts, against a backdrop of demolition sites,[61] arguing that the Tories had brought industrial collapse, and that the only way to stop that destruction was to vote Labour. The party had rebuilt Britain, post-1945, and he said that it would make great investment in many areas and create employment. In a speech on 30 May, Smith claimed that 125 people in Scotland had lost their jobs every day since Mrs Thatcher had come to power in 1979. On 9 June, Smith comfortably won his redrawn seat of Monklands East, polling over 50 per cent of the vote but, nationally, Mrs Thatcher was returned to power with a majority of 144, and a majority over the Labour Party of 188.[62]

Three days after polling day, Michael Foot announced his resignation as leader, provoking Labour's first ever extra-parliamentary battle for the Labour leadership. As a result of the Wembley conference reforms, the unions, the CLPs, together with the party's MPs each held a share of votes in the complicated electoral college (in a ratio of 40:30:30). The two main contenders were Neil Kinnock, from the left of the Party, and Roy Hattersley, hailing from the right.

Hattersley, who had been pondering whether to stand against Neil Kinnock for the leadership of the party, received a telephone message from John Smith saying in effect that 'even if no one votes for you, I will'. Hattersley also had to decide whether to stand for the deputy leadership as well as the leadership, and he was left with little choice in the matter when Smith telephoned again to say: 'You've been nominated for the deputy leadership. I've forged your nomination papers.'[63] Hattersley faced a determined challenge for the deputy leadership from Michael Meacher, a left-winger. While Smith headed Hattersley's campaign team, Robin Cook garnered votes for Meacher. Both Smith and Cook tried to avoid a repeat of the bitter 1981 deputy leadership contest between Tony Benn and Denis Healey. In the words of Kinnock's biographer, Martin Westlake, Smith and Cook met regularly to 'ensure that neither candidate damaged the public standing of the other'.[64]

As the day of the leadership ballot neared, it became clear that Roy was not going to defeat Neil for the leadership. Smith admitted as much in a press interview: 'We don't want to take second place, but yes, we'll take it.'[65] David Basnett of the Municipal Workers' Union had been instructed by his union to vote for Roy Hattersley in the leadership contest, but contacted Roy to say he wanted to switch to Neil Kinnock. When Smith heard about Basnett's intention to switch allegiance, he was furious, not least because Basnett was a fellow boilermaker. Using unrepeatable language, Smith told Basnett that his union wasn't going to change its vote.[66] Despite Smith's efforts, Hattersley was well beaten in the leadership contest, polling only 19 per cent of the total, some way ahead of Eric Heffer and Peter Shore, but miles behind Neil Kinnock on 71 per cent. However, Hattersley easily beat Meacher for the deputy leadership by 67 per cent to 27 per cent.[67]

In the shadow Cabinet elections of October 1983, Smith polled 97 votes, finishing in fourth place. He was promoted to the Labour Party's Employment spokesperson, following the decision of Eric Varley to leave Parliament, in order to become chief executive of the Coalite company.[68] Much later on, John Reid revealed that when he had been a special adviser to Neil Kinnock (1983–5), Smith had lobbied for the job of Employment spokesperson, on the following grounds: 'Tell Neil, Tebbit is a bastard, and tell him I'm a bigger bastard.'[69] Unfortunately for Smith, Norman Tebbit moved on to Trade and Industry just as Smith moved to Employment. Nevertheless, Smith respected Tebbit as a political opponent, and was one of the first hospital visitors after Tebbit was badly injured in the Brighton bombing of October 1984.[70]

Smith spent a considerable amount of the 1983–4 session opposing the fine print of the Trade Union Bill, impressing the unions with his opposition to compulsory ballots. Gordon Brown and fellow newcomer Tony Blair observed Smith's deft parliamentary tactics as he argued through sessions of the Bill's committee stage in standing committee F,[71] with both Brown and Blair playing supporting roles.[72] Brown and Blair were very much in John Smith's mould inasmuch as they were workaholics who virtually lived in the House of Commons, from nine in the morning until around midnight. Indeed, Smith and Norman Hogg often gave Gordon Brown a lift into the Commons in the mornings.[73]

At this point, Brown had turned down his first job offer from Kinnock, fearing that he would become stuck interminably in a Scottish portfolio.[74] On Roy Hattersley's recommendation, Blair became a junior Treasury spokesperson in November 1984. A year later, Brown became Smith's number two at Trade and Industry, dealing with regional affairs, and would remain more or less at Smith's side until 1994.[75] John Rentoul comments that, whereas Brown pursued a career path of 'sticking as closely as possible to John Smith', Blair's strategy was much closer to that of John Major, then junior Social Security minister, namely 'openness to all strands of opinion within the Party'.[76] Or as James Naughtie puts it, whereas Smith had acted only as 'an opener of doors' for Blair, he had been 'a benign boss to Brown'.[77]

Smith's main non-legislative issue at the end of 1983 concerned the ongoing industrial dispute between Eddie Shah, owner of the Messenger Group of newspapers in Warrington, and local members of the print workers union, the National Graphical Association (NGA). In November 1983, pickets from the NGA were engaged in violent struggles with police outside the *Stockport Messenger*. Smith condemned the violence, but claimed that the situation had occurred because Mrs Thatcher's negligence had left the situation to be taken care of by the courts. Shah had made no concessions, and sought confrontation rather than conciliation.[78]

Some Kinnock supporters claim that Smith sat back and did nothing during the difficult miners' strike 1984–5. This is inaccurate. Technically, Stan Orme was the shadow Cabinet minister directly responsible for energy matters when the strike started. On 28 March 1983, while Smith was still Energy spokesperson, he had described Ian MacGregor's appointment as the new Coal Board chairman as 'divisive', and that a Labour government would be opposed to working with him.[79] At the beginning of the strike, Smith appeared on *Question Time* with Norman Tebbit, the Secretary of State for Industry and President of the Board of Trade. When asked whether the Government was being intransigent in the miners' strike, Tebbit simply denied that it was a national strike because Arthur Scargill, the president of the National Union of Mineworkers, had not held a ballot for industrial action, while Smith claimed the government was abdicating its duty to the nation by its policy of nonintervention. He also opposed the use of the law courts in the dispute.[80] Neil Kinnock's mistake – which he now describes as 'the greatest regret of my whole life'[81] – was not to call upon Scargill to hold a democratic ballot early on in the dispute. Kinnock and Stan Orme tried to broker a resolution to the dispute, which MacGregor accepted, but Scargill rejected. Kinnock grew to detest Scargill's arrogance.[82] The miners' strike revealed Neil Kinnock's central weaknesses as Labour leader: in order to make Labour electable, he had to renounce most of his left-wing past. Smith had no such problem since he always hailed from the right.

In the October 1984 shadow Cabinet elections, Kinnock gave Smith the shadow Trade and Industry portfolio in preference to Robin Cook.[83] According to Cook's biographer, John Kampfner, Kinnock developed a habit of not promoting his former allies. Cook had made the mistake of opposing his leader's ill-fated attempts at the October 1984 conference to introduce one member, one vote in CLPs for the reselection of Labour MPs, and had to settle for the role of campaigns co-ordinator.[84]

One of Smith's most important tasks at Trade and Industry was figuring out how best to disentangle Labour from its commitment, first outlined in 1982, to return all privatised utilities to the public sector. Labour had also committed itself to the principle of 'no speculative gain', meaning that compensation to Thatcher's newly enriched shareholders, who had made a fast buck with the privatisation of British Telecom or British Gas, would be minimal and highly unpopular. When the BBC journalist Selina Scott asked John Smith how he would persuade people to buy shares in British Telecom if Labour intended to bring it back into public ownership, Smith replied in typically high-minded fashion: 'We will appeal to reason.'[85] While Neil Kinnock was anxious to engage in a reversal of the policy of 'no speculative gain', the wider Labour movement, particularly the public sector unions and the left of the party, still regarded nationalisation as a cherished policy not to be tampered with. Accordingly, the NEC's 1984 statement, A Future That Works, had left the party's policy virtually unaltered.[86]

In 1986, Smith headed a working party to look not only into the issue of shareholder compensation, but also the wider issue of public ownership, working alongside David Blunkett, then a member of the soft left. Together the two men drafted a document entitled Social Ownership.[87] Smith agreed to the re-nationalisation of all the public utilities, but offered full compensation to shareholders, as well as a commitment that Labour would acquire a strategic stake in vital national industries: oil, steel, pharmaceuticals and construction. The changes meant that Labour went into the 1987 general election committed to restoring most of the privatised utilities to the public sector, but on improved terms for shareholders as compared with 1983.[88] Only after the 1987 election would the party radically altered its policy on nationalisation.[89]

Smith had shown once again that he could work well with a figure on the left of the party (although at the time of writing it seems incredible to think of David Blunkett as once hailing from the left), just as he had with Benn, then Foot in the 1970s. It also provides another indication of Smith's favoured political style:

> We managed to change these [policies on nationalisation] without any row. We worked hard for that. I think we can achieve the same sort of unanimity on other issues, but you must set about it patiently. The people in charge just can't announce policies . . . I've no time for excessive policies which you have no hope of carrying through.[90]

While Smith was shadow Trade and Industry spokesperson, he settled on a consistent theme that would characterise his economic beliefs for the rest of his political career: that an efficient economy and a fair society were not mutually exclusive pursuits. Smith was impressed and inspired by Robert Kuttner's book, *The Economic Illusion*.[91] Kuttner challenged the prevailing orthodoxy of new right ideas prevalent in America in the early 1980s that a more egalitarian distribution of incomes and services was only achievable at the expense of an efficient economy. But nor did Kuttner agree with the old utopian, state-centred views of the left, believing that they had not paid sufficient attention in the past to the pursuit of economic growth and investment in the long term.

Smith's ideas on this subject came together most impressively when he gave the Eighth John Mackintosh Memorial Lecture on May Day 1987.[92] Specifically, Smith argued that: '. . . prosperity, broadly defined as a steadily increasing standard of living in an efficient and productive economy, is not only consistent with a socially just and caring society, but that in an intelligently organised community, prosperity and social justice mutually reinforce each other.'[93] Government, he argued, should become the engine of economic growth through co-ordinated investment in education and training, research and development and a regional industrial policy. Public and private sectors would 'pull together in a positive sum game'.[94]

Many of Smith's views in this area of policy chimed with those of Labour-supporting members of the business community. Simon Haskel had been a founder member of the 1972 Industry Group, a group of people involved in business and industry who felt that Labour was too influenced by trade unions and who wished instead to put the view of management in order to achieve a balance between 'both sides of industry', although both Haskel and Smith hated that phrase. The group's aim was to make contact with Labour front benchers, and for businessmen to talk to them about their views relating to business and industry. To this end, they organised meetings, seminars, events and speakers, mainly at the House of Commons.

By the mid-1970s, the fashionable view among monetarist economists and many leading members of industry was that clever accountancy automatically equalled good business practice, that one of the prices of low inflation was persistently high unemployment, that low taxation was required to provide incentives to entrepreneurs, and that productivity could be enhanced if workers had as few rights as possible. Simon Haskel recalls that members of the group were critical of that view, particularly the easy hire and fire of staff.[95] One of Haskel's, and indeed John Smith's, closest friends, Michael Montague, a self-made entrepreneur, led the way in challenging this prevailing orthodoxy.

Of Jewish background, Montague had set up his own electrical firm at the age of only 26. He rose rapidly to become head of the American company, Valor and Yale plc.[96]

With his distinctive moustache and balding head, Montague looked more like an old army general, than a discreetly gay businessman. Smith liked Montague's eccentricity. Over the years, Smith became an occasional visitor to River Willows, Montague's Oxfordshire home. Despite being a very rich man, Montague preferred to travel by public transport, and cycled at weekends, rather than use his Rolls-Royce. He was never ashamed to be a Labour supporter. Nor was he man who held back from speaking his mind. Famously, as chairman of the English Tourist Board, 1979–84, he attacked 'second rate' hoteliers and 'greedy' seaside impresarios.[97] Montague developed a taste for championing the rights of the customer, and went on to head the National Consumers' Council.[98] Rather unfairly, Montague was portrayed as one of 'Tony's cronies' in being elevated to the peerage as Lord Montague of Oxford on Labour's landslide in 1997. His closest ally was John Smith, rather than Tony Blair.

The truth is that Montague had helped out several generations of Labour politicians long before Blair came on the scene. Montague and Simon Haskel concurred with Smith that a healthy economy and a fair society went hand in hand. Haskel likes to think that John Smith vigorously took up these ideas in the 1980s, partly as a result of his regular contact with the members of the group, now renamed the Labour Finance and Industry Group. Up until Smith had read Kuttner's book, he had been uncomfortable with the economics both of business (which was seen as fair to the bosses, but not to the workers), and the left of his own party, which he saw as too biased in favour of working people. Smith had to believe what he was saying in order to espouse it, and once convinced that a strong economy equals a fair society, he ran with it, blossoming as a politician, gradually increasing his profile on the Labour front bench. Haskel adds: 'Once he [Smith] knew what he believed, he could sell it.'[99] Just as importantly for the long term, Smith persuaded other members of the shadow Cabinet to work closely with business people. At his instigation, Gordon Brown and Tony Blair later met key members of the group. In many respects, New Labour's connections with business existed long before Tony Blair's period as leader, and both Blair and Gordon Brown are indebted to Smith for establishing these close links. Montague's name, along with other stalwarts like Simon Haskel, John Gregson and Swarj Paul, rarely appear in histories of the Labour Party because they were deliberately discreet and sought neither fame nor favour. As a result, Montague's current place in historical footnotes is confined to a piece of political trivia, that he collapsed and died on 5 November 1999, the last day that the hereditary peers sat in the House of Lords.[100]

John Smith and Michael Montague also shared the same views on wealth and opportunity. Simon Haskel later recalled that whenever anyone asked Montague how he could be both a Labour supporter and ride around in a Rolls-Royce, he replied: 'I don't want everyone to ride around in a cheap car. I want everyone to ride around in a Rolls.'[101] John Smith did not have a downer on wealth and good living. Donald MacCormick recalls holidaying with Smith at Charente-Maritime in 1981, when the Smiths stayed at the house of a French socialist deputy. What struck MacCormick was not only John's 'relish in seeking to emulate the French political style', but more importantly that John was:

> . . . the kind of socialist who thought and felt in the French manner – regarding wine and good food, restaurants and music and opera not as dubious frivolities but as valued parts of normal living. He had a passionate wish that these pleasures should be spread and enjoyed by the greatest number of people possible.[102]

*

In April 1985, Smith took part in Labour's Jobs and Industry campaign. The main public aim of the campaign was to highlight the plight of Britain's three million unemployed. Innovative campaigning methods included a Jobs Roadshow in marginal constituencies, a 'Jobs for Youth' rock tour led by Billy Bragg, complete with banners and T-shirts, and a poster competition, all designed to appeal to young voters. Smith's involvement was not really noteworthy, although he formally approved the main working document, *Working Together for Britain*, which launched the campaign on 2 April,[103] and appeared in the campaign video (as part of an introductory campaign pack sent out to party workers in February 1985), claiming, 'Labour will put Britain back to work by building a stronger economy.' However, Smith's other main message to Labour's activists in the video was anything but upbeat, stressing: 'We cannot pretend that it will be easy to get Britain back to work.' The underlying message of the campaign video, outlined by Tony Manwaring of Labour's Research Department, was hairshirt rather than hopeful, stressing Labour's need to get its economic act together: 'The campaign must change the mental picture that people have of Labour's economic strategy. Labour must be seen as the Party of production, enterprise and wealth creation – and not as some well-meaning Party that prints money to solve each and every problem.'[104]

Whilst an doubted improvement on the debacle of 1983, the Jobs and Industry campaign still fell well short of the slick presentation that would later characterise Labour's 1987 general election campaign. Opinions differ as to the success of the campaign. Looking back John Prescott's allies fondly refer to it as 'BM – before Mandelson'.[105] Mandelson's appointment as Labour's new director of Campaigns and Communications a few months later heralded a rapid expansion of Labour's new drive to improve its campaigning techniques, leading eventually to a highly professional general election campaign in 1987.

However, as Mark Wickham-Jones rightly points out, the greatest significance of the Jobs and Industry campaign was that: 'For the first time in over fifteen years, moderate members of the shadow Cabinet played a central role in the formation of Labour party economic policy.'[106] Smith and Hattersley had also been assisted for the first time (at least in a major way) by Labour's research department staff (later known as the party's Policy Directorate), while John Eatwell, Neil Kinnock's new economics adviser, liaised with members of the shadow Cabinet, as well as drafting the leader's speeches on economic policy.[107]

Towards the end of this quiet phase in Smith's political career, one journalist dubbed him 'the tortoise of Labour politics', but the commentator was wise enough to add that Smith had amply demonstrated to the 'seemingly faster hares that the race does not necessarily go to the swift – or the noisiest runner'.[108] Perhaps Smith's undiminished energy is better caricatured by Simon Hoggart's later description of Smith 'steaming down the Committee Corridor like a small rhinoceros',[109] unflattering though it may be.

Certain lifelong convictions do not fit the chronology of biography. What of John Smith's conservative views on conscience issues, especially abortion, and the closely related issue of embryo research? In July 1979, John Corrie, the Scottish Tory back bencher, introduced a private members' Bill that sought to amend the Abortion Act 1967 and the Infant Life (Preservation) Act 1929 in several respects, most notably introducing a time limit of 20 weeks for abortions, rather than the legal maximum of 28 weeks. During the Bill's passage, Smith voted against an amendment in the name of Ian Mikardo, the Labour MP for Bow and Poplar, that sought to leave out the 20 weeks provision, inserting 'twenty-four weeks or less' instead. On a free vote, Labour back benchers split 171 to 43, with Smith joining the minority grouping.[110] Corrie's Bill failed due to lack of parliamentary time and filibustering.[111] On 21 January 1988, Smith supported the Second Reading of the private members' Bill in the name of David Alton, the Liberal MP for Mossley Hill, which sought to reduce the upper time limit for legal abortion to eighteen weeks from 28 weeks.[112] However, Smith's support for the principle of the Bill was on the understanding that the Bill's committee stage would see votes on options other than eighteen weeks. Alton's Bill, like the others before it, fell due to filibustering and lack of government time.

However, in April 1990, the House of Commons again voted conclusively on the abortion time limits, as part of the consideration of the far-reaching Human Fertilisation and Embryology Bill. Geoffrey Howe, the Leader of the House, moved initially that the new time limit for abortion should be set at 24 weeks, which was passed by a majority of 206, and thereafter, the House of Commons voted to reject a series of other options, which were moved in 'pendulum fashion'[113] – eighteen weeks, 28 weeks, 20 weeks, 26 weeks and 22 weeks. John Smith did not vote on eighteen weeks and 20 weeks, but voted in favour of 22 weeks (which fell by 46 votes, the narrowest margin of the options other than 24 weeks), and against 26 and 28 weeks,[114] suggesting that he was never an anti-abortion hardliner. Murray Elder recalls that Smith paid close heed to what the prevailing medical evidence said about the sustainability of an infant's life at a given number of weeks when weighing up how to vote.[115]

Smith's conservative stance on abortion had the potential to cause him problems when he became leader of a political party that was 80–90 per cent pro-choice. Indeed, when Smith was elected leader, one liberal commentator in the *New Statesman & Society* highlighted the fact that Smith had supported Alton's Bill, and demanded that he 'must be asked at every opportunity what the party line should be on the issue of women's control over their own fertility'.[116] A week later, Steve Platt, the editor of the *New Statesman & Society*, responded to a considerable number of letters on the subject by disagreeing with his columnist's article:

Some issues are not, as Sean French suggests, matters for an imposed 'party line', but for personal – and often very difficult choices of conscience. Smith would support increased restrictions on the availability of abortion. So be it. The great majority of Labour MPs would not. It is their numbers, not Smith's individual conscience, that would determine any future Labour government's policy. And that is party line enough.[117]

Platt was right. The simple solution for any political leader whose strong views on a matter of conscience differ from his or her party, is to allow the MPs concerned a free vote in the House of Commons, which Smith almost certainly would have done.[118]

Smith took a pragmatic line on the law relating to divorce. As early as January 1971, he had supported divorce law reform in Scotland, recognising that there was no point in carrying on marriages 'when in reality, the marriage has long been dead and buried'.[119] He did not believe that divorce law reform would adversely affect the institution of marriage, an institution which he revered: in later life, Smith would often intone to his work colleagues: 'You should be married.'[120]

Despite his traditional Scottish upbringing, Smith consistently voted in favour of the lowering the age of homosexual consent.[121] Murray Elder believes that Smith did so primarily on the grounds of equity rather than on the basis of his personal morality.[122] On 21 February 1994, 39 Labour MPs, including David Blunkett, shadow Health secretary, Ann Taylor, shadow Education spokesperson, as well as the Chief Whip (Derek Foster), the Deputy Chief Whip (Don Dixon) and the Pairing Whip (Ray Powell) voted against Edwina Currie's amendment to the Criminal Justice and Public Order Bill that aimed to reduce the age of consent for homosexual sex from 21 to sixteen.[123] On this occasion, the *New Statesman & Society*'s editorial diverted from the sensible line it had taken over Smith's views on abortion several months before, questioning whether 'opposition to equal rights for gay men is compatible with senior office in the party', and speculated whether Smith should ask these front benchers if 'their consciences allow them to continue to serve under his leadership'.[124]

Ten
CHOPPERS AND WHOPPERS

HE DETAILS SURROUNDING the Westland Affair are well documented
elsewhere.[1] This account seeks merely to highlight John Smith's
impressive role in harrying the government on the issue, and its positive
impact on his future political career (and conversely the negative impact on
Neil Kinnock's career).

John Smith sensed from any early stage in the Westland affair, as he put it,
that 'something was fishy'. Roy Hattersley rang Smith during the Christmas
recess of 1986 to sound out his shadow Cabinet colleague on what he thought
of the crisis that was brewing. Labour had a spare supply day on 15 January,
and the two agreed to run with a debate on Westland.[2]

On 9 January 1986, Michael Heseltine, the Defence Secretary, resigned from
the Cabinet over the apparent failure of the Prime Minister to consider a
European takeover bid for the ailing Westland Helicopter Company based in
Yeovil, but it was Leon Brittan, the Secretary of State for Trade and Industry
who fell into the opposition's firing line because of his (and indeed Mrs
Thatcher's) apparent favouritism towards Sikorsky-Fiat, a rival American bid.

At 3.41 pm on Monday, 13 January 1986, Leon Brittan gave an all-too-brief
statement to the House of Commons on the background to the Westland
affair.[3] As soon as the Secretary of State for Trade and Industry sat down, John
Smith asked why on 8 January Brittan had met with Sir Raymond Lygo, the
chief executive of British Aerospace, despite the fact that ministers had agreed
before Christmas not to lobby on either consortium's behalf, and to leave the
matter for Westland shareholders to decide:

> Does the right hon. and learned Gentleman not understand that unless he
> gives a full account of what was said to Sir Raymond Lygo the impression
> will continue to circulate widely in Britain that the right hon. and learned
> Gentleman was saying one thing to Parliament, that he was even-handed,
> and doing another thing in practice and seeking to influence the outcome
> of the deal?[4]

Brittan then reluctantly gave an account of his meeting with Lygo on 8
January, at which Lygo had expressed concern that British Aerospace might

lose substantial orders to the United States for the European Airbus (A320) if it backed the European consortium bid, and that a successful European bid might provoke US retaliation in the form of protectionist measures. Brittan had therefore indicated that it was in the national interest that the Westland issue did not drag on.[5]

However, the real damage was done by Michael Heseltine, who asked Brittan whether he had received any letters from British Aerospace, giving its views of the meeting between Brittan and Lygo. Heseltine knew perfectly well that a letter existed – from Sir Austin Pearce, chairman of British Aerospace, to the Prime Minister – so his question was not asked in innocence. Instead of admitting the existence of this letter (and indeed, palming off queries about it on the grounds that it had been marked 'Private and Confidential'), Brittan chose evasion, claiming he had not received any such letter.[6] When Dennis Skinner asked Brittan again whether he had received any letters from the chairman of British Aerospace, Brittan replied that he was 'not aware of any letter from Sir Raymond Lygo to anyone else either'.[7] Of course he wasn't; the chairman was Sir Austin Pearce, and the chief executive was Sir Raymond Lygo – technically the government had received a letter from the former; all Brittan's grubby reply indicated was that he had not received one from the latter.

Even more damning was the fact that throughout this exchange, the Prime Minister sat on the government front bench and said nothing. Indeed, while Brittan got himself tied up in knots, Mrs Thatcher ordered that Pearce be contacted so that, with his clearance, Downing Street could make known the existence of the Pearce letter. Having watched the Channel Four news coverage of Brittan's statement earlier in the day, Gerald Malone, the Secretary of State's parliamentary private secretary, realised that his boss would have to go back to the House to retract his earlier statement.[8] At 10.27 pm, Brittan was forced to apologise unreservedly for misleading the House earlier in the day, but he did not perform even that task very honourably because he claimed he had been protecting the confidentiality of Austin Pearce.[9] John Smith not only highlighted Brittan's failure to make an unreserved apology, he also engaged in a cross-examination of Brittan's misleading replies earlier in the day to chants of 'Resign' from Labour back benchers.[10]

Having dealt with Leon Brittan, Smith then laid a large portion of the blame for Westland at the feet of the Prime Minister:

> Throughout the whole of that performance this afternoon, the Prime Minister sat in silence. She had more knowledge than any other hon. Member because she was the recipient of that letter and, no doubt, had read

it before she came across to the House of Commons. In that circumstance, why did the Prime Minister not even lean across to the Secretary of State, who was within inches of her throughout the debate, and correct him if he was at some stage misleading the House? I ask the Prime Minister to apologise to the House tonight or tomorrow for what was said by the Secretary of State.[11]

Brittan tried to recover the situation through repeated apologies (six in all), but when back benchers in the House of Commons sense weakness, they go in for the kill. Roy Jenkins described Brittan's behaviour as 'pathetic', attacked the Prime Minister for allowing her minister to mislead the House for half an hour, and claimed that although what Brittan had said 'may just be within the formal bounds of truth, the margin is so narrow that we shall count our spoons quickly whenever they [Brittan and Thatcher] are together again'.[12] Patrick Cormack, a Tory back bencher never to be underestimated for his ability to wound a stricken minister, asked the Secretary of State: 'Does he not accept that his inglorious part in this long and unhappy chapter should come to an end?'[13] Then, Dennis Skinner, one of those who had been misled, claimed Brittan had 'no alternative but to go – and take the Lady with him'.[14]

Six years later, Edward Pearce, the political columnist for the *New Statesman*, pithily summed up the secret behind Smith's parliamentary triumph over Westland: 'Mr Smith's genius, exemplified over Westland, is to catalogue wrongdoing with a twitch of the eyebrow or nostril as if such things defied belief, but evidently have happened. Poor, rap-taking Leon Brittan was to look then, like the prisoner in the dock.'[15]

On 15 January 1986, the opposition had its first chance to inflict real political damage on Mrs Thatcher. As described, an opposition day debate had been selected before the Christmas recess. It is now forgotten that on this occasion, Neil Kinnock performed very well, successfully pinning the blame for the crisis on Mrs Thatcher:

> Only one question remains in my mind about the Secretary of State for Trade and Industry: is he a culprit, or a victim, in this matter? The Prime Minister sits next to him today, as she did on Monday. Is he her agent or has he been acting on his own? That is the question that the Prime Minister must answer. She must answer it, honestly, now.[16]

Only an hour before his wind-up speech, Smith had seen the contents of a leaked letter, originally written by the Solicitor-General, Patrick Mayhew,[17] in which Mayhew had criticised the conduct of Michael Heseltine for making 'material inaccuracies' about the European bid. Smith asked how had the

Solicitor-General come to write such a letter, and who was responsible for the leak:

> While the first matter is important, the second is sinister. If it is the case that one Department of this Government deliberately organised a leak to frustrate a Minister in the same Government, that is not only dirty tricks but a habit that is inimical to the practice of good government in this country.[18]

By this stage, Mrs Thatcher had instigated a Whitehall inquiry into the leaked letter, during the course of which Colette Bowe, an official in the Department of Trade and Industry, was identified as the culprit.

In the course of the next ten days, Smith tried to keep up the pressure on the government by making a large number of media appearances. After the opposition day debate on 15 January, Smith told Donald MacCormick on *Newsnight* that the Westland issue was 'a graphic illustration of the way the Government sacrifices the public interest to its own ideology'.[19] That weekend, Smith emphasised that Thatcher and Brittan had not behaved in an even-handed way over the two rival bids; indeed, difficulties had been put in the way of the European bid. There seemed to be government 'by leakage and misunderstanding', increasing the public's perception of Thatcher's dictatorial style of government.[20] On Wednesday, 22 January 1986, Smith again appeared on *Newsnight*, this time arguing that if Mrs Thatcher gave a 'blow-by-blow' account of what had happened, it would go some way to pacifying the House of Commons, but worries were still being openly expressed. In particular, the 'Big Question' was whether there was ministerial involvement in the leak, and whether the guilty party would be prosecuted: 'This is a different kind of leak than usual because it was done deliberately to damage a colleague.' The whole Westland business had been 'a shabby affair'.[21]

On Thursday, 23 January, Mrs Thatcher suggested that her office did not seek her agreement for the leak of the Mayhew letter, but she added: 'Had I been consulted, I should have said that a different way must be found of making the relevant facts known.'[22] Alex Fletcher, the Conservative MP for Edinburgh Central asked the Prime Minister whether she was satisfied that the statement she had just given had enhanced the integrity of the government.[23] The following day, Smith appeared yet again on *Newsnight*, commenting: 'I don't think I have ever heard a shiftier statement made to the House of Commons than the one the Prime Minister made.'[24] Tom King, the Northern Ireland secretary, was wheeled out on behalf of the government, claiming that he felt 'nausea at the sanctimonious approach of John Smith'.[25] It was the only effective blow landed on Smith during the whole affair. Nevertheless, by the next day Leon Brittan had resigned as Trade and Industry secretary.

The opposition's best chance to unseat Mrs Thatcher came on Monday, 27 January 1986 when they tabled an emergency debate in the House of Commons. Unbeknown to the opposition, leading members of the Cabinet – the 'greybeards' or 'men in grey suits' – had got together earlier in the day, and 'helped' the Prime Minister draft her speech that evening so as to provide a plausible explanation as to why the blame for the leaked letter could not be pinned directly at the door of No. 10.[26] Neil Kinnock delivered one of the most verbose and mistimed speeches of the Thatcher era. After hostile interventions from Tory back benchers, the leader of the opposition was forced to withdraw allegations of dishonesty against the Prime Minister. Then, he made a slip about bids being made for Heseltine instead of Westland.[27] Kinnock rambled on, quickly losing the attention of his audience. Admittedly, he was not helped by the constant, and seemingly orchestrated, chattering on the Tory back benches, but it was pitiful that the Labour back bencher George Foulkes had to intervene to ask the Speaker to 'do something about the giggling schoolgirls opposite'.[28]

Once Kinnock had sat down, all Mrs Thatcher had to do was to play a straight bat, which she did, merely reading out her carefully prepared statement, steadfastly refusing to take interventions, especially from the dogged Tam Dalyell.[29] Later on in the debate, Michael Heseltine saw which way the wind was blowing, and rallied behind the Prime Minister,[30] provoking a stinging attack from Michael Foot, who quoted Sir Winston Churchill: 'It's all right to rat, but you can't re-rat.'[31]

Smith's wind-up speech came too late to topple Margaret Thatcher, but he revelled in the drama of the occasion: 'At times, it was a bit like a courtroom. It was exciting.'[32] Like the great advocate that he was, Smith still managed to land an effective blow on the Prime Minister by focusing on the best part of the opposition's case: what was the precise extent of Mrs Thatcher's involvement in the leaked Mayhew letter? Smith quoted Mrs Thatcher's inadequate statement of 23 January, in which she had said, in reply to a question from Cranley Onslow, chairman of the 1922 Committee, that it was 'vital to have accurate information in the public domain because we knew that judgements might be founded upon that . . . It was to get that accurate information to the public domain that I gave my consent.'[33] Smith therefore asked: 'Why did the Prime Minister tell us last Thursday that she gave her consent to the leaking of the letter into the public domain?'[34] Did the Prime Minister mean consent to the leak or consent to the inquiry? To Smith, the answer was clear:

It is obvious for everyone to see [in *Hansard*] that the Prime Minister did not mean that [consent to the inquiry]. So she either gave us the wrong answer then [23 January] or today. Which one was it? On the record in *Hansard* the Prime Minister admits that she gave her consent to the leaking of the information. Until she publicly corrects that account and answers the particular allegation that I have made, the question will remain unanswered.[35]

Smith knew he had hit his target when Mrs Thatcher twice intervened to claim that she did not give her consent to the leaking of the information.[36] He later recalled the moment: '*She* interrupted me, eyes blazing, she was so angry! I was delighted because it seemed to me to be a sign of weakness.'[37] Smith went on:

If we are to accept the Prime Minister's statement that she did not give her consent, she was remarkably foolish to say so when she answered the question to the House. It takes me back to my days in the criminal courts. When some people gave unfortunate answers when required to do so about their activities they did not always get such an understanding response. 'I made a mistake', said the Prime Minister. Did the Prime Minister make a mistake? That is one of the unanswered questions, and there are more.[38]

Smith concluded by taking a swipe at the 'steadily deteriorating' standards of good government in Britain under Mrs Thatcher:

I hope that the time will come soon in this House of Commons when Ministers, including the Prime Minister, when asked straight questions will give honest answers; when we will have a Government in whose competence, as well as in whose integrity, we can have confidence.

The problem is this: if we accept the explanation given to us, it is a sorry tale of woeful incompetence. If we cannot accept it, the whole integrity of this Administration is suspect.[39]

It remains an article of faith to some Labour back bench MPs that if only John Smith had led for the opposition instead of Neil Kinnock, Mrs Thatcher might have fallen. After all, Mrs Thatcher had said earlier in the day: 'I may not be Prime Minister by six o'clock tonight.'[40] On balance, however, Thatcher survived because of the last minute intervention of leading members of the Cabinet, ironically a rare reassertion of collective Cabinet responsibility.[41]

Only days later, Smith made the government look shifty again, this time attacking its attempts to sell off British Leyland's car division, Austin Rover, to the American-owned Ford motor company, and British Leyland's Truck, Bus and Land Rover Divisions to General Motors. Paul Channon, Leon Brittan's replacement as Trade and Industry secretary, argued that these companies were costing the taxpayer a fortune, that there was no way that people could keep putting their 'heads in the sand', and that this sort of joint venture was the way forward. Smith, however, argued that the country was 'shocked at the casual way the Government has gone about this matter', and portrayed the proposed sell-off as 'blind dogmatism that prefers a foreign private sector solution to a British National Interest'.[42]

Labour's Trade and Industry spokesperson always seemed to know when best to strike. Smith had got wind of the secret Rover deals some weeks before, but he persuaded Kinnock to hang fire to gain the maximum political capital over Westland before moving on to the next target.[43] Smith repeated the tactic that he had deployed during Westland of asking the Secretary of State a series of specific questions.[44] Channon made a steady, honourable attempt, but was no match for Smith. Other back bench Tories accused Smith of unnecessarily stirring up anti-US feeling without offering a viable alternative. In fact, Smith supported a credible British Leyland management buy-out plan, in which BL Trucks and Bedford vans would have merged, keeping control of the company in the United Kingdom. Moreover, Smith had a deep-seated attachment to the fate of British manufacturing industry. As he pointed out to David Dimbleby, British Leyland had just produced a new range of vehicles, and was beginning to turn things around after a very difficult trading period. At this point, Britain shouldn't be selling its key industries to its major competitors.[45] And even if Smith was being opportunistic, his primary responsibility was to harry the government of the day, a task that he had once again performed with great skill. On 6 February, the government backed down. A month later, talks collapsed between the government and General Motors over the Trucks and Land Rover sell-off.

Up until this point, John Smith's stock had always been very high in the House of Commons among Labour MPs, but not outside. Commentators and columnists, if they referred to him at all, sometimes asked 'John Who?' Westland wasn't exactly a turning point, because Smith's star had already been rising, but his great performances undoubtedly made him better known with the general public. Smith's emergence from relative anonymity gave him a fresh appeal, a kind of newness that wasn't entirely warranted, given his previous brief spell of media attention as a Cabinet minister at the end of the Callaghan government. The columnist Edward Pearce likened Smith's quiet phase to Charles II's comment about Sidney Godolphin – 'never in the way, never out of the way'.[46] It was a good comparison because Godolphin's reliability as an administrator was the secret of his rise through the ranks,[47] as it had been in Smith's case.

A series of largely favourable press profiles followed Smith's Westland success.[48] For instance, Peter Riddell, then political editor of the *Financial Times*, profiling Smith in *The Listener*, accurately predicted that the shadow Trade secretary would become shadow Chancellor, describing him as 'the indispensable Labour figure of his generation'.[49] Other reviews were not quite so flattering. John Sweeney, for instance, nicknamed Smith 'MacBuddha', likening him to the Dalai Lama:

> Both have the same physical characteristics: stolid frames turning to podge, topped off with inscrutable, beatific physiognomies. Both wear glasses. Both are emphatic moderates. Both come from hilly countries, oppressed by a larger and more populous neighbouring land. And both represent unfashionable faiths – socialism and Tantric Buddhism respectively – downtrodden, for the moment at least, by the reigning ideologies in London and Peking, with a warmth which earns them respect.[50]

Frequent appearances on *Newsnight*, BBC *Breakfast Time*, *This Week*, *Next Week* (then hosted by David Dimbleby) and *Question Time* had raised Smith's public profile. By the autumn of 1986, Smith and his family were even profiled in *Woman's Own*, where the shadow Trade secretary revealed how he kept his ego intact. The previous Christmas, the three teenage Smith girls had given him a notice to pin on the wall of his House of Commons office: 'The trouble with political jokes is that they get elected.'[51]

It had been an outstanding year. The only blemish occurred in February 1986 when Smith was fined £60 at Dumfries Sheriff Court after admitting driving at 98mph on the A74 Glasgow-Carlisle road.[52] Nevertheless, by November 1986, Smith concluded: 'I've been in the House of Commons for sixteen years, but it's only this year that I've been noticed outside it.'[53] His stock was also rising still further inside the House of Commons. In October 1986, he finished in second place in the shadow Cabinet elections (a considerable improvement on his fifth place a year before), just behind Gerald Kaufman.

On Wednesday, 19 November 1986, Smith won the coveted *Spectator/ Highland Park* Parliamentarian of the Year award at a luncheon in the River Room at the Savoy Hotel. Charles Moore, then editor of *The Spectator*, read out the judges'[54] citation:

> Westland was one of those occasions where the Opposition needs not a cloud of elevated eloquence, but a fund of fierce commonsense. It found it in John Smith, its trade and industry spokesman. Instead of generalised denunciations of the Government, Smith preferred chapter and verse. With his lawyer's acumen and his Scottish bluntness, he harried the

Government through its disasters and used his victories to further later campaigns. Westland, Austin-Rover, Land-Rover – if Mr Smith were a regiment, these names would be emblazoned on his colours. He knows when to press on and, even more difficult, when to stop. He displays good nature without weakness and good speaking without frills. The judges had no difficulty in agreeing that his was the outstanding parliamentary achievement of the year.[55]

Smith's short acceptance speech perfectly captured the traditional ribaldry of the occasion. (Free samples of whisky were handed out at the luncheon.) He read out a letter from an anonymous member of the public, who had complained about a recent Smith speech on privatisation. Part of it read: '. . . you bald, owl-looking Scotch bastard. So get back to Scotland and get that other twit Kinnock back to Wales.' The following day, Frank Johnson, then a columnist for *The Times*, quipped: 'Mr Roy Hattersley, the shadow Chancellor, must accept that he has now lost the battle over a future Labour Government's attitude to privatisation. He really must stop writing to shadow Cabinet colleagues in this way.'[56]

But, as Smith received his award of a silver quaich[57] from John Biffen, the previous year's winner, it would hardly have been possible to have listened to the citation's reference to 'a cloud of elevated eloquence' without reflecting that had he been up to the relatively straightforward task of taking advantage of an open goal, Neil Kinnock, rather than John Smith, should have been collecting the award. Instead, the hard and bitter reality was that Kinnock had stumbled appallingly when it had mattered most. In retrospect, if Westland was the point where Smith's political career in opposition really took off, it was also the first unshakeable doubt in Kinnock's structurally unsound efforts to resemble the future Prime Minister. Moreover, for all the subsequent claims that Smith didn't offer his full-hearted support to Kinnock's leadership, from Westland onwards large sections of the PLP and hostile commentators in the media couldn't *avoid* comparing the parliamentary strengths of Smith (and therefore his leadership credentials) with the weaknesses of Kinnock in this sphere. It is in the nature of the competitive bear-pit that is the House of Commons that such comparisons are made. Smith's star had risen to a point where he now looked and sounded like a future leader of the Labour Party, and it must have been very hard for the incumbent of the post to have failed on an issue where one of the pretenders to the throne had succeeded.

It must have become difficult for Smith to retain his respect for a leader when he had demonstrated that he could do the job better. Indeed, Hattersley recalls that John was 'bad-tempered' about Neil's poor performance over

Westland.[58] From Westland onwards, the two men kept their distance. Smith, bound by loyalty to his party, refused to challenge Kinnock openly, despite periodic approaches from anti-Kinnock Labour MPs. But by the same token, he privately let off steam at Kinnock's weaknesses. Kinnock, meanwhile, refused to confront his indispensable subordinate. It set the pattern of the relationship between the two men for the next six years.

As a result of his political success at the dispatch box, Smith's diary began filling up with more meaningful events. In November 1986, he deputised for Neil Kinnock at a conference held by West Germany's trade union bank, and in the same month spoke at a fringe meeting at the Confederation of British Industry's annual conference. Significantly, he had finally started giving up at least some weekends with his family, something he had previously been very reluctant to do.[59] It had seemed pointless with all Labour's infighting in the early 1980s. But now his career was on an upward path, there at least seemed some point in such personal sacrifice.

The task of arranging all these extra diary commitments fell to Ann Barrett, who became Smith's secretary in January 1987. Barrett, an Irish woman, had worked for businessmen in Belfast before moving abroad as a secretary attached to the diplomatic service. After running a bookshop in Limerick in the West of Ireland, she became a secretary for the PLP, taking shadow Cabinet minutes on a Wednesday afternoon. Ann organised Smith's diary as Trade and Industry spokesperson, sharing John's tiny office, roughly twelve foot by seven foot. It was so small that John had to ask Ann to move out of her seat so that he could get documents out of the desk drawers.[60]

Smith took part in meetings of the leader's committee, set up by Kinnock in 1986, and comprising members of the shadow Cabinet, the NEC and the trade unions. He was part of the Labour team charged with drafting Labour's 1987 general election manifesto, *Britain Will Win*, and was one of the heavyweight shadow Cabinet speakers deployed to give key speeches in various parts of the country during the campaign. Smith's main role during the 1987 election campaign was to plug Labour's very patriotic industrial strategy. On 24 March 1987, a few weeks before the campaign got underway, he launched Labour's industrial policy document, *New Industrial Strength for Britain*. As with the attack on the Land Rover sale a few months earlier, the aim was to build trust in Labour by identifying the party as being pro-British. To that end, on 27 May Smith took part in a *Newsnight* discussion on the fate of British industry, hosted by his old friend, Donald MacCormick, where he debated the issues with Paul Channon and Ian Wrigglesworth, the SDP/Liberal Alliance's spokesperson on Trade and Industry, after a film report from Will Hutton extolling the virtues of Germany's emphasis on research and development.[61] On 1 June, Smith led Labour's morning press conference, at which he was surrounded by television and video equipment, a bicycle and a fridge, and announced the number of job losses in these industries. Labour, he said, would support a 'Buy British' policy.[62]

However, Smith's worst moment on the campaign trail came on 27 May 1987, during *Election Call*, a BBC phone-in programme hosted by Sir Robin Day (and simultaneously broadcast on Radio Four). A man claiming to be an old soldier posed Smith a scenario whereby the West's conventional weapons were doing well against Soviet ones, but then the Soviets used nuclear weapons: the questioner asked what would a Labour government do if it had disbanded all its nuclear weapons, as Labour proposed? Smith replied that in that situation the Ministry of Defence would have to consider the situation, but he believed it was wrong to have battlefield nuclear weapons, which were likely to be used at an early stage of any conflict. Probably, Smith had answered the question about as well as it could have been done, in terms of trying to defend his party's position. In their famous general election series, David Butler and Dennis Kavanagh claim that Smith 'fumbled badly'. [63] At any rate, it was a lawyer's answer.

Like his political hero Hugh Gaitskell, Smith believed in multilateral nuclear disarmament, but since his party's policy was unilateral nuclear disarmament, he had a circle to square if he was to abide by the collective responsibility of the shadow Cabinet. Smith undoubtedly achieved this through sophistry. Andy McSmith unearthed an interview with Smith in a left-wing magazine called *Radical Scotland* in February 1983, where Smith claimed that: 'There is no great moral gulf between a unilateralist and a multilateralist if they are both genuine disarmers.' Smith added: 'What is needed is good timing so that a unilateral initiative has the maximum multilateral effect.' There was no reason why Britain should be an independent nuclear power.[64]

Nevertheless, Smith's 1987 general election reply to the old soldier stuck in the throat of Dick Mabon, an SDP defector. In Mabon's eyes, Smith and his allies on the Labour right 'trembled at unilaterialism': the unilateralists were 'cowards' and 'appeasers' who were willing to lay down Britain's arms as an example to the rest of the world, as if that gesture would have made any difference to the cause of world peace: 'They were nuts,' he adds. Mabon also could not believe that pro-European politicians like Smith had defended the earlier 1983 general election pledge to withdraw from the EEC, especially since Smith had been one of the 69 rebels to vote with the Conservatives in favour of European entry in October 1971 (see chapter 5). Of course, deep down,

Smith had not changed his views either on the need for an independent
nuclear deterrent or the merits of EEC membership, but Mabon's view is that
Smith's support for the shadow Cabinet line was the price he had to pay for
promotion.[65] Perhaps the inevitable demands of adhering to collective shadow
Cabinet responsibility loomed larger in Smith's mind.

Rather like 1959, Labour fought a highly professional campaign at the 1987
general election, vastly improved in presentational terms from the previous
election, but with very little to show for it in terms of seats gained from the
Conservatives. The best illustration of the new professionalism came with the
famous party election broadcast on 21 May 1987 made by Colin Welland and
Hugh Hudson of *Chariots of Fire* renown, featuring Neil and Glenys Kinnock
hand-in-hand on the cliff-tops of North Wales. Less convincing was Smith's
short contribution in which he 'praised' Kinnock's handling of Militant.[66]
Labour's Industry spokesperson performed far better during Labour's final
party political broadcast on 8 June, when he was filmed on a station platform,
arguing that Labour's first priority was to reduce unemployment by one
million.[67] Three days later, Smith began election night by claiming that the
contest was still wide open, that Labour would do well in the key marginals.
But even at this stage, he knew the game was up, and had recourse to his innate
high-mindedness, claiming that the better off had turned their backs on their
fellow citizens. By the time he was filmed being returned as the member for
Monklands East, Smith was claiming the end of Thatcherism and that deep
divisions would be wrought in the country in her third term.[68]

Smith never bought into the invulnerability of Margaret Thatcher and what
he viewed as her misguided philosophy. He always thought that the pendulum
would eventually turn in Labour's favour.[69] John was incredulous that the
electorate did not share his point of view. For instance, John later spoke with
pride about a conversation with a wealthy neighbour outside his plush
Morningside home. When Smith had asked the neighbour whether the
windfall from the Tory's proposed poll tax (which cut bills for those owning
big houses) would be sufficient to change his vote to the Conservatives, the
neighbour indignantly replied: 'I am not about to be bought for £1,000 a year.'
The man then snorted that he would be voting Labour for social reasons.
Perhaps Smith's most endearing feature was to believe, quite genuinely, that
such a sense of social conscience existed amongst Englishmen who owned
similarly big houses.[70]

Eleven
EVERYBODY NEEDS GOOD NEIGHBOURS

THE 1987 SHADOW Cabinet elections held on 25 June witnessed the rise of Tribune, the waning of Solidarity, and the decimation of the Campaign Group. In all, 42 Labour back benchers contested fifteen places.[1] Tribune endorsed fourteen candidates, of whom eight were successful. Solidarity fielded eighteen candidates, but only six were elected. Long-standing moderates like Peter Shore and Giles Radice were voted off the shadow Cabinet. Meanwhile, the Campaign Group put up nine candidates, but only one – Jo Richardson (a joint Campaign and Tribune Group member) – was elected.[2] John Smith finished fifth in the poll, behind three members of the Tribune Group – Bryan Gould (163), John Prescott (130) and Michael Meacher (127) – and one fellow Solidarity member, Gerald Kaufman (115).[3] Solidarity had fought and won many of the crucial battles of the early 1980s – as secretary Mary Goudie says, 'We set the scene.'[4] But now came a new breed of more aggressive politician under the Tribune banner, demanding swifter modernisation of the party.

Peter Shore and Denis Healey returned to the back benches, leaving Neil Kinnock a modest amount of room to reshape his shadow Cabinet team. John Smith was appointed shadow Chancellor, replacing Roy Hattersley, who was shifted sideways to become shadow Home Secretary.[5] Hattersley had been widely criticised for his presentation of Labour's taxation policies during the 1987 election. His strategy was very different from that which Smith would operate in his shadow Budget in 1992 (see chapter 16). Instead of coming out with full details of Labour's tax plans, Hattersley wanted to keep them as vague as possible. Labour only committed itself to saying that no one earning less than £25,000 a year would be worse off under Labour. The policy held until the final week of the campaign when Kinnock admitted that removing the upper earnings limit (UEL) on national insurance contributions (NICs) might result in people who earned more than £15,000 paying 'a few pence more'. On the Saturday before polling day, Hattersley stoically stuck to the original policy during a heated BBC television interview with Martyn Lewis.[6] In his memoirs,

Hattersley recalls telephoning Smith afterwards. 'Was it as bad as I think?' Hattersley ventured. Smith replied: 'Worse.'[7]

Bryan Gould's top spot in the shadow Cabinet poll led to press speculation that he could choose the post he wanted, namely the shadow Chancellorship. According to Gould, Smith 'regarded himself as the natural heir to the job', while suspecting that a campaign was being orchestrated on Gould's behalf. Apparently, Smith was 'very rude' (within earshot of Gould's research assistant on the House of Commons terrace), saying that he was 'not about to be muscled out of his rightful inheritance by an upstart like Gould'.[8] According to Donald Macintyre, Gould badly wanted to replace Hattersley, but Kinnock told Gould that Hattersley had insisted on Smith as his successor.[9] Hattersley concurs with this version of events, adding that Kinnock initially replied to every point that Hattersley made with 'But Bryan came top', to which Hattersley is said to have reminded his leader that John Prescott had polled second place, but that didn't put him in the running for the post of shadow Foreign Secretary.[10] Gould admitted to being 'a little disappointed' to have been made shadow Trade and Industry Secretary.[11]

Elsewhere, Gerald Kaufman replaced Denis Healey as shadow Foreign Secretary, while Michael Meacher's good poll showing earned him the post of Employment spokesperson, in preference to Prescott, who had to settle reluctantly for the Energy portfolio.[12] At the suggestion of John Smith, Gordon Brown, (then aged 36, having polled 88 votes in the shadow Cabinet elections) became shadow Chief Secretary to the Treasury, and Smith's new deputy. Moreover, Kinnock, in an effort to tackle the Conservatives jibes on Labour's tax and spending, made the post of shadow Chief Secretary to the Treasury one that qualified for shadow Cabinet rank. Brown's role was to stop shadow Cabinet colleagues from making uncosted spending commitments which the Tories could exploit.[13]

Smith's promotion to shadow Chancellor marked the end of his legal career. Until that point, he had taken a few cases during the House of Commons' long summer recess,[14] but now he felt that pressures of time and possible conflicts of interests meant that his career as an advocate had to be, if not given up forever, then at least put in cold storage. John McCluskey also believes that Smith felt that 'defending guilty men was not good for his image'.[15] Smith's last civil case involved defending clients who had miscalculated when converting Jordanian dinars into pound sterling.[16] That the new shadow Chancelllor was defending someone who didn't know how to convert dinars into pounds was an ironic private joke at the Scottish Bar.[17]

Archibald, Sarah and
John Smith

Archibald, Sarah, John, Anne and
Mary Smith on holiday in Dublin

John Smith in 1953

GLASGOW TEAM WIN "THE SCOTSMAN" TROPHY

Mr John Smith, of Glasgow University, receives "The Scotsman" Trophy from Mr G. Fraser Cowley, an Assistant Editor of the paper, at the end of the inter-university debating contest in the Marischal College, Aberdeen, last night. With Mr Smith is his colleague, Mr Donald Dewar.

The Glasgow University team of John Smith and Donald Dewar win the *Scotsman* debating trophy, 11 February 1961. © *Scotsman*.

John Smith speaking at the Glasgow University Union, Donald Dewar is on the left.

INVOICE

PLEASE QUOTE THIS REF. No. AND DATE **K 189060**

Grants of St. James's
LIMITED

IMPORTERS AND BONDERS OF WINES, SPIRITS AND CIGARS
LONDON, S.W. 1

The Secretary,
Students Representative Council,
University of Glasgow,
Peano Lodge,
University Ave.,
GLASGOW. W.2.

24/42= 66

Dispatched from	Agency	Ledger	Dispatched
39	*	0.3.	Invoiced 20/9/62

* FOR DEPOT REFERENCE NUMBERS PLEASE SEE OVER

Bot.	¼'s	¼'s	Min.		PRICE	£	s.	d.
1				Black and White	430/6	21	10	6
1				Gordon's Gin	409/6	20	9	6
6/12				Smirnoff Vodka White	406/-	10	3	-
1				Cognac Planquette	458/-	22	18	-
6/12				Noilly Prat French	174/-	4	7	-
6/12				Martini Sweet	168/-	4	4	-
1				Regency Dry	154/-	7	14	-
	8 Splits			Ginger Ale	8/3	3	6	-
	8 Splits			Lemonade	7/11	3	3	4
			4	Tomato Juice	12/1	2	8	4
3 Syphons				Soda.	105/7	15	16	9
				11 cases	3/-	1	13	-
				Deliver to:-				
				Rectorial Head Quarters, 132, Byres Road, GLASGOW. W.2.				

Grants of St. James's, Ltd.,

69, Royston Road,

GLASGOW. N.1.

FOR CONDITIONS OF SALE SEE OVER

E. & O. E.

Total £ | 117 | 13 | 5

CHARGED CASES

The invoice showing all the booze belonging to the Rosebery camp in the Glasgow Rectorial campaign of 1962. (Printed by Geo. C. Fairservice Ltd. Glasgow for the Albert Lutuli Rectorial Campaign Committee.)

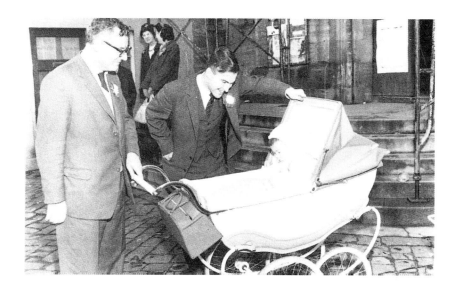

The East Fife by-election, November 1961

John Smith marries Elizabeth Bennett, 5 July 1967

John Smith, advocate

Sarah, Elizabeth, Catherine, Jane and John Smith outside their Morningside home, 1974

'So who won the point?' John McCluskey playing tennis with John Smith. It was a battle every time. (Kindly supplied by Lord McCluskey.)

John on the by-election trail with George Robertson (centre), Hamilton, May 1978, and a lady collecting for the Red Cross. (Reproduced by kind permission of Lord Robertson of Port Ellen.)

Hacking into a rubber tree at the Guthrie Plantation, Malaysia, January 1979, with Neville Gaffin (bearded) looking on in the background. (Reproduced by kind permission of Sir Thomas Harris.)

A Cabinet minister busily sifting through the Red Boxes while abroad in Malaysia, January 1979. (Supplied by Sir Thomas Harris.)

Shortly after he was appointed, Smith sought the advice of former Chancellor, Denis Healey. They had always been quite close. After John's death, Healey got to know Elizabeth Smith well because of their mutual interest in Russia.[18] Elizabeth promoted cultural and business links through her work for the St Andrews' Foundation.[19]

Initially, the shadow Chancellor's 'team' consisted of Ann Barrett, and Smith's researcher Bill Jones, a former official at the DTI. Smith's new office was situated in the basement of the House of Commons, opposite the staff canteen. The room regularly reeked of boiled cabbage. Visiting City slickers were aghast that the shadow Chancellor worked in such cramped conditions, until Smith pointed out that it was palatial compared with his previous office.[20]

In 1988, Bill Jones indicated his intention to leave, meaning that Smith required a new researcher. David Ward, co-ordinator of the PLP's campaign activities from 1985–7 had stood unsuccessfully as a Labour candidate in the Tory safe seat of Chelsea in 1987. Later, he was appointed head of communications at UNICEF.[21] After brief contact in 1987, assisting Smith in a visit to the IMF and the World Bank,[22] Ward met up with Smith again at a party, during which Smith enquired as to how Ward was getting on at UNICEF. Ward replied, jokingly: 'Oh fine, but I'm only working there because you haven't made me a better offer.' Smith made the offer, and Ward became the shadow Chancellor's researcher. During Ward's first week, Smith suffered his first heart attack.[23]

Establishing a good working relationship between a Prime Minister and his or her Chancellor is vital in ensuring the long-term survival of any government, but the relationship between a shadow Chancellor and his or her leader of the opposition has rarely been explored because the economic stakes are much lower. Yet such a relationship may be important for the future economic prospects of the nation if the opposition is seen as a likely potential government.

John Smith and Neil Kinnock did not disagree fundamentally on most aspects of economic policy, but their chilly relationship precluded regular discussion. By contrast, for the most part, Neil Kinnock and Roy Hattersley had a fairly regular system of consulting one another.[24] John Smith told Neil things about economic policy far less frequently.

In public, Smith always stayed loyal to Kinnock, but privately he harboured doubts about the leader's abilities on the economic front. According to Murray Elder, Smith believed that the party 'owed a huge amount to Neil' post-1983, and the shadow Chancellor took the view that Kinnock was entitled to a second election after the achievements of the 1983–7 period.[25] Chris Smith (then a member of the shadow Treasury team) believes that John 'remained ultimately completely loyal to Neil', but that John was 'sometimes frustrated by his belief that Neil didn't grasp entirely the economic agenda'.[26]

From 1987 onwards, Neil Kinnock's continued failure to press home Labour's advantage in the House of Commons when presented with open goals led a number of union leaders and MPs to make clandestine approaches to John to stand against him, or for John to ask Neil to step aside. There were two major problems with any Smith challenge: one could be overcome, but the other could not. Firstly, Smith was firmly identified with the right of the Party. But apparently, that need not have hampered Smith's cause. He was told at the time that most of the Campaign Group as well as his natural supporters on the right would back him if he stood against Kinnock.

The insurmountable obstacle was that it went against Smith's nature to challenge Kinnock for the leadership. As Chris Smith points out, 'John was 100 per cent not contemplating a coup to oust Neil, but people were pushing him to do so.'[27] One such person was Barry Sheerman, then Labour MP for Huddersfield. In the latter half of 1987, Smith and David Ward were in Washington DC, when by chance they met Sheerman and his wife in a restaurant. What started as a pleasant encounter ended up as a thoroughly unpleasant lunch, during which Smith sat through Sheerman's diatribe against Kinnock, and his maladriot attempt to urge Smith to stand against Kinnock for the Labour leadership. The lunch ended in acrimony, with Smith eventually telling Sheerman to 'shut-up', or words to that effect.[28]

Peter Mandelson's account of his own encounter with John Smith in August 1987 has been documented elsewhere.[29] Mandelson had been attending the Edinburgh Television Festival, and the Smiths had invited him to stay, along with the Hattersleys, at their home in Morningside.[30] Donald Dewar joined the group. Late into the evening, long after Elizabeth and Molly had gone to bed, and after many whiskies, John made some disparaging remarks about Neil Kinnock's leadership. According to Peter Mandelson's version of events, Smith complained that he never knew where he stood with Kinnock, and it was almost impossible to gain access to him. Smith respected Kinnock for his barnstorming speeches during election campaigns, but felt these lacked substance, and were, according to Mandelson's version of what Smith said, 'froth, pure froth'.[31] Mandelson then half-defended Neil Kinnock. In his biography of Mandelson, Donald Macintyre does not reveal his source, but it is fairly clear that this is Mandelson's account of what happened. Roy Hattersley admits that this is a truthful account, recalling that John got 'very strong' with Mandelson and turned on him.[32]

It seems therefore that Mandelson and Smith had a major falling out, and the relationship between them never recovered. Elizabeth remembers that this was 'the one and only time that *he* [Mandelson] was allowed into our house', and that that evening's events marked 'the beginning of the end' of John's relationship with him.[33] The outcome – Smith's fury – appears very apocalyptic, given the supposed content of the conversation, but all we have is one side of the story. Everyone had had lots to drink and Smith was perfectly entitled to say what he liked within the confines of his own house. Moreover, Chris Smith recalls that John was careful not to raise his tensions with Neil in public.[34]

The real problem with John and Neil's relationship is that they were, in Roy Hattersley's words, 'chalk and cheese'.[35] There existed what David Ward characterises as 'a communication gap' between them.[36] John had enormous intellectual self-confidence, which jarred with Neil's insecurity. Neil was not intellectually weak (far from it), but he was enormously interested in ideas, and restless to express them, whereas John, the advocate, was more prosaic – a processor of ideas and decisions. John occasionally found Neil exasperating, and Neil wanted more help from John in his drive to reform the Labour Party. Instead of sorting out their differences, they would avoid doing so on the grounds that it was just too hard.

Neil's political style was highly successful in the country. He developed a real flair as a party organiser, and became a great platform orator. In contrast, John spent most of his time in the House of Commons. Neil also had a history as a rebellious left-winger in the Callaghan government, opposing Smith's devolution plans. Neil rarely mixed socially with other senior shadow Cabinet members, so was never part of that camaraderie that subsequently developed between some of its members. When John became shadow Chancellor, 'there was no hinterland for John and Neil to build on', as one Smith insider puts it.[37]

Battered by press comments about his leadership after the 1987 election,[38] the Labour leader had withdrawn into his office in the House of Commons, surrounded by a cabal of loyal advisers.[39] Among them was Charles Clarke, his chief of staff, whom Smith thought insubstantial. Relations between Kinnock's office and John Smith's team did not improve when Kinnock's office effectively turned itself into a bunker. Once, David Ward met with Julie Hall, Kinnock's press secretary, and suggested that Neil and John should attend more events together. Neil's office did not respond.[40]

Meanwhile, the question of the Labour leadership remained on the political agenda for nearly the whole of the 1987–92 Parliament. Most notably, in October 1988, Tony Benn challenged Neil Kinnock for the leadership, while

John Prescott and Eric Heffer challenged Roy Hattersley for the deputy leadership. Kinnock and Hattersley, known by the media as Labour's 'dream ticket' since their joint election in 1983, immediately appointed joint campaign managers: Robin Cook, then shadow Health minister, a natural left-winger, tried to shore up the left-wing vote for Kinnock, while John Smith attempted to secure the votes from the centre and the right of the party for Hattersley.

Hattersley claims that he tried to persuade Smith to take over his job as deputy leader. Five years of performing the role of the deputy leader had not changed Hattersley's low view of the job: 'I didn't want to stand.' Hattersley remembers that Smith quite rightly saw the deputy leadership as 'a kiss of death', and moreover, he [Smith] 'didn't want to be associated with that leadership'.[41] Smith is said to have replied: 'Nobody you approve of wants the job. You can't escape. It's either you or Prescott.' So Hattersley had to stick with it, and make sure he was not defeated by Prescott, otherwise, he claims, Kinnock would have resigned.[42]

The Kinnock-Hattersley campaign started well when Ron Todd, the general secretary of the huge Transport and General Workers Union (TGWU)[43] personally backed the Kinnock-Hattersley ticket. However, in June 1988, Denzil Davies resigned as Labour's Defence spokesperson after Kinnock gave a television interview in which he suggested that Labour need not be stuck with 'something-for-nothing' unilateralism. Davies complained that Kinnock hadn't consulted him, and afterwards Ron Todd refused to repeat his union's endorsement of the Kinnock-Hattersley ticket until the Blackpool Labour Party conference in October. Matters took a turn for the worse at the TUC conference in Bournemouth in September when the Electrical, Electronic Telecommunications and Plumbing Union (EEPTPU) was expelled from the TUC.[44]

Suddenly, John Prescott's challenge for the deputy leadership gained a new credibility. Not only could the discontented left of the party register its disapproval of the policy review (see chapter 12) by voting for Prescott, but also people in the party's mainstream were increasingly tempted into viewing a vote for Prescott as a way of registering their opposition to Kinnock's abrasive style of leadership, and perhaps even getting rid of him before the general election.

Voting for the leadership and deputy leadership contests took place on Sunday, 2 October, the first evening of Labour's annual conference. That night, in a *Newsnight* special, John Smith claimed that Benn had been irresponsible in standing for the leadership since he stood no chance of winning.[45] Smith was vindicated: Kinnock annihilated his opponent, taking

88.6 per cent of the votes. Meanwhile, Roy Hattersley polled 66.8 per cent, beating off the challenges of John Prescott (23.7 per cent) and Eric Heffer (9.5 per cent).[46] It seemed at the time that the sheer scale of Kinnock's victory ruled out any question of a more serious challenge from John Smith (or possibly Bryan Gould) before the general election. In any event, Kinnock's opponents knew that he would stand and fight if cornered, making any leadership contest very bloody indeed. Also, while the PLP was divided over his future, Kinnock still enjoyed high levels of support amongst the constituency party and the trade union components of Labour's electoral college.

Such support for Kinnock did not stop leaders of some of the big unions putting pressure on Smith to stand against him. It had been a stressful conference week. During a radio interview, John had been asked to comment on Roy Hattersley's alleged remarks a few days before about introducing a wealth tax, and abolishing private health care and fee-paying schools. Smith had told the interviewer, Peter Deeley, 'I don't know where you get these ideas from . . . Good morning', and with that walked out of the interview room.[47]

When John returned home that weekend he complained of feeling ill, after a night out at the opera in Glasgow.[48] On the Sunday, Elizabeth persuaded him to miss his two o'clock flight back to London. The following day a GP friend and neighbour, Dr Mike Ryan, was called to examine Smith, and arranged for him to go to Edinburgh Royal Infirmary. An electro-cardiogram revealed nothing wrong, and the registrar on duty famously said, 'Whatever it is, it's not your heart.' Several of Scotland's leading cardiac consultants were also present, as befits an examination of one of the country's leading polticians. (It wasn't an emergency admission.) Just as John was tying his shoelaces, he went 'into the dark' as he later put it.[49] His next recollection was of waking up on the trolley going into the intensive care unit.[50] Shortly afterwards, John told his friend Ruth Wishart that, ever since his father had died of a heart attack (back in 1981, aged 73), he had been curious as to the sensation. Having gone through it, John described it as 'like being hit by a very large bus going at high speed'.[51]

John initially stayed in the coronary care unit, recalling that for the first couple of days he was 'almost euphoric, talking endlessly to my family just out of relief at being alive'. After the initial euphoria, he experienced moments of 'acute depression because I was not sure what I would be able to do. Those thoughts crowd in on you in the intensive care ward. Despite all the bustle, it can be very lonely.'[52] Eight days gradual recuperating on a general ward followed. Being the restless and demanding type, John was 'not a great patient', but he tried to occupy himself reading the dozens of climbing and art books that friends had brought him.[53]

When John finally got home, he felt very vulnerable, wondering whether he could get up the stairs.[54] He convalesced for about a week at Derry Irvine's house on West Loch Tarbert, about ten miles south of Tarbert Loch Fyne. Smith abstained from alcohol, surviving instead on Barr's Irn Bru, and long walks, despite the lashing rain.[55] Derry's house became very special to John. Once, he described it to a friend as 'just a little bit of heaven'.[56]

While he was still weak and recovering, Smith briefly considered giving up politics and returning to the law. He could reason with himself that he was after all a first-class advocate and he could have made a good living out of it. At one point, he was offered a judgeship, but turned it down.[57] Malcolm Rifkind, then Secretary of State for Scotland, only has a very vague recollection of the offer, but remembers being 'broadly sympathetic' to the idea.[58] Lord Fraser of Carmyllie, the then Lord Advocate, has a better recollection:

> I had known John well at the Scottish Bar and was well aware of his calibre. I had been troubled by his ill-health and had indeed sought to communicate to him that if he wanted to go to the Scottish Bench I would so advise. At that time my advice would have been followed without question.
>
> John did not take my advice, not, I hope, because he feared there was some conspiracy to sideline him at the height of his powers, but because he correctly reckoned that his political influence was still at its peak.[59]

Had Smith left politics and pursued a career as a QC, John McCluskey believes that he had 'the brains, the capacity, the style and the contacts to be successful'. Moreover, Smith often said to McCluskey that he loved the working ambience of Parliament House, the library next to the Court of Session in Edinburgh, and found it a more appealing place to work than the Palace of Westminster.[60] Ranald MacLean believes that Smith would have been a good judge because 'John wasn't a bad listener', but feels that ultimately Smith 'wouldn't have liked to have been tied down. The role would have stemmed John's natural adrenalin.'[61] Lord Fraser reflects:

> Had he taken up my offer, I would like to think he would still be alive today, but he was always too big a political giant to head off to Airdrie for a day's criminal trials. Still, it is a matter of abiding regret to me that I was not more direct or persuasive in prompting him towards a later less stressful career.[62]

As John grew stronger, Elizabeth Smith recalls that her husband increasingly saw falling back on his old legal career as the easy option, and that he would have been miserable had he not gone back into politics.[63]

By the end of October 1988 (less than a month after his heart attack), John was able to write to his old friend Elizabeth Thomas, Michael Foot's special adviser from his days at the Privy Council office, that he was 'now much better and recovering steadily'. He had received a 'get well soon' message from Michael Foot, which was 'a real tonic'. In the letter, Smith expressed his appreciation for the 'superb medical attention' he had received, something for which he was always enormously grateful. But John confessed to being 'under rigorous supervision – diet, rest, exercise etc.' Already, he had plans to return to frontline politics 'all being well' by January 1989. Even in convalescence, he informed his former Privy Council office colleague: 'I regard – like most of my countrymen – devolution as unfinished business. It will be done yet.'[64]

John had tried to diet before, but as a member of the Commons club for the well-proportioned, he had never come close to winning the annual prize – a magnum of champagne – for losing the most weight. Now, he took it more seriously. Elizabeth and the Smith girls would goad John on, posting less than flattering pictures of him on the fridge door to remind him that snacking was outlawed.[65] Initially, John set himself a strict daily total of 1,000 calories plus vegetables. If Smith broke his own strict rules, he sometimes initiated a day's starvation, as a penance.[66] For a very short time, he even tried to convert people to non-alcoholic low-calorie wine, but that didn't last long: Ruth Wishart recalls it tasted 'absolutely awful'.[67]

In retrospect, John's dieting regime was too severe to be sustainable. Jimmy Gordon recalls that subsequently John would spend six-week stints without drink and on a strict diet, as his doctor had ordered.[68] John had admitted to himself shortly after his heart attack, 'walking is fun, but dieting is not'. In a rare newspaper article, he admitted that 'alcohol is not a friend. My one serious lapse – as my friends will not be surprised to hear – came from that quarter.'[69] Nevertheless, in the space of three months, John went from 15 stones, 5 pounds to 12 stones, 11 pounds. He became quite a public figure in terms of public health campaigns, starring in a Family Heart Association video to convince heart attack victims that a full recovery was possible;[70] *The Sun* ran a full-page diet special featuring the shadow Chancellor;[71] and he even appeared on *Kilroy*, as one of many people with experience of recovering from heart attacks.[72]

Inevitably, as John had time on his hands, he needed something to keep him busy. In the past, he had four main hobbies – sailing, music, tennis, and walking in the Scottish countryside. John owned a sailing dinghy that he took on to the water at South Queensferry. (Neil MacCormick helped to crew it, before he got his own boat.)[73] Sometimes John took his dinghy all the way to Iona on holidays. Once, in the shallow waters off the white beaches, the Smith dinghy went hopelessly aground on the rocks in a dropping tide.[74]

John's musical tastes were eclectic: from the Gaelic tunes of his youth to Country and Western. Indeed, when John appeared on *Desert Island Discs*, he chose 'I've Loved and Lost Again' by Patsy Cline.[75] Beforehand, John had discussed his selections with Ruth Wishart, and her immediate reaction had been 'Not you too!',[76] but as John explained on the programme, when the Smith girls were younger, they were devoted to Country and Western music, blasting it out in the car on family holidays. 'The Easter Hymn' from *Cavellaria Rusticana*, and 'The Prisoner's Song' from Beethoven's *Fidelio* also found a place in the Desert Island repertoire.[77] In later life, John and Elizabeth were enthusiastic about opera, and had a season ticket in Row B at the Theatre Royal, Glasgow. Ruth Wishart feels that John was 'determined to use it as a way of keeping hold of his hinterland', maintaining his old student association with Glasgow, as well as a means of chilling out.[78]

Smith had previously enjoyed his ferocious battles with John McCluskey on the tennis court, but after his heart attack, tennis was considered to be too strenuous, and he gave it up. Instead, he took up walking again. McCluskey believes that John wasn't the same after he gave up tennis and was not able to eat and drink as he wished: 'John was someone with great gusto. He reminded me of Pavarotti in a way. He functioned best when he was full of fun.'[79] 'If anything, John's abstemiousness seemed to make him less ebullient than before.'[80] Perhaps there is something in the observation that Smith's dieting robbed him of his energy and his resolution. Did a less Rabelaisian John Smith emerge from his first heart attack? Or maybe McCluskey just missed the sparring company of his pal.

John had always loved Scotland's hills and mountains, but he did not show any real interest in walking until 1974 when he walked across the Lairig Ghru (the ancient right of way through the Cairngorms that passes between Ben Macdui and Braeriach). Ranald MacLean, who was then an advocate depute, put together a party made up of John Smith, Alastair Cameron (now Lord Abernethy), Colin McEachran (who was called to the Bar a year after John, but also did his law at Glasgow; still a practising QC), and Derek Patterson, then secretary of Scottish and Newcastle Brewers, with whom MacLean planned the trip. At the time, John had been working as parliamentary private secretary to Willie Ross, the Secretary of State for Scotland. Smith lacked all the proper kit for walking, and had to borrow a rucksack from Ross's principal private secretary, Peter Mackay,[81] a pair of boots from Ranald MacLean (or perhaps the other way round), and a pair of knitted socks from his old pal, Neil MacCormick.[82] At any rate, John then embarked on a longer walk than he had ever done in his life.[83]

From then on, Smith developed a taste for walking. Annual summer expeditions were arranged, normally by Ranald MacLean, where the walking party would rent rooms in a hotel, have a meal on a Friday night, ascend a not too strenuous hill on the Saturday, and return back to the hotel for another meal, drinks and conviviality.[84]

What began as an advocates' activity eventually mushroomed into a much larger political gathering known, from about 1989 onwards, as the 'Radical Ramblers'. MacLean recalls that the Radical Ramblers were a 'loose grouping – the only qualification was that none of us ever voted Tory'.[85] Other regular walkers included Murray Elder, Jimmy Gordon, Donald MacCormick, Menzies Campbell, Gordon Brown, and Alan Haworth (later secretary of the PLP). In time, Menzies Campbell remembers that the walks became less focused as the number of participants swelled.[86] Gavin Laird agrees: 'It grew like Topsy – husbands, wives, sweethearts – even the dog came along.'[87] John really got to know and like Gavin Laird, often describing him as 'a real gent of the old school'.[88] In August 1982, Laird joined a large group of walkers who once again followed the route of the Lairig Ghru, south to north.[89]

John sometimes walked in the Pentland hills on Boxing Day or after Hogmanay as part of the usual post-Christmas detox fad, along with attempting to give up drink for January. But up until his heart attack, Smith's rambling forays had neither been regular nor that serious: one year the Radical Ramblers had even gone up Cairngorm, but in the chairlift. Alan Haworth recalls: 'The walk was slightly incidental to the party afterwards.'[90] During a trip to the Isle of Arran in August 1983, they climbed Goat Fell, the morning after a convivial dinner. Although not a Munro, Goat Fell is the largest hill on the island, and only slightly short of 3,000 feet in height. Some members of the group, including Ranald MacLean, Menzies Campbell and Donald Mackay, reached the top within a couple of hours. Well over an hour later there was still no sign of Smith. Word eventually reached the summit that he had stopped for morning coffee on the way up.[91]

After John's heart attack, he became much more serious about walking, and in line with almost every other challenge in his political and personal life, he entered into the task with great enthusiasm, determination and a strong sense of purpose. This time around, the target became climbing all 277 Munros.[92] Munro-baggers take their hobby extremely seriously. The exact number of Munros is a subject of intense debate and scrutiny. In the early 1980s, the number of Munros was revised upwards from 276 to 277 (explaining why journalists writing about Smith could never decide which was the accurate figure), and then as a result of a re-survey by the Scottish Mountaineering

Club in 1997, the number of Munros enjoyed a net gain of seven. The present total stands at 284.[93]

Murray Elder, Dr Mike Ryan (Smith's family doctor), Chris Smith and Alan Haworth were among those urging Smith to take up Munro-bagging. Haworth remembers saying, 'You live in Edinburgh – I manage to do it from London.'[94] Chris Smith recalls: 'John carried on with the Munros not just for show, but mainly because he enjoyed it, much to his initial surprise, and the doctors had told him it would be good for him.'[95]

Alan Haworth (occasionally accompanied by his wife, Maggie), Chris Smith and Gordon Brown and Doug Henderson[96] became his regular climbing companions, as did Dr Lewis Moonie,[97] Ranald MacLean, and occasionally Alan Alexander, a contemporary of John's at Glasgow University and Dr Mike Ryan. Catherine Smith joined her father on five occasions, Jane once, and Elizabeth bagged three Munros in one day in March 1989. John kept a Munro diary, written out in longhand. John also bought a '3,000-plus' Munroist map to record all the Munros he had bagged. On John's death, when his office was being cleared, Hilary Coffman, a press officer, came across the map. Haworth meticulously took out the red pins, and noted down the names of all the 108 Munros that John had bagged, and then several years later compiled a complete database. Elizabeth Smith now keeps John's Munro map at her Edinburgh home.

On Saturday, 15 April 1989, John climbed his first ever Munro, Beinn Dorain, in the Orchy group, his favourite hill, and he did it on his own. He came unstuck after bagging numbers 33 and 34, Beinn Ghlas and Ben Lawers, both in the Lawers group. At 9.30 am on 23 December 1989, John set out from the National Trust Visitors' Centre. On the way up, the weather deteriorated, with heavier snow falling. He was about to turn back down the hill when he fell in with four walkers, including a former fellow student at Glasgow University. The group knew the hill better than John, and were far better equipped: unlike John, they had come with ice axes. John's ice axe was lying wrapped under the Christmas tree in Morningside, waiting to be opened. The party of five moved doggedly up the icy slopes in whiteout conditions. Disaster struck between the two peaks when Smith struck off to the right on a path that looked easier to avoid an icy slope. Unfortunately, he started sliding, then 'gathered speed, hurtling, up in air, very frightened, saw river a long way below; must have slid 1,000 feet, ended up 2–300 yards from the foot of corrie. Quite shocked.'[98]

Another figure hurtled down the mountain, 100 yards to the north. At the time, Smith didn't know who it was. The figure lying motionless was his friend from Glasgow. Fortunately, a doctor in the party attended to the man. While his friend was taken off to a hospital in Glasgow, Smith drove with some difficulty, due to the large swelling that had developed on his right buttock. Plans for more Munro-bagging were temporarily put on hold. John had had a miraculous escape; his friend had suffered two fractured arms, two broken ribs, a head wound, and was hospitalised for a week. Smith noted in his diary: 'I did not have my ice axe, which might have helped me. Perhaps a crucial warning.'[99] Alan Haworth recalls that John didn't want this incident in the newspapers, and indeed, attempts were made to hush it up, although it still made the diary columns of the newspapers and walking magazines.[100]

Another climbing expedition also involved concealment from the press. In 1990, John was filmed climbing Bynack More, part of the Cairngorms group. Or rather he wasn't filmed climbing it. The trip was part of a 'Climb for the World' charity day, during which mountaineers all over the world would unfurl the UNICEF flag as they reached the summit of their respective mountains. John, together with Murray Elder, Chris Smith, Alan Haworth and Douglas Boynton, had gathered at the Glenmore Lodge Outdoor Centre. However, the television crews indicated that they were not going to lug their camera equipment all the way up the mountain, so John and his climbing party were asked to stand over some tussocks of grass dressed in their UNICEF sweatshirts. All the TV crews then packed their bags and went home, except for one journalist who completed a portion of the walk, but turned back in order to meet his copy deadline for a Sunday newspaper. Two-thirds of the way up the Munro, the weather turned very, very bad, with rain sheeting down. John remained dogged. Eventually, there was a revolt. People began to say things like: 'This is mad. We're going to be hypothermic.' John argued vehemently that the walk was not for show; it was for a good cause. Also, what if they turned back, and were caught out by the press? Chris Smith argued that the press ridicule would be as nothing if somewhere the newspaper headlines read, 'shadow Chancellor imperils Mountain Rescue'. Alan Haworth recalls that John was the most reluctant of the lot to turn back, but the argument about the Mountain Rescue clinched it, and the party returned to Aviemore to hide in the 'Happy Haggis' chip shop for fear of being rumbled.[101]

On 21 July 1990, Murray Elder accompanied John up Ben Cruachan, and later recalled that for all his love of the Scottish hills, John's single favourite day – and one of Murray's happiest memories – came when they looked down from the summit on John's native county of Argyll.[102]

John shared with most Munro-baggers a fierce determination to get to the summit. On 14 April 1991, Gordon Brown injured his leg during a second walk up Meall nan Tarmachan, part of the Lawers group of Munros. As the party neared the summit, Gordon fell on to his ice axe, piercing his thigh. Fortunately, the party included Dr Lewis Moonie, who was medically qualified to attend to Gordon's minor wound. Although Gordon was off work for a week, his injury was not serious. As both Murray Elder and John were near the top, they both carried on to the summit, before returning back to descend with the casualty.[103]

During Smith's convalescence, Gordon Brown had taken over the shadow Chancellor's brief, assisted by Ann Barrett and David Ward. Brown put in a good performance in reply to the Chancellor's autumn statement.[104] John was sitting up in bed at home, watching the debate on television, and 'quietly cheering on Gordon', as he 'hammered Lawson in that first debate'.[105] Gordon Brown had performed so brilliantly that he began to be seen by political commentators as a potential leader. Brown's rise to prominence was reinforced in November 1988 when he topped the poll at the shadow Cabinet elections with 155, finishing just ahead of his boss John Smith, on 144 votes.[106] Indeed, Brown had the unenviable task of conveying these results to Smith while he convalesced in Edinburgh.[107]

In early January 1989, Smith felt well enough to make his first constituency speech in front of the local AGM of the Citizen's Advice Bureau. Tom Clarke, who tended to alternate with Smith as speaker on this occasion, recalls his neighbouring MP in sparkling form: 'You could tell that John was itching to get back to work. It was the most brilliant speech I've ever heard on the NHS . . . John was always the best informed when he needed to be.'[108]

John Smith officially returned to work during January 1989, looking refreshed and tanned, the Smiths having taken a recuperative holiday to the Gambia. Smith occasionally walked the three miles from the Barbican complex to Westminster with Norman Hogg. He also resolved to say goodbye to many of his old working habits:

> . . . that chronic inability to say 'no' to work engagements however logistically improbable they were . . . that stupid Calvinist obsession with work which made me guilty if I took any leisure time. I'm going to go back to work with a motto given to me by Sam Galbraith,[109] who's not only a fine doctor, but a knowledgeable politician. He's determined I'll make my contribution on the Floor [of the House] and on television rather than scampering up and down the countryside and so he told me: 'Do less to do more.' I'm listening to him.[110]

But Smith began his official comeback in London on an uncertain note by making a very dull speech in Park Lane, which somebody else had written for him. After the speech, Ann Barrett remembers commenting: 'That was awful, John.' Smith replied: 'I know. I thought I might have said at the end of the speech, "Now I'm going to ask you all for a summary of what I've just said."' Barrett feels that Smith's speeches were always best when he had personal control over their construction.[111]

In his natural home, the House of Commons, Smith was soon back to his sparkling best on 9 February 1989. The occasion was a debate on the White Paper on the government's latest expenditure plans. Smith had unearthed a Department of Transport White Paper,[112] which revealed that Britain's road maintenance was better under Labour and worse under the Tories:

> The Chart usefully plots the progress or otherwise of maintenance for both local and national roads. It shows a sharp improvement in both until just after 1979, followed by a dramatic decline thereafter. Most helpful of all the chart is bisected by a line; above the line is marked 'better', below the line 'worse'.
>
> I'm happy to confirm to the House that according to the White Paper the roads were better under Labour and worse under the Tories.
>
> It is hoped that other departments will now follow Transport's lead. Perhaps the DTI's monthly trade figures could be similarly presented with trade surpluses appearing above the line marked 'better' and trade deficits marked 'worse'.
>
> But even when the government reverts to the practice of being economic with the truth the White Paper cannot conceal the continuing decline in public investment.[113]

Smith spent quite a bit of time projecting his own image in a non-political way in magazines and on television. Press articles highlighted the fact that Smith had lost 36 pounds, and had taken up hillwalking.[114] He also turned out, perhaps against expectations, to be a fairly good television performer, appearing three times on *Wogan*.[115]

Academic research evidence conducted by Patrick Seyd and Paul Whiteley, two of Britain's leading experts on party membership, also shows that the shadow Chancellor was proving popular with Labour Party members in this period. When Seyd and Whiteley asked Labour's rank-and-file before the 1992 general election to speculate on who they would most like to succeed Kinnock, one-third of respondents opted for Smith and only three other MPs – Tony Benn, Gordon Brown and Roy Hattersley – attracted over 10 per cent.[116] Seyd and Whiteley also asked Labour Party members to rate senior party figures on a scale from zero to one hundred. Smith attracted exactly the same level of personal support (73 out of 100) as

Kinnock. The survey also revealed that Smith was less disliked than Kinnock, but as Seyd and Whiteley point out, this finding is understandable since Kinnock attracted more criticism than Smith who, at the time, was not associated with the party's internal reforms nor even a member of the NEC.[117] However, the research shows that Smith's relatively low party profile (and indeed in the media) didn't stop the party members from rating him highly: they were no doubt impressed by his formidable performances in the House of Commons.[118]

It seemed that John Smith had made a full recovery from his heart attack, and more importantly, had successfully *demonstrated* that he had made a full recovery. Commentators did not suggest, in public at least, that Smith's health might debar him from the Labour leadership, although Smith had jokingly threatened to sue anyone who said that.[119]

In May 1989, Labour won the Vale of Glamorgan by-election with the biggest swing against the Tories in 54 years. The by-election also saw the emergence of another John Smith, that is John P. Smith, rather than Rt Hon. John Smith QC MP. Unsurprisingly, having two Labour MPs named John Smith caused great confusion, especially when John P. Smith ran for the NEC, picking up the votes of 72 constituency parties, despite the fact that he was a virtual unknown.[120] On another memorable occasion, the Carlton Club invited 'our' John Smith instead of Sir John Smith, then of Coutts and Rolls-Royce, to speak in their esteemed establishment. Delighted, 'our' fearless John Smith wrote back, accepting the invitation with relish, but to their shame, the Carlton Club did not stand by their mistake.[121]

The downturn in the British economy was mirrored by a marked downturn in the relationship between Nigel Lawson on the one side and Sir Alan Walters and Mrs Thatcher on the other. The Chancellor wanted Britain to join the Exchange Rate Mechanism (ERM) of the European Monetary System (EMS) in order to defend the value of the pound in the volatile exchange rate markets, and to give Britain an anti-inflationary anchor.[122] Walters, Mrs Thatcher's economic adviser from 1981–3, still had the ear of the Prime Minister in 1989, and they both shared a deep dislike of fixed or 'pegged' exchange rates.[123]

On 7 June 1989, John Smith used the opportunity of an opposition day debate to highlight both the deteriorating state of the economy, and the deteriorating state of relations between the Chancellor of the Exchequer and the Prime Minister. The shadow Chancellor began with a carefully prepared set of Lawson quotations from 1988, in which the Chancellor had claimed Britain was experiencing an economic miracle. But, Smith argued, this kind of 'self-congratulation' had proved to be short-lived because it was based on 'blissful ignorance, the sort of ignorance demonstrated by a man on the top of a ladder who does not know he is about to fall off'.[124]

After the line-by-line demolition of the government's economic policy came the devastating mockery of Lawson's increasingly strained relationship with Mrs Thatcher. The Prime Minister had told the *Glasgow Herald* that 'Nigel is a very good neighbour of mine, and a very good Chancellor'.[125] Smith pointed out that good neighbourliness was 'highly relevant to the confusion and disarray which lies at the heart of Government policy':

> After all, when he [the Chancellor] picks up the telephone and wants to get through to No. 10, it must be rather disconcerting to be told, 'Walters here. Would you like to speak to [Brian] Griffiths?'[126] It is not clear who the real Chancellor of the Exchequer is. We have here the nominal Chancellor of the Exchequer.[127]

Smith mercilessly mocked Lawson by singing the sugar-sweet theme song of *Neighbours*, the Australian soap opera.[128] The opposition bench fell about laughing, as the Tory MPs, and especially Lawson, looked straight ahead in stony silence. Elizabeth Smith recalls the delight of her three daughters, who were fanatical fans of *Neighbours*, at their dad's singing performance.[129] David Ward, then Smith's researcher, cannot remember whose idea it was to use *Neighbours* – John certainly didn't watch the programme – but asked Ann Barrett to watch the opening credits of the soap to double-check the lyrics.[130]

'Good neighbours' contained the two main components of every great John Smith speech: the carefully built up case for the prosecution, followed by the devastating use of mockery to ram home the advantage. Smith also excelled when coming back on an intervention. He benefited even more once the political columnists and commentators *thought* he was good. The belief carried its own momentum.[131]

Michael Foot recalls how Smith had by this stage become 'a past master' of the House of Commons:

> Nye Bevan was the best ever, but John had Nye's gift of going for the strongest part of the opponent's case, rather than the weakest part, and demolishing it. In this way, John was always turning the debate to our advantage, and was good on the big occasions. The House of Commons came to see him do it. He was top class, and he became the best of the lot at it.[132]

But whereas John was prepared to take more risks on his feet, he was very prosaic when it came to committing his thoughts on paper. In a *Sunday Times* article in August 1988, Smith opened with five percentages and three dates in six lines.[133] John believed that anything he wrote down as shadow Chancellor could have an effect on opinion in the City of London or worried middle-income earners. It also had something to do with his Scottish Presbyterian background – the written word was somehow different, and to be treated with caution.[134] The result was that John wrote very few articles in journals – for example, he wrote only one piece for the *New Statesman* between 1988–91 – and even the few that he did write were carefully placed.

Smith's command and control of the House of Commons were shown again on 24 October, when he effectively told the Chancellor to issue a 'Back me, or sack me' ultimatum to the Prime Minister over the growing influence of Sir Alan Walters, the 'unelected, unappointed, alternative chancellor'.[135] Smith began by outlining the Prime Minister's growing isolation with the rest of Europe, the Commonwealth (following her famous Kuala Lumpur outburst) and domestically within her Cabinet. The shadow Chancellor struck effective blows at the Chancellor where he must have known that his opposite number was right: Smith spoke scathingly of the 'deference and lack of courage of a Cabinet who dare to challenge her [Mrs Thatcher's] overwhelming pretensions'.[136]

The shadow Chancellor then concluded on a stark note: 'I advise the Chancellor to make an early decision on the important question of whether he will jump or be pushed . . . It is time he said, "Either back me or sack me."'[137] Lawson was virtually isolated on his own side: only three Cabinet colleagues chose to sit with him on the Tory front bench during the debate.[138] A day later, on 25 October, Lawson had resigned. Had Smith pushed the Chancellor over the edge? The idea is ridiculous, but perhaps Smith had eloquently articulated in public what an increasingly fed-up Chancellor had been thinking for some time in private. Moreover, Smith had spotted that the crucial working relationship between a Prime Minister and his or her Chancellor had broken down completely, and deep down Lawson knew that. It was typical of Lawson that he didn't hold any grudges. Indeed, eight months later, he paid Smith a backhanded compliment on *Question Time*, claiming that one of the reasons the Conservatives would win the forthcoming general election 'is the fact it is not John Smith but Neil Kinnock leading the Labour Party'.[139]

After the fall of Lawson, several commentators drew comparisons with Smith's earlier scalp of Leon Brittan during the Westland crisis three years before (see chapter 10).[140] Writing in *The Independent*, Peter Jenkins was especially effusive: 'It requires no great stretch of the imagination to see Chancellor Smith rising to present his budget. For his party at this juncture this makes him a precious asset.'[141] Smith was upbeat: 'You don't hear people saying we do not have an opposition now, do you?'[142]

On 31 October 1989, Smith took on John Major, the new Chancellor of the Exchequer, and former Chief Secretary to the Treasury, in an opposition debate on the government's economic policy. Smith performed reasonably well, despite wrecking tactics by Government back benchers,[143] but Major's response showed that he would be no pushover: 'The right Hon. and learned Member for Monklands East made his usual forceful speech, both forceful and his usual speech. It was good music hall. He has become the Jasper Carrott of parliamentary debate. For all the humour, however, it was an empty speech.'[144]

Major had spotted one of Smith's few potential weaknesses as a parliamentary debater – the danger of being seen as too frivolous. Years of sitting behind and later beside Callaghan had taught Smith that appearing statesman-like was more important than raising a laugh from back benchers in the Chamber, but Major's comments were a timely reminder.

On 21 November 1989, the House of Commons entered the television age, as the cameras were allowed in for the first time. The following day, Smith celebrated his successful return to the Labour front bench by picking up for the second time the *Spectator*/Highland Park Parliamentarian of the Year award, on this occasion from Lord Hailsham, the guest of honour at the Savoy Hotel. Charles Moore, again the chairman of the judges'[145] read out Smith's citation, dubbing the shadow Chancellor 'the leading discomfiter of the Government'. In the view of the judges, whilst Smith had undoubtedly benefited from a bad year for the British economy, he had 'moved in for the kill' and successfully riled Lawson over his deteriorating relationship with Sir Alan Walters.[146]

Largely because of his House of Commons performances, Smith continued to command a huge following among fellow Labour MPs. In the shadow Cabinet elections in November 1989, he again finished second on 153 votes, only two down on the previous year. Gordon Brown once again topped the poll on 165 votes.[147]

As Chancellor of the Exchequer, John Major could not have been more different than Lawson: whereas Lawson was bold and sometimes arrogant, Major came across as modest and consensual. Not only was Major far more subtle than Lawson in debate, making it more difficult for Smith to go on the attack,[148] but also Major started to ease the public expenditure purse strings in his November 1989 Autumn Statement.[149] Chris Smith recalls that the Treasury team held discussions on how to deal with the new Chancellor's more consensual style, but in terms of responding to Conservative Budgets and affecting the course of Labour's economic policy, Major's arrival on the scene changed little.[150] Nevertheless, both the policy content and the presentation of the Autumn Statement should have acted as an early warning signal for the coming year, when the much-underestimated Chancellor of the Exchequer was to take everyone by surprise.

The day after Major's first Budget, Smith spoke about the government's neglect of the manufacturing sector, but he didn't really land any effective blows on Major.[151] Then, on Monday, 8 October, Major finally announced Britain's entry into the ERM at the alarmingly high rate of DM 2.95. Mrs Thatcher had insisted upon an accompanying interest rate cut timed to coincide with the Conservative Party conference. Smith felt that such a political stunt was economically inept because it lost the confidence of the foreign exchange markets from a very early stage. The whole point of entering the ERM was to take the politics out of exchange rate management, thereby convincing the currency markets that Britain was serious about achieving exchange rate stability. Secondly, Britain's ERM entry was a disaster in diplomatic terms; the Germans had not been consulted, while the Italian Treasury minister first heard about it in the middle of his boating holiday.[152]

But John Major had stolen yet another one of the opposition's policies, and the two main political parties now had virtually the same anti-inflationary strategy. Once again, John Major had left Smith with very little to say in response to a policy that he broadly agreed with. Worse still, Labour could hardly publicly criticise the Tories for entering the ERM at the wrong rate, for 'raw political reasons', as Neil Kinnock puts it.[153] Meanwhile, the reliable sage, Anthony Howard drew attention to the fact that Labour's still healthy opinion poll lead over the Conservatives might disappear: after all the party had been in a similar position in 1985–6, only to lose the general election in 1987.[154]

No doubt many a celebratory glass was downed following the demise of Mrs Thatcher on 22 November 1990, but after the initial euphoria in the Parliamentary Labour Party died down, Labour back benchers suddenly realised that John Major posed a serious threat. Major also had a 'good' Gulf War (although all the substantive decisions had been taken by Mrs Thatcher before her downfall), while the Labour leadership strained (it was said, with no help from Smith) to keep its left wing at bay on the issue. In the New Year, the government announced above-inflation pay increases for public sector workers such as teachers.

And if John Major proved a formidable political operator as Prime Minister, then Norman Lamont, his successor as shadow Chancellor, proved equally adept at blunting the opposition's attacks on economic matters. In a bold move, Lamont used his first Budget in March 1991 to cut poll tax bills by an average of £140 a person, to be funded by a 2.5 per cent increase in Value Added Tax (VAT). To Labour's dismay, the Chancellor had successfully lanced the boil of the poll tax in one go: the hated tax would still remain until after the election, the VAT increase would be fairly unpopular, as were the hefty rises on spirits, petrol and cigarettes, but the Conservatives under John Major were signalling to the electorate at the very least a cosmetic (and, as it turned out, a temporary) break from their Thatcherite past. The Chancellor even took some money from the better off by limiting mortgage interest rate relief to the standard rate of tax, by increasing the tax on company cars, and by launching a crackdown on offshore tax avoidance (stealing one of John Smith's ideas). In short, it was a highly political Budget, designed to shift the Major government towards the centre ground, and to leave open the option of a June 1991 election. It also had Labour rattled. One front bencher admitted at the time: 'This makes things a bit awkward.'[155]

Chris Smith admits that Labour's Treasury team was caught unawares by Lamont's 1991 Budget. The Chancellor's decision to increase VAT to alleviate the worst effects of the poll tax came 'like a bolt from the blue'. The first reaction of Labour's Treasury team was: 'He's switched from one regressive form of taxation (the poll tax) to another (VAT).' Unfortunately, deeper analysis by John Hills at the LSE revealed that the VAT increase was not particularly regressive: because it was zero-rated on such items as children's clothes and food, the poorest in society spent most of their money on these items rather than on goods and services that were subject to VAT.[156]

Overall, the measures in the 1991 Budget increasingly demonstrated that there was little difference on economic policy between the two main parties, and the question undoubtedly began to occur in the minds of the electorate: why bother switching to Labour if the evil dragon has been slain, when this gentle new knight is promising to banish the poll tax from the land, and is shifting the Tories back to the centre ground?

Twelve
NOT MAKING ALL THE CHANGES

L ABOUR'S POLICY REVIEW process from 1987–91, including its deliberation, refinement and presentation, saw the party transform itself into a
sober-suited credible alternative to the Conservatives. The party's main
task in 1987 was to begin a major policy re-think in light of their second
massive electoral defeat. Their highly professional election campaign had
raised Kinnock's profile, but the floating voters were still unhappy with the
party's policies on taxation, spending, defence, and nationalisation. Large
swathes of the electorate still feared that Labour would be beholden to the
unions, and vulnerable to challenges from the hard left.

In order to change party policy, the Labour leadership set about over-
turning a whole raft of conference resolutions carried by the hard left in the
period from 1983–6. In order to achieve this, seven policy review groups were
established, whose members were drawn jointly from the NEC and the
shadow Cabinet.[1] Each group was expected to produce a statement of broad
themes in time for discussion at Labour's Blackpool conference in 1988, as a
softening-up process for real policy change the following year.

As shadow Chancellor, Smith had to be content with convening the
'Economic Equality' review group (jointly with Diana Jeuda of the Union of
Shop Distributive and Allied Workers) dealing mainly with Labour's tax
policies. Initially, Bryan Gould, shadow spokesperson for Trade and Industry,
chaired the 'Productive and Competitive Economy' review group, covering
subjects such as training, investment and whether to renationalise the public
utilities. Thus, the shadow Chancellor was in charge of tax and spending, but
half his job was in the hands of someone else, and moreover someone with
very different economic views from Smith. Gould's review group would
produce some quite interventionist ideas on trade and industry. With typical
understatement, Chris Smith, then a junior member of Smith's Treasury
team, recalls 'frissons of difference' between the two policy review groups.[2]

A further design fault at the heart of the policy review process was that all
seven groups beavered away producing policy ideas and spending commitments without any overall macro-economic framework or 'public

expenditure' review. In 1988 and again in 1989, a prospective Labour Chancellor of the Exchequer (and, indeed the real Chancellor, Nigel Lawson) had a huge Budget surplus to play with, which permitted some very sloppy thinking on the policy review groups that Labour would be able to afford large increases in pensions and benefits. What was needed was a chief secretary of the Treasury figure to develop the whole process in a co-ordinated way and, more importantly, to put a lid on the spending commitments. No such system was put in place until too late in the day.

In terms of detailed personal input into the economic equality group's deliberations, a Smith insider recalls that Neil Kinnock took 'a back seat'.[3] However, a member of Neil Kinnock's office sat in on each review group to monitor its progress.[4] John Eatwell, Neil Kinnock's economic adviser, was one such person. Eatwell helped to co-ordinate a group of economists that met regularly to exchange information, worked closely with the economic secretariat, and also organised meetings of the economic policy sub-committee, the lattermost a monthly meeting of ministers that Neil Kinnock sat in on (all three groups are discussed below) as well as being in 'continuous dialogue' with the leader. Eatwell also met regularly with Smith, crucial since the leader of the opposition and the shadow Chancellor 'did not meet that often'. Fortunately, Eatwell and Smith got on very well. Shortly after Smith was made shadow Chancellor, he invited Eatwell and his wife for a weekend in Edinburgh. Eatwell was unprepared for the vision that greeted him on the Sunday morning on entering the Smiths' kitchen. There was the shadow Chancellor, dressed only in a short dressing gown, stirring the porridge: 'To this day, it's my abiding image of John.'[5]

In terms of published material, the policy review process kicked off with a document entitled A Statement of Democratic Socialist Aims and Values. The review paper was very much the baby of Roy Hattersley, who argued that, although the levying of 'fair taxes' would not guarantee the abolition of poverty, it would ensure, so the theory went, that everyone would have the opportunity to reach their potential through access to education and training.[6] Smith supported Aims and Values, but Bryan Gould felt that it was too fulsome in its praise of the market at the expense of state intervention.

One of the main difficulties of being a shadow Chancellor is that the Chancellor of the Exchequer constantly wields the power to shift the goal posts by altering the level of taxation and spending. Opposition policy reviews do not operate in a vacuum: they can rapidly be overtaken by events. This problem was most starkly illustrated in Nigel Lawson's March 1988 Budget. The Chancellor cut the basic rate of income tax from 27 per cent to 25 per cent, but his most dramatic move was to abolish four of the five higher bands of income tax (ranging from 40–60 per cent), leaving only the 40 per cent tax band. For most of the 1980s, the highest earners had paid 60 per cent in tax, but in one bold stroke Lawson created a whole new set of benchmarks on tax, so much so that by the time it came to Smith's shadow Budget in 1992, putting income tax up to 50 per cent seemed to go against the prevailing trend. But in the shorter term, Labour MPs were outraged: left-wingers disrupted Lawson's speech, and Kinnock told his own side, 'Do not get mad, get even.'[7]

Shortly after Lawson's Budget, Smith spoke to a group of merchant bankers who confessed to him that they didn't know what to do with the Chancellor's tax cut. This admission did not go down well with the shadow Chancellor: as Smith later put it, back in his Monklands East constituency 'I had pensioners in tears'.[8] Smith's more dispassionate view on Lawson's Budget was that with the available money – a huge budget surplus of £14 billion was forecast – resources could have been far better allocated, rather than squandering it on tax cuts for the better off.[9]

On Wednesday, 25 May 1988, Smith's 'Economic Equality' review group came up with a basic sketch of Labour's economic policy for consideration at the NEC. The shadow Chancellor's paper proposed avoiding the punitive tax rates of the past – taxes should be no higher than in the rest of Europe – but people should still be persuaded of the need for fairness in taxation. The reduction of inflation replaced the reduction of unemployment as Labour's number one priority. The NEC accepted Smith's draft proposals by a very wide margin of 20 votes to three, with Ken Livingstone abstaining.[10]

A year later, the fruits of Labour's two-year policy review process were published in *Meet the Challenge, Make the Change: A New Agenda for Britain.*[11] The leadership announced the abandonment of the party's policy on unilateral nuclear disarmament, ditched the notion of punitive rates of taxation, and began to embrace the idea of the market economy. Neil Kinnock deserves a great deal of the credit for driving these changes through the NEC, but it still represented an uneasy compromise between interventionists like Bryan Gould, and a more market-orientated approach supported by Kinnock and Smith.[12]

Throughout his period as shadow Chancellor, John Smith was anxious that Labour should not trumpet its policies too early on tax and spending. Believing that these areas represented Labour's Achilles' heel, he did not want to expose his weakest flank to unnecessary enemy fire. One means of deflection was to lead the media up the garden path, which Smith was not averse to doing. For instance, David Ward believes that Smith's advocacy of credit controls was 'a vaguely plausible debating tool designed to avoid discussing more important aspects of Labour's economic policy'.[13] Most politicians appeared on Brian Walden's *Weekend World* on ITV, *Frost on Sunday* (then on TVam) or *On the Record* (on BBC1) with the express aim of attracting attention for a new policy idea. By contrast, Smith very often appeared on these shows with the deliberate intention of *not* making news.[14] As David Ward points out, one of the reasons why John Smith made an excellent shadow Chancellor of the Exchequer was because he was 'good at doing boring'.[15]

Nevertheless, Smith did not rule out using credit controls. Indeed, at the time Neil Kinnock was receiving advice from economists to do so.[16] The principle was to keep interest rates lower by asking the banks and building societies to restrain lending to individuals. Smith argued that mild forms of credit control were used across the rest of Europe.[17] In February 1990, the shadow Chancellor claimed that 'credit controls are a useful touch on the brake decelerating consumer demand. They don't have to be comprehensive or hermetically sealed.'[18] The flaw, as Peter Rodgers of *The Independent* pointed out, was that Labour was 'investing controls on bank lending with all sorts of magical properties that they do not in fact possess'.[19] Little did the economic commentators realise that Smith had got them expending column inches discussing something that he never seriously considered implementing.

By contrast, Smith had a deep and passionate commitment to introducing the national minimum wage. As shadow Chancellor, he deployed all his backroom cajoling tactics to ensure that Labour's policy was introduced in the teeth of union opposition. One opponent was John Smith's friend, Gavin Laird, general secretary of the AEU since 1982, mostly on the grounds of differentials: that whatever level the minimum wage was set at, skilled workers further up the wage scale would demand incremental increases. Matters came to a head at the 1988 Labour Party conference in Blackpool when Laird recalls: 'We had a blazing row, a violent argument just short of fisticuffs . . . John had a short temper . . . but half an hour later, we were standing having a drink together. That was John . . . I loved the man.'[20]

But even after Labour had agreed to the broad outline of the policy, certain unions remained opposed to it. On 24 July 1989, Eric Hammond of the EEPTU penned a letter addressed to the chairman of the economic equality review group (Smith) to articulate his union's opposition. Immediately, Smith wrote back to Hammond: 'If, as appears from your letter, your organisation has major reservations on our proposals, it would be more helpful if we had been advised of these views during the period when the proposals in the Report were being actively considered.'[21]

Eventually, the national minimum wage policy was firmed up in *Opportunity Britain* in April 1991: 'We will introduce a national minimum wage, starting at a level of 50 per cent of median men's earnings [Stage One] ... Over time we will increase the minimum wage as a proportion of earnings to a point where no-one is paid less than two thirds of the median male hourly rate [Stage Two].'[22]

Gavin Laird was still opposed: 'It's never worked in the past, there's no logic for it, it doesn't work in any other country and it certainly will not work in Great Britain.'[23] Hammond concurred: '[The minimum wage is] so fundamentally wrong that it will increasingly threaten Labour's prospect of a national victory.'[24] Smith brushed off these attacks, claiming on *Newsnight* 'one or two might lose their jobs'.[25]

During the long run-up to the 1992 general election campaign, Michael Howard, then the Conservative Employment spokesperson, waged war against Labour's minimum wage policy. On 4 July 1991, he launched a pamphlet entitled, *Labour's axe on jobs*. Tony Blair, by then Labour's Employment spokesperson, quickly responded to this attack, claiming the Tory document was 'a tissue of distortion and fabrication', and pointing out that every other country in Europe had a minimum wage.[26] John Smith was even more emphatic about his adhesion to the policy: 'Absolutely disgraceful that we've not had it long before now.'[27]

With hindsight, Gavin Laird graciously acknowledges that it was untenable to deny a minimum wage to the poorest paid workers in society. The fears about differentials never materialised.[28] Even the Conservatives later dropped their opposition to a national minimum wage under William Hague.

In November 1989, Neil Kinnock reshuffled his shadow Cabinet, shifting Bryan Gould from Trade and Industry to Environment (at Smith's suggestion),[29] promoting Gordon Brown to Gould's old job, and replacing Michael Meacher with Tony Blair as Employment spokesperson.[30] Bryan Gould was understandably bitter at his dismissal, later claiming in his memoirs: 'It seemed to me that those who could not win the argument had nevertheless contrived to have me removed from a position of influence.'[31]

Out of the unwieldy policy review process, 1987–9, emerged new structures and new personalities whose cumulative effect would be to shift control of policy making back into the hands of the shadow Cabinet, where it had resided until the Bennite revolution of the early 1980s. Mark Wickham-Jones, the key academic in this area of Labour history, quite rightly points out that: 'By 1990 economic policy initiatives stemmed from the leaders of the PLP.'[32] Chris Smith recalls that control had shifted to the shadow Chancellor's hands, so much so that 'if John wanted to push forward an idea, he could have done'.[33] How had this come about?

By this stage, Smith had gathered around him a group of around a dozen City economists and academics whose activities were co-ordinated by Andrew Graham, a Fellow and tutor in economics at Balliol College, Oxford and a former economic adviser to Harold Wilson from 1966–9, and again from 1974–6, when Graham became the main policy adviser in Wilson's Policy Unit. In late 1984, Neil Kinnock had suggested to Lord Kaldor, the Hungarian economist, that he should form a group of economists who could help the Labour Party. Initially, the group was known as the Kaldor Group, but in February 1985, it became known as the Labour Economic Policy Group (LEPG), and was chaired by Andrew Graham. In the early summer of 1988, John Smith rang Graham, and invited him to become his main economic adviser, but on a part-time basis so that Graham could continue to teach and research at Balliol. During Smith's period off work following his heart attack, Graham worked for Gordon Brown. When Smith returned to work in January 1989, Graham set up a small group of economic advisers who met every three to four weeks in order to discuss and advise Smith on aspects of Labour's economic policy on a freelance basis. Graham played a leading role, sending out the invitations, setting the agenda, organising and chairing the meetings, and writing most of the papers. John Eatwell, Kinnock's economic adviser, also played a leading role. As more people were added to the group, it became known as the Treasury Advisers Group (TAG). Smith would also ask Graham to prepare his briefing for the counter-attacks on the Budget.[34] Meghnad Desai, one of the advisory group's members, recalls Smith's frequent requests for ammunition with which to attack the Government: 'Let's have some jokes.'[35]

Desai was professor of economics at the LSE, and became a Labour peer in 1991. Other prominent economists on the advisory group included: Chris Allsopp, editor of the *Oxford Review of Economics* and later on the Bank of England's Monetary Policy Committee; David Currie, professor of economics at the London Business School;[36] the City analyst Neil Mackinnon; John Hills from the LSE, dealing with public expenditure and macro-economic issues; and Gerald Holtham, a former Organisation for Economic Co-operation and Development (OECD) economist, who later became director of the Institute of Public Policy Research in 1994. Dan Corry, Labour's economic policy adviser, who later became chief economist at the Institute for Public Policy Research and later a special adviser at the Department of Trade and Industry completed the list of key contributors.[37] Corry proved to be a valuable source of expertise. In a letter to Neil Kinnock (undated, but clearly from 1990), Chris Smith enclosed inflation forecasts from Corry for 1991, describing Corry in the covering letter as someone who 'very much knows his stuff and can – at the drop of a hat – get more'.[38] Gavyn Davies, then chief UK economist at the City analyst Goldman Sachs, occasionally wrote briefing papers on important economic subjects such as the ERM, but almost exclusively for Neil Kinnock.

Members of the advisory group argued that in the modern world of global capitalism Labour Chancellors could no longer resort to old-fashioned spending to haul Britain out of recession because foreign capital would flow out of Britain overnight and the pound would go into freefall. The new orthodoxy, focusing as it did on supply-side reforms (like investment in research and development, education and training) saw the abandonment of Keynesian macro-economic demand management, which was perceived to have failed in the 1970s.[39] Bryan Gould's economic ideas were put in the dustbin. In a rare interview for *Tribune* in September 1990, Smith observed:

> In a sense, we have moved on from the Keynesian concept. We live in an interdependent world, but it is also a very unstable world, where capital movements in Tokyo, New York and London can subvert the economic policies of nation states. That is why I am looking for control mechanisms to give us a little bit more stability.[40]

The major objective became creating a stable economic environment in Britain in which companies would have the confidence to invest.[41] To this end, the pursuit of inflation became the government's primary goal. Smith needed an anti-inflationary anchor to prevent the usual flight of capital overseas when Labour returned to government. He found it in the shape of the ERM. Economists such as Meghnad Desai were crucial in convincing him that the ERM would be a good idea. Desai recalls: 'After the Lawson boom, it became essential to have this straitjacket to keep inflation under control, but we had so much hassle from gung-ho Keynesians like Bryan Gould.'[42] In some respects, as Tudor Jones argues, the changes resembled the Croslandite and Gaitskellite revisionism of the 1950s in that they sought to revise Labour's policies in the light of changing economic and social circumstances.[43]

In a speech to the German Chamber of Commerce on 19 June 1991, Smith rejected the unfettered markets approach and 'minimalist social provision' that had characterised Thatcherism. Such a philosophy, Smith argued, had produced 'not so much a European Social Market Economy as a Casino

Economy in which markets run riot'. By contrast, the German approach had 'produced a highly skilled, highly invested, highly innovative and highly productive economy' because of its 'commitment to the long-term, to macro-economic stability, to an economic environment that encourages investment and innovation, and to a financial system that is geared to the needs of industry'. While the Conservatives could not reconcile their free market dogma with the 'reality of the developing European Community', Labour could because while it supported markets it did not elevate them 'into a theological obsession'. Markets often failed to achieve economic efficiency and they certainly did not produce social justice. The solution lay in 'a partnership in which markets can be made to work better and more efficiently, if the public sector plays its proper role'.'[44]

Smith always retained a core belief in the value of public service and the dangers of a wholly free market approach. He applied this philosophy in his own backyard. When the Royal Mail letterbox near his Edinburgh home was threatened with closure through lack of use, the public-spirited Smith ensured its survival by hauling up bags of mail on the train from his House of Commons office to Edinburgh, and then stuffing them through the threatened mailbox.[45]

Another innovation at this time was the creation of the Economic Secretariat. The secretariat, chaired by the shadow chief secretary to the Treasury (for most of this period, Margaret Beckett), met every week, and comprised all the researchers from the policy review groups. Apart from David Ward, the main members of the secretariat were Dan Corry, Cathy Ashley and Emma Maclennan, Ward's partner. The team operated out of an office in St Stephen's House on Victoria Embankment. Emma took maternity leave twice, in 1989 and 1991. In the first instance, Sheila Watson was her replacement. Watson went on to work for Margaret Beckett, and has done so ever since. In 1991, Nick Pecorelli was appointed as Emma's second replacement. John Eatwell also attended the discussions, forming an important link with the Labour leadership.

The Economic Secretariat discussed current economic issues, tried to co-ordinate the work of the policy review groups, and to anticipate the news agenda, issuing regular draft press releases and briefing papers,[46] although it had no formal policy making role.

One of the secretariat's most useful functions was to supply Labour front benchers with ammunition or 'devastating facts'. For example, in 1988 the secretariat linked up with John Hills at the LSE and Holly Sutherland, who had a computer-based tax and modelling programme at Cambridge that could calculate income changes arising from the 1988 Budget. Working in tandem with John Eatwell, and Cathy Ashley and Emma Maclennan operating out of Walworth Road, the secretariat was able to supply an overnight briefing for Labour back benchers, which went down so well that they gave John Smith and Gordon Brown a standing ovation at the weekly meeting of the PLP.[47] A similar exercise was carried out a year later.[48]

Yvette Cooper is one bright prospect in the Blair era. However, she began her political career as an economic researcher to John Smith in 1990. Andrew Graham recommended Cooper for the job, which she planned to decline. David Ward persuaded her she was mad to turn down the chance of working for the shadow Chancellor.[49] Much later, she (wisely) used the fact that she had worked with John Smith during her battle to be selected for the ultra-safe Labour seat of Pontefract and Castleford.

Emma Maclennan recalls that Smith 'liked to have a clever team around him'. If a junior member of the staff like Karen Gardiner at the LSE had an idea, Smith respected her opinion, let her run with it, and, unusually among senior politicians, gave credit where it was due. Smith also liked the fact that he had a politically correct Treasury team, including Paul Boateng (black), Chris Smith (gay), Margaret Beckett (female), and John Marek (Welsh).[50]

Nevertheless, with no disrespect to Smith's highly competent Treasury team, the key shadow Cabinet members in terms of the development of economic policy were John Smith, Gordon Brown at Trade and Industry and Tony Blair at Employment. In April 1990, *The Economist* commented that having the triumvirate of Smith, Brown and Blair in charge of economic policy gave a more reassuring message to worried fund managers in the City of London than, say, their predecessors, Roy Hattersley, Bryan Gould and Michael Meacher would have done.[51]

However, another figure of importance should be added when assessing the efficacy of Smith's economic team – that of Margaret Beckett, who was elected on to the shadow Cabinet for the first time in November 1989, and became John Smith's deputy as shadow chief secretary to the Treasury. Up until that point, Beckett had chaired the Health and Social Security Policy review group. Both Neil Kinnock and John Smith wanted Margaret for the job. Beckett recalls that when Kinnock offered her the job, he told her: 'You were my choice, but I told John I had somebody in mind. He asked me who it was, and John said he would have chosen you as well.'[52] David Ward recalls: 'Margaret was the ideal person to suppress demands for higher expenditure from shadow Cabinet colleagues, and quickly developed a reputation as a bit of a Rottweiler . . . John and Margaret's relationship was really cemented at that point.'[53]

John Kampfner is therefore nearer to the mark than *The Economist* when he refers to Smith's 'economic foursome that would steer policy for the next few years'.[54] To their rivals, they became known as the 'favoured four'.[55] And partly in an effort to deflect the electorate away from deep-seated doubts about Kinnock's leadership skills, the party projected this economic foursome into the media spotlight.[56] As Eric Shaw puts it, all four were 'able to convey an aura of authority, expertise and prudence'. He adds: 'Smith, in particular – with his air of the canny, shrewd and utterly reliable Scottish solicitor (or bank manager) – increasingly became a key figure in Labour's exposition of its economic case.'[57]

The main task facing Labour's economic team at the end of 1989 was to plug the many holes in the policy review. As early as June 1989, Dan Corry had pointed out a central weakness: 'Given the nature of the review and the way it has divided up subjects, it is not that easy to gain an overall view of the new Labour economic policy.'[58] In February 1990, Corry wrote: 'We cannot so much wrap up our spending plans in a vague idea of boosting demand and claim that it all pays for itself as the economy grows.' Corry actually did what David Mellor, the Tory Chief Secretary of the Treasury subsequently did, namely undertake a costings exercise of the policy review, adding up all Labour's spending commitments and producing a headline figure to scare the voters.[59] Corry was especially qualified to undertake such a task because he had worked as a civil servant economist at the Treasury from 1986–9, and had been involved in the costing exercise undertaken by the Treasury for the Conservative government in the run-up to the 1987 general election. He recalls: 'If nothing else, it meant I knew how what some might see as vague aspirational statements could be costed – unless you were very careful on how you phrased them.'[60] David Ward believes that although David Mellor's interpretation of Labour's spending plans was malicious, it was not totally false in that it exploited the major weakness of a lack of overall control of public spending.[61]

Gordon Brown, Beckett's predecessor as shadow chief secretary to the Treasury, had spotted the need for fiscal prudence, as his briefing paper (dated roughly 1990) to Neil Kinnock reveals: 'We have to be seen to be *unified* and *firm*; ie capable of saying no to things that may be desirable but not affordable.'[62]

In early 1990, Margaret Beckett, with the aid of Dan Corry, limited Labour's spending to just two hard commitments on pensions and child benefit, and to stop all the rest of the pledges from being counted, introduced an 'as resources allow' formula: no further spending unless financed by economic growth. It became known as 'Beckett's Law'.[63] However, David Ward compares the exercise to the little Dutch boy putting his finger in the dyke to hold back the water: 'a retrospective attempt to impose discipline on a process that was inherently undisciplined'.[64] Margaret Beckett agrees, arguing that Labour's spending commitments had not been 'scientifically conceived', but adds that they were 'the result of a party process conducted through the policy review'.[65] The retained pledges had therefore become so entrenched that they could not be dropped. In the absence of committing the party to higher public borrowing (which Neil Kinnock would not countenance), Labour's tax proposals had to be drawn up to meet these demands, and that ended up being the decision to remove the upper earnings limit on national insurance contributions, a key part of the 1992 shadow Budget.

In May 1990, Labour published *Looking to the Future*.[66] The whole tone of the document was moderate and business-like ('business where possible, government where necessary'). The main difference between it and *Meet the Challenge, Make the Change* in terms of economic policy was that it ditched most of Labour's commitments to bring the major privatised utilities back into public ownership (except the water industry).[67] But the main focus turned inevitably on Labour's tax and spending plans. Smith formally pledged to increase child benefit by 30 pence a week for the first child, and £2.15 for others, and to increase pensions by £5 for a single pensioner and £5 a week for a pensioner couple.[68] To finance these plans Smith proposed abolishing the upper earnings limit on national insurance contributions, introducing a series of tax bands from 20 per cent to 50 per cent, abolishing the married couples allowance (but increasing child benefit) and ending higher-rate relief for mortgage interest.

The political problem with these tax policies? They clobbered middle-income earners in three different ways all at the same time. Firstly, ending the married couples allowance and mortgage interest rate relief for higher earners might be excellent free market economics since both schemes were in effect middle-class subsidies that distorted the workings of the free market,[69] but politically they would hurt financially the very middle-income, middle-class voters that Labour was attempting to win over. Secondly, increasing the top rate of income tax from 40 to 50 per cent was equally politically dangerous. Thirdly, the abolition of the upper earnings limit on national insurance contributions meant that all earnings above £20,280 would be subject to national insurance. With income tax (50 per cent) and national insurance (9 per cent), this would mean a marginal top rate of tax of 59 per cent.[70]

Labour's tax and spending plans were subjected to the most rigorous scrutiny (and the greatest downright distortion) ever seen in the run-up to a post-war British general election campaign. David Mellor, in cahoots with Kenneth Baker, the Conservative Party chairman, set to work a team of people to cost every spending pledge uttered by a Labour front bench spokesperson since the 1987 election (something, as we have seen, that Corry had conducted privately, and more honestly, for Labour). No spending commitment was left unturned in accumulating the imaginary total extra public expenditure – set at £35 billion – that an incoming Labour government would incur. As soon as *Looking to the Future* was published, Kenneth Baker promptly launched his 'Summer Heat on Labour' campaign, one of the aims of which was to make voters believe that the election of a Labour government would lead to higher taxes because of Labour's high public spending.[71] The Tories kept up this message for nearly two years (see chapters 15 and 16), eventually eating into Labour's opinion poll lead.

The next phase of the policy review process required Labour leadership to sharpen, refine and co-ordinate Labour's economic strategy,[72] transforming policy documents into campaigning tools for a general election.[73] In order to achieve these aims, the three original policy review groups – Smith's economic equality group, Brown's productive and competitive economy group (formerly under Gould) and Tony Blair's employment team (originally 'People at Work' under Michael Meacher) – coalesced into a single economic review group headed by John Smith called the Economic Policy Sub-Committee.

The new aims of the sub-committee were formally agreed on 29 January 1990:

> (a) to highlight and 'fill-out' those areas of policy dealt within the policy review which best illustrate the content of the Party's economic policy; (b) to examine those areas of policy which need to be developed in the light of changing events; (c) to provide guidance on the drafting of the 1990 Conference Statement [*Looking to the Future*].[74]

The Labour leadership wanted to shift policy making from the review groups to the new sub-committee, which would be more tightly controlled by the senior members of the NEC and the shadow Cabinet.[75] As Margaret Beckett puts it, the Economic Policy Sub-Committee was the 'forum within which the really tight decisions were taken'.[76]

Paper-givers were asked to keep their submissions to the sub-committee brief, focused, and in a standard format.[77] On 16 January 1990, prior to a meeting of the sub-committee, John Eatwell outlined the main purpose of these 'campaigning documents':

... to ensure that everyone is singing the same song (the ERM brief was a great success in this respect) and to provide the confidence that goes with background briefing and 'detail in reserve' . . . The importance of having these documents was illustrated by the effects of the slight divergences on matters of taxation over the holidays.[78]

Meetings of the Economic Policy Sub-Committee were then held roughly fortnightly thereafter. From an early stage, the sub-committee took on a policy making rather than just a policy-tightening role. For example, in February 1990, the sub-committee came out in favour of ERM membership, subject to certain conditions.[79] At another meeting, it agreed 'not to rule out the role of private capital to finance investment in marketable public services, such as transport'.[80] At subsequent meetings, however, other important issues, such as the future role of the National Economic Development Council (NEDC – often known as 'Neddy') and measures to control public sector pay, were not resolved.[81] There were other problems with the sub-committee: Neil Kinnock used to speak a lot at the meetings, which would annoy John Smith: 'Neil would tend to go off on a long discourse, much to John's annoyance, so much so that when it came to John's turn, his interventions would be monosyllabic and spectacularly short.'[82]

A classic example of the Economic Policy Sub-Committee's growing influence over policy came when Smith and others emerged victorious in their disagreement with Bryan Gould, Labour's Environment spokesperson over Gould's proposed alternative to the rates. When Gould took over the Environment portfolio from Jack Cunningham,[83] Labour's previous policy had been fairly vague – supporting a part property tax and a part local income tax. David Blunkett, Cunningham's number two who had come up with this new idea – in *A Modern Democracy* – stayed on in his post. But Gould, his new boss, while acknowledging Blunkett's experience in local government,[84] considered it unworkable and electorally unpopular, and sought an alternative.

Gould's argument with Smith rested on how best to revise the rebates system. The former wanted to introduce something called 'an automatic adjustment of liability to rates', calculated according to a person's taxable income, operated through the Inland Revenue tax code structure.[85] Smith's new Treasury team were opposed to the idea, fearing that it would raise problems, as Gould puts it, 'of confidentiality and complexity'.[86] The Treasury team got its way, as Labour adopted a 'Fair Rates' strategy, but the story of how the policy was abandoned is a matter of dispute between Bryan Gould on the one hand and almost everyone else involved.[87]

Smith, with the help of John Eatwell, Henry Neuberger, a former economic adviser to Neil Kinnock, and Gordon Brown (who also considered the scheme too complicated), ditched Bryan Gould's scheme.[88] Margaret Beckett also claims that she and Jack Straw engaged in a 'huge fight' to get the scheme changed.[89] In a briefing paper prior to a meeting of the Economic Policy Sub-Committee on 30 January 1990, Eatwell had described Gould's poll tax alternative as: '. . . very complex, and would be virtually incomprehensible to anyone without an accountancy qualification. John Smith will attack it, and urge a system akin to rates, though based on capital valuation. I tend to agree with John. Simplicity is the key.'[90]

Then, on 21 May 1990, Eatwell briefed Neil Kinnock, prior to a scheduled meeting between Kinnock and Gould, suggesting 'some detailed amendments' to Gould's paper:

> I guess he [Gould] is proposing a two-stage process – an immediate return to the rates at the old valuations but with an enhanced system of rebates, coupled with legislation which can then proceed at a more leisurely pace and which can relate re-valued rates to the ability to pay through the Inland Revenue tax code structure. This may be the most sensible set of options in *technical* [Eatwell's emphasis] terms, but the politics of offering two changes to local government finance may not be so easy.[91]

Eatwell was concerned that 'our proposals are still very inadequately tested in a technical sense', preferring 'something which is not just easy to understand but whose implementation can also be easily explained'. Eatwell then suggested to Kinnock the means by which Gould's proposals could be changed:

> The crucial thing is that the Economic Policy Sub [-Committee] should be the door by which the Treasury team get involved. The draft proposals urgently need to be knocked about in a rigorous way by the Treasury people and by a select few in local government who can probe all the technically weak points. This should have been done but has not been done.[92]

Getting wind of what was happening, the press deduced correctly that Smith had demonstrated his growing grip over Labour's economic policy.[93] Margaret Beckett sees the method by which Labour eventually handled its alternative to the poll tax as a forerunner to how they dealt with the shadow Budget. According to Beckett, once Bryan Gould and David Blunkett had been persuaded to give up their overly complicated scheme, they did 'a brilliant job' of setting out clearly and precisely what the rates would cost under Labour. 'Up until that point, the Tories kept challenging us, "Tell us what the rates will cost." The Chartered Institute of Public Finance and Accountancy (CIPFA) then validated Labour's figures.' The overall effect of Labour's simpler, revised scheme was to blunt the constant Tory refrain that Labour's poll tax alternative didn't add up. John Smith and Margaret Beckett felt that one of the lessons learned from the poll tax episode was that Labour could repeat the trick of validating their tax and spending figures by saying, 'Here is our [carefully costed] shadow Budget.'[94]

In structural terms, the Economic Policy Sub-Committee had handled one of those 'really tight decisions' to which Beckett has already referred. It would also play a vital role in changing Labour's policies on Europe, a subject close to the hearts of both John Smith and Neil Kinnock.

Thirteen

LE GRAND PROJET

THE COURSE OF the 1987 Parliament saw the partial fulfilment of Neil Kinnock's vision of bringing the Labour Party into the European fold. A huge part of this process involved Labour's conversion to the Exchange Rate Mechanism of the European Monetary System. Despite differences on other aspects of economic policy, Kinnock and Smith both shared a strong belief in the European project. David Ward describes Smith as 'an engaged European':[1] he liked the European style of dialogue, and its methods of negotiation suited his political skills.

In economic terms, the shadow Chancellor was instinctively in favour of the ERM because it involved governments managing currency movements through intervention in the workings of the free market. On 22 March 1989, in a speech at the Intercontinental Hotel in London, Smith attacked the notion of unfettered free foreign exchange markets, citing the decision of James Baker, US Treasury Secretary, to agree to the Plaza Accord in September 1985:[2] 'The significance of the Plaza meeting was the recognition by governments even of a radical laissez-faire persuasion that the operations of the free-floating currency market could be to quote Mr Lawson "destabilising and disruptive".'[3]

Managed exchange rates became *de rigueur* in this period. At the Louvre in Paris in February 1987,[4] measures were agreed to halt the US dollar's downward path, again with the broader aim of stabilising exchange rates, and in February 1989, the Group of 7[5] meeting in Washington had also taken measures to reduce exchange rate instability. The shadow Chancellor con-cluded: 'I believe that exchange rate management and policy co-ordination need to be strengthened in the 1990s.'[6]

A key moment in Labour's pro-European journey had been the speech of Jacques Delors, the President of the European Commission, to the TUC conference in September 1988. Unfortunately, that week *The Sun* ran with its 'Up Yours Delors' headline. But such flagrant displays of xenophobia did not deter the leaders of the major unions from warming to the European Community. One or two union leaders, including Ron Todd of the TGWU, believed that they might be able to recover worker rights from Brussels lost as a result of Mrs Thatcher's trade union laws in the 1980s. In party terms, the guarantee of trade union support offered Kinnock and Smith a means of pushing through pro-European resolutions at party conferences against the wishes of the old Keynesians and some, though not all, the left of the party.

John Smith believed that committing the Labour Party to joining the ERM would enhance the credibility of the party's economic policy by giving it an anti-inflationary anchor, but he wasn't prepared to countenance independence for the Bank of England nor an independent European Central Bank (ECB).[7] Entering the ERM could also be portrayed as yet another way of Labour ditching the anti-European, anti-capitalist policies of 1983 that had proved to be so disastrous in electoral terms.[8] The constraints imposed on ERM membership would also virtually guarantee that a future Labour government would not spend too much in office.

Smith and Kinnock first tried to push for a commitment to join the ERM during the final stages of *Meet the Challenge, Make the Change*, but Bryan Gould's opposition prevailed.[9] Gould had emerged as the main opponent of ERM entry.[10] Others, including Peter Shore and Austin Mitchell, still held to traditional Keynesian economics – stimulating demand in a recession through increasing public spending – something which Britain's entry into the ERM would curtail.

In June 1989, Neil Kinnock and John Eatwell compiled a paper outlining Labour's conditions for entering the ERM: (1) Central Bank collaboration; (2) a co-ordinated European-wide growth strategy; (3) sufficient structural funds to support regional projects; but at Bryan Gould's insistence, they had to add 'condition (4)' – entry at a competitive rate.[11] On 28 June, the shadow Cabinet accepted Gould's tough conditions,[12] which he calculated would render Britain's entry virtually impossible. This painstakingly agreed formula lasted until the autumn of 1989.

Meanwhile, the Conservatives were having huge internal debates of their own on the issue of whether or not to join the ERM. Nigel Lawson, the Chancellor of the Exchequer and Geoffrey Howe, the Foreign Secretary, had corralled Mrs Thatcher, making her promise that Britain would join the ERM when certain conditions were met,[13] but everyone knew she was instinctively against the idea. In July 1989, Mrs Thatcher relieved Geoffrey Howe of his beloved Foreign Secretaryship as payback. Once Lawson had resigned in October 1989, John Major bravely ran with a modified plan. The 'hard' ecu would become a thirteenth currency, circulated freely within the European Community member countries. The other currencies would not be abolished,

LE GRAND PROJET   181

but rather the free market would determine which currencies would survive.[14] Smith not only enjoyed demolishing the government's hard ecu plan,[15] he also used the opportunity to wind up the Conservative Euro-sceptics in the House of Commons by airing the possibility that the hard ecu might eventually lead to a single currency.[16] While the Conservative government kept arguing that their hard ecu plan was working, Labour's numerous sources in European capitals informed Smith's office that it was not making any progress whatsoever.[17] Most European governments and central bankers rubbished the idea.[18]

The demotion of Bryan Gould in the autumn of 1989 – the demise of what Frank Dobson derides as 'the New Zealand lamb' view of Europe[19] – cleared the path for Kinnock and Smith to move away from the rather negative language on the ERM outlined in *Meet the Challenge, Make the Change*, towards a stance which made ERM entry 'an early objective of Government policy'.[20]

In October 1989, leading members of Labour's Treasury front bench team visited Paris, Frankfurt and Brussels in a carefully orchestrated attempt to force the pace on ERM membership. Smith met with Jacques Delors, the European Commission President, to discuss the Delors Plan on Economic and Monetary Union, and Delors conceded that his report was 'not the final word' in the debate on that subject.[21]

Smith then addressed a meeting of the European socialist group in the European Parliament, telling MEPs that Labour was 'eager to negotiate early entry into the Exchange Rate Mechanism of the EMS' and 'keen to plan a full and constructive part in the debate on progress towards Economic and Monetary Union'.[22]

When the Treasury team arrived in Paris, Ewan Fergusson, the British Ambassador to France from 1987–92, allowed the use of his Rolls-Royce to ferry Labour's team about the city. This decision led to a complaint from Margaret Thatcher.[23] More importantly, Smith met Michel Rocard at Matignon, the French Prime Minister's residence in Paris. According to the press version of the meeting, Rocard clapped and exclaimed 'Bravo' when Smith expressed his enthusiasm for implementing the European Social Chapter.[24] David Ward's notes of the meeting *seem* to show that Rocard was agreeing with Smith's support for a politically accountable European Central Bank:

JOHN SMITH: We don't want a Bundesbank model – we want more political control.
MICHEL ROCARD: Bravo – please keep on this line . . . There can be no fully

independent Central Bank. The legitimacy of the Bank is gained from the
Executive.[25]

It appears that Rocard must have said 'Bravo' on two occasions, accounting
for the difference between the press account and David Ward's contem-
poraneous account, which only noted one 'Bravo'.[26]

Ward's notes of Smith's subsequent meeting in Frankfurt with Karl Otto
Pohl, chairman of the Bundesbank, reveal that, even in late 1989, the Germans
were warning Britain not to enter the ERM at too high a rate, and that tensions
in the system might require a realignment of the ERM, which the Bundesbank
supported:

> KARL OTTO POHL: Pound should be in [ERM] otherwise UK will be isolated
> ... Bank wants a realignment to reduce domestic inflationary pressure. But
> the French don't want it and neither does the FRG government. I wouldn't
> exclude the possibility of collapse ... If the UK joined it could be a good
> pretext for a realignment. But don't join at the wrong rate – even a little
> under valued [off the record: DM 2:60].[27]

Michael Jones, political editor of *The Sunday Times*, summarised the
significance of the Treasury team's visit in grandiose terms: 'All this puts them
[Labour] light years ahead of Mrs Thatcher down the federalist road. It
represents a huge transformation in British politics.'[28] Writing in *The
Guardian*, Martin Kettle agreed, though less emphatically:

> John Smith's visit to three European countries this week ... is a pregnant
> symbol of a rapidly shifting political development in Europe and Britain ...
> Western European governments are realising not only that Labour is back
> in political business at home, but that a potential Labour government will
> be a pro-European force with which they can do business on the wider EC
> stage.[29]

Smith ran with the new policy enthusiastically. He was especially keen on
emulating 'the German model'. In March 1990, he even said: 'I am a nut about
Germany. They have a decent decentralised constitution and I would like to
see our economy as strong as theirs. First they equip the West and now they
have the whole of the East to equip as well – lucky sods.'[30]

On 6 May 1990, in an interview with the Christopher Hulme, economics
editor of *The Independent on Sunday*, the shadow Chancellor claimed that
ERM membership would provide 'counter-inflationary discipline' and that
'devaluation will not really be an option' for British businesses seeking a
competitive advantage. Such companies would now have to keep an eye on
their wage demands. Smith even conceded that if employers did not keep

wages down to a competitive level, 'there would be unemployment, wouldn't there?'[31]

Andrew Graham had advised Smith from an early stage (indeed Neil Kinnock, as far back as July 1986) that ERM membership carried with it certain dangers.[32] Chris Allsopp, an economist at New College, Oxford, warned in February 1990 that if Britain entered at too high a rate – creating what he termed 'a non-credible system' – large increases in interest rates might be needed to convince the financial markets of the government's commitment to maintaining the rate within the ERM. Even then, the financial markets might see sterling as a one-way bet in a downward direction.[33] Nor was ERM membership an immediate guarantor of low inflation. As Gavyn Davies pointed out to Neil Kinnock, the counter-inflationary impact of ERM membership 'will only build up gradually over time. It will not occur immediately'.[34] A proper anti-inflationary strategy, Davies argued, also required strict control over public sector pay[35] and limiting future spending commitments 'as much as possible', not just so that long-term investment in industry could be achieved, but also so that the 'persistent Conservative question "where are you going to get the money to finance your spending programme"' could be answered without recourse to excessively high taxes or increased public borrowing.[36] Andrew Graham agreed: 'Everyone can see that we cannot afford a large public expenditure programme in the first year of a new Labour Government so it is in our interest to emphasise that a significant part of macro[economic] policy is (and should be) medium term.'[37]

Such economic constraints, imposed by ERM membership, explain why Smith put so much emphasis in speeches at this time on investment for the medium and long term. As he candidly told a business conference in Newcastle in September 1991:

> [The ERM] provides a framework for currency and price stability and that in itself should help to secure an economic environment that encourages investment. But the ERM is simply a framework and much depends on what is done within it. And that is why supply-side policies are more important than ever before.[38]

The Labour hierarchy had committed itself to membership of the ERM as 'inevitable and desirable' without consulting the wider Labour Party. Although the 1990 Labour Party conference endorsed the relevant policy document – *Looking to the Future* – they were rubber-stamping a change of policy that had already been thrashed out in the Economic Policy Sub-Committee of the shadow Cabinet.

*

By early 1990, Neil Kinnock and John Eatwell were already making moves to commit the Labour Party to joining the single currency. At a key meeting of the Economic Policy Sub-Committee in February 1990, Kinnock and Eatwell were rebuffed by more sceptical shadow Cabinet members such as Michael Meacher and Frank Dobson. David Ward summed up the key objections to supporting the Euro in a paper submitted before the meeting:

> The problems of democratic accountability and fiscal controls are substantial and could become a source of intense debate within the Party. At a time when the Conservatives are deeply divided over Europe we should minimise the risks of reopening the old European arguments that have dogged the Party in the past.[39]

However, the political imperative for Labour to agree a line on monetary union came from the ongoing intergovernmental negotiations during 1990 and 1991 that would lead eventually to the Maastricht Treaty.

Many of the problematic issues associated with Labour's possible endorsement of a single currency were aired at a meeting of the shadow Cabinet on 7 November 1990. Kinnock's own notes of the meeting reveal that he saw Labour's acceptance of a single currency at this stage as 'qualitatively different' from the ERM, indeed a 'Rubicon' to be crossed. The political problem for Labour (and indeed, the Conservatives) was to avoid becoming isolated in Europe. Thus, Labour *had* to come up with some sort of line on the single currency. However, Labour could not agree to the idea outright because of their support for some form of democratic accountability for the European Central Bank, and the economic dimension – the perceived need for convergence. Kinnock's notes are also a fascinating insight into the divergent views expressed by various members of the shadow Cabinet on EMU, including Smith's caution.

> J[ohn] Smith – 'season of comment' . . . Central Bankers 'opening bid' . . . Can't say when and whether move to irrevocable monetary union and single currency; J[ack] Cunningham – Yes if, conds[conditions] 1. Regions – fundamental change. 2. Convergence – feelings in other countries.[40]

Frank Dobson, author of two mildly Euro-sceptical papers at the time,[41] recalls his main problem with the EMU proposals as drafted – that while the central bankers would work full-time in the day-to-day running of the ECB, the ministers and officials involved in ECOFIN, the Council of Economic and Finance Ministers of the European Community, were essentially 'amateurs meeting once a month', making it impossible to achieve adequate political accountability.[42]

The shadow Cabinet discussion led to a position paper on EMU, which called for a more democratically accountable ECB than the one being proposed by the European Commission. Labour also called for a 'substantial degree of convergence' of growth rates and levels of employment between the European economies before the Euro was established to prevent 'unbearable strains within the Community' which would 'probably culminate in fragmentation rather than closer integration'. Finally, the paper also warned that the single currency might create deflationary pressures in the weaker regions of the EC, and therefore supported 'an enhanced role for regional transfers'.[43] This cautious view of EMU was endorsed at the NEC on 28 November 1990.[44] Anderson and Mann rightly call Labour's policy on the Euro 'a fudge'.[45]

The PLP's substantial number of Euro-sceptics were livid. This grouping coalesced around the Labour Common Market Safeguards Committee, chaired by Nigel Spearing, who wrote to Kinnock claiming that: 'New policy is now made on the hoof by spokesmen who are pushing the Party into commitments it never made and cannot accept.'[46]

In a speech to the Royal Institute of International Affairs on 29 January 1991, Smith fleshed out the cautious line on EMU that had been hammered out by the Economic Policy Sub-Committee, the shadow Cabinet and the NEC the previous November. Most senior shadow Cabinet members realised, as Smith did, that 'the move towards economic and monetary union is solidly based and is widely supported by the majority of the Community' and was going to happen. However, what was not certain in early 1991 was whether the 'German tradition' of an independent Central Bank or the 'Franco-British tradition' of a politically accountable Central Bank would triumph in the Maastricht negotiations. Smith publicly supported the French idea of making the European Central Bank subject to political control, arguing that 'the key issue in the whole debate about monetary union . . . is what form of accountability should exist for Community financial institutions', and that 'the present Commission's proposals, which envisage a basically independent central banking system' were not satisfactory. Instead, Smith proposed the strengthening of ECOFIN:

> In effect, it [ECOFIN] should become the political supervisory body, with its own secretariat and permanent representatives, capable of adding an effective political dimension to the conduct of monetary policy and the external exchange policy of the Community. We believe this proposal would also ensure that a line of accountability to national parliaments would be preserved.[47]

By mid 1991, Neil Kinnock and John Eatwell again began to argue privately that Labour should come out more strongly in favour of the Euro, believing that Britain should not exclude itself from such an important development in European integration.[48] Eatwell drafted an NEC statement (which would be discussed on 8 July 1991)[49] that would have pushed 'the position on [the Euro] gently but firmly linking the "desirability" of monetary union to the "desirability of convergence" '.[50] However, Smith favoured a more cautious line. In a letter dated 1 July 1991, quoted partially by Martin Westlake in his biography of Kinnock, Smith informed Eatwell that, while he was not opposed to the single currency, coming out in favour would be 'seized upon by the press to help the Tories, by saying both parties are divided'.[51] 'While I am all for exploiting the difficulties which arise for Major and his colleagues from divisions in their Party, we should be clear that if we demand definition from them, the media will require it from us.'[52]

The debate over Euro tactics contrasts the political styles of Kinnock and Smith. Frank Dobson recalls, 'whereas Neil liked to nut an issue head on, John normally preferred to politic his way around a problem'.[53] Smith also thought that there was still plenty of time 'before the December crunch [the Maastricht summit] . . . it does not seem wise to commit ourselves now when we do not know the form of a proposal which may change in the negotiations between now and December.'[54] In this, Smith was right – the outcome of the negotiations at Maastricht were not pre-cooked.[55]

On 30 August 1991, the Labour Party's Economic Policy Sub-Committee, meeting in Edinburgh for the first time,[56] recommended acceptance of Economic and Monetary Union in principle, but with many pre-conditions attached.

For the rest of the year, shadow Cabinet members held to the line of welcoming the possible benefits of Britain joining the single currency, while also pointing out the Labour Party's specific objections to it. Smith repeated his key reservation to the EMU in a speech to the Deutsche Bank Seminar in Berlin on Thursday, 12 September 1991:

> I do not believe that it is satisfactory for there to be such vague political accountability as is contained in the present proposals . . . It should be recognised that monetary union influences all aspects of economic life and therefore cannot (and in my opinion should not) be detached from democratic decision making.[57]

However, word started to flow in from the Labour Party's wide range of contacts in European capitals during the latter half of 1991 that most of the other European leaders now saw the establishment of a single currency and an independent Central Bank along the German model, rather than the French vision, as inevitable. George Robertson, Labour's spokesperson on European Affairs since 1985, was among those who warned the Labour leadership to this effect just before Maastricht.[58] The bottom line was that EMU was not being shaped in the way that Labour wanted.

Chris Smith was responsible for the international aspects of economic policy on John Smith's Treasury team: 'I must be one of the few members of the House of Commons to have read the Maastricht Treaty.' During the Maastricht negotiations, Treasury officials were under political direction from the Major government not to tell Labour anything of the status of the negotiations, in contrast to many of the opposition parties in Europe. Smith's team found a way round this because the German CDU would tell their SPD opposition what was going on, and they in turn would pass on information to the Labour Party in Britain. Smith's office also had good relations at the time with the socialists in France[59] and the Netherlands, as well as in the European Commission and the Bundesbank.

Late into the night on which the Maastricht negotiations concluded, people working in Wim Kock's office kindly sent the newly finalised text of the Treaty to David Ward's office. Unfortunately, the resources of Her Majesty's opposition being limited, Ward's office had a cheap and cheerful fax machine, the blade cutters of which tended to jam. The following morning, Ward walked in on a massive ream of fax paper, constituting the entire text of the Maastricht Treaty. With Ann Barrett, he spent the next couple of hours cutting the Treaty into pages.[60]

As George Robertson had forewarned, the French backed down in their support for a politically accountable European Central Bank, acceding to the German preference for an independent Central Bank.[61] The French decision temporarily left Smith without a means to argue that the Central Bank would be subject to some sort of democratic control. However, in a key speech in Paris in February 1992, the shadow Chancellor renewed his call for an enhanced role for ECOFIN as 'the effective political counterpart' to the ECB otherwise, he argued, the ECB would 'operate in an uncertain political vacuum'.[62]

Neil Kinnock has since complained that he and John Eatwell had taken the lead in selling the merits of Britain's possible the membership of the Euro to the party when Smith should have been doing more of the work.[63] Smith realised the perils of committing Labour too enthusiastically and too soon. Labour's rather hesitant line on the Euro has remained essentially the same for the last fourteen years. Nevertheless, the conversion to Europe became the centrepiece of Labour's transformation into a respectable mainstream, European socialist party. John Smith's other important role was to convince businessmen in Britain, and Labour's former critics abroad, that the Labour Party really had changed.

Fourteen
THE ORIGINAL MR PRUDENCE

MICHAEL HESELTINE DERIDED it as 'the prawn cocktail offensive'.[1] Chris Smith complains: 'I never had a prawn cocktail.'[2] Paul Boateng recalls he must have eaten a prawn, but stuck to lots of rocket salad to watch his waistline.[3] Mo Mowlam, Gordon Brown's number two at Trade, referred to it as 'eating for Labour'.[4] Whichever phrase is used, Labour embarked upon a series of seminars and lunches in the City of London to demonstrate to business people its new financial competence. But as Chris Smith puts it: 'It was a familiarisation rather than a persuading process.'[5] Paul Boateng recalls: 'It wasn't about persuading City folk to put out the bunting the day after a Labour victory; it was stopping them from throwing themselves out of the windows.'[6] Or as John Smith said at the time: 'I am not in the business of seeking the City's endorsement. Our policies are for society and not for the City. I do not want to make enemies out of them but I am not going round hawking for approval.'[7] Ironically, at the end of the process, Labour would pull off the astonishing coup of getting the *Financial Times* to urge its readers to vote Labour in 1992.[8]

By the autumn of 1989, especially after the demise of Nigel Lawson, the political climate had changed. The economy went from boom to bust. Labour quickly emerged as the likely next government. Industry started 'battering down' Smith's door because it sniffed political change.[9]

Initially, the shadow Chancellor dined with senior people from major City firms such as Lehman Brothers or Goldman Sachs. Afterwards, more junior executives would hold follow-up meetings with Dan Corry and other members of Smith's Treasury team. Another side benefit was that Labour received top-rate briefings from respected City economists free of charge when such information would normally have cost them.[10]

Gradually, the message started to get through: Labour (or at least its leadership) were not as frighteningly left-wing as they had first feared. Simon Haskel recalls that before business people met John, they expected to be on the receiving end of left-wing rhetoric, but after meeting him, they were surprised: John listened to them (he was good at that), and gave the impression that he was genuinely interested in what they had to say. Moreover, he had a balanced view of the rights and responsibilities of employers on the one hand, and workers on the other. Haskel recalls: 'He used to say, "We're all in this together".'[11]

Such Labour lunches in the City had a positive effect on general attitudes to the party's economic policies, and faith in John Smith's abilities in particular. In April 1990, a survey of 77 economists for *The Economist* revealed that 45 per cent thought Smith would make the best Chancellor of the Exchequer, compared with 25 per cent for John Major, with 30 per cent undecided. Some 68 per cent of respondents believed that a future Labour government was capable of controlling public spending, while 62 per cent felt that Labour's tax plans were good, compared with only 18 per cent who thought they were bad. They believed that a Labour government would be far better for dealing with unemployment (60 per cent compared with 21 per cent for the Conservatives), marginally better for economic growth (36 per cent to 33 per cent), but only 9 per cent felt that Labour would be better than the Conservatives for controlling inflation (and some 61 per cent felt the opposite). However, as a rule, academic economists were more favourable to Labour than City economists.[12] Nevertheless, a measure of how far Labour had come since the dark days of 1983 could be seen in the statistic that 57 per cent of City economists believed that Labour would either be good for the economy or make no difference.[13]

The central question remained: would these generally positive signals from the City of London survive the pressure to support the Conservative government during an election campaign? A survey of City fund managers for the *Sunday Correspondent* in April 1990 worryingly revealed that 55 per cent intended to move their money overseas if Labour won the election.[14]

Fortunately for Smith, the aforementioned *Economist* poll also coincided with the shadow Chancellor's high-profile visit to Washington, which David Ward describes as 'an international extension of the prawn cocktail offensive'.[15] It was the first trip to the United States by a senior Labour figure since Neil Kinnock's disastrous trip before the 1987 election. On that occasion, Denis Healey and Neil Kinnock emerged from an all-too-brief meeting in the Oval Office crest-fallen, after Ronald Reagan expressed his disapproval of Labour's defence policy. One of the main reasons why Smith received a better reception was the Bush administration's greater pragmatism compared with the Reagan administration. On 17 April 1990, President George Bush indicated that America's good relations with Britain would not be altered if Labour came to power. Henry Catto, the US Ambassador in London, persuaded Bush both that Labour had changed, and that, with a 20-point lead in the opinion polls, it stood a good chance of gaining power.[16]

In Washington DC, the shadow Chancellor delivered a lecture to the America-Community Association, in which he welcomed and endorsed 'the dynamism, efficiency and realism which markets can provide' and underlined Labour's commitment to enter into the ERM as a means to achieving currency stability and low inflation. Nor would Labour spend more than the country could afford, or go for an old-fashioned 'dash for growth'.[17]

Smith's visit received generally favourable press coverage in Britain, including comments such as 'Showman Smith',[18] 'Leave it to Smith',[19] and rather implausibly in the *Daily Mirror*, 'Yankee Bosses are Voting for Labour'.[20] More realistically, David Hughes, writing in *The Sunday Times*, described the shadow Chancellor as 'the man who has done more than any other individual to swing Britain's economic establishment away from mortal terror of a Labour government'.[21] Only *The Independent* remained sceptical: 'Mr Smith can cut a dash on the American lunch and conference circuits, but a more detailed examination of Labour's policies might raise rather than resolve doubts.'[22]

Inevitably, the Tory tabloids picked holes in Smith's visit, remarking that it had not merited a single mention in an American newspaper or a television or radio programme. George Gordon, a reporter from the *Daily Mail*, bagged a quote from an unnamed foreign policy expert at the Brookings Institution, describing the Washington people that saw Smith as 'very much an outing with the Second XI'. At Senator Sam Nunn's office, a staff member expressed surprise that Smith had not even seen Vice-President Dan Quayle, adding: 'I mean, Quayle turns out for banana republics.'[23] David Ward recollection differs: 'It wasn't that we didn't *get* to see Dan Quayle; we didn't *want* Dan Quayle!'[24]

But would business people and the electorate swallow Labour's plans on personal taxation? One incident illustrates just how far the shadow Chancellor had to go in convincing businessmen of his policies in this area. After one lunch, during which the topic of general taxation was discussed, Smith descended in a lift with a very well paid company chairman who asked about the effect Labour's plans would have on his personal taxation. This seemed to be his main worry.[25]

A year later, Smith and David Ward visited Japan, along with Michael Montague, who had substantial financial interests there. Labour's press release emphasised the fact that the visit built on talks the previous year in Washington with senior members of the Bush administration.[26]

The trip started in chaotic fashion. Smith was supposed to be met by the British Ambassador as soon as he arrived in Tokyo, but this meeting was put in jeopardy because Smith's connecting flight from Edinburgh to London was delayed. The Japanese Airlines staff were concerned that the shadow Chancellor might miss his Heathrow to Tokyo flight, which would have meant Smith arriving in Japan a full day late. Much to their astonishment, the British Transport Police organised a 'tarmac transfer' in a car speeding across runways between the aeroplanes. However, when the car arrived, there was no stepladder to get Smith down from the Edinburgh aircraft. At one point, John is said to have offered to jump. In the end, a ladder appeared and he just made the flight.[27]

On Monday, 8 April, Smith had a round of meetings with important Japanese business leaders, including Mr Ishihara, chairman of Nissan, and Mr Morita, chairman of Sony, and a long-time friend of former Prime Minister, James Callaghan. Smith also visited a geisha house in order to meet up with members of the Japanese Diet, the country's legislative assembly. Ward and Smith sat cross-legged for hours in agony as they ate 30 courses, and had their glasses refilled with saki and beer by geisha girls.[28]

When the shadow Chancellor visited the Imperial Palace on 9 April, Smith wanted to discuss important matters of trade between Britain and Japan, but the Crown Prince of Japan, who'd been educated in Britain, quizzed the Labour leader on His Imperial Highness's specialised subject at university – the Inland Waterways of the United Kingdom.[29] Two days later, Smith delivered a fairly dull but reassuring message about Labour's desire to achieve macro-economic stability to a gathering of the Japan-European Committee of the Keidanren, Japan's leading business federation. Once again, he used Labour's new pro-European outlook, and its support for the ERM as a badge of financial respectability.[30] Back in Britain, Smith's visit was received positively.[31]

In the first half of 1991, the general message from a series of reports from leading firms of City economists showed quite clearly that the City of London was no longer frightened by the prospect of a Labour government. Even the worst report predicted that under Labour inflation might be 1 or 2 per cent higher at the end of five years than under the Conservatives. A Goldman Sachs report (May 1991) praised Labour's training and investment programmes; James Capel (June 1991) saw no real likelihood of a run on the pound if and when Labour was elected. The Japanese analysts, Nomura (May 1991), even criticised the Tories' attempt to compile a 'shopping list' of Labour's proposals – adding them all up, and producing figures implying large tax increases or unsustainably higher borrowing – as 'absurd'.[32]

THE ORIGINAL MR PRUDENCE

In November 1991, Smith went to Brussels to speak with European Labour MEPs and Bruce Millan, one of Britain's European Commissioners. He then had meetings with, amongst others, Jacques Delors, all designed to show Labour's pro-European credentials.[33] Symbolically, a week later, Sir Alexander Graham, the Lord Mayor of London, invited Smith to the Chancellor, Norman Lamont's, annual Guildhall speech. Lamont had not been consulted about Smith's invitation. The shadow Chancellor took full political advantage, telling reporters: 'It's a proper idea to invite the opposition spokesperson with an election imminent. It was a very good opportunity for me to survey the scene and prepare my own speech for next year.'[34]

In early February 1992, several members of Labour's economic team (John Smith, Margaret Beckett, Tony Blair, David Ward and Sheila Watson as assistant to Margaret Beckett) embarked upon a tour of three European cities – Bonn, Brussels and Paris. The press release issued before the trip reveals the extent to which Labour was trying to create the impression that it was preparing to enter government.[35]

In Bonn on 2 and 3 February, the economic team met with Federal Minister, Frederick Bohl, Head of the Chancellery, and attended a dinner hosted by leading members of the SPD, Labour's sister party in Germany. In Brussels, Gordon Brown, then Labour's Trade and Industry spokesperson, joined the Treasury team, and Smith had meetings with Jacques Delors and several other European Commissioners, among them Bruce Millan and Sir Leon Brittan, the Vice-President of the Commission. Smith also spoke to John Kerr, then the United Kingdom's representative to the European Community, and later permanent under-secretary at the Foreign Office from 1997–2002. Margaret Beckett recalls Kerr commenting to Smith that reform of the Common Agricultural Policy was perfectly possible. John agreed: 'If the Berlin Wall can come down then CAP can be reformed.'[36] The following day, David Ward, Margaret Beckett and John Smith travelled on to Paris, where they stayed at the British Embassy.[37] The three deliberately had their picture taken outside the British Embassy on the exact spot where Thatcher made her desperate 'I fight on, I fight to win' remarks during the November 1990 leadership contest.[38]

The main item on the itinerary for 6 February was a working lunch with the French Finance Minister, Pierre Beregovoy[39] at the Finance Ministry in Bercy. At about 12.15 pm, a ministerial bateau ferried Smith and Beckett from the Place de la Concorde in central Paris down the Seine to the Finance Ministry building, during which John telephoned Elizabeth excitedly on his mobile: 'You'll never guess where I'm 'phoning from?'[40]

The presence of John Smith as shadow Chancellor undoubtedly helped to reinforce Labour's message of economic prudence. As Lord Desai recalls, in the course of the previous five years, 'John had established himself as "John, the Prudent Chancellor".'[41] Indeed, Gordon Brown's whole subsequent pose as Mr Prudence owes much to his mentor. Paul Boateng agrees that one of John Smith's greatest gifts to the Labour Party was to build a reputation for prudence, and that Gordon Brown and Tony Blair have built on that legacy of developing a sound macro-economic policy.[42] The down side was Smith's perpetual portrayal in the media as a dour, cautious Presbyterian bank manager, when in fact he was the life and soul of any gathering. Smith's caution was real, but it was a caution born of the desire to get Labour back into power, not to be mistaken for dourness.

Nevertheless, presenting the international financial community, the City of London and the electorate with a 'safe pair of hands' tended to squeeze out anything too radical or distinctive, diminishing any positive sense of what the Labour Party actually stood for.[43] Two differing views had emerged in the period 1987–92, between what Bryan Gould referred to as the 'safety-first' approach, supported by most of the right, most notably Smith, and on the other side, people including Gould and Hattersley (for once not supporting Smith), who wanted a bolder approach.[44]

Much of the contemporary criticism of the policy review process agreed with Gould that Labour played it too safe,[45] and failed to offer a sufficiently radical alternative to the Conservatives – a deficiency which became ever more apparent with the advent of John Major. Eric Shaw, an experienced observer of the Labour Party, is particularly critical of the policy review. In his chapter entitled, 'A Paler Shade of Pink'[46] Shaw argues that Labour paid a heavy price at the 1992 election 'for its "play-safe" strategy which had always held that it was sounder to concentrate on establishing prudence and moderation, rather than risk sailing into more controversial waters'.[47] Ironically, despite painful policy and party reforms, and for all John Smith's growing reputation for prudence, Labour risked being portrayed as a pale imitation of the Conservatives.

Fifteen
TAXING PROBLEMS

IT WAS JOHN Smith and Margaret Beckett's idea to present a shadow Budget. They firmly believed that Labour had to set out definitively its tax and spending plans, and that the ambiguity of not doing so would expose Labour to the familiar Tory attacks of 'where is the money going to come from?'[1] Perceived vulnerability on tax meant that there was a real danger of the party not being able to sustain a prolonged battle with the Tories on this subject. The best chance was to challenge the Tories, as Margaret Beckett puts it, 'Budget to Budget'.[2] David Hill, then Labour's director of campaigns and communications, also recalls that it was 'vital that John Smith should set out the fact that Labour had a rational alternative view to that set out in Norman Lamont's Budget'.[3] Smith reasoned that if Labour announced their plans too early, the Tories would simply hold the Budget and wreck Labour's carefully crafted proposals, forcing the shadow Chancellor into another modification of his plans. It was therefore better not to reveal Labour's hand until the last minute.[4] More broadly, the Tories had all the advantages of government in terms of the timing of their Budget, and the general election that would inevitably follow it.

The idea of a shadow Budget was not entirely new. Smith had used similar language in the media to attack Lawson's 1989 Budget.[5] The shadow Chancellor's thoughts on these matters had been evident as early as 1990, as is revealed by Neil Kinnock's notes of John Smith's contribution to a shadow Cabinet discussion:

> Too early to make commitments . . . 1. Terrible uncertainty; 2. Public finances: is cupboard going to be empty? Will the Tories spend it before election? . . . 9. [Kenneth Baker, Conservative Party Chairman] cannot get at us . . . *Objectives*: 1. Enhance credibility of party; 2. Enlarge area of support; 3. Economic policy ready to be a plus – cut a draw on tax . . . 4. Strong economy, fair society.[6]

In short, Smith's view was that the best Labour could do was to 'cut a draw on tax'.

Charles Clarke, Neil Kinnock, John Eatwell and Philip Gould agreed with the idea of a shadow Budget, but wanted John to make big speeches on tax much earlier to give time for Labour's message to get across. John Eatwell explains:

> There was a very increasing tension from the autumn of 1991 to January/February 1992 arising from John's persistent refusal to make a big speech on taxation. It was a straightforward political disagreement, a significant difference of opinion, between Neil and John, between David Ward and Charles Clarke and between Andrew Graham and me.[7]

But the modernisers' concerns about the shadow Budget went far deeper. From an early stage, Labour's pollsters had been warning about the electoral implications of raising too high a level of tax from middle-income earners. As far back as December 1989, Boase, Massami and Pollitt (BMP), an advertising agency that supplied information to the shadow Communications Agency (SCA), had highlighted the concept of the 'aspirational classes', hard-pressed working-class achievers and members of the lower middle classes, who were said to be highly sensitive to Labour's tax rises.[8]

The SCA, headed by Philip Gould, began to question the whole idea of Labour's 'foolish' pledges to increase pensions and child benefit, and the abolition of the upper earnings limit on national insurance contributions to pay for these measures.[9] Patricia Hewitt is emphatic: 'As early as 1988 we were stuffed on tax for the next election.'[10] In his biography of Kinnock, Martin Westlake argues: 'The dynamics would have been very different if he [Smith] had added his weight and authority to the modernisers' cause'.[11] Conceivably, the new Economic Policy Sub-Committee could have been used as the forum to dump the pledges, just as it had been used to commit the party to the ERM.

In party political terms, however, removing the benefit increases altogether was never an option. For good or for ill, the proposals were the result of a detailed policy review that had gained the support of the bulk of the Labour Party (see chapter 12). David Ward recalls that there had been 'quite a battle' to get the top rate of income tax down to 50 per cent because many other left-leaning shadow Cabinet members wanted 60 per cent.[12] Margaret Beckett also remembers that there had been a 'big fight' to resist the left's call to inflation-proof the pledges.[13] However, Patricia Hewitt is scathing about Smith's achievement in stopping uprating: Smith thought 'he'd pulled off an amazing piece of modernisation' and that such an outcome was 'the most you could possibly expect the Party to agree to'.[14]

Roy Hattersley believes that in theory, shadow Cabinet ministers, usually with the backing of the leader, could change party policy, but in practice, and for most of the time, they couldn't challenge the party.[15] Smith had to fight to get the spending commitments down, suggesting that in party terms, this was

about as much as could be wrung out, especially in view of all the other major
Kinnock reforms prior to the 1992 election. Chris Smith also believes that the
spending pledges were:

> agreed party policy, enshrined in stone. Nowadays, if Labour wants to
> come up with a new policy, they just announce it, but in those days it had
> to go through the Party as a whole. The spending commitments were an
> agreed set of proposals, and departing from it meant departing from an
> agreed formula.[16]

Margaret Beckett identifies another political danger of doing so: 'David Mellor
[the Tory Chief Secretary to the Treasury] would have said, "We told you so –
Labour's numbers don't add up."'[17] Andy McSmith agrees: 'To have altered
another major element of party policy at a late stage might have added to the
impression of unreliability and panic under fire.'[18]

Almost every Labour politician interviewed now about the shadow Budget is
negative about the party's spending commitments. Tony Blair's present Chief
Whip, Hilary Armstrong, believes that Smith had no option but to present a
shadow Budget – 'nothing stacked up otherwise' – but agrees with Nick Brown
that the Labour Party had been stuck with 'daft commitments' on pensions and
child benefit very early on which were 'unsustainable' against the backdrop of an
economic recession.[19] Chris Smith agrees, believing that the Economic Equality
group got it wrong, leaving little room for manoeuvre elsewhere.[20] Roy
Hattersley also admits that shadow Cabinet ministers would produce impressive
looking policy proposals in the policy review committees, which would be
approved by the NEC, but no consideration was given to the overall costs,
leaving Smith and his Treasury team to figure out how to pay for it.[21]

Despite some of the retrospective negativity, Larry Whitty, then the general
secretary of the party, recalls: 'They [the spending commitments] were very
popular in the Party and in core vote terms.'[22] Paul Boateng agrees, arguing
that 'to the Party, they were totemic'.[23] Meghnad Desai still thinks that the
policy was a good idea, and remembers how big a positive impact it made
before the Conservatives began to attack it.[24]

Nevertheless, it benefited the Tory strategists enormously to know that
'Labour were inextricably bound by these [spending] commitments'.[25] In May
1991, David Mellor, the Tory Chief Secretary to the Treasury, argued that
taxpayers would be 'led over the threshold more times than Elizabeth Taylor and
Zsa Zsa Gabor'.[26] A month later, Mellor was outrageously claiming that Labour
needed to raise an extra £35 billion in order to meet all its spending pledges.[27]

According to Philip Gould, John Smith resisted any major changes in his tax
policies, believing 'as a matter of faith in the moral case for increasing benefits'

and that 'his [Smith's] reputation for integrity was essential to our chances of re-election'. Gould even claims that Smith said: 'All we have in politics is our integrity, and if we lose that we lose everything . . . Neil's changed so much, I can't change at all.'[28]

The shadow Communications Agency conducted more polling in June 1990 which seemed to support Gould and Hewitt's case that Labour's tax policy, together with the leadership question, were the two main impediments dissuading floating voters and middle-class voters in the south of England from switching to Labour. But when they presented these findings to Smith, he allegedly said that he wouldn't be lectured to by 'admen and pollsters'.[29] Philip Gould and the modernisers weren't the kind of people to let things drop. In the autumn of 1991, Patricia Hewitt prepared another briefing paper, this time for Labour's Campaign Advisory Team (CAT), outlining the voters' concerns on tax.[30] When Hewitt presented her findings to Charles Clarke, Kinnock's Chief of Staff, he ordered all copies of it to be destroyed for fear of upsetting Smith, allegedly telling Hewitt: 'You don't fucking understand. We can't discuss it.'[31] Charles Clarke believes that Smith relied too heavily on the idea that 'the policy of "just leave it to him and he could busk it" would carry us through' and that 'everyone else was a combination of stupid or tactically inept'.[32] According to Gould, Clarke had had a blazing row with Smith at a shadow Cabinet away day in January 1991, leading Clarke to feel 'very nervous' about his relationship with the shadow Chancellor. Allegedly, Neil Kinnock considered sacking John Smith, but the former didn't feel he was in a strong enough position to do this, and the latter knew he was strong enough to resist: 'I think it was a straight stand-off'.[33] In fact, a Labour leader cannot sack a shadow Cabinet member when in opposition. (Technically, they can be removed from their portfolio, but they cannot be stopped from attending meetings of the shadow Cabinet.) Neil Kinnock strenuously denies he ever considered it.[34]

However, it *is* the case that Kinnock felt that Smith could have done more in the run-up to the election to sell his own tax policies and to attack the Conservatives' economic record.[35] Kinnock wanted Smith to come out of his corner and fight, but Smith wouldn't budge. Gould claims 'His [Smith's] view was that tax for Labour was rather like the NHS for the Conservatives – if you raise the issue, it just gets worse.'[36] Moreover, as Chris Smith argues: 'Neil wanted John to present an image as a fiery, passionate denouncer of Tory extravagance, but that approach wouldn't have suited the image that John was trying to project.'[37] Finally, Gould gave up: 'To my eternal discredit, in the face of John Smith's stubbornness and Clarke's antagonism, I lost heart.'[38]

Perhaps Philip Gould and Labour's other pollsters should have spent more of their time coming up with possible solutions to deal with Kinnock's woeful personal standing in the polls, rather than constantly focusing on tax. John Smith continued to make outward protestations of loyalty to Kinnock, but these seemed half-hearted and unconvincing. When the shadow Chancellor had appeared in a Labour party political broadcast in April 1991, the floating voters were impressed by Smith's message on long-term investment in British industry, but when he uttered the following sentence – 'I think Neil Kinnock turned the Labour Party right round, and gave it a sense of purpose; and was courageous enough to make the Labour Party face up to problems and solve them.' – the people-metering[39] ratings plummeted.[40] Stories continued to circulate that Smith was prone to occasional private, but never public, outbursts in which he railed against Kinnock's leadership. During the year, Smith had allegedly remarked to a colleague that 'just because we're working for a lunatic doesn't mean we all have to behave like lunatics'.[41]

Around January 1992, the idea of 'the Australian option' was aired, replacing Kinnock with Smith, just as Australia's Labour Party had replaced William Hayden with Bob Hawke just before the 1983 election.[42] The only circumstances where Smith would have stood for the leadership was if Kinnock could be persuaded voluntarily to step down, and Smith would be elected by acclaim. He would not have been short of support. However, replacing an incumbent leader so close to an election carried huge risks. The PLP resigned itself to sticking with Neil Kinnock.

Some Kinnock supporters have even suggested that Smith deliberately sat on the political fence in the run-up to the 1992 election in order to secure the succession that he rightly felt would be his.[43] This is doubtful. Firstly, like everyone else, Smith had suffered thirteen years in opposition (a period which he loathed) and above all else, he wanted a Labour government. Secondly, David Ward argues that 'John didn't go into the 1992 election thinking we'd lose. He was totally mentally engaged with the prospect of becoming Chancellor of the Exchequer.'[44] Thirdly, can we really suppose that Smith, a Labour Party man since the age of sixteen, deliberately sat back and watched Kinnock go down to defeat in 1992 to serve his own personal ends? Roy Hattersley rightly dismisses the idea as 'nonsense'.[45]

What is more credible is that Smith took care not to offend the left while Kinnock was still leader. The source of Neil Kinnock's frustration was understandable. As Frank Dobson puts it: 'Neil felt he was really going out on a limb' reforming the party, while John was 'a bit careful about who he chose to offend'. One of the Scottish Labour MPs at the time compared Smith's method of picking up allies on the left as akin to 'climbing a mountain, leaving a bit of iron rations at staging posts along the way'.[46] Smith had once said: 'A moderate in a left-wing party is the best thing to be.'[47] David Ward prefers to believe that it was not so much a case of Smith taking care not to offend the left, as that it was inherent for Smith to be magnanimous.[48] There is certainly something in the fact that Smith's whole political style and moreover his natural predilection was not to pick up unnecessary enemies.

During what subsequently became known as 'the near term campaign'[49] or pre-election campaign, Conservative posters warned of Labour's 'Tax Bombshell', claiming taxpayers would pay an extra one thousand pounds in tax per year under Labour, as a result of the so-called 'Double Whammy' – higher rates of income tax combined with increased national insurance contributions for middle-income earners. Labour's lead started to slip in the opinion polls. John Eatwell argues that from the moment the Tories delivered their double whammy, Labour was always on the defensive, partly because there hadn't been the big presentation; it was 'the dog that didn't bark'.[50]

On 7 January 1992, Labour launched its pre-election campaign. John Smith and Gordon Brown, Labour's Trade and Industry spokesperson, unveiled the party's first main poster, a 'Made in Britain' logo 'suspended' by a piece of string, together with the punch-line, 'The only string attached to our policies.' The day after, Edwina Currie contrasted her party's poor presentation on tax with Smith 'looking the soul of Scottish rectitude, smart and sleek and with a bright flowery tie that spoke of a modern outlook and confidence'.[51]

However, such positive coverage was obscured the following day when the *Daily Express* ran with a private memorandum written by Chris Smith purporting to show that Labour intended to spend £35 billion. It was an old document, a think piece setting out various options, written shortly after the 1987 election, and out of context. In the hands of the rottweilers at the *Daily Express*, the £35 billion figure became the amount that Labour intended to spend in government after the 1992 election. Chris Smith still has no idea who got hold of his document, but suspects that someone must have been sitting on it for years,[52] ready to wheel it out at election time.

On 27 January, John Smith, Margaret Beckett, and Jack Cunningham, Labour's campaign co-ordinator, responded to the Conservatives' attack on tax by unveiling a 'Vatman' poster, depicting Norman Lamont in a Batman suit. The economic secretariat undertook a lot of work to reinforce the twin themes of pinning the blame on the Tories for the recession,[53] and predicting more VAT increases (possibly to 22 per cent) if the Tories were re-elected.[54] The secretariat also defended Smith's tax plans, highlighting how many people would gain from them.[55] They even tried to launch a counter-attack on what they saw as the Tory tax lies, quoting an article by Jo Rogaly in the *Financial Times*, claiming that: 'Voters have been frightened by blatant, ruthless and lying propaganda into believing that Labour will increase taxes for ordinary wage earners.'[56]

But, it is much harder for opposition parties than it is for the government to make news that the media is willing to report.[57] During the course of January and February 1992, Labour mounted a credible defence of its tax and economic strategy, but was steamrollered by the sheer weight of the Conservative propaganda onslaught. As Larry Whitty later observed: '[The Tory onslaught on tax] was crude, but it worked. And we did not successfully counter it either before the campaign or during.'[58]

Worse still for Labour was the fact that it lost its key campaigns and communications people. Colin Byrne, Kinnock's chief press officer, had resigned in the autumn of 1991, as had John Underwood, Labour's director of campaigns and communications, four months earlier.[59] Moreover, Peter Mandelson no longer worked at the heart of the party's propaganda machine, having been selected as the Labour candidate for Hartlepool. In the absence of these key people, Kinnock's relationship with the press deteriorated in the run-up to the election, and Labour lacked a set of sharp suits to counter the Tory attacks on tax.

Neil Kinnock, backed up by further polling evidence from SCA (an ICM poll had put Labour behind the Conservatives after the latter's tax offensive), was now tempted to interfere in Smith's tax strategy. Ominously, he had interfered at least twice before. Kinnock's thirst for exploring new ideas had plunged Smith's Treasury team into chaos in April 1989. He had suggested in a BBC radio interview that Labour would impose the top rate of tax at £40,000 and above, forcing Smith's team to completely re-do all their calculations.[60]

Then, in July 1990, Kinnock had suggested a new standard rate of income tax of 12 per cent, with the remaining 13 per cent (the standard rate of income tax was then 25 per cent) to be hypothecated[61] for the NHS. Chris Smith recalls that hypothecation was something that Neil occasionally floated as an idea, but John was 'highly sceptical'. Although hypothecation might increase public acceptance of the tax being imposed, Smith argued that it reduced a Chancellor's flexibility in setting tax policy, introducing rigidities into the system. It is significant that every Treasury under every government since the war has rejected the idea: 'John did not see it as a runner and never regarded it as a serious proposition.'[62] Smith's way of dealing with Kinnock's ideas, with which he disagreed, was to say little, and indicate he would think it over. In any case, the Gulf War intervened, everyone assumed that a general election was imminent, and the idea never saw the light of day.[63] In January 1992, Kinnock interfered for a third time on Smith's turf, this time with disastrous consequences.

The setting was Luigi's restaurant in Covent Garden. Since his falling-out with the tabloid press in 1987, Kinnock restricted himself to informal dinners with handpicked groups of journalists. On Tuesday, 14 January 1992,[64] six middle-ranking journalists from *The Times*, the *Financial Times*, *The Guardian*, the *Mirror*, the BBC and ITN[65] dined with Neil and Glenys, Adam Ingram, Neil's PPS, and Julie Hall, his press secretary. During the meal, Neil put forward the idea that Labour intended to phase in its proposed increases in national insurance contributions.

There are three possible interpretations of the Luigi's episode. One possibility is that Neil Kinnock, never the most economically literate of Labour leaders, simply got trapped by a far more economically literate *Financial Times* journalist into making a straightforward error. Rather than saying nothing that might incriminate him, he let rip on a subject about which he knew little. In this scenario, Kinnock could have padded away a non-committal response or refused to answer, and asked John Smith later to clarify the details. But, as one insider puts it, 'Neil was incapable of asking John . . . that would have been humiliation beyond death.'[66] Such an interpretation has the 'advantage' of demonstrating that Neil's actions were not deliberate, and that he was 'only' guilty of talking loosely. However, this portrays Kinnock as a fool, which he manifestly was not.

The second interpretation appears to have the weight of hard background evidence behind it. Neil Kinnock wrote to John Smith on the morning of 14 January – the day of the Luigi's episode – outlining his support for phasing-in the rises in national insurance contributions:

> In preparing my speech for the rally in York [12 January 1992] I worked through our economic policy documents, and I was particularly struck by a recurrent theme in the discussion of tax and national insurance policies, namely the argument that any significant changes would be phased in.[67]

Kinnock then reproduced relevant supporting quotes from three of Labour's recent policy documents, two of which suggested that tax and national insurance reforms could be introduced gradually,[68] and one which indicated they might be 'carefully phased in so as to cushion the impact on personal incomes'.[69]

John Eatwell argues that the idea of phasing-in was 'always implicit' in every document Labour had produced on tax and spending. As early as January

1990, Eatwell had aired the pros and cons of phasing-in.[70] A month later, Eatwell expressed his concerns about the electoral implications on middle-income earners of Labour's proposed abolition of the upper earnings limit (UEL) for national insurance contributions (NICs):

> The mystery of what exactly will happen to those above the UEL when it is abolished remains a big gap – are the tax bands to be set so that they [middle-income earners] don't lose anything? In addition, it is unclear whether the idea is to bring the tax and the NI changes in over a Parliament or over a shorter period.[71]

Thus, Kinnock was not announcing a change of policy in suggesting phasing-in.[72] His emerging opinion was that the removal of the ceiling on NICs would have 'an impact on personal incomes', adding: 'It is clear that lifting the NICs ceiling does significantly increase the tax burden on the £21,000 and £30,000 band . . . It is also clear that phasing-in would not only be reasonable, but might make the policy more attractive to this group – especially in London and the South East.'[73] He then outlined the main political danger of phasing-in; that it might be 'portrayed as a change of position from one we have taken in recent weeks – although I haven't yet found a quotation from any of us saying that we would *not* [Kinnock's emphasis] phase in our changes'.[74]

The whole tone of Kinnock's letter was worded in support of phasing-in: he even enclosed the relevant passages from *Opportunity Britain*, as well as a supportive piece written by Andrew Dilnot, director of the Institute for Fiscal Studies.[75]

Neil Kinnock's letter of 14 January shows that the Labour leader had thought about all aspects of phasing-in, and was fully aware of the arguments from every conceivable angle. We also know that he and his closest advisers had been itching for months to get Smith to make a big speech on tax. In effect, Kinnock's letter set out what that big speech should contain – a pledge to phase in the removal of the UEL – in order to alleviate the concerns of the voters who were telling the party's pollsters that they were worried about tax increases. Indeed, John Eatwell claims that Luigi's arose because the 'big speech' on taxation had never been made, and Neil was trying to 'present party policy'.[76] (Although announcing that the Labour Party intended to phase in some of its tax plans hardly amounts to 'a big speech'.)

According to David Ward, John Smith was not unhappy about the letter, and was not opposed to ameliorating the effects of the abolition of the NICs ceiling. Retaining the option of phasing-in might have proved useful to Smith in shaping his shadow Budget plans (and indeed, his first Budget as Chancellor of the Exchequer), but his leader's ill-advised intervention and subsequent public blurting-out ruled it out as a policy option.[77] John Eatwell reflects: 'I've always felt since that *de jure* we were right, but *de facto* maybe we weren't. The spending commitments were undoubtedly too generous. The problem for Neil was his suggestion of phasing-in was seen by the press as a new idea.'[78]

As we have already seen, Smith frequently balanced his loyalty to his party with his doubts about Kinnock's leadership by saying that he'd think things over, but he rarely changed policy after these discussions. Had Kinnock ever pulled rank, and insisted upon a change of policy, Smith would have deferred to the authority of his leader, but Kinnock always backed off from a full confrontation. As Kinnock later put it to his biographer, Martin Westlake: 'I certainly had no interest in having blazing rows with him [Smith]. They could never have remained secret, and the results of stories of basic disagreement would obviously have been disastrous.'[79] So, typically, after Kinnock wrote his letter on the Tuesday morning, the matter was left hanging. In any case, the details of NICs were due to be discussed formally at a meeting between John Eatwell and Smith's Treasury team on the Wednesday (15 January).

From the available evidence, one can rule out version one of the Luigi incident: although Neil Kinnock may not always have grasped every nuance of economic policy, on this occasion, his handwritten letter to Smith demonstrates conclusively that he knew precisely what he was proposing. But that does not necessarily prove – à la version two – that he was acting deliberately in revealing his phasing-in idea to journalists. It seems inconceivable that Neil would have used such an incompetent means of seeking to change the tax policy. Therefore, the most convincing explanation – version three – is that Kinnock did not mean to say what he said to the journalists, although he strongly supported the concept of phasing-in the national insurance increases. His forever fertile mind had been moving in the direction of such a policy change for some time, maybe partly because of what his pollsters in the SCA had been telling him. It was rolling about in his mind; he had written to Smith that very morning about the issue.

Initially, most of the journalists present were not sufficiently au fait with previous Labour Party documents on the subject to discern on the night if Kinnock was announcing a change in tax policy or not. David Ward believes that Julie Hall may have inadvertently drawn the attention of some of the journalists to Neil's throwaway comments in the back of one of the taxis that drove the guests home after the meal.[80] For one reason or another, the most economically literate of the journalists, Alison Smith of the *Financial Times*, seems to have persuaded her editors to lead with a piece on Kinnock's remarks, but not until Thursday, 16 January.[81]

Meanwhile, on Wednesday, 15 January, Smith's Treasury team met up for the pre-arranged meeting with John Eatwell. None of them, including Eatwell, knew anything about their leader's comments the previous evening (strengthening further the view that Kinnock had not acted deliberately, since Eatwell had helped Kinnock compile the case for phasing-in). Smith only got wind that something was up when he was interrupted during lunch at the French Embassy. He discovered that Jon Sopel, later one of Blair's biographers, but then a BBC journalist who had attended the dinner at Luigi's, was running with a mysterious story on the BBC lunchtime news that Labour, apparently panicked by an ICM poll the previous day putting the Tories back in the lead,[82] was about to announce a change in its tax policy.

When challenged by a lobby journalist earlier in the day, Margaret Beckett, also oblivious to Kinnock's gaffe, denied the story. The plot thickened when first a *Financial Times* journalist telephoned a bemused member of Smith's Treasury team asking about phasing-in, and then Smith learned that Julie Hall had also telephoned one of Smith's team that morning to check up on Labour's official line.[83] (If Hall did indeed call Smith's office, then it appears to show that she knew far less than Kinnock about the phasing-in idea.) This evidence, though unsubstantiated, perhaps suggests that Hall was searching for a means of backing up her boss's injudicious remarks. The shadow Cabinet met that afternoon for its routine weekly meeting. Tax policy was not discussed, and it can be reasonably assumed that no one present except Kinnock knew about his remarks the previous evening. When Bryan Gould was asked by reporters as he left the meeting whether there had been any change to Labour's tax plans, he, like Beckett, denied it, and even told the journalist that whoever was putting about that story was being mischievous, not knowing that the mischief-maker was his own leader![84]

By the Thursday morning (16 January), it looked as if Labour had got away with it. Only *The Times* and the *Financial Times* ran with the story on their front pages,[85] and the BBC dropped the item from its bulletins. It was only when Tim Collins,[86] Conservative Central Office's new parliamentary officer, took up the story, that it blew up in Labour's face. The Tory propaganda machine fed stories back to the press claiming that Labour, panicked by the new opinion polls, had made a *volte-face* on tax. At Prime Minister's Question Time later that day, John Major branded Neil Kinnock 'a tax dodger'.[87]

The following day, the story of Luigi's was all over the newspapers. Unsurprisingly, the *Daily Mail* took full advantage of Kinnock's own goal, giving its readers a photograph of the interior of the restaurant. They even reproduced the menu, and calculated that the bill had come to £400.[88]

Chris Smith recalls that 'John was most exercised after Luigi's.'[89] That is something of an understatement. In fact, according to David Ward: 'John was seething, saying things along the lines of "I can't work with this guy", and "I'm going to tell him what I think of him", except in much more colourful terms.'[90] John believed that Neil had deliberately interfered on his patch and, according to Roy Hattersley, wouldn't see Neil for two days. Again, according to Hattersley, David Hill became so anxious about the impasse that at one stage he tried to get to speak to Hattersley behind the Speaker's Chair in the House of Commons, but had to be held back by the Serjeant at Arms. Hill told Hattersley: 'You've got to get them together. John won't see him'.[91] David Ward's strong recollection is that there was no two-day impasse. He is certain that Neil and John saw each other later that afternoon.[92]

After the stand-off (however long it lasted), it seems that John and Neil met in Neil's office, with Roy Hattersley acting as intermediary.[93] Smith was very angry, but there was no blazing row because a couple of minutes into the meeting, Neil, to his credit, admitted he was wrong, and apologised, thereby defusing the tension. Kinnock again pointed to the fact that *Looking to the Future* had referred to phasing-in, but he had not realised the damaging effects that his musings at Luigi's would have. Only Julie Hall tried to persuade Kinnock to stick to his guns over phasing-in.[94]

Neil resolved not to interfere again. In a narrow sense, the post-Luigi's agreement helped in that at least from then on it appeared to be clear that, as Larry Whitty recalls: 'John was always in control of economic policy. Luigi's was a flash in the pan, and afterwards John was back in charge.'[95] Little did Whitty and Smith know that Kinnock would yet again interfere on economic policy, this time on the sensitive issue of the realignment of the pound within the ERM of the EMS (see chapter 16).

One effect of 'Luigi-gate' was that any nuances of difference on tax between Labour shadow Cabinet members were now blown up into blazing rows. Two weeks later, Roy Hattersley fell into the trap of agreeing to a lunch with lobby journalists. He revealed that he had privately pressed John Smith to defend the idea of introducing the national insurance increase in one go. According to Hattersley, Smith had taken the old-fashioned view that he couldn't undermine his leader. If Kinnock really wanted to go ahead with phased increases, and Smith had overruled him, the party would have been damaged. There was no blazing row between Hattersley and Smith, but the press made it into one, and Hattersley felt he had been stitched up.[96] Smith's high reputation also suffered a temporary blip. During February 1992, allies of the modernisers spun anti-Smith stories in the media, attacking Smith for being too conservative and too cautious.[97]

After the 1992 election, Michael Portillo, the new Chief Secretary to the Treasury, penned a piece of Conservative Central Office propaganda entitled, *The Economics of John Smith*. It suggested that Smith had stopped Kinnock from phasing in the increases. Portillo then wrote: 'Mr Kinnock dined in vain. The clever Mr Smith had committed a blunder which the less intellectual Mr Kinnock had striven valiantly to avoid.'[98]

When Ken Livingstone sought to stand against Smith in April 1992 for the Labour leadership (see chapter 17), he cited the fact that taxing so heavily over £20,000 was particularly harsh for people living in London, faced with higher than average house prices and a higher cost of living in general.[99] Margaret Beckett recalls a meeting of the PLP shortly after the election when Ken Livingstone complained that abolishing the national insurance ceiling was a big mistake because it affected too many people. Shouldn't Labour, he argued, have come up with proposals in the shadow Budget that only affected 16 per cent of the population? 'John and I exploded at the same time, saying it *did* only affect 16 per cent of the population.'[100]

Clearly, the whole Luigi's episode damaged Labour's credibility on tax for a few years after 1992, and it caused a further deterioration in the already strained relationship between Smith and Kinnock. Roy Hattersley feels that Kinnock had never been engaged in anything other than 'loose talk', but that Smith believed it to be 'calculated sabotage'.[101] Philip Gould claims to have written in his diary after the general election:

> This was a core disability at the heart of the Kinnock leadership, because the fact that he and Smith did not get on meant they never got to grips with the tax problem. If, before the election, they had been able to discuss it, they might have been able to solve it. But the relationship was not there and instead they accepted an uneasy compromise, their advisers kept them apart, and we were left with no big economic story to tell the voters.[102]

Sixteen
SHADOW BUDGET

NORMAN LAMONT'S MARCH 1992 Budget was primarily a political exercise designed to win the general election. On 10 March, the Chancellor of the Exchequer took everyone by surprise (including John Smith) by announcing the creation of a new 20 per cent band of income tax, but only on the first £2,000 of taxable income. In economic terms, the measure disproportionately helped the low-paid, but its primary aim was political: Labour would now be forced to come up with a shadow Budget at least as fair to the poor as the Conservatives. Moreover, Lamont knew that because of the deteriorating state of the public finances, there was only a certain amount of money to go around. If Smith wasn't prepared to add to the Public Sector Borrowing Requirement (PSBR) by increasing public borrowing (and the shadow Chancellor had said several times in public that he wasn't), and was committed to his spending increases (which Smith was) then he had very little room for manoeuvre.[1]

Smith and his team had expected Lamont to announce a cut in the basic rate of income tax from 25 per cent to 24 per cent. The immediate effect of Lamont's Budget was to plunge Labour's plans into disarray. Lamont remembers seeing 'frantic conversations taking place between Neil Kinnock and John Smith' on the Labour front bench 'who were plainly very discomfited and confused'.[2] While Labour's Treasury team engaged in 'hurried consultations',[3] Kinnock had to reply immediately on behalf of the opposition. John Eatwell, his economic adviser, watching the debate on television in the shadow Cabinet room, flung his papers all over the table and said: 'We can't respond to that. That's it. It's all over. We've got no money to spend. Neil's got no speech.'[4] John Eatwell recollects: ' [Lamont's Budget] was a quite deliberate device to embarrass Labour.'[5] Despite having 'no speech', Neil Kinnock was still able to attack Norman Lamont quite effectively for increasing the PSBR instead of tackling the recession.[6]

Smith and Kinnock met immediately after the Budget and agreed firstly to delay their shadow Budget launch (originally planned for the following day), and secondly not to opt for further borrowing to match the Tory tax cuts. The cuts would have to be reversed. Politically, Labour would have been on thin ice had Kinnock and Smith elected to borrow. John Eatwell recalls: 'There was this atmosphere in the press of economic probity. If we'd spent an extra £100,000, they'd have attacked us as a spendthrift party. We had to accept the fiscal balance.'[7]

That is not the full story of Labour's anguish. Margaret Beckett had earlier had a 'huge row' with John over whether Labour should increase borrowing. Whereas Beckett felt that borrowing would undermine the opposition's case, John felt that it was credible,[8] and David Ward agreed.[9] The next morning, Margaret said to John, 'I've been thinking about what you said, and yours is the right decision.' John replied, '*I've* been thinking about what *you* said, and I think *yours* is the right decision.' Beckett argues that nobody spotted the real extent of the black hole in the public finances – around £50 billion – until *after* the election.[10] Eventually, Margaret's original view, shared by Neil Kinnock, prevailed. In his reply to the Budget, John Smith accused the government of 'borrowing money they do not have to buy votes that they do not deserve'.[11]

Smith and Kinnock met again to seek ways of making their shadow Budget benefit the poor more than Lamont's Budget. Without recourse to borrowing, there was insufficient money both to rectify the effect of the new 20 pence tax band, and to cut national insurance to help middle-income earners.[12] The shadow Chancellor eventually came up with the idea of raising personal allowances (the amount that an individual may earn before incurring income tax) for everyone by 10 per cent. Labour calculated that the measure exempted an extra 740,000 low-income earners from paying tax altogether.

Elizabeth Smith remembers that John very much saw the shadow Budget as 'his unique selling point'. He was 'chuffed about it like a child pleased with something special'.[13] Jimmy Gordon recalls: 'John was proud of the intellectual honesty of it. He felt that one should be open about these things. He had this naïve belief in the attitudes of the average man in the street.'[14]

Given Kinnock's damaging interference at Luigi's, the delicate matter of whether the leader should attend the launch of the shadow Budget needed to be addressed. Philip Gould alleges that when he and David Hill, Labour's director of campaigns and communications, told Smith that Kinnock wanted to attend the launch, Smith replied sharply: 'Dressed as a waiter from Luigi's?'[15]

When John Smith unveiled his shadow Budget on Monday, 16 March, everything was done to show Labour's economic team as a Treasury-team in waiting. They gathered on the steps of the Treasury for a photo opportunity, and from there decamped to the official launch held at the Institute of Civil

Engineers in Parliament Square. Smith's opening line sounded just like the real thing: 'The Labour Budget proposals – which I am announcing today – will promote recovery from recession and reform the tax and national insurance system.' Smith had decided against holding up a dummy red box, but the whole language deployed had an authentic feel – 'I now turn to the reform of the personal tax and benefits systems'.[16]

After Smith sat down, several journalists tried to catch out Neil Kinnock on points of economic detail. David Hare recalls in his election diary:

> Kinnock sits beside Smith, letting him rip. The Press want to trip Kinnock up and address questions to him, hoping he will demonstrate his ignorance of economics. But Kinnock refuses to speak, deferring all the time to Smith, whose classlessness is much helped by his being a Scot. All the politicians in this election are pretending to be bank managers. John Smith is very definitely trying to be an area manager, and what's more, with Barclays, not the Midland.[17]

Smith's main selling point was that his shadow Budget would result in eight out of ten taxpayers being better off than with the Conservatives. Lord Desai believes that the shadow Budget was 'a brilliant idea, an absolutely beautiful document' that balanced the books.[18] Even Tony Benn was complimentary: 'Very clever, attacking the rich and with plans to help the poor. Excellent, good socialist Budget.'[19] John Eatwell recalls: 'On the day, it felt like a triumph. It was brilliantly presented, it looked good, made sense . . . but it reinforced the tax issue.'[20]

The real problem was that while the poorest in society gained quite a bit under Smith's Budget, those earning between £7,000–£20,000 gained very, very little (some estimates calculated this income group's gain as little as 10 pence), while it could be argued that a small but electorally vital group of middle-income earners were clobbered quite hard by the removal of the upper earnings limit on national insurance contributions. Against this, Smith set the threshold for the new top rate of tax (50 per cent) at the relatively high income level of £36,375, a measure which affected less than 10 per cent of the population.[21]

Business opinion was divided fairly evenly. On 18 March, 40 industrialists backed the shadow Budget in a letter to *The Times*,[22] nearly matching the number of top Tory industrialists – 44 to be exact – that had backed the Conservatives the previous day.[23]

In terms of television coverage, at least, the shadow Budget launch was a success. Not only were the Liberal Democrats furious that their manifesto launch,[24] scheduled for the same day, had been relegated to the second item on the news agenda, but also the BBC's *Nine O'clock News* devoted nineteen minutes of airtime to the shadow Budget.[25]

That evening Smith got the better of Lamont in a television debate, the latter having accepted a challenge from the former without consulting John Major. With his characteristic lack of grace, Lamont claims in his memoirs that he didn't think he had done that badly, and felt that Smith was 'rather pompous and arrogant'. Allegedly, during drinks afterwards, the shadow Chancellor commented to his opposite number: 'It must be hard to be about to lose your job and your house.'[26]

Shaun Woodward, a Conservative strategist at the time (though now a Labour MP), acknowledges that: 'The media's praise for John Smith's shadow Budget had a sapping effect on Conservative Party morale.'[27] Characteristically, Lamont blames an official in the Treasury for the four-day delay in producing a response to the shadow Budget.[28] Even when Lamont finally appeared on the Friday, he was inept enough to pick the same day as the unemployment figures were released, showing 40,200 more people had joined the dole queues in February.[29] Mid-campaign, *The Economist* felt that Michael Heseltine and Smith had been 'the star turns in the two campaigns, outperforming their leaders' but that the television focus on the two leaders meant that 'the two stars have not been seen that much'.[30]

Press coverage of Smith's shadow Budget was far more negative than on television. Only the traditional Labour tabloid, the *Mirror*, and the left-leaning broadsheet, *The Guardian*, gave Smith's tax plans a positive response. Meanwhile, the Tory tabloids exploited the tax issue to the full.[31] On 7 April, the *Daily Mail* ran with a front-page headline: 'Warning. Mr Smith's budget would at a stroke turn recession to slump. If you make it, they'll take it', accompanied by five pages of hostile coverage. The rest of the Tory supporting press, including *The Sun* and *The Times*, were also aghast at Labour's tax plans. The *Daily Express* claimed that Labour was 'waging a class war on the middle class'. Even *The Independent* warned: 'If Labour fails to oust this unpopular government, it will largely be because yesterday Mr Smith refused to think again.'[32]

But even more appalling was the outpouring of middle-class angst from columnists and commentators at the prospect of higher taxes. The *Daily Mail* enlisted the ultra-rich Andrew Lloyd Webber to argue, somewhat implausibly, that 'the trouble with the Labour Party is that it has this absurd notion that high earners are rich'. Frank Johnson, then writing for the *Sunday Telegraph*, declared 'Mr Smith means the end of civilisation'.[33] Meanwhile, in *The Spectator*, Edward Whitley compiled a guide to tax havens in the event of a

Labour victory.[34] Unfortunately, no unlikeable celebrities carried out their threats to leave the country.

Margaret Beckett believes that Labour were victims of their own success: 'John was ultimately right in that the shadow Budget added up. The Treasury demolition never happened. Judith Chaplin said that for four days they had tried to find its flaws, until Maurice Saatchi intervened, said forget it, and took the decision to go back to the propaganda on tax.'[35] In effect, the Tories, not knowing how to respond properly, chose to run the campaign – based on Labour's tax bombshell – they were going to run with anyway, as though Smith had never delivered a detailed accounting of Labour's tax and spending plans. They invented a figure of £37.9 billion for Labour's spending plans.[36] Chris Patten, the Conservative Party chairman, claimed that 'dogs bark, cats meow and Labour puts up taxes',[37] while his party officials at Conservative Central Office ran with the slogan, 'The Price of Labour – £1,250 a Year for Every Family'. Roy Hattersley maintains, 'had Smith not opened his mouth during the campaign, the Conservative Party would still have invented something like the "Double Whammy" '.[38]

Larry Whitty recalls that although the shadow Budget had been originally well-received, 'the *Daily Mail* coverage with all the [tax] tables was a travesty.'[39] One example will suffice. They deliberately left out of their calculations the positive impact that Smith's proposed increases in child benefit would have had on the incomes of most families.[40] The columnists in the respectable broadsheets showed barely more restraint.[41]

Members of Smith's Treasury team, together with the economic secretariat and the brilliant team of economists such as John Hills and Holly Sutherland, tried to rebut some of these claims. Karen Gardiner from the LSE compiled a set of 'Points we want to Address'.[42] Andrew Graham pointed out that Labour was being blamed for tax rises that had happened over the Tory years.[43] Yvette Cooper pointed out: 'Only those earning more than £420 per week will lose under Labour's proposals. Contrary to the views of various journalists, middle incomes, and even "middle class" incomes do not fall into this category.'[44] The economic secretariat also produced numerous briefing papers rebutting the Tory claims.[45]

With the benefit of hindsight, Emma Maclennan wonders if Labour could have done more to rebut many of these inaccuracies.[46] John Eatwell also feels that the economic secretariat placed too much faith in the persuasive power of their economic arguments at the expense of establishing stronger links between it and Labour's communications team.[47] On Tuesday, 24 March, David Hare describes a 'markedly bad-tempered' Labour press conference 'as

John Smith tries to prove tax has actually increased during the 13 years of Tory rule'.[48] Murray Elder believes that Neil Kinnock and John Smith should have held a joint press conference, saying emphatically that Labour would not spend any more than it had promised without economic growth.[49] But the relationship between Smith and Kinnock was probably so tense as to have ruled out such a press conference, and it would have risked sounding wholly unconvincing.

The Conservatives successfully rammed home their exaggerated message about Labour's tax plans, but at no point did they question the personal abilities of John Smith as a potential Chancellor of the Exchequer. And any doubts the electorate had about Labour in 1992 were surely not about the competence or otherwise of John Smith. As *The Economist* put it just before the 1992 election: 'If the Conservatives, in a moment of lunacy, put up posters of Messrs Smith and Brown, with the caption, "Can you trust them?" the average passer-by would say yes.'[50]

For the duration of the 1992 election campaign, Michael Montague provided his Waterloo office near the Old Vic. John Smith and Ann Barrett were in one room, with Gordon Brown ensconced in another. Helen Liddell, on sabbatical from the board of the *Daily Record*, kept John in constant touch with the leader's office and Labour's campaign team, led by Jack Cunningham. Liddell was specially chosen as John's minder as someone who 'wouldn't cramp his style', but nevertheless someone who would keep an eye on him.[51] Her nickname became the 'whirling dervisher'. Elizabeth featured more after the shadow Budget than prior to it. She based herself at the Kensington Hotel (and, once again, Montague footed the bill). Helen Liddell recalls that Elizabeth was 'good at keeping John calm' and that he deferred to her.[52]

According to Liddell, John's great weakness on the campaign trail, which Liddell shared, was for an early morning fry-up. Such indulgences were supposedly banned by Elizabeth, but John and Helen occasionally sneaked off to a greasy spoon café in Waterloo. On another occasion, John caught the sleeper to Glasgow for an early morning television appearance in Scotland. Liddell accompanied him, and asked him to promise that he would stay in his berth and get some sleep. 'Aye,' John replied, 'I've taken a wee pill.' Unconvinced, she later found the shadow Chancellor in the lounge car with his great pal, Murdo Maclean, drinking whisky and singing Gaelic hymns. Liddell was only allowed to stay on condition that she matched John and Murdo drink for drink. Liddell stayed, she says, because 'I couldn't afford to let him [John] out of my sight.'[53]

For much of the campaign, however, Smith travelled not by train but by helicopter. Helen Liddell proved to be a bad traveller, and John was continually passing the sick bag: 'You could tell if he [John] was in a good mood because he'd tried to keep my mind off things by counting the number of swimming pools below, but if he was in a bad mood, he'd tell me to read the *Financial Times*, which would make me feel ill.'[54]

Liddell also had to cope with John's 'appalling temper'.[55] One morning, David Ward, Helen Liddell and Ann Barrett gathered in Helen's room in the Kensington Hotel to draw lots as to who would knock on John's door to retrieve the leader's briefcase (Helen had left it in John's suite). Smith had been short-tempered that morning because he'd been constantly harassed by people. Ann broke the tension by announcing: 'I've been elected to come into the lion's den.'[56] Liddell also recalls: 'John could be robust and cutting. You had to be as tough as he was to cope with him.'[57]

The most exciting moment of Smith's campaign trail apparently came when it emerged that Lou Kirby, a former editor of the *Evening Standard*, but now a reporter with the *Daily Mail*, had uncovered two discussion papers between Smith and his economic advisers dating from 1990, one of which had advised that public sector wages might need to rise by 1 per cent above inflation to reduce the pay gap between the private and the public sectors. The story did not amount to a row of beans, and Smith was advised to ignore requests from Kirby for an interview.[58] However, Anna Healey, Labour's press officer, telephoned from the car behind Smith to say they were being followed. Smith and Liddell had to speed away from the chasing journalists. 'It was like the Keystone Cops . . . fairly hairy stuff,' recalls Liddell.[59] 'John thought it was great fun – talked about it for months.'[60]

Such was the expectation of a Labour victory that civil servants from the Treasury kept in regular touch with John Smith's office. Martha Kearney, from BBC1's *On The Record* programme, contacted Smith's office before the election result to ask if she could film Smith's proposed office in the Treasury. Smith's people refused on the legitimate grounds that Labour hadn't won yet.[61]

Terry Burns, Permanent Secretary to the Treasury, was nervous about a possible run on the pound following a likely Labour victory, so John Eatwell and Treasury officials agreed to an election night statement that Smith would read out.[62] Two scenarios were catered for: a Labour government with an overall majority, and a minority Labour government ready to form a coalition with the Liberal Democrats. Despite the differing scenarios, the two 'Labour Chancellor of the Exchequer' statements are remarkably similar:

We are on course to form a majority Government with a strong mandate to lead the country out of recession. We are committed to prudent economic management. We will do whatever it is necessary to sustain the value of the sterling in the ERM, with, in due course, movement to narrow bands at the existing parity. We are also committed to a strong supply side policy. Those are the policies which will build recovery out of recession.

We are on course to form the next Government. We will present policies to the House of Commons and to the country to take Britain out of recession, to make families and pensioners better off, and to invest in the Health Service and in education. There is a broad consensus in the country which supports these policies. We are committed to prudent economic management. We will do whatever is necessary to sustain the value of the sterling in the ERM, with, in due course, movement to narrow bands at the existing parity. We are also committed to a strong supply side policy. Those are the policies which will build recovery out of recession.[63]

What the Treasury didn't know, but the Bank of England did, was that these statements would never have been issued,[64] and that Labour was planning an immediate realignment of the pound within the ERM, worth about 8–10 per cent. Eatwell had secretly held conversations with Bank of England officials in order to find out precisely how to arrange a realignment. Had Labour won, Eatwell 'wasn't looking forward to having that conversation' with Terry Burns, having to dissemble to him. Nor was he looking forward to telling John Smith because he didn't know about the realignment plan either! Eatwell admits: 'If I'd done that and we'd won, John would have been fed up, very angry and quite reasonably so.' Charles Clarke, John Eatwell, and Neil Kinnock knew about the realignment plan.[65] Labour's economic advisory group – particularly Andrew Graham and Meghnad Desai – had long agreed that the pound was overvalued. Indeed, Desai joked that Smith's economic advisory group should have been called the 'Ten to Three Club', disguising the fact that they supported a realignment of the pound within the ERM at DM 2.50.[66] Desai claims that when he and Eatwell met on the Monday before the general election to attend Neil Kinnock's speech on economic policy, they chatted informally afterwards that Labour was probably headed for victory, and Desai argued that in such circumstances it was likely that the incoming government would raise interest rates by 2 per cent to defend the pound, and begin realignment negotiations immediately.[67] Desai was not party to the realignment plan, but he assumed that some sort of plan would be implemented, and that John Smith would have been informed about it.[68]

Such was the secrecy involved in the realignment plan that Neil Kinnock
had indicated via a letter written by Charles Clarke that everything connected
with the Treasury dialogue should be directed through Neil's private office.
However, David Ward was never shown a copy of the letter, nor had anyone
informed him about these arrangements, so that when John Smith asked
Ward to get in touch with Treasury officials to arrange a meeting, Ward did as
he was told. Clarke was furious with Ward for telephoning the Treasury, but
the feeling was reciprocated because Clarke hadn't told Ward about Neil
Kinnock's wishes. Ward took the view that Neil and his office were perfectly
entitled to seek to control a matter such as this (Neil was leader after all), but
surely Neil's office needed to establish a decent working relationship with
John's team so that important wires did not get crossed, which happened in
this case.[69] It is little wonder that Clarke did not want Ward to be involved.

The main defence for those plotting the realignment plan is that the
shadow Chancellor, and indeed Treasury officials, had to remain convinced
that there would be no run on the pound in the event of a Labour election
victory. One of the best ways of convincing the international money markets
was for Smith to sound convincing: he certainly would be if he believed what
he was saying. However, could not Smith, the brilliant advocate, have been
told in advance, and still sounded convincing? Twice in the space of four
months, the leader of the opposition and his closest advisers had directly
interfered, and actively sought to change a central aspect of economic policy
without consulting the shadow Chancellor. Neil Kinnock defends his
decision not to tell Smith:

> It would have been seriously unfair if I'd said to John weeks before the
> election that I wanted realignment simply because it was essential that
> when he gave assurances against devaluation as shadow Chancellor he was
> confidently and genuinely telling the truth. If he and I had agreed to my
> intentions, if he had still had to give assurances against devaluation, and if
> we had won (at best minority) government, and then pursued realignment
> it would have seriously damaged John from the outset. No-one doubts
> John's barrister skills but it would have been utterly wrong for me to have
> asked him to give assurances against devaluation, whilst sharing the
> knowledge of intentions to cut interest rates and make the exchange level
> of sterling more rational and competitive.[70]

On the Monday before polling day, Smith met with Terry Burns. Still
completely oblivious to what Eatwell had been up to, Smith looked at the
government finances as a precursor to a Labour victory. Helen Liddell recalls
that John had been buoyed up by that, but Liddell tried to tell him: ' "We're

not going to win." John bawled me out, and said I was being defeatist, but Alan Donnelly, our advance man agreed. I recall him saying, "We've not won."[71]

On election morning, Smith left his Edinburgh home for his Monklands East constituency, claiming that when he returned, he would be Chancellor of the Exchequer.[72] The Smith girls had even decorated the house for John's triumphant return, and the police were standing guard outside. Smith's confidence in Labour's victory held right throughout polling day as he greeted constituents outside the polling stations. Helen Liddell and Alan Donnelly had to take Smith to one side during his constituency count to tell him that the 'plane waiting to take him to London as the Labour's first Chancellor of the Exchequer in thirteen years would no longer be required.[73] According to Liddell, 'John took it hard.'[74]

Typically, within a few days John bounced back, telling Martin Dempsey, then a councillor in Monklands District Council not to worry:

He picked the [local] Party up because a number of long-term members of the Labour Party were not going to renew their membership. We had tae face the District Council elections in two or three weeks, and we couldna' get the people out tae campaign. John told them, 'There's always another day, we fight, we go back to the electorate – that's democracy.'[75]

John Major had won with an overall majority of 21 seats. In the aftermath of a fourth election defeat in a row, it didn't take long for figures inside the Labour Party to begin the inevitable round of blame and recriminations.

Various explanations have been offered for Labour's defeat in 1992. Some accounts put the blame on Kinnock's performance at the famous Sheffield Rally. The rally was undoubtedly mistimed, having hoped to create the impression of lift-off at the end of a Labour campaign that had never reached such dizzy heights.[76] The television coverage of the event was unfair in that it only showed Kinnock's cringe-making 'well, all right!' comments, rather than the fine speech that he delivered that evening. However, although Sheffield was subsequently interpreted as emblematic, Labour's post-election polling showed that many voters did not even recall watching the rally.[77] Others cite the party's decision to air the idea of proportional representation in the last week of the campaign as the price of co-operation with the Liberal Democrats in a hung Parliament, the theory being that talk of coalitions led to a late swing back to the Tories. Rightly or wrongly, Labour was perceived as willing to embrace a coalition in order to get into government.

Labour may have squandered its strongest card on health with the 'War of

Jennifer's Ear'. Philip Gould, seeking a means of counter-attacking the Tories in one of their weakest areas (and keeping Labour's tax plans off the news headlines), sought to highlight the fact that Tory tax cuts also meant NHS cuts.[78] A party political broadcast, directed by Mike Newell, depicted a little girl being turned away from Great Ormond Street hospital for a 'glue ear' operation. The Tories reacted angrily to the broadcast, but the real problem for Labour occurred when Jennifer's mother objected to her daughter's case being used in the broadcast. Gould's misjudgement (which he now prefers to gloss over) meant the argument on the health service became, as Larry Whitty put it, 'not a little grubby', mired in claim and counter-claim.[79]

But the single most common explanation is that John Smith's shadow Budget cost Labour the election. In his biography of Robin Cook, John Kampfner describes Smith's Budget as 'a public relations disaster',[80] while, more recently, James Naughtie agrees: 'By common consent in the shadow Cabinet afterwards, it [the shadow Budget] had been a disaster.' He even adds: 'The sight of the Labour Treasury team posing on the steps of the Treasury – a most un-Smith-like piece of PR – had seemed hubristic, and so it proved.[81] Smith's old friend, Donald MacCormick argues that the shadow Budget 'failed to take account of aspirations in the more affluent south, and set the tax bite too deep. It contributed to Labour's loss.'[82] A member of Smith's Treasury team feels that £20,080, while a large amount in Smith's constituency, was not in the South-East, and John did not fully appreciate that: 'Although 80 per cent of people would not be earning that amount, 75 per cent aspired to earn that amount.'[83] In his biography of Kinnock, Martin Westlake goes further, claiming that the shadow Budget was 'almost certainly the biggest factor in Labour's, and Kinnock's, 1992 downfall'.[84] To this day the abiding myth remains – especially prevalent in the Murdoch press – that the shadow Budget snatched defeat from the jaws of victory.[85] It seems a very bold statement to make that the shadow Budget could have loomed so large at the very top of voter concerns. On the other side of the debate, Roy Hattersley now claims that the shadow Budget 'didn't lose us a single vote', although he admits he might be exaggerating.[86]

John Smith was unrepentant about his shadow Budget. Chris Smith agrees that John 'very strongly believed in it. He was entirely happy with the idea that higher earners should pay more in tax. He did have doubts about the spending priorities, but that was set in stone as part of the party process with the policy review.'[87] Writing in *The Herald* on the day after John died, Brian Wilson accurately summed up Smith's consistent beliefs in this area:

> I recall his irritation when his tax proposals came under criticism within the

Labour Party prior to the last election [in 1992]. He, the supposed right-winger, remained firmly committed to the redistributionist principle, while some fainter hearts fled from it at the first whiff of grapeshot.

John Smith straightforwardly believed that we had to go out and tell people that if they wanted a society which offered work and homes and education and a decent National Health Service to everyone, then it had to be at some cost to those who could afford it. To pretend otherwise was an affront to his morality, as well as to the electoral intellect.[88]

Helen Liddell agrees: 'John could be quite high-minded. He didn't change his views on tax.'[89] Smith wasn't naïve enough to think that no further change was necessary after 1992 in order to get Labour elected but, as he put it: 'I am not going to turn my heel on them [the public] now. I don't think the public have any respect for people who say, "Oh well, if you don't like that set [of policies] we will give you a wholly new set."'[90]

Gallup's private polling for the Conservatives shows that 80 per cent of people believed in January 1992 that their taxes would go up under a Labour government, whereas 75 per cent thought so by March 1992. Against this, the figures for November 1991 were 61 per cent, strengthening Kinnock's belief that Labour (and especially Smith) should have expounded his tax plans earlier to stem the Tory attacks on tax. As Clive Soley put it after the election: 'We can not win the tax argument in a 4-week campaign.'[91]

It may be that as the general election loomed closer, middle-income voters started to get out their little calculators to see how much more tax they would be paying under Labour. As Butler and Kavanagh point out: 'After the election, people were more willing to admit the economic reasons for their vote.' Depressingly for Smith, a Harris ITN exit poll found that 30 per cent of voters felt they would be personally better off under Labour's tax plans, compared with 49 per cent of voters who thought they would be worse off.[92] However, in their recent examination of New Labour, Anthony Heath, Roger Jowell and John Curtice argue that 'there is not a shred of evidence that Labour's popularity declined in 1992 in the immediate aftermath of John Smith's shadow Budget and the furore over his proposed tax increases'.[93] And they add that despite this fact, 'the belief that voters will not tolerate increases in tax has now become a shared article of faith among Conservative and Labour leaders'.[94]

Did Kinnock lose the election for Labour, and could Smith have done better? The wider media likes to embrace the theory that leaders of political parties are crucial to winning elections (and *The Sun* famously tried to claim that 'It was

The Sun "wot" won it' in 1992), but political scientists are far less emphatic. A detailed study conducted by Ivor Crewe and Anthony King into the 1992 election found that neither the personality of Neil Kinnock nor that of John Major *directly* affected the outcome.[95] The difficulty with such studies, as the experts readily admit, is that they only deal with pure or *direct* effects. So the impact that Kinnock had on the image of his party, and its policies and ideas, can't be accurately measured. These *indirect* effects may be as important or indeed more so than direct leadership effects. Secondly, while one can prove that Kinnock consistently polled worse than Major when voters were asked who would make the best Prime Minister,[96] it is not necessarily the case that a strong dislike of Kinnock's personality was the primary reason for Labour's defeat. The same logic applies when political scientists have tried without success to prove Kinnock's own claim that the Tory press's character assassination of him led to Labour's defeat.[97]

At a superficial level, it seems as though John Smith would have performed better than Neil Kinnock at the 1992 election: a Mori poll conducted the week before the election showed that Labour's lead over the Tories could have increased from 7 points to 16 points if John Smith had been leader.[98] The NOP/BBC exit poll on the night of the election revealed that twice as many people thought that Smith would be the best Labour leader as thought Kinnock would.[99] A shadow Cabinet insider even claims that Labour's own pollsters had put the names of six prominent Labour politicians into their computers, and the test revealed all six would have won, all except Neil. The insider claims that 'Neil was the problem'. The Tory newspapers had done Neil Kinnock's reputation so much damage that 'they [the electorate] wouldn't have Neil'.[100] Another insider claims that Labour's pollsters knew that Neil was the problem but they didn't tell the leader,[101] fearing it would dent his already fragile confidence.

Larry Whitty was pretty near the mark when he pointed out that 'the long-running attack on the leader of the Party did have a considerable effect upon the general unease about Labour and its fitness to govern'.[102] Anecdotally, people would point to the fact that Kinnock lacked gravitas and was verbose. By contrast, John Smith's public image seemed to represent everything that the voters wanted from Labour, even if neither caricature was accurate.

After the election, Ivor Crewe and Anthony King tried to test whether Smith might have done better by asking actual voters in 1992 how they would have voted if Smith not Kinnock had been Labour leader. The hypothetical difference was +5 per cent for Smith. In other words, 8 per cent of voters who did not vote Labour claimed they would have done so if Smith had been leader, compared with only 3 per cent of voters who did vote Labour, but would not have done so had Smith been leader. The major problems with these findings are that they asked voters after the event, the questions took no account of the different set of political circumstances that would have pertained had Smith been leader, and the results may only tell us that the voters *think* they are influenced by party leaders, when this may not be the case.[103]

We are still left without a satisfactory answer as to why Labour lost in 1992. David Hill has come up with the best, and most depressing explanation, and it had very little to do with John Smith's shadow Budget. Common sense would suggest that the political party which the public thinks will win the Election (which in this case was Labour) would end up winning it. Not so in 1992. It appears that 'the more people considered the prospect of a Labour victory [as the opinion polls appeared to show], the more they were worried by it'.[104] After the 1992 defeat, Philip Gould successfully proved, using Labour's own private NOP polling, together with Gallup's findings, that 'the belief that Labour would win continued to grow right through the final week of the campaign'. He correctly predicted that this finding spelt trouble for Labour:

> We do now have to be careful, because now that people understand that Labour may win, there will undoubtedly be a shift back to the Conservatives. Electoral history is littered with campaigns which were ahead on Friday and lost the following Thursday. And the Conservatives will now hit the tax thing very hard . . . It does make people uneasy that we're ahead.[105]

Gould was (and is) firmly of the view that this widely-held belief that Labour would win, together with rogue polls showing a Labour landslide, helped to scare ex-Tory Liberal voters in the last week of the campaign.[106] More broadly, he drew the conclusion that 'They [the voters] couldn't bring themselves to [vote Labour] because they believe Labour is outdated and doesn't understand modern aspirations . . . the word "Labour" appears to many people to belong to the past.'[107]

Labour therefore lost in 1992 because the floating voters did not yet trust it to run the country. Labour's own inquest into its defeat highlighted this fact as the most important reason. In retrospect, John Eatwell[108] and Margaret Beckett are in agreement with Gould's analysis: 'We thought that if we had detailed policies, accurately costed and utterly defensible, that would answer the question of trust. But it didn't. They still didn't trust us. It was an emotional thing; it wasn't based on the figures.'[109]

John Smith's shadow Budget, or rather broader concerns over tax, were merely a symptom rather than a cause of the Labour Party's electoral defeat. Chris Smith argues: 'Tax was part of the jigsaw, not a determining factor in Labour's defeat.' Labour lost because people were still not ready to vote Labour.[110] Larry Whitty agrees. In one sense, people had asked themselves, 'How much is it going to cost me to vote Labour?', but wavering voters had always asked themselves that when pondering whether to elect a Labour government. At a personal level, the voters regarded John Smith as someone who looked and sounded competent and reassuring, but this personal regard for Smith was not underpinned by a general trust in Labour.[111]

Despite all Neil Kinnock's attempts to broaden Labour's electoral appeal beyond its traditional working-class base, the middle classes had adopted a highly materialistic agenda, which Labour was only edging towards. As Roy Hattersley ruefully puts it, in 1992 the middle classes had 'ceased to care – or at least to care enough to risk their new-found and, they imagined, precarious prosperity by supporting policies which helped the poor'. Against the backdrop of the recession: 'The nervous motto of the middle classes was "what we have, we hold".'[112] The choice for Labour ever since 1992 has been about accepting that 'fact', reforming itself accordingly in the quest for power (as propounded by New Labour), or seeking to convert people to the idea of social justice and modest wealth redistribution, running the risk of remaining permanently in opposition (ideas still held by remnants of the old right and the left).

The demise of Margaret Thatcher in November 1990 also dissipated much of the animosity that had been building up in the country towards the Conservatives. When the more conciliatory John Major took her place, the general mood for a change of government had been satisfied without a General Election. Larry Whitty agrees that this more medium-term factor was responsible for Labour losing the massive leads it had enjoyed over the Tories during 1990, and had the effect during the course of 1991 of making it clear to people inside Walworth Road that Labour was not going to coast the election.[113] In his observations on the 1992 defeat, David Hill largely agrees: '. . . It must be recognised that the replacement of Margaret Thatcher by John Major could be depicted as enough change for those many voters who were very uncertain whether they could risk a change of party.'[114]

Seventeen
VERY NEARLY A SHOE-IN

Neil Kinnock [May 1992]:

> I was in a terrible situation for the first full eight years for all the time, I was
> trying to get the Party back to respectability . . . The Labour party is full of
> superior people who can't be bothered to work out how to beat the Tories.
> Of course, when Smithy gets in it will be easier. Things won't be as hard.
> They'll never be as hard as they were.[1]

Philip Gould [May 1992]:

> Getting Neil in would have been wonderful. It would have shaken the
> whole bloody country. Getting John Smith in won't be the same.[2]

Friday, 10 April 1992 is etched in every Labour Party member's memory. At 5
am, Neil Kinnock gave his speech conceding defeat. At lunchtime, members
of the Treasury team met for a pre-planned victory celebration,[3] which now
resembled a wake. Smith was applauded as he entered the room. He made a
short speech expressing gratitude to everyone for all their hard work. He tried
to lift everyone's spirits, reminding the young people gathered there that,
above all, they should maintain their commitment to the Labour Party
because they could still change things in the future.[4]

The following morning, John Smith telephoned Roy Hattersley, expressing
his concern that Kinnock might not stand down in time for a leadership
election to be held by the autumn. Smith still hadn't forgiven Kinnock for the
Luigi's episode, and feared that Kinnock would support Bryan Gould for the
leadership. He sought and gained an assurance from Hattersley that if
Kinnock stalled about going, Hattersley would 'tell Neil where his duty (and
self-interest) lay'.[5] While it seemed fairly certain that Kinnock would step
down in the coming months, no one outside the incumbent leader's office
knew the timescale of Kinnock's departure.

Over the weekend of 11–12 April, and with unseemly haste, trade union
leaders almost fell over themselves in their attempts to endorse John Smith as
the Labour Party's fourteenth leader, even before Kinnock formally stood
down. John Edmonds, the leader of the GMB union, said there was 'one name

on everybody's lips'.[6] Larry Whitty recalls that Edmonds's comments didn't help matters: 'I remember him 'phoning me that weekend, saying, "John should walk it."'[7] The Amalgamated Engineering Union (AEU), the Transport and General Workers Union (TGWU), and the Electrical, Electronic Telecommunications and Plumbing Union (EETPU) all followed Edmonds's lead. These four unions constituted at least one fifth of the total votes in Labour's electoral college.[8] Of the large trade unions, only the National Union of Public Employees (NUPE) had failed to declare for Smith without the need for an election. It was alleged at the time that the union barons were arranging a 'shoe-in'[9] for Smith.

Such manoeuvrings seem very undemocratic, but perhaps inevitable, given that, as Larry Whitty recalls, 'John was so much the heir apparent.'[10] It was also felt that resolving the leadership issue quickly would help maintain party unity after such a wounding fourth election defeat.

On Saturday, 11 April, reports were carried in the media that John Smith and Margaret Beckett would be running as a team. Initially, Margaret had not the slightest wish to be deputy leader. She rang the BBC: 'I'm not running.' Margaret then rang Gordon Brown and Tony Blair to tell them: 'This [story] is not true,' assuming either Gordon or Tony might be deputy leader. Gordon commented that it would not be good to have two Scots in the leadership team, but Margaret replied that that would 'not necessarily be the case with you [Gordon]'.[11] All the manoeuvring and soundings that followed stemmed from the fact that Beckett had seemingly ruled herself out.

In such circumstances, it is unsurprising that Smith sounded out Tony Blair as to whether he might stand. However, Blair made it clear on the Monday through David Ward that he was reluctant to stand, citing his young family. When Ward contacted Blair again, Blair's response was: 'We think it should be Gordon.'[12] According to Rentoul, Blair and Brown had discussed the matter, and agreed if either of them had to stand, it should be Brown, and since that would create an unbalanced Scottish leadership ticket, Blair was effectively arguing that neither man should stand.[13] Much eyewash has been written about Brown and Blair's possible candidatures for the leadership in 1992.[14] Roy Hattersley goes so far as to suggest that the idea that Tony and Gordon considered standing for the leadership in 1992 against Smith is 'nonsense' and 'pure legend', invented by Peter Mandelson. If so, that must include Blair's supposed view that Brown had had his chance in 1992 and flunked it.[15]

Because he eventually became Labour leader, all Blair's actions are given far more retrospective attention by journalistic biographers than they merit historically. Blair wasn't as big a player as Gordon Brown in 1992. If Blair had any support at all, it came from Kinnock people, who were now largely sidelined. Nor would Blair have had any meaningful support among the trade union bosses. Brown was also ahead of Blair in terms of the PLP: Blair didn't even feature in a *Sunday Times* poll of 138 Labour MPs conducted immediately after the general election.[16]

Two anonymous allies of Blair suggest in Donald Macintyre's biography of Peter Mandelson that Brown should have stood against Smith in 1992. The 'plan' would have been a Brown-Blair leadership ticket, attacking Smith as representing the 'old order', responsible for the 1992 defeat through his supposedly disastrous shadow Budget. Yet, as Macintyre rightly states, Brown had more support in the PLP than Blair, though it amounted to a fraction of the support that Smith enjoyed.[17] There is little doubt that Smith would have beaten Brown decisively.[18] In any case, Brown was totally loyal to Smith, having served as his understudy for so many years.[19] Moreover, according to Donald Macintyre, Brown had made an undertaking less than a year earlier not to stand against Smith.[20] Only Peter Mandelson, it seems, considered a Brown-Blair leadership ticket as a viable option.[21]

In reality, John Smith was left with only one realistic option: he needed to persuade Margaret Beckett to change her mind. As it turns out, that proved unnecessary. Having 'killed' the story on the Saturday, the Becketts' telephone had started to ring all day Sunday, as parliamentary colleagues urged Margaret to stand for the deputy leadership.[22] On the Tuesday morning (14 April), John Smith bounded up the stairs to Margaret Beckett, and declared: 'I gather you've decided to run – David Ward has already told me.'[23] Meanwhile, Nick Brown had been despatched to see Beckett on behalf of Brown and Blair. As Nick Brown arrived at Beckett's office, Smith was already leaving the building. He allegedly said to Nick Brown, 'Margaret has decided to stand, and I think this is a very good idea.'[24] The following day, Beckett executed her public U-turn. Smith had not shoved or cajoled Beckett to stand, she had simply changed her mind, having been swept along by the high level of support she had received from parliamentary colleagues.

On Monday, 13 April, Neil Kinnock formally announced his intention to stand down as Labour leader. Kinnock also indicated that Roy Hattersley wished to stand down as deputy leader, and that Hattersley shared the leader's views on the early timing of the elections. Hattersley's departure made John Smith the only member of Callaghan's Cabinet left in the shadow Cabinet.[25]

It appeared that a combination of Neil Kinnock's determination to step down quickly and the union barons' desire to see a swift shoe-in for Smith would lead to a very precipitous leadership contest, or perhaps no contest at all. But there was a huge backlash in the party against rushing into things. On 19 April, John Prescott summed up the mood of many malcontents in the Labour Party when he appeared on *Frost on Sunday*, claiming that the constituency parties were getting angry 'that somehow it is being settled even before the MPs have met'.[26] Five days later, Clare Short wrote in *Tribune* that she was 'stunned and angry' that the party had not even had a chance to 'mourn' its defeat, and yet it had been 'told the result of the next leadership election'.[27]

There were also more practical considerations leading many to call for a pause for breath: there were local government elections to be fought in May; the new Parliament was not due to begin until 6 May, meaning that leadership candidates would not have sufficient time to canvass fellow MPs;[28] the unions needed time to consult with their members; and the constituencies had to hold ballots.[29]

There was also something of a backlash against Smith personally. In an emotionally charged letter to *The Guardian*, Colin Byrne, Kinnock's former chief press officer, made the extraordinary claim that a conspiracy had existed to make Smith leader if Kinnock lost the election. This conspiracy, Byrne claimed, had included a whispering campaign against Kinnock in the run-up to the election, thus ensuring that Smith became leader.[30]

Byrne had left Labour's employment in the autumn of 1991, complaining that people in Labour's office were trying to position themselves for jobs after the election, which he felt Labour couldn't win.[31] His partner, Julie Hall, Kinnock's press officer, had suffered terribly at the hands of the press during the election campaign when the Tory press discovered that members of her family had used private health care.[32] Paul Routledge also claims that Smith had taken a dislike to Hall, dating back to the time of Smith's heart attack in October 1988. Hall, then an ITN reporter, had tried to get a sickbed interview, much to Smith's distaste.[33]

Were the modernisers behind the Byrne letter? According to John Rentoul, Mandelson, Blair and Brown all knew about the letter, and tried to persuade Byrne not to fax it to *The Guardian*.[34] The most credible interpretation of Byrne's letter is that it simply represented the bitter ramblings of a committed moderniser who feared that the Labour Party would get stuck in a rut if Smith took over, or as Edward Pearce succinctly put it at the time, 'the rage of an outgoing apparatchik, now detached from outer-office authority, denouncing authority and the doings of apparatchiks'.[35]

In any case, the more widespread and growing feeling in the Labour Party at the time was that the proper constitutional processes of the party should be followed. John Smith was in full agreement,[36] as were Roy Hattersley and Margaret Beckett.[37] In 1963, after Hugh Gaitskell's death, several candidates put their hats in the ring, and there followed a comradely contest which did the Party a lot of good: Beckett saw no reason why this should not happen again.[38]

On Tuesday, 14 April, the NEC blocked, by a margin of fifteen votes to ten, Kinnock's idea of a special conference to elect a new leader on 27 June.[39] Charles Clarke briefed Neil Kinnock beforehand, and it is quite clear that the departing chief of staff shared his leader's sense of urgency:

> It would be a failure of opposition if a leader was not elected and functioning as a proper Opposition until the beginning of 1993 which would be the case if not elected until October (getting office set up, having shadow cabinet elections, learning their portfolios until they were ready to tackle their opposite numbers).[40]

Neil Kinnock's rough notes of the NEC meeting on 14 April 1992 reveal the other main arguments he deployed in support of an early contest:

> Case. *Simple.* L'ship election 2 months or 6 months . . . Labour pre-occupied, 'divided' . . . Tories 6 months off; latter *cannot* be justified . . . Pressures . . . entitled. Stay in post – Oct . . . 1983 – election was in *June* . . . unions running Labour Party . . . leadership and deputy leadership – maximum support.[41]

However, it soon becomes clear to Kinnock that he is losing the argument – at one point he notes down, 'gave [give?] me back my *dignity*' – as increasingly, his fellow NEC colleagues begin to raise their objections to an early contest: '*Robin* [Cook] rulebook . . . John Prescott "rush"? . . . Skinner *Cost*; Blunkett Conf [erence].' After Kinnock writes down 'Joan', signifying Joan Lestor, his notes end, presumably as he realises that he will not be able to garner enough votes for a quick contest, and that his former authority as leader is now swiftly draining away from him.[42] The NEC rejected, by the decisive margin of eighteen votes to seven, a motion deferring the contest until the party conference in October 1992. Instead, the meeting voted by fifteen votes to ten in favour of an amendment in the name of David Blunkett, delaying a contest until 18 July.[43]

After Kinnock's formal resignation statement, Bryan Gould had been first to announce his intention to stand both for the Labour leadership and the deputy leadership. Although Kinnock did not formally support Gould (Kinnock abstained on both the leadership and deputy leadership ballots), it was pretty clear where his allegiances lay. During the 1992 general election campaign, he had let slip to David Hare: 'In every profile of Brian [sic] Gould you read they now say he's back with Kinnock again. He was never out. But it's become a fact. All along he was my best bloody friend.'[44]

After the election, Kinnock had tried to persuade Gould to stand only for the deputy leadership, because 'Smithy has got it [the leadership] all sewn up'. He warned Gould that he would only get 'a fraction of the vote. Better to let him [Smith] have it. He won't last the course. It's important that you're there to pick up the pieces.' Gould was unsure whether Kinnock's reference to Smith 'not lasting the course' meant that Smith would encounter political or health problems.[45]

Gould denies that by standing for both the leadership and the deputy leadership, he scuppered his chances of winning the deputy leadership. Gould had precedent on his side: Hattersley had stood for both positions in 1983, albeit with limited success. More importantly, had Gould only stood for the deputy leadership, Smith might have won the leadership without a contest.[46] It was important that Smith faced a credible challenge. Gould had disagreed with the leadership for quite some time, and knew that if he didn't speak out now, even though he stood no chance winning, then the party could not debate fully why it had lost. As he put it: 'We would have faced another five years of iron discipline and emphasis on unity.'[47] David Blunkett became Gould's campaign manager, and (like Kinnock) tried to persuade Gould to stand only for the deputy leadership, but to no avail.

Early on, Gordon Brown volunteered to be Beckett's campaign manager. Did Smith ask Brown to make this offer? Beckett doesn't know, and Brown hasn't commented on the matter. Beckett's candidature was immediately endorsed by 'a bevy of shadow Cabinet members who had already declared their support for Smith',[48] including Jack Straw, Tony Blair and Gerald Kaufman.

One side-effect of Margaret Beckett's change of mind was that it put paid to John Prescott's chances of winning the deputy leadership. An unsuccessful deputy leadership candidate against Roy Hattersley in 1988, Prescott had only stood on the premise that Beckett was not going to compete.[49] Unfortunately, Prescott announced his intention to stand for the deputy leadership the same day as Beckett, and had already enlisted the help of Richard Caborn, the Labour member for Sheffield Central as his campaign manager.[50] Having entered the contest, Prescott couldn't really withdraw. Ann Clwyd announced her intention to stand for the deputy leadership on that same day. Ken Livingstone, the former leader of the Greater London Council (GLC) added his name to the leadership contenders, and Bernie Grant came on side as his running mate.

Very soon after Kinnock's resignation, Smith asked Robin Cook to be his campaign manager. The two men had disagreed frequently over policy issues in the past: they'd clashed on devolution when Smith had been a junior minister in the 1970s (see chapter 6), and Cook had for a long time been opposed to Britain's membership of the Common Market, as well as being a supporter of unilateral nuclear disarmament. Apparently, Smith was often heard to say, 'Wee Cookie's an odd one right enough.'[51] But having Cook on board meant Smith could shore up his support on the left of the PLP.[52]

In his first press conference, Smith trotted out some old chestnuts such as 'an efficient economy and a fair society go together' and 'I believe that Britain's future lies in Europe.'[53] He answered questions cagily on electoral reform and Labour's relationship with the unions. The general consensus was that Smith had performed poorly: David Ward recalls Smith and his team's exhaustion after the general election. There had only been one day to organise the press conference.[54]

That weekend, the newspapers ran with stories, almost certainly concocted by Peter Mandelson, that the faltering Smith campaign had been saved by the modernisers.[55] Donald Macintyre claims that Mandelson met with Cook for lunch at the Red Lion pub in Whitehall, and suggested that, in addition to enlisting the help of Gordon Brown and Tony Blair, Smith should undertake a national tour, emphasising the differences with Gould over Europe, and neutralising the doubts from Kinnock's people about Smith's stamina. Mandelson took little subsequent part in the campaign, but characteristically couldn't keep his nose out. Even on holiday with the Blairs at Derry Irvine's house in West Loch Tarbert over Easter, his host chastised him: 'What's it got to do with you? Get off the 'phone, Mandelson.' In reality, whether he liked it or not, Mandelson would be out of the inner loop of the Labour leadership for the next two years,[56] although that did not stop him from filtering his modernising message through to journalists.

Initially, Smith's team had seen its task as gathering such a massive level of support in the PLP as to create a bandwagon effect, which might have made a leadership contest unnecessary. However, from a very early stage, Smith's supporters (particularly Robin Cook) realised that it would be politically damaging for Smith to be elected unopposed, ever open to accusations of being carried to power on the back of an old-fashioned trade union stitch-up. Such a perception had also gathered momentum in the media. Cook therefore wrote a letter to all Labour MPs stating that the purpose of gathering the highest possible support in the PLP was to 'rebut the media attempt to portray the leadership election as a union fix'. For the same reason, the Smith team also made it clear that it welcomed a full secret ballot of the CLPs (introduced as a result of party reforms in 1989) as a means of demonstrating just how much support the shadow Chancellor had in the wider party.[57] It was also important to avoid accusations of complacency. Frank Dobson recalls that 'taking it seriously' was part of John's public image. One of John's great strengths during the 1992 leadership contest was that he successfully presented himself as someone who would not only carry on Neil Kinnock's legacy, but also had the necessary gravitas and appeal to the general public that Kinnock apparently lacked.[58]

By Wednesday, 22 April, the Smith camp could claim the support of fourteen out of eighteen of shadow Cabinet members, leaving the Gould camp with only the support of David Blunkett, Michael Meacher and Clive Soley, Labour's Housing and Planning spokesperson. Soley, and to a lesser extent his boss, Meacher, had had a disagreement with Smith just before the 1992 general election campaign. Soley had called for a relaxation of Treasury rules on the Public Sector Borrowing Requirement (PSBR), so that money from council house sales could be released to finance the construction of new council houses. However, he had been forced to retract the statement[59] due to Smith's intervention, and the issue still rankled with him.[60] Meanwhile, Clare Short, chair of the Tribune Group and the NEC's Women's Committee, took the view that Smith was almost certainly going to win the leadership contest, but she backed Gould for the deputy leadership on the grounds that the party needed a balanced ticket.[61] Peter Hain also openly backed Gould for the deputy leadership, largely on ideological grounds because they were both old Keynesians opposed to the ERM and the Maastricht Treaty.[62]

The first hurdle for the Smith camp – gathering nominations from at least 20 per cent of the PLP (in effect 55 MPs) – posed no problems.[63] He quickly garnered the support of more than half of the PLP, leaving very few votes to go around among the remaining candidates if they were to reach the 20 per cent threshold. Margaret Beckett and John Prescott easily cleared the hurdle for the deputy leadership, but Bryan Gould, Bernie Grant and Ann Clwyd were struggling, as were the two leadership hopefuls, Bryan Gould and Ken Livingstone.

Andy McSmith claims that Bryan Gould did not have the necessary signatures for the deputy leadership, and had to appeal to Ann Clwyd backers to reach the 20 per cent threshold.[64] On Wednesday, 22 April, Gould claimed he had garnered 35 nominations for the deputy leadership and 'slightly more' for the leadership, but said he was confident of making the 55-MP threshold for both contests.[65] However, he couldn't have been *that* confident because he consulted Joyce Gould,[66] Labour's director of organisation (no relation to Bryan), to check whether MPs could submit duplicate nomination papers, stating their second preferences.

On Friday, 24 April, Joyce Gould issued a statement to the effect that if a candidate did not receive 20 per cent of the vote, then the duplicate forms would stand. In effect, she was proposing an exhaustive ballot. The Prescott camp immediately denounced what they termed 'a last-minute rule-change' as 'highly suspicious'. Rumours circulated the following day that Robin Cook was offering the Gould camp a deal on nomination papers to ensure that a leadership contest took place. The Gould camp angrily denied the story, claiming they had reached the threshold without any 'help' from the Smith camp.[67]

The next day, David Hill, Labour's director of communications, cast doubt on the validity of Joyce Gould's earlier statement by announcing that no change of the rules could be made until the NEC met on 28 April, the deadline for nominations.[68] Larry Whitty also differed slightly with Joyce Gould over how the duplicate forms would come into play.[69] On Monday, 27 April, during the first full meeting of the new PLP, Whitty announced a sensible compromise, stating that no system of second preferences or transferable nomination for Labour leadership and deputy leadership elections was permissible under existing rules. MPs could, however, withdraw their first set of nomination papers and submit an alternative set if they expected their first choice of candidate to fall short of the 20 per cent minimum threshold.[70]

The main 'victim' of Whitty's clarification was Ann Clwyd, because everyone could see that Bryan Gould needed more votes to be certain of reaching the required threshold to stand for both contests. An unknown number of MPs seemed to have switched away from Clwyd and towards Gould, and this led to Clwyd's support haemorrhaging, so much so that she pulled out the contest altogether the following day.[71]

On 7 May, the MPs' nominations for the leadership and deputy leadership were announced: Smith gained a massive 162 nominations (60 per cent of the PLP), compared with only 63 for Bryan Gould and thirteen for Ken Livingstone. Meanwhile, Margaret Beckett headed the deputy leadership nominations with 89 votes, followed by Gould on 69 and John Prescott on 64, with Bernie Grant on only fifteen.[72] The standard bearers of the left, Ken Livingstone and his running mate, Bernie Grant, had failed to gain the necessary signatures, and were duly eliminated. Thereafter, many MPs on the left opted for Smith over Bryan Gould, preferring, as Tony Benn did 'a right-winger who had to work with the left, than a so-called left-winger who had to prove his responsibility by swinging to the right'.[73]

On Wednesday, 3 June 1992, the two surviving leadership contenders – Bryan Gould and John Smith – spoke in front of the whole PLP and, a week later, the three remaining deputy leadership candidates – Gould, Beckett and Prescott – held a hustings meeting in front of their fellow MPs.[74] No detailed record remains of these meetings: the minutes merely list some of the names of the MPs who asked questions to the candidates. It is important to remember that this was the first occasion when leadership and deputy leadership candidates had addressed the PLP (something that would be repeated in 1994). Alan Haworth, secretary of the PLP, felt that candidates should not be bound in any way in the future by what they had said in a private meeting of the PLP.[75] The only alternative record of the meeting is to be found in Tony Benn's diary. Apparently, Smith emphasised the importance of reforming the policy and organisation of the party, stressed his long-held view of a strong economy going together with a fair society, and defended his shadow Budget, claiming that Labour had to be a party of redistribution.[76]

As the clear front-runner, Smith's campaign strategy was to avoid banana skins. His glossy A5-size election pamphlet, though only stretching to four pages, reveals much of the policy themes and the overall tone that Smith wanted to convey. The front cover depicted Smith as a reassuring bank manager figure, holding a Parker pen. The back cover pictured Smith with Mo Mowlam, Janet Anderson, Kate Hoey and Harriet Harman, stressing his commitment to addressing the gender gap,[77] and the picture inside showed Smith dealing with a Tory intervention, emphasising the shadow Chancellor's debating strengths in the House of Commons. More significantly, a copy of Smith's own Edinburgh South CLP membership card was reproduced, accompanied with the message (in large lettering): 'I believe most members of the Labour Party joined for reasons similar to my own. I saw the Labour Party then, and see it now, as a movement to deliver social justice and to create an open society.'[78] Smith's main themes were fleshed out in greater detail in his election address, *New Paths to Victory*.

> There is no point in our debating whether our policies were right for 1992, because we will not be asked to fight the 1992 General Election for a second time . . . It is also vital that the work begun by Neil Kinnock, of modernising the structures and procedures of the Party, be carried forward. In a democratic party like ours participation by individual members is its lifeblood . . . In all our activities – policy making, campaigning, election to

office – we should encourage the widest possible involvement in our membership. [Suffering four election defeats] is an experience which demands a radical response. We cannot address the next five years on the basis of business as before. We must find fresh directions for Labour and offer a new vision to Britain.[79]

Various accounts have suggested that Tony Blair and Gordon Brown assisted Robin Cook in drafting *New Paths*.[80] In fact, the document was almost solely the work of Cook.[81] As an interesting footnote in Labour history, Patricia Hewitt contributed a thirteen-page, 2,880 word draft statement, but, according to David Ward, Smith stopped reading it after the first paragraph,[82] which read '... the results on April 9th made it quite clear that we have not yet completed the task of becoming a modern, radical, European social democratic party'.[83] The phrase reminded Smith of the SDP he hadn't joined in 1981, and summed up the fear on both the traditional right and the left of the party that the modernisers intended to turn the party into 'SDP Mark II'.

Philip Gould, one of the architects of the Blair revolution, later claimed: 'John Smith wanted to heal the Party, not reform it. His instinct was for consolidation, not modernisation.'[84] However, the centrepiece of *New Paths to Victory*, and the major exception to its theme of consolidation based on past policies, was the promise to establish a Special Commission on Social Justice to examine Labour's policies on welfare, taxation and the redistribution of wealth. While Labour would take the lead in the work of the commission, it would be willing to accept ideas from outside organisations, the overall aim being to empower people to make their own way out of poverty.[85]

New Paths to Victory was mildly radical. While some of the green policies had been aired before,[86] they were now considered as part of a coherent fiscal green package. In a section entitled 'A New Constitution for a New Century', Smith wholeheartedly endorsed much of the Charter 88 agenda:[87] a Bill of Rights, a Freedom of Information Act, an elected Second Chamber, the decentralisation of power to Scotland and Wales and the English regions, and fixed term Parliaments. However, while Smith promised that Labour should be free to reach its own conclusions on proportional representation, he expressed his personal wish to 'preserve the link between elector and constituency Member of Parliament which is a strength of the British tradition', and ruled out electoral pacts.[88]

In a section entitled 'A New Structure for a Modern Party', Smith, while acknowledging the 'immense historic debt' that the Labour Party owed to the trade union movement, nevertheless expressed a belief that 'the future of the Labour Party must be founded on the clear principle that its major decisions must be taken by its membership on the basis of one member, one vote [OMOV] ballots'. Specifically, Smith floated the idea of changing the rules for the election of the leader so that the CLPs and the PLP each be given a 50 per cent share in future leadership contests, with no formal role for the trade unions. He also claimed that he wished to 'look again' and apply the principle of OMOV to the selection and reselection of Labour parliamentary candidates, and to seek a reduction in the union block vote at Labour Party conferences.[89] Such moves led John Rentoul to claim that Smith became 'a sort of honorary moderniser for the purposes of the leadership campaign'.[90]

Bryan Gould's campaign was frantic and media-oriented: *The Times* calculated after the contest was over that he had travelled more than 7,000 miles, published 50,000 words worth of speeches and articles, speaking on podiums for 35 hours.[91] Nor did Gould's campaign hold back from attacking large parts of Labour Party policy. As he told an interviewer, he had 'loyally not opened up on any of these issues over the past three years' because the party had placed a premium on unity to try to win the 1992 election. But now that election had been lost, the party 'ought not to go back into purdah'.[92] Gould declared from the outset: 'We challenge the "one more heave" brigade. We will not win on the policies that lost in 1992 in four years' time.'[93] He also claimed that Smith's shadow Budget had sealed Labour's fate in April 1992 by putting 'a cap on the aspirations' of the middle classes.[94] This group of voters had changed, and Labour, he argued, should continue the process of modernisation in order to gain their trust and to appeal to their aspirations. Bryan Gould was not opposed to tax redistribution, but in a cutting phrase directed at Smith, he claimed that 'a cleverer package' could have been put together.[95] Gould also profoundly disagreed with Smith over Britain's continued membership of the ERM. Such a policy meant handing over control of macro-economic policy to an outside body – the European Central Bank.[96]

From an early stage in the campaign, Gould also called for 'a move to one member, one vote whenever possible, but at the same time giving levy-paying trade unionists the opportunity to opt in to full party membership'.[97] Gould had got his mention of OMOV in first, making Smith's ideas (see above) look like a belated response. On 5 July 1992, Smith appeared to backtrack on the BBC's *On the Record* programme by calling for changes to OMOV, which were 'consistent with organisations being in the Labour Party'.[98] The GMB would eventually oppose the idea of no formal role for the unions in leadership contests (see chapter 22), and it never saw the light of day.[99]

The Fabian Society organised a debate on 20 May at which Gould again went on the attack, claiming that Labour needed a leader who knew what it meant 'to fight and win in those areas outside our heartlands'. Since Smith had represented two safe Scottish constituencies (Monklands East and Lanarkshire North) and Gould had gained and then lost the marginal seat of Southampton Test[100] and won in marginal Dagenham in 1983, Gould's remarks carried a certain edge.

Meanwhile, Smith focused both on his support for devolution and for OMOV, arguing that 'strengthening the Labour Party's democracy does not mean weakening our relationship with the trade union movement'.[101] Smith, however, delivered a far more interesting statement of his basic morality in reply to a question from the audience, when someone postulated that Labour might be unelectable in an individualistic society:

> Labour is about altruism. The philosophy of democratic socialism is based on a moral view of life, and that must shine through everything we do. We start from moral principles and go out to devise practical policies to implement them. If there is no morality it is not worth having . . . on this I would not shift an inch.[102]

Tribune, which had earlier come out in support of Bryan Gould, while acknowledging that a Smith-Gould ticket was more realistic,[103] organised a debate jointly with the Labour co-ordinating committee on 26 June, at which Smith promised that no changes would be made relating to OMOV until the 1993 party conference (see chapter 22). Reports from that debate typified the pattern of the contest: while Smith 'gave a bank managerish speech lacking in passion and ideas', the only interesting contribution came from the man who stood no chance of winning – Bryan Gould.[104]

John Smith and Margaret Beckett explicitly did not run as a 'dream ticket' in the same way as Roy Hattersley and Neil Kinnock had supposedly done in 1988.[105] Beckett ran her campaign independently from Smith partly because 'John had to work with whoever won', but also because Beckett had a quite different history with the party than Smith.[106] During her campaign, Beckett stressed her CND and trade union roots, the contribution she could make as a woman towards addressing the gender gap, and her opposition to immediate reform of one member, one vote.[107]

Smith and Beckett expressed nuances of difference on policy grounds, but both made supportive statements about each other. Smith gave a few interviews making positive comments about Beckett, although he maintained, rather unconvincingly, that he did not have an official running mate. Meanwhile, Beckett's *Modernisation Manifesto* pictured her sitting by John Smith, and welcomed his proposal for a Social Justice Commission.[108] During the campaign, Beckett's support for Smith was almost sugary: 'From my own point of view, when I sat down and thought about the next general election, it was my very clear view that I could not think of anyone in the Parliamentary Labour Party better than John Smith to rekindle hope, confidence and trust.'[109]

Despite all the sincere attempts by Labour's affiliated organisations to support debates, and Gould's admirable huff-and-puff, the media soon lost interest in the 1992 Labour leadership contest because everyone knew the outcome. The problem for Gould was that nobody was listening in what Alan Watkins later described as 'this sleepy contest'.[110] The bookies offered odds of 1/6 for Smith, with Gould on 6/1 against. Such odds now seem generous. In Gould's words, the Smith campaign 'gained the impression of an unstoppable momentum' because successive trade unions released the results of their consultations in the run-up to the final vote.[111] Gould's decision to stand for both the leadership and the deputy leadership had also proved to be a serious mistake. Margaret Beckett made all the running, securing the backing of the TGWU, who controlled some 8 per cent of the total electoral college votes. Even by mid-June, the outcome of the deputy leadership contest was not in doubt, though Prescott still hoped (with the welcome support of NUPE), to deny Beckett an outright majority, thus forcing the contest to a second ballot.[112]

On Saturday, 18 July, the delegates gathered at the Royal Horticultural Hall in London to elect their new leader. Smith won a crushing victory over Gould, polling 90.9 per cent of the electoral college votes.[113] Meanwhile, Margaret Beckett won the deputy leadership polling 56.8 per cent, comfortably beating off the challenge of John Prescott (28.4 per cent), with Gould finishing in a poor third on 14.7 per cent.[114] The only following Gould seems to have had is with women Labour MPs; of the 34 Labour women in 1992, eighteen backed Smith only narrowly beating Gould's total of sixteen votes, including Clare Short and Jo Richardson.[115]

In his acceptance speech, Smith told delegates that Labour was 'embarking on a great journey: a journey to eliminate poverty, injustice and homelessness, and a journey to build a lasting and sustainable prosperity'. Interviewed afterwards, the delighted new Labour leader told reporters: 'I've been a member of the Labour Party all my life and this is the greatest moment, the greatest honour they could have done me.'[116] He meant it. Ruth Wishart recalls that 'you could have touched the pride factor in John that day'.[117]

To mark his election as Labour leader, John Smith agreed to a photo opportunity in St James's Park with Elizabeth, and their three daughters – Sarah (23), Jane (20) and Catherine (19). The police blocked off the bridge over the lake so that the Smiths could have their picture taken. The story goes that bemused foreign tourists waiting either side of the bridge had remarked: 'What's the bald guy doing with three models?' (Elizabeth Smith looked stunning too.) According to the gossip columns, at any rate, it was 'Smith's proudest moment'.[118]

In the immediate aftermath of his leadership victory, most of the Tory press portrayed Smith as a man dependent on his union paymasters for his political and financial support.[119] Smith's previous heart attack was considered to be a fair subject for discussion, albeit at the tabloid end of the newspaper market. Exercising its usual capacity for tastelessness, The Sun ran with the headline: 'He's fat, he's 53, he's had a heart attack and he's taken on a stress-loaded job. He may be leader, but Smith can't get life insurance.' The Sun had asked six top life insurers to cost a life insurance policy for the new Labour leader, based on a man of his age, health record and workload. 'One refused to have him on their books, another said yes but trebled his premium, and the rest wanted to make him pay far more than a fit man of his age.'[120]

That summer, John and Elizabeth celebrated their silver wedding anniversary, which they combined with Jane's 21st birthday party. It would be a happy occasion, but there was a huge discussion beforehand over whether to invite both Derry Irvine and Donald Dewar. In the end, John and Elizabeth invited both of them, despite the fact that Derry had married Alison, Donald's ex-wife. The day's celebration began in the garden with champagne and speeches: John paid a touching personal tribute to his family, and Jimmy Gordon toasted the happy couple, but meanwhile, family friends watched as Donald and Derry performed 'an amusing cabaret act', avoiding each other at opposite ends of the garden.[121]

Eighteen
HEALING THE WOUNDS

ESPITE NEIL KINNOCK's impressive legacy of turning the Labour Party into a more electable force than it had been since the early days of Harold Wilson, his immediate legacy was one of electoral defeat. When Smith's team took over, morale was low both in Walworth Road and in the country. The transition from the Kinnock regime to the Smith regime was not an easy one. Ann Barrett was given no assistance from the Kinnock people. 'It was a complete blank. I had to start everything from scratch.'[1]

In terms of the physical layout, secretaries dominated the ground floor of the new leader's office, including Elizabeth Barlow and Jenny Stringer (the latter having previously worked for Michael Foot), who both proved a great help relieving the burden on Ann Barrett. Above them, the press team (David Hill, Hilary Coffman and Mike Elrick) and policy team (Pat McFadden, Delyth Evans[2] and David Ward) worked in a mezzanine area. John Smith had his office on the floor above, together with his secretary, Ann Barrett. Remarkably, regular members of Smith's team numbered only about a dozen, with certain people like Meta Ramsay being brought in from time to time to assist the policy unit on foreign affairs issues. The clear benefit of having a small office was that one-to-one contact was manageable: colleagues could 'go up stairs' if they needed to see John.

The leader of the opposition's private office would be vastly expanded under Tony Blair in terms of expense and scale. Smith's period as Labour leader coincided with the first two years of a new Parliament immediately after an election when resources are limited. Murray Elder points out: 'They always compare Neil's high profile in the run up to the 1992 General Election with John's two years after that election. They are two completely different parts of the electoral cycle.'[3] Smith's office was therefore necessarily small, and many of its members had to double-up. Most people were expected to be there from eight in the morning until at least nine o'clock at night and as Meta Ramsay recalls: 'It was a case of all hands to the pump. Anyone that was available would accompany John on trips, or form part of his entourage at Party Conferences.'[4] However, in retrospect, Ann Barrett feels that 'small was definitely better'.[5] Considering the size of the team that was up against the might of the government machine, John's office performed very well. Had Smith lived, Murray Elder planned to expand the leader's office in the two years running up to the general election, although it is safe to assume that Smith would have resisted it mushrooming as it did under Blair.[6]

John Smith's leadership victory led to a considerable reorganisation of staff in the leader's office. The biggest single casualty of Smith's clear-out of Kinnock people was Charles Clarke. With Kinnock gone, Clarke's power disappeared overnight.[7] Nearly a decade later, in 2001, Clarke entered the Cabinet as Minister Without Portfolio and party chairman. Smith made Murray Elder his new chief of staff. Elder left the Bank of England in the 1970s to assist members of the shadow Cabinet in 1980: first Denis Healey, and then John Smith. Elder had a heart transplant before Smith had his heart attack,[8] and Elder, the more experienced mountaineer, had persuaded Smith to go Munro-bagging as part of his recovery (see chapter 11). Since 1984, Elder had worked for the Labour Party in Scotland (having lost out at the 1983 general election to a very youthful Charles Kennedy in Ross, Cromarty and Skye),[9] and was general secretary of the Labour Party in Scotland from 1988–92, by which time he had become a major player in the Scottish Constitutional Convention. Elder's two main jobs were liaising with other members of the shadow Cabinet on policy matters and managing the delicate negotiations in the run-up to the crucial OMOV in the autumn of 1993 (see chapter 22).[10]

The policy unit comprised David Ward, Pat McFadden (from the spring of 1993 onwards, having worked with Donald Dewar) and Delyth Evans.[11] Ward dealt mainly with policy development, and with crafting speeches for John, alongside Delyth. McFadden would be at Murray Elder's side in the battle for OMOV. David Hill was an obvious choice to become the leader's chief spokesperson. He had headed Hattersley's deputy leader's office from 1983–91, before being made director of campaigns and communications. Under Smith, Hill undertook the role of both Labour's chief spokesperson and the leader's chief spokesperson (the first time that had ever happened), splitting his time between Labour's press office and Smith's press office. The thinking was that it would save conflict between the leader's press office and Walworth Road. Hilary Coffman, coincidentally David Hill's partner, accompanied Smith on many of his trips. Coffman, who had once worked for Michael Foot, was the only other survivor from Kinnock's period as leader. In May 1993, Hill's roles in charge of press and presentation were clearly delineated from the party's campaigning and elections functions, which were headed by Sally Morgan.

Mike Elrick completed the press office team, working as an assistant both to

Coffman and Smith. He had chaired the Kincardine and Deeside Labour Party, and came to the attention of Murray Elder during the by-election there in November 1991. After Labour's defeat in 1992, Elrick became the youngest member of the leader's office, aged only 25. Partly because Elrick was Scottish, partly because he shared Smith's love of hillwalking, and partly because they got on well together on regional tours, Elrick saw a different side to John, and found he could say things to his boss that some of the others wouldn't dream of saying. Smith appreciated that he had someone who did not always tell him he was doing the right thing. Elrick compared his role to that of the man who whispered in the Roman general's ear at the victory parade in front of the Forum: 'Remember you are mortal.'[12]

Similarly, if Smith's secretary disagreed with him, she said so: 'If you answered him [John] back, he was fine.'[13] Ann Barrett had no personal political ambitions and felt that John welcomed her views at staff meetings, knowing them to be disinterested. She now regrets that she did not make more use of the opportunity to represent the view of 'ordinary voters'.[14] Her main task was to manage the leader's diary. John tended not to interfere, but he had an endless fascination for railway timetables: 'John was completely obsessed about how to get from a to b at the cheapest rate. Eventually, I didn't tell him about his travel plans, and presented him with the ticket before departure.'[15] On paper, Ann also dealt with invitations and handled the book-keeping relating to the leader's office, but in practice she had to deal with a lot more than that. Often, John would ring her at 6 am: 'Ann, can you sort this out?' It never occurred to John to apologise to one of his staff for ringing them up so early (or so late, sometimes midnight); his attitude was always 'I'm up, so you should be up as well.' Ann sorted everything out for John. And because Ann's office led into John's office, she also became the leader's gatekeeper, and tightly controlled the amount of time that each person spent with John.[16]

John did not get on well with his first driver, Ted, an ex-policeman. Everything was too much trouble for Ted. His failings were cruelly exposed one day when Ann Barrett was off work due to illness. Ted was sent over in the leader of the opposition's car to collect the keys from Ann's first-floor flat. However, while in the flat, he left the car keys in the ignition, and when he returned the leader of the opposition's car was gone. That night, the BBC's *Six o'Clock News* reported the theft. As a result of the episode, Ted was sacked. By contrast, his replacement Terry Rayner, was 'a jewel'.[17] At six foot four, he towered above everyone else. Sadly, Terry would later find John lying dead at the Barbican. He later served as Tony Blair's driver.

One other point of continuity with the Kinnock era was Larry Whitty, who

remained as general secretary of the Labour Party, a post he had held since
1985. Whitty presided over a party that was in drastic need of an economy
drive after the huge expenditure of a general election. This reality formed part
of his reasoning when he put some of Walworth Road's paid positions out for
competitive interview during the course of 1993. However, as Whitty recalls,
the restructuring of Walworth Road post-1992 was not just about the bottom
line – 'the Party was more broke after 1987 and after 1997 than 1992' – but also
about increasing its efficiency.[18] Murray Elder sees the opening up of
directorate posts to fully competitive tender as 'a New Labour exercise before
New Labour', showing that Labour had become more professionally minded.
However, both Walworth Road and the leader's office were disappointed by
the paucity of high quality applications they received from people outside the
existing party machine.[19] Perhaps such an outcome was not surprising:
Labour had been in opposition for a very long period and the pay, though not
derisory, compared poorly with the private sector.

Sally Morgan's aforementioned appointment as campaigns director was
very much Larry Whitty's preferred choice. John Smith and Murray Elder had
hoped to attract high flyers with proven business backgrounds but, for the
reasons outlined above, there was less competition for the posts than the Party
had expected. Also as part of the reorganisation, Peter Coleman took over as
director of organisation from Joyce Gould.[20] Around the same time, Geoff
Bish also retired (or more accurately, 'walked') as head of the research
department, and was replaced by Roland Wales. An economics graduate from
Glasgow University, he had also had a spell as a personal assistant to the chief
economist at the Bank of England. He impressed not only John Smith, but also
Murray Elder who had worked with Wales at the Bank of England. Roland was
'the candidate that John felt comfortable with', and the leader's view prevailed,
meaning that Tony Benn's son Hilary lost out for the post.[21]

Hilary Armstrong recalls being 'quite surprised' to be chosen as Smith's
parliamentary private secretary (PPS), or 'bag-carrier'. Although politically
close to John's position on the right of the Party, she didn't know him that
well. Hilary had entered Parliament in 1987 as the Labour MP for North West
Durham, and a year later had been appointed as a junior opposition
spokesperson on Education. Armstrong is not clear why she was chosen by
Smith, but her immediate boss, Jack Straw at Education, had apparently
informed Smith that Hilary was 'good at getting gossip in, but not gossiping',
ideal requirements for a PPS, and also for a Chief Whip, which Armstrong
eventually became in 2001. She recalls that 'John loved the gossip at all levels'.
In those days, on the opposition side, only the leader had a PPS, so Armstrong

had very little rubric to go on as to her exact role, but her main job was to keep John closely in touch with the PLP.[22]

Armstrong recalls that if John wanted advice on the way through a political problem, he often went to Donald Dewar, seeing him as '*the* one who understood how to get there'. While he enjoyed Derry Irvine's company, 'At that time Derry did not have quite the same political nous as Donald.' Still, John met regularly with Derry to discuss matters both personal and political. On Scottish issues, Murray Elder feels that Donald Dewar's influence on John was 'huge', even after Donald stopped being shadow secretary of State for Scotland. Quite simply, 'John trusted Donald not to do anything daft on Scotland.'[23] Or, as Ruth Wishart points out, 'John always knew that Donald would stay on message.'[24] Later, Dewar became vitally important to John in monitoring the work of the Social Justice Commission (see chapter 21). Elder recalls that in terms of someone with whom John would have a chat, Dewar's influence was also considerable, but in terms of day-to-day decisions, John was 'more of a loner', and someone who kept his counsel within the leader's office.[25] As Hilary Armstrong puts it, 'Nobody ran John.'[26] But Murray Elder is being too modest; his counsel was also very important.[27]

The other person whom John regularly sought out for advice was his deputy, Margaret Beckett. Early on, John had said to Margaret: 'I want you to be a real deputy. Take that over, deal with it . . . I'll leave it to you . . . John had a clear view that there were certain things that only the leader could do, including taking the major strategic decisions, and that he should free himself from the other things he didn't have to do.'[28] Margaret and John held weekly one-to-one discussions. Both were long-gamers, mapping out the political territory. Margaret recalls: 'John felt there was no need to commit himself to policies too early, ahead of when he was ready to do it.' Beckett feels she acquired her fair share of enemies outside Smith's office, people who disliked the role she played, and the amount of responsibility that Smith gave her.[29]

One or two people, while not always physically in John's office, briefed him regularly. Meta Ramsay (having been a senior diplomat) briefed John and accompanied him to meetings with foreign leaders: 'He liked receiving briefings. I think it was the advocate in him.'[30] Andrew Graham, working mainly at Balliol College, Oxford, sent Smith regular briefings either by fax or by post, and he and Smith had regular chats over the telephone.[31] Meanwhile, Simon Haskel, among others, continued to keep the leadership informed about the ongoing relationship between business and industry and the Labour Party. The work that had been done before 1992 (see chapters 9 and 14) was to some extent carried on after it. On the third Tuesday of every month, Haskel had a regular slot an hour before Prime Minister's Questions, during which he chatted to Smith about matters relating to business and industry.[32] Smith also kept in close touch with Michael Montague and his old friend Gavin Laird, who by this stage sat on the board of several private companies as well as being general secretary of the AEU. Laird actively assisted the Labour leadership, particularly Gordon Brown, in tapping into the business community in Scotland.[33]

John Smith's leadership style differed markedly from that of Neil Kinnock. Partly, the difference came down to their contrasting characters. Michael Foot recalls that criticisms of Smith never really got through to their target because John's character was 'so strong, he was so skilful . . . he was not hurt by such things'. He adds: 'John was stronger than Neil. Neil would have made a fine Prime Minister. He had the passion, but John had the lot.'[34] Derek Foster feels Smith had 'an attractive self-assurance'.[35] Hilary Armstrong thought John 'one of the most self-confident people I've ever known' whereas 'Neil needed more reassurance'. John, she remembers, was also someone who could 'deal with the truth'. He knew when he had done too much the night before, or when (rarely) his performances in the House of Commons had not been up to scratch.[36]

Frank Dobson, on the other hand, feels that although Kinnock had a more sensitive personality than Smith to start with, 'John had never been done over', whereas Neil had had 'more kickings from the press'.[37] Neil Kinnock's previously flamboyant style also influenced Smith's own style as leader: the priority became to appear as 'un-Kinnock' as possible, as Simon Hoggart once put it.[38] Frank Dobson also feels that Smith benefited from the contrast drawn between himself and Neil – the frugal bank manager following on from the lightweight, though neither caricature was true.[39] Smith was very comfortable with his chosen political style, modelling himself on unshowy political heroes such as Clement Attlee and Harry Truman,[40] who might be characterised as low-profile, but nevertheless effective team leaders.[41] 'I think in terms of achievement. Attlee was a formidable figure, although he would not be regarded as a class act by modern standards. Now he would be considered as rather reserved and perhaps a little grumpy, but he led a good team.'[42]

James Callaghan was also someone whose political style John had watched and learned a great deal from. Leo Beckett feels that John copied much of his leadership style from Jim Callaghan,[43] but Margaret Beckett sees John as 'much more of an ideas man than Jim'.[44]

The paradox was that the reassuring image that Smith deliberately cultivated, both as shadow Chancellor and as Labour leader, concealed the real man underneath. Derek Foster states: 'Whereas you'd expect Neil to be passionate, John was economical with his passion.'[45] It was sometimes very different in private. When a Labour back bencher tried to put a motion on a controversial matter to the PLP, Doug Hoyle, the PLP chairman, failed to dissuade him. Smith said to Hoyle he'd handle it. To Hoyle's surprise, the back bencher backed down, and Hoyle asked Smith, 'How on earth did you do that?' Smith apparently replied: 'I threatened to throw the wardrobe at him.'[46]

Neil had relied on a very small group of loyal advisers; Smith tried to involve people, rather than treating them as enemies. Overall, there was a greater toleration of alternative points of view. Members of Smith's team deliberately attempted to avoid the heavy-handed approach associated with Kinnock's private office when it came to dealings with outsiders, be they researchers or journalists.[47] Very quickly, visitors to Smith's office appreciated the change of atmosphere.[48]

But there was a rationale behind Neil Kinnock's abrasive leader's office. Neil Stewart, a member of Kinnock's office, whose difficult task it was to represent the leader's views to the PLP and to Walworth Road, sums up the need for a thrusting, cajoling leader's office in conversation with David Hare both during and after the 1992 general election campaign: 'Have you asked yourself why the leader's office needs to exist? Why does Kinnock have to have his own staff group? Why doesn't the Labour Party run the campaign itself? Why is there this strategy group? Because things wouldn't get done. Because Neil's determination would get diluted.'[49] Stewart's other great insight (after the 1992 election) concerned the traditionally fractious nature of the party that Kinnock had attempted to lead for nearly a decade: 'We [Labour] are instinctively anti-leadership. Labour is the dissident party and the activists are the deviants within that. The Party has often had splits. Deference plays little part.'[50] Or as Neil Kinnock has put it more recently: 'It is important that the Leader likes (or loves) the Party enough to maximise its chance of winning. Sometimes the affection can only properly be transmitted through a firm grip on the back of the Party's neck.'[51]

The problem with this kind of juggernaut, or cudgel, style of leadership is that it has a limited lifespan. Too many people get upset. And yet, after what might be termed the Smith pause for breath, Tony Blair essentially resumed Kinnock's 'reform or die' leadership style.

Smith saw the necessity of continuing the party's process of modernisation, but a combination of Neil Kinnock's style and the painful but necessary process of modernising the party had upset many people, leaving sections of the party feeling insecure about what the party stood for. As Frank Dobson recalls: 'John's great strength lay in repairing the relationship between the leader and the PLP which had become strained by Neil Kinnock's wholly necessary reforms of the Party.'[52] Larry Whitty agrees: 'Neil had broken very bitterly with the left. I remember John saying, "I've got to get away from this business of treating people as outcasts." John even had a good word to say about Ken Livingstone.'[53]

After the upheavals of the Kinnock reforms, the Party needed a healer. In practical terms, this meant rebuilding links between the leader's office and large parts of the Labour movement. In September 1992, Larry Whitty wrote to Murray Elder with suggestions about how best Smith might re-establish those links:

> It was clear from my vantage point that over the latter years of Neil Kinnock's leadership there were serious breakdowns in communication and empathy between the Leader and various key elements of the Party. This was, for the most part, not due to any deliberate decision to reduce contacts but just that they got squeezed out.
>
> It seems to me it is very important in the new era for the Leader's diary to give some priority to contacts with these key elements. In most cases they would not require more than a quarterly or half yearly meeting, but those meetings should be given virtual absolute priority once they are in the diary.
>
> In many of the following cases the officers or leading members of the groups concerned have complained to me over the years, and may well be complaining to you now. In which case I am reinforcing their pleas. The loyalty of these groups to the Leadership is, for the most part, unquestioned, but the enthusiasm with which they pursue that loyalty can be greatly enhanced by short, regular meetings.[54]

What emerges from the rest of Whitty's document is the sheer extent to which various Party groups felt left out during Kinnock's leadership. For example, Whitty described the junior members of the Labour front bench as 'a severely neglected group', adding, 'I think Neil only met them perhaps twice in six years as a collective'; while Whitty did not recall Kinnock having met the Labour Group in the House of Lords at all.[55] Many other groups felt the same. Whitty predicted that the resumption of such contacts would 'pay enormous dividends in terms of goodwill, hard work, loyalty and in some cases money from all the groups concerned'.[56]

Unlike Kinnock and Blair (and indeed, Gaitskell), Smith was especially tolerant when dealing with those on the left of the Party. In a way, it was harder to forgive Neil Kinnock, a figure originally from the left for getting rid of cherished left-wing policies. John's relationship with the left was helped enormously by the fact that, although he hailed from the right, because of his consistency on most issues, the left knew where they stood with him.[57] As an anonymous observer remarked adroitly at the time: 'The people who like Smith most are those he disagrees with.'[58]

John Smith indulged Tony Benn, at least while Benn remained on the NEC, probably more than he should have done. By the middle of 1993, Benn concluded: 'I get on well with John Smith, but he is a very right-wing figure.'[59] Despite disagreements over policy, the two men still retained a mutual affection for one another, based on their days together at the Department of Energy (see chapter 5). On the publication of Andy McSmith's biography of John Smith, *Playing the Long Game* in 1993, Smith signed Benn's copy with the words 'To My Old Friend and Mentor'.[60]

Smith also retained a high regard for his other former boss, Michael Foot. The feeling was mutual. In July 1993, Smith visited Foot's Hampstead home for his 80th birthday party. The late Paul Foot, Michael's nephew and John's old adversary from the Woodside selection battle (see chapter 3), recalled it as 'a very jolly occasion':

> I remember John saying to me, 'Well, Paul, I suppose that neither of us have changed an inch since we first met thirty years ago' – and that was quite true. I also remember Michael waving a knife around before cutting the birthday cake and making a little speech in which he urged John Smith on to election victory 'so we can organise a Left-wing opposition to him!'[61]

Michael Foot also remembers that 80th birthday party fondly, but more significantly, adds that Smith had 'a great understanding of all the other strands of the Party' and saw his role as re-uniting the party. 'He was never pretentious with the Party or the unions.'[62]

Shortly after Smith became leader, Murray Elder talked to Dennis Skinner, and he replied that no one from the leader's office had done that in years.[63] On another occasion, Skinner telephoned the leader's office demanding to know what Smith was doing to stop Michael Heseltine's pit closure programme (see chapter 20), and was surprised to gain a meeting with Smith the very same day.[64] However, Skinner shared Tony Benn's loathing for Neil Kinnock, and one of the reasons he liked Smith, and indeed Tony Blair[65] was simply the fact that they were persons other than Neil Kinnock. When Murray Elder went with the Labour Party delegation to a Socialist International gathering in Athens, he told Clare Short that John Smith wanted to see her in his room so that Labour's full delegation could have a meeting before the conference started. Short expressed her pleasure and astonishment.[66]

Hilary Armstrong recalls that 'all the awkward squad used to talk to him', citing Lynne Jones, Alice Mahon and Jeremy Corbyn, the so-called 'usual suspects' in the present Blair era.[67] Derek Foster argues that whereas Neil . Kinnock had seen at first hand how dangerous the left could be, John Smith was 'innocent of the left – He was never seized of how powerful they could be.'[68] Leading members of Smith's office disagree that Smith was ever innocent of the left. Smith certainly took time to listen to the views of the left, but that doesn't mean he was innocent about them.[69] Larry Whitty also remembers that some of the figures on the old right of the PLP were 'a bit iffy' about the extent to which John was prepared to talk with people on the left of the party.[70]

Margaret Beckett argues that John always made a sharp differential between those people who were elected and those who were not. The elective principle was important to him. Every elected Labour member had a contribution to make. He used to say to Alice Mahon, 'Here's my little elected representative to the NATO Assembly.'[71]

There were limits, however, even to Smith's tolerance of mavericks, such as the time when George Galloway was absent without permission for a Second Reading vote on the Local Government (etc) (Scotland) Bill in January 1994,[72] forcing the Chief Whip to respond in front of a full meeting of the PLP that Galloway had been 'severely reprimanded and issued with a final warning with regard to discipline'.[73] *Plus ça change.*

As has been documented many times before, much of Smith's politics was conducted in the tearoom or the smoking room of the House of Commons, sitting down with a few back benchers. Derek Foster recalls that, although Neil Kinnock was a naturally gregarious person, with a good sense of humour, his office was reluctant for their boss to go into the tearooms (presumably thinking the leader had better things to do with his time). The Chief Whip therefore became frustrated when Kinnock did not make appearances as often as Foster would have liked. Whereas:

> John did it without having to be told or prompted. Indeed, he would often wander down on his own without an entourage for a dram and a tale with almost every colleague in the Smoking Room. On these occasions, John was in his element – he liked his colleagues. He was the ultimate House of Commons man. He loved the place.[74]

By contrast, Derek Foster found in his one year as Chief Whip under Blair (and subsequently as a back bencher) that it was 'almost impossible to get Tony to come into the tearooms – he doesn't enjoy doing that.'[75] Frank Dobson agrees: 'John was more at home in the House of Commons, had more time for the Commons and more time for the PLP than either Kinnock or Blair.'[76]

Smith realised that an important part of party leadership in the House of

Commons is being seen as someone willing to listen to the concerns and gripes of lowly back bench MPs. Very often, ordinary Labour MPs (in common with most back benchers from all parties) just want someone to chat to, to let off steam, or to feel part of the wider team. Smith was always willing to listen and to make Labour back benchers feel wanted, regardless of which section of the party they hailed from. As Frank Dobson points out: 'John was a talkaholic; you could distract John just by having a chat with him.'[77] Beyond the House of Commons, it also greatly helped that Smith was a thoroughly social animal, whose special skill lay in networking in large rooms of people, particularly at Labour Party and trade union conferences.

Although Hilary Armstrong tried to keep a constant eye on her leader, Smith would often try to lose his PPS during the working day (and more especially, the working night) in the House of Commons. People would 'phone up asking for his whereabouts, and Armstrong would usually find him in the tearoom or the smoking room 'talking with the most unlikely person'.[78] Ann Barrett has similar recollections.[79] Leo Beckett recollects that later on at night, Smith would pretend he'd gone home in the leader's car, but 'would sneak back into the House of Commons . . . He wanted to be himself.'[80]

One major accusation levelled by the modernisers against Smith is that he neglected the organisational duties of the party leader: 'Smith thought all you had to do was balance out the traditional right with the traditional left, and there you had traditional party management.'[81] A corollary of this argument was that the left had already been marginalised, so that it was irrelevant to see party management in terms of balancing left and right, and what Smith should have been doing was balancing modernisers and traditionalists. In fact, Smith did both: he kept the left happy, while mediating between the modernisers and the traditionalists.[82]

However, it is accurate that Smith did not know a great deal about the NEC. Derek Foster recalls: 'Neil knew the geography of the Party, where power was diffused within the unions . . . John was never terribly interested in that side of the Party, didn't understand how the Party operated, and therefore he occasionally got impatient with the NEC.'[83] Foster remembers arriving late for an NEC meeting, and entering a furore. Loyalist trade union representatives were angry with the new leader. Foster sat down next to Robin Cook and asked what was going on. Cook pointed to a copy of Smith's resolution:

> John partly expected that the trade unions would weigh in behind his resolution, and he seemed surprised and hurt that they hadn't. Neil would never have been caught in that way. He knew all about the legwork that needed to be done in advance of such a meeting. Charles Clarke was a

crucial part of that operation, especially in terms of the organisation of the Party Conference.[84]

Murray Elder has no recollection of Smith causing any astonishment at any NEC meeting, but remembers union leaders being astonished when Smith moved his resolution on the Trade Union Review Links Group at the last minute on 19 May 1993 (see chapter 22). On a normal day-to-day basis, Murray Elder kept Gordon Colling, the trade union side co-ordinator, informed about what was happening.[85] But in any case, Smith's inexperience of the workings of the NEC mattered little because Kinnock had fought and won many of the hardest battles against the hard left. The NEC was now a different animal from the early 1980s. Votes were regularly won by 21 votes to 2, with only Dennis Skinner and Tony Benn voting against Smith's line. Even these two figures on the left were clinging for their survival: Skinner was voted off in 1992 (as was Bryan Gould, while Tony Blair and Gordon Brown were voted on) and Benn lost his place in 1993, after 34 years. Whitty concurs that it helped Smith enormously that he was never short of a majority on the NEC, and that the party was now in calmer times: 'Whereas John didn't want to interfere, Neil had to.'[86]

In the summer of 1992, when it became clear that he would be elected leader, Smith had a long conversation with Larry Whitty in which he indicated that he wanted party matters to be dealt with without the leader necessarily having to intervene.[87] Given his inexperience, Smith left Murray Elder in charge of co-ordinating the main trade union elements in the NEC. However, whereas Kinnock would never have dreamt of allowing Charles Clarke to attend NEC meetings, there was no objection to the idea of Murray Elder attending them. But while Smith was perfectly prepared to listen, and pursued a policy of non-interference, he was keen not to second-guess the views of individual NEC members (especially the union representatives). Used to doing Kinnock's bidding, they had now to figure it out for themselves. On Thursday, 23 July 1992, after Smith's first NEC meeting, Tony Benn commented: 'I got the feeling that John Smith was listening', but this was mostly due to the fact that 'It was just so nice not to have Kinnock there.'[88]

The NEC now met only occasionally and it had precious little say on policy, control over the latter having shifted to the policy review groups, the new joint policy committees (JPC), and the National Policy Forum (NPF).[89] At the 1992 Labour Party conference, delegates voted to endorse *Agenda for Change*. A short policy document, it appears at first sight based on Smith's *New Paths to Victory* leadership manifesto, but in reality was an idea first conceived under Neil Kinnock.[90] However, these reforms were not triggered until after the 1992 Labour Party conference. The NPF and the JPC were therefore yet more Kinnock reforms from which Smith benefited enormously.

Since the National Policy Forum had no power to initiate policy, and could only recommend changes to JPC positions, and since Smith chaired the JPC, power had shifted away from the NEC, and into the hands of the leader. Writing in 1993, Peter Shore rightly concluded: 'No previous leader has enjoyed such personal and institutionalised control over party policy.'[91] Mark Wickham-Jones agrees that the main effect of Kinnock's reforms to the party's policy making structure was that 'John Smith inherited a party structure in 1992 in which the authority of the leader was once again paramount'.[92] This factor had an important consequence. As Steven Fielding rightly argues: 'there was now little need to alter the constitution [of the Party] as the leader's effective autonomy had been restored.'[93]

Despite the National Policy Forum's lack of teeth, when it held its inaugural meeting in Hammersmith in November 1992, Smith sat through the whole of the day's proceedings. 'No leader in the next century is ever likely to show as much interest as Smith did that day,' remarks Larry Whitty.[94]

Occasionally, Smith's big tent policy was a shade too tolerant of wayward viewpoints, at the expense of cohesion. In May 1993, Meghnad Desai was sacked from his job as Labour's front bench economic spokesperson in the House of Lords, after writing an article for *Tribune* in which he argued in favour of raising the higher band of income tax (from 40 to 50 per cent) and removing the upper earnings limit on national insurance contributions that had formed a large part of Labour's shadow Budget in 1992. Desai compounded his offence by stating that, if these policies could not be kept, he personally favoured removing the zero rating for VAT on all items, including food and children's clothes, and simultaneously doubling all entitlements, including child benefit, unemployment benefit and pensions.[95]

Desai, a member of Labour's economic advisory group, had first mentioned the idea of removing zero rating for VAT on all items during a discussion hosted by Sue Cameron on *Newsnight* in July 1992. The following March, when the Tories introduced VAT on domestic fuel, they brought up the fact that Desai favoured zero rating on all items. By this time, Desai had been appointed as Labour's economics spokesperson in the Lords, but when the story broke he was abroad in India, and so he wrote a letter apologising to Smith, pointing out that when he had made the remarks back in July 1992, he had been on the back benches.[96] Desai's letter became important later on, because it imprinted in Smith's memory that Desai was not on the front bench when he had made these comments.

However, Desai made the mistake of repeating his views on zero rating in the *Tribune* article, where he wrote a regular column: 'I was doing another one of my economics lessons.'[97] And yet, Smith's office failed to spot the potential damage that Desai's article might cause. Three factors compounded Labour's eventual blunder. Firstly, Bruce Anderson later told Desai that Conservative Central Office, knowing that Desai was prone to make controversial remarks, had dedicated a person to keep a track of everything he wrote. Secondly, the editors of *Tribune*, keen to promote their special issue, trailed it to the press on the Wednesday night (5 May), two days before publication. Thirdly, and probably as a consequence of the *Tribune* press release the night before, Norman Lamont was able to taunt Gordon Brown with Desai's article at Treasury Questions on the Thursday morning.[98] Despite this, no Labour Whip reported Brown's discomfiture to the leader's office. As a result, 'all hell broke loose' that afternoon, as Desai puts it, at Prime Minister's Questions: 'John got slaughtered.'[99]

Smith began well by attacking the government for its increases in VAT on fuel and national insurance, which he claimed would cost the average family an extra £8.50 per week in tax. However, Major was primed with a quote: 'I favour the higher band income tax and the removal of the ceiling on national insurance contributions that Labour's 1992 shadow Budget proposed. Failing that, I would remove zero rating for VAT on all items.'[100] Major then revealed that the quote came from Desai. Smith replied that 'the noble Lord was on the back benches when he said what he said'. Smith thought he was in the clear, recalling from his letter two months before from Desai, in which Desai had said he was not an opposition spokesperson. Seeing his prey in trouble, John Major converted an open goal: 'Clearly the right hon. and learned Gentleman [John Smith] has lost touch with his own party. The quote that I used, far from being elderly, is in *Tribune* today.'[101] It was one of the rare occasions that John Smith was thoroughly worsted by John Major in the House of Commons.

The following day, Desai was relieved of his post. Desai recalls: 'Charles Clarke later told me that had he been in charge, I'd have been sacked on the Wednesday night.'[102] The following week, *Tribune* ran with a headline 'Desai sacked to save Smith blushes',[103] when that was not the real reason for his dismissal. Desai acknowledges: 'I entirely deserved to be sacked due to my incompetence. I had no intention of putting Smith in a position where he appeared to have no idea who his spokesman was. I made a fundamental mistake. No sensible politician should have done that.'[104]

There was no ill feeling on Desai's part, and Smith also forgave him. Indeed,

Desai subsequently became a Labour whip in the Lords, but remained accident prone, and was sacked again in late January 1994 when he suggested that Labour should balance any reflationary package with a more progressive tax system.[105]

With the retirement of both Roy Hattersley and Gerald Kaufman from the Labour front bench, Smith had some scope to make changes in the senior end of the shadow Cabinet. Having finished top of the shadow Cabinet poll (on 23 July) with 165 votes, and having served under Smith in various economic portfolios for eight years, Gordon Brown had by far the strongest claim to the shadow Chancellorship, even if Robin Cook, John's campaign manager (who finished third in the shadow Cabinet elections) had made it known that he wanted the job. Nor did Cook possess the same pro-European and fiscally orthodox views that Brown and Smith shared. Cook had to settle for Trade and Industry, while his old job at Health was handed to David Blunkett. Tony Blair, second in the poll on 150 votes, replaced Hattersley as shadow Home Secretary. In addition to her duties as deputy leader, Smith appointed Margaret Beckett shadow Leader of the House and campaign co-ordinator. John Prescott, Beckett's nearest challenger in the deputy leadership contest, stayed on at Transport, but Bryan Gould, crushed by his dire performance in the leadership contest, was given the backwater post of shadow Heritage Secretary, although he claims to have been offered a choice of Heritage, Health and Education.[106]

By appointing fellow right-winger and pro-European Jack Cunningham as his shadow Foreign Secretary, and by retaining the equally right-wing and equally pro-European George Robertson as the Party's European Affairs spokesperson, Smith signalled that there would be no change in the Party's cautiously pro-European stance.

Smith's long-time friend Donald Dewar was at last released from his long stint as shadow Secretary of State for Scotland (1983–92), and became shadow Social Security spokesperson, with responsibility for the Social Justice Commission. Smith had released Donald from his Scottish responsibilities partly as 'an act of charity'[107] – eleven years in that job deserved a George Cross, let alone a change of scene – but it was also in Dewar's own career interests to get out of Scotland. Murray Elder says that, even at the time of his switch of portfolios, Dewar was grateful for the break from his frontline Scottish job, and later always felt that without it he would never have been Secretary of State for Scotland and then First Minister, his life's ambition.[108] However, Norman Hogg suggests that Dewar, who had only ever really been interested in Scottish affairs, deeply resented being switched to Social

Security.[109] Dewar's replacement was Tom Clarke, Smith's neighbouring MP in Monklands West.

Among the junior ranks, Mo Mowlam was landed with the combined Citizen's Charter and Women's portfolios, and left Smith's office in 'floods of tears',[110] having failed to gain promotion, despite polling joint sixth place in the shadow Cabinet elections.[111] Harriet Harman had pipped her for the plum post of Gordon Brown's deputy. Chris Smith was appointed Labour's Environmental Protection spokesperson, a post that had assumed shadow Cabinet rank.[112] Chris believes that he was elected partly due to John's partronage.[113]

The overall political complexion of Smith's shadow Cabinet resembles much more that of a team put together by Harold Wilson or James Callaghan than one shaped by Neil Kinnock or Tony Blair in the sense of seeing the need to balance the left and right of the party. Hilary Armstrong sees Smith as 'an acute politician' who was part of that tradition of Labour Party figures, like Wilson and Callaghan, who regarded party unity as vital. Smith had seen the party nearly implode in the early 1980s.[114] Tony Benn also recalls:

Neil Kinnock surrounded himself with cronies. Tony Blair was worse. If Blair had been around at the time of the Wilson Government, I wouldn't have been in the Party. But John Smith realised that the strength of the Party lay in its diversity. Like Wilson and Callaghan, he carefully balanced the team, and used the breadth of the Party.[115]

Margaret Beckett sums up best why John succeeded in welding their diverse personalities into an effective team:

John was an unusual mixture of a team player and a team leader. There was no doubt that he was the one in charge. He had that rare quality of absolute self-confidence, but it was a naturally unassuming self-confidence. He was so confident in his own abilities, so secure in himself that he didn't feel challenged by anyone else in the team.[116]

Chris Smith remembers that John liked to hear alternative points of view, and would 'quiz a case strenuously' so that he could marshal the arguments for and against in a logical order.[117] Hilary Armstrong agrees, recalling that after an honest and frank exchange of views, Smith would go away, weigh up the arguments, and come back with his own mind made up.[118] By treating people as part of a team rather then as subordinates, Smith was able to inspire great loyalty, but the price he demanded in return was absolute loyalty.

The upper echelons of the shadow Cabinet now comprised people as diverse as Robin Cook, Gordon Brown and John Prescott, none of whom got on particularly well with one another, but all of whom, quite remarkably, served reasonably happily under Smith. John Prescott, who had been very much an outsider under Kinnock, felt 'immensely comfortable' in Smith's team.[119] As Prescott's biographer points out: 'He had reached an understanding with Smith, and felt Smith's respect, which he had not felt before from a leader of the Party.'[120] Prescott was also pleased that Mandelson and his ilk had been sidelined. He 'felt listened to', and it was probably the most comfortable time that he enjoyed in relation to the party leader, certainly before, and arguably ever since.[121] Prescott was allowed to develop his own distinctive policies on regional government and was at the forefront of moves to ensure that a future Labour government used private capital to finance large railway infrastructure projects, a policy that John Smith had strongly supported for several years.[122] For example, had Labour been elected in 1992, Prescott had secured an agreement with rolling stock manufacturers that would have permitted £150 million of rolling stock leasing 'virtually from day one of a Labour Government'.[123]

Robin Cook also felt more relaxed under John Smith's leadership than he had under Neil Kinnock, recalling those two years as 'blissfully happy'.[124] Both Cook, now in charge of Trade and Industry, and John Prescott dealing with Employment policy from October 1993, at least now *felt* that they had a say in economic policy. Such input was formalised by Cook and Prescott's membership of the 'Q' economic committee, alongside Margaret Beckett and Gordon Brown.[125] Murray Elder comments that both Cook and Prescott felt they'd 'got an in', and that 'it wasn't just the shadow Chancellor running economic policy'. However, he adds: 'One of Smith's great strengths was that he made people feel that they had an input even if he was backing the other side.'[126] Frank Dobson also felt that he had 'an in' under John Smith's leadership, and was yet another shadow Cabinet member who felt 'very, very comfortable' with John's leadership.[127]

In the autumn of 1992, former Labour leaders were invited to a reception in the shadow Cabinet room to mark Cledwyn Hughes's retirement as leader of the Labour Peers.[128] Smith joined Neil Kinnock, Michael Foot, James Callaghan and Harold and Mary Wilson. Wilson was by then a very sick man, with diminished powers of memory. Nevertheless, Smith made a special point of talking to Wilson. Afterwards, Mary Wilson said to Mike Elrick: 'Thanks for remembering us. We don't get invited to things anymore.'[129] And that is how Smith viewed the Labour Party. He didn't forget its roots.

Nineteen
A DEVALUED PRIME MINISTER

A FTER A LARGELY anonymous summer as leader, Smith was presented
with an open goal: on 16 September 1992 – 'Black Wednesday' – Britain
was forced to withdraw from the Exchange Rate Mechanism (ERM) of
the European Monetary System (EMS). Major's government had raised
interest rates from 10 per cent to 15 per cent in one day in a desperate attempt
to defend the pound, but had been forced into a humiliating devaluation. Both
Major's economic policy (ERM membership as a means of keeping down
inflation), and his foreign policy (securing the ratification of the European
Communities (Amendment) Bill or Maastricht Treaty) seemed ruined.

Little mention was made of the fact that John Smith, and his new shadow
Chancellor Gordon Brown had enthusiastically supported ERM entry, and
that they had both, up until this point, supported the ratification of the
Maastricht Treaty. In a way, Labour's economic and foreign policies lay in
ruins too. Bryan Gould had been right to warn during the leadership election
of the perils of remaining in the ERM. On the eve of the ERM's collapse, Tony
Benn didn't think that 'Smith the lawyer, the conservative Scottish lawyer,
utterly committed to Europe, is going to be able to achieve very much'.[1]
As Benn recalls: 'The Opposition couldn't attack the Tories because we
supported it.'[2]

Throughout the summer, Gordon Brown had taken a hard public line that
Britain should not devalue or engage in an agreed realignment within the
ERM. Brown had studied his economic and political history and could see that
one of Labour's weaknesses was a perception in the financial markets (and
among the electorate) that it had a tendency to countenance devaluation
(Stafford Cripps in 1949, and James Callaghan in 1967). Brown believed that a
future Labour Chancellor had to demonstrate willingness at least publicly to
defend the value of the pound to avoid being seen as the party of devaluation.

In contrast, when the Tories got into real difficulty defending the value of
sterling over the summer of 1992, John Smith advocated a managed realignment of sterling downwards against the deutschmark, but leaving sterling's
value against all other ERM currencies unchanged. At no point did Smith

advocate full, old-fashioned devaluation of the pound. Such a move, as Joe Rogaly of the *Financial Times* pointed out, would have been contrary to Smith's cautious nature.[3] However, a managed realignment of the pound within the ERM had become the emerging consensus among Labour's economic advisers.[4]

Smith told Labour MEPs in Strasbourg:

> Membership of what is, after all, a fixed but adjustable system does not preclude the possibility of a general realignment. I believe that such a realignment is indeed likely . . . Such a realignment could permit a reduction in German interest rates leading to similar reductions through-out the Community . . .[5]

It was no slip of the tongue: Smith issued a press release of his speech,[6] and made similar comments in an interview for *Tribune* ten days later.[7] Again, in the House of Commons on 2 July, Smith repeated his description of the ERM as 'a fixed but also an adjustable system'.[8]

At this point, other key figures in the Labour Party supported Smith's desire for a realignment. One of Neil Kinnock's final acts as Labour leader was to argue for a British realignment within the ERM in a letter to the *Financial Times*.[9] David Ward also wrote to Smith around the same time, advising exactly the same line.[10] At some point that summer, Smith also telephoned John Eatwell, Neil Kinnock's former economic adviser, to seek his views:

> SMITH: What are the best arguments for a realignment of the pound?
> EATWELL: That it is inevitable.
> SMITH: That's good enough for me.[11]

Then on 24 July, Andrew Graham recommended 'a multilateral realignment with the emphasis on a D-mark revaluation'. In short, he argued that German deflationary policies were being exported to the rest of the EC, causing unemployment. Graham not only believed that a general realignment would bring interest rates down across Europe – which made economic sense – he also argued that for Labour to advocate such a policy made political sense in two respects:

> First, if we do not argue for this position we will be identical to the Conservatives on most macro policy . . . Second, there is little danger of us being labelled at the next election as the devaluation party because within not more than a year or so from now either a realignment will have happened or it will no longer be relevant because the fundamental error in Germany will have worked through and interest rates will be lower.[12]

David Ward also became worried because John Edmonds' GMB union was due to call for an old-fashioned devaluation of the pound at the TUC. Pressure was mounting for this demand to be incorporated into an NEC statement to be considered at the Labour Party conference. On Saturday 5 September, Ward wrote a confidential note to Smith warning that Gordon Brown's stance on the ERM was being overtaken by events:

> I am not sure we are well positioned on the ERM and think it is possibly a mistake to have stopped making any reference to the possibility of DM realignment. I know Gordon and Murray disagree with this (and would have preferred that we had not raised the issue during the leadership election). They certainly have a coherent argument for their position. But the alternative is not stupid either and they just might be wrong.[13]

Ward was not for one moment supporting what he termed 'a [Bryan] Gould style devaluation', but rather an upward movement of the deutschmark against all other currencies. He outlined the advantages of pursuing such an approach:

> Restating this argument would enable us to differentiate ourselves more clearly from the Tories, point out more forcefully the weaknesses of the EC economy, and gain some favourable reporting of our new found flexibility (which happened after your speeches in the leadership election, but have been lost since).[14]

Ward then summarised Brown's concerns:

> Gordon's worries about all this are that we run the risk of being called the party of devaluation (wanting to join the so-called 'Club Med' currencies), and that our arguments for a boost to the domestic economy will be sidetracked by the dealignment debate which the public don't understand.[15]

However, Ward predicted that the Major government would not be able to stick to DM 2.95 for the duration of the Parliament, and that in such circumstances, it would be beneficial in policy and media coverage terms if Labour were seen to be leading the debate. More pressingly, Ward reminded Smith of 'the problem of the GMB's realignment motion to Conference which John Edmonds is reluctant to drop'. Ward therefore suggested amending the wording of the NEC document to highlight the benefits of an upward realignment of the deutschmark, but repeated: 'Gordon is very reluctant to consider this and certainly will not [agree] unless you insist.' Two days later, after consulting Margaret Beckett, Ward produced a suggested form of words for the NEC document.[16]

At one point, the differences between Gordon and John became quite pronounced. On Tuesday, 1 September, Brown made it plain that Labour was not calling for a realignment of the pound.[17] Seven days later, Smith, on the other hand, commented that while he was 'not in favour' of devaluation, he did not think that 'the Community can rule out a realignment of the Deutschmark against the other currencies in the system'.[18] By the following day, Brown was saying: 'It [devaluation] was not our policy at the last election, is not our policy now and will not be our policy at the next election.' But he seemed to backtrack on his earlier hard line, indicating that although he did not want Britain to take the initiative in a realignment of the pound within the ERM, if Germany took the lead, he would seriously consider the proposal.[19]

But the shadow Chancellor apparently told the PLP the following day that: 'Our policy is not one of devaluation, nor is it one of revaluation or realignment.'[20] Paul Routledge suggests there was friction between Smith and Brown over the extent to which they should press Lamont to realign/devalue,[21] while John Rentoul claims that 'a public rift opened when Brown ruled realignment out and Smith ruled it in'.[22] In the face of arguments in shadow Cabinet on 10 September from Robin Cook, Bryan Gould, Michael Meacher and David Blunkett (who made a call for a comprehensive realignment the previous day) that the pound had been overvalued and had to be realigned, Brown and Smith had apparently stood firm.[23]

On 14 September 1992, only two days before the pound fell out of the ERM, Andrew Graham wrote to Gordon Brown and John Smith bemoaning the fact that the British government had 'completely bungled' its attempt to gain the Bundesbank's agreement for a revaluation of the deutschmark against the other EC countries,[24] believing the devaluation of sterling might have been averted as 'the bankers and the finance ministers would have been seen to act together'.[25]

The day after Black Wednesday, Andrew Graham sent round a note entitled 'Thoughts on the currency crisis' to members of Smith's team:

> In the space of a week the cause of European integration has been put back ten years . . . The market has again been made the master and not the servant of economic policy. The scope for a rational, cooperative, internationally agreed set of exchange rates has been extraordinarily damaged.

Thousands of millions of pounds had been wasted in a futile attempt to defend the value of the pound. John Major and Norman Lamont had committed 'a cock-up of monumental proportions'. Graham also foresaw that Britain's fall-out from the ERM made a two-speed Europe a reality.[26]

In the immediate aftermath of Black Wednesday, the NEC met to debate the consequences of withdrawal from the ERM. Labour reiterated its long-run support for the single currency, provided 'real economic convergence' – particularly on growth and employment – could be achieved.[27] An amendment in the name of Dennis Skinner calling for Britain to withdraw permanently from the ERM and for a referendum on Maastricht, backed by Benn's idea of a Treaty of Maastricht (Referendum) Bill, was decisively rejected, but Bryan Gould also argued that the ERM was flawed and had caused the recession.[28]

On Thursday, 24 September, Parliament was recalled from the summer recess to discuss the growing economic crisis. John Smith's gave a brilliant parliamentary performance, which had the effect of putting on the backburner Labour divisions over Europe and the ERM.

When Judith Chaplin, the Conservative MP for Newbury[29] intervened and had the audacity to suggest that the leader of the opposition had undermined sterling by calling for interest rates to be cut three days prior to Britain's exit, Smith pounced:

> I was waiting for someone to blame me for the devaluation last week. The hon. Lady has not disappointed me. Of all the charges that could have been laid against me and of all the comment that there has been in recent weeks, the argument that I have been undermining sterling is the most far-fetched that I have ever heard. It shows that, whatever one says or does not say, some on the Conservative Benches will find it unacceptable. [*Interruption.*] It seems that there is a new charge: that any criticism of the Government undermines sterling, but sterling has already been undermined by those who are in charge of our affairs.[30]

With one salvo, Smith had blasted the Tory challenge out of the water. After one or two successful ripostes his adrenalin was pumping so much that he was 'virtually airborne'.[31] So effective did Smith become at this form of counter-attack that the No. 10 political office later asked the whips' office to discourage Tory back benchers from intervening during his speeches.[32]

Smith's conclusion was devastating. Major, he argued was the 'devalued Prime Minister of a devalued Government'.[33] In his autobiography, even John Major recognises Smith gave 'a brilliant debating performance' and that, 'Presented with an open goal, he joyfully smashed the ball into the net.' However, Major also admired the new leader of the opposition's 'brass neck', since as shadow Chancellor, Smith had supported ERM entry. Major listened to what he later called 'a riot of freewheeling hypocrisy', but he had been given 'ample evidence that here was a man of flexible opinions who would be a formidable opponent'.[34]

Even the *Daily Mail* praised Smith's performance: 'Smith did not muff his golden opportunity. Yesterday was the day Her Majesty's Opposition found its voice.'[35] In *The Times*, Peter Riddell wrote: 'John Smith fulfilled all his Party's hopes in a powerful Commons debut as Labour leader.'[36] Meanwhile, *The Times* editorial brutally painted the contrast between Smith and his predecessor:

> What a difference a change of leader makes! As soon as John Smith rose to his feet it was clear that the Conservative leader would never again be able to rely, as Mrs Thatcher under pressure always could, on the weak advocacy of the man across the aisle. Mr Smith deployed his forensic skills to batter Mr Major for lame excuses and absent apologies.[37]

Writing in *The Independent*, Matthew Symonds compared Smith to the great barrister, George Carman QC: 'George Carman would have been proud of Smith. Without anything very useful to say about the Government's policies on either the ERM or Europe, Mr Smith sensibly opted for lawyerly ridicule. Unless it is Mr Carman, nobody does this sort of knockabout better than Mr Smith.'[38]

It is less well known that Smith liked to have two to three pre-prepared jokes for set-piece speeches. David Ward and Delyth Evans provided Smith with factual raw material for their leader's House of Commons speeches and some ideas for jokes, and helped work out a skeleton of political arguments. Smith would then write out what he wanted to say by hand. A 40 minute speech might take him a whole day.[39]

Smith's speeches generally followed a discernible pattern: some initial hard-hitting facts were nearly always followed up with humorous swipes at the government. Smith and his team had learned from comedy writers that good jokes came in threes: the first joke to 'tickle' the audience, the second to achieve the big laugh, and, with the audience is in the palm of one's hand, a third unexpected gag, which is convulsively effective.[40] One of the best examples was deployed on 9 June 1993 during a big set-piece debate on the government's economic and social policy when Smith referred to the plummeting unpopularity of the government, and the Prime Minister's 'botched' reshuffle, following the resignation of Norman Lamont:[41]

> If we were to offer that tale of events to the BBC light entertainment department as a script for a programme, I think that the producers of *Yes, Minister* would have it turned down as hopelessly over-the-top. It might have even been too much for *Some Mothers Do 'Ave 'Em*.[42]
>
> The tragedy for us all is that it is really happening – it is fact, not fiction. The man with the non-Midas touch is in charge. It is no wonder that we live

in a country where the Grand National does not start and hotels fall into the sea.[43]

Delyth Evans came up with the BBC light entertainment part, John thought of *Some Mothers Do 'Ave 'Em*, and David Ward thought of hotels falling into the sea. John used to rehearse these ideas with Ward and Ann Barrett.[44]

Smith had started off so well, and so humorously, that there was always quite a pressure on the leader and his 'comedy' team to keep delivering, and a certain amount of worry that they might run out of ideas.[45] Smith was always on the search for fresh jokes. On the day of Smith's death, Dennis Skinner recalled: 'He used to come to me on occasions and say, "Have you got any good jokes for my speech tomorrow?"'[46]

Although having the ability to perform well in the House of Commons is not the only attribute required of a leader of the opposition – as William Hague discovered to his cost from 1997–2001 – Hilary Armstrong points out, 'performance is a lot of the job'.[47] Michael Foot agrees that, especially in a situation where there is no immediate prospect of a return to government, 'getting the Labour Party in a good mood [in the House of Commons] is an essential part of the role'.[48] And if a leader is commanding in the House, then the back benchers can have confidence in him (or her). Frank Dobson recalls that John Smith 'exuded an air of competence, always looked like he would cope, was unlikely to lose an argument in the House of Commons, and was perceived as a winner'.[49] Clare Short also remembers: 'When we sat behind John we always knew that he would be good. This immensely strengthens a party and the respect in which it is held.'[50] By contrast, Hilary Armstrong recalls that 'Neil could either be brilliant or dreadful, but the problem was that people never remembered the good performances'.[51] But Murray Elder sums it up best:

> John's whole adult life, whether as a debater at Glasgow winding up a long debate, as a criminal lawyer persuading a jury that a man was not guilty of murder, or in the Commons in the 1970s making devolution policy on the hoof from the Dispatch Box, had taught him how to be convincing in front of an audience.[52]

Whereas John excelled in the House of Commons, 'living on his sharpness', as Murray Elder claims, 'put him on a conference platform in a big hall with a prepared speech and he was much, much more dull'.[53] The political commentator Anthony Howard also recollects Smith making a warm-up speech for Neil Kinnock in Birmingham Town Hall in the spring of 1989: 'He had a model text, but his delivery was hopeless. He swung from side to side like a metronome, and the effect of his words on his audience was almost that of a lullaby . . . the platform was never his metier, any more than the House of Commons was Neil Kinnock's.'[54]

The contrast was starkly illustrated only five days after his demolition of Major when the Labour leader made his first conference speech as leader. Making a good conference speech involves getting the jokes right and getting people to laugh and applaud at the right times – it was all too pre-prepared to suit John's impromptu style of speaking and debating. For example, when Smith criticised the Prime Minister in the following terms, it sounded too contrived: 'We were promised a *New Statesman*, and what have we got instead? A *Spectator*.'[55] Other jokes fell flat, including Smith's response to Major's excuse for the ERM debacle – that the markets were irrational – 'That is a case of the pot calling the kettle grey.'[56] John might have gained a better audience reaction if he'd told them about the pair of jokey tartan boxer shorts he was wearing underneath, given to him by Elizabeth and the three Smith girls to celebrate his first conference speech as Labour leader.[57]

Meanwhile, Tony Benn noted that Smith was 'uncharismatic but so much better and more honest than Kinnock, who looked like a man in a mask with a fixed smile and no expression'.[58] Although Smith did not come across well to his audience in the conference hall, he did at least look and sound better on television, and he realised that such things mattered.

Remarkably, until he became leader, no one accompanied John Smith to Labour Party conferences. 'John didn't like an entourage. He didn't feel he needed anyone around him to bolster his ego,' remembers Ann Barrett. Instead, he loved wandering off on his own, especially on trains, and bumping into ordinary people who would recognise him.[59] Leo Beckett agrees that John 'actively didn't like an entourage'. He fondly recalls:

> When we were going anywhere from the courtyard of the House of Commons [in the Leader of the Opposition's car], John would sometimes run about trying to find the driver: 'I'll go and fetch the driver.' I'd say: '*I'll* go – that's what *I* do! You're not supposed to do that. You're the Leader of the Opposition.' He'd always say: 'Where's Leo? Is he coming with us?' John wouldn't leave me behind. He'd squeeze in the back [of the car] with Margaret and the others. John was different. We lost something [when he died].[60]

In Smith's view, party leaders should be accessible to the general public. But such an outlook was difficult to maintain at conferences, where security guards and members of his team had to accompany him from venue to venue. Even the leader of the opposition's wife had to have a minder, so at the 1992 conference, Ann Barrett was charged with accompanying Elizabeth everywhere. Reporters from the *Daily Mail* followed Ann and Elizabeth, and kept their readers informed about every item that Elizabeth had purchased.[61]

The 1992 Labour Party conference had begun on a sour note. Bryan Gould chose an eve of conference speech to the Labour Common Market Safeguards Campaign to announce his resignation from the shadow Cabinet. Gould claims that he had delivered his resignation letter to Smith before his speech, and that he intended his leader to see it before he spoke.[62] Gould neglects to mention in his memoirs that he had himself filmed by a TV crew as he handed his letter of resignation into the hotel reception. By complete accident, one of Smith's press team witnessed Gould's resignation stunt at first hand. After Gould left the hotel reception desk, Mike Elrick delivered the letter to John Smith and Murray Elder. A discussion ensued about how Smith should respond. Meanwhile, Elrick went along with other Labour colleagues to hear what Gould had to say at the fringe meeting. As it happens, Gould gave an extremely anodyne speech, but he was quite unsettled over Smith's swift response to his resignation letter.[63]

Gould's behaviour that day merely confirmed Smith's view of him, that he was both precious and pretentious. Three years earlier, at the Labour Party conference, 'a shadow [Cabinet] minister', probably John Smith, made disparaging remarks about Gould while chatting with Bruce Anderson along the seafront at Brighton: 'These days, everyone except Mr Bryan Gould has grasped the fact that it is no longer necessary to say one thing to the voters and something entirely different to a party audience.' Since the shadow minister was talking about the right to drink champagne at a Labour Party event without worrying about who was watching, it had to be Smith, although in typical Smith fashion, he made sure that such comments were not attributed directly to him.[64]

By the end of the conference week in 1992, Gould had been heavily defeated in the NEC elections. By February 1994, he had announced his resignation from Parliament to take up an academic appointment in his native New Zealand.[65] Since then, he has virtually disappeared from the British political scene, and yet his influence on Labour politics from 1987 onwards, at least until he lost the leadership to John Smith in 1992, was considerable.[66]

In his House of Commons tribute immediately after Smith's death, John Major claimed that 'we met often and amiably', that they would 'share a drink – sometimes tea, sometimes not tea' and that their meetings would 'extend far beyond the time that was immediately scheduled for them'.[67] While the two men indeed met occasionally behind the Speaker's Chair for two-minute chats, Smith and Major's formal meetings were very infrequent. Murray Elder suggests (slightly tongue in cheek) that perhaps Major was being treated so appallingly by his own back benchers at the time that he was glad to meet someone who was at least civil to him. Smith was being civil to the Prime Minister, but the former was 'a tad bewildered' and 'not interested' in the latter's expressions of how much he appreciated these chats.[68] As Simon Hoggart later put it: 'He [Smith] didn't dislike Major in particular, but had little time or affection for him. "There's nothing to like or dislike," he once said.'[69]

Some routine matters of business, such as Labour's representation on the new National Lottery Millennium Commission, passed off without controversy. Smith accepted Major's suggestion that one Labour figure should sit on the commission – which ended up being John's great business friend, Michael Montague – alongside two government members, the Secretary of State for National Heritage (then Peter Brooke) and Michael Heseltine.[70]

Nevertheless, Hilary Armstrong recalls that John Smith 'didn't think that much of John Major', not respecting him as a senior politician.[71] Moreover, both Armstrong and Murray Elder agree that there was 'a lack of complete trust on Smith's part'.[72] The relationship had got off to a bad start. During the summer recess, shortly after Smith became leader, John Major briefed Smith, on Privy Council terms, about the creation of a no-fly zone over Bosnia agreed at the London conference in August 1992, which Major had chaired. According to Murray Elder, Major implied that Smith had been consulted and agreed, when in fact Smith had only been informed about events in Bosnia. Smith felt 'badly misused'. On the next occasion, Smith made sure that at least one other person was listening on the telephone when the Prime Minister rang so that he had a witness present to listen to what was actually agreed.[73]

A similar problem appears to have occurred when Major sent aircraft to Iraq, specifically to patrol the air exclusion zone in the 22nd parallel to protect the Shi'ites from being bombed by Saddam Hussein. Tony Benn had written a letter to the Prime Minister on Tuesday, 18 August, requesting a recall of Parliament to debate the issue of Iraq, but he received a letter from the Prime Minister on Tuesday, 1 September, saying that 'he [Major] did not think it necessary to recall Parliament and that he had briefed John Smith fully'.[74]

On Northern Ireland policy, however, Smith generally supported Major's attempts to secure a lasting peace. The Prime Minister regularly briefed the leader of the opposition on the negotiations with the Irish government over the Downing Street Declaration. According to Major, Smith took 'a cheery and cynical view' that he had 'no qualms about supporting us . . . because no one would ever win votes in mainland Britain through Northern Ireland.'[75] Labour's stance on Northern Ireland had become a little unbalanced during the latter period of Neil Kinnock's leadership because the appointment of Kevin McNamara in 1987 meant that both the leader and his chief Northern Ireland spokesperson were decidedly pro-Nationalist in their views on the future constitutional position on Northern Ireland. John's election as Labour leader gave the Unionists in the Province someone to look to on the Labour side for reassurance. Indeed, Smith made a visit to Northern Ireland in December 1992 with the express aim of reassuring the Unionist community, but just before he arrived for meetings with trade unionists, church leaders and security chiefs, the IRA fired three mortars at a police station at Markethill in County Armagh.[76] Although Smith came from the Protestant tradition, he shared his party's belief in a united Ireland if it could be achieved by consent. He also saw the merits of achieving a balance between the largely Republican views of most of his Labour back benchers (adequately represented by McNamara), and his own capacity to ease some of the fears about Labour that were current in the Unionist community at the time.

Smith respected the secrecy involved in Northern Ireland issues, such as keeping it quiet that the government was negotiating with the IRA, but he always remained wary in case on general Northern Ireland issues (and indeed on other issues) the Prime Minister should unnecessarily 'tie him in' to a bi-partisan policy.[77] Tony Blair, the shadow Home Secretary, had conducted a review of Labour's policy towards the Prevention of Terrorism Act (PTA), which the Labour government had introduced in 1976. On 16 February 1994, Blair sent John Smith a synopsis of Labour's three major objections to the PTA. Labour would not vote against the annual renewal of the PTA in the House of Commons if a judge and not the Home Secretary had the power to extend the period of detention for questioning without charge beyond 48 hours, if the government set up an independent review of exclusion orders,[78] and if interviews with suspects held in Northern Ireland were recorded, as was standard practice on the mainland. According to Blair's letter to Smith, Labour's Northern Ireland spokesperson, Kevin McNamara, was 'agreeable' to this stance, and Blair suggested to Smith that 'perhaps we could sit down in the next ten days or so and work out tactics'.[79] Within a few weeks, it seems that Blair's team joined Smith in secret talks with Downing Street on the future of the PTA.

However, someone working in Whitehall opposed to the Northern Ireland peace process appears to have leaked the fact that secret negotiations were taking place between the Prime Minister and the leader of the opposition to Charles Lewington, a journalist working for the *Sunday Express*. No. 10 took the view that the leak must have come from Smith's office or one of Tony Blair's advisers, while the opposition in turn felt certain that someone in the government must have been responsible. A sharp exchange of letters then ensued between Major and Smith. On 7 March 1994, John Smith wrote to the Prime Minister complaining about the leak. Three days later, Major wrote back, complaining about Smith's remarks on the BBC *Nine o'Clock News* on 9 March. The Prime Minister quoted the remarks attributed to Smith, claiming: 'They seem to indicate that you are simply out to make party political capital.'[80] The BBC report had said: 'Mr Major is tonight facing new complaints from Labour leader John Smith that he is not safe to talk to on Privy Council terms after the leaking of their secret talks last week . . . Mr Smith, after what he regards as a cursory leak enquiry failed to find the mole, wants assurances before talking again.'[81]

John Major asked Smith to repudiate these comments, 'specifically the allegation that you do not believe it is safe to talk to the Prime Minister on Privy Council terms'. The Prime Minister also denied that he had made 'cursory' inquiries about the source of the leak, adding:

> I personally made inquiries of the very few people in Number 10 who knew of our conversation, and am fully satisfied that the leak did not come from here. I then asked those Ministers whom I had consulted to make inquiries in their own departments. They have now done so, and have told me they are satisfied their departments were not responsible for the leak.[82]

If the Prime Minister had left it at that, John Smith's ire would not have been raised, but instead Major ended his letter thus:

> As well as the Ministers and civil servants, there must have been members of your staff and no doubt some of Tony Blair's advisers who knew of our meeting. You know as well as I do that leaks can be made for a variety of motives. I don't know whether you have yet made inquiries of your staff and advisers, but I should be grateful if you would do so and let me know the outcome. I can then consider whether it would be appropriate for any further inquiries to be made.[83]

The very same day (10 March), Smith fired back an angry letter to the Prime Minister, in which he picked up immediately on the last paragraph of Major's letter:

> You cannot be serious in making the suggestion in the last paragraph that someone on my staff or on Tony Blair's staff leaked my confidential

discussions with you to the *Sunday Express*. If you read the story again it was designed to cause us embarrassment. It did not in fact succeed in its objective, but that was clearly the intention of a newspaper whose loyalties to your party cannot be doubted. You might also take note that 'a Ministerial source' was referred to in the body of the story. I assume it is not being suggested that this reference was invented by Mr Charles Lewington.[84]

Smith went on to point that he had only heard about Major's inquiry into the leak as a result of the Prime Minister's remarks on Radio Two's *Jimmy Young Show*. After being approached by the press, Smith's office had issued the following statement:

> Frankly, it is hard to believe that this inquiry – carried out in little more than 24 hours – could have been as thorough and comprehensive as such a serious breach of confidence merited, and that I requested. I remain deeply disturbed at the leak and at Mr Major's failure to discover its source. Mr Major should either hold a proper inquiry or put arrangements in place to make sure that the confidence of any future discussions is properly safeguarded.[85]

The leader of the opposition's statement then formed the basis for the BBC's report that evening, the exact wording for which Smith could not be held responsible. In his concluding remarks to Major, Smith returned to the matter of substance: 'I hope you have not lost sight of the fact that the existence of what should have been a confidential discussion was leaked and I am fully entitled to be aggrieved.' Finally, Smith indicated a willingness to continue the discussions because they were 'clearly in the public interest', but that if people in the government immediately outside the Prime Minister's office were to be consulted in the future about such talks, then 'some account will need to be taken of this unfortunate experience'.[86]

For the leader of the opposition Tuesdays and Thursdays were defined by Prime Minister's Questions (PMQs).[87] Both Hilary Armstrong and Murray Elder recall that an inordinate amount of time was spent reading up and preparing questions.[88] During the morning, advisers would pore over the newspapers, meeting again at lunchtime to talk over what questions might be asked, before a final meeting was held an hour beforehand to hone and research the leader's questions.[89]

John Smith strongly disliked PMQs: its dry format, and absence of spontaneous debate.[90] Hilary Armstrong also recalls that PMQs 'used to drive him insane'.[91] Simon Hoggart once asked Smith why he didn't deploy his wit more often as leader of the opposition against Major. Smith replied: 'I must always appear statesmanlike.' As Hoggart puts it: 'He was holding back the bubble of his own high spirits.'[92] And yet, as we have seen, when it came to big set-piece speeches, Smith couldn't stop his natural exuberance from surfacing. The end result was that, as Anthony Seldon points out, 'Smith had not turned out to be as effective at Question Time as Number Ten feared, though he proved better in debate than they had anticipated.'[93] After what would be Smith's last ever Question Time on 10 May 1994, Robert Hardman, then the Commons sketch-writer for the *Daily Telegraph,* observed: 'Unlike the solar variety . . . eclipses of the Opposition leader are occurring with surprising regularity on Tuesday and Thursday afternoons at Prime Minister's Question Time.'[94]

However, Smith did score effective blows against the Prime Minister on occasion, so much so that Major sometimes lost his cool afterwards. Smith liked to return to the subject of the Tory broken pledges on tax. After one particular Smith attack on this subject, the two Johns walked out of the Chamber via the back of the Speaker's Chair. Major stopped Smith in the corridor and engaged in an animated and agitated conversation for fully 20 minutes, in full view of passing MPs. Eventually, Smith prised himself free and privately expressed incredulity to Hilary Armstrong along the lines of 'You'll never guess, he's just had a go at me for attacking him on the broken election pledges on tax, claims I'm being disrespectful and bringing down the Office of the Prime Minister.'[95] For the Prime Minister to be seen to be berating the leader of the opposition in front of other MPs outside the Chamber does seem to demonstrate acute sensitivity, given that Smith was perfectly entitled to bring up the issue at PMQs. By this stage, Major had convinced himself that everyone was against him, not just his political opponents.[96]

In his biography of Major, Anthony Seldon does not mention the effectiveness of Smith's tax jibes and their capacity to cause the Prime Minister to lose his cool in such a public way, but he rightly emphasises that Major also resented the way that Smith attacked the probity of government ministers and their links with big business.[97] Smith generally focused his attacks on the lucrative private sector appointments taken up by ministers on their retirement from high office, rather than the almost weekly sexual scandals that ruined the Prime Minister's widely misinterpreted, yet ill-judged Victorian-style 'Back to Basics' campaign. Major admits that Smith's campaign 'succeeded in sowing the seeds of doubt'[98] in the public's mind concerning sleaze.

Major became extremely touchy about Smith's attacks on the probity of his government, as letters between the two Johns reveal. On 24 March 1994, for example, Major objected to Smith's reference the previous week to the use of cars by staff from the Kingston Hospital and St James's University Hospital Trusts: 'Both Trust have publicly shown the figures you use to be misleading. I suggest you withdraw them forthwith.'[99]

In January 1994, Smith buttonholed Tony Benn in the lobby after a dinner with American correspondents, and discussed the recent spate of Tory scandals. Benn warned that 'Scandal could work both ways', but Smith, who had 'a slight alcoholic enthusiasm about him' replied: 'Oh no, the Labour Party is made up of people with happy marriages.'[100] Hugh Macpherson, a contemporary of Smith's at Glasgow University, later pointed out the amusing irony that just at the time when the Tories were 'dreaming up an electoral wheeze that lauded Victorian family values, in a party rent with adulterers and fornicators, John [Smith] and his family stood as the very exemplar of all that the Conservatives were supposed to be advocating'.[101]

Major's most public attack on John Smith came during the Qualified Majority Voting (QMV) crisis in March 1994. The British government was then battling to defend Britain's 'blocking minority' in the Council of Ministers.[102] At this crucial point in the negotiations, John Major committed a major blunder on Tuesday, 22 March. In reply to a Commons question from the pro-European Labour MP Giles Radice, Major blurted out: 'The right hon. and learned Member for Monklands East (Mr Smith) is the man who likes to say yes in Europe – Monsieur Oui, the poodle of Brussels'.[103]

For several months, the Conservatives had been attacking Smith's decision to sign up to the Party of European Socialists' (PES) manifesto, one of the main party groups in the European Parliament, in the run-up to the 1994 European Parliamentary elections. The manifesto pledged, among many other things, to cut the average working week to 35 hours. John Smith had responded by saying that the 35 hour week wasn't a firm Labour commitment, but subsequently distanced himself from the PES manifesto: it was now portrayed as a broad set of goals that all European socialists wanted to achieve, rather than a firm set of proposals.[104] Under the heading of 'democracy', the PES manifesto proposed that more decisions should be taken jointly between the European Parliament and the Council of Ministers (known as 'co-decision'); and called for majority voting to become the norm in the Council of Ministers, the main decision-making body of the European Community. The Conservatives used these phrases to peddle the notion that Labour was intent on abandoning Britain's veto. Indeed, in February 1994 John Major attacked Smith at Prime Minister's Questions over his decision to sign the PES manifesto.[105] It was in this political context that the Prime Minister made his remarks.

In his memoirs, John Major admits that the 'Monsieur Oui' comment was 'a gratuitous and graceless accusation, and I knew it as soon as the words left my lips in the heat of an exchange'.[106] His biographer, Anthony Seldon agrees that 'Major's judgement let him down'. As soon as the Prime Minister returned to his room in the House of Commons, 'he knew he had gone too far'. The cheap jibe had been discussed, and rejected at a meeting of officials in No. 10 that morning, but the phrase had stuck in the Prime Minister's mind.[107] In fact, Smith did not take any offence. However, Douglas Hurd, the Foreign Secretary, was very cross at the time and feels John Major 'dug us all in deeper'. The Prime Minister had been kept fully informed of the negotiations and the difficulties that Hurd was experiencing, and yet he had made this unscripted remark.[108]

The political effects of Major's remarks were disastrous. He had chosen the wrong ground on which to stand and fight on Europe. He had stoked up Tory back bench feeling on the issue, and he mistakenly believed he could have gained a better deal for Britain. Hurd negotiated a sensible compromise at Ioannina in Greece, but Major was savaged by the press and by his own back benchers, including Tony Marlow, who called on the Prime Minister to resign, the first time a Tory back bencher had done so since 1963. Smith mocked the Prime Minister's 'vainglorious assertions of "no surrender"'.[109] By this stage, John Major's authority had sapped considerably as a result of the prolonged parliamentary ratification of the Maastricht Treaty.

Twenty
A FIGHTING OPPOSITION

THE PASSAGE OF the European Communities (Amendment) Bill, or the Maastricht Bill as it became known, was designed to bring into effect the European Treaty negotiated in the Dutch town of Maastricht in December 1991. The British ratification process began in the House of Commons on 1 May 1992 with the Bill's Second Reading. Three hundred and eighty-four days later, after 210 hours of parliamentary debate, the Bill finally had its Third Reading. Mulling over the events, David Baker and his academic colleagues rightly concluded that in terms of Conservative rebellions 'the passage of the Maastricht Bill was an exceptional episode in parliamentary history'.[1]

It is often forgotten, however, that Labour was more divided over the Maastricht Bill than the Conservatives. Research at the Centre for Legislative Studies at the University of Hull conducted by Philip Norton and Philip Cowley, and assisted by the author and Matthew Bailey, reveals that while a total of 49 Conservatives voted against the Maastricht Bill, 138 Labour MPs, or nearly half the PLP, defied that Labour whip at some point during its passage. While there were 64 separate Conservative rebellions on the Bill, compared with 40 Labour rebellions, the average number of Labour rebels per rebellion was 33, compared with only 18 for the Conservatives.[2] As Tony Benn recalls: 'The idea that the Party was united in favour of Europe was a complete illusion', although he is just plain wrong to claim that 'the European policy was never put to the Party'.[3] This is characteristically inaccurate: what Benn really means is that a referendum on the Treaty was never put to the country.[4]

Under Neil Kinnock's leadership, the PLP had to decide how to vote on the Second Reading of the Maastricht Bill, which was due to be debated on 20 and 21 May. Four options were up for consideration: abstention on Second Reading; outright opposition; a reasoned amendment, followed by an abstention on Second Reading; and a reasoned amendment followed by a vote against. At a meeting of the PLP on Wednesday 13 May, Gerald Kaufman, still Labour's shadow Foreign Secretary, argued that there was no chance of defeating the government as the Liberal Democrats and the minor parties had agreed to vote with it.[5] Besides, Labour supported many aspects of the Treaty, especially the inclusion of the Social Chapter.[6] They should therefore adopt a reasoned amendment calling for the inclusion of the chapter in the Treaty, which he argued would have the added benefit of uniting the party. At the end of the debate, Neil Kinnock warned:

> ... the British public are not going to vote for any party which turns its back on Europe ... We must not take a holier than thou stance which is what voting against the Second Reading means ... We are in Europe to stay ... It would be political suicide; a source of virility next week, but a source of mortality in the years to come.[7]

The sheer extent of Labour back bench hostility to the Treaty was shown the following week when Dennis Skinner revealed that his 'round robin', urging outright opposition on Second Reading had gathered 85 signatures, but that it was 'not for publication'.[8] On the Bill's Second Reading the following day, some 61 Labour MPs (including tellers) voted against the government, defying the Labour line to abstain, voting alongside 22 Conservative rebels.[9]

On 2 June 1992, the Danes voted against ratification in their Maastricht referendum. This event provoked a large group of Conservative MPs to call on Major to abandon the Treaty.[10] Major chose to delay ratification until the autumn against the advice of the whips. On Wednesday, 10 June 1992, the PLP debated three propositions: a motion in the name of Tony Benn calling for a referendum on the Treaty;[11] a leadership motion in the name of Gerald Kaufman calling on the PLP to keep its tactical options open on the Bill; and a Tribune Group motion moved by Peter Hain opposing any government attempt to reintroduce the Maastricht Treaty, and proposing a radically different Treaty to include a democratically accountable European Central Bank (ECB) and a strengthened Social Chapter.[12] Press reports the following day described the meeting as 'distinctly rowdy'.[13] They were accurate.

Tony Benn argued that Maastricht had profound constitutional effects, and should be put to a referendum. On behalf of the leadership, Gerald Kaufman claimed that agreeing to a referendum would split the party; Major was tempted to agree to a referendum, Kaufman claimed, because it would unite his party 'and split ours' – 'That is why we should not be impaled on this question.' The Bill was not before the Labour Party: 'It is their Waterloo, not ours.' Peter Hain argued that it would be premature to divide over the issue of a referendum, but the party should not close the door to the possibility. He described the shadow Cabinet's amendment as about 'as clear and dynamic as a bucket of blancmange'.[14]

With typical understatement, Alan Haworth, the secretary of the PLP, records in the minutes of the meeting: 'An extensive discussion then took place.' John Reid argued that the question was not: 'Is Labour for or against a referendum?' but 'Is it split?' Supporting a referendum would 'take the heat off the Tories', George Robertson stressed that although Maastricht had its faults, it was not a Tory Treaty. Critics of the Treaty included Jean-Marie Le Pen, Margaret Thatcher and Norman Tebbit. In reply, Neil Kinnock argued that the party should 'wait until there is a Bill to vote upon'. Above all, it should not fall into a position which showed Labour as divided. At the end of the debate, David Blunkett then moved that all three motions be remitted, and that the shadow Cabinet bring forward a further statement at a later date. His motion was carried by an overwhelming majority.[15]

The first major test for Smith's leadership on Maastricht came at the Labour Party conference. Tony Benn sought to attract support for a referendum on the Treaty. Smith opposed the idea of a referendum on Maastricht because, according to James Naughtie, he thought that the answer would be 'No'.[16]

The trade unions played a helpful role in stifling the demand in the party that had been building up in favour of a referendum. The majority of trade unions supported Maastricht: its Qualified Majority Voting (QMV) in the Council of Ministers on such matters as working conditions, and information and consultation of workers. But the unions were keenest of all on the Social Chapter or Protocol, as this statement adopted by the TUC General Council on 22 July 1992 reveals:

> Had the British government signed up to the Social Protocol there can be almost no doubt that that, in itself, would have been sufficient reason for the trade union movement to advocate ratification of the Treaty. The social protocol constitutes the building material for a genuine EC social dimension.[17]

At the September 1992 conference, the leadership, with the aid of the unions inflicted, in the words of Tony Benn, 'a crushing defeat for the opposition to Maastricht and a crushing defeat for the referendum'.[18] John Smith secured backing for an NEC Statement – *Europe: Our Economic Future* – that explicitly ruled out a referendum and endorsed the Maastricht Treaty as 'the best agreement that can currently be achieved',[19] confirming the decision of the Parliamentary Committee and the NEC that there should be no referendum. In relation to the September 1993 Labour conference, Larry Whitty was able to reassure Smith as far in advance as March 1993 regarding the unions' stance that, 'On Maastricht etc. there should be no problem'.[20]

When Labour MPs returned to the House of Commons in October 1992 at
least they had an issue to unite around, temporarily obscuring their divisions.
A huge and sudden row had erupted over Michael Heseltine, the president of
the Board of Trade's decision to close 30 coalmines. One hundred thousand
people marched in the centre of London to protest at the redundancies, and
Labour launched a swift and effective national petition organised from
Walworth Road.[21] The opposition, fronted by Robin Cook, the shadow Trade
spokesperson, with the help of a small number of Conservative rebels, secured
a temporary retreat on the part of the government when Heseltine launched a
review under Lord Wakeham, and cut Major's majority to just 13 when the
issue was debated in the House.[22]   Smith twice raised the matter at Prime
Minister's Questions.[23] But the large threatened Tory rebellion of the previous
autumn petered out, as Smith had feared.[24] By the following January, the
government easily won the Second Reading vote on the Coal Bill, which
privatised the coal industry.[25]

The other main issue vexing the PLP under John Smith's leadership was the
rapid disintegration of the former Yugoslavia. Jack Cunningham, Labour's
shadow Foreign Secretary, broadly supported the government's policy of nonintervention in Bosnia. Cunningham's predecessor, Gerald Kaufman, had
harried the Foreign Secretary, Douglas Hurd, pretty furiously over what he
saw as Hurd's caving-in to Germany's demand for the recognition of Croatia
and Slovenia in return for British opt-outs on the single currency and the
Social Chapter at Maastricht. Kaufman argued that endorsing Croat and
Slovene independence gave the green light to the Bosnian Serbs to declare
independence, provoking a three-sided civil war with the Bosnian Muslims
and the Bosnian Croats.[26]

A relatively small but highly vocal section of the PLP had called for an
immediate halt to the ethnic cleansing, and strongly supported sanctions
against Serbia. On 16 November 1992, sixteen Labour MPs, including Kate
Hoey and Clare Short, had voted in favour of a Liberal Democrat opposition
day motion that supported these sentiments.[27] Two days later, Max Madden,
one of the sixteen rebels, moved a motion calling on the PLP to express its total
opposition to the threatened partition of Bosnia-Herzegovina, and urging the
opposition front bench to bring forward an opposition day motion in the
Commons to debate the merits of military deployment to protect humanitarian convoys. Jack Cunningham replied that while he supported the broad
sentiments in Madden's motion, troops could only be sent as part of a United
Nations-authorised intervention.[28]

During the spring of 1993, Bosnia experienced one of its periodic moments of high tension with the Serb shelling of Srebenica, one of the so-called UN 'safe areas'. On 17 April 1993, eighteen Labour back benchers wrote an open letter to *The Guardian* denouncing the government's policy as appeasement and supporting the possible active engagement of ground troops against the Serbs to halt the shelling of Srebrenica. A decade later, in March 2003, after resigning as Minister of State at the Home Office over the issue of Iraq, John Denham delivered his resignation speech, during which he reminded the House that he was not a pacifist and had supported armed intervention in Bosnia:

> I shall never forget the surprised and bemused expression on John Smith's face when some twenty newly elected Labour Members of Parliament went to see him to demand Labour support for a foreign war. I believe that we should have supported it, and that, had we done so, Balkan history might be different.[29]

Was Smith swayed to some extent by the strength of feeling on his back benches? On the weekend of 17-18 April he issued a statement calling for the UN to issue an ultimatum to Serbia, that unless a ceasefire was made effective, the UN would authorise air strikes against Serbian lines of communication in Bosnia-Herzegovina.[30] However, on 19 April, Jack Cunningham appeared to contradict that view, largely agreeing with Douglas Hurd that air strikes against the Bosnian Serbs might damage the UN's humanitarian effort.[31]

On Wednesday, 21 April 1993, a planned PLP discussion on the Plant Report into Electoral Reform (see chapter 21) was shelved to allow a full debate on the situation in Bosnia. Several newly elected Labour back benchers supported military action, and others argued that military intervention was necessary to prevent the conflict from spreading. Bernie Grant went even further: 'The Moslems will be annihilated if we wait for sanctions to work.' However, there were plenty of people on the left opposed to military action, including Alice Mahon, who was worried about 'being sucked into a whole scale war in the Balkans', while Robert Wareing, chairman of the All-Party British-Yugoslavia Parliamentary Group, took a passionately pro-Serb view, claiming that ethnic cleansing was also being carried out by the Croats, and that 'Military intervention will make a Balkan war more, not less likely'. Replying to the debate, Cunningham argued sensibly that there was no way that existing UN troops could be turned into fighting troops. Moreover, he rightly argued that 'as things stand, there is no international support for massive ground forces intervening in Bosnia'. President Bill Clinton, especially, would not agree to that. Cunningham reluctantly supported air strikes if the authority of the UN was further flouted, although he continued to share Douglas Hurd's view that it would be wrong to lift the UN arms embargo, describing Margaret

Thatcher's suggestion (and her rare point of concurrence with Bernie Grant) of arming the Bosnian Muslims as 'absurd'.[32]

In the subsequent shadow Cabinet elections of October 1993, Cunningham achieved the lowest vote of any successful candidate. But Smith and Cunningham went back 22 years, having entered the House of Commons at the same time, and few were surprised when Smith retained Cunningham as his shadow Foreign Secretary. After Smith's death, Cunningham's successor, Robin Cook, proved far more incisive in attacking Douglas Hurd on the ineffectiveness of the UN safe areas.[33]

Despite Bosnia, the issue of Maastricht dwarfed all others during the 1992–3 session. Back in 1977–8, Smith had gained invaluable parliamentary experience defending clause after clause of the Scotland Bill from a group of persistent Labour rebels, whose behaviour helped to drain the life from the Callaghan government (see chapter 6). Now, fifteen years later, Smith was on the other side of the House of Commons trying to sap the authority of a beleaguered government by keeping it up night after night discussing clause after clause of the Maastricht Bill. Derek Foster, Smith's Chief Whip recalls:

> The Callaghan Government had only survived by the competence of the Whips, [and] John realised the importance of the Whips. Once he was assured of my competence, he left me to it, and we developed the most trusting relationship that I enjoyed in the whole of my ten years as Chief Whip.[34]

But Maastricht posed a serious dilemma for Smith: how did a principled, long-standing pro-European secure the passage of a Treaty he largely supported, while at the same time trying to maximise internal Tory divisions? Apparently, the late Roy Jenkins remarked to Charles Kennedy at the time that Smith was '"doing a Harold Wilson" – ducking and weaving' to appease both factions. Kennedy accuses Smith of focusing disproportionately on the Social Chapter – 'the one element of Maastricht that every Labour Member agreed with' in order to 'maintain an impression of party unity, without making any substantial steps towards ratification'.[35] Kennedy's charge is unrealistic and plain wrong. If Smith wasn't being entirely consistent, the fact remains that no leader of the opposition worthy of the position would have turned down the opportunity to take advantage of the government's growing divisions. Moreover, those in charge of Labour's tactics never had any intention of endangering the ratification of the Treaty. Day-to-day tactics on the Maastricht Treaty were left to George Robertson: 'John trusted me to harry the Government but not to lose the Treaty, and I reported to him regularly, and to the shadow Cabinet, while Jack Cunningham took care of the big things.'[36]

The Labour whips' office colluded with the Conservative Maastricht rebels to maximise the chances of defeating the government. It was 'a constant source of amazement' to George Robertson that 26 Conservative MPs, including Iain Duncan Smith, were prepared to vote against their own government: 'It was not a normal, casual rebellion. They were there and available. We had a formal arrangement. If I could contrive a situation to defeat the government, they would co-operate.'[37] Long after the event, John Major told Derek Foster that he 'never understood how they [the Tory Maastricht rebels] could be prepared to do that'.[38]

By the summer of 1992, Britain had taken over the six-monthly presidency of the European Council, and that autumn Major introduced a 'paving motion' to signal the resumption of the parliamentary ratification of Maastricht. There can be little doubt that Major assumed he would have the support of Labour and, through an overwhelming vote in favour of the motion, would be able to demonstrate to his fellow European leaders that the government was pressing ahead with the ratification process. What went wrong? Why did Smith not support Major on the paving motion?

When Smith struck deals, he stuck by them, and expected reciprocity. When John Major agreed that Neil Kinnock should succeed Bruce Millan to be the next European Commissioner from Britain, Smith took him at his word. Mary Goudie recalls: 'John thought he had done the deal . . . nobody ever said "no" to John.'[39] The strength of Smith's backing for Kinnock is clear from a letter that Smith penned to John Major on 6 October 1992: 'When we met I strongly urged you to appoint Neil Kinnock as the second Commissioner and I take this opportunity to reassert that view as forcefully as I can. As I understand it, we do not differ on his abilities or suitability for the post.'[40]

Initially, Tristan Garel-Jones had asked George Robertson if he wanted to do the job, but John Smith vetoed even the idea on the grounds that he didn't want Labour to fight another potentially tricky by-election against the SNP in Scotland.[41] Also, Smith wanted to deliver something for Neil in recognition of his achievements in turning the Labour Party round. George Robertson had therefore approached Bruce Millan to say that Neil Kinnock was interested in the post. Millan said he certainly had no objection, and he would be supportive of Neil succeeding him, especially as Neil Kinnock had nominated him for the position originally. Kinnock's appointment would only have been a two-year interim one until 1994, since the next set of European elections would have seen the posts of European Commissioners swap around again for fresh five-year terms.[42]

However, due to behind-the-scenes pressure on Major from his own side, the Prime Minister reneged on his agreement with Smith. Neil Kinnock is very self-effacing when speculating as to the reasoning behind the Prime Minister's change of mind: 'The arguments put to him [John Major] in July 1992 were rather prosaic in political terms: I think Tories said to him: "How can we send Kinnock to Brussels as Commissioner when we were telling everyone that he couldn't run a whelk stall just a few months ago?"'[43] Technically, Major was perfectly entitled not to accept the opposition's nomination and, obviously, Neil Kinnock could not press his own case. The convention was that the two European Commissioners from the United Kingdom would be drawn from the government and the opposition. In practice, this meant one Conservative and one Labour appointee, but in each case the decision rested with the Prime Minister. If Labour created too much of a fuss, there was a real danger that the Prime Minister might have broken that convention.[44]

Having changed his mind, John Major telephoned Bruce Millan to say that he wanted him to continue for another two years. Millan pointed out that the Labour Party had wanted Kinnock, but accepted the Prime Minister's decision with reluctance.[45] Neil Kinnock recalls Major informing him of his decision: 'Major told me, rather apologetically, that it was taken because of the advantages of the "continuity" of Bruce staying in the Commission.'[46] George Robertson remembers Smith's reaction on hearing the news: 'John was wild. He believed that Major was breaking a solemn agreement. He regarded the issue as a matter of honour.' Tristan Garel-Jones understood just how damaging this decision would be, and went to the trouble of tracking down Robertson by mobile phone in Calais, where Robertson was staying with his daughter in a bed and breakfast. Robertson's reaction was: 'John is going to be livid.'[47] Neil Kinnock recalls: 'John was certainly very brassed off.'[48]

But was Major's decision to call off the Kinnock deal the decisive factor in Smith's decision to oppose the paving motion on Maastricht in November 1992? Smith took the view that the Tories didn't care about Labour, and that they had lost the last of their purchasing power with the opposition. As Robertson puts it: 'all bets were off.'[49] While it was one motivating factor, it is hardly likely that is was *the* decisive factor.

At this stage, it was not the opposition's job to make life easy for the government. As Neil Kinnock points out: 'The debate, remember, was about a month after Black Wednesday and it was pretty natural that the Leader of the Opposition would want to inflict harm on a seriously wounded Tory Government.'[50] Moreover, both Millan and Kinnock feel that Smith would have had difficulties with his own back benchers in terms of the large number of Labour MPs who wanted to oppose the paving motion for tactical partisan reasons.[51] Nevertheless, the spat over the European Commission post further damaged the relationship between Smith and Major.

In late October 1992, Derek Foster, as Labour Chief Whip, was aware that his side was just as divided as the Tories. He called on Smith to say that, ideally, he would like Labour to vote against the paving motion. The Chief Whip was therefore 'euphoric' when Smith agreed: 'It solved all of my problems [in party management terms], and put Major, who then had a majority of only 22, and more than that number of Maastricht rebels, on the spot.' Foster argues that Neil Kinnock would not have been able to take the decision to oppose the Treaty because he had started out as anti-European and changed his position, but because Smith had been consistently pro-European, no one was going to seriously doubt his continuing pro-European credentials.[52] This reasoning is doubtful: Kinnock could and probably would have done the same as Smith.

The PLP debated the decision to oppose the paving motion on Thursday, 29 October. Even though the exact wording of the Government's motion was not then known, Smith told his colleagues that they would be voting against it, and in terms of any amendment would seek to make support for the Government as difficult as possible in relation to its own rebels, whilst ensuring that all Labour MPs entered the same lobby.[53]

Labour therefore put down an amendment to the paving motion on 4 November 1992. The government won the first division by 6 votes, largely due to the votes of the Liberal Democrats, but 26 Conservative MPs voted for Labour's amendment in the opposing lobby.[54] Then, the government squeaked home by only 3 votes on its main paving motion.[55] Perhaps it was opportunism on Smith's part, but it was a classic example of what oppositions are supposed to do in the British parliamentary system, namely oppose. The fact that the opposition had come so close to defeating the government undoubtedly lifted the spirits of the PLP, and gave back benchers a renewed sense of purpose. Moreover, the decision to oppose the paving motion was, as Derek Foster puts it, 'merely the opening salvo in what proved to be ten months of acute embarrassment to the Tories'. The opposition's aim, he claims, was 'to prolong the government's agony for as long as possible'.[56]

All sorts of parliamentary devices were deployed to this end, including preventing the government from moving its Business Motion at ten o'clock, which would have allowed it to carry on debating the Bill until the small hours of the morning. These tactics, whilst effective, were also at the same time unsociable and inane. On one occasion, Diane Abbott complained to the leadership at a meeting of the PLP: 'Is it not becoming a charade, and if so why should she be staying here until late hours, when she could be putting her baby to bed?'[57]

Repeatedly, the Chief Whip had to reassure Labour MPs that they were not being kept there unnecessarily, and to praise them for their continued co-operation.[58] On one occasion, Foster told a gathering of the PLP that it would be 'grossly incompetent of the Party to forfeit the possibility of a victory over the Government . . . because of "little local difficulties"', in this case the prospect of a rail strike (and the resultant problems in Labour MPs being able to return to their constituencies on a Friday).[59] However, Foster recalls: 'Had we not done this, the Tories would have been able to complete more quickly far more clauses in the Bill.'[60] And as always, Dennis Skinner strongly supported this kind of combative approach: 'We keep the Government enfeebled if we turn up in such strength at 10 o'clock that they do not move the motion. Even without a vote we have defeated the Government.'[61]

The other main procedural tactic during the Bill's committee stage was for the opposition to put down 'probing amendments', raising an issue for debate, but then not pressing it to a vote.[62] On 26 November 1992, five days before the beginning of the committee stage, Robertson explained the leadership's reasoning for the probing amendments to a meeting of the PLP: 'We are not out to wreck the Maastricht Treaty. We will call our votes in pursuit of our objectives, not Liberal objectives or right-wing nationalist objectives. Nor are we attempting any filibuster; this Bill needs to be carefully considered in its entirety, and over a lengthy period.'[63]

Many of the Labour Euro-sceptics were unhappy with these tactics. Dennis Skinner wanted to filibuster continuously, seeing the dangers of Labour being seen to wound but not to strike. Ken Livingstone felt the opposition's aim should be to bring down the government. George Howarth felt that Labour's credibility would be undermined if the amendments were debated then simply withdrawn. Nigel Spearing objected to Robertson's choice of language, claiming that not all Euro-sceptics were right-wing nationalists; many were sincere constitutionalists. However, on the pro-European side, Giles Radice saw it as 'entirely legitimate' to put down amendments and to debate them, but not necessarily vote on them. It was not the party's policy to wreck the Bill, nor to time waste: 'That would be to abandon our pro-European position.' Replying to the debate, Robertson emphasised the need to stand united, while leaving the Tories in disarray.[64] That hope, however, soon dissipated. By the New Year of 1993, Jack Cunningham had to admit: 'When it comes to votes, the reality is that there are some people who will do whatever they like, but we must, as a Party, seek to come out of this whole exercise with as much unity and coherence as possible.'[65]

While Smith wanted to cause his own government maximum embarrassment over the parliamentary ratification of the Maastricht Treaty, he hoped that Poul Nyrup Rasmussen, the Prime Minister of Denmark, would be able to secure a favourable second referendum result, negotiated after the compromise agreed at the Edinburgh Summit in December 1992.[66] While most of this account of Maastricht deals with Labour's parliamentary tactics on the Bill, it is important to point out that these tactics were not central to what Labour was doing in terms of policy development on Europe. Labour remained a pro-European party with strong links with European leaders. Smith especially enjoyed a good working relationship with many of the socialist leaders. The parliamentary aim, however, was to embarrass the Tories, not to bring down the Treaty.

On 19 May 1993, Smith met with President Mitterand at the Elysée Palace in Paris. The French President feared that a combination of the Tory rebels and the Labour Party's insistence on the inclusion of the Social Chapter might lead Britain to blocking the ratification of Maastricht, upsetting his joint European project with Chancellor Kohl of Germany. Mitterand asked Smith: 'You're not going to take any risks with the Treaty?' Smith replied: 'I didn't take half the risks that you did, holding a referendum.'[67] Smith then reassured Mitterand that Labour was merely 'playing for as long as we can' in terms of giving the government a hard time in the House of Commons.[68] Smith was right. Ultimately, by holding a referendum the French government took the greatest risk with the fate of the Maastricht Treaty.[69]

Increasingly, the Labour front bench's tactics provoked growing complaints from ardent pro-Europeans who became frustrated that the leadership was unnecessarily dragging out the ratification process. After the Edinburgh Summit, some 90 Labour MPs, excluding members of the shadow Cabinet, but including Neil Kinnock and Gerald Kaufman, signed a motion in the name of Peter Mandelson backing the Treaty as the 'best available', and supporting the rapid completion of the ratification process.[70] At a meeting of the PLP on 20 January 1993, Giles Radice warned that the party was 'in danger of letting tactics determine strategy'. He added: 'We should not support time wasting by Tory rebels.'[71] According to George Robertson, these pro-European MPs were 'constantly in need of reassurance' that the Labour front bench did not intend to wreck the Treaty. Ultimately, he claims, the pro-Europeans trusted Smith because of his consistent pro-European credentials.[72]

According to Derek Foster, the whole exercise of harrying the government became 'a great unifying factor' in the PLP.[73] Not everyone agreed. On 21 April 1993, Bryan Gould condemned 'a Parliament in which the Labour Party

Opposition front bench spokesmen have tacitly agreed to ease the passage of the Bill'.[74] A few weeks later, Peter Shore attacked George Robertson for not opposing a Treaty that 'handed over great chunks of British power to decision making in the European institutions', adding: 'If my hon. Friend [Robertson] cannot understand that, he is not fit to speak for my party.'[75]

It is exceptionally rare for the PLP to vote on motions to determine party policy. In opposition, the shadow Cabinet normally agrees the whip on legislation after merely consulting the PLP, but within the space of one month, two important issues relating to Labour's stance on the Maastricht Bill were fully debated in the PLP, and subject to a democratic vote.

On 17 February 1993, the PLP debated the pros and cons of the European Central Bank (ECB). Roger Berry moved that: 'The PLP, in line with party policy, opposes the establishment of an independent European Central Bank.' The leader moved a much longer amendment which argued that Maastricht 'while not perfect is the best agreement that can currently be achieved'.[76] Roger Berry concluded: 'The Maastricht proposals are clearly undemocratic, and are deliberately deflationary. Labour should oppose, and oppose vigorously, an Independent Central Bank.'[77]

Moving the amendment, Smith stressed that the move to European Monetary Union (EMU) would be 'considerably delayed'. While he admitted that the Central Bank was 'deeply embedded' in the Treaty, he pointed to other articles that committed the bank to achieving non-inflationary growth and high levels of employment. The effect of the rebel motion would be to wreck the Treaty: 'Perhaps that is their motive.' Speaking candidly, Smith admitted that he would have preferred that the French and British socialist model of a more democratically accountable ECB had prevailed at Maastricht. However, the unavoidable reality of the European Community was that there had to be compromises, and 'it is completely hopeless to suggest that we can always get all our points in full'. In conclusion, he held out the possibility of a new Labour government in 1996, arguing its vision for EMU at an inter-governmental conference: 'By then we will have hardly got to the point some colleagues fear. It is sometimes a mistake to treat all these things as if they are in concrete forever.'[78]

Peter Shore felt that the issue was about the 'the future of our country' because control over monetary policy was being handed over to the ECB. He rubbished Smith's earlier arguments, claiming that the Franco-British position wasn't 'worth a damn, if it ever existed'. He concluded: 'The Frontbench hasn't got the guts to stand up for Britain, and if this amendment is carried today it will go down as a day of infamy in the history of the Labour Party.' Bryan Gould argued that whenever the bankers had prevailed they had always brought recession and unemployment. The Treaty was 'an outstandingly audacious statement of the bankers' ambition to achieve power'.[79]

Replying to the debate, John Smith said that Bryan Gould's remark that Europe should be forced to start again surely encapsulated an idea which could not be supported; every single sister socialist and social democratic party in Europe would be opposed to this line. The leadership amendment was carried by 112 votes to 46.[80]

On 8 March 1993, Labour's internal divisions were temporarily eclipsed when it defeated the Major government for the first time. Amendment 28, relating to the method of selection for the United Kingdom's 24 members of the European Union's Committee of the Regions, was carried by 314 votes to 292, with 26 Conservatives backing Labour. The decisive feature of the vote was that eighteen Liberal Democrats switched sides, supporting Labour.[81] George Robertson had got what he wanted: an opportunity to inflict a considerable humiliation on the government – John Major's first House of Commons defeat – without wrecking the Treaty.

However, Labour Party unity continued to be difficult to maintain as, once again, the PLP voted on a key aspect of the Bill, this time on the EC's plan to limit the amount that member states could run up Budget deficits to 3 per cent of GDP. On Wednesday, 10 March 1993, Denzil Davies moved a motion rejecting the relevant clause in the Treaty,[82] and calling on the Labour leadership to press its probing amendment 119 to a vote during the committee stage of the Bill.[83]

The Labour leadership attached a very long amendment to the rebel amendment.[84] John Smith re-emphasised the 'not perfect but best available' mantra. He also emphasised that running excessive Budget deficits was not a good thing. Moreover, he pointed out:

> The view that we can still operate economic self-government has had its day. It is out of date and is not apt for the vicissitudes of the times. We must co-operate with others; and co-operation involved compromises. That is the nature of a multi-national, multi-party European Community. It is in the Council of Ministers that we will have to make our economic alliances.[85]

An extensive discussion then took place, during which Giles Radice made the case for a single currency. David Winnick, on the other hand, argued that a future Labour government would be 'imprisoned' by the deficit restrictions.

Predictably, Austin Mitchell claimed: 'The Treaty is a Charter for Central
Bank rule, on a monetarist basis . . . how much more will we swallow?'
Replying to the debate, Smith claimed that the Treaty did not have the
imprisoning features that were being alleged. The leadership amendment was
then carried by 94 votes for to 35 against.[86] The great debate over Budget
deficits really matters in terms of the history of New Labour because, as a
direct result of this meeting we see the genesis of Gordon Brown's so-called
five economic tests, conditions that would have to be met before a future
Labour government would contemplate joining the Euro.[87]

The very fact that Smith allowed these votes to take place demonstrates that
he paid proper attention to the concerns of the PLP. David Ward recalls Peter
Hain, one of the leading rebels on Maastricht, saying after one of these
meetings: 'We've lost, but at least we've been listened to.'[88] But the rebels were
not content to leave the issue within the confines of the PLP; Tory back bench
amendments opposing the establishment of the ECB attracted sizeable Labour
rebellions in the division lobbies, when the Labour front bench abstained.[89]

The same pattern of vigorous debate in the full PLP followed by large
Labour rebellions in the House of Commons against the front bench line of
abstention continued over the Third Reading of the Maastricht Bill. During
the private debate in the full PLP, the Labour Euro-sceptics expressed their
deep and profound opposition to the leadership's line. Dennis Skinner's
reaction to the shadow Cabinet's decision was 'in John McEnroe's words, you
cannot be serious'. Peter Shore claimed: 'This is the largest single issue in our
lifetime, yet we can't muster a view.' Nigel Spearing felt that the Maastricht
Treaty was 'against what the Party was founded to do – to battle against
bankers' forces.' On the other side of the debate, Giles Radice argued that
Labour Party policy was in favour of Maastricht, that the abstention on
Second Reading was due to the omission of the Social Chapter, and that,
having gained a victory on that subject, there was now a strong case for a yes
vote on Third Reading.[90]

A good number of back benchers were willing to argue for the leadership
line. For instance, Dale Campbell-Savours acknowledged that many Labour
back benchers held passionate views, but urged colleagues to sink them in the
interests of party unity. Replying to the debate, Jack Cunningham pointed to
the five major amendments conceded by the government – the Committee of
the Regions, the two amendments on the Social Chapter, and the others on
ECOFIN and the Bank of England. Having abstained on Second Reading, the
only consistent approach was to go for another abstention on Third Reading.
But apart from the gains he had already mentioned, 'the other major objective

has been to stop the party dividing over Maastricht', while letting the view prevail that the Tories were deeply divided.[91]

Despite appeals for unity, some 68 Labour MPs voted against the Third Reading on 20 May 1993, joining 41 Conservatives in the no lobby, while five Labour MPs supported the Conservatives.[92] In the aftermath of the vote, John Smith sacked Kate Hoey, then the party's junior spokesperson on the citizens' charter and women for defying the Labour whip.[93]

Ever since February 1993, Robertson had set a 'ticking time bomb', originally known as Amendment 27, a device to show that Labour wished to ratify the Treaty, but only if the British government signed up to the Social Chapter. It all came down to parliamentary procedure: how to engineer a vote that embarrassed the Conservatives without bringing down the Treaty. The amendment did not prevent the Bill from becoming law, but it forced the government to hold a vote on the Social Chapter before the Treaty could be officially ratified. George Robertson was very proud of his ticking time bomb, but he concedes that two of Labour's rising stars, Geoff Hoon and Stephen Byers, both from legal backgrounds, together with some helpful clerks from the House of Commons, helped to develop the idea.[94]

Controversially, the Deputy Speaker failed to select Amendment 27 for debate during the committee stage of the Bill.[95] Jack Cunningham protested in 'the strongest possible terms' about this decision,[96] and it eventually reappeared at report stage as New Clause 2. This time, the Speaker accepted it for debate (after discussions with Cunningham, George Robertson and Derek Foster).[97] The government was cornered: it knew it would be defeated if the new clause was put to a vote, so it accepted it, leaving it to lie dormant until the very end of the parliamentary process.[98]

The ticking time bomb went off on 22 July 1993. That day, Major performed very well at Question Time,[99] and opened quite effectively the Social Chapter debate by attacking both John Smith and Paddy Ashdown for playing party political games with the Treaty.[100] Smith, stuck with a formal speech, performed poorly.[101] The first vote on Labour's amendment was supposedly tied at 317 votes to 317, with Betty Boothroyd bound by convention to support the government.[102] However, the government then lost its own motion rejecting the Social Chapter by 8 votes, by 324 votes to 316.[103] Having been defeated, John Major chose what became known as the 'nuclear option', in effect telling his MPs to support the Treaty without the Social Chapter, or face the prospect of a general election. The following day, the House voted again, and this time the government won comfortably, as the Tory rebels stared over the precipice, and fell back into line. George Robertson was jubilant: '. . . it will not be that press-ganged victory which will be etched into the public memory, it will be the ashen Tory faces of the night before as they were defeated resoundingly by 324 votes to 316 votes. It was the beginning of the end for Major.'[104]

Yet, even in his moment of triumph after the Social Protocol vote, Robertson recalls that Smith was reluctant to speak to the press, and he had to persuade him that he had to make a few comments after such a body-blow to the government. Smith was a House of Commons man, and saw Labour's Maastricht victory primarily as a House of Commons triumph.[105]

The following morning, when the House returned to vote through the Treaty, Smith thrived on being under-prepared, relying on only a few notes, and spoke well. Biographer Anthony Seldon also feels that the Labour leader 'completely upstaged' Major on 23 July, having 'recovered the form that had deserted him the day before'.[106] Major agrees with Seldon's view: 'I spoke poorly. John Smith did rather better.'[107]

George Robertson argues that Labour's opposition to the Maastricht Bill was 'a guerrilla campaign of huge proportions', and that the Labour Party had succeeded in inflicting a major defeat on the Major government. So proud was Robertson of his Maastricht campaign that he had a limited edition commemorative mug produced.[108] Derek Foster accurately sums up the vote's significance:

> The Government defeat in July 1993 was merely the culmination of a prolonged exercise that had begun with the paving motion. It was an enormous parliamentary success, both strategically and tactically, and John deserves much of the credit for that inspired decision to oppose the paving motion.[109]

In a wider sense, Labour's guerrilla tactics meant that ministers were deprived of time for the other workings of government. George Robertson had argued in front of the PLP a few months before: 'Every day that is spent on this legislation is a day which is not spent on some other item in their legislative programme.'[110] Moreover, the authority of the government drained away. Robertson recalls: 'John knew the damage he was inflicting because he had been in Government. We were draining away the lifeblood from the Tories.'[111] Nevertheless, the biggest single reason for the Tories' woes lay with their own rebellious back benchers, who were prepared to damage their own side to the point of distraction.

John Smith manifestly did not lead a united PLP on Maastricht, but his tactics kept Labour Party divisions within bounds, while making the Tories seem the more divided party. European enthusiasts and sceptics alike had been allowed to have their say within the PLP, acting as a safety valve. Moreover, the authority of the Major government had been sapped night after night without ever really endangering the Treaty, or damaging the close diplomatic links that Labour enjoyed in Europe.

In December 1993, the opposition pressed home its parliamentary advantage by beginning a five-month-long period of parliamentary non-co-operation. The government had announced that all the stages of the Statutory Sick Pay Bill (which transferred the responsibility for sick pay to employers) and the Social Security (Contributions) Bill (implementing a 1 per cent increase in national insurance) would be guillotined all in one day the following week. According to Derek Foster, John Smith was 'incandescent with rage' at the lack of consultation and parliamentary scrutiny. When Foster suggested that the opposition should withdraw from the normal behind-the-scenes channels of communication between the two front benches, Smith gave the go-ahead, and issued a press release to that effect.[112] It is not clear whether Smith was genuinely angry about the government's attempt to restrict debate on these two measures, or whether he saw clear political advantage in highlighting the Tory tax rises, especially in the run-up to a crucial year of local and European elections, and invented these spurious reasons. At any rate, the effect was that the opposition broke off nearly all links with the government. Henceforth, there would be no pairing for any purpose, and 'every possible parliamentary advantage would be exploited to disrupt the Government's legislative programme' until further notice.[113]

Night after night, Labour back benchers kept two to three hundred Tories out of their beds. It didn't take much organising either because MPs like Dennis Skinner and Bob Cryer loved such exercises (having engaged in similar assiduous opposition in the early 1980s). Skinner and Cryer acted as tellers, as the opposition divided the House on nearly everything, even non-contentious legislation.[114] On Thursday, 13 January 1994, the Chief Whip announced to the PLP that non-co-operation was being extended to pairing on select committees, and then thanked colleagues for their support, making it clear that there would be no attempts to keep colleagues at Westminster unnecessarily. The aim was to 'harass and detain the Tories'.[115]

In retrospect, Derek Foster claims that not only were Labour left-wingers kept busy (and therefore not stirring up trouble), it also made the opposition look effective to the party membership outside Parliament.[116] Not everyone in the PLP agreed with the strategy, however. Certain figures in the party became unhappy about the way that the Labour leadership had gone into the dispute without a clear objective, or a means of extricating itself from it. In January 1994, Ken Purchase asked what the exit strategy was, and what was 'the ulterior motive in the present campaign'. The Chief Whip replied that the aim was to stop the government 'riding roughshod over the House of Commons', and said he would keep the campaign going 'until they [the Government] came to us to seek a reasonable way of conducting the business of the House'.[117]

The ultimate problem with non-co-operation was, having started it, how did you call it off? Derek Foster and his deputy, Don Dixon, had great difficulty persuading a reluctant John Smith to wind the exercise down. It took several weeks to convince Smith. In late April 1994, Foster and Dixon eventually came up with a cosmetic package of measures in John Smith's name that he could present before the PLP along the lines of 'but for our period of non-co-operation, such-and-such wouldn't have happened'.[118] On Thursday, 28 April, the Chief Whip announced to the PLP that a number of concessions had been obtained from the government, and that the 'usual channels' had been re-opened.[119]

Derek Foster recalls his two years serving under Smith as 'the most efficient whipping system in my hands in the ten years that I was Chief Whip. It was probably the Opposition at its best.'[120] To those who claim that Smith did nothing in his first year, he had successfully harried the government over Maastricht to such an extent that their authority to govern had been sapped. Morale in the PLP had been restored, Labour back benchers had got behind their leader, and the opposition had demonstrated its fighting qualities. Yet, despite all these successes on the parliamentary front, the modernisers felt that Smith was adopting too low a public profile and failing to modernise the party sufficiently to secure guaranteed victory at a general election.

Twenty-One
JUST ONE MORE HEAVE?

WO YEARS AFTER Smith's death, Peter Mandelson upset many people
T when he claimed that John Smith believed in 'party unity, almost at any
cost, even if it meant not facing up to one or two awkward choices'.
According to Mandelson, there was a sort of '"one last heave" . . . mentality
creeping into the Party'.[1] Was John Smith's leadership, in terms of its policy,
ideology, image, style and profile all about one more heave?

Peter Mandelson was sidelined under the leadership of John Smith, who
was strongly of the view that Mandelson should serve his apprenticeship on
the back benches like everyone else. As a result of their mutual distrust,
Mandelson's talents were deployed at the margins. Newspaper stories
appeared in the summer and autumn of 1992 suggesting that Blair and Brown
should lead the party, while Smith and Beckett were 'presented as dull and
inadequate'.[2] Smith was widely portrayed as the man who should have fought
the 1992 election, but not the man for 1996–7. The media speculated endlessly
as to whether Labour should now 'skip a generation', as the Conservatives had
done in selecting John Major.[3] 'Friends' of Tony Blair were quoted, nearly
always anonymously. As one anonymous front bencher put it: 'It will be our
bank manager versus their bank manager [John Major]. The question I ask is:
how do we persuade the public to risk moving their accounts?'[4] In fact, John
Smith was *ideally* suited for a battle with John Major on the centre ground of
British politics, but that didn't stop Mandelson from spinning his stories,
which had the effect of winding up both wings of the party.

At Smith's very first NEC meeting on becoming leader, it was agreed that
members of the national executive would wind up the debates. According to
Tony Benn, Dennis Skinner had commented 'very sarcastically': '"What about
the beautiful people? Aren't they going to be allowed on the platform? Tony
Blair surely because he's after John Smith's job." Clare Short said, "We know
he's after John's job, we all know that".'[5]

Setting aside the question of 'spin', Peter Mandelson's principled belief,
shared by an impressive array of people in the party, including Kinnock, Blair,
Brown, Jack Straw and Philip Gould, was that unless Labour's modernisation

accelerated, it risked being beaten yet again at the next general election.[6] A fifth defeat in a row might finish the party for good. As Tony Blair put it in an article for *Fabian Review*:

> The sun of opinion polls comes out and warms its back. The sky looks cloudless. The breeze of public hostility is now gentle. Why go through the hassle and uncertainty of moving to unfamiliar territory? So it puts its feet up and relaxes. And it waits. Until the next shower. It was his determination to break this pattern that led Neil Kinnock to push through party reform.[7]

In private, Patricia Hewitt recalls Blair saying: 'We have to make changes *now* and be vocal about it despite our leader, because otherwise there will be nothing to inherit.'[8] Peter Mandelson therefore seems to have chivvied Gordon Brown and Tony Blair to speak up in favour of the modernisation agenda at shadow Cabinet and NEC meetings.

Neil Kinnock couldn't interfere too much in case Smith's people accused him of disloyalty. Smith's genuine anger over Neil Kinnock's intervention at Luigi's had taken some months to subside. But apart from his enthusiastic letter to the *Financial Times* calling for Labour to support the single currency (see chapter 19), Kinnock stayed out of the fray during the 1992 leadership contest. Thereafter Kinnock encouraged Blair and Brown behind the scenes, persuading them to press Smith to pursue more vigorously the modernisation agenda that he considered to be his legacy, and necessary to winning the election. Charles Clarke claims that Neil Kinnock thought Brown and Blair were too loyal to Smith, adding, 'and yes, there were a number of occasions when Tony and Gordon agreed with Neil's analysis, but wouldn't say so'.[9]

All along Neil Kinnock's basic objection to John was that he thought John was lazy. Just after Neil stood down from the leadership, Neil thought what a rare treat it would be to go the cinema in the afternoon. As Neil and Glenys sat down to watch the film, Neil noticed a man in front of him eating an ice cream. It was John Smith.[10] However, from the moment Smith became leader, Kinnock gave him his full loyalty. Indeed, Roy Hattersley claims that in the last year of his life Smith became 'a great Kinnock admirer, fatally won over by the impeccable loyalty which the old leader showed to the new'.[11]

Nevertheless, allies of Kinnock pressed for further and faster modernisation. In November 1992, Nick Raynsford wrote an article for *Fabian Review*, entitled 'Sleepwalking into Oblivion?', criticising Smith's soporific leadership, and urging a more radical approach.[12] Stuart Hall was more fundamental in his criticisms:

Mr Smith is an able technician. He does not have any feel for how strategy and the construction of social constituencies of support match up, or for wider social and cultural themes. He is unlikely to drive through the Party the change in the culture of Labourism that would give realignment depth and substance.[13]

One didn't need to be a moderniser to be a critic of John Smith's leadership. The journalist Colin Brown claimed there was a widespread view in the party that Smith was, 'too conservative, too old-fashioned – too Scottish – to carry the South of England with Labour'.[14] Writing in 1993, Peter Shore considered Smith's 'Scottishness' a potential flaw:

It is difficult indeed for Scots, in their almost Nordic political culture where Labour and social democracy are still dominant, to realise the extent of the alienation in middle and southern England that still exists between the Labour Party and the electorate. In Scotland it may well be that 'one more heave' at the next election is all that is required – particularly under a more confident and experienced Leader, a man of settled convictions and natural moderation – whereas in England, a new breakthrough based on the appeal of new policies and a restatement of purpose is urgently required. In Scotland, Labour has conquered politically. But in England, the pursuit of power cannot be successful without first winning hearts and minds.[15]

Partly based on his own bitter experiences at the hands of the English electorate, Neil Kinnock also believed that Smith's 'Scottishness' 'would prove his greatest weakness'.[16] Even Smith's great ally, Roy Hattersley describes him as 'an emotional Scotsman'.[17] On one occasion, John and Roy were in Haymarket for the Edinburgh Festival, and Roy commented that he had never realised before just how continental Edinburgh was, and how he could now see the difference between Scotland and England. Smith's reply is said to have been: 'If you didn't know that you must be a f****** idiot!'[18] When criticised by what he referred to as 'the London papers' for promoting too many Scots to senior shadow Cabinet posts, Smith had once declared, 'There's no such thing as too many Scots.'[19]

Could Labour convert its electoral success with the middle classes in Scotland to winning them over south of the border? In September 1990, Smith seemed less than emphatic: 'The Party in Scotland has shown that we can win over areas as prosperous as those in England which we need to win over. People are wondering whether we can develop a southern strategy. I think we can.'[20]

Writing in July 1993, Peter Riddell argued that because the Labour leader had grown up in the Scottish Labour establishment, 'At heart, Smith believes that everything would be all right if England were like Scotland.'[21]

Another group of Smith's critics emerged on Labour's soft left, where people wanted to break free from the perceived shackles of the Kinnock period, and have a real discussion over policy. Much ideological discussion took place in the Tribune Group. Peter Hain and Roger Berry called for an abandonment of the monetarist orthodoxies inherent in the Maastricht Treaty.[22] In July 1993, the Tribune Group of Labour MPs gave the go-ahead to a Keynesian economic strategy document – *What's Left? The Future of Labour* – by Hain and Berry, but publication was delayed because of explicit criticism of the shadow Cabinet team in earlier drafts. By November 1993, loyalist elements in the Tribune Group exacted their revenge on Hain, ousting him from his position as secretary.[23] Hain claimed he was a victim of a battle being fought in the party between 'those who think we can slip into power by default and by not offending anybody and those who think we have to offer a radical alternative'.[24]

Bryan Gould shared Hain's view that Labour was being insufficiently radical in the wake of its fourth electoral defeat.[25] Gould established the Full Employment Forum, officially launched on Saturday, 3 July 1993, with the help of John Edmonds, economists from Cambridge, and other Keynesian parliamentarians such as Austin Mitchell.[26] The Full Employment Forum made very little headway.

Two very important factors impinge. Firstly, Smith's time as Labour leader was in the first half of a Parliament, when the leader of the opposition's main priorities are regrouping his or her party, before the second half of a Parliament when the policies of the opposition begin to be sold to the wider electorate.[27] Both phases were planned for under Smith's leadership, but sadly, only one was implemented. Secondly, those who criticised Smith's low profile, especially during the summer recesses, came mainly from the metropolitan elite based in London, who never fully appreciated the fact that Smith lived and worked in Scotland.[28]

In truth, Smith did have a strategy for his first two years as Labour leader. In the first year, his speeches focused on constitutional change. In the second year, the main public thrust was economic, culminating in accusations that Major had deceived the public during the 1992 general election campaign by promising not to increase taxes. Gordon Brown played a key part in the VAT on fuel campaign in the summer of 1993.[29] In the autumn, Brown fleshed out Labour's economic alternative in a series of speeches and press conferences, backed up by extensive opinion polling. The overall aim was to develop a 'central positive, long term message' on the economy.[30] The next phase, due to start in June 1994, setting out Labour's values to the electorate, would have been far more positive, and far more directed to the country at large. Smith died before that phase got under way. Privately, just before John died, he and Margaret Beckett had both agreed to take on a higher public profile: 'That was the next step,' she recalls.[31]

Only two weeks after Labour's shattering 1992 defeat, Smith re-emphasised his continued commitment to a devolved settlement in Scotland. In a speech to the Scottish Trades Union Congress (STUC) general council dinner, he argued that 75 per cent of the Scottish electorate had voted for political parties committed to constitutional change at the 1992 election:

> I believe, as the election indicated, that there is a strong and consistent majority for the proposals for a Scottish Parliament advanced in the [Scottish Constitutional] Convention. It must be our continuing commitment to see these proposals brought to active fulfilment. For me, in a personal sense, it is very much unfinished business. I had the privilege and the responsibility under the last Labour Government, of piloting the Scotland Act through the House of Commons.[32]

But Smith's plans for constitutional change went far beyond Scotland, and were to be extended across the whole country. He elaborated on this theme in a speech to Charter 88 on 1 March 1993, in which he attacked the 'relentless centralisation of power' under the Conservatives that had rendered Westminster 'dictatorial and remote'.[33] His proposals – including incorporating the European Convention on Human Rights into British law, devolution for Scotland and Wales, House of Lords reform, a freedom of information bill and regional government – were quite radical, with the possible exception of electoral reform. Smith awaited the outcome of a working party on electoral reform, which had been established under the leadership of Neil Kinnock in December 1990, under the chairmanship of Raymond Plant, professor of politics at Southampton University.[34]

In the run-up to the 1992 general election, political imperatives alone might have driven Kinnock and Smith to seek possible accommodations with the Liberal Democrats. Andy McSmith claims that Smith (as shadow Chancellor) spoke to Paddy Ashdown in a taxi in May 1991 on the way to a television studio, and said he was willing to concede electoral reform for the House of Commons in return for Liberal Democrat support in the event of a hung Parliament.[35] But there is no record of the meeting in Ashdown's published diaries. Indeed, during a gathering of the Bilderberg Group in Spain in May 1989, during which Ashdown and Smith drank copious amounts of brandy, the shadow Chancellor rejected the idea of electoral pacts, believing that Labour would win in its own right.[36]

However, Smith was not entirely comfortable with the first-past-the-post system. During his campaign for the leadership in 1992, Smith indicated that he did not like the one-party system in the south of England (Conservative dominance) and in central Scotland (Labour dominance) produced by the voting system, but made clear that he wanted to maintain the constituency link.[37] Later on, he was particularly annoyed after one Prime Minister's Questions when John Major had claimed that the first-past-the-post system was 'satisfactory' when the Prime Minister had been elected on only 42 per cent of the vote; while Smith agreed with first-past-the-post at Westminster, he thought it was absolutely the right of the electorate, not the politicians, to decide whether they thought it 'satisfactory' through a referendum.[38] But in his first eight months as leader, Smith held to the view that electoral reform was 'more complicated' than other aspects of constitutional change and that: 'There's a good and healthy debate going on within the Party and I don't want to prejudge it.'[39]

Jeff Rooker, Labour MP for Birmingham Perry Barr, chairman of the Labour Campaign for Electoral Reform, and a member of the Plant Commission,[40] had unsuccessfully argued for a top-up system of about 100–150 members to make the supplementary vote system more proportional. In December 1992, Rooker and Smith engaged in a robust exchange of letters. Having discovered from an article in the *Financial Times* that Smith was intent on making a major speech attacking Britain's 'creaking constitution'[41] (Smith's aforementioned speech to Charter 88), Rooker wrote expressing concern that his leader might omit any reference to possible reform of the electoral system: 'I am not looking for you to be specific but I genuinely believe that your comments will not carry weight unless you at least refer to the matter – which you neglected to do at Annual Conference [1992].'[42]

On 15 December 1992, Smith wrote back complaining that Rooker's letter had been given to the press, adding curtly: 'I do not really think this is how you should communicate with me.'[43] Rooker sent Smith's letter straight back, and scribbled on it angrily: 'The only copy is in my office – no press or colleague has seen it – so who's peddling this nonsense?'[44] In October 1993, Rooker was dropped from his post as Labour's higher education spokesperson for advocating charging students for tuition fees, turning down Smith's offer of a defence portfolio.[45]

Smith's decision not to refer too closely to the thorny issue of electoral reform also left him open to Tory attack. On 19 March 1993, after the Charter 88 speech, John Patten, the Education Secretary, of all people wrote to the Labour leader to 'complain':

You skate over the whole issue of electoral reform – devoting only one paragraph of your speech to the issue – conveniently hiding behind the Plant Commission enquiry. Yet this has not deterred a number of your shadow cabinet members from speaking out either in favour or against electoral reform. What is your view please? I think people will take a dim view of a party leader who offers a new constitutional settlement yet can't make up his mind on whether or not he favours electoral reform.[46]

As with many other controversial issues such as Maastricht and Bosnia, the PLP debated electoral reform and the findings of the Plant Report thoroughly. Proponents of electoral reform, including Dr Tony Wright, the Birmingham academic-turned Labour MP, argued that 'to retreat now from the point we have reached – that first-past-the-post is no longer good enough – would be an act of electoral suicide'.[47] On the other side of the debate, Derek Fatchett,[48] chairman of the first-past-the-post group of Labour MPs, warned of 'coalition by stealth'. Gerald Kaufman argued that the party was 'spending too much time on irrelevancies such as this'. Moreover: 'Who is going to volunteer to be replaced in a Labour Cabinet to make way for coalition partners?' Meanwhile, John Spellar[49] and Bruce Grocott[50] appeared to compete to see who could condemn PR in the bluntest fashion, the former arguing that 'it is not our job to prop up the Liberals', while the latter left no doubt as to his views: 'Let us kill the debate stone dead.'[51]

John Smith's response to Plant, according to Tony Benn's diaries, was that 'The House of Commons should be left as it is'.[52] On 19 May 1993, after an NEC meeting,[53] Smith pledged publicly that a future Labour government would put the issue of electoral reform to a binding national referendum, but he also added: 'As the Plant Committee acknowledges, there is no intrinsically superior electoral system and I see no reason why we should make a change unless the alternative is clearly preferable. I remain unconvinced of the need for a change in the system of voting for the House of Commons.'[54]

Any subsequent confusion or lack of clarity over Smith's position on electoral reform arose from the fact that he simultaneously supported a referendum on PR while remaining personally opposed to it.[55] Smith did not want to rule out electoral reform altogether because powerful figures in his party, particularly Robin Cook, supported it enthusiastically. Nor did he want to alienate Liberal Democrat voters. So his solution was to support the idea of a referendum, and Margaret Beckett seems to have played a key role in persuading John to agree to this policy.[56] Paddy Ashdown was unimpressed, dubbing the referendum pledge a 'fudge'.[57] It probably was, but it needed to be, given the extent of the splits in the PLP over the issue.[58]

However, Smith was far more relaxed about conceding a form of proportional representation system in Scotland, partly because he knew he could
rely on Donald Dewar and Murray Elder (heavily involved in the Scottish
Constitutional Convention) not to do anything 'too daft'. Dewar also
supported first-past-the-post but, like Smith, he had been scarred by the 1979
referendum result. Dewar was keen to achieve a system that gave adequate
representation to the rest of Scotland outside Glasgow and Edinburgh.[59]
Labour eventually supported the Additional Member System (AMS),
combining 73 first-past-the-post seats (comprising the 72 Westminster
constituencies, plus one constituency for Orkney and Shetland, rather than
the combined constituency of Orkney and Shetland for Westminster
elections), and 56 regional top-up seats, seven for each of Scotland's eight
European electoral regions.[60]

Andy McSmith argues that during the 'Smith interregnum', very little
happened in the area of developing party policy: 'This was a deliberate tactic
on Smith's part. Supremely confident of winning, he decided to proceed by
setting up a network of commissions and committees to work on ideas.'[61]
Smith's main policy initiative in his first year as leader was to establish the
Social Justice Commission. He had first alluded to the idea of a commission at
the start of his leadership campaign on 30 April 1992, foreseeing an
independent body comprised of 'specialists and representatives of the
majority of the public who want a fairer society' and to 'identify a fairer tax
and benefits system that will stand the test of time'.[62]

In autumn 1992, Donald Dewar, now Labour's shadow social security
spokesperson, invited Gordon Borrie to become chairman of the Social Justice
Commission.[63] Borrie had worked as director general of the Office of Fair
Trading (OFT), and came into contact with Smith after 1979 when Smith was
appointed shadow spokesperson on Trade. His clearest memory of Smith
dates from November 1991, when the two accompanied Michael Montague to
a Royal Command Performance. During the evening, Diana Ross came down
from the stage and introduced herself to several members of the audience.
Borrie recalls Smith cringing in the front row, 'cowering with shyness. It was
clear that light entertainment was not his thing.'[64]

Donald Dewar indicated to Borrie that he and Smith wanted to appoint
Patricia Hewitt as his deputy. Hewitt, formerly of the shadow
Communications Agency (see chapter 15), had become deputy director at the
Institute for Public Policy Research (IPPR), and possessed a great deal of
expertise in the field of welfare reform.[65] Her Labour Party background was in

contrast to Borrie's perceived 'independence'. Borrie was dyed-in-the-wool Labour, but independent in that he was not wedded to one view.[66] Borrie had fourteen colleagues on the commission – or fifteen if its diligent and influential secretary, David Miliband, son of the radical socialist Ralph Miliband is included – drawn from all sectors of the professional world: two professors of economics, two Liberals, one representative each from business and the unions, a vicar, a journalist, a philosopher, two social policy experts, and three people associated with welfare pressure groups.[67]

Borrie recalls that he wanted a wide-ranging review, adding: 'Nothing was off-limits – even the future of universality was considered a subject for debate.'[68] The thinking was that major economic and social changes had occurred since the Beveridge Report 50 years before, and the commission wanted to reflect this changing world. For example, occupational pensions did not feature prominently in Beveridge's day, but they became important by the early 1990s. As the commission's blurb put it, its aim was to promote social justice[69] by developing a long-term strategy to cope with the three major revolutions – economic, social and political – that had altered Britain's society over the previous thirty years.[70] Borrie reflects: 'We were not providing a Party manifesto, but we wanted to produce a well researched, detailed background paper on a range of subjects.'[71] The Social Justice Commission was formally launched at a small press conference on 17 December 1992, attended by John Smith, Margaret Beckett and the other commission members.

Borrie and Hewitt maintained regular contact with Donald Dewar, and with Pat McFadden, whose portfolio in Smith's policy unit included social security and employment issues, but neither interfered directly – they 'never banged the table'.[72] Nor did Smith interfere once he was reassured that the commission was working away satisfactorily. After two interim reports were published in July 1993, Smith expressed his enthusiasm for them, and recommended that members of the shadow Cabinet should read them. Both *The Justice Gap* and *Social Justice in a Changing World* were very slim documents, merely outlining broad principles, rather than going into great detail. Borrie believes Smith wanted a broad outline all along, because when they met up again in the autumn of 1993, his 'strong recollection' is that Smith became afraid that 'the devil might lie in the detail' of the final report. Borrie feels that Smith feared the political dangers that lay in appearing to commit the party to specific policies.[73] Smith's eyebrows were raised when the commission produced a series of issue papers in advance of the final report, mentioning such specific things as the suggested level of child benefit, and recommending that it should be taxed when received by the better off.[74] The commission's broad set of conclusions – set out in *Social Justice: Strategies of National Renewal* – were published in October 1994, five months after Smith's death. Its view chimed with Smith's belief that social justice and economic efficiency could go hand in hand.

Subsequently, Borrie has found that the Blair government have not viewed his report as a valuable resource. 'He [Blair] has not said anything against it, but it never gets mentioned.' By contrast, Borrie feels that Gordon Brown's 'genuine preference' is that social justice and economic prosperity should go hand in hand, and that Brown is much more of an upholder of social justice than Tony Blair.[75]

Just as the Labour leader was offended by social injustice at home, so abroad Smith wanted to close the gap between the rich industrialised North and the poorer countries in the South by updating some of the ideas first expressed in the Brandt Commission Report.[76] The Socialist International had asked Smith to prepare a report along these lines, and the Labour leader was very keen to do so. Indeed, the leader's office was increased in size to make it possible.[77] Smith aimed to outline a series of reforms to international institutions in the form of a Penguin paperback. One of his most radical ideas was to call for the Group of Seven (G7) (now known as the Group of Eight or G8 following the addition of Russia) industrialised countries to become a permanent core of an economic equivalent of the UN Security Council, expanding its membership to include some of the larger Asian-Pacific and Latin American countries. Smith also advocated merging two of the Bretton Woods institutions (the global economic structures established in 1944) – the International Monetary Fund (IMF) and the World Bank – under the wing of this new Economic Council. However, after Smith died, David Ward was informed that Tony Blair did not want to run with these ideas.[78]

On 4 November 1993, while giving the Robert Kennedy Memorial Lecture in the Oxford Union, Smith gave vent to another innovative policy idea, suggesting that the permanent membership of the UN Security Council be increased to include Germany and Japan, and possibly India, Brazil and Nigeria.[79]

On the domestic front, Smith supported the creation of a Ministry of Justice to bring legal issues under the same department, and often repeated his intention of enshrining the independence of the Central Statistical Office in statute. Before he died, Smith had also agreed to the idea of a Monetary Policy Committee, which would provide 'open and transparent' advice to the Chancellor of the Exchequer, rather than the present system where the 'seven wise men' give guidance to the Governor of the Bank of England.[80] It also seems likely that Smith would have been more radical than Blair in opening up government, especially in the area of reform of the Official Secrets Act.

In June 1993, John Smith established an Environmental Commission to look into green issues.[81] It was not a party commission, nor was it an independent commission along the lines of the Social Justice Commission, but rather a hybrid of both: Chris Smith, Labour's environmental protection spokesperson, chaired a nineteen-strong committee whose secretariat comprised Chris's staff, but also included environmental experts without party affiliations as well as MEPs, MPs, trade unionists, NEC members and Labour councillors. The Labour Party also made submissions to the Commission. Chris recalls that John was 'very willing to delegate', and describes him as being 'interested, but not super-interested' in green issues.[82] But it says something for Smith's commitment to the process that he attended the launch of the commission, and indeed opened the all-day discussion on 7 June 1993.[83]

Far from having a cupboard bare, by the time John Smith died, and as Anderson and Mann point out, Labour had 'more-or-less comprehensive policies' on constitutional reform, Europe, education, transport, defence, and the work of the Social Justice Commission was nearing completion.[84] By the early spring of 1994, Andrew Graham, now re-engaged more fully as Smith's economic adviser having dealt with internal college commitments at Balliol (see chapter 18), had begun to have detailed policy discussions with Smith, Robin Cook and John Prescott as lead-ins to meetings of the Joint Policy Committee.[85] Everybody was getting geared up for the two-year lead-up to the general election when John Smith died.

Anderson and Mann conclude that New Labour's policies, with the major exception of education, were 'different only in small ways from what Labour would have produced had Smith not died'.[86] In July 1993, when the NEC debated a statement on higher education, Smith and Gordon Brown defended the idea of student grants rather than loans or a graduate tax, while Kinnock felt that student loans should be part of the debate. Smith's more cautious line prevailed.[87] However, in her controversial Green Paper on higher education, Ann Taylor, Labour's education spokesperson, aired various ideas, including introducing student loans, but within an appendix 'to distance the Party from them'. Unfortunately, the paper was leaked to the press, attracting a fair amount of controversy. According to the Minutes of the Joint Policy Committee:

> There was considerable concern that, even as drafted, the paper leaned too heavily against the grant-based approach which Labour had long

advocated. Grants, it was argued, were desirable because they were a targeted benefit, socially just, and an important means of access to less wealthy students.

It was recognised that there was a need to be able to float new ideas, and stimulate debate, without undermining support, and committing to policies before they had been fully considered.[88]

The two main historical debates concerning Labour's economic policy after 1992, as they relate to John Smith, are the extent to which Gordon Brown, the new shadow Chancellor, was in control of economic policy after 1992, and the degree to which there was disagreement (and indeed agreement) between the two men on how to proceed. From the outset, Smith appointed Brown chairman of the Economic Policy Commission, a joint committee comprising shadow Cabinet and NEC members. The EPC would determine the direction of Labour's economic policy.[89]

Hilary Armstrong believes that after 1992, 'John and Gordon worked closely together, but Gordon did get frustrated that John was too slow'.[90] Murray Elder agrees, and believes that, had Smith lived, there would have been 'very considerable tensions' between John and Gordon over whether to commit the Labour Party to freeze public spending at Tory levels in the first two years of a Labour government. John was much more of the view that incoming ministers in a new Labour government would need a bit of money to spend after eighteen years, whereas Gordon would have fought that view 'tooth and nail . . . there would have been a fierce battle'. Labour needed to be 'much fiercer'.[91] Hilary Armstrong rightly sums up Gordon's reaction to the 1992 shadow Budget as being 'they'll [the Tories] get us come what may', so he was determined that there would be no early commitments on spending.[92] Brown understood the central lesson about the 1992 shadow Budget: Labour could not afford to be explicit about what it intended to do in terms of public spending commitments. His whole strategy relied upon building confidence among the electorate and the money markets in Labour's ability to run the economy.[93]

Gordon Brown claims that on becoming shadow Chancellor he told Smith that he was scrapping the shadow Budget. Paul Routledge's account, based on an interview with Brown in July 1997, is carefully phrased. Cryptically, Brown pointed out that 'people were very resistant to change'.[94] One of 'those people' must have included Smith, because in June 1992 he had been telling interviewers: 'I don't retreat an inch from the shadow Budget' and 'I'm slightly puzzled when it has come from people allegedly on the left.'[95]

Roy Hattersley argues that it would have been in John's temperament to have interfered on Gordon's patch: John had been shadow Chancellor immediately before, and had been Gordon's boss as shadow Chief Secretary to the Treasury, from 1987–9.[96] Lord Desai firmly believes that John Smith was in charge of economic policy after 1992: 'As Prime Minister, Blair has behaved as an extra Foreign Secretary. If John had lived, he would have been an extra shadow Chancellor – Gordon wouldn't have got away with it.'[97] Desai also believes that, had John Smith lived, there would have been no need to stick to the Tory spending limits: 'He [Smith] may have believed in progressive taxation in a Croslandite sense but he was a fiscally prudent person – fiscal prudence was John's other name.'[98]

So much of the macro-economic strategy of New Labour has been about the need to control spending, rather than grasping the nettle in relation to redistribution. Once the voters were persuaded of Labour's economic competence, and as economic growth was achieved, Brown implemented mildly redistributive tax policies without too many people noticing, but he has resolutely not touched the basic rate of income tax, and any discussion on this subject has been closed down instantly.[99]

John Smith retained a moral view that the better off should pay more in income tax. Indeed, David Ward argues that Smith would have eventually agreed to ditch the other aspects of his shadow Budget – including the spending limits – in return for a top rate of income tax of 50 per cent.[100] But Brown saw all too clearly the political dangers of committing Labour too early in the 1992 Parliament to a higher top rate of tax. As he told a special pre-Budget meeting of the PLP in November 1993: 'If we committed ourselves now to raising the top rate of income tax, it would pre-empt other policy decisions and future events, and also the Tories would seize on it and say Labour was committed to higher taxes. We should convince people that we would tax for specific purposes.'[101]

Brown therefore spent a lot of time downplaying the idea of Labour as a high-tax party. On 9 November 1992, Brown had launched Labour's *Campaign for Recovery*, a series of measures to combat the recession, but he made a point of saying that he had scrapped the 1992 shadow Budget when he said 'we are not proposing to raise tax and national insurance at this stage.'[102] By 26 January 1994, Brown was telling Radio Four's *Today* programme: 'We will only spend what we can afford to spend.'[103] Smith backed him up by warning shadow Cabinet colleagues not to make unauthorised spending commitments. Brown's unswerving financial rectitude dented his chances of becoming leader in preference to Blair, because the shadow Chancellor's pronouncements in defence of the ERM and on taxes and spending alienated both the left and the traditionalists in the party, while it was altogether easier for Blair to posture about tackling not just crime, but the causes of crime.[104] In the autumn of 1993, Brown had for the first time failed to gain one of the two top spots in the shadow Cabinet elections.[105]

The other part of Brown's strategy was to try to shift Labour's emphasis on tax away from increasing tax rates to closing tax loopholes. In *Campaign for Recovery*, the shadow Chancellor proposed the introduction a 'windfall tax', a one-off grab of the profits of the privatised utilities. According to Brown, Smith backed the idea in the face of opposition from 'most of my shadow Cabinet colleagues'.[106]

Would Smith have supported Brown's eventual policy of Bank of England independence? Chris Smith believes that while John would have resisted an independent Bank of England in 1994, he feels it is an open question whether Gordon Brown would have convinced him some time in the run-up to the 1997 general election.[107] It seems unlikely that John Smith would have been comfortable with the idea of giving away so much economic power, given his strong previous attachment to the idea of democratic oversight of Central Bank decisions (see chapter 13). Roy Hattersley agrees that John wouldn't have been keen on the idea of an independent Bank of England, though Hattersley is now a convert.[108] Lord Desai adds: 'John's principles were at a deeper level. He was not an instrumentalist. In 1994, he would have been opposed, but who knows what his position would have been by 1997.'[109] With the benefit of hindsight, Gordon Brown's decision to hand over independence to the Bank of England has proved to be a great success.

Smith also supported the idea of moving the party away from its old policy of nationalisation. In March 1993, Tony Benn noted in his diary after an encounter in the House of Commons tearoom with three Scottish Labour MPs[110] that 'Smith is cutting up very rough with any Scottish front bencher who disagrees with him about public ownership.'[111] Smith also embraced enthusiastically the idea of public-private partnerships. In February 1993, in a speech to the Local Government conference in Bournemouth, Smith referred to the need for 'an active and creative partnership between the public and private sectors'.[112] A year later, on 20 February 1994, Gordon Brown, Robin Cook (Trade and Industry) and John Prescott (Employment) launched *Financing Infrastructure Investment*. The 6,000-word document proposed introducing public-private partnership for investment in the National Health Service. All remaining state-owned industries would become 'public-interest companies', but operating according to the normal demands of the private sector.[113]

Under Smith's leadership, Brown had dropped the shadow Budget (without saying precisely what Labour's tax plans were), and shadow Cabinet colleagues were more or less forbidden to make any spending commitments. As Paul Anderson and Nyta Mann point out: 'Gordon Brown had firmly established both the broad outline of economic policy and much of its detail.'[114] Brown was the economic architect of New Labour before the term was invented, the man who drafted the initial drawings, submitted the necessary planning applications, but the question remains, would he have got all his ideas past Smith, the planning officer?[115]

Patrick Seyd and Paul Whiteley maintain that Smith would not have agreed to stick to the Conservative's spending commitments in Labour's first two years in office. Nor, they believe would Smith have ruled out raising income tax rates for the lifetime of a Parliament. They conclude: 'Overall, it is fairly clear that Smith's Labour Party was not New Labour.'[116] It is very difficult to tell what Smith would have done, especially on the spending commitments: of course, no one in 1994 (before Smith died) was arguing that the Conservative spending commitments for 1996–7 and beyond should be adhered to. On Seyd and Whiteley's second point, Murray Elder believes that Smith might have ruled out further income tax increases during the lifetime of a Parliament after an initial 50 per cent top rate of tax had been introduced.[117]

The other main criticism of Smith as leader is that he lacked a really coherent intellectual vision, a defining set of ideas. Shortly after Smith's death, Ben Pimlott argued that, while Smith had 'certainly made the Labour Party a more united and happier place than it had been for a generation', there had been 'quite a lot of reason for disquiet'. Pimlott remarked upon an anecdote from Martin Gilbert's multi-volume biography of Churchill,[118] when Churchill sent back a pudding to a chef: 'The trouble with this pudding is that it has no theme.' Labour, Pimlott argued, lacked 'a politically and intellectually satisfactory theme'.[119] He could hardly have been more wrong.

Three of the four books written about John Smith since his death have attempted to draw together his political ideas into a coherent whole. Just before Smith died, Christopher Bryant[120] edited a series of philosophical essays based around the idea of Smith's Christian Socialism, taking its title, *Reclaiming the Ground,* from Smith's famous Tawney lecture (see below).[121] Secondly, shortly after Smith's death, Gordon Brown, in *Life and Soul of the Party,* summarised 'John Smith's Socialism' through a careful analysis of his writings and speeches.[122] Thirdly, in 2001, Brian Brivati compiled a collection of his speeches entitled *Guiding Light.* In a sense, all three contributions seek to continue Smith's legacy by emphasising, quite rightly, his commitment to social justice.

But is there John Smithism? The short answer to this question is no. Smith was a political pragmatist by temperament and training. John McCluskey points out: 'If you are an advocate, you can't allow yourself to dwell on a case. Indeed, after a case, you get rid of the papers and send them back.'[123] Murray Elder was constantly frustrated after John had given a good speech on a subject. When he asked his leader, ' "Shouldn't you follow that up?", John would say "It's finished, dealt with." His mind was always on the next issue.'[124] Moreover, whenever John had been asked as a politician to expound his 'big idea', he had nearly always replied, 'A Labour Government'.[125]

John Smith had learned a very simple yet fundamental set of values on his father's knee, such as the idea that the better off should pay considerably more in tax, and that children were best educated in the comprehensive system. He had also encountered ordinary people in his childhood, as an advocate and as the MP for a deprived area, and took the straightforward view that it was intolerable that there was such a thing as the stinking rich when the poor were so poor. Smith saw these values represented in the Labour Party's socialist approach, and joined the party at an early age because he felt it would best forward the idea of social justice, even if Smith had not yet enunciated that term. These gut convictions meant that Smith was someone who never doubted that Thatcherism was just plain wrong, and that socialism could provide a viable alternative.

What constituted Smith's religious beliefs? Derry Irvine is firmly of the view that John was 'always a Christian', and that he saw his faith as 'an effective operational way of life'.[126] Jimmy Gordon, a Roman Catholic, agrees that John had always been religiously minded. Both Derry and Jimmy acknowledge that John was not devout at Glasgow University, and only turned to the Kirk in later life.[127] Nevertheless, Smith developed a high regard for Scottish Presbyterianism in general, seeing the Kirk both as a democratic institution and an historical force for good in such areas as social work.[128]

Friends agree that for most of his life, John, like most good Scots Presbyterians, saw religion as largely a private matter between himself and God.[129] It is not widely known that Elizabeth and the three girls did not accompany him to church on Sundays (although the three girls had all gone to the local Sunday school at that period of John's life when he personally was not a regular attender). In later life though, Elizabeth recalls that John would pop out of the house at five minutes to eleven and come back from Cluny church at twelve o'clock. Religion was such an intensely personal thing for

'It grew like Topsy – husbands, wives, sweethearts – even the dog came along.' A large walking party, Arran, August 1983, including (back row from left): Menzies Campbell, Dr Mike Ryan, John Smith, Murray Elder, Jimmy Gordon. Middle row: Elizabeth, Jane, Catherine and Sarah Smith. Front row: Gavin Laird, Gordon Brown, Maggie Rae, Alan Haworth. (Supplied by Lord MacLean.)

John's office (1987–88) was so small he had to ask his secretary Ann Barrett to move out of her seat so that he could get documents out of the drawers. (With kind permission of Ann Barrett.)

John meeting with the Japanese Prime Minister, Mr Toshiki Kaifu in his office in Tokyo, January 1991. (Reproduced by kind permission of David Ward.)

Margaret Beckett, David Ward and John Smith outside the entrance to the British Embassy in Paris (Rue Faubourg St Honore) standing at the spot 'where Mrs Thatcher fell', February 1992. (Supplied by David Ward.)

Trying to be cheerful after the disappointment of the 1992 General Election. John Smith at a thank you lunch for the Shadow Treasury campaign staff on 10 April 1992. From left: Emma Maclennan, Sheila Watson, John Smith, Margaret Baeckett, David Ward, Yvette Cooper, Nick Pecorelli, Karen Gardiner, Dan Corry and Andrew Graham. (Supplied by David Ward.)

John on his 100th Munro ascent, chatting to climbers on their way down the Buachaille Etive Mor, September 1992. (Supplied by Ranald MacLean.)

With the whole family at St James's Park on becoming Labour leader in July 1992.
From left: Catherine, Elizabeth, Jane, John and Sarah.
(Courtesy of Russell Boyce/Reuter.)

Former Labour leaders – James Callaghan, Michael Foot and Harold Wilson – join
John Smith to mark the retirement of Cledwyn Hughes (centre) as the Labour
leader in the Lords, autumn 1992. (David Clark is in the background on the extreme
left.) (Reproduced by kind permission of Lord Graham of Edmonton.)

John with Ivor Richard, the new opposition leader in the Lords, autumn 1992 (James Callaghan is in the background on the left of the picture). (Supplied by Lord Graham of Edmonton.)

David Blunkett and John, autumn 1992. (Supplied by Lord Graham of Edmonton.)

At Madame Tussaud's, 1993. From left: David Hill, Meta Ramsay, Ann Barrett, Jenny Stringer, John Smith, wax model, Hilary Coffman, Delyth Evans, Pat McFadden, Elizabeth Barlow, David Ward (hidden). (Supplied by Ann Barrett.)

Jack Cunningham and John Smith meet their hero, Nelson Mandela, May 1993. (Courtesy of empics.)

John's last Sunday, spent with Lanarkshire politicians past and present at the Blantyre Miners' Welfare Club, 8 May 1994. Standing (left to right): Dr Jeremy Bray MP (Motherwell South), William McKelvey MP (Kilmarnock), Dr John Reid MP (Motherwell North), John Smith MP (Monklands East), Tommy McAvoy MP (Rutherglen), Tom Clarke MP (Monklands West), Adam Ingram MP (East Kilbride), George Robertson MP (Hamilton). Front (seated): Rt Hon Peggy Herbison (Smith's predecessor in Lanarkshire North) and Ken Collins MEP (Strathclyde East).
(Supplied by Lord Robertson of Port Ellen, © Contrast Photography.)

The late Scottish First Minister Donald Dewar accompanied by Baroness Elizabeth Smith, widow of former Labour Leader John Smith, visit the grave of John Smith in the graveyard of the Abbey on the Isle of Iona. The grave bears the inscription 'An honest man's the noblest work of God'.
(Courtesy of empics.)

John Smith speaks at the Labour Party Conference in Brighton, 28 September 1993. (Courtesy of empics.)

John that his daughters would later ask their father why they had not been brought up in the Church. Elizabeth recalls that John was strongly of the view that religion and politics should be kept separate. Christians did not *have* to be socialists, nor should socialists assume ownership of Christianity for socialism. Smith also cautioned against the idea of politics becoming a crusade, or turning into a religion, becoming too important in the lives of men and women at the expense of other things in their lives.[130]

But being Labour leader almost required one to set out the moral basis of one's beliefs. In March 1993, Smith gave the Christian Socialist R.H. Tawney Lecture, which became known as *Reclaiming the Ground*. Smith took the matter very seriously. Norman Hogg recalls it was 'a big day for John' and Donald Dewar complaining that John was spending ages in its preparation.[131] Hogg recalls that Smith regarded *Reclaiming the Ground* as 'an important beacon on where he stood, and where he was likely to take the Labour Party'.[132]

John drew on the ideas of Archbishop William Temple, who believed in the notion of Christian fellowship, that people had an obligation or a duty to one another.[133] In politics, that meant a duty to serve one's community and one's nation. Smith attacked the right's notion of individualism: 'This thesis grotesquely ignores the intrinsically social nature of human beings and fails to recognise the capabilities that all people have to act in response to commitments and beliefs that clearly transcend any narrow calculation of personal advantage.'[134]

Instead, Smith shared Temple and Tawney's view that individuals were social animals, not merely interested in commercial transactions, but bound together to cooperate within strong communities.[135] Surprisingly, Smith called on people to look more closely at the early writings of Adam Smith, including his *Theory of Moral Sentiments*, where he argued that however selfish a man might be, there were some principles in his nature which interested him in the fortunes of others.[136]

British politics hadn't seen anything like it since Margaret Thatcher made her ill-judged speech to the General Assembly of the Church of Scotland in 1988. But unlike Thatcher, Smith's comments resonated with the basic values of a much higher percentage of Scots. As the journalist Ivo Dawnay had spotted, even before Smith became leader, the man from Argyll espoused 'a very Scottish species of practical Christian socialism'.[137] John Battle recalls that for years, utopians in the Labour Party had sought for high ideals without reference to the real world. Now, here was Smith marrying social justice on the one hand, and economic efficiency on the other. Battle recalls that for John

Smith 'the politics of pragmatism was not about sell-out, but about getting a deal with benefits for everyone'.[138] The other important impact of Smith's speech was that it created space for other Christian Socialists such as Battle, Paul Boateng, Tony Blair, Hilary Armstrong and Chris Smith to 'assert the importance of a certain strand of Labour's thinking, to say, "This is legitimate, and we can express it"'.[139]

Smith also had to judge how best to respond to the apparent success of political ideas emanating from across the Atlantic. There is no doubt that Bill Clinton's victory in the American presidential elections in 1992 had a worldwide impact on the future of social democracy. Brown and Blair were 'captivated' by the success of the New Democrats, and they both looked to the United States as 'a hotbed of ideas and new thinking'.[140]

Was Smith in favour of drawing from this hotbed of ideas, the so-called 'Clintonisation' of the Labour Party? Tudor Jones argues not – rather that Smith was a consistent believer in social democracy along the lines of continental Europe.[141] Ben Clift agrees that whereas both Smith and Kinnock were more in the social democratic, European mould, Blair was more Atlanticist and closer to Bill Clinton on economic issues.[142] However, what the academics (and the modernisers) apparently ignore is Smith's pragmatism. He was perfectly relaxed about ideas coming from anywhere. As Frank Dobson puts it: 'He didn't care about sire and dam, as long as it was a sound horse.'[143] Murray Elder claims that John was 'entirely comfortable' with Tony and Gordon looking to America for ideas.[144] Dobson recalls that Smith was comfortable with the ideas of Robert Reich,[145] who looked at new ways of getting the unemployed back to work.[146] But while Smith may have borrowed a few good ideas from whatever source, he remained, as Murray Elder acknowledges 'hugely committed' to Europe.[147]

In one sense, the political closeness between British and European Socialists at this time was inevitable. The Party of European Socialists (PES), then the largest grouping in the European Parliament, officially met twice a year, but since they also held 'emergency' meetings, Elder recalls that it 'seemed a lot more than that, and it often was'. There was therefore 'a lot of coming and going on the European side'. That meant John knew and was very comfortable with the PES leaders, and that would have greatly influenced the way he thought.[148] Frank Dobson agrees that on anything technically related to Europe, John Smith was 'at the races', but that in other matters he felt the Labour leader was an 'instinctive Atlanticist'.[149] Only Smith knew how committed he was to Europe vis à vis America, and his political colleagues' views of his level of commitment either way depends to a large extent on their own pro-European views, and/or pro-Democrat leanings.

During Neil Kinnock's nine years as leader, the Labour Party had moved, with John Smith's support, firmly into the mainstream of European democratic socialist thinking. As shadow Chancellor, Smith had been especially keen to promote European capitalism along the 'German model' (see chapter 13). Unfortunately, Smith's relatively short period as Labour leader occurred at a time when Europe experienced a period of economic crisis as a result of the fall of the Berlin Wall and the political and economic costs of German reunification, the latter responsible for European-wide currency instability in the latter half of 1992. More or less simultaneously, many Labour figures, including Tony Blair, returned from the States enthused by the electoral success of the Clinton campaign. (In government, Blair has further strengthened the links between the United Kingdom and the United States.) Smith, the consistent pro-European, had to cope with both the political and economic crisis in Europe, and a flood of new thinking coming from across the Atlantic.

Clive (later Lord) Hollick was one such messenger of this new thinking. He wrote a paper entitled *Campaign '96* arguing for 'a new Labour Party, new policies and trade union links'. These findings were presented to Smith, Murray Elder and David Ward. According to Philip Gould, Smith was unimpressed: 'This is all very interesting, but I think you will find that it will be our turn next time.'[150] In January 1993, Blair and Brown visited the United States for talks with Clinton's staff. Jonathan Powell, political secretary at the British Embassy in Washington, and soon to be Blair's chief of staff, organised the trip.[151] Meanwhile, on 9 January 1993, Philip Gould organised a one-day conference on 'Clintonomics' at the Queen Elizabeth II Conference Centre in Westminster. Gould also co-authored an article in *Renewal* with Patricia Hewitt calling on Labour to emulate Clinton's success in ditching the Democrats' image as 'a party of the poor and of the past' by forging 'a populism of the centre rather than the left'.[152] Apparently, Smith sent Gould private messages 'asking me not to be disruptive',[153] while Clare Short publicly warned in *Tribune* on 15 January that the 'Modernisers want to destroy Labour's soul'.

By Wednesday, 27 January 1993, Smith was warning the NEC against 'all the sniping that's going on' by 'parliamentary prima donnas'. At first Tony Benn was not clear to whom Smith was referring. Smith made some elliptical references and then said: 'This idea about "Clintonisation" is absurd. We've got to study experience from elsewhere.' The party had to stop indulging in

'Oppositionitis'.[154] Benn's account supports the view that Smith did not have a problem with borrowing ideas from the New Democrats.[155] But while it may appear that Smith was attacking Blair and Brown, in fact he was probably having a swipe at Clare Short in an effort to maintain party unity.

Short was clear about what it all meant: 'The hint we get is "dump the poor".'[156] John Prescott also railed against the modernisers, claiming the Party was becoming 'obsessed with image' and that they 'would draw exactly the wrong conclusions from the Clinton victory'.[157] While Blair and Brown were in the United States, Mandelson claims that Smith rang him and said: 'All this Clintonisation business, it's just upsetting everyone. Stop boat-rocking with all this talk of change and modernisation. It will just divide the party. If we remained united we'll win. Do just shut up.'[158] According to James Naughtie, 'this was an angrier Smith than Mandelson had ever experienced'.[159] Such warnings from Smith don't seem to have stopped Tony Blair from publicly drawing comparisons between Clinton's ability to reach beyond the Democrats' declining base of support and 'the problems that Labour has faced here. The Clinton campaign reached out to a broader section of the population and we've got to do that too.'[160]

Hugh MacPherson argues that John Smith challenged the notion that a political party should merely conduct opinion polls to ascertain what the voters wanted and then advocate the views of the median voters in order to obtain office.[161] Rather, Smith belonged to a different generation, believing that the primary role of a politician was to convince the electorate that your view, and that of your party, was the right one. Early in Smith's leadership, Philip Gould, Kinnock's (and later Blair's) polling guru, gave a talk based on focus group findings. Afterwards, Smith commented to Ann Barrett: 'We'll not have them back.'[162] After the 1992 election campaign, Smith dispensed with the services of Gould's shadow communications agency,[163] and brought in a new advertising agency, Butterfield, Day, Devito, Hockney.[164]

How were the practicalities of opinions polls and political campaigning handled under Smith's leadership? Smith put Margaret Beckett in sole charge of campaigning, including developing all the party political broadcasts, working alongside David Hill, Labour's director of communications, and they were later joined by Sally Morgan, the campaigns director.[165] The deputy leader also headed a new Campaigns and Elections Committee, an NEC body which had two main tasks: rebuilding the party and restoring morale, and shaping the nature of the debate in the country.[166] Contrary to popular belief, opinion polling was carried on under Smith's leadership. Labour appointed psephologist Roger Jowell and his NOP polling group to run a series of focus groups over time (referred to in psephological jargon as 'a quantitative tracking study'),[167] and to report regularly to the relevant party committees.[168] Jowell argued, based on evidence from the Clinton campaign in 1992, that too much polling in Britain had been conducted in the immediate run-up to a general election. Instead, Jowell succeeded in introducing tracking polls for the *duration* of the electoral cycle.[169]

The leader was taken to one of these focus groups, where he sat in a room with a false glass wall, listening to the views in the other room. Mike Elrick recalls:

> John sat through it dismissively, listening to the views of the group, some of which were horrific – some suggested bringing back hanging. I remember looking across at John, as he mechanically stuffed peanuts into his mouth. You could tell it was an exercise that he felt that he had to go through with.[170]

On another occasion, the pollsters sent Smith a list of 'Vocabulary That Worked Well', and conversely, 'Vocabulary That Didn't Work Well'. The favourable buzz-words and phrases included: 'Tough on crime: tough on the causes of crime'; 'Investing in education, investing in the future'; 'Life would be less taxing with Labour'; and 'Labour's vision for Britain' – all language strikingly similar to that deployed subsequently by Tony Blair and New Labour – while the supposedly unfavourable sound bites included: 'High skill, high wage economy'; 'Honest Government'; 'Full and fulfilling employment'; and 'Labour won't tax for its own sake'[171] – all messages associated both with Smith's period as shadow Chancellor and Labour's economic campaign launched in the summer of 1993.

Margaret Beckett paid quite close heed to the advice of the pollsters, including Philip Gould, believing that the Labour Party owed him a great deal. Indeed, Gould continued to provide much of his valuable information, especially in the run-up to the European elections, free of charge. Beckett saw that a balance needed to be achieved in the relationship between polling and policy. It would have been 'mad' not to pay some heed to polling evidence, but on the other hand polling should not be allowed to drive the long-term strategic development of policy.[172]

Although Smith's gut reaction to focus groups and attempts to tailor his message to pander to the voters was sceptical, Margaret Beckett believes it would be misleading to suggest that Smith was totally hostile to opinion polls: 'John was playing for the next election from the day he became leader ... John took account of the information passed to him.'[173] Murray Elder essentially

agrees, arguing that the polling evidence was always kept in proportion: 'We
[the Labour Party] went mad on polls after John's death.' Smith reluctantly
agreed to the use of polling evidence as part of his overall campaigning
strategy, as a tool to find out what people were thinking about him, and how
favourably he was perceived as party leader. If his poll ratings in certain areas
were not going well, he would ask himself what he needed to do to improve
them, and how he might justify his actions better, but he would not alter his
basic beliefs or opinions on the basis of unfavourable polling evidence.[174]

The messages on polling do seem to have got across to Smith, as is shown
by his remarks to a gathering of the PLP in December 1993. Even though the
PLP minutes are a semi-verbatim account of what Smith said, the points come
across clearly enough:

> The Party must be ready to take every opportunity to get its message across
> in 1994, which would be a pivotal year . . . The Tories were at their lowest
> ebb for 12 years, and the public no longer trusted them on tax or running
> the economy. There would be a major campaigning effort in 1994 to bring
> home even more vividly these points – building up to the April tax
> increases . . . The Parliamentary Committee had identified a number of
> clear themes which must be repeated and repeated again with ruthless
> determination and self-confidence.[175]

George Robertson remembers an occasion, on the eve of the European
elections, when Smith took him aside in the smoking room, and informed him
that apart from attending one or two events in the first weekend of the
campaign, he was not going to do much personal campaigning in Scotland.
The leader told his shadow Secretary of State for Scotland that he needed to
spend his time convincing voters in the south of England that Labour was fit
to govern: 'I've got to focus on these voters.'[176] Even though Smith may not
have liked focus groups, he knew precisely what was required of him and the
Labour Party if it was to win a general election.

However, Smith came under quite a lot of pressure from people inside his
own office to develop a more clearly defined strategy. Around January 1993
David Ward wrote a note to Smith expressing concern that the leader's office
was 'very hierarchical and communication channels are weak'. Ward
suggested the formation of a strategic planning group, covering press, policy
and political management, comprising Smith, Ward, David Hill, Murray
Elder and Hilary Armstrong. Its role would have been 'to try to structure our
activity according to a strategic plan rather than being driven by events'.[177] In
June 1993, Delyth Evans wrote a confidential memorandum to Smith, which,
among other things, suggested:

3. Regular strategy meetings . . . I think one of the main failings of the office at the moment is that we do not meet as a team to discuss our strategy for the coming weeks/months . . . I would suggest that you should build up a team of key advisers . . . who can meet together every three months or so . . . Unless you are prepared to invest real time, on a regular basis, in thinking, discussing, arguing with people you trust and whose opinions you value, you will always be operating from day to day with no broader sense of priorities or objectives . . . David Puttnam has a beautiful house in Wiltshire which he is more than happy to put at your disposal for weekend conferences of this sort.[178]

Meta Ramsay, having been a senior diplomat, was used to hierarchical structures, and had regularly attended management courses. Frustrated, she suggested to Simon Haskel that he ask John if he would gather members of his office together for a day with a management consultant. As Murray Elder sat through a series of flow charts and explanations of line management, it was clear that he hated it. Afterwards, a discussion took place on what changes might take place in the structure of the office, but nothing was acted upon.[179]

Similarly, in late 1992, David Ward, Delyth Evans and Andrew Graham compiled a note for Smith, entitled, *Agenda 1993: Themes for the 21st Century*, in an attempt to establish key themes and 'priorities for a Labour Government':

1. Knowledge is power and education is wealth creation . . . research and development, skills, industrial policy
2. Open Society and Open Government
3. Active Government and Dynamic Markets (intervention in the market)
4. Value of Society and People to Work Together (cohesive society)
5. Britain's Leadership Role (language, UN, environment)[180]

The three advisers suggested a series of speeches, round tables and conferences at which Smith would reinforce these key themes. It didn't happen.

Murray Elder feels that the small size of the office meant that it did not require a clear managerial structure. Despite everyone's private suggestions (and there never were any criticisms of the leader's abilities), each person in the office had a personal line of influence to John. For instance, David Ward and Delyth Evans influenced his speechwriting; Meta Ramsay and Andrew Graham supplied their own policy ideas; Murray rarely sat in on a press meeting with Hilary Coffman, David Hill, Mike Elrick, and so on.[181] Moreover, as Elder recalls: 'John disliked meetings where people aired their latest grand designs. John was not a worrier, nor a re-worker of ideas.'[182] It wasn't that Smith didn't know where he was headed, it was just that, very often only he and Murray Elder, and separately, he and Margaret Beckett, and to some extent, David Ward and Pat McFadden, in terms of policy development, knew part of what the overall strategy was. It was all in Smith's head.

Operating from the sidelines, Philip Gould wanted to increase John Smith's profile, partly because he knew that Labour's greatest asset from 1992–4 was John Smith. Smith's personal ratings were generally good from the autumn of 1993 onwards (74 per cent thought he was caring, and 69 per cent considered him to be competent),[183] but focus group evidence suggested that the Labour leader wasn't sufficiently visible, and people did not really know what he and the Labour Party stood for.[184] Although the Conservatives had suffered a dramatic loss of credibility in the wake of the ERM debacle, the voters, despite Labour's substantial opinion poll lead during 1993, said that they expected the Conservatives to win the next election.[185] Gould identified a deep pessimism among disillusioned Tory voters; that it didn't matter which party came to power, no one was capable of solving Britain's economic problems. In such a cynical political climate, Gould feared that the voters would turn back to the devil they knew – the Conservatives (especially if the economy improved) – rather than risking it with Labour. As he put it: 'Modern electorates are insecure, uncertain and anxious. They are more afraid of things getting worse than they are hopeful of things getting better.'[186] Labour also still carried a considerable amount of baggage from its previous period in government, which the Tories could successfully exploit by questioning Labour's fitness to govern. For instance, at least two thirds of voters still believed that Labour was 'under the thumb of the unions' and that a future Labour government would increase taxes by 'a lot'.[187]

Several people in Smith's office agreed with Gould's analysis, including Hilary Coffman and David Hill. Partly, they felt that they couldn't do their job of promoting the leader without the leader taking a higher profile. Hill echoed Gould's fears about Labour's future electoral prospects in a paper entitled, *What the Electorate Think of Us*, based on the findings of two focus groups (comprising Tory 'waverers') conducted in the south-east of England. Not one of those interviewed had indicated that they would vote Labour:

> Little in terms of the electorate's perception [of Labour] has changed since before 1987. Labour has no clear identity. As a result people tend to fill this void by recycling their past prejudices. This explains why the same old fears are still so strongly in evidence . . . This programme needs to be presented in a single-minded and consistent way – its effect must be noticed and believed or respondents will 'fall back' on long held negative views, and 'play safe' electorally again.[188]

However, David Hill and Hilary Coffman sometimes made the mistake of trying to change their leader's mind in too direct and immediate a way. The tactic occasionally backfired. Ann Barrett knew from the way Smith said 'Good morning' what kind of mood he was in. From years of experience, she discovered the best way of handling her leader when he was in a foul mood was to give him a coffee and leave him for an hour or so to come to. Hill and Coffman occasionally ignored Ann's advice not to interrupt John: 'They would charge in, and after thirty seconds, they were out.'[189]

It wasn't just Smith's media team who urged upon him the need for a stronger public profile. In David Ward's aforementioned note to Smith in January 1993, he also remarked upon the leader's 'extreme caution' when considering interview requests, adding: 'There is a wide perception that you are being held unnecessarily under wraps . . . I think it is easy to fall into a strategy of saying no to everything. Eventually, this results in only accepting the interviews we can't avoid like the *Frost* programme.'[190]

Ward argued that even the events that Smith hosted, particularly the launch of the Joint Policy Commission in November 1992, and the Social Justice Commission launch a month later, went 'under-reported' in the media, in marked contrast to Kinnock's high-profile policy review document launches from 1989–91.[191]

Delyth Evans, hailing from a media background, also argued that Smith 'must not shy away from the media'. Evans was very supportive throughout John's leadership, but her memorandum of June 1993 is strikingly similar to Ward's earlier constructive criticism: Smith had 'wasted some good opportunities to present many of your leadership achievements to date', including the launch of the Social Justice Commission (December 1992), the Charter 88 and Tawney speeches (March 1993), and the leader's announcement on electoral reform (May 1993) in terms of publicity:

> Each of these events represented an important element in your leadership agenda, and potentially had a very wide appeal, but we failed to maximise their impact. They provided good opportunities for lengthy interviews, but we missed them . . . In my view you have been shielded far too much in the past year, a strategy which has been almost entirely counter-productive. You have been made to look defensive, accused of inaction and of being remote. None of these are true. The valid criticism is that you have not presented yourself or your achievements effectively.[192]

Apart from the call for strategy meetings mentioned earlier, Evans made several other positive suggestions to Smith:

1. More media exposure. There is no reason to run away from heavy TV interviews. You come across extremely well on television.
2. Cut down on diary engagements. I believe you are doing too many unnecessary things, wasting valuable time that could be used more effectively. I think you have to be absolutely ruthless in responding to invitations – asking 'what do I gain by doing' rather than 'oh, I might as well go.'
3. Regular strategy meetings. [See above]
4. Decide on your image. People still do not have a clear idea of who you are or what you stand for. I do not believe it is simply enough to hope they will eventually build up their own reasonably accurate impression of you. I think we need to decide on three or four key messages about you that we want most of all to get across, and concentrate on promoting those few messages. Everything you do, your whole public demeanour, should give expression to those key messages.[193]

After listing a set of 'summer priorities', Evans warned, 'If we do not fill their pages/programmes for them, our opponents will.'[194]

In January 1994, Andrew Marr, then writing for *The Independent*, penned an intelligent piece, in which he compared Smith's strategy to that of the Russian commander, Kutuzov, in Tolstoy's *War and Peace*. Kutuzov became notorious for his lack of enthusiasm for engaging the French in battle. His generals would continually press him to attack the enemy, but Kutuzov believed that the Russian army could not destroy the French army nearly as effectively as the French were destroying themselves. Marr pointed out that: 'Mr Smith clearly believes that the Conservatives are doing a splendid job of self-destruction.' The Labour leader had 'merely ambled into the odd studio to express mild surprise about how shabby the Government is, and made a few obvious points, rather gently, across the Dispatch Box'. Of course, as Marr pointed out, Kutuzov was proved right, but unlike the Russian commander, the Labour leader would still have had to fight the crucial pitched battle on tax and the Labour Party still had to 'persuade harassed, worried middle-income Britain that it will be better off under socialism'. Labour, in other words, lacked a sense of urgency and despite the Tory's disarray risked losing its fifth election in a row.[195]

On 16 April 1993, Bill Rodgers, one of the four founding members of the SDP wrote to Smith warning him that without an accommodation with the Liberal Democrats, there was no chance of a centre-left government in the last decade of the twentieth century. He wrote 'entirely in a personal capacity'. Nevertheless, he cited Heath, Jowell and Curtice's *How Britain Votes*[196] as evidence that the electorate was being 'steadily changed by fundamental

economic, social and cultural factors', including industrial decline and
unemployment (leading to a shrinking of Labour's traditional support base),
and a rise in the number of young people entering higher education. Rodgers
believed that Labour, which 'for half-a-century has been a conservative rather
than a radical party' would simply not 'get there in time', in other words make
the necessary changes to attract sufficient support to win in its own right.
Predictably, Rodgers suggested that Smith should acknowledge that the
Liberal Democrats formed part of a three-party system, and that he should
make an alliance with the forces on the centre-left in order to defeat the Tories.
He concluded: 'All these issues are being debated in public, and nothing I have
said is new. But I am deeply worried that the need to get rid of this government
is not at present reflected in the realism and urgency of your leadership.'[197]

An old ally of Smith's, a true Gaitskellite, was telling Smith to his face that
Labour, on their present course, were not going to defeat the Tories on their
own. Occasionally, Rodgers liked to clear his own mind on an issue by setting
out his position on paper, but the letter he produced to Smith, though genuine
and personal and intended for noone else, he admits was 'too clever, too tidy,
and didn't have the flavour of a personal letter'. In retrospect, Rodgers feels he
had made the mistake of not talking to Smith directly. Looking back, he stands
by the content of the letter, arguing that 'Blairism was right for 1997, but John
wouldn't have been right enough'.[198]

Smith was not ignorant about the demands of media publicity, nor was he
being deliberately awkward. But he wanted to be himself. The day after
Smith's leadership election victory, he met with the President of Mexico first
thing in the morning, a fairly conventional appointment for a leader of the
opposition. There followed a far more typical 'Smith' engagement, in which
John had agreed to open a constituency party office for his friend and close
colleague Chris Smith in Islington. John Smith's meeting with the Mexican
President had finished early, so Meta Ramsay and John had time to kill before
meeting Chris Smith. To have arrived early would have thrown the local
organisers into an unnecessary panic, so Smith and Ramsay went into an
Islington pub. Smith insisted on paying for the coffee, and gave his autograph
on the bill. Looking back, Meta recognises the potential damage had a
photographer taken a picture of John Smith, leader of the opposition, walking
into a pub at 11 am.[199]

Smith was what he was: there was no sense in trying to package him a
different way. When Jon Sopel, one of Blair's biographers, asked Roy
Hattersley if he had ever persuaded Smith to change his mind, the former
deputy leader just laughed, and said: 'John Smith hasn't changed his mind on

anything since he was seven years old.'²⁰⁰ Alastair Campbell also recalls that 'Ach' was one of Smith's favourite words: 'It was his way of dismissing "fancy notions". It was a stance born of supreme self-confidence . . . He *was* [Campbell's emphasis] old-fashioned in many ways, and saw no reason to apologise for it. He was, above all, a man of integrity.'²⁰¹

There was also an element of touching naïvety about John Smith. Because he was such a House of Commons man, Smith was not always au fait with what was happening outside Westminster. Ann Barrett recalls one occasion when John announced that he and Simon Haskel were going to see David Hare's play, *The Absence of War*. Ann was horrified. '"You can't go to that, John. It portrays you in a damaging light. The press would have a field day if they saw you there." You see, John didn't know.'²⁰² In fact, although the character of George Jones in *The Absence of War* is modelled quite closely on Neil Kinnock, the character of Malcolm Pryce was not intended by Hare to represent John Smith.²⁰³

But for all his loathing of image-makers, Smith deliberately cultivated his own image – as the careful bank manager, statesmanlike figure – because he felt certain he would be Prime Minister, and he needed to behave in a Prime Ministerial way. There were real political dangers, as Neil Kinnock had learned to his cost, of being seen as too ebullient. Smith therefore curbed his natural exuberance, and didn't always project his real personality in public. There were plenty of times when he could have made a funny story out of his encounters as leader of the opposition, or let them leak out in order to paint himself in a more interesting light, but either he did he not feel the need, or he also actively stopped these anecdotes from seeing the light of day in case they damaged his statesmanlike pose. On one occasion, the Labour Party had had the misfortune to organise a gathering in the Queen Elizabeth II Conference Centre at the same time as a Star Trek Convention. As David Ward and John Smith entered the lift on the ground floor of the conference centre, 'Mr Spock' walked in beside them. Ward could not resist saying: 'I suppose, it's a case of "Beam me up, Scottie".' 'Mr Spock' replied: 'That would be entirely logical.' Afterwards, Smith said to Ward, 'Don't you dare let that story appear in the *Times Diary*!'²⁰⁴

John Smith was devoid of the insecurities that bedevil most politicians. What mattered to John was the political substance of a story on the front page, not the person communicating the story. According to David Hill, Smith had 'an innate detestation of trickiness with the press', and that was a large part of the reason he disliked Peter Mandelson.²⁰⁵ In the unlikeliest of places, in *Woman's Own*, Smith spoke out against 'the black art of public relations that's

JUST ONE MORE HEAVE 317

taken over politics. We're talking about the government of the country – not the entertainment industry.'[206] The most legitimate argument in favour of a high media profile is that in today's 24 hour media age politicians need to make themselves permanently available. If a minister does not appear on a news programme, then, so the argument runs, someone with a contrary view will be given the vacated airtime.

Elizabeth Smith remembers that John liked to think that he had no protective screen around him. He was not hidden away by advisers and spin-doctors. Perhaps he was failing to recognise the growing importance of the media, living in a dream world, and such a stance as leader of the opposition would almost certainly have been impossible to maintain as Prime Minister.[207] But by doing it *his* way, Smith set his own agenda for the media, not the other way about. In truth, Smith had a perfectly user-friendly relationship with journalists, but he was not fixated or obsessed by it, in the way that New Labour became. Smith took the view that if the press wanted to contact him at weekends, then he was accessible. According to Elizabeth, every Fleet Street editor had his Edinburgh telephone number. If they dared to telephone on a Sunday morning, they would get a flea in their ear for being intrusive, but they knew where he was.[208]

But the most important difference between John Smith and New Labour with regard to the media is that Smith had no time at all for Rupert Murdoch. Ann Barrett recalls: 'He [Murdoch] was a no-no.' Just before his death, Hilary Coffman arranged for Andrew Neil, then editor of *The Sunday Times*, to interview John Smith without first consulting him. Barrett recalls Smith's reaction when he heard about the interview: 'I thought he [John] was going to explode. But he wouldn't have let his staff down by cancelling it, so Andrew Neil became the last journalist ever to interview John Smith.'[209]

It was later said, at least in a work of fiction, that Smith thought that 'Newsnight was the most watched programme on television'.[210] Apocryphal or not, the Labour leader certainly took an old-fashioned view of the need for quality news coverage, as demonstrated during the autumn of 1993 when he opposed switching ITN broadcasts from 5.30 pm and 10 pm to 6.30 pm and 11 pm. Michael Brunson, ITN's political editor, had contacted David Hill to gain the Labour leader's support in the campaign to save *News at Ten*. Smith wrote a stern letter to Sir George Russell, the chairman of the Independent Television Commission, then the final arbiter of the ITV schedules, arguing that if the plan went ahead 'it would be a major blow to coverage of news and current affairs on British television'. Smith then revealed just how high-minded he was when he claimed that were the 5.30 pm slot to move to 6.30 pm, many viewers would 'be left without any access to a serious news bulletin at any time during the day' on ITV, implying that ITN's lunchtime and early-evening broadcasts didn't constitute serious news bulletins. However, Smith's intervention, and more especially that of John Major, may have contributed to *News at Ten* gaining a temporary stay of execution.[211] The ITV bosses eventually got their way in November 1998, and the schedules were fiddled about with, with disastrous consequences, such that the ITN news has now been given a definite slot in the schedules at 10.30 pm.

Is John Rentoul therefore correct to argue that the whole idea of New Labour was 'proposed and rejected under Smith'?[212] The modernisers can't have it both ways. They can't argue simultaneously that Smith rejected modern-isation *and* that Brown and Blair were successfully pressing on Smith a modernisation agenda during his leadership. Jon Sopel, John Rentoul, Philip Gould and Paul Routledge all claim that by 1993, Brown was ditching 'tax and spend', while Blair promised that Labour would be 'tough on crime, tough on the causes of crime'.[213] Indeed, Routledge uses an anonymous quote from a moderniser at the time: 'Gordon and Tony are like two sturdy oxen pulling an occasionally reluctant plough.'[214] The moderniser/traditionalist dichotomy just won't do.

Instead of seeing the debate as one fought between modernisers and traditionalists, Alastair Campbell is right to describe the nuances of difference at the time as being between 'those frantic for change and those happy to play a longer game'. The 'frantics' included Blair, Brown and Jack Straw, while the 'long-gamers' included Smith, Beckett and Prescott.[215] In an interview for ITN at the end of 1992, Smith revealed the reasoning behind his caution:

> I don't believe that you should rush forward and put everything in your shop window for next Wednesday. I think you've got to do the patient and careful work, taking some original thoughts, working them through in practical ways, and when you're ready to do so, presenting them to the public in a way which commands and maximises not only the support for the policies but for the Party.[216]

Roy Hattersley argues that Smith mostly definitely did not belong to the 'one more heave' school. Rather, he was 'determined to modernise his party. But he wanted to bring the old principles up to date, not replace them. He looked for intellectual improvements, not ideological alternatives.'[217]

But some of Smith's biggest critics don't even think Smith had a long game. They don't buy the idea that he had a clear set of policy ideas in mind for the latter half of the Parliament in the run-up to the election, and feel that Smith was so sure of his own abilities that, if it was possible to get away with it, he would have got by on an ad hoc dual strategy of preserving party unity and hammering the Tories in Parliament. Maybe Smith's critics should remember his greatest reform of all – the introduction of one member, one vote.

Twenty-Two
OMOV AND CLAUSE IV

JOHN SMITH GAMBLED his leadership of the Labour Party on the outcome of the OMOV vote in late September 1993. Donald Macintyre rightly calls it 'a stupendous gamble . . . No other Labour leader has ever taken such a risk.'[1] And yet the mythology propounded by the modernisers is that Smith should never have had to gamble his leadership in 1993, because he should have pushed through the changes a year earlier, and that the changes Smith introduced were too modest. Are these claims accurate?

After Labour's 1992 defeat, Neil Kinnock firmly believed that *his* project needed to carry on at a breakneck pace otherwise Labour was doomed to perpetual electoral defeat. 'We must not go back on the policy or organisational changes, but we must make policies fit for 1996, not 1992.'[2] And a large part of not going back on those organisational changes meant reforming OMOV. Charles Clarke, Kinnock's most loyal lieutenant, shared this view, as an undated briefing note (probably from 1991) from Clarke to Kinnock reveals. As Kinnock prepares for a meeting with John Edmonds, leader of the GMB union, Clarke argues: 'We know this reform is a key trust issue for the electorate. It is probably the last Achilles' heel of Labour. It is a reform on which your authority and credibility is at stake – you will not and cannot back down or compromise.'[3]

By the late spring of 1992, Kinnock had already declared his intention to stand down as Labour leader, yet he was still trying to chivvy colleagues into further reform. Kinnock's thinking is revealed in a covering letter attached to a memorandum dated Wednesday, 20 May 1992 and put to the NEC's Organisation Committee the following Monday: 'There are some colleagues who will doubtless say we should "take more time" before making a final decision. I have to tell them that *we do not have that luxury of more time* [Kinnock's emphasis].'[4] Kinnock then proposed in his motion to the NEC's Organisation Committee that a new system of rules for the selection and reselection of parliamentary candidates should be put to the 1992 conference, rather than being delayed a year, otherwise no Labour candidates would be in place until the summer or autumn of 1994.[5] Throughout the document,

Kinnock comes across as a man in a hurry.[6] The ground was already being cut from under his feet.

Tom Sawyer, the deputy general secretary of NUPE, in conjunction with Larry Whitty, the general secretary of the Labour Party, made moves to consult the Party membership and the unions more widely on OMOV, thereby slowing down the reform process. The NEC meeting of 27 May received a letter from Sawyer proposing that the party should deal with issues relating to OMOV in 'a considered and constructive way', and attacked Kinnock's desire for rapid change.[7] Sawyer then proposed that Larry Whitty should come up with proposals, to be put before the NEC in June on how best to proceed with OMOV. It is clear from the minutes that Labour's general secretary also favoured a slower and wider pace of reform.[8] The main point of difference between the modernisers on the one hand, and Tom Sawyer and Larry Whitty on the other, was not so much timing as the fact that the former group wanted a simple OMOV change, and the latter group wanted a wider redefinition of the trade union relationship with the Labour Party.[9]

After the NEC meeting, Charles Clarke expresses a growing frustration that the OMOV reforms have become stalled:

> All this review talk is a[n] excuse for having not a clue what to do and reacting defensively to exagurated [sic] press reports about attempts to break the link . . . There is a total vacum [sic] in the affairs of the Party at present, which was clear in the discussion with [John] Edmonds . . . Neither Larry Whitty nor any of the trade union leaders has a clue what to do.[10]

The modernisers allege that John Smith somehow interfered in Neil Kinnock's last NEC as leader on 24 June 1992 to stall the OMOV process. The claim was made that Robin Cook, Smith's campaign manager, acting on Smith's behalf, succeeded in getting a motion passed at the NEC to delay discussion of OMOV until the 1993 party conference. Smith wasn't even a member of the NEC until he was officially elected leader in July. Larry Whitty denies that Robin Cook was in some way acting for Smith 'but he [Cook] did represent a widespread view amongst the unions and the soft left that the OMOV issue should not be dealt with in isolation from other union-related matters'.[11] Kinnock's former authority over his NEC colleagues had been diminished.[12] On 24 June 1992, John Prescott, Clare Short and John Edmonds of the GMB backed Cook's proposal, and it was carried by thirteen votes to eight. Kinnock's sub-committee became a review group on links between trade unions and the Labour Party, as had been suggested by Larry Whitty.[13]

Charles Clarke warned against delaying a vote on OMOV for another year: 'The *new leadership will therefore start off with a crisis which will hang over them for a year* [Clarke's emphasis].'[14] Neil Kinnock is also convinced that John Smith faced 'an unnecessary drama'[15] because of his stalling in 1992.[16] This argument forms the heart of the modernisers' case against John Smith, which is best summarised by John Rentoul (one of Blair's biographers): '[Smith] allowed the traditionalist forces to regroup over the next twelve months' because they appealed to the party's emotional loyalty to the trade unions, and their suspicions of turning the party into an 'SDP Mark Two'.[17]

Murray Elder believes that Kinnock is mistaken in maintaining that Smith could have got through OMOV at the 1992 Labour Party conference for two main reasons. Firstly, Elder believes that Kinnock confuses the immense power of a Labour leader in the run-up to an election with the diminished power of a defeated leader in the immediate post-election period. It is conceivable that Kinnock could have won the OMOV vote in 1991 had he 'held a gun to the party's head', demanding unity so close to an election. Post-election, even though Smith was a new leader with a new mandate, he lacked that same powerful lever.[18] Derek Foster believes that had Neil Kinnock been leader in 1992, then he could have got OMOV through. As soon as Kinnock declared his intention to stand down, 'all bets were off' in terms of any deal that he may or may not have been able to cut with union leaders over OMOV. Smith's likely election as leader meant that there was 'a new game in town'.[19]

Secondly, Murray Elder believes that one of the two biggest unions opposed to OMOV – the TGWU and the GMB – would have had to back down for the vote to have been won on OMOV under the old block voting rules still in place in 1992.[20] Even Charles Clarke admitted at the time that: 'The only proposition is simple OMOV, but this depends on [the] GMB changing their vote in its favour.' Moreover, Clarke recognised that John Edmonds would not budge: 'Plenty of elements are available but compromise on OMOV for reselection is not one of them.' Indeed, Clarke's position appears contradictory: it was 'very important there is no messing around because even though everyone is espousing the principle [of OMOV] there are two or three versions none of which command majority support'.[21] He, too, like Elder, realised that 'there is no majority for a proposition [on the selection and reselection of candidates] at this year's [1992] Conference.'[22]

The key leadership achievement at the 1992 conference was the reduction of the union block from 90 per cent to 70 per cent, yet another one of Neil Kinnock's valuable reforms. Elder believes that such was the basic arithmetic that this was 'an essential prerequisite' of winning the vote on OMOV in 1993. If the two biggest union block votes were against Smith, and he had charged ahead, he would have lost in 1992 – 'a catastrophic start to Smith's leadership'.[23] Larry Whitty's view is that most probably if OMOV had been pushed in 1992, it would have been defeated, but he feels there is just the possibility that a proposal such as that reached in 1993 could have been bulldozed through a year earlier.[24]

Derek Foster rightly comments: 'John did not initially realise the legwork involved in getting OMOV through.'[25] Smith had no previous experience of the NEC. Although he knew many of the trade union leaders well, he did not have an intimate knowledge of the Labour Party rulebook, and relied hugely on Murray Elder and Larry Whitty.

Frank Dobson, a self-confessed long-gamer on most issues, sees the differing tactics over OMOV as reflecting the contrasting leadership styles between Neil Kinnock and John Smith: 'Neil had long since given up on playing a long game and preferred to head butt his way to get things done.' By contrast, charging ahead with OMOV immediately on becoming leader 'wasn't John's way of doing it'.[26] David Ward agrees, recalling that Smith liked to see himself as cat-like, making a series of light steps and then pouncing with devastating effect on his prey. The other analogy Smith loved to use was altogether more vulgar, and therefore wholly typical of the new Labour leader: two bulls, one young the other a good bit older, are in a field, eyeing up some cows on a hillside. The young bull suggests to the older bull: 'Let's run up the hill and shag one of them!' The older bull has a better idea: 'No, let's walk up the hill and shag the lot of them!'[27]

However, the cows (in this case the unions) were still frightened in 1992. At the Labour Party conference in Blackpool, traditionalists won a card vote rejecting 'proposals which undermine the historic and essential link between the industrial and political wings of the Party' and, specifically, conference reaffirmed its support for trade union representation 'at every stage in the selection of parliamentary candidates by Constituency Labour Parties'.[28]

The search for a way forward on OMOV was now the responsibility of the Union Links Review Group, which initially comprised NEC members John Prescott, Clare Short, Bryan Gould, Robin Cook, Margaret Beckett and John Evans, alongside eight union representatives.[29] Lewis Minkin, author of *The Contentious Alliance*, a history of the links between the Labour Party and the trade unions, joined the discussions, as did Larry Whitty, and Joyce Gould, Labour's director of organisation.[30] Whitty was largely responsible for the composition of the working party,[31] but claims the inclusion of so many trade unionists was 'not a deliberate anti-OMOV move'.[32] In effect, three sub-groups emerged within the Review Group: those in favour of the status quo (the conservatives), those who wanted an OMOV system for both leadership and deputy leadership elections and selection of parliamentary candidates (the modernisers), and those who wanted a wider review of the relationship between the unions and the Labour Party. As well as Larry Whitty, this third group included Tom Sawyer, Tom Burlison, Lewis Minkin, Bryan Gould and Tony Manwaring, secretary to the Union Review Links Group. It wasn't ever a simple matter of conservatives versus modernisers, as many existing accounts of OMOV have supposed. In the end, the eventual compromise would be hammered out between the modernisers and those seeking a wider transformation of the union relationship with the party.[33]

When Bryan Gould resigned from the shadow Cabinet on the eve of the 1992 Labour Party conference, John Smith appointed Tony Blair in his place on the Union Links Review Group.[34] Larry Whitty originally proposed Blair, and recalls that Blair was initially hesitant about filling Gould's vacant chair.[35] Perhaps Blair's reservations were well founded, for he quickly became iconic of the 'pure' or radical view on OMOV: that only union members who had actually joined the Labour Party should be allowed to vote in the party's elections.

Joyce Gould believes that Blair behaved naïvely on the review group by floating the idea of permanent referenda and postal ballots for every issue.[36] Such ballots were incredibly expensive, and Blair's over-ambitious ideas were rejected out of hand.[37] Even Rentoul, Blair's sympathetic biographer, admits that when Blair 'arrived in the middle of the debate . . . there was an edge of intellectual arrogance to his impatience'.[38] And yet both Rentoul and Sopel portray Blair as the man bravely sticking his neck out in favour of a pure version of OMOV.[39]

A fundamental difference of opinion began to develop between Blair and Smith over the future of the trade union movement's relationship with the Labour Party. Smith believed the unions were integral to the Labour movement, and the institutional links should remain, though they should be made more democratic. He genuinely believed that ordinary union members were the bedrock of the Labour movement. He never tired of telling Murray Elder and Hilary Armstrong that his inspiration for shifting to OMOV had been a check-in clerk at Edinburgh Airport, who mentioned that she had just voted for him in one of the ballots for the 1992 leadership election. The clerk added: 'That's the way it should be not just for me, but [for] everyone in the Labour Party.'[40] Smith saw that a simple ballot paper could change people's experiences.[41] On the tenth anniversary of Smith becoming leader, Hilary Armstrong recalled: 'I can't tell you how often I heard that story. It was anecdotes like that which drove him and reinforced his gut instinct. That's how he worked.'[42]

Conversely, Blair wanted to weaken, though not wholly sever, the institutional link, believing the unions represented 'vested interests': Labour Party members should provide the link between the party and the people in the country. It is particularly galling to listen from the vantage point of 2005 to Blair's self-proclaimed purity on OMOV when he benefited hugely from it in his own leadership contest in 1994, and subsequently abandoned it in the selection process for Labour's candidate for the Welsh Assembly and London mayoral elections, in favour of good old-fashioned trade union stitch-ups. In any event, pure OMOV was never a starter in 1992–3. Rather, as a result of the discussions in the review group, around December 1992, Tom Burlison of the GMB came out with the idea of a Registered Supporters' Scheme, also known as the Registered Members' Scheme.

The Registered Supporters' Scheme proposed creating a new class of Labour Party member: a registered member within an affiliated organisation – mostly belonging to a trade union – who would make a reduced membership payment to the Party to reflect the fact that they already belonged to an affiliated organisation. These members would then have full membership rights for selections of parliamentary candidates and the election of the leader and deputy leader,[43] but their votes would never be allowed to count for more than two-fifths of the total in such elections. When Blair arrived on the review Committee, Burlison's plan seemed to represent the best chance of getting an agreement between the recalcitrant unions – the GMB and the TGWU – and the modernisers, as Rentoul phrases it,[44] or more accurately, between those wishing a wider redefinition of the trade union relationship with the Labour Party and the modernisers.

Andy McSmith claims: 'By the time Blair arrived, the cause of one member, one vote was almost dead.'[45] Certainly, Nigel Harris of the AEEU was the only member of the review group before Blair came along to support a 'pure version' of OMOV.[46] The moderniser legend has it that Blair 'still had the upper hand in the Battle for John Smith's Ear'.[47] Blair was extremely unhappy about the pace of modernisation under Smith's leadership and would supposedly tell friends (or 'helpful' people like Peter Mandelson, who spread the story around) on several occasions: 'John is just so cautious. It's a disaster.'[48] Blair stretched the boundaries of shadow Cabinet loyalty to its limits on 17 January 1993 during a BBC *On the Record* interview about OMOV. Afterwards, Smith is said to have warned Blair that he might be endangering his chances of ever becoming leader.[49] In an interview with *Tribune* at the end of January, Blair again expressed his objections to the Registered Supporters' Scheme, and stressed that Smith needed to speed up the modernisation process:

> More generally, Labour now has to embrace the idea that it will have to change its approach in the run-up to the next election . . . We've got to realise that, three or four years down the road, Labour, under John Smith's leadership, has got to be in a position to ensure what has happened at the last four elections is not repeated.[50]

In February 1993, the Union Links Review Group reported its interim findings to the NEC. The group listed three options for reform of leadership elections.[51] It seems that at this point Smith went through a period, as Larry Whitty puts it, where he 'wasn't sure about where he wanted to go', but not everyone would agree with Whitty's analysis that 'he [Smith] hadn't really thought it through' from the very beginning.[52] Contrary to the moderniser view of history, Tony Blair had very little to do with finding a way through the impasse. He was marginalised because his approach to OMOV was unrealistically radical. The debate had long since moved away from the 'pure' version of OMOV that Blair espoused. Rather, Larry Whitty seems to have been far more influential in convincing Smith that he needed to modify his plans. On 23 March 1993, he wrote a confidential note to Smith, outlining the sheer scale of trade union hostility to the leader's proposals:

> The original aim was of course to produce a report with a single and consistent package of recommendations which would receive largely consensus support from most unions and could be voted through as a package, although individual votes would be needed on each of the constitutional amendments. Instead we may well need to find a way of getting through areas covered by the [Trade Union Review Group] report on a more piecemeal basis.[53]

Whitty also attached a detailed assessment of the positions of the various unions on the crucial issue of the selection of parliamentary candidates, and predicted (accurately as it happens) in his covering letter to Smith: 'To be certain of winning on OMOV [at the party conference] one major union will have to be persuaded into at least abstaining; even then it is tight.'[54]

Whitty also claimed that it was impossible to implement Burlison's Registered Supporters' Scheme in time to choose parliamentary candidates for the general election.[55] Smith therefore chose to postpone the Registered Supporters' Scheme, which in effect killed it. But finding another acceptable package with which to replace it proved difficult.

Tom Sawyer, the deputy general secretary of NUPE, and that union's representative on the review group, provided a way out of the stalemate.[56] Sawyer had been a key moderniser in the Kinnock era, but Smith left him largely out of the loop.[57] (On Blair's election as leader, Sawyer took over from Larry Whitty as general secretary of the Labour Party.) Sawyer made an unlikely person to emerge with a compromise, having coined the slogan, 'No say, no pay' at NUPE's annual conference in June 1992.[58] Protracted negotiations followed that ended up with the levy-plus compromise which traded a significant say for the unions in leadership and deputy leadership elections for levy-plus for parliamentary candidate selection: trade union members would pay an extra £3 on top of the political levy they paid to the union in return for voting rights on the selection of parliamentary candidates at constituency Labour parties, as long as they declared that they supported Labour, while union members would be encouraged, though not forced, to join the Labour Party.

Doubts surround the original authorship of levy-plus. A very similar concept had been discussed by Gordon Brown in a *Tribune* pamphlet as early as 1987, although Phil Wilson, Blair's assistant in Sedgefield, coined the phrase 'levy-plus' in a report to Blair in 1992.[59] John Prescott had also supported the levy-plus system in his 1988 deputy leadership challenge, and he put his considerable weight behind Sawyer's proposal.[60]

Some accounts of OMOV suggest that on Wednesday, 19 May 1993, Smith gained agreement for the levy-plus compromise at a meeting of the review group.[61] In fact, no consensus was reached at the meeting, but Smith had avoided a stalemate by simply refusing to have a vote. At a press conference after the NEC meeting, he announced: 'These are new proposals which have not yet been considered by the Labour movement. I recommend them.'[62] The document outlining the levy-plus compromise – presented on one sheet of A4 – was not open to amendment. One furious union member of the NEC railed: 'This is not the way to do business. If we'd been asked to agree, I suspect there would have been a serious split, and they [the proposals] would have gone down the pan.' Unsurprisingly, Tony Benn wasn't happy either: 'I described it as a speech from the throne. I suppose all we can do is move a humble address. There is no debate on the NEC now; you read it in *The Guardian* and when you get there it's all been decided.'[63] John Rentoul sees the levy-plus compromise as a reverse for the cause of modernisation: 'For all Blair's boldness at the start of the year, he had taken John Smith's warning seriously, and kept his head low while he watched the tanks roll on to Smith's lawn.'[64]

Smith now put his levy-plus proposals out to the party and the wider Labour movement for a summer of consultation, but in the end it turned into more a summer of uncertainty for Labour, as splits over the proposals occurred inside the PLP, within the unions and the party membership, and even between the leader and his general secretary.

At the end of 28 May 1993, 44 Labour MPs, including Clare Short, Michael Meacher and John Prescott, put their names to a 'Keep the Link' motion, expressing their opposition to people in the Labour Party 'who would like to see Labour wholly divorced from the unions. They want to sever the trade union link and replace it with a system of private influence and personal patronage.'[65] Meanwhile, John Spellar, the right-wing Labour MP for Warley West, headed the 'Labour First' group that campaigned independently both of the leadership and the soft left Labour Co-ordinating Committee[66] in favour of OMOV.

Just as poised was the balance of opinion in the constituency Labour parties. On 27 June 1993, BBC1's *On the Record* programme revealed the results of a survey of 180 constituency secretaries: 93 secretaries supported union participation in candidate selection, while 82 preferred OMOV. The leadership's attempt to introduce OMOV in this area was therefore very evenly balanced in terms of CLP support. But what also emerged from the survey was that 109 constituency secretaries wanted to maintain a union say in leadership and deputy leadership elections, compared with only 61 that favoured OMOV.[67] On 11 July, again appearing on BBC's *On the Record* programme, Smith retreated on his earlier insistence that the unions could not participate in leadership elections in the hope that in return they would back him on levy-plus for the selection of parliamentary candidates.[68]

Meanwhile, Larry Whitty and Smith clashed over the extent of trade union engagement vis-à-vis parliamentary candidate selection. Whitty, probably the best general secretary the Labour Party has ever had, was prepared and able to have an open and honest argument with the leader if he disagreed with him. Whitty hailed from a GMB background, and his principal objection to levy-plus was that it appeared to 'cut out the trade union role altogether' in terms of the selection and reselection of parliamentary candidates. Union involvement also gave a degree of stability to candidates during the selection process and, perhaps more importantly, to MPs when it came to their reselection process each Parliament.[69]

By early July 1993, Whitty had concluded that Smith was heading for defeat at conference on levy-plus because of union opposition. He therefore actively engaged in negotiations with the union leaders for a compromise solution based on some sort of phasing-in either of the levy-plus or the Registered Members' Scheme, his personal preference being for the latter. He was never disloyal to Smith, and wrote to his leader setting out exactly what he was doing:

> I am now actively pursuing a position which runs along the attached lines. If this becomes public, it will no doubt be seen as a move to thwart OMOV and hence an attack on you.
>
> In fact, I think it is my responsibility as quietly as possible to get a solution which minimises damage both to you in the immediate term and to the Party/trade union relationship in the medium term. There is no doubt that the present conflict has . . . been extremely damaging to Party morale and effectiveness, and trade union attitudes to the Party.[70]

Also in July 1993, Andy McSmith published *Playing the Long Game*, a commendable biography of Smith. However, the accompanying articles in the newspapers were less measured, including Paul Routledge and Andy McSmith's article in *The Observer* portraying Smith as a Godfather figure who surrounded himself with a MacMafia, and claiming: 'As "one member, one vote" threatens Labour unity, resentment boils up over private office.'[71] Around the time of Smith's first anniversary as leader, Michael White wrote in *The Guardian*: 'Many people who wanted Kinnock to be more like Smith now want facets of the Kinnock personality to be grafted on to his successor.'[72] Peter Riddell, reviewing McSmith's biography in *The Times*, picked up on the fact that, less than a year into Smith's leadership, 'he has failed to inspire either his party or the public'. Smith had many virtues, including 'patience, detachment from day-to-day criticism, and a long view. The trouble is that he can appear too detached.' Nevertheless, Riddell recognised that the real test of Smith's strategy had yet to come over OMOV.[73]

No agreement was reached on levy-plus at the final meeting of the Union Links Review Group on Wednesday, 14 July, but five days later, the NEC met in special session to discuss the party's consultation exercise, and voted by a margin of 20 votes to seven[74] in favour of an electoral college system for leadership elections, while trade unionists would have to pay an additional, though greatly reduced, levy for the privilege of participating in parliamentary selection contests.[75]

By this stage, Smith had begun a spring and summer campaign trying to appeal directly to the trade unions at their various annual conferences. In the words of Robin Cook, Smith needed an orchestrated OMOV campaign 'to establish that OMOV is a strong, personal commitment of the leader'.[76] However, Murray Elder did not see the need to act on Cook's idea of a committee to co-ordinate the campaign.[77]

John Rentoul describes Smith's union charm offensive as 'one of the least successful episodes of his leadership, as he went up and down the country stirring up hostility, and hardening opposition to this plan'.[78] Certainly, Smith lost many of the actual votes on OMOV at which he spoke.[79] But one advantage of Smith agreeing to speak was that it got the relevant trade union general secretary off the conference platform. It also gave the leader a chance to set out the positive case for strong trade unions. For example, at the Fire Brigades' Union (FBU) annual conference in May 1993, Smith stressed 'the proud and deep links between trade unions, their members and the Labour Party'.[80]

Having helped to keep the row over OMOV just within bounds during the spring and the summer, Smith really began to turn the tide at the TUC on Tuesday, 7 September. During his speech, he made no direct reference to OMOV, but instead aired a clever but genuine defence of trade unionism: 'We need as never before strong trade unions to fight for jobs and social justice . . . it is through the collective strength of trade unions that workers have the best hope of defending their interests.'[81] He also committed himself and his party to the goal of full employment:

> The goal of full employment remains at the heart of Labour's vision for Britain. Labour's economic strategy will ensure that all instruments of macroeconomic management, whether it concerns interest rates, the exchange rates or the levels of borrowing, will be geared to sustained growth and rising employment.[82]

Frank Dobson, Labour's shadow employment spokesperson, had raised the banner of full employment at other union conferences prior to Smith's speech. He still treasures a handwritten note from John thanking him for helping him write it.[83] John Prescott and his allies, very much trade union MPs, connected to the speech 'like a bolt of electricity'.[84] *Tribune* agreed: 'The strained mood that has characterised Labour Party and trade union relations in recent months appears to have lifted . . . As the speech came to an end it seemed that two previously arguing partners had visited the marriage guidance counsellor and decided to patch things up.'[85]

Even Tony Benn was delighted that the speech 'knocked everybody sideways' and it was 'an interesting confirmation that only the Right-wing leaders can do that'.[86] But the speech 'infuriated the modernisers' because it represented a real rejection of the modernising agenda.[87] Jon Sopel claims that the unions considered it 'payola' and 'to the Modernisers it smelt like a sell-out to save John Smith's skin'. Sopel also argues that Smith's TUC speech contained unattainable policy pledges about which Blair was 'furious'. [88] Smith had talked about full employment, a national minimum wage, implementing the Social Chapter of the Maastricht Treaty, and introducing a new charter putting part-time and full-time workers on the same legal footing. According to Frank Dobson, Gordon Brown was also 'unhappy' at that point with John's endorsement of the goal of full employment, partly because it was too ambitious.[89] However, within a month, whatever their apparent disagreements, Brown had published a pamphlet in time for the Labour Party conference entitled *How We Can Conquer Unemployment*, in which he argued that full employment could be secured through 'demand management as an integral part of structural policy'.[90] And despite all the criticism of Smith's TUC speech from the modernisers, New Labour subsequently implemented every policy item that Smith mentioned in his speech during its first term in office,[91] including attaining the supposedly unrealistic goal of full employment as expressed by the classic definition – 3 per cent of the workforce not currently in employment.

Hilary Armstrong believes that while Smith's TUC speech was 'too over-the-top', it was still 'an important ingredient in getting OMOV'.[92] John Edmonds of the GMB talked in a more conciliatory language after Smith's speech, claiming that the Labour leader's address had 'improved the mood marvellously' and saying: 'We all want a solution.'[93] However, he didn't budge an inch on the issue of Labour candidate selection.[94]

Overall, Armstrong recalls that John Smith became 'hugely frustrated' that he kept making significant concessions, only to see them pocketed by the union leaders: 'People got fundamental about their stance.' Armstrong may be letting distance lend disenchantment, but she is certainly correct that the union leaders opposed to OMOV presented it as breaking the link entirely, something that Smith would never have done.[95] It would be wrong, however, to see the debate over OMOV among the union leaders merely in terms of every union baron stubbornly holding out against the leadership. Bill Morris's position, as head of the TGWU, had a certain honesty to it because he knew that he simply could not persuade his executive to change its mind, and that therefore there was no point in trying.[96]

It is not accurate, as Sopel suggests, that Smith was aloof and did not bring senior trade union officials like John Edmonds into his confidence:[97] many meet-and-greet sessions were held with trade union executives at the relevant union conferences and at Westminster. The source of this story is almost certainly Edmonds himself, who became annoyed with Murray Elder that he was not maintaining constant contact with him. But Elder didn't see the point when Edmonds was not prepared to make any meaningful concessions.[98] Instead, the negotiations took place directly between the two Johns.

Murray Elder recalls that on OMOV, Smith experienced 'huge frustration' with John Edmonds. Larry Whitty concurs that John Smith was 'utterly and totally' frustrated by Edmonds' attitude.[99] The negotiations between the two Johns were interminable. Smith's 'acute disappointment' with Edmonds arose not merely from the fact that the GMB was Smith's own union (albeit by virtue of the fact that Smith had been a boilermaker), but also that Edmonds, like Smith, had been a moderate centrist figure in the Labour movement.[100] The Labour leader felt that when the crunch came over OMOV, Edmonds was playing games. One particular meeting between the two Johns lasted four hours, during which Smith had been 'driven demented'. After the meeting, Murray Elder recalls that Smith staggered into the office, exhausted and frustrated that there had been no progress.[101] A decade on from OMOV, Edmonds had the barefaced cheek to invoke the Smith era (*Independent* editorial, 9 June 2003) as an example of how the Labour Party should be run.

On the other hand, Edmonds always claimed he was not opposed to modernisation of the unions' relationship with the Labour Party. He could point to the fact that he had moved the resolution at the Labour Party conference in 1988 calling for an end to the block vote. Nor was he opposed to the idea of one member, one vote, but rather he felt very strongly that 'everyone who contributes should have the right to participate in Labour Party democracy. Not just the 200,000 individual members, but also the four million who back the Party through their political levy payments.' Specifically, he felt that local union members who paid the political levy should also be able to cast individual votes (amounting to no more than a third of the total) in the selection of parliamentary candidates.[102]

John Smith revealed in a letter to his former colleague, Elizabeth Thomas, in the middle of September 1993: 'I'm learning fast about how the Labour Party needs to be led.' He added: 'With a bit of luck, I think we can carry through the reforms which are needed.'[103] Smith should have written that a *lot* of luck would be needed.

During one tortuous discussion with Edmonds, Smith had informed him that if the vote over OMOV had been lost at conference, he had a plan B. Smith would have gone to the NEC that evening, and said something along the lines: 'OK, the game's a bogey. This is now a matter of confidence. I want another conference motion later in the week on OMOV, and if I don't win, I will resign.' In these circumstances, Edmonds promised (though nothing was written down) that the GMB would have backed down and supported the leadership on the confidence motion. Murray Elder recalls: 'It was handy for John to have this plan in his back pocket should things go wrong.' However, the negative side was that it meant that Edmonds' speech to the conference on OMOV was more intransigent than it otherwise would have been. The GMB leader felt he could play hard to get.[104] Smith allegedly told Edmonds that, unlike most members of the shadow Cabinet, he could enjoy a comfortable life as a QC if his political career fell through,[105] although we should take what Edmonds says with a pinch of salt. Smith had deliberately not made the first OMOV vote a vote of confidence, having seen Major's damaging use of the 'nuclear option' over Maastricht in July 1993 (see chapter 20).[106]

As with so many of the most important political decisions in his life, Smith discussed the whole issue a few days before the vote with Derry Irvine, the future Lord Chancellor.[107] But it seems that Larry Whitty first mooted the idea of a confidence vote on OMOV. On 9 August 1993, he wrote to Smith predicting that he was almost certain to lose: 'Only if the GMB (or TGWU) shift will any others start to shift except on a clear confidence vote for and against the Leader.'[108] In the attached assessment, he concluded:

> If defeated, I am *not* in favour of delaying to a Special Conference or a Ballot (which is now being publicly talked about). If it is an issue of confidence then the emergency NEC meeting should *either* put the issue of confidence to *this* Conference, *or* accept the decision and come up with its own procedure under its own powers in due course. I favour the latter option, but the former – though high-risk – would give you a clearer cut victory, though in my view at a heavy price.[109]

So Whitty, who had been opposed to Smith's plans to abandon union involvement in the selection of parliamentary candidates, and had tried privately to reach a compromise solution with the union leaders, in the final analysis realised that his leader's mind was made up, and therefore that he should do everything possible to ensure a victory for the leader.

For days in the run-up to the big vote, Smith kept asking for bits of paper so he could tally up how many votes he had on his side of the argument.[110] Elizabeth Smith recalls that 'ever since he was first married to me, John loved writing on the backs of envelopes'. She adds that 'John had this phrase: "The currency of politics is votes."'[111] But in the case of OMOV, it didn't matter how often (and it was very often!) Smith totted up the votes for and against, with the undecideds at the bottom, he came up with the same depressing answer: defeat.

Smith desperately needed to win over the Union for Manufacturing, Science, Finance (MSF) delegation, headed by Ken Gill. The MSF delegation had met on the eve of the conference on the Sunday. Hilary Armstrong, not only Smith's PPS but also an MSF delegate, recalls that had a vote of the MSF delegates been taken on that Sunday night, it would have been anti-OMOV, but in the end delegates were persuaded not to put the matter to a vote.[112] The leadership needed to find a way to get the MSF delegation to change its mind.

David Gardner, Labour's National Constitutional Officer, was responsible for combining the NEC proposed rule changes on OMOV, endorsed at the last NEC in London the week before conference, with one supporting the introduction of a quota system for women, requiring half of all winnable seats with no sitting Labour MP to choose a woman candidate, into one single rule change, which became known as rule change E. He did so because he wanted to maximise the breadth of support for the whole package of reforms, both from CLP and union delegations. Separate votes would have allowed cherry-picking and possible defeat for both vital elements.[113] There was also a technical importance to the resolution because the platform had to come out with the right sequence of votes and it had to group the votes together in such a way as to prevent one vote leaving the rest of the OMOV package in tatters. Larry Whitty's recollection is that he had only agreed to the combined rule change as a conscious means of maximising the vote from the CLPs. He saw the constituency vote as being 'soft', but felt that the unions had largely made up their minds. He was not aware of how tight the position was with the MSF, and that their possible abstention was attainable.[114]

Unknown to Whitty, Anne Gibson (a key MSF delegate)[115] and Hilary Armstrong were trying to cook up a way of turning the all-women's short-lists' inclusion in the resolution to swing an MSF abstention. The pair spent several minutes going up and down in a lift to the puzzlement of fellow delegates. Eventually, they came up with the fairly disingenuous argument that the only honourable thing for MSF to do, given their long-standing commitment to all-women short-lists, was to abstain on rule change E. It was agreed that Gibson should do all the speaking at the MSF meeting arranged for the Wednesday lunchtime because Armstrong was obviously too closely associated with Smith.[116]

But on Wednesday morning, when John Smith stood up to open the debate on OMOV, his second conference speech in just nineteen hours,[117] the abstention from MSF was not yet forthcoming. The leader was up-front with the delegates about his reasoning for pushing the OMOV reforms:

> What millions of trade union members and Labour Party supporters all over this country want above all else is a Labour Government. As Leader of our Party, charged with the responsibility for securing that victory, I say to

this Conference that the changes I propose today are vital – absolutely central – to our strategy for winning power. I ask you to unite behind them.[118]

In the debate that followed, Bill Jordan, of the Amalgamated Electrical and Engineering Union, followed the leadership line, claiming that 'the electorate are watching. Your vote today will answer a question they are entitled to ask: who really leads the Labour Party? Tell them it is John Smith.'[119] However, the atmosphere of the conference had turned against the leadership by lunchtime. Murray Elder had expected that Tom Sawyer or Rodney Bickerstaffe would speak in support of the platform on behalf of NUPE. Instead, Maggie Jones, senior political officer at NUPE, ended up by adopting too antagonistic a tone with the union leaders opposed to OMOV.[120] John Edmonds likened Smith's reforms to 'an iceberg – the little bit you see above the surface looks benign enough. It even flashes in the sunshine. But it is the nasty bit below the surface that does the damage.'[121] Bill Morris then made an effective defence of the TGWU's position, arguing that the debate was not about giving rights to constituencies, it was about taking away the rights of four million levy-paying members.[122]

At this stage, two unions were showing some signs of movement: the Union of Communication Workers, and MSF. If a deal could be struck then Smith knew he would be 'home and dry', but at lunchtime, they had not yet secured an MSF abstention. Smith had already met with Roger Lyons, general secretary of MSF, only to hear Lyons report that he had failed to win over his delegation. The Labour leader's reply is said to have been to tell Lyons to go back and 'f****** well try again'.[123] Hilary Armstrong also met Lyons that morning and offered him a way out, suggesting the all-women short-lists route that she had cooked up earlier with Anne Gibson. She got into 'a real strop' when he refused to show 'a bit of leadership' and take up the idea, and claims that 'he didn't understand it'.[124]

Sally Morgan and Murray Elder discussed the changing atmosphere and agreed that John Prescott should be asked to give the closing speech on behalf of the platform. Larry Whitty was scheduled to wind up the debate, but he was in that slot in case John Smith wanted to speak again. John had already spoken in the morning, but that didn't necessarily preclude him from doing so again in the afternoon.[125] But in Elder's view 'it had to be John [Prescott]'.[126] If mandated constituency delegates were indeed to change their vote, then they would need a pretty convincing explanation to give to their fellow party members back in the CLPs as to why they had changed their minds: John Prescott's powers of persuasion and pull with the party was about as good a

reason as they could ever come up with. Moreover, from the beginning of
Smith's leadership, Prescott had been the strongest and most consistent
supporter of OMOV.

Meanwhile, Margaret Beckett was against the whole idea of OMOV:

> I felt that the Party didn't need to make so great a change. John had floated
> ideas about reform of OMOV in his leadership campaign. People assumed
> the leader had committed himself. He hadn't. It all ended up being very
> risky, causing difficulties in the Party because it was seen as breaking the
> link [with the unions]. John would never have tried to do that, but it was
> seen as a totem, and we had a difficult period.[127]

Labour's deputy leader was concerned that people were telling John that it was
going to be easy to win, which was 'not true'. From an early stage, Beckett was
not part of the conversations on OMOV (although she was a member of the
Union Links Review Group), the only time during John's leadership that she
was left out of key discussions of policy.[128]

On the Saturday before the big OMOV vote, Beckett appeared on the *Today*
programme and described OMOV as 'not the most burning issue of the
week'.[129] Then she miscalculated the day before the vote by failing wholeheartedly to endorse the leadership line in a BBC interview. Asked whether she
thought Smith would win, she replied: 'I very much hope that we will be able
to reach a decision.'[130] She even sympathised with delegates opposed to rule
change E, claiming some of them were not really opposed to OMOV.[131]
Beckett's stance subsequently did her great harm, both in her relationship with
John, and the other John – John Prescott – who was able to defeat her in the
deputy leadership contest in 1994. But even with the benefit of hindsight,
Beckett does not regret her decision not to support John on OMOV: 'Deputy
leaders down the years have taken different stances from their leaders. I
believed I was very loyal to John. But I felt that great errors were being made.
I did not express dissent or encourage people to vote against the platform.'[132]

At about eleven o'clock, John Prescott was called away from the conference
platform for a quick meeting with Murray Elder and John Smith. Prescott said
he would do it, provided Margaret Beckett was on board, and that Larry
Whitty, who was due to wind up the debate, also agreed.[133] Prescott did it his
way, and none of the delegates knew until the last minute that he was going to
close the debate.

Meanwhile, the MSF delegation had met in secret, successfully avoiding the
journalists because a pre-booked church hall had been their venue. It also
helped the leadership's cause (whether by accident or by design) that one of
the hardliners couldn't find the venue and failed to turn up.[134] At the meeting,

Anne Gibson's speech (prearranged with Hilary Armstrong) did the trick because it placed MSF delegates in a dilemma: either they had to renege on their promise to improve women's representation in Parliament or they had to back down on OMOV. Faced with such a dilemma, the only 'honourable course' was to abstain. Dr Lynne Jones, an MSF member and a leading member of the Campaign Group of Labour MPs, did not like the way the two motions had been combined into one rule change, but did not allow the episode to damage her high regard for John Smith.[135]

The MSF delegation voted narrowly by nineteen votes to seventeen to abstain.[136] Hilary Armstrong told Smith the news that he'd won.[137] But John Prescott, who was about to speak, wasn't informed in case it put him off his vital speech.[138] David Hill, Smith's press officer, argues that the morning's debate had seen a slippage of support among the CLP delegates, and that Prescott's speech was therefore pivotal in shoring up that part of the electoral college.[139] On examining the arithmetic of the union block votes, it might at first seem that Prescott's speech was not crucial in tipping the vote the leadership's way because the MSF abstention accounted for a sizeable and, in terms of winning the vote, pivotal 4.5 per cent of the block vote. There would have had to have been a fairly substantial fall-off in constituency support for the leadership to have lost the vote, given that they eventually won by a margin of 3.1 per cent.

However, the CLP element in the OMOV vote was crucial in democratic terms. Groups of Labour MPs, party officials and members of Smith's office worked tirelessly to try to persuade the CLP delegates at the conference to change their minds. Indeed, the leader's office kept a tally of which CLP delegates were in favour, those firmly opposed, and those who were undecided, and therefore persuadable.[140] (Such attempts to win over delegates set a precedent, and were deployed by Tony Blair's leadership in the period 1994–5 to win Clause IV.) Smith was sending a vitally important message to ordinary party members that their votes mattered. Hilary Armstrong rightly points out that 'Prescott's speech went with the flow of that'.[141]

Smith might have survived the initial blow of defeat on OMOV, provided that he had carried the CLPs with him. In such a circumstance, he would then have been able to argue that the ordinary party members were with him, and that the result was undemocratic, the result of votes cast by union barons, who had mostly not balloted their members.[142] Such an outcome would have, in some ways, echoed Hugh Gaitskell's finest achievement when he narrowly lost a vote on unilateralism at the Scarborough conference in October 1960, but could argue that 65 per cent of the CLPs had voted for the leadership's stance, making the trade unions' victory a pyrrhic one.[143]

However, what has not emerged from any of the accounts of OMOV so far
is that Larry Whitty, as the Labour Party's general secretary, was very reluctant
to allow Labour Party staff to be used to help to deliver constituency votes on
OMOV. On the preceding Saturday night, at a meeting in Whitty's room at
the conference hotel with Murray Elder and Sally Morgan, Whitty agreed to
this happening, 'after quite a heavy – if not heated – discussion'.[144] Whitty
recalls: 'I would not use Party staff up until that point. I wouldn't normally
have done so on a point of principle.' The primary reason for Whitty's
conversion was that, although he was not a fan of Smith's version of OMOV,
he preferred it to seeing the leader defeated. He finally agreed, seeing it 'as a
unique exercise to ensure that the Leader had the best chance of winning'.[145]
Subsequently, Whitty felt that the use of party staff may have 'set an
unfortunate precedent'.[146]

John Prescott's closing speech in the OMOV debate marked the culmin-
ation of the canvassing of delegates on the floor of conference. According to
Prescott, Smith told him that morning of the confidence vote plan.
Interestingly, Prescott claims he would have opposed his leader, adding: 'You
cannot ask the conference to stand on its head. They won't do it.'[147] If anyone
actually tries to read Prescott's speech, they will not find a proper sentence in
it. The poor party conference transcribers did their best:

> Trade unionist argue with the fervour that they have about this issue, that
> their Conference has made a decision, and we perhaps are a little bit
> annoyed they cannot change to a different one. That should not be a reason
> for attacking them for defending a democratically-arrived-at decision in
> the movement. Let us be in accord, and recognise the right of each
> constituent part of the movement. It is important.[148]

Prescott reminded delegates of Smith's fervent defence of trade unions at the
TUC conference a few weeks before, and concluded:

> There is no doubt that this man, our Leader, put his head on the block by
> saying, basically: "*I fervently believe*" – because that is what he believes – "*in
> the relationship between the trade unions and the Labour Party*". He has put
> his head on the block. Now is our time to vote. Give us a bit of trust and let
> us vote to support him.[149]

Even this tidied-up transcription of Prescott's speech is tortuous. Despite the
grammar, everyone in that conference hall knew how much Prescott cared
about the unions. Writing in *Tribune*, Bill Hagerty described Prescott's speech
as 'electrifying' and the debate as 'a show of shows with John Prescott the
star'.[150] Pauline Prescott said afterwards to Alastair Campbell: 'If he [John

Prescott] does nothing else in his life, that speech had everything.'¹⁵¹ While one might concur with Donald Macinytre's assessment that Prescott's speech had not changed the outcome of the vote on OMOV, few would disagree with his conclusion that 'it transformed what would have been a sullen, and perhaps reversible, vote in favour of OMOV into a tumultuous endorsement both of the leadership and of change in the Party'.¹⁵² It was unquestionably one of the most impressive party conference speeches of the decade. And as Denis Healey rightly points out, Smith had achieved OMOV 'with a lot of support from John Prescott . . . both [Johns] share the credit'.¹⁵³

OMOV had been high-tension stuff and, as James Naughtie puts it, after the vote, Smith 'had the high spirits of a man who had been spared the gallows'.¹⁵⁴ This elation at winning the vote was spoilt somewhat when Anna Ford asked him on BBC1's *Six o'Clock News* whether it hadn't been a 'stupid idea' to push the issue of OMOV to the point where his leadership was put on the line. He was so annoyed that he refused to be interviewed for the *Nine o'Clock News*.¹⁵⁵

But not even the BBC could put a damper on the celebration party that night. For the first time, Smith's whole family attended to lend moral support. 'We were like that,' says Elizabeth, 'pulling together as a family when it mattered.'¹⁵⁶ During the day, the three Smith daughters sat in the front row of the conference hall. Up in the suite that evening, basking in victory and surrounded by political friends and family, Sarah recalls that there were 'a lot of us, and lots of bottles of champagne'.¹⁵⁷

John Smith loved champagne. When Sue Lawley had asked Smith (as shadow Chancellor) on *Desert Island Discs* which luxury he would take with him on a desert island, Smith replied: 'I would take a case of champagne. I would enjoy drinking it and then I would send messages out in the bottles.'¹⁵⁸ A few days later, Smith's office received a rude letter from someone pointing out that it was impossible to put champagne corks back in their bottles after they had been popped open.¹⁵⁹ Hilary Armstrong recalls that Smith had a tankard in the members' smoking room, which most people assumed was filled with beer, when it frequently contained champagne.¹⁶⁰

Unsurprisingly, it was a struggle to get up the next morning. When Mike Elrick entered the plush five-room suite that the Grand Hotel had laid on for the leader, he knocked on his leader's bedroom door to borrow an iron. He was greeted by a bleary-eyed John Smith dressed only in vest, socks and underpants.¹⁶¹ Smith had to make an appearance on the conference platform (though he didn't have to give a speech) within half an hour. Not wanting to risk Smith being interviewed at the front entrance to the hotel, he, Smith and the members of Special Branch assigned to Smith took a back route, only to encounter a locked door. Eventually, they got the leader into the conference centre. After about an hour on the platform, Smith made his excuses and left.[162]

Everyone knew that John Smith believed in the Labour Party and in the trade unions, and, albeit by the skin of his teeth, he had brought the party and the Labour movement with him in introducing a difficult change. His victory did not result in a massive backlash or a great aftershock from the trade unions, and in that sense it was a vindication of his whole style of leadership. There had been rancour, but even at its height (in the spring and summer of 1993), it had not got totally out of hand, at least not by Labour Party standards.

Nonetheless, Smith's OMOV victory came at a price in terms of party funding. Shortly afterwards, Bill Morris told Larry Whitty that 'it would no longer be "business as usual"'. The TGWU and the GMB chose to cut their affiliation fees to the party, meaning a shortfall to party funds of £290,000. On 1 December 1993, Whitty, forever the pessimist, wrote to Murray Elder:

> I can no longer produce anything out of a hat. If this goes on, we will stagger through 1994, and Party finances are likely to collapse in 1995 or 1996 *unless* we use the general election Fund in that period (which is difficult constitutionally in any case) and take our chance on a low media spend on the general election itself. That is not a course I would seriously advise, but we may have to face up to it.[163]

It is a moot point whether the bruising experience over OMOV would have incurred long-term damage to Smith's relationship with the trade union leaders had he become Prime Minister. In September 1990, Smith had indicated during the TUC's annual conference in Blackpool that 'should a Labour government be elected, it will not lock out trade unions from consideration of economic and social policy as happened through the Thatcher years'.[164] Gavin Laird feels that John would have sought closer links with the unions in government, but wouldn't have 'bowed the knee'.[165] Some of the union barons – particularly John Edmonds – had, in Smith's view, behaved so badly that 'Prime Minister' Smith might have behaved in a tougher way with them in government. Smith had encountered all too vividly that tendency among trade union leaders to bank concessions from Labour leaders, and then to come back with another set of demands without giving anything in return, as if no concessions had been made in the first place.

But for every John Edmonds there was a Rodney Bickerstaffe or a Gavin Laird, moderate union leaders who had helped to sway the vote on OMOV in Smith's favour. On 15 October, John wrote to thank Laird:

Without your steadying and encouraging support, we could not have done it. It was an important challenge for Labour and we are now a much better party for having made the changes. I think there is no doubt that we have increased our attractiveness to both potential members and the voting public.

Hope to see you on the hills before too long.

Yours ever

John[166]

Whatever interpretation one draws, only a man respected by the unions could have secured such a major change at that time in Labour's history. Victory had been achieved without the support of his deputy Margaret Beckett, in the teeth of opposition from John Edmonds, Smith's supposed kingmaker, and without the active support of Tony Blair, who positioned himself (like Beckett) in case his leader fell.

According to David Ward, John Smith and Tony Blair met to patch up their differences at a private dinner in January 1994,[167] after an extended period of coolness between them throughout the autumn of 1993. Tony thought that John had been too timid and compromised too much over OMOV. As a result of this meeting, Smith suggested that Ward have lunch with Blair to involve him more closely in the post-OMOV policy thinking. At the lunch, held in Vitello D'Oro, an Italian restaurant next to Church House, Ward recalls impressing upon Blair the need to improve his relations with Smith, and discussing in outline various ideas for speeches.[168] Derry Irvine, however, denies that relations became tense between Tony and John, adding that 'John ran the show then'.[169] And that was that.

At any rate, Blair's failure to lend his leader support in his time of need can be seen in retrospect as a tactical error, for it allowed the rise of John Prescott who loyally stood by Smith. In the subsequent shadow Cabinet reshuffle in October 1993, Smith gave Prescott the Employment portfolio he coveted. Frank Dobson, another keen supporter of OMOV, reluctantly accepted Prescott's old job at Transport, but as a sweetener he also gained additional responsibility for London. But, Larry Whitty is the real unsung hero of OMOV. Even though he had a proper falling-out with Smith over the content of the reform package, Labour's general secretary charted a way through, coming up with the confidence vote idea, and backing the leader when it really mattered, endorsing (albeit reluctantly) the canvassing of the CLP on the floor of conference.

Contrary to the views of Kinnock and the modernisers, Smith had done the right thing in not charging ahead with changes to OMOV in 1992 instead of

1993. After the bruising reforms of the Kinnock period, the party was not ready for another bout of huge change. The system agreed wasn't pure OMOV, as Blair wanted, but it was a workable OMOV.[170] The unions had to ballot their members for leadership and deputy leadership elections, and no longer had such a big say in the selection of parliamentary candidates. As Denis Healey argues: 'OMOV broke the union barons' hold.'[171] Roy Hattersley goes so far as to argue that Smith should 'take credit for the most important reform in the party's post-war history'.[172] But that means it was a more important reform than Clause IV, a claim that requires close examination.

The accusation from the modernisers is that a shocked and relieved Smith put up the shutters on any further modernisation of the party after his bruising experiences over OMOV.[173] Post-OMOV, Hilary Armstrong recalls that John did feel it was necessary to 'give people a rest' because he felt he had 'pushed things a long way'. But she is not one of the people in the party who believe that Smith would have done nothing else. Moreover, the OMOV episode showed that 'he did take risks'.[174] But how did this approach relate to possible reform of Clause IV?

On the face of it, the debate over whether to rewrite Clause IV mattered little. In straightforward policy terms, Labour has never implemented its famous Section Four – worker control of industry – when in government. First adopted in 1918, it enunciated Labour's main aim as:

> To secure for the workers by hand or by brain the full fruits of their industry and the most equitable distribution thereof that may be possible, upon the basis of the common ownership of the means of production, distribution and exchange, and the best obtainable system of popular administration and control of each industry and service.[175]

In November 1959, John Smith's hero, Hugh Gaitskell, had discovered to his cost the huge symbolic importance of the clause to the Labour movement after his conference defeat over the issue. Smith faced calls from Jack Straw (in May 1993)[176] and Neil Kinnock (February 1994)[177] to completely rewrite Clause IV. Hilary Armstrong recalls that Smith was 'irritated' by Straw's intervention on the issue.[178] In fact, it went beyond mere irritation. As early as 12 September 1992, Straw had sent a draft report of his analysis of Labour's 1992 general election defeat to the leader's office. Straw's basic analysis (in a very wordy paper) was that Labour had lost because people believed 'you can't trust Labour' and that 'implied that we ourselves were not clear what we stood for, what we believed in'. In a section entitled 'Policy and Ideology', Straw concluded:

It will now be apparent that I think that a change to Clause 4 is needed if we are to refresh our appeal to the electorate as a governing party which takes Britain into the 21st century, and the second millennium. Clause 4 will celebrate its 25th anniversary at the end of next February [1993], so this may be a fitting moment to begin that recasting of the clause.[179]

After Straw had written his initial draft report, John and Jack spoke on the telephone, an occasion that Straw vividly recalls:

He told me that I was wrong in arguing that Clause IV should be rewritten, I would stir up a hornets' nest ('look at what had happened to Gaitskell'), and as a result would damage my own political standing and very possibly lose my seat on the shadow Cabinet in the next year's PLP election (a prospect which evidently caused him no great anxiety). I asked him whether he agreed with Clause IV. No, he said, but it should be allowed simply to 'wither on the vine'. It was 'a sentimental souvenir, best ignored'. I quoted these words, but without attribution, when I set out the 'case against change' in my *Policy and Ideology* pamphlet.[180] I told John that I respected his views but did not agree with them, and that I did not intend to give up on my campaign. He was not pleased.[181]

Straw then turned his long paper into a short pamphlet. Partly because of Smith's warning, Straw thought it wise to get his local Labour Party in Blackburn explicitly on board, and officers of the Blackburn CLP agreed that he could publish the pamphlet, although it was stressed by John Roberts (chair) and Phil Riley (secretary) in the eventual publication that: 'This pamphlet contains Jack's personal views. They have not been endorsed by the Blackburn Constituency Labour Party.'[182] Straw admits his actions were only retrospectively endorsed by his general management committee, and even then on a close vote.[183]

Straw then sent his leader a draft of *Policy and Ideology* some time over the Christmas 1992/New Year 1993 period and, soon after, Straw asked to see Smith. Apparently, the meeting 'began in a frosty atmosphere, and went from bad to worse':[184]

John had great charm and wit, and this was the side which the public saw. But he also had a temper . . . and was intolerant of those who persisted in disagreeing with him. John was aggressive in our meeting, something which I thought could be put down to an understanding by him that he was vulnerable on the issue of modernisation – or the lack of it – of the Party.[185]

Indeed, there couldn't be a better set-piece illustration of the fundamental difference that emerged between Smith and the modernisers, namely that while Smith thought reform of OMOV was sufficient to get Labour elected, modernisers like Straw wanted to go much further. Straw is fairly disparaging of Smith's strategy:

> Although John engaged in some change in the Party (principally OMOV), he essentially had an 'ins and outs' view of politics, that there would come a moment when it was 'our turn'. Meanwhile the best thing the Party could do was to get behind him, and on no account rock the boat. This view was not shared by Neil Kinnock, nor by Tony Blair; and late in 1993 and early 1994 some of this criticism surfaced. Meanwhile, I think I was some sort of lightning conductor for John's concern.[186]

During their meeting, Smith again reiterated his position that Straw would be stirring up a hornets' nest, and that he might well lose his seat on the shadow Cabinet 'because of the unpopularity I would bring on my head'. Straw responded by saying that he 'disagreed with his [Smith's] analysis totally'. The Labour Party, he argued had to have 'the confidence to acknowledge that what was right in October 1917 (when Clause 4 was drafted) was not necessarily right in 1993'. Straw said to Smith that he would have to accept the consequences, including the loss of his seat in the shadow Cabinet if the pamphlet were not to be well received: 'I had taken the matter too far in my head to back off now.' Straw had been alone with Smith for getting on for an hour. Smith lost his temper: 'Amidst raised voices, I sought to take my leave. "You can take this with you too," he shouted, as he threw the envelope containing my pamphlet at me. I left.'[187]

On John Smith's death, Jack Straw wrote a tribute in *The Times* in which he described Smith as 'the toughest politician I have ever encountered . . . Some learnt their lessons from John the easy way, others the hard way.'[188]

Roy Hattersley claims that Smith had considered sacking Jack Straw: 'I had to intervene to point out that the young man didn't mean any harm.'[189] In fact, it wasn't in the Labour leader's power to sack Straw in the sense of removing him from the shadow Cabinet, as when Labour is in opposition, the PLP elects the shadow Cabinet annually. However, the allocation of shadow portfolios *was* within his gift. Theoretically, Straw could have had his portfolio withdrawn, and yet still sat and argued his piece at shadow Cabinet meetings. As it was, Smith had already shown his displeasure with Straw by giving him 'a limited lower-grade portfolio shadowing two-thirds of the Department of the Environment'.[190]

As early as 1960, John Smith had described Clause IV to his friend Kenneth Munro as a 'shibboleth'. John had also said that the ability to exercise economic control was much more important than ownership.[191] It was another Smith view that didn't really change as the years progressed. In February 1994, Smith described the debate about getting rid of Clause IV as 'academic'[192] – the question of who owned British industry had ceased to be relevant. It was a diversion from more important tasks. Straw is correct in his analysis that privately at least Smith felt that it would be damaging to party unity if he took on the issues of OMOV and Clause IV at the same time.[193] Frank Dobson believes that John realised that getting rid of Clause IV was 'more trouble than it was worth'.[194] David Ward agrees. In a rare use of a religious analogy, Smith commented to Ward: 'People need their icons, their altars. You can't make people change everything all of the time.'[195] According to Murray Elder, Smith had been explaining his attitude towards Clause IV to a group of Russians. Clause IV was like an icon that for years had been placed at the centre of the church. Smith said he wanted to move it to the side of the church because it was no longer central, but people could still go and see it if they wished.[196]

Had Smith lived, he would have put his own imprint on Clause IV, but he wouldn't have completely rewritten it. The journalist Colin Brown argued, not naming his source, that one of Smith's last ideas before he died was to issue a statement outlining his own Christian Socialist beliefs, based on his R. H. Tawney Lecture, *Reclaiming the Ground*, of 20 March 1993.[197] The statement would have been issued in June 1995, and put to the party conference for October of that year. It would have been laid alongside Clause IV, rather than seeking to replace it. David Ward, Smith's chief policy adviser, has since confirmed that this would have happened.[198] Smith's intended statement of aims echoed Gaitskell's 'New Testament' aims of February 1960, except that Gaitskell had been forced to come up with his version as a result of the conference defeat on the rewriting of Clause IV that he had suffered three months earlier.[199]

At the October 1994 Labour Party conference, delegates voted to retain Clause IV.[200] Even when Blair tackled the issue head-on about six months later, he recognised the importance of involving the broader party before contemplating change: the archetypal party man, John Prescott, was brought on board to sell the idea, and the entire membership was balloted in a referendum to bind the whole party into the decision. The result was overwhelming: at the special conference on 29 April 1995, only three out of 500 constituencies that balloted their members voted against the change to Clause IV.[201] It is ironic that the reduction in the union block vote to only 49 per cent, as a result of Smith's 1993 OMOV reforms, greatly assisted Blair in his efforts to secure the change.

The greatest single merit of Blair's rewriting of Clause IV is that it positioned New Labour as close as possible to the views of the median voter. Panel evidence from the British election Study conducted by Heath, Jowell and Curtice shows that a disproportionate number of Conservative voters switched across to Labour as a direct result of Blair's ideological repositioning of the Labour Party on economic issues.[202]

Historically, OMOV was probably a more important change than Clause IV, the latter being a cosmetic exercise, a piece of symbolism designed to appeal to disaffected Tory voters pondering whether to switch to Labour. Smith's reform, on the other hand, took away real power from the union leaders, more so than at any time since 1918, especially in relation to the selection of parliamentary candidates, and gave it back to ordinary party members, and indeed ordinary trade unionists, many of whom subsequently became Labour Party members. The union leaders could no longer fix things as they had done in the past. OMOV was also probably the most important single reform in Labour's history, but not as important as the Kinnock reforms taken as a whole.

Such a conclusion is open to debate, but perhaps modernisers and long-gamers can at least agree on one point: as Murray Elder argues, Smith's OMOV victory cleared the way for Blair's eventual reform of Clause IV, for the hardest battle of all had already been fought and won by Smith.[203]

Twenty-Three
STRESSES AND STRAINS

HILARY ARMSTRONG RECALLS that John Smith would come into Parliament for his breakfast and would be there until midnight at least. 'It was the kind of existence where there was often no milk to make a cup of tea in the flat.'[1] Jimmy Gordon describes John Smith as 'indefatigable', travelling from London to Edinburgh and back again, as well as campaigning elsewhere: 'They say that hard work doesn't kill you, but bad transport can, standing at platforms waiting for a train at 2 am.'[2]

In the early 1990s, Labour was continuing an intense period in its history. For the leader, there was a brutal assault course of NEC meetings, speech preparation, including rewrites right up until the last minute, not to mention the formidable round of receptions in the evenings. Smith's ability to be the life and soul of any party helped him to excel on these occasions, but they were very tiring, meaning that the whole conference experience could be pretty gruelling. And the leader of the Labour Party wasn't just required to attend the annual Labour conference: special conferences, the seasonal conferences, the Scottish and Welsh conferences, and of course, the TUC conferences – as well as many of the individual union conferences – were all part of the round. Frank Dobson recalls that during these union conferences, Smith would stay in the bar chatting until late. He would remind John to get to his bed, not because he was looking ill, but because he had to be up early in the morning. No one can keep on doing that indefinitely.[3]

Most functions include the inevitable buffet. John's particular weakness was peanuts.[4] Ann Barrett remembers: 'John was a nibbler. He spent six to nine months after his heart attack being careful about what he ate, then he reverted to old habits. You can't change a person's basic outlook on life.'[5] The author's abiding image of Smith is of him being caught on camera eating a Mars bar, and the sheepish look on his face as he tries to hide the wrapper. Ann once chastised John for drinking too much from a bottle of whisky. Puzzled, Smith asked: 'How did you know that?' Ann replied: 'I marked it!'[6] On another occasion, John went to the House of Commons gym where the leader of the opposition debuted in black gym shoes and vest; hardly the latest sports wear.

By chance, he spotted his press officer, Mike Elrick, and for the rest of their respective workouts the two men studiously attempted to avoid each other's gaze.[7]

John spent more time in London with Elizabeth after he became Labour leader because of the huge number of official engagements that they both had to attend. Odd evenings were set aside for going to the cinema, or just flopping in front of the television, but fewer than they would have liked. Only hillwalking provided Smith with any meaningful relaxation. However, if you are leader of the opposition, freeing up the necessary time to go hillwalking can be extremely stressful in itself. It's a telling fact that while John had conquered around 96 Munros from April 1989 until July 1992 as shadow Chancellor, he managed a mere dozen in his 22 months as leader of the opposition.[8]

Nevertheless, John bagged his 100th Munro – Stob Dearg, part of the Buachaille Etive Mor group – on Saturday, 12 September 1992, celebrating his birthday weekend with Murray Elder, Mike Elrick, Alan Haworth, Ranald MacLean, and Dr Mike Ryan (the doctor who had taken Smith into the old Royal Hospital in Edinburgh back in 1988).[9] John had gone to considerable lengths in the previous couple of weeks to get himself into a position where he could tackle his 100th Munro. On Thursday, 27 August, he went up on the hills on his own as 'part of bid to get to 12th September', climbing his 97th Munro, Meall Bhuidhe in the Rannoch-Glen Lyon range. However, he did not set off until 4.45 pm, and got down only as darkness was falling at about 11 pm. The weather had been bad for weeks, and John went east to the Mounth group to get better weather, and the tactic worked, but only just. On the way up, John spotted 'Balmoral stalkers – perhaps royalty', but the weather turned nasty. Although he bagged Cairn Bannoch (No. 98), he had to shelter behind a cairn, and was on the point of turning back when he spotted two members of the Grampian Police Mountain Rescue Team, who were out walking socially. John fell in with the two policemen, bagging Cairn Bannoch, his 99th Munro.[10] Alan Howarth believes that 'The gods smiled on John Smith that day.'[11]

Haworth admits: 'While he was a joy to be with, and was very enthusiastic, I wouldn't have liked to have been on a hill with John directing the way.'[12] In August 1989, John, Alan Haworth and Murray Elder had climbed Sgurr na Ciche. John jumped enthusiastically to the next ledge, digging his heels in as he landed. Alan Haworth reflects: 'I remember saying to John, "Have a care!" . . . Had we been roped up, we could have all gone down the hill like skittles.'[13] Unlike most of his friends, John had not begun his hillwalking career at university, and his lack of experience occasionally showed.

However, the hills still had that capacity to soothe Smith's soul, as conveyed when he wrote the foreword to Peter Drummond and Ian Mitchell's biography of the Reverend Archibald Eneas Robertson (1870–1958), *First Munroist*, published in the summer of 1993. Drummond was a constituent of John's.[14] On this occasion, the normally prosaic Smith gave vent to a very rare bout of flowery language to describe the day – 28 December 1992 – when he climbed Beinn Challum, part of the Mamlorn group, John's 101st Munro:

> About a 1,000 feet up we broke through the cloud inversion and entered a magical world. The sky was blue, the sunlight reflected on the snow, and above an all-encompassing sea of cloud all we could see in every direction was mountains. To the south the Crianlarich Hills and the Arrochar Alps, to the east the Lawers group, to the west Cruachan, and to the north and north-west Ben Nevis itself and the Mamore hills. I do not believe there was a better place to be on the face of the earth that winter's day than on the top of a Scottish mountain.[15]

But even precious moments intended for relaxation and leisure could not guarantee relief from the stresses and strains of being leader of the opposition. One weekend in May 1993, when Smith was about to go walking in the hills (to celebrate Gavin Laird's 60th birthday)[16] panned out thus: first Joe Gormley, former president of the National Union of Mineworkers died,[17] then John Major sacked Norman Lamont as Chancellor of the Exchequer.[18] Smith had to do a series of impromptu interviews in his Edinburgh home, making him pressed for time. Disaster struck as Smith discovered that the zip of his suitcase had broken. Then he got into his aged B-reg. Ford Sierra that proved to be a nightmare, always emitting clouds of poisonous fumes. The following day, Smith and his party of walkers took on the fairly arduous 20-mile walk over the Lairig Ghru.[19] On this occasion, however, John failed to complete the walk: feeling unwell at less than halfway, he turned back.[20]

Nor did an official trip abroad provide much in the way of hoped-for relaxation. Over Christmas 1993, Smith went to Israel accompanied by Elizabeth, their three daughters, Mike Elrick and Meta Ramsay. Meta felt it was important to foster the Jewish vote and improve links with Labour's sister party in Israel, including its leader and Prime Minister, Yitzhak Rabin. Israel was chosen in preference to India, where Smith would have visited the following year, had he lived.[21] The leader of the opposition made only one official visit abroad in 22 months.

From 20–26 December, the Smith family stayed in Jerusalem. When the Smiths arrived at the Church of the Nativity in Bethlehem on Christmas Eve for an Anglican carol service (as guests of the Anglican Bishop of Jerusalem, who was an Arab), they were not permitted to use the church, and had to stand on the top of the roof, as the only place where the Anglicans had permission to stand. Smith greatly enjoyed a Christmas Day service in St Andrew's church in Jerusalem as the guest of the Scottish minister there. He also had excellent individual meetings with Prime Minister Rabin, and Shimon Peres, the Israeli Foreign Minister, both of whom he knew from meetings of the Socialist International.[22]

The rest of the visit was not a great success in terms of generating publicity. Smith grew increasingly irritated with his minder, whom he considered patronising. He was also unhappy with the briefing he received from a senior Israeli security spokesperson. Mike Elrick recalls: 'John didn't suffer fools gladly, and he felt insulted by the bog standard briefing, believing that he had not been given the respect that a Leader of the opposition from Britain deserved.' However, a Christmas Party on the night of 29 December with the British Ambassador, Andrew Burns, at his residency in Tel Aviv proved enjoyable.[23]

Back in Scotland, stories were coming out of Monklands District Council (MDC) in John Smith's constituency, which further added to his concerns. Monklands Council had come into being in 1974. There was no specific place called 'Monklands'. Rather, most of the council comprised the towns of Airdrie (wholly situated in Smith's Monklands East constituency), and Coatbridge (which was mainly Catholic, and mostly located in the neighbouring Monklands West, save for approximately 8,000 voters). Lanarkshire politics has always been tribal, but it became much more accentuated in the post-war era when the lack of electoral competition caused the emergence effectively of one-party states, especially in and around Glasgow. One interpretation of the root causes of the problems in Monklands is that, deprived of battles with their political opponents, parochial local councillors engaged not so much in wholesale corruption (no evidence was ever found of *criminal* ongoings in Monklands) as occasional malpractice. The councillors wielded great power: in the depressed areas of the central belt of Scotland the local authority was often the area's major employer. Allegations of nepotism were rife. It was said that if a person joined the Labour Party and voted the councillors back into positions of power every year, then favours were returned – a job would be found in the council, or someone would move miraculously up the housing list. The line between the local party machinery and the local authority bureaucracy apparently became blurred. Helen Liddell puts it more strongly: 'It was tribalism at its worst.'[24] And yet, as George

Robertson recalls: 'many of the local councillors did not believe they were doing anything wrong, partly because they had been in power for such a long time.'[25] Matters were long left untouched by Labour's hierarchy in Scotland, the problems being seen as just too ingrained. If Smith was guilty of not intervening, then plenty of other Scottish Labour MPs were guilty of the same reluctance to get embroiled.

The Monklands allegations during Smith's period as Labour leader were threefold. Firstly, it was alleged that Labour councillors from mainly Catholic Coatbridge had kept control of nearly all the top jobs in MDC at the expense of the people in mainly Protestant Airdrie. However, the religious divide between the two towns did not play any part in this story as some commentators have supposed: virtually all of the people who fell out with one another were Catholics.[26] This was a falling-out between brothers of the same religion and of the same political party.

Secondly, it was alleged that major spending projects had been allocated disproportionately to Coatbridge rather than Airdrie, including prestigious but loss-making developments such as the massive £12 million 'Time Capsule' sports and leisure complex, the Summerlee Industrial Heritage Museum, the Drumpellier Lochs Visitors Centre and the Quandrant Shopping Centre: Coatbridge received £21 million in capital projects, Airdrie had only been given £2.5 million. The difficulty in comparing this apparently huge disparity in funding is two-fold. The comparison is of dissimilar areas: Coatbridge had most of the available derelict land on which building could take place.[27] If large capital projects are excluded from the totals (and they included over 70 per cent of total spending in this area), then Airdrie and Coatbridge received about the same sums of money.[28]

Thirdly, the council was accused of operating a two-tier system for job applications, or at the very least, not following standard practice in its recruitment policies. The dispute started in August 1992 when four rebel Airdrie Labour councillors, Tommy Morgan, Brian Brady, Peter Sullivan and Jim Logue, revealed the existence of green job application forms – apparently only available to councillors – and pink forms for the general public.[29] The Labour Party eventually suspended all four rebel Labour councillors.[30]

In its defence, MDC accurately pointed out that green forms were freely available to the public from council buildings, whereas job centres issued pink forms.[31] Provost[32] Bob Gilson described the allegations as 'utter lies and complete fabrication'.[33] Council Labour group leader, Jim Brooks, even described the four rebels as 'political pop stars intent on promoting their own egos'.[34] Many of Brooks's comments in this period went over then top. In reality, the four Airdrie rebels were very bright people, deserving of advancement within MDC's hierarchy. Could much of the fuss that followed have been avoided had Brooks shared power more widely with these very talented individuals, rather than seeking to hold power in his own hands? By failing to do so, it could be argued that he created an artificial division between the representatives of Airdrie and Coatbridge, the latter feeling that they had been excluded from positions of power.

Matters escalated when Eileen McAuley, a local reporter for the *Airdrie and Coatbridge Advertiser*, delved more deeply into the matter, revealing cases not only of dozens of people who had filled in pink forms that had failed to get jobs with MDC, but, much more damagingly, that 22 relatives of Labour councillors were employed on the local authority's payroll. Close relatives were also apparently given seasonal jobs without being interviewed.[35]

But one flaw in the argument about alleged nepotism in Monklands is cultural. In former times when the pits and the steel works were the main employers in Coatbridge, there was a long tradition and source of pride of family members working in the same factory. Extended families could be so large that not every cousin knew every other cousin's name, or indeed all the names of the people to whom these cousins were married. It is therefore unsurprising that when the pits and the steel works all closed, making the council the largest employer in the area, that many council workers were related to one another. Coatbridge was a relatively small town with a largely closed population: few people left the area to find work. Lastly, it is fair to say that until the controversy erupted, very few people in the local community would have seen anything wrong in the ties of kith and kin evident in their local council.

The reports about the job application forms heralded a two-year campaign by the *Airdrie and Coatbridge Advertiser* against MDC and, by implication, against John Smith and Tom Clarke, the Labour MPs for Monklands East and Monklands West respectively. Indeed, in November 1992, MDC sued the *Advertiser* for defamation, and then refused to display council advertisements in the *Advertiser*, instead publishing its own *Monklands News*. John Smith even sent a congratulatory message to MDC on the launch of *Monklands News* in November 1992, and his warm endorsement appeared on the front page of the first issue.[36]

Labour's Scottish National Executive in Keir Hardie House could not ignore the growing clamour for an investigation into the affair. Jack McConnell, then Labour's general secretary, intervened, holding a series of meetings with MDC councillors to 'get to the bottom' of the affair. At the time, McConnell defended the decision of John Smith and Tom Clarke not to intervene: 'This has got more to do with Labour Party headquarters than to do with the local MPs. Quite rightly, they are detached from the accusations because of their parliamentary duties. This is an internal Labour Party matter and it needs to be dealt with accordingly.'[37] But by this stage, the issue had become a national one, and was grabbed with both hands by the media.[38] On Tuesday, 3 November 1992, the *Daily Record* entered the fray, devoting its front page, an opinion piece and a two-page spread to the Monklands affair. Media interest in the story grew, and it mushroomed out of all proportion to its importance in the body politic.

John Smith and Tom Clarke (who was also shadow Secretary of State for Scotland) tried to maintain a strict silence on the basis that it was a local authority matter. George Robertson, Clarke's successor as shadow Secretary of State for Scotland, points out: 'Most MPs knew these were grossly unfair attacks because there is no mechanism for a local MP to interfere in the workings of the local authority.'[39]

Perhaps the pacifier in Smith, the unifier, the politician who had never sought to create unnecessary enemies, didn't want to get involved. The only time Smith had ever interfered in a local constituency matter – as a naïve law student in the famous Woodside incident (see chapter 3) – he had emerged with his fingers burnt. Some of the key players in this story were very close allies of Smith. Eddie Cairns, chairman of the Monklands East Labour Party, had been Smith's election agent for fifteen years. Moreover, Cairns and Jim Brooks, the Labour group leader, had delivered on Smith's behalf in the past. In 1983, Lanarkshire North disappeared as a result of Boundary Commission changes. The very large constituency of Coatbridge and Airdrie was split into Monklands East and Monklands West. Local Labour Party people like Cairns ensured that Smith emerged unchallenged as the Labour candidate in the newly created seat of Monklands East, despite the fact that Smith had never lived in the constituency.

Mike Elrick believes that Smith feared that if he interfered in such a running sore, he risked adversely affecting his political relationships in his own backyard.[40] Smith also had to act on the basis of proof, rather than what he viewed as a constant swirl of unsubstantiated smears. There was also a danger of giving these stories a credence they didn't deserve: the involvement of the leader at a national level might have seen the whole business escalate way beyond its actual importance, and that did not suit the statesmanlike, Prime Minister-in-waiting pose that Smith was understandably keen to cultivate.

However, the Scottish media and the other political parties took predictable advantage of the situation, increasingly arguing that, as Labour leader, Smith needed to ensure that his party was completely free from accusations of sleaze. How could he attack the Conservative government for its failure to preserve high standards in public life at Prime Minister's Question Time, so the argument ran, if there were allegations of cronyism in his own backyard? Moreover, if Smith was really committed to helping the lives of ordinary people (which he clearly was), didn't that include intervening on behalf of those denied life opportunities by allegedly unfair MDC recruitment practices?[41]

John Smith and Tom Clarke tried valiantly to stress the positive aspects of Lanarkshire. For instance, in September 1992, Smith was photographed in the *Advertiser* as the committed constituency MP giving his backing to the launch of the 'Lanarkshire Civic Pride Campaign', sponsored by the Lanarkshire Development Agency. Smith admitted that the 'deep pride' in Lanarkshire had been 'knocked by recent events'.[42]

In November 1992, the Scottish Labour Party finally set up an inquiry, chaired by Anne McGuire,[43] into MDC's recruitment and selection procedures.[44] And a month later, John Broadfoot, Scotland's Controller of Audit, began extensive inquiries to see if public money had been misappropriated or misspent in any way.[45]

Meanwhile, a renegade English Tory back bencher seized hold of the Monklands issue as something akin to manna from heaven. David Shaw, the Conservative MP for Dover, raised the issue repeatedly at Scottish Questions. Initially, Ian Lang, the Secretary of State for Scotland, studiously refused, as he put it, to 'pry into [Labour's] private grief'.[46] The furore in the House of Commons started on Wednesday, 16 December 1992 when Shaw asked:

> Is my right hon. Friend aware that many Scottish people in my constituency have been shocked to learn that 22 relatives of Labour councillors are employed by Monklands District Council? . . . Is my right hon. Friend aware that the people of Airdrie and Coatbridge believe that they can obtain houses, council house transfers and repairs only if they have the approval of the ruling Labour families on the council?[47]

Lang replied that his powers to intervene were limited by statute: Section 211 of the Local Authority (Scotland) Act 1973 gave him discretionary power to order a local inquiry only if a local authority had failed to carry out its statutory duty.[48] Scottish Labour back benchers were incensed at these allegations being raised at Scottish Questions by an English Tory MP. John Maxton, the Labour MP for Glasgow Cathcart, demanded that Lang dissociate himself from Shaw's 'irresponsible and unscrupulous campaign', and challenged Shaw to repeat his allegations outside the Chamber 'where he is not covered by parliamentary privilege'.[49] Later that day, George Galloway, the Labour Member for Glasgow Hillhead, also came to the aid of Smith, accusing English Tory MPs of hijacking Scottish Questions in order to 'spread foul smears against my right hon. and learned friend the Leader of the Opposition', and against councillors from an area that most Tory MPs could not locate on a map.[50]

Undaunted, David Shaw tabled a number of hostile Early Day Motions,[51] demanding a Commons debate into 'the conduct of the leader of the Opposition' with regard to the affairs of MDC, claiming Smith's reluctance to become involved was 'not in the public interest' and was 'wholly inadequate for someone who has been so closely associated with his local council for the past nine years'.[52] In January 1993, Shaw, along with Phil Gallie, the Tory MP for Ayr, even mischievously visited Airdrie on a so-called 'fact-finding mission'. Gallie commented to reporters: 'John Smith and Tom Clarke could conceivably be Prime Minister and Scottish Secretary respectively and they don't seem to be able to clean up their own backyard.'[53]

In January 1993, John Smith told party activists that he wanted the Labour Party inquiry to clear the matter up as quickly as possible. However, after the meeting of the Monklands East Constituency Labour Party, opinion was divided over whether Smith had behaved impartially. One member claimed Smith had adopted an 'overtly aggressive' attitude: 'He was extremely angry and appeared to be attacking those who have been campaigning for change, including those regarded as moderates . . . his approach verged on the venomous at times and he seemed very clearly to think this whole affair was our fault.'[54] Other activists saw it differently, describing Smith as 'non-committal' and even 'sympathetic' towards the Airdrie rebels.[55]

But at the same time, Tom Clarke chose to speak out, publicly defending the conduct of Coatbridge councillors in his constituency.[56] Clarke had just returned from an enforced three-week break from his duties as shadow Scottish Secretary,[57] during which Clarke was suffering from ME, and came under a great deal of attack from the Scottish media over Monklands, despite the fact that he had not been Provost of Monklands since 1982. During Clarke's illness, John had said: 'Don't bother your backside about what they're saying. People only notice the Scottish newspapers when they next buy a fish supper.' Nevertheless, when Clarke had recovered from his illness, he wanted to clarify his position that there should be a public inquiry. That being done, he hoped that would be the end of the matter.[58]

Clarke denies outright that his comments caused Smith to move him from
the Scottish portfolio to International Development in the October 1993
shadow Cabinet reshuffle, despite the fact that he had moved up from
seventeenth to thirteenth in the shadow Cabinet elections. Superficially, the
move, which saw George Robertson take over as shadow Secretary of State for
Scotland, seems to have come as a shock to Clarke because before the
announcement, he indicated he would be 'greatly surprised if moved'.[59] In
fact, Clarke argues that no one is going to admit publicly that they expect to be
shifted from one shadow Cabinet position to another. Secondly, George
Robertson had been elected on to the shadow Cabinet for the first time, having
done such a great job over harrying the Government on the Maastricht Treaty
(see chapter 20). Smith was therefore faced with a problem over 'what to do
with all these Scots'. Clarke claims he had always wanted the International
Development portfolio, and was 'extremely happy' to be switched from
responsibility for Scottish issues. Privately, Clarke twice offered to resign from
the Labour front bench due to his illness, but Smith wouldn't wear it: 'So
you're a doctor, are you?' The doctors indicated that Clarke would recover
from his ME in time, and Smith accepted that view, loyally sticking by Clarke
at every turn.[60]

On Thursday, 4 March 1993, Labour's internal inquiry report recommended a major overhaul of MDC's recruitment procedures.[61] However, the
inquiry was widely accused in the Scottish press of sidestepping the central
allegations of 'jobs for the boys', as well as ignoring claims of alleged financial
impropriety. For instance, the editorial of the *Daily Record* ran with headlines
such as 'Clean up the Monklands Mess' and 'If something's wrong – hush it
up',[62] while the *Evening Times* (Glasgow's main evening newspaper) led with
'It's a whitewash' on its front page.[63] The following week, *The Sunday Times*
editorial felt that the electorate had been 'Taken for a ride'.[64] The Labour
inquiry was also accused of shooting itself in the foot by criticising reporters
from the *Airdrie and Coatbridge Advertiser* for going 'beyond reasonable
bounds' in their coverage of the affair. As the *Daily Record* put it, it looked like
a case of 'If the News is Bad, Blame the Messenger'.[65]

At one level, it is understandable that Labour's hierarchy shied away from
delving any further into the recruitment practices of MDC. The proper route
for any disgruntled former employee was to take his or her case to an
industrial tribunal. Indeed, Jack McConnell took legal advice that it was not
possible to investigate past appointment allegations.[66]

Probably the worst moment for Smith came at a monthly constituency
surgery in April 1993, when he had to face down 40 Labour activists protesting

outside the Airdrie Arts Centre, all filmed by a Scottish Television camera crew. The Labour leader was very angry at the disrespect shown to him, but agreed to meet two of the dissidents, local branch chairmen, John Turnbull and Ian McNeil. In their short meeting, 'truths were spoken', and Smith promised to implement the findings of Labour's review.[67] John Smith may have been under siege, but he was no coward. Deputy manageress Diane Stein recollects that although his surgery had a back door, Smith never used it: 'He always went out to face them.'[68] On leaving his surgery, Smith brusquely told reporters that he did 'not approve of being asked questions in this manner' and asked to be allowed to get to his waiting car.[69]

Meanwhile, the Tories made hay. In May 1993, at the Scottish Tory Party conference debate on local government reform, Allan Stewart, Parliamentary Under-Secretary of State for Scotland, exploited Smith's discomfiture to the full, attacking his 'self-imposed purdah' on the subject of Monklands:

> The three wise monkeys of Monklands are quietly sitting it out, wringing their hands, wishing they could just click their heels and it will all go away. We have Jack McConnell who sees no evil, Tom Clarke who hears no evil, and John Smith who speaks no evil, speaks no good, speaks not at all . . . Smith preaches about Christian socialism, but actions speak louder than words. And his silence on Monklands speaks volumes.[70]

It soon got to the stage where Smith could not make *any* speech in the House of Commons without David Shaw making interruptions, such as: 'What are you frightened about?' and 'Why will you not answer a question on the nepotism and corruption on Monklands District Council?' Shaw was threatened with disciplinary action by the Speaker before resuming his seat.[71]

Shaw was just nuisance value, but the Monklands controversy made it much harder for Smith to make his planned speeches calling for the reform of Britain's democracy, including reform of local government, and much harder to attack examples of Tory sleaze. On 13 January 1994, Smith attacked the Prime Minister over alleged Conservative gerrymandering in Westminster City Council.[72] A few days later, Sir Norman Fowler, the Conservative Party chairman wrote to Smith asking him to respond to the allegations in his own constituency before attacking Conservative councillors in Westminster.[73]

In early February 1994, John Smith wrote to Ian Lang, calling him to order an inquiry under section 211 of the Local Government (Scotland) Act 1973. However, Lang replied that such specific allegations were not provided for under the aforementioned Act. He also called on Smith to release all the material accumulated by the Labour Party as a result of its internal inquiry.

This provoked another letter from Smith in which he reiterated that an inquiry should be instigated, this time citing section 7 of the Local Government and Housing Act 1989, which imposed a statutory duty on all Scottish local authorities to appoint all staff on the basis of merit, and also Section 95 of the aforementioned 1973 Act, which imposed on every local authority an obligation to make arrangements for the proper administration of their financial affairs.[74] This was the basis upon which the later Nimmo Smith inquiry (see chapter 25) was conducted, but Lang chose not to act.

The growing political importance of Monklands and the extent to which it was now damaging Labour were illustrated at a full meeting of the PLP in February 1994, when Dale Campbell-Savours asked about issues that might be raised in the forthcoming debate on Scottish democracy,[75] 'in view of the fact the Tories were liable to use this as an opportunity to further their smear campaign about MDC'. George Robertson, the new shadow Secretary of State for Scotland, then outlined 'Labour's robust response to the continuing smears', and the Chief Whip drew attention to EDM 527, and urged colleagues to sign it.[76] On 3 February 1994, John Smith's great friend and constituency neighbour, Norman Hogg, had tabled the EDM deploring MPs who make allegations under cover of parliamentary privilege, and claiming that because the Scottish Office had not ordered an inquiry, there was 'no valid complaint against MDC'. Around a hundred Labour back benchers signed it, including 25 Scottish Labour MPs. As Campbell-Savours had predicted, a Tory back bencher, this time George Kynoch, the Conservative MP for Kincardine and Deeside, raised the issue of Smith's letter the previous week to Lang, but this time John Maxton was ready for him:

> Does he [Kynoch] associate the name of the Secretary of State for National Heritage, the right hon. Member for Westminster North (Sir John Wheeler) with Westminster Council in the same way he so glibly associates my right hon. and learned Friend the Member for Monklands East with Monklands Council?[77]

Either Maxton and/or the *Hansard* report made two errors. The question *should* have been referring to Peter Brooke, who was Secretary of State for National Heritage, and MP for City of London and Westminster South. Sir John Wheeler was the neighbouring Conservative MP for Westminster North, and certainly never served as Secretary of State for National Heritage. But the overall point stands. Few politicians or media commentators at the time claimed that Mr Brooke should seek to interfere in the controversy surrounding Westminster City Council, but they kept haranguing John Smith to embroil himself in the affairs of Monklands District Council.

Meanwhile, in Monklands, the power balance within the council had begun to change dramatically. On Sunday, 27 June 1993, many of the well-established figures in the Monklands East CLP had been ousted from positions of power at the constituency's AGM. After a secret ballot, chairman Hugh Lucas was narrowly ousted after twelve years, and replaced by Peter Veldon, and then Smith's election agent Eddie Cairns was also narrowly ditched as secretary after three decades in the post. Cathy Dick, a local councillor, took his place.[78] On Sunday, 27 February 1994, the rebels further consolidated their position, this time in the District Labour Party executive, winning another six places, taking their total to nine, although the old guard still held a majority overall with eleven. Councillor Jim Brooks led a walk-out of about a third of those present, complaining about the entitlement of seventeen TGWU delegates to vote at the meeting. Symbolically, the old guard were leaving, and those that remained were glad, some singing 'Cheerio, cheerio'.[79] In the end, disaffected local people had taken matters into their own hands to effect change.

In early April 1994, Tom McFarlane, a foreman at an MDC depot, won an industrial tribunal for unfair dismissal. McFarlane's case had been supported throughout by three of the four Airdrie rebels.[80] The case hinged on the fact that the aforementioned senior members of MDC were involved 'in all levels of recruitment' and therefore they were capable of getting involved with the dismissal of an employee, rather than a properly constituted council committee.[81] In a highly controversial move, Brian Brady had taped a conversation with James Dempsey, director of Leisure and Recreation, which directly related to the McFarlane case.[82]

McFarlane claimed that his dismissal dated back to February 1992, and the failure of his wife to be included by the Monklands East CLP in the lists of interviews for possible candidates at the local elections. McFarlane appealed to the Scottish Labour Executive, won his case, and his wife called upon the secretary of the District Labour Party to resign. In response, Eddie Cairns had allegedly said to McFarlane that it would be 'bad for him' if he called for the secretary's resignation, but undeterred Macfarlane went ahead and did precisely that on 4 March 1992. McFarlane had also voted against Jim Brooks's allies at a series of votes at the AGM of the Monklands East Constituency Labour Party in 1991. Brooks had allegedly said that those who voted against him would be 'sorted out'.[83] Peter Sullivan, another of the Airdrie rebels, backed up this account, recalling that Brooks had said after the 1991 AGM that 'certain people's cards were marked and that they would be remembered'.[84]

On Saturday, 4 July 1992 McFarlane received his redundancy notice, hand delivered by James Dempsey.[85] No efforts were made to re-deploy McFarlane, despite available alternatives.[86] For his part, James Dempsey claimed during the tribunal that McFarlane's redundancy was part of an incomplete rationalisation begun two years earlier, that there were no other suitable jobs for the foreman, and that he had turned down an offer of early retirement.[87]

The industrial tribunal found that McFarlane had been unfairly dismissed. However, it rejected any suggestion that Dempsey had said that the applicant was dismissed for political reasons, and was quite satisfied that Dempsey did not in any way tailor his report with the ulterior motive of getting rid of MacFarlane. Nor was Dempsey put under any pressure to produce a report that would have ensured McFarlane's dismissal. Nevertheless, the tribunal concluded that changes to an official council report about plans to sack Mr McFarlane were 'politically motivated because the issue of the compulsory redundancy of the respondents' employees was politically sensitive'. Furthermore, the decision to dismiss McFarlane had taken place at the aforementioned 'corridor meeting' of Jim Brooks, Eddie Cairns, Jim Smith, the Manpower Services director, and James Dempsey, and not at any official or recognised committee. The tribunal essentially confirmed what the earlier Scottish Labour Party inquiry had discovered that, contrary to normal local authority practice, elected officials dealt with the hire and fire of even the lowliest members of council staff. It also emerged that leading members of the council operated a redundancy policy without that policy ever having been ratified by a duly constituted meeting of the full council.[88] Standard local authority procedures had not been followed; in today's speak 'good governance' was lacking.

When the McFarlane story broke, Mike Elrick got wind of Michael Crick's (the biographer and *Newsnight* journalist) intention to doorstep Smith in his Monklands constituency. Crick had been rooting around the constituency for several weeks, and had chatted extensively to the Airdrie rebels.[89] On that Friday afternoon, Elrick drafted a press release and debated with John Smith the merits of coming out in support of McFarlane. Smith reluctantly agreed to do that, and thus the story of Smith's backing for McFarlane made the first editions on the Saturday morning in Airdrie.[90]

Michael Crick recalls that he fixed up a pre-arranged doorstep with Smith: 'It looks like you've done it by surprise, but they know they're going to be doorstepped.'[91] Smith refused a formal interview, but David Hill informed Crick that his leader would answer a few questions if Crick just happened to be outside Smith's monthly constituency surgery on the Saturday morning (2

April).[92] Crick's diary entry from that day reads: 'Before Smith arrived, a press officer [Elrick] turned up, who [had] travelled all the way from London, and began pumping us for questions. I gave nothing away . . .'[93] Elrick recalls that he could have guessed what Crick would have doorstepped Smith with, and had no real expectation that Crick, like any reporter worth his salt, would tell him what he was about to say, but he went through the motions of quizzing Crick about what he intended to ask, as any press officer would do.[94]

In his diary, Crick admits that when Smith arrived, 'I rather cocked up the interview by not pressing the point that his constituents are demanding he do something about Monklands Council.'[95] In the rest of the 'interview', Smith expressed frustration that many unsubstantiated allegations about Monklands had been made by Conservative MPs under the cover of parliamentary privilege. The Labour leader then reminded Crick that he had already asked Ian Lang to consider holding an inquiry. Crick pressed Smith on his failure to act on behalf of his constituents, and the following set-piece exchange ensued:

> SMITH: I'm going to see my constituents just at the moment in my surgery. I'll be dealing with their real problems, real problems of unemployment, social security and all other matters which with many other communities, we have to suffer. Now if you'll excuse me.
> CRICK: Do you think Monklands is a model for how a Labour government would operate?
> [Smith goes into surgery].[96]

The subsequent Crick television report focused on the McFarlane case as an example of MDC creating an atmosphere among those who dared to speak out against the system of 'jobs for the boys'. But interestingly, McFarlane's own testimony reveals that while he agreed that Monklands was a source of continuing embarrassment to Smith – 'his Achilles' heel for some time to come' – McFarlane did not agree that Smith should have intervened in the affair a lot earlier. It is worth repeating McFarlane's comments at length, from the original Crick transcript:

> CRICK: But shouldn't he have done something about it a lot earlier?
> MCFARLANE: I have got to say 'No'. John Smith is our MP. Apart from the fact that he's the leader of the group and leader of the Party, he's only our MP here in Monklands. And as such, any other MP, any MP, no matter which party they belong to, cannot come back to the constituency and tell them what they want.
> CRICK: What would have happened if he did?
> MCFARLANE: Well, they might just have told him to mind his own business.
> CRICK : That seems extraordinary, that the leader of the Labour Party can't

come and tell his own party to behave.

MCFARLANE: The leader of the Party is a nice man; I know him quite well; he's a personal friend, but it's difficult. He's only the leader of the Party when he's down in the Commons. You know, up here he's just John Smith, the MP, and as such there are other people in this area who are the leader of the Party, and he just does what he's told, and that would be incumbent on any MP from any political persuasion.[97]

Mcfarlane had squared the pertinent circle as to why Smith had been so reluctant to get involved. In the West of Scotland context, the party leader was not necessarily the boss when it came to local fiefdoms. Rather, the local (mostly, but not exclusively) Labour MPs relied hugely upon on the continued loyalty and support of long-established power barons on the ground.

Mike Elrick feels that, if Smith had lived, Monklands would not have gone away, and agrees with McFarlane that it was Smith's 'Achilles' heel, a thorn in his side'. He feels that his leader should have 'read the Riot Act', but is also critical of the Scottish Labour Party machine, particularly Jack McConnell, for failing to deal with the matter effectively.[98]

Smith's handling of Monklands can be contrasted with the effective and ruthless way in which the Labour Party under Neil Kinnock rooted out the Militant Tendency in the 1980s, especially from Liverpool, and begs the question: should Smith have adopted similarly bold tactics in Monklands?[99] There were obvious dangers in provoking a local bloodbath that might have distracted attention away from Smith's national leadership, but equally Kinnock showed that clamping down on Labour extremism locally, provided everything was done following legally tight procedures, could improve the Labour Party's standing nationally. Smith's consensual style of leadership may have worked wonders with a potentially fractious PLP and shadow Cabinet at Westminster, and with the trade unions, always keen to cry 'betrayal', but perhaps a pressing need to preserve loyal allies, and a desire not to make unnecessary enemies, led him not to interfere in his own backyard.

However, in contrast to 1980s' Merseyside, the vast majority of the Monklands allegations were proved to be completely unfounded in the subsequent Nimmo Smith inquiry. Labour's internal inquiry had also resulted in job application procedures being changed for the better.

What was disgraceful about the whole affair was its inflation by the press, egged on by the activities David Shaw, who engaged in a straightforward Tory smear campaign against the Labour leader of the opposition. Nor did senior members of the Conservative government do anything to stop the antics of their back benchers. Alex Salmond, commenting after John Smith's death, concluded: 'I have always had the sneaking suspicion, certainly when John Smith was alive, Government ministers felt that keeping this row simmering was overwhelmingly in their party's interest.'[100]

John Smith felt he knew exactly what the Tories were up to in Monklands. As the much maligned Jim Brooks said in his testimony to the Nimmo Smith inquiry:

> The Labour Party was conscious of the fact, along with everyone else in the country, that we had a future Prime Minister in the community, John Smith. To that end, the Tory guns from Central Office were trained firmly on this area – we had to be seen to be angels . . . John Smith said to me two weeks before he won the nomination as leader that anything which happened in Monklands would be magnified 1,000 times . . . I was a bit sceptical when he said that, but now I am absolutely sure he was right.[101]

Many of the journalists, like Eileen McAuley and Michael Crick, were just doing their jobs,[102] as McAuley told the Nimmo Smith inquiry:

> We were pursuing matters of legitimate public interest and concern, and as a local paper it was our responsibility to subject the council's decision-making process to robust scrutiny . . . We did expect the late John Smith, as Labour leader to comment on the scandal raging in his own political backyard, and I make no apologies for that. He was answerable to his local constituents and his policy of silence was ill-conceived and counter-productive from his own and his party's point of view.[103]

However, neither Crick nor McAuley found any evidence of wrongdoing on the part of Monklands councillors, and certainly not on the part of Smith. Michael Crick is honourable enough to admit that he feels 'a bit guilty' about pursuing Smith, only a few weeks before the Labour leader died.[104]

The greatest irony about the whole affair is that MDC disappeared into North Lanarkshire Council as part of the local government reorganisation of Scotland, implemented shortly after Smith's death. Sadly, that wasn't the end of the matter, as the bitter Monklands East by-election of June 1994 and the two subsequent inquiries into the matter would show (see chapter 25).

On Wednesday, 6 April 1994, John Smith, Chris Smith, Murray Elder and Mike Elrick began their ascent of Eididh nan Clach Geala in the Deargs range.[105] The party encountered blizzard conditions. On the descent, whilst crossing a peat bog south of Ullapool, John twisted his ankle and landed in a heap. On his arrival back in Edinburgh, he had had no medical attention for three hours, and couldn't stop fidgeting. According to Donald MacCormick, he tried to dull the pain with a combination of medicinal whisky, and a bag of frozen peas on his foot.[106]

Unwisely, John carried out constituency engagements on the Thursday and Friday. One of the most memorable if unwelcome photographs of Smith was taken the day after he twisted his ankle. A team from *Panorama*, who were filming a programme about Monklands District Council, photographed Smith touring a Boots factory in Lanarkshire wearing an extremely unflattering hairnet and limping around on a stick.[107]

On the Saturday, Elizabeth and Kenneth Munro had Donald and Lizzie MacCormick and their five-year-old son John staying for the weekend. Also in the household was the Munro's six-year-old grandson Callum. John and Elizabeth were invited along the road to join them for supper. Elizabeth Munro had a look at the swollen ankle and immediately went to her freezer and took out a bag of frozen peas. She taped these to John's ankle and, after a short time, he announced some relief from the pain. The relief was sufficient to enable John to leave the adults' party and to hop upstairs to read the boys a bedtime story. As they chatted, John and Callum discovered that they had the same birthday, 13 September, and agreed to have a joint birthday party the following September when Callum would be seven and John 56.[108]

Michael Foot recalls Smith hobbling on to the stage at Jo Richardson's[109] memorial meeting. When Foot warned him to take care of his injured foot, Smith replied: 'But my heart's all right.'[110] Smith was more concerned that his doctor had ordered him not to put his ankle under strain for six weeks, which John noted in his Munro Diary would rule out hillwalking during the Whitsun recess. He had high hopes, however, of joining Alan Haworth in his attempt to climb Haworth's 200th Munro on 16 July 1994.[111]

The next time the Kenneth Munros saw John at his home he was still hirpling, but he was all enthused because he'd just had satellite television installed. Catherine Smith whispered to Kenneth and Elizabeth as they went in through the door, 'He'll tell you it's all shite!', and sure enough Smith flicked through all the channels, commenting: 'There's the soft porn one – it's shite . . . there's the shopping channel . . . it's all a load of shite!'[112]

Mike Elrick recalls that he and others had become concerned about his boss's health and his workload for some time before he died. But no one had been able to slow him down – such was his nature. Donald Dewar was exactly the same (and a similar fate befell him in 2000.) Secondly, as Elrick points out: 'If you are leader of the Opposition, you are either in frontline politics, or you're not.'[113] On recovering from his first heart attack back in

1988, Smith told his great friend, Bob McLaughlan, that he had no alternative to doing what he did, that frontline politics required an energetic commitment.[114]

Smith's greatest strength in running the party – his approachability and willingness to listen to almost every MP – also put an enormous added weight on to his diary. Perhaps there were aspects of John's extremely onerous diary that could have been passed on to subordinates, but that would have changed the way he ran the Labour Party, and there was no changing him.

For some time, Elizabeth Smith had asked another Labour MP, who happened to live in the same Barbican complex as the Smiths, to keep an eye on her husband to check that he did not have too many late nights.[115] Indeed, during the later gala dinner evening, Elizabeth confided to David Blunkett that her husband was pushing himself too hard.[116]

Smith had chest pains on Friday (6 May), during and after attending the official opening ceremony of the Channel Tunnel,[117] but he pressed ahead with Labour's European election campaign. The Labour leader's state of health could not have been helped either by the anger he experienced that day over the questionable behaviour of the government, and specifically, Nicholas Scott, the Minister for Social Security and Disabled People. The previous week (Friday, 29 April), the House of Commons had carried unanimously a motion calling upon the government to give more parliamentary time to Roger Berry's Civil Rights (Disabled Persons) Bill.[118] John Hannam, the chairman of the All-Party Disablement Group, who supported Berry's Bill, had come under immense pressure from the government not to put down his motion, but had stuck to his guns.[119]

However, by the following Friday, Conservative back benchers had tabled blocking amendments to the Bill, with the connivance of Nicholas Scott. Scott was then forced to apologise to the House for denying that anyone in his department had been involved in drafting these amendments.[120] Scott had misled the House, but three points are worth adding in partial mitigation of the government's behaviour. Firstly, the government fully intended to bring forward legislation of its own on the subject, and could legitimately argue that this approach would produce a better outcome than a Private Members' Bill. Secondly, Labour back benchers were actively encouraged at two separate meetings of the PLP to attend the Friday debates on the Bill by the Chief Whip and Barry Sheerman, Labour's spokesperson on disabled rights.[121] The issue therefore took on a highly party political flavour, even if the Bill attracted support from all three main political parties. The third, and most relevant point, was conceded by Derek Foster in the PLP, namely that the government would not normally be formally required to take heed of such a motion; it merely had moral force.[122]

Smith reacted to Nick Scott's antics with undisguised private fury. Either that night, or soon after, a journalist interviewed Smith in his office. The Labour leader just sat there swearing, saying over and over again that it was 'a f****** disgrace!' The journalist was not sure how to respond, or how best to write up the interview, and Mike Elrick had to tell him that Smith was just genuinely upset at the injustice of the government's actions.[123] In his generous tribute to Smith, Alastair Campbell recalled Smith's anger at Scott's refusal to resign over the wrecking of that Bill to help the disabled, adding: 'He [Smith] had an intense belief in right and wrong, instilled by a strict but loving Presbyterian upbringing, and an almost evangelical loathing of poverty. He was intensely Scottish.'[124] Simon Hoggart described it as an 'act of deceit which went against everything he [Smith] had ever learned'.[125]

On Sunday, 8 May, Smith turned out for the launch of the Strathclyde East European election campaign at the Blantyre Miners' Welfare Club. George Robertson was pleased in the sense that Smith had come to help out Kenneth Collins, the local MEP,[126] and MPs from the Lanarkshire area also attended the event, as did Peggy Herbison, John's predecessor in his old Lanarkshire North constituency. (The gathering also marked the 47th birthday of John Reid, Labour MP for Motherwell North, but Smith refused to be photographed eating a slice of cake.)[127] But it wasn't just a case of turning up and shaking a few hands, then leaving, it was a whole afternoon, where John had to be 'a total person'. As ever, Smith did the glad-handing very well, but at a price. He had given up a precious Sunday, as it turns out his last Sunday, his only rest day to help out in a part of the country in which Labour was certain to win anyway.[128]

On Monday, 9 May, Smith split his day in Edinburgh, campaigning with Robin Cook and David Martin MEP, then took the Shuttle to London with Robin Cook and Mike Elrick for another stint of Euro campaigning in the capital. That evening, Smith attended a meeting of the Joint Policy Committee, spoke with David Clark about the situation in Bosnia, and then voted on EC documents dealing with Italian steel, which was subject to a three-line whip.[129]

The following morning (Tuesday), the leader of the opposition held a half-hour meeting with Jack Straw at 11 am to discuss the Local Government Review, before having his photograph taken with Denis MacShane, Labour's victor in the Rotherham by-election, held on 5 May 1994.[130] Smith briefly visited the South African Embassy in London to celebrate Nelson Mandela's election victory. Much to everyone's surprise, the leader of the opposition, despite his sore ankle, suddenly broke into a little dance, akin to the South African toyi-toyi, such was his glee at Mandela's triumph.[131] Thirty years after successfully campaigning for the election of the anti-apartheid campaigner, Albert Luthuli (see chapter 3), Smith was delighted to witness the final death throes of apartheid.

The rest of the early afternoon was taken up, as usual, with preparing for Prime Minister's Questions. Smith claimed that Tory back bench calls for a referendum on the single currency showed that the Conservatives were 'hopelessly divided' on Europe. Major, on this occasion, got the better of Smith, by arguing that a decision on a single currency was a long way off, and that he would not want to commit future Parliaments to a referendum on the issue[132] (although he committed his party to the idea in April 1996).[133]

Smith then flew back up to Edinburgh on the Tuesday afternoon because he felt he simply had to attend a meeting of the Boundary Commission concerning his Monklands East constituency, which started at 10 am on the Wednesday morning.[134] Smith had asked his old flatmate Norman Hogg, Labour MP for Cumbernauld and Kilsyth, to stay and watch for the duration of the inquiry, held at the City Halls in Glasgow.[135] Smith also worked closely with his neighbouring MP, Tom Clarke, who later commented in his tribute to Smith: 'Remarkably, on the last two days before he died I was to be in John's company for longer periods than at any time since he became leader.'[136] Every outstanding issue was clarified between them, and any previous minor differences were settled.[137] In the end, Smith's advocacy proved successful. Before he died, John heard that the reaction from the inquiry had been good, although he never lived to see the constituency changes: Airdrie and Shotts looks much more like Smith's old seat of Lanarkshire North.[138]

John Smith, a man with a known heart condition, then flew back down to Heathrow from Glasgow, for a further series of official meetings, and then the gala dinner. All this travelling up and down the country in such a short space of time for a man with a sore ankle.

On his return to Westminster, Smith's anger at the government's behaviour over the Civil Rights (Disabled Persons) Bill was still evident in front of the television cameras: 'This Government does not know the difference between the Conservative Party interest and the national interest, and it's time that we had a Government that did.'[139]

By the time John set off for the dinner he was not in the best of tempers because, despite his office issuing a clear note rescheduling the shadow Cabinet meeting to 4.30 pm, all members arrived at 5 pm. Added to this, he had mislaid his speech. Fortunately, Ann Barrett, who was acting as minder that evening, had anticipated this, and was carrying a spare copy.[140]

However, by the time Smith's car arrived at the hotel, the tensions of the day had been put to one side. For all the previous criticisms about Smith's supposed low public profile (see chapter 21) and his apparent lack of media savvy, his last photo-call transmitted all the right messages that public relations people dream about. John's great friend, Menzies Campbell, though a political opponent, commented the following night that the fact that John and Elizabeth held hands as they walked inside sent out a powerful image that here was a man at peace with himself and his family, the self-confident leader of the Labour Party, a man on top of his brief, communicating his confidence to the party and the wider electorate.[141] All Smith's previous efforts since he'd been shadow Chancellor to reassure the electorate about Labour's (and his own) capacity to govern, to regain their trust, came together at that one moment.

Twenty-Four
A WEEK-LONG WAKE

A T 8.05 AM on Thursday, 12 May, John Smith died after an early morning shower in his Barbican flat. He had suffered a second, massive heart attack. From 8.05 am until 8.11 am, Elizabeth attempted mouth-to-mouth resuscitation and heart massage. Also present were Hilary Armstrong, Smith's Parliamentary Private Secretary and Hilary Coffman, Smith's press officer. They had been ready to accompany Smith to Basildon as part of campaigning for the European elections. At 8.16 am, a motorcycle paramedic, who had been diverted to help out, arrived first on the scene. Smith was not breathing. A minute later, the ambulance team arrived with emergency equipment. Paramedics gave Smith three electric shocks with a heart defibrillator, and injected him with adrenalin and atropine in an attempt to restart his heart.[1] Further attempts were made to revive the Labour leader during a desperate dash to St Bartholomew's Hospital, which by a terrible irony Smith had visited only a few weeks earlier as part of a campaign to keep open the hospital's Accident and Emergency Department. Dr Roworth Spurrell and his cardiac team worked for more than half an hour, trying to revive Smith, but to no avail. Smith was pronounced dead at 9.15 am.

The official announcement of Smith's death was delayed until 10.30 am so that Smith's eldest daughter, Sarah, then holidaying in the United States, could be informed of the tragic news. Despite the official embargo, by this stage, less than scrupulous journalists were telephoning Labour politicians relaying the morbid news, while in the leader's office, Smith's secretary tried to keep the reporters at bay. At 10.40 am, Mike Besser, professor of medicine, who had showed Smith around the threatened A&E Department only two weeks before, formally announced the death of John Smith.

Individual testimonies help convey the sense of confusion and the shock of that awful day. Hilary Armstrong recalls that she arrived at the flat at about the same time as Smith's driver, Terry Rayner. She knew something was wrong by the agitated reaction of the man at the reception desk. Terry tried to resuscitate John. Elizabeth went with John in the ambulance, while Hilary Armstrong and Hilary Coffman went separately to Barts in a taxi. Armstrong then rang Betty

Boothroyd, the Speaker of the House of Commons, before taking Elizabeth back home so that the girls could be contacted.[2]

John Smith's great pal, Jimmy Gordon, first heard the news of John's heart attack when his mobile phone went off at Hyde Park Corner. He was so 'poleaxed' by the news that, having done one television interview, he headed home to Glasgow.[3] Derry Irvine, who had attended the fundraising dinner the previous evening, recalls that Smith had given a good, strong speech, scarcely using notes, but that his voice seemed odd and fracturing by the end of the night. The following morning, John's youngest daughter Catherine telephoned Derry to tell him the news that his best friend was dead. Derry was so cut up about it that he took two-and-a-half days off work, something that a workhorse like Irvine had never done before.[4]

Very early on, George Robertson's Millbank office came under siege as journalist after journalist telephoned him asking him to comment as shadow Secretary of State for Scotland on John's death before it had been officially confirmed. Most of the Scottish political reporters were in Inverness to cover the Scottish Conservative and Unionist Party conference, but had quickly got wind of what had happened. Robertson spent the rest of the day dealing with the huge Scottish media interest in the story. The following day, he visited the Smith family home.[5]

Mike Elrick was the first member of Smith's press team to arrive in the office on that Thursday morning. Elrick knew something had happened to John as soon as the secretaries asked him to handle calls coming in from journalists. Elrick pleaded ignorance and said he couldn't confirm that Smith had taken ill. It was from Hilary Coffman that he learned that John had died. The first politician he met was Jack Cunningham with whom he shared an embrace.[6] Cunningham was later filmed on the news hugging a distraught Paul Boateng, one of Smith's former Treasury team when shadow Chancellor. Rarely can there have been a British political death that provoked so many men to shed so many tears in one day. Simon Hoggart recalled: 'I have never known the Commons have the genuine sense of grief we saw yesterday . . . It has knocked the guts out of Westminster.'[7] Later on, Margaret Beckett came into the office looking visibly upset, and gave a brief speech to the secretaries.[8]

Meta Ramsay, still tired from the gala dinner the night before, met David Clark, Labour's defence spokesperson, and was told that John had had a heart attack. She half-ran across to the leader's office, wondering how serious his condition was: unlike many people that day when they heard the news, it never entered her head that John had actually died. It was only when she entered the leader's office that she realised the awfulness of what had happened.[9]

At this point, Donald Dewar (who'd been told the news by a journalist) made the decision to go to the hospital with Meta. As their taxi arrived at Barts, they were met by a sea of photographers and journalists which the police escorted them through.[10] Later, while Elizabeth and Meta left in an unmarked police car out of the back of Barts, Donald, the two Hilarys and Terry drove out the front in the official car to distract the media scrum.

No one succeeded in photographing Elizabeth and Meta as they arrived back at the Barbican either, because the police arranged for the gates to be opened at the back of the complex.[11] In the flat, Donald, the two Hilarys, Meta, Terry and a policewoman sat around in a state of shock. Understandably, Elizabeth now insisted on flying to Edinburgh to be with Jane and Catherine, who were by this stage being comforted by Kenneth and Elizabeth Munro, old family friends, as well as Ruth Wishart and Helen Liddell.[12] There, Elizabeth and Kenneth Munro telephoned every conceivable friend of Sarah's in an attempt to track her down in California. Kenneth put a stop on Sarah's credit card, meaning that the next time she tried to use it, she would know something was wrong.[13] Meanwhile, the Foreign Office got in touch with the nearest consul general. The foremost task then became ensuring Sarah's swift passage to Edinburgh, free from press intrusion.[14] By late morning the journalists gathered outside the Smith family home were 'getting tetchy' with lunchtime deadlines looming. After discussion, Liddell made a short statement.[15]

Back in the leader's office, Ann Barrett organised plane tickets to Edinburgh (for 2 pm). Once again, the police got Elizabeth and Meta to their destination unseen. The cameramen were held back at an observation point, and the police escorted Elizabeth to the waiting plane. When Meta, Mike Elrick and Elizabeth boarded the plane, they were met by utter silence.[16] Malcolm Rifkind was on the flight, and en route he came over and kissed Elizabeth, expressed his sorrow, and told her that she had to be strong.[17] On arrival in Edinburgh, no other passengers moved until Elizabeth stood up, one of the first of many moving examples of the great respect shown to the Smith family on that day, and in the subsequent week. Deputy Chief Inspector Robert Swanson of Special Branch met Elizabeth at the airport and personally drove her home. (Several hours later, Swanson met Sarah off the plane on her arrival from the United States.) Helen Liddell had laid down the law to journalists, saying that she was making an imaginary line beyond which they were not to cross on Elizabeth's arrival. If they transgressed, she would telephone their proprietors, never mind their editors. In the end, the press were 'fantastic', mostly because so many of them had known John for such a long time, and they too were genuinely distraught.[18]

Shelley, the family cat, sat on the window-sill waiting for his master to come home. In the hallway, Elizabeth would have passed a picture of the last Labour Cabinet, taken inside No. 10 Downing Street, with John standing behind a seated Tony Benn. Ruth Wishart recalls that she and Meta Ramsay sat through the wall-to-wall coverage on the television with the two girls: 'It was mesmeric, a small domestic equivalent of the Twin Towers, and especially chilling watching it with the family.'[19]

ITV (though curiously not the BBC) suspended all regular news programmes and ran with open-ended news coverage. Michael Brunson, then ITN's political editor, gave a very heartfelt tribute to Smith as chairman of the Parliamentary Lobby Journalists. ITN's sombre coverage earned it a Royal Television Society award, attended fittingly both by Elizabeth Smith, two days before she took her seat in the House of Lords, and by Sarah, then working for BBC Television.[20]

That night, David Dimbleby chaired a special *Question Time* from Edinburgh. Although its venue was as planned, the programme's format was changed so that friends and political acquaintances could come along to pay their tributes to John Smith. The panel comprised Malcolm Rifkind, Secretary of State for Defence (who was the only member of the scheduled panel to take part), George Robertson, shadow Secretary of State for Scotland, like John, a former pupil at Dunoon Grammar, standing in for Donald Dewar, and Menzies Campbell, representing the Liberal Democrats, and recalling his friendship with John at Glasgow. Ludovic Kennedy graciously sat in the studio audience to allow Campbell his place. Alex Salmond, leader of the SNP, stood in for Margaret Ewing.

Other members of the audience that night included: John McCluskey and Ross Harper from John's time in the legal world; Neil MacCormick who told tales of John's student days on the Clyde puffers (much to the bemusement of Dimbleby, who didn't seem to know what puffers were); Jack McConnell, general secretary of the Scottish Labour Party, and Rosemary McKenna, Chairman of the Convention of Scottish Local Authorities (COSLA). Both spoke of John Smith's last day as Labour Party leader. Bob Thomson of the General Municipal and Boilermakers Union talked of John's long association with his sponsoring union; and Peter Veldon, chairman of Monklands Constituency Labour Party, and Martin Dempsey, an ex-councillor on Monklands District Council, stressed John's commitment to his constituents.[21]

Murray Elder was in hospital in Scotland convalescing from an operation. He thus had little knowledge of what was going on when he was paged by Alex

Allan, the Prime Minister's Private Secretary.[22] John Major had been at breakfast when informed of Smith's death, and had asked for a few minutes alone to absorb the news. He tried to pen a note to Elizabeth Smith, but scrunched up an inadequate first draft.[23] Later, he and his Cabinet colleagues agreed to cancel normal House of Commons business as a mark of respect.[24] Meanwhile, Murray Elder, discharged from hospital, went to Edinburgh, organising the funeral at Elizabeth's request.[25]

Within hours of Smith's death, Saltires and Union Jacks flew at half-mast all across Scotland. In Smith's constituency, Provost Robert Gilson called a minute's silence before suspending the business of Monklands District Council for the day, and making arrangement to set up books of condolence at Sir John Wilson Town Hall in Airdrie, and in the Municipal Buildings in Coatbridge. At Airdrie Arts Centre, where Smith held his monthly surgeries on the first Saturday of each month, deputy manageress Diane Stein recalled receiving 'wee mindings'[26] at Christmas from Smith.[27] Only the *Airdrie and Coatbridge Advertiser* was less than effusive in their tribute to Smith: print deadlines meant their Friday, 13 May edition was unable to make any mention of Smith's death, while the following week, the newspaper's editorial brought up the Monklands affair: 'It's no secret, that for the past couple of years John and *the Advertiser* were on opposite sides of the fence regarding the Monklandsgate affair. He chose, publicly at least, to keep his own counsel on an issue, which, both in its content and timing, must have caused him concern.'[28]

At the Scottish Conservative and Unionist Party Conference in Inverness, at 10.50 am, delegates had just finished debating the economy, when a note was passed to the platform that read, 'John Smith is dead.' Adrian Shinwell, the president of the Scottish Conservatives, made the announcement to a blue-rinsed gasp from across the auditorium of the Eden Court Theatre. A minute's silence preceded the suspension of conference business. In one of the most poignant moments of the day, an ashen-faced Ian Lang, Secretary of State for Scotland, gave an impromptu tribute outside the conference hall, describing Smith as 'a fine parliamentarian, a fair, decent and good man, and a great patriot, a man who loved Scotland'.[29] The Conservative conference resumed at 2.15 pm, allowing Lang, who had now regained his composure, to give a brief appreciation of Smith's 'quicksilver mind':

> Because our parliamentary system is an adversarial one, it was inevitable that to us, in the party political battle, he personified the other side, but we could respect, and we now mourn alongside his own party a leader who honoured democracy and who loved his country and served it with distinction.[30]

Lang then formally suspended the rest of the day's platform proceedings.

At 2.30 pm, Betty Boothroyd, the Speaker of the House of Commons, her voice almost breaking, formally announced the death of the Rt Hon. John Smith QC MP. She suspended the sitting of the House until 3.30 pm, when tributes could be moved to Smith in the form of an Adjournment debate. John Major opened the tributes, Margaret Beckett, acting leader of the Labour Party, followed the Prime Minister. Memorably, she quoted the end of Smith's speech the night before (see Prologue), adding that it should stand as his epitaph.[31] Paddy Ashdown praised Smith's 'dogged determination in the face of adversity and challenge'.[32] Menzies Campbell recalled: 'It seemed to John Smith's friends that he never failed at anything to which he set his hand.'[33] Neil Kinnock's grief had been doubled by the death of his mother-in-law the previous night. John had held 'conviction without obsession; his principles were for application, not for decoration; and his superb intelligence was for practical use, not for adornment.' But what glowed above everything else was John's sense of humour, which was 'a product of his ability to put life into perspective. It showed resilience under pressure and determination in adversity.'[34]

Some of the most glowing tributes came from the left of the party, with whom Smith had always enjoyed good relations. Alice Mahon was in tears. Dennis Canavan judged that Smith's greatest ability was 'to unite people'.[35] Tony Benn spoke for only 45 seconds, but his tribute drew out two of Smith's best qualities:

> Inside him burned the flame of anger against injustice, and the flame of hope that we could build a better world. That was what moved him. Secondly, he was a man who always said the same, wherever he was. Whether one heard him in public at a meeting or in private, whether one heard him in the Cabinet or in the House of Commons, he always said the same thing. For that reason, he was trusted. He was a lovely man, and I hope that his family will gain something from the knowledge that their grief is shared by us.[36]

Dennis Skinner spoke thus: 'I speak today because I come from a different wing of the Party, yet we never had words in anger. It is incredible that throughout the whole of that period, we were able to remain friends.'[37]

Before the House adjourned, Betty Boothroyd rounded off the tributes, describing Smith as 'a dedicated politician. He played a hard game when it was necessary, but as the Prime Minister said, there was never any malice in his attacks . . . I knew he was a good man.'[38] The House adjourned at 4.11 pm. Up until that point Chris Smith had been relatively composed, but when he ran into Ann Taylor after the tributes, he broke down and wept.[39]

Margaret Beckett spoke to a meeting of the shadow Cabinet that afternoon:

> I told them the Party had a huge duty to fight the European elections
> without losing any ground so that John's legacy would not be diminished
> . . . John had built up a team, a strong team, which was better person for
> person than our opponents. We needed to prove it. It was 'the team' that
> was going on.[40]

At 6 pm, the whole PLP stood in silence in honour of their fallen leader, and
then Doug Hoyle, the chair of the PLP, announced that were would be an
opportunity for colleagues to express their tributes to Smith at the meeting of
the PLP the following Wednesday morning (18 May). As acting leader of the
Labour Party, Beckett then indicated that representations would be made to
the government with a view to rearranging the Business of the House so that
Labour MPs could attend John's funeral in Edinburgh the following Friday.
She then announced that the campaigning activities of the party would be
suspended until after the funeral. She informed back benchers that the shadow
Cabinet had been 'determined and single-minded that once the electoral fray
was resumed, it should be returned to with vigour in order that on 9 June the
Party should achieve results at the polls which would do John proud, and that
no other considerations should get in the way of this'.[41]

At Labour Party headquarters at Walworth Road, Larry Whitty not only
had to cope with 'the most shattering day of my life' in terms of personal grief,
but also with the 'massive outpouring'[42] from members of the public. He
hastily organised a 'condolence room': a monochrome photograph of Smith
was set on a table, and a plain condolence book, nothing fancy, quickly
became surrounded mainly by red carnations and red roses. But very soon the
20-foot by twelve-foot room was unable to cope with the deluge of flowers,
and the caretaker needed all his time to clear the floors.[43]

As the day wore on, tributes came in from home and abroad. The
Archbishop of Canterbury, George Carey, described Smith as a man
'passionately committed to building a society both prosperous and just'. John
Monks, general secretary of the TUC, described Smith as 'a friend to people at
work . . . with his concern for a better life for everyone in society'.[44] Heartfelt
messages also came from many of the European socialist leaders, with whom
Smith had got on so well. Dick Spring, Irish Foreign Minister, Deputy Prime
Minister (Tanaiste), and leader of the Irish Labour Party, described Smith as
'a man of deep and abiding vision and a complete master of every brief he
studied'.[45] Across the Channel, *Le Monde* ran with an editorial on its
prestigious front page, describing Smith as '*un renovateur prudent*' (a 'prudent
reformer').[46] *Le Figaro* devoted nearly a page to Smith's death.[47] The Belgian

Willy Claes, president of the Party of European Socialists, commented: 'We have lost not just a good friend but a convinced, and convincing, European,'[48] and Felipe Gonzalez, Prime Minister of Spain, expressed similar sentiments.[49] The following day, the *Daily Mirror* ran with, 'The Best Prime Minister We Never Had', devoting fourteen pages to the aftermath of Smith's death.[50] *The Independent* reminded its readers that Labour had lost a leader 'who restored party morale after a humiliating fourth general election defeat'.[51] *The Guardian*'s Hugo Young stated: 'There has not been a less divisive leader, and none had fewer enemies.'[52] Tony Benn agreed, arguing that Smith had 'played a notable part in healing the personal breaches that had opened up during the Eighties', and had 'laid fresh foundations for the good will and co-operation between left and right that existed under Clem Attlee and Harold Wilson'.[53]

During the eight days between Smith's death and the funeral, Elizabeth received a constant stream of friends and family at her Edinburgh home, as a policeman kept guard at the gate. Tony Blair, Gordon Brown, George Robertson, Simon Haskel, Michael Montague and Jack Cunningham all came up from London. Blair told Meta and Elizabeth that one of the things he most admired about John was his willingness to listen to everybody, and bring everyone into shadow Cabinet discussions.[54]

Many of John's university friends also came, including Menzies Campbell, Bob McLaughlan, Derry Irvine, Neil and Donald MacCormick, and Donald Dewar. The three girls wanted to hear about their dad at university, especially the mounting anecdotes that proved he was quite a wild student. Meanwhile, John's two sisters, Annie Kelly (from Aberdour, with her husband, Alex Kelly, a headmaster in Fife) and Mary McCulloch (living in Canada with husband Jack) recalled their time together as arts students at Glasgow.[55]

A pattern soon developed that whoever was in the house around 7 pm (usually numbering around ten to fourteen people) would sit round the big table in the kitchen for the one proper meal of the day. A steady stream of family friends supplied sustenance: Elspeth Campbell (wife of Menzies) emptied her freezer into two baskets; Flora MacCormick, wife of Neil, brought a tureen of homemade soup; an Italian family, next door neighbours of the Munros who owned a pasta shop, donated huge trays of lasagne; while Bill Taylor QC[56] had the presence of mind to gift a case of white wine.[57] Elizabeth Munro dealt with replies from the funeral invitations.[58] Anne Gordon, Jimmy's wife, organised the flowers at the Smith family home.

It was a strange existence for Ruth Wishart, living in the attic with Meta, taking care of the grieving family, performing the role of Mrs Bridges, and dealing with the comings and goings downstairs that resembled Piccadilly

Circus. Wishart, a member of the press, now found herself under siege from the journalists gathered at the front of the house.[59]

Laughter was never far away around the kitchen table as everyone recalled how John would shop from the Innovations catalogue, debating what were John's worst buys. He had recently bought a large circle of wood that fitted on top of his small round dining table, enlarging his table space. This particular 'innovation' promised to 'end small table misery now'. Everyone recalled how enormously enthusiastic John would be about his latest gadget (whether it was his electronic Filofax or satellite TV) or project (one year, growing tomatoes in grow bags in nearly every window of the house).[60]

The Smith family home had become 'warmly cocooned in a week-long wake'[61] that ended up being an important source of comfort for Elizabeth and the girls.

Among the thousands of letters of condolence received by Elizabeth Smith was a personal message of sympathy from the Queen. Others tried to get in touch. At one point, Elizabeth had just gone for a lie down when the telephone rang: it was Diana, Princess of Wales, could she speak to Elizabeth?[62] Diana invited Elizabeth and her three daughters to Kensington Palace for the day, an offer that they took up a few months later. She also sent an informal bunch of flowers with a handwritten note. By contrast, Charles, Prince of Wales, initially sent a pretty formal fax. Perhaps the Prince of Wales's officials realised their mistake, because they followed up the dry fax with a second letter, although even this typed version contrasted markedly with Diana's effortless informality.

Even political opponents felt moved to send messages of condolence. Chris Patten, the former Tory Party chairman, wrote a beautiful letter to Elizabeth, from the perspective of a father of three girls, and someone who had also suffered from heart trouble himself.

Elizabeth rightly describes the sheer outpouring of emotion on John's death in the form of thousands of cards and letters as 'a phenomenon'.[63] Jack Cunningham told of Labour Party offices around the country receiving bouquets of flowers around the clock. On one occasion, a smartly dressed woman knocked on the door at Elizabeth's home, armed with a bunch of flowers. Meta Ramsay answered the door, half suspecting that it was a friend of one of the girls. Instead, the lady, a complete stranger, poured out her story. She'd been walking around her house in Dundee crying, and felt an impulse to get into her car, and pay her respects personally. She did not want to intrude, she explained, so she just handed over the flowers and left.[64]

Elizabeth tried to reply to as many people as she could in her own hand, but the number of letters proved so vast that she was unable to cope. The Labour

Party supplied secretarial support, compiling a letter that encapsulated her feelings, which was sent out to many of those who had sent their condolences:

> It was kind of you to write to me about John. The whole family is deriving comfort from the sincere expressions of grief and loss expressed by so many people in this country and abroad.
>
> Our loss is enormous, but as time passes we will come to treasure the way in which countless people have experienced something akin to our own shock, bewilderment and bereavement, and have found ways to tell us what they feel.
>
> The public response encourages me to hope that the example of John's life, and the universal dismay at his dying, may serve to advance the noble causes to which he so wholeheartedly gave his life.[65]

Ann Barrett received a letter of condolence from Shirley Sheppard, a former secretary to Hugh Gaitskell, recalling her own moment of grief back in 1963 when another Labour leader's life had been cut short: 'My heart goes out to you at this moment. The loyalty we give our bosses and the emotion we feel is very different from all others. The closeness experienced with them is unique; the hours spent with them together watching their moods and dilemmas are not repeated with others.'[66]

Tony Blair was the first MP to send a personal note to Ann Barrett:

> This is just a line to say how deeply, deeply sorry we all are and how we are thinking of you. John absolutely worshipped the ground you walked on, as you know. He was immensely proud of you and would often, in your absence of course (!) comment on how lucky he was. All our prayers are with you. Yours ever, Tony.'[67]

Back at the House of Commons, the PLP met for a special tribute on the Wednesday morning (18 May). After standing in silent tribute, Doug Hoyle, the chair of the PLP, read out John's obituary, which had been prepared (as with all fallen Labour figures) by the secretary of the PLP, Alan Haworth.[68] Tom Clarke began the tributes, as John's nearest parliamentary neighbour, quoting a verse from Robert Burns:

> Few hearts like his, with virtue warmed
> Few heads, with knowledge so informed
> If there's another world he lives in bliss
> If there is none, he made the best of this.[69]

Neil Kinnock spoke about John's qualities of leadership, particularly the awesome self-confidence, while Chris Mullin stressed John's absolute lack of malice. Jean Corston said that a leader at ease with himself had helped create a party at ease with itself, adding: 'We could do with more feminists like John Smith.'[70] Acting leader, Margaret Beckett rounded off the tributes, stressing what John knew: that the 'broad church' of the Labour Party is about the whole, not just the individual. It was vital to conduct the forthcoming leadership contest with dignity and mutual respect. She concluded by saying that although she was only too aware of the extent of shock within the party arising from John's death, the party should be as professional as John had been, act responsibly, and get on with the work.[71]

Having been asked by Elizabeth to arrange the funeral, Murray Elder had to work without modern precedent for dealing with a leader of the opposition's funeral, not since the death of Gaitskell 30 years before anyway. In terms of protocol, it was necessary to avoid a situation where the Prime Minister was the most important person attending the funeral. This outcome was achieved when James Callaghan agreed to represent the Queen, meaning that everyone else, apart from the immediate Smith family, had to be in the kirk before him.[72]

Just before 11.30 am on Friday, 20 May,[73] around 900 invited guests crowded into the large, red sandstone church at Cluny, where Smith had been an elder of the kirk. Many other mourners packed into the Church Centre to watch a special televised relay of the funeral. Congregations also gathered around the country, at Westminster Central Hall, and in cathedrals in Liverpool, Manchester, Birmingham, Bristol, Newcastle and Cardiff. Outside the church, a few hundred people gathered to pay their respects, despite the chill wind. Floral tributes were piled on the banks of grass around the kirk:[74] Ian Lang and the Scottish Office had sent gold blooms; another wreath came from the Ambassador of the Russian Federation; Glenda Jackson left a small posy of white freesias; the Co-operative Movement sent an emblem worked like an old trade union banner in white and purple petals; there was also a saltire of blue and white flowers, with a note: 'Remembering John, "Hairy" to his childhood friends from Ardrishaig'.[75]

Lord Callaghan, dressed in his tails, Lady Wilson (wife of Harold), and Edward Heath attended, as did Betty Boothroyd, the Speaker of the House of Commons. Members of the government, including John and Norma Major, Sir Norman Fowler (Conservative Party chairman), Malcolm Rifkind (Secretary of State for Defence), Ian Lang (Secretary of State for Scotland), Lord MacKay of Clashfern (Lord Chancellor), and Lord James Douglas Hamilton (Scottish Office Minister) sat in the fifth row, the rows in front being reserved for close friends and family. John's personal staff members were given a special pew. Other party leaders included Paddy Ashdown, Alex Salmond, Rev. Ian Paisley and John Hume. The former Liberal leader David Steel was also in attendance. They were joined by figures from the media such as Jon Snow, Melvyn Bragg, and Robin Butler, the Cabinet Secretary. John's old legal chum, Sir Nicholas Fairbairn, arrived dressed eccentrically in a grey frock coat and top hat, the full mourning rig of a Victorian undertaker, complete with a red carnation. Glenys Kinnock held Michael Foot's hand as they approached the gates of the church, with the whole of the shadow Cabinet trooping behind in twos. Approximately half the Parliamentary Labour Party attended.

The Rev. George Munro, Cluny's minister, began by commenting that John had died on Ascension Day, and that that coming Sunday was the Festival of Pentecost in which many nations under heaven had gathered in one place. So it was true on the day of John Smith's funeral. Senior government ministers and socialist leaders came from the United States, Israel, South Africa and from across Europe.

After a short prayer, John McCluskey read in a clear, commanding voice from 1 Corinthians 13, Paul's great hymn to Christian love.[76] Jimmy Gordon, managing director of Radio Clyde, who had been Smith's best man, delivered the first of three tributes, pointing to the cruelty and injustice of death.[77] Margaret Beckett, Labour's acting leader, read from Matthew 5, verses 1–12, her voice nearly breaking as she uttered the part about, 'Blessed are they that mourn, for they shall be comforted.' But her voice regained strength with: 'Blessed are the peacemakers, for they shall be called the sons of God.'

Then, in a beautifully clear, confident voice, Derry Irvine spoke. He recalled his continuous friendship with John, beginning in 1959 at Glasgow University. He described John as 'a Highlander, a romantic, a Presbyterian, not a puritan' who had a set of moral imperatives that attached equal value to every human being, as free from snobbery as it was possible for any man to be, and someone who relished the absurd. Throughout his life, John had given his friends fierce loyalty, and his friends had given theirs in return. Derry concluded: 'We shall cherish his memory until our times are come.'[78]

The congregation then heard Kenna Campbell, a solo soprano, sing the prose version of Psalm 23 unaccompanied in Gaelic. A friend of Donald Dewar's had suggested Kenna to John's sister, Mary: 'Time was of the essence. It was up to Elizabeth to decide what she wanted, but once she had agreed, I listened to Kenna sing over the 'phone.'[79] The haunting and beautiful performance at the kirk, recalling Smith's Highland roots, was undoubtedly the highlight of the funeral.[80]

Donald Dewar gave the last of the three eulogies. As usual, he'd left his preparation to the very last minute. Meta Ramsay had found an old copy of the 1959 Glasgow University Handbook in her London flat (where she had returned briefly to pick up some black clothes, before flying back to Edinburgh), dating from the time that John had been chair of the Labour Club.[81] The night before the funeral, Elizabeth Munro heard Donald rehearsing his speech at 3 am.[82] On the day, Donald rose to the occasion, stressing John's consistency of purpose, and the fact that his principles lasted throughout his life, as well as raising a laugh or two in the audience. In the aforementioned GU Handbook, John had strangely proclaimed that 'in this Club we think it valuable occasionally to indulge in political activities such as canvassing'. Donald commented: 'Not even in my most Presbyterian moments would I describe canvassing as an indulgence – a penance perhaps, never an indulgence. Given his work rate then and through the years it must have been a case of breaking bad news gently.'[83]

John had set out his 'credo': that 'the opportunity of each individual to lead a complete and civilised life should be as equal as far as is possible to that of his neighbour', and there followed a plea for a more just distribution of material wealth. These principles had remained with John all his life. For John, achieving political power, said Donald, was all about helping people who could not help themselves: 'Consistency was at the core of him. Politics a series of practical problems to be overcome. Square, determined, sometimes thrawn,[84] always probing, pushing for a way forward.' Those who depicted John as 'douce, dark suited and safe knew not the man'. 'John could start a party in any empty room, and often did – filling it with good cheer, Gaelic songs and argument.' 'He enjoyed people and loyalty was a prime virtue, and never with John a one-way process.' Dewar concluded: 'The people know they have lost a friend – someone who was on their side and they knew it.'[85]

At the end of the service, the coffin was borne out of the church, and taken on its way to Iona (John's favourite holiday escape), to be buried near the graves of Scotland's ancient kings.[86] In her sensitive commentary of the service for the BBC, Jane Franchi ended with a quote from one of John's constituents: 'Forbye[87] being a politician, he was a good man.'[88]

The wake was held at the Signet Library,[89] Old Parliament House, on the High Street. The choice of venue reflected the fact that Smith had remained well liked at the Bar. On the morning of Smith's death, John's friends read with sadness the note posted by the Dean above the fireplace in the Robing Room of Parliament House, announcing, with regret, the death of the Rt Hon. John Smith QC MP. John and Norma Major stayed at the wake for an hour and a half, right until the end, and kindly gave Tony Benn a lift in their 'plane on the way back to London.[90] The only unexpected drama of the day occurred when a pane of glass from a dome skylight in the reception hallway crashed to the floor.[91]

After the wake, a convoy of vehicles set off on the long trip from Edinburgh across to Iona. Only close Scottish friends and family attended the Iona part of the funeral, and Elizabeth drew up a list of the people that she wanted to attend. Elizabeth was also firmly of the view that John would have wanted to have been buried on Iona. This presented a problem. Because of Iona's special position, many seek to be buried there, but space is scarce and the ground is rocky. (Natives may be buried within the Reilig Odhrain itself, but residents who are not natives have a special area, where Smith now lies.) But Smith was a well-known figure on the island, and became one of the members of the congregation in the Iona Community when he visited.[92] Indeed, Joanna Anderson, one of the leaders, remarked: 'Every night he was here, he was on his knees in the abbey church. You don't see that very much.'[93] The only quite understandable fear the Iona people had was that the Smith's family's request might lead to a flood of similar requests. They need not have feared. The special permission granted, was treated as an all-time one-off.

Murray Elder had contacted Norman Shanks, a member of the Iona Community since 1980 and later its leader from 1995–2002. Shanks had worked for fifteen years as a civil servant in the Scottish Office, including two years (from 1975–7) as Private Secretary to the Secretary of State for Scotland (Willie Ross, then Bruce Millan). From 1989–97, after becoming a Church of Scotland minister, Shanks had regular contact with leading Scottish politicians as the kirk's representative on the Scottish Constitutional Convention.[94] Elder asked Shanks if he would be willing to deal with the matter of gaining permission, and to conduct the short committal ceremony. Shanks agreed.[95] He then contacted the then chief executive of Strathclyde Regional Council, Michael Gossip. After consultations with the local councillor and the Community Council on Iona, special permission was granted. The fact that Smith was a native of Argyll and a regular visitor to Iona, played much more with the council than the fact he was a prominent politician.[96]

By this stage, Jimmy Gordon had taken charge of the logistical side of the funeral party's trip to Iona. On a Friday, the Caledonian MacBrayne (CalMac) ferries only left at 4 pm or 11 pm. The funeral party couldn't get there in time for four o'clock, and everyone would have been just too emotionally and physically exhausted to take the later ferry. In the end, the director of CalMac proved a star. Jimmy Gordon was able to charter a small ferry from Oban to Mull. He also organised a minibus to meet the funeral party for those not travelling by car. Accommodation was also arranged at local hotels and bed and breakfasts. In a very touching gesture, Jimmy gave the whole logistical exercise the name, *Operation Para Handy*, recalling John's great love of Neil Munro's book about the puffers that had sailed up and down the islands off the West Coast of Scotland.[97] During the week of funeral preparations, Ruth Wishart and the Smith girls dubbed Jimmy Gordon '*Para Handy*'.[98]

Police outriders on motorcycles accompanied the funeral party across Scotland from Edinburgh to Mull, stopping traffic at roundabouts, thereby ensuring that the convoy stayed intact. As the vehicles reached Erskine Bridge, they were waved through without paying the toll (then 60 pence per car).[99] As the cortege did so, a Ford Escort snuck across with them without paying.[100]

On arrival in Oban, on a beautiful May evening, the ferry made its crossing to Mull. Jimmy Gordon had even organised a carry-out, and when he took it down from the roof-rack of his car, everyone gratefully fell on the drink.[101] Jimmy phoned ahead for (and Derry Irvine financed) a couple of dozen fish suppers from Craignure Inn on Mull.[102] Ruth Wishart remembers Derry going into the kitchen to explain to the staff how the meals should be prepared, and who wanted sauce with what.[103] Meta Ramsay recalls: 'It was the best fish and chips I've ever tasted in my life.'[104] The funeral party boarded the Fionnphort passenger ferry for the very short trip from Mull to Iona. By this stage, it was twilight, and with Iona people waiting silently and respectfully on the jetty it made a beautiful, surreal scene. When they reached the island, the Columba Hotel had laid on bowls of soup and sandwiches, which were ravenously devoured by the entire party who had eaten nothing since breakfast, except the fish supper from Craignure.[105]

The short service the following day was timed to start before the first ferry of tourists arrived. Derry Irvine, Donald Dewar, Jimmy Gordon, John McCluskey and John's two brothers-in-law acted as the pallbearers, removing the coffin from Saint Oran's chapel where it had lain overnight. The funeral party gasped as Donald Dewar momentarily stumbled on the cobbled stones.[106] Norman Shanks, presiding over the short service, likened the journey of the mourners to 'a kind of pilgrimage to this special place'. He added: 'We know Heaven has been enriched immensely by the presence of someone who is already looking for a cause to fight and friends new and old with whom to share a good talk and a good time.' Smith's coffin was committed to the ground[107] as Neil MacCormick played two tunes on the bagpipes, Robert Burns's 'A Man's A Man, For A' That', followed by a Gaelic lament, 'Caol Muile', known as the hymn of St Columba.[108]

After the service, two of the pallbearers, Donald Dewar and Derry Irvine, engaged in a long, forced conversation, for the first time in years, as the funeral party made its way down to the hotel. Afterwards, Ruth Wishart asked Dewar what on earth they had managed to talk about. Donald replied: 'Art.'[109] At the hotel, Ruth Wishart handed over an autographed copy of *Tales of Para Handy* to Jimmy Gordon, signed by all the other members of the funeral party in appreciation of his organisational skills.[110] As Neil MacCormick looked across from Iona to the hills of Mull, he spontaneously broke into a Gaelic song, 'An t-eilean muileach', 'The Isle of Mull', one of John's favourites, written by Dugald MacPhail, one of whose descendants was present representing the islanders of Iona.[111] Both John's sisters, Mary and Annie, joined in.[112] The singing brought to an end ten days of close bonding between John's friends and immediate family.

John's grave is situated in a different area of the graveyard from the historical side. One follows a gravel path at the end of which Smith's grave is set just in front of a stone wall with a view out to the sea. However, the writing on the headstone was obscure from the path, and eventually, the headstone was turned around so that people could look at it without trampling in the graveyard. For the tenth anniversary, the inscription was repainted in gold lettering: It reads: 'John Smith, September 1938–May 1994. An Honest Man's the Noblest Work of God.'

In the week after Iona, smaller services were held across the country,[113] including a memorial service at the Sir John Wilson Town Hall in Airdrie in the Monklands East constituency on Friday, 27 May 1994. Elizabeth and the three girls attended, as did Robin Cook and Gordon Brown. During the service, the Rev. Peter Gordon referred to Smith 'as one of the most distinguished Scots of our time'.[114] George Robertson, Eddie Cairns and Jack Cunningham delivered eulogies, Donald Dewar read Burns – 'A Man's A Man, For A' That' – and Tom Clarke read scripture.[115]

The main national (British) memorial service took place at Westminster Abbey on 14 July.[116] The Archbishop of Canterbury, Dr George Carey, had carefully researched his eulogy, having asked Ann Barrett to fax him a copy of the three tributes from Donald Dewar, Jimmy Gordon and Derry Irvine that had been delivered at Cluny two months earlier:[117] The archbishop said:

> John Smith is the name of everyman. That is fitting because everyman is what John Smith the political leader stood and worked for . . . Social justice was his cause, rooted in his fierce and instinctive commitment to the worth of every person made in the image of God.[118]

Twenty-Five
CONSEQUENCES

Those wishing merely to read a biography of John Smith should read
no further. This chapter disobeys the advice of the late Roy Jenkins on
how to finish a biography. Jenkins cited the King's instruction to the
White Rabbit in *Alice's Adventures in Wonderland*: 'Begin at the beginning,
and go on till you come to the end; then stop.'[1] Jenkins adds: 'And the way to
stop is to describe the end of the subject's life, put him in his grave, and if you
can think of a succinct epitaph, give it a headstone.'[2]

Unfulfilled promise leads to fascination and speculation: 'Labour . . . for the
first time for years seemed to have overcome its obsessional complex about its
inner self, appearing more outward-looking and healthy.' The number of
voters believing he had been a good leader had risen above 50 per cent, and his
average lead over the Prime Minister was an impressive 20 per cent. A Gallup
opinion poll showed that Labour now had a comfortable lead, no longer just
due to Conservative weakness.'[3] Moreover: 'Within the previous year he had
become accepted by the public as the right and inevitable next Prime
Minister.'[4] One of his shadow Cabinet colleagues wrote that one of the most
fascinating developments of the year had been 'the almost invisible transfer of
the nation's confidence, from the man with real power in Downing Street to
the man with shadow power in Opposition'.[5] In his diaries, Tony Benn noted:
'It has dominated the press and television in an astonishing way. It is a terrible
personal tragedy for him as he was closer to Downing Street than at any time
in his life.'[6]

However, these comments refer not to John Smith's death, but that of Hugh
Gaitskell, aged 56, on 18 January 1963. Just like Smith, a Labour leader had been
cut down in his prime when it looked fairly certain that he would become
Prime Minister after a long period in opposition. Writing only a day after
Smith's death, Joe Haines, former press secretary to Harold Wilson, drew out
many of the similarities between the untimely deaths of Smith and Gaitskell:
they were of a similar age when they died (Gaitskell 56, Smith 55); both were
on the brink of becoming Prime Minister because the Prime Minister of the
day (Macmillan/Major) was a spent force; and both had suffered a coronary

thrombosis before they became leader, and had seemed to make a full recovery.[7]

Politically, there were both similarities and differences between Gaitskell and Smith. Although Smith considered Gaitskell to be one of his early political heroes, and shared his views on multilateral nuclear disarmament, Smith was consistently pro-European whereas Gaitskell famously warned that European federation would mean 'the end of Britain as an independent European state' and 'the end of a thousand years of history'[8] at the Labour Party conference in Brighton in October 1962. Smith was very much a conciliator, ruling from the centre of the Labour Party, whereas Gaitskell was much more a preacher and teacher.[9] Most notably, whereas at the Winter Gardens in Blackpool in November 1959, Gaitskell had tried and failed to alter Clause IV, against the sage advice of Tony Crosland that it would cause far more trouble than it was worth,[10] Smith wisely left that particular Pandora's box unopened. As Hugh Macpherson rightly point out: 'John was different from Gaitskell in one vital regard: he had the capacity to unite the Labour Party whereas Gaitskell, to succeed, had to defeat a section of it'.[11]

With the benefit of hindsight, perhaps the closest historical comparison is with Donald Dewar, who died six years after Smith on 11 October 2000: once again, Scotland, and also the United Kingdom, witnessed the untimely death of a huge Scottish political figure who had apparently recovered from his initial serious illness;[12] commentators and politicians praised both Dewar and Smith for their long-standing commitment to social justice;[13] both were key figures in the long struggle for Scottish home rule;[14] the huge public funeral, one in Glasgow, the other in Edinburgh, observed by a largely respectful press;[15] and the final tranquil place of rest, Smith buried on Iona, Dewar having his ashes scattered in Lochgilphead. Despite being very different characters, one diffident and awkward, the other easy and outgoing, both men had learned their political craft as student politicians while debating weighty issues in the Glasgow Union. Most of all, John Smith and Donald Dewar shared a common circle of close acquaintances, who had to endure the double blow of losing another dear friend.[16]

Elsewhere, this author has explored the question, 'What if John Smith had lived?'[17] I have argued that Smith would have won the 1997 election comfortably, but not by as much as Tony Blair.[18] He would have paid closer attention to the PLP and the Labour movement at the expense of a high media profile, and increased income tax a bit. He might have gone into the Euro and kept Britain out of war in Iraq. At the time of the tenth anniversary of Smith's death, quite a few journalists and politicians also wheeled out the 'what might have been' articles.[19] Similarly, Philip Williams includes an epilogue at the end of his biography of Gaitskell, in which he explores, quite reasonably, the '[Gaitskell] Government that Never Was', and 'The Promise Unfulfilled'.[20]

Politicians have to move with the times, and Smith, more than most, understood the politics of pragmatism. Therefore, who can really tell what he would have done in government?[21] For instance, how long would Smith's long-standing opposition have lasted to the idea of an independent Central Bank (both in Europe and in the United Kingdom)? Who now thinks that Gordon Brown was wrong to hand over power of interest rates to the Bank of England on day one of the New Labour government in May 1997? At what level would Smith have set the national minimum wage? Which of the recommendations of the Social Justice Commission would he have accepted (and which would he have rejected)? These would have been tough choices to make for the leader of the party in the two to three years before the general election.

What has been missed in previous accounts of this period is that Smith's death had three other unintended leadership effects, two of which concerned the Conservative Party, and one of which had to do with Labour: put crudely, Smith's death saved John Major, ended Michael Heseltine's leadership ambitions, and gave the Labour Party its first ever woman leader.

Indirectly, John Smith's death spared John Major an immediate leadership challenge.[22] Before Smith died, the European Parliament elections, due to be held on 9 June, were being widely referred to as a referendum on the Prime Minister's future. All the media focus shifted to the Labour Party after John's death, in terms of both their grieving, and the fevered speculation over the Labour leadership contest due to be held on 21 July, with the short-term effect of drawing media attention away from the divisions in the Conservative Party.

Smith's death inevitably took some of the political edge off of the European elections. Normal campaigning was suspended until after his funeral. Conservative Central Office hastily removed several personal attacks from their European election Manifesto – *A Strong Britain in A Strong Europe*, including:

His [Smith's] judgement has been entirely wrong on all the key decisions he had had to make in the last decade. (p. 662).

Mr Smith's first eighteen months in office have been characterised by ineffectual and visionless leadership. (p. 662).

Mr Smith has been evasive ... [his] first eighteen months have managed to make Mr Kinnock look like a first-rate leader. (p. 663).[23]

Researchers in Conservative Central Office had also been busy compiling a dossier on Monklands, entitled *Monklands: Not in My Backyard*, first published on 11 April 1994, which regurgitated many of the unsubstantiated allegations surrounding MDC (see chapter 23), and which claimed: 'Mr Smith has seemingly abdicated responsibility for sorting out the situation in his own backyard, passing the buck to the Scottish Office, or even back to his constituents, rather than tackling the issue head-on. (p. 1)'[24]

And yet, the day after Smith's death, Major made a relatively apolitical speech to the Scottish Conservative and Unionist Party Conference in Inverness in which he again paid tribute to Smith, and called for a higher quality of debate and an end to 'knocking, carping and sneering' politics.[25] It is very difficult to separate out Major's genuine consideration to the Smith family at their sad loss, and the Prime Minister's political imperative to survive the European elections.

The European election results were disastrous for the Conservatives, but not catastrophic.[26] As the academic experts put it at the time: 'John Major had escaped the threatened wipe-out by a very narrow margin, but he *had* escaped it.'[27] It is possible therefore to argue that John Smith's death probably afforded John Major temporary relief on the leadership front,[28] before he had to tell his own critics in June 1995 to 'put up or shut up'.

But if Major had received a temporary reprieve, then Michael Heseltine's last remaining hopes of becoming Tory leader had been dashed. Heseltine had suffered a heart attack the previous June. Smith had sent Heseltine a handwritten note, which had apparently given the president of the Board of Trade 'hope and encouragement'.[29] The weekend after Smith's death, Heseltine gave a series of interviews in which he denied that he lacked sufficiently good health to succeed John Major.[30] But Smith's fate meant the media were forever destined to speculate that a similar fate might befall Heseltine.[31]

The third leadership effect (and the one that is currently obscured by the Brown/Blair business) is that Margaret Beckett became the first woman leader of the Labour Party.[32] Beckett led the Labour Party with composed dignity in the weeks immediately after Smith's death. As well as taking on Smith's role (including non-stop campaigning and taking Prime Minister's Questions), the acting leader also operated without a deputy leader.[33]

Uniquely in Labour's history, in the three months between Smith's death and Tony Blair's election as leader, Margaret Beckett had to work with a leader's office that was not of her own creation.[34] Some members of Smith's old team had a slightly awkward time working for Margaret Beckett. It wasn't that she was a difficult person to deal with (far from it), but important people kept telephoning the office asking to arrange a meeting with Tony Blair, and Smith's old team had to point out that Beckett was the leader, and out of protocol they had to see her and not Blair, the likely winner of the leadership contest. This included enforcing protocol on Bill Clinton at the time of the 50th anniversary of the D-Day landings when the White House let it be known that they wanted to see Blair.[35] Eventually, Beckett and Clinton met for 40 minutes at Hartwell House in Oxfordshire.[36]

Margaret Beckett says of her decision to stand both for the leadership and the deputy leadership of the party: 'I had discovered [during my period] as acting leader that I had the capacity to lead the party. I was not prepared to run just as deputy leader.'[37]

Beckett was also determined (and this was a view strongly shared by Larry Whitty) to avoid the party having to hold two contests, a leadership contest in the summer, and a deputy leadership contest at the party conference in the autumn, both potentially divisive and expensive. Finally, Beckett made her decision in the full knowledge that she might not win either contest: 'I recognised that there was a strong possibility of a new leadership team for a new era, and I hadn't the slightest intention of standing in their way.'[38] One of Beckett's comments during the 1994 leadership campaign stands out: 'One of my women colleagues said to me: "They buried you with John."'[39]

Paul Routledge argues that Margaret Beckett's decision to stand for the leadership 'made the task of assembling the right coalition of support for Brown practically impossible'.[40] But Routledge appears to get the chronology wrong. Brown chose to stand down in favour of Blair. Had he run against Blair, then Beckett would have made a good running mate. The idea is not as far-fetched as it now seems: the two colleagues were politically very close: Brown had been Beckett's campaign manager in the 1992 deputy leadership contest (see chapter 17). Leo Beckett recalls that many of the Scottish Labour MPs were saying, 'It's Gordon and Margaret.'[41] Beckett could also count on the support of one or two of the big unions, including the TGWU. Overall, however, Beckett's decision to stand both for the leadership and the deputy leadership was a miscalculation which virtually ensured that John Prescott was elected deputy leader.[42]

A more obvious consequence of Smith's death was that it provoked a by-election in Monklands East, reawakening all the unwelcome controversies that had surrounded Monklands District Council (MDC) during John Smith's leadership (see chapter 23). Very quickly after John's death, Helen Liddell's name was mentioned as a likely successor to John,[43] but she claims she was extremely reluctant to stand: 'I hated London, hated Parliament, I was a Chief Executive [of the Business Venture Programme], I had a nine-year-old daughter and a sixteen-year-old son about to do his Highers. I had a good life.' She had therefore hidden herself away in the week before the funeral, only slipping into the back of Cluny church at the last minute. Then she sat listening to Donald Dewar's oration about the value of public service. Eventually, she succumbed, after 'considerable pressure' exerted by George Robertson and Donald Dewar.[44] Other Scottish Labour luminaries disagree fundamentally with Liddell's interpretation of how she came to be selected for the constituency, claiming that she was desperate to be selected.[45] Whichever is the more accurate version of events, the unavoidable fact for Liddell was that she fitted the bill; she had been brought up in Coatbridge, and she was certainly tough enough to deal with the well-known problems in the constituency.[46] She needed to be.

It came as no surprise when Liddell was selected on the first ballot as Labour's candidate.[47] According to one insider, Labour's canvassers quickly discovered on the doorsteps of Airdrie that the disquiet over the MDC, fuelled by the hostile national press coverage, had become the defining issue of the campaign. The feeling was in the Scottish Labour Party hierarchy that if that level of hostility continued on the doorstep, then the by-election was going to be lost.[48] Others fundamentally disagree. For good or for ill, Helen Liddell chose to depart from the Smith-Clarke line on Monklands, which had been to call upon the Secretary of State for Scotland to instigate a public inquiry if there were allegations to answer. On the weekend of 17–18 June, Liddell declared: 'It's my job to fight for the people of Monklands East, regardless of whom I have to take on, be it the district council or the regional council. I will fight for everyone from Downing Street to Dunbeth Road, and every other point in between.'[49] Liddell had asked Maurice Hart, MDC's chief executive to provide her with a set of figures on the alleged spending disparities between Coatbridge and Airdrie. On 21 June, Liddell stuck her neck out: 'The figures produced by the district council prove that expenditure on major projects has been concentrated in one part of the district. This is unacceptable to local people and unacceptable to me.'[50]

The main problem with Liddell's new strategy was that it risked upsetting the 8,000 voters from Coatbridge who formed a small but still crucial part of the Monklands East constituency. As soon as she made her remarks, all the Labour Party workers in Coatbridge downed tools. The committee rooms in Coatbridge were bare. On the Sunday before the election, Tom Clarke MP spent all day telephoning Coatbridge party members to try to get them back on board. Then, on the Monday he returned to London to learn of good news. The Smith-Clarke plan for investment in Lanarkshire had borne fruit. The Scottish Office announced that the Scottish Development Agency was going to pump large sums of money into Lanarkshire. On that basis, Clarke spoke to a reporter from BBC *Reporting Scotland*. However, the reporter asked Clarke to comment on Liddell's paper. Kay Ullrich, the SNP candidate, had also reiterated her charge about Smith and Clarke's lack of intervention in the Monklands Affair to journalists.[51]

Having been told about these developments, perhaps Clarke should have refused to do the interview. However, Monklands was such a controversial issue that, if you didn't say something, it was taken to mean that you had something to hide. (Eddie Cairns had been doorstepped by the media, and jumped into a car. It looked sheepish and guilty.) Moreover, Clarke had spent the whole weekend trying to win back the Labour Party workers in Coatbridge,[52] so he dismissed Ullrich's allegations as 'largely McCarthyite smears, mythology' in the interview, which was broadcast on the Monday night.[53] Clarke also made the following comments: 'If an inquiry had been held, the accusations would have been laughed out of court . . . I do not know what figures Helen Liddell has seen. What I do know is that John Smith and myself were fighting very hard, to make sure we got the resources to both towns.'[54]

Helen Liddell then issued a terse statement: 'I am the candidate for Monklands East. I called for these figures and I am more than satisfied of the need to redress the balance of spending in the district.'[55] Adam Ingram, the Labour MP for East Kilbride, then went on the media claiming that Clarke must have seen Liddell's figures when in fact Clarke had never set eyes on Liddell's paper (and still hasn't).[56] George Robertson attempted to defuse matters, claiming that Clarke was just fighting his constituency corner.[57] Jimmy Wray, the Labour MP for Glasgow Provan,[58] and then convener of the Scottish Group of Labour MPs, came to Clarke's defence: 'He [Clarke] responded to an attack the candidate had made. No candidate should ever make any attack . . . until such time as it can be substantiated.' However, Wray, after a conversation with the Labour leadership, issued a statement claiming that he had now seen Liddell's paper on the spending figures, that they revealed an imbalance in expenditure, and that 'Helen Liddell is absolutely right to find this unacceptable.'[59]

The spin put on the *Reporting Scotland* story did Tom Clarke a great deal of temporary damage. That autumn (1994), he was voted off the shadow Cabinet, but once he and his allies, Jimmy Wray and Jim Cunningham (Coatbridge

born, but Labour MP for Coventry South East since 1992),[60] had explained
Clarke's position to colleagues, Clarke was voted back on to the shadow
Cabinet for the next two years. But, at the time, Clarke was perhaps unfairly
portrayed as the man who nearly lost Labour Monklands East when in fact
he'd gone into councillor Jim Brooks' office on the Tuesday afternoon before
polling and pleaded with him to make the necessary 'phone calls to the
Coatbridge workers to get them back on polling day.[61]

Given the absence of ward returns for the by-election, it is not possible to
say definitively whether the Coatbridge factor was decisive in winning the by-
election, or whether Liddell's attempts to deal with the Monklands issue won
back a key group of disillusioned Airdrie voters. At any rate, on 30 June 1994,
Liddell only just held on, as the SNP slashed Smith's 1992 general election
majority from around 16,000 to 1,640. Labour's total vote had been just above
John Smith's majority in 1992.[62] Meanwhile, the Coatbridge Labour Party
workers apparently hadn't even been invited to the count, so they held their
own 'victory' celebration, during which Tom Clarke was given a standing
ovation.[63]

It had been a bruising encounter. Nicholas Wood of *The Times* described it
as 'one of the dirtiest by-election campaigns of recent times'.[64] In her victory
speech, Liddell claimed that SNP and Tory canvassers had 'played the Orange
card', a charge that Alex Salmond, the SNP leader, vigorously denied.[65] Mild
hysteria between Protestants and Catholics, which had never been at the heart
of the controversy, erupted in a thoroughly unseemly way. On the night of the
count, Liddell was spat on, and had to endure jeers and cries of 'scum' and
'Fenian bastard' from banner-waving Nationalists. Kay Ullrich was hit on the
side of the head with a bag of chips.[66]

The Monklands controversy did not die down after the by-election. Liddell
said she was putting the MDC councillors 'on probation'.[67] She also got her
own back on David Shaw, the Tory MP who had caused so much trouble for
Smith (see chapter 23), when she visited his Dover constituency to draw
attentions to all his supposed failings, and was delighted when Shaw lost his
seat in the Labour landslide.[68] But in the shorter term, the Scottish Labour
Party hardened its line, calling upon the ruling Labour group to re-admit the
rebel Airdrie councillors by the end of September 1994, or face the
consequences.[69]

In October 1994, MDC voted to hold its own inquiry[70] under Professor
Robert Black, QC, chair of Scots law at Edinburgh University, against the
reservations of three council officials.[71] The inquiry was weak: it was not held
in public; individuals were free to submit evidence without being under oath;

the names of those taking part were never revealed; and it was starved of resources, MDC having set a limit of £50,000. Moreover, Black merely published the evidence, rather than coming to a definitive set of conclusions. Helen Liddell said that she felt 'very angry' and 'appalled' at some of the findings.[72] Subsequently, the Labour Party suspended all seventeen Labour councillors pending its own internal investigation under Mike Penn, the National Constitutional Officer.[73]

Shortly afterwards, Tom Clarke met a distraught Eddie Cairns, one of the suspended councillors and Smith's long-time election agent. In one pocket he had a letter from John Smith saying, 'I want you to carry on as my agent', and the other had news of his suspension as a Labour councillor.[74] Cairns died a disillusioned and heartbroken man. Whatever else can be said of John Smith, he wouldn't have let that happen to Cairns: loyalty meant everything to both men. As if to underline that the old order was on its way out, Provost Bob Gilson died in November 1994.[75]

A week after the publication of the Black Report, Ian Lang finally agreed to John Smith's original request for a full inquiry into Monklands – a section 211 inquiry – concentrating exclusively on whether MDC had failed to comply with the statutory obligation[76] to appoint staff on merit, not looking at the alleged spending or housing bias. In contrast to Professor Black's investigation, William Nimmo Smith QC was given full powers to summon witnesses.

The allegations against MDC began to fall apart when Professor Robert Black admitted that, had there been a court case, MDC would have been found not guilty of nepotism charges. He also admitted that his report was 'bland', and not thoroughly investigated. Factual errors were also found in his report.[77]

Nimmo Smith's 83-page report concluded:

> There is no evidence that any appointment to paid office or employment with the Council in the period since 16 January 1990 has been made otherwise than on merit, and accordingly the Council have not failed to comply with the duty imposed on them by section 7 of the Local Government and Housing Act 1989.[78]

Nimmo Smith also criticised the questionable behaviour of David Shaw MP, finding that Shaw had: 'No evidence of substance to offer . . . I regarded his attitude as irresponsible.'[79] Nimmo Smith only made gentle criticisms of Jim Brooks's handling of the council:

> I had a strong impression that there was substance to the perception that political power was exercised by a small number of Coatbridge councillors.

Councillor Brooks in particular struck me as a strong-willed man who liked
to control the exercise of power . . . If power is exercised in such a way as to
lead to a sense of exclusion, suspicions are more readily aroused and
rumours and allegations gain currency.[80]

Both Tom Clarke and Helen Liddell welcomed Nimmo Smith's report: Clarke
said he wasn't surprised by its findings, while Liddell made the prescient
remark: 'I wish it [the inquiry] had been done three years ago when John
Smith first called for it. It would have saved my constituents a lot of anxiety.'[81]

Published just before Christmas 1995, the findings of the Nimmo Smith
report were largely overlooked: the investigative journalists had long since
disappeared from Lanarkshire, hunting elsewhere for fresh quarry. The facts
are that Smith had called for a public inquiry, and that once that inquiry was
eventually held, no evidence of wrongdoing was found to have taken place.

The most important consequence of Smith's death is that it provoked a
Labour leadership contest in which Tony Blair emerged as leader instead of
Gordon Brown. For years, the debate has raged about whether Gordon Brown
is the true inheritor of John Smith.

Had Gordon Brown become Labour leader in 1994, instead of Tony Blair,
he would have pursued a modernising agenda very similar to Blair, but there
would have been more references to Labour's past, and that very much
included John Smith's vision of economic efficiency and social justice going
hand in hand. On 29 May 1994, Brown very movingly invoked the spirit of
John Smith in a rousing address in Swansea. All the language deployed
suggested that Brown felt that he carried Smith's torch: 'The flame still burns,
the work continues, the passion for justice endures, and the vision will never
fade: the vision of Labour in power.'[82]

Brown and Smith came from similar Scottish Presbyterian backgrounds, the
latter brought up in the headmaster's house, the former in the manse.
Fundamentally, for all his prudence, Brown still believes in rooting out injustice
and tackling greed. But there are many points of difference: Smith was utterly
secure about the person he was; Brown is far less secure. Brown has developed
Euro-sceptical credentials, calling for wholesale deregulation in Europe, and
looks much more to America for his inspiration, whereas Smith always looked
to Europe, extolling the virtues of the German model of capitalism.

The debate as to whether Smith favoured Brown or Blair as his successor has
poisoned the upper echelons of the Labour Party, obsessed the media and had
the effect of obscuring John Smith's legacy for over a decade. Is there a case for
either stance?

Firstly, I put the evidence supporting the belief that Tony Blair was Smith's chosen successor. In his biography of Tony Blair, John Rentoul recalls a conversation between John Smith and David Ward on Monday, 9 May, three days before Smith died. Smith told Ward that he had a bet with Mike Elrick, his press officer, to encourage Smith to lose more weight. Ward had said something to Smith along the lines of, 'Wouldn't it be awful if anything happened to you?' Smith had replied with a question: 'What would happen?' and then apparently answered his own question by saying: 'It's got to be Tony, hasn't it?'[83] Early in the week between Smith's death and funeral, Ward told Blair of this chat.

If Ward's recollection is accurate, it appears to remove one of the principal claims made by Gordon Brown's supporters that in standing for the Labour leadership in 1994, Blair was acting contrary to Smith's wishes. In the words of a Blair supporter: 'It shows that Tony knew at the time that this whole stuff about Gordon being Smith's "favourite son" was rubbish. There was no betrayal.'[84]

In December 2002, Ward brought up this story again some eight years after it appeared in John Rentoul's biography of Blair. Ward recalls that on a Friday afternoon he was caught unprepared by a reporter from the *Sunday Telegraph*, who seemed not to have read the Rentoul book. When asked whether Blair knew that Smith wanted to succeed him, Ward replied: 'I told him.' According to Ward, it seems that someone in Downing Street had started the ball rolling as part of the continuing war between the Brown and Blair camps.[85]

Independently of Ward, Derry Irvine also states: 'During the last six months of his life, John Smith made it clear to me on several occasions that he favoured Tony as his successor.'[86] And it also seems that shortly before Smith's death, Irvine had informed Blair of Smith's preference.[87] Irvine has 'no doubt at all' that his version of events on the Blairite succession is the truth.[88] Early in 1994, two other colleagues claim to have heard Smith musing in the leader's office to similar effect.[89]

Roy Hattersley has a completely different version of events. When, in April 1994, he informed his leader that he was standing down from the House of Commons, Hattersley claims they had a brief chat about the leadership, albeit indirectly. John had been cross with Gordon over the introduction of a windfall tax. John supported it, as did the shadow Cabinet, but, according to Roy, colleagues had been annoyed that Gordon had announced it without first gaining their agreement. John was therefore cursing Gordon. Hattersley then said something to the effect that Blair looked like the probable successor. Smith replied that there was no vacancy, but that Blair would probably win if a leadership election were held tomorrow. However, it was Gordon who would prevail in the end.[90] James Naughtie, in *The Rivals*, concludes unconvincingly: 'Smith was probably being mischievously ambiguous but his long-term prediction has not yet been put to the test.'[91] Hattersley is adamant as to the truth of his story: 'With John, you would know who he wanted.'[92]

So was it Gordon or Tony? In fact, there is a third plausible explanation, namely that Smith could have told some people that Gordon was the chosen one, and others that Tony was also the one to succeed him. Derry Irvine feels that it was 'impossible that "honest John" would say different things to different people'.[93] Mike Elrick agrees that such duplicity was impossible.[94] Was Smith capable of such behaviour? It would have been in his interests not to have committed himself. Derek Foster claims he would be incredulous if Smith *hadn't* said different things to different people: 'Every good persuader in the House of Commons adjusts his or her words when seeking to influence different people. Certain phrases work better with one person than another'. Foster does not see such activity as evidence of deceit on the part of Smith, but as 'part of a politician's quiver full of arrows. Often such skills are required to create and maintain Party unity.'[95] The fact that everyone is so adamant about what Smith told them suggests there is at least a possibility that he told different things to different people, but it is only that, a possibility.

Before he died, Smith was certainly weighing up the relative merits of Blair and Brown. In early 1994 Smith had asked Derek Foster, his Chief Whip, to compile an honest assessment of how the members of the shadow Cabinet were performing.[96] Foster recalls that the document was 'for his eyes and my eyes only'. Security was tight: Foster later removed the confidential paper from Smith's office one or two days after Smith's death, lest anyone use the information during the leadership contest.[97]

The Labour Chief Whip recalls that although he was 'a huge fan of Gordon Brown', when writing up the dossier he had to admit that in the previous twelve months Gordon had been 'plodging[98] through treacle' in his attempts to persuade the Labour movement of a tougher stance on economic policy. By contrast, Foster wrote that Tony Blair had to be given credit for improving Labour's image with the voters on law and order, an issue where the party traditionally trailed behind the Tories. He is also is firmly of the view that 'John wanted Gordon' and that the PLP was so certain that Gordon would be John's successor: 'it was almost unspoken, it was so certain.'[99]

In the absence of documentary evidence, and with such diametrically opposing accounts, it will remain impossible to verify which version of events is correct. However, all accounts concur on two separate points. Firstly, in

May 1994 Blair was ahead of Brown in the future leadership stakes. Smith's replies to Roy Hattersley, Derry Irvine and David Ward are consistent with this view. Secondly, there is sufficient evidence from Hattersley, Irvine, Ward and Foster to prove conclusively that Smith did ask several different people in the months before he died who should succeed him.

Smith may also have been contemplating his own demise. On one occasion, he confessed to David Ward, 'I know how I'm going to die.'[100] But that doesn't necessarily mean that Smith had such a morbid thought at the front of his mind at every minute of the day. Mike Elrick argues: 'If he was genuinely worried about dying, why would he go out hillwalking? He wasn't that reckless. John genuinely thought he would form a Labour Government.'[101]

However, it wasn't in Smith's gift, or any other Labour leader, to hand over the leadership to anyone else. The debate matters hugely to Gordon Brown who sees himself as Smith's natural inheritor. It matters also to the Blair people anxious to prove that Brown's talk of being John's chosen heir was nonsense from the start.

When a political leader dies, after the initial shock (which was profound in this case) thoughts inevitably turn to the succession: to deny such mind processes is to deny what parliamentary politics is all about. It is necessary to move quickly in case political ground is lost. As James Naughtie puts it: 'It was not a choice between one and the other, mourning and scheming.'[102]

By the time Tony Blair made his comments that Smith's death would 'devastate everyone who knew him', he had already rung Peter Mandelson to discuss what his next move should be.[103] On the evening of Smith's death, Alastair Campbell, by now political editor of *Today*, was caught out at the end of an interview by Mark Mardell when giving tributes to John Smith. When asked who should succeed Smith, Campbell replied, 'Tony Blair, no doubt about it.'[104] A phalanx of journalists also lined up to back the Blair bandwagon in their newspaper columns.[105] Within hours of Smith's death, it had therefore become the accepted view in the party and the London media that both modernisers could not stand against each other for the leadership – that would endanger 'The Project' – and that Blair was in such a strong position that it would have to be Brown that stood aside.[106] Supporters of Gordon Brown felt that a tide of southern metropolitan comment in the media, fuelled by the modernising MPs, had done for their man. Such resentment has bubbled away for the last ten years.

While Blair's people were already putting together a leadership campaign team headed by Jack Straw, Gordon Brown was still genuinely distraught. According to Charlie Whelan, Brown's new press secretary, the shadow

Chancellor spent the day writing obituaries, including for the *Daily Mirror*. 'Everybody was asking, "Where's Gordon Brown?"'[107] In television interviews, Brown said Smith would have been a reforming and radical Prime Minister who would have remained true to his great Christian principles, and expressed the hope that the Labour Party would continue the work Smith had started.[108]

A huge amount of controversy surrounds the role of Peter Mandelson. Donald Macintyre is probably right to argue that initially Mandelson had been uncertain whether to back Gordon or Tony.[109] On the day of Smith's death, Derry Irvine bumped into Mandelson and asked him about the succession: Mandelson merely mumbled, whereas Irvine said, 'It has to be Tony.' Mandelson replied, 'I am not persuaded of that.' Irvine then told the Blair camp that Mandelson seemed to be favouring Brown.[110] John Rentoul entertains the possibility that Mandelson, knowing his value to Blair, was playing hard to get, and knew the message would get through to Blair.[111]

Blair and Brown had made a 'secret pact' that they would not stand against each other, but because Blair's people were off and running, the inference was made in the media that Brown should be the man to stand down. Publicly, Mandelson commented on Channel Four's *A Week in Politics* on Saturday, 14 May that Labour had to consider 'who will play best at the box office, not simply appeal to the traditional supporters and customers of the Labour Party'.[112] A *Sunday Times* poll then showed Blair well ahead of Brown, and Mandelson claims that the holding formula – that neither modernising candidate would stand against the other – blew up in Brown's face. Supposedly, the polls showed an unstoppable momentum towards Blair, just as John Major had achieved in the 1990 Conservative leadership contest.[113]

Paul Routledge, Brown's biographer, places a good deal of emphasis on Mandelson's letter to Brown on 16 May, in which Mandelson wrote that Gordon might split the party if he stood against Blair, but nevertheless offering to support Brown if he chose to stand. Brown did not reply to the letter.[114] Brown's supporters remained deeply suspicious and resentful about Mandelson's supposed role in promoting Blair's candidacy. Mandelson claims that even this late in the day, he was still engaged in a painful choice over whom to back.[115] Donald Macintyre agrees that Mandelson was 'genuinely torn by his loyalties to both men'.[116] Donald Dewar, a friend to both Blair and Brown, though he'd probably have backed Gordon Brown in any contest, saw Mandelson's letter before it was sent, and summed up the terrible dilemma that many people faced at the time: 'It's all most unfortunate. Most unfortunate.'[117]

Eventually, at least a week after Smith's death, Mandelson publicly plumped for Blair, but after a meeting with Brown to ensure that Brown was 'airlifted out of this situation before his people did him and us any more damage'. Mandelson felt he had made 'an enemy for life'.[118] The difficulty, however, in relying upon Peter Mandelson's version of events is that, remarkably enough, Peter is seen as being at the forefront of organising everything, what Paul Routledge terms the 'Mandyfication' of history.[119] Commentators need to realise that Peter's influence is entirely dependant on the continued endorsement and patronage of Tony Blair: without it, he is nothing.

On 27 May, *The Scotsman* produced a survey of Scottish Labour MPs: fifteen backed Brown, six Blair, but six other Brown supporters wanted their man to stand aside for Blair. The story appeared in such a way as to suggest that, even on his own patch, Brown's support would not hold back the sheer force of the Blair juggernaut. Whatever the extent of Mandelson's fingerprints on spinning *The Scotsman* findings (and the anger they fuelled in the Brown camp), the momentum behind Blair was proving unstoppable. On 29 May, a survey for BBC's *On the Record* showed Blair with a clear lead in all three sections of Labour's electoral college. Two days later, Gordon Brown formally announced that he would not be contesting the leadership.

Blairite legend has it that Brown and Blair hammered out the leadership question in Granita, a then trendy but now defunct restaurant in Islington. Brown's supporters, however, claim Brown had made his mind up the night before at a 'Last Supper' in Joe Allen's, a basement restaurant in Covent Garden, attended by Murray Elder, Nick Brown and Charlie Whelan. Brown believed he could have won,[120] but he did not want to damage the party's modernisation process by standing against Tony Blair. Charlie Whelan brutally sums it up: 'The idea that Tony and Gordon would ever fight it out at the end was always complete bollocks. As simple as that.'[121]

The debate over what was said and agreed at Granita is a classic example of the near impossibility of compiling an accurate historical account of anything to do with New Labour. The only two witnesses – Blair and Brown – will not testify, leaving their rival gangs of supporters to fill the void with what they think their man would have said, leaving ample time, of course, to rubbish the other side's version of events.

The nominations for the leadership and deputy leadership contests closed at 4 pm on Thursday, 16 June 1994. Two hours later, the results were announced at a meeting of the PLP: Margaret Beckett gained 42 nominations from her fellow MPs for the leadership, neck-and-neck with John Prescott on 46, but with Blair way ahead on 154. Denzil Davies was eliminated from the contest for the leadership, having polled seven votes, way short of the 12.5 per cent threshold (or 34 MPs) set under the leadership rules. Meanwhile, on the deputy leadership, Beckett reversed positions with Prescott, nudging ahead with 106 nominations to 101.[122] The three remaining leadership contenders then took part in a leader's hustings meeting of the PLP on Wednesday, 6 July 1994[123] for only the second time in Labour's history, the first time having been back in June 1992 (see chapter 17). Then, on 21 July 1994, Blair won the leadership with 57 per cent, with Prescott second on 24 per cent, and Beckett finishing a poor third on 19 per cent. Prescott won the deputy leadership contest comfortably, polling 56.5 per cent to 43.5 per cent for Margaret Beckett.[124] In his acceptance speech, Blair claimed that John Smith had 'showed the British people that public service is still an ideal that can breathe hope into a politics grown weary and cynical'.[125]

At his first PLP meeting as leader, Tony Blair made it clear that the Labour Party was on 'a war footing from now on', and that there was 'absolutely no room for complacency'. If Labour was to win, 'The messages needed to be hammered home on every occasion, and every day.' The new broom approach was signalled as Tom Sawyer replaced Larry Whitty as the party's new general secretary. In an apparent swipe at Smith's efforts at leader, Blair told his colleagues bluntly that what was important was not 'the little battles in Parliament, or within the Parliamentary Party, but the great battle outside'. The aim was 'not just to win for a term, but to put the Tories out for a generation', but he warned: 'The Tories could be relied upon to be ruthless in their counterattack and Labour should match them with equal determination.'[126]

Some of Tony Blair's allies sought to distort and belittle Smith's legacy. the *Sunday Times* editorial on the weekend after John Smith's death was typical:

> An era of Labour history has ended with John Smith's death. As the last opposition front bencher to sit in James Callaghan's Labour Cabinet, he bridged the gap with Labour's last unhappy period in office and was, to those who remember it, vulnerable on that score. Labour's new leadership will be a greenfield development, divorced, we hope, from the corporate state approach that dominated Labour thinking during John Smith's ministerial career in the 1970s, and light years from Clause IV's commitment to 'common ownership' that shaped Labour's programmes for more than 50 years. John Smith underpinned Labour's revival as a mainstream party on whose shoulders the responsibilities of office no longer seemed implausible. Tony Blair should lead Labour's bid for government in a new era of British politics. Those in the Labour Party who balk at being led by a youthful, public school-educated moderate who rarely uses the language of

traditional socialism would do well to realise that such a prospect is now the Tories' worst nightmare.[127]

Philip Gould's analysis of the impact of Smith's death on the electorate is extraordinary:

> John's death had a profound effect on the British electorate. Not really connecting with him when he was leader, they missed him greatly when he had gone, and they recognised him as a politician who commanded enormous, widespread respect. In death the public revered him and through his death they started to feel differently about the Labour Party. They saw once again its deeper, finer qualities, so long submerged by failure and strife. John Smith healed a party that had become ill at ease with itself. He widened democracy in the Party. But most of all, through the extraordinary national response to his death, he gave back to Labour the confidence and pride it had lost for so long.[128]

Smith's biographer, Andy McSmith, also deals with this issue: 'It was as if, when tragedy turned everyone's attention to the Labour Party, observers suddenly recognized it as a potential party of government. Whereas in 1992 the Party had chosen a new leader of the opposition, this time it could be electing a Prime Minister.'[129]

As a result of Smith's death, there wasn't just a personal outpouring of emotion for the death of a good man who would have become Prime Minister, there was also, as Gould and McSmith try to explain (the latter a shade more subtly than the former), an extraordinary emotional reconnection between sections of the electorate and the Labour Party – perhaps for the first time since 1964. This positivity towards New Labour directly benefited Tony Blair in what became known by pollsters as the 'Blair effect'.[130]

Some Labour figures believed that they had been subject of a coup d'état. Tony Benn views New Labour as 'a complete corruption'. Modernisers had 'infiltrated' the Labour Party 'like Trotskyites', building a 'theory' that Tony Blair was the only man who could win in 1997.[131] Quite how Benn has the gall to criticise the use of Trotskyite tactics, given his methods in the early 1980s, is unclear. However, he argues that Smith's death had the effect of clearing the way for the modernisers.[132] According to Patrick Seyd and Paul Whiteley, the Blairites believed that 'nothing less than the complete abandonment of the old social democratic norms – interventionist government, redistribution, working class support – was necessary'[133] in order to gain power. New Labour transformed itself into 'a catch-all party', representing not sectional or vested interests, but a broader range of viewpoints and interests, primarily those of big business.[134] Smith was equally keen on courting big business, but he placed equal weight in developing a good working relationship with the Labour movement, whereas Blair has sought to distance himself from the unions.

Only a week after Smith's death, on 18 May 1994, Gould wrote a memo to Peter Mandelson: 'Post John Smith there is only one viable strategic opportunity for Labour, and that is to become a party of change, momentum and dynamism. This is most certainly the mood of the country, and probably of a majority of the Party.'[135]

Not so. In reality, the mood of the country in 1994 was that the Tories were finished, and a majority of the electorate were deeply moved by Smith's death because he reminded them of what Labour stood for – fairness and social justice. What the electorate certainly did not envisage, or were not calling for at the time, was the creation of an entirely new political party.

Many academics disagree that Blair's changes represent a rejection of Labour's past. In their admirable study of New Labour, Steve Ludlam and Martin Smith, with the help of around a dozen other academics, have ploughed through an exhaustive number of policies to conclude that 'Blair's success cannot be divorced from the process of party adaption that occurred under Kinnock and Smith'.[136] Andrew Gamble and Gavin Kelly also argue that there existed a great deal of continuity on macro-economic policy between Kinnock, Smith and Blair. All three leaders, they rightly point out, had emphasised the importance of developing Britain's skills base, regional policy and accepting most of Thatcher's industrial relations reforms. Moreover, they all realised that in the new global economy 'national economic protection is no longer politically or economically viable'. Gamble and Kelly therefore conclude that New Labour did not operate outside the Labour tradition, but rather 'squarely in the long tradition of economic revisionism which has been such a distinctive feature in the evolution of the party in the last fifty years'.[137]

Ludlam and Smith also draw on continuities between other Labour revisionists, most notably between Hugh Gaitskell and Blair and Harold Wilson and Blair. However, the book overlooks the fact that any new party leader, however reform-minded, will have recourse to past policies partly to justify them, and partly because political necessity will often require them to keep traditionalists on board until such time as the leader can stamp his or her authority on the party. But that doesn't mean they are not seeking in the long-term to reject the past. Only in second and third terms do party leaders (if they are lucky enough to survive that long) generally reveal their true policy intentions. Moreover, Ludlam and Smith tend to bracket Kinnock and Smith together, while almost exclusively going on to discuss Kinnock. For instance,

they argue: 'Kinnock laid the groundwork for Blair and it seems unlikely, although unknowable, that Blair could have been elected without Kinnock.'[138]
But if Ludlam, Smith, Gamble and Kelly and many others are correct in thinking that New Labour did not reject Labour's past, then why was there all the resentment from allies of John Smith? The answer partly lies in the overblown claims made by the modernisers on behalf of New Labour: that history effectively started in 1994, and the period beforehand was Labour's 'unelectable period'. For the idea of a new party to appear plausible, the *whole* of Labour's past needed to be rejected. In 1996, Peter Mandelson and Roger Liddle wrote *The Blair Revolution: Can New Labour Deliver?*, in which they bracketed Smith and Kinnock's periods together as 'essentially . . . a ground-clearing operation' with Blair being seen as *the* person pushing 'wholesale modernisation'.[139] Shortly after the 1997 election, Mandelson wrote: 'We're doing so well because we got our act together as a would-be government three years ago',[140] strongly suggesting that such a condition had not existed pre-1994. Larry Whitty feels that some of this 'year zero' stuff was 'a bit brutal'.[141] It seems therefore that Tony Blair's election as leader hastened the extent to which Smith's period as leader of the Labour Party became obscured. Partly that was unavoidable, but certain Blair supporters deliberately set out to make it the case.

There is an alternative analysis. No consummate politician, faced with similar circumstances to Blair, would have turned down the chance to start with a relatively clean state, presenting a fresh face to the electorate. Blair doesn't live in anyone's shadow. Major lived in the shadow of Thatcher, but in no sense has Blair lived in the shadow of Smith.[142]

But the overall effect of the understandable media obsession with Blair and Brown has been to obscure John Smith's legacy. As if to show how little impact Smith's legacy had on Blair, 28 contributors to Anthony Seldon's *The Blair Effect*[143] mention Smith's name only eighteen times: seven of which concerned devolution; four mentioned 'Kinnock and Smith' is as if they were one and the same; and four remarked upon Smith's death.

Shortly after Smith's death, Labour's headquarters at Walworth Road was renamed 'John Smith House' at the suggestion of Joan Lestor,[144] but within a year, New Labour's campaign headquarters were set up at Millbank Tower on the banks of the Thames. Millbank was not redesignated John Smith House. Most of Labour's staff moved there in the run-up to the 1997 election and, by January 1998, almost all Labour's operation had been moved from John Smith House. Symbolically, at least, the Smith era had been largely erased from Labour's memory.

On Tuesday, 29 April 1997, during the closing phase of Labour's 1997 general election campaign, Smith's memory was invoked only once by the Labour Party as a campaigning tool, when Blair referred to the last line of Smith's 'opportunity to serve' speech.[145] Then, just before polling day, while the London-based *Mirror* ran with a headlined article by Alastair Campbell, Blair's press secretary, its sister paper in Scotland, the *Daily Record* ran with a sombre black-bordered picture of the late John Smith, and an impassioned plea from Elizabeth Smith, headlined, 'Win it for John'.[146]

And what happened to John Smith's 'unfinished business'? On 15 July 1994, just before he became leader, Tony Blair gave a speech in Cardiff in which he reaffirmed his party's pledge to introduce devolution for Scotland and Wales during the first year of a Labour government.[147] Although the constitutional convention process was still ongoing when Smith died, the widespread expectation, and the convention's position, was that an incoming Labour (or Lib-Lab coalition government) would simply have legislated to bring the Parliament into being. Key figures inside the Labour Party hierarchy began to think differently.

In late 1995, it seems that the Labour Party had established a committee headed by Derry Irvine, the shadow Lord Chancellor, to plan the mechanics of how it intended to bring forward devolution legislation on coming to power.[148] The committee is said to have comprised, amongst others, Donald Dewar, then Chief Whip, Ann Taylor, shadow Leader of the House, Jack Straw, shadow Home Secretary, and George Robertson, shadow Secretary of State for Scotland, with Pat McFadden serving as its secretary.[149]

The committee's deliberations were set against an unfavourable backdrop. Michael Forsyth, the Secretary of State for Scotland, had chosen to attack the convention's plans to vary the standard rate of income tax up or down by three pence in the pound. He labelled it 'the tartan tax', and plugged it remorselessly. Somehow, Labour needed to find a way of responding to that highly effective 'tartan tax' campaign. Secondly, almost everyone expected an incoming Labour government to be operating with a small, or possibly no, majority. Thirdly, in such circumstances, the party hierarchy would have had to persuade northern English Labour MPs that the first Labour government in eighteen years would spend most of the first session of Parliament, not legislating on health and education, but on creating a Parliament in Scotland and an Assembly in Wales. Fourthly, judging from the experience of 1977–8, the Labour government might have faced a hostile House of Lords. As a result of such pressure, Labour might have been forced to concede a referendum.[150] For all these reasons, the committee supported the idea of a pre-legislative referendum, and also a separate vote on whether to have a tax-varying power. George Robertson claims that he and Donald Dewar agreed that this new policy was the only way to guarantee getting the legislation through Parliament.[151]

However, to Robertson's surprise, in March 1996 at the time of the Dunblane tragedy, Tony Blair indicated that he wanted the new policy announced in June 1996, in time for the whole of Labour's draft manifesto to be put to the party membership. Blair felt for 'utterly logical reasons' that he could not allow the party to decide, and then change the devolution policy in September. Critics would have said, 'What is Blair going to change next?'[152]

From that point on, Robertson's faced a huge battle in the Scottish Labour Executive to get the plan through. Confusion seemed to reign for several months. At one point, the Labour Party indicated it supported two separate referendums on the tax-varying power (one at the pre-legislative stage, and one if proposals were brought forward to increase income tax by the new Scottish government) – the policy lasted six days. Eventually, the policy was simplified to a two-question pre-legislative referendum on the merits of a Scottish Parliament and the tax-varying power. John McAllion, Labour's Scottish Constitutional Affairs spokesperson resigned, claiming that he had not been consulted. The perception in much of the Scottish Labour Party was that Blair had tinkered with the Scottish constitutional convention's plans for a devolved Scotland, when it appears that many of the key Scots in the shadow Cabinet, including George Robertson, and possibly Donald Dewar, agreed with the policy, if not the timing of its announcement. From then on, the Scottish media became suspicious of Blair's enthusiasm for devolution. Matters came to a head at the launch of Labour's Scottish manifesto in April 1997 when Blair seemed to compare the tax-varying powers of the Scottish Parliament with those of 'the smallest English parish council', and declared that 'sovereignty rests with me as an English MP and that's the way that it will stay'.[153] In fact, Blair had been asked if he supported the tax-varying power, and replied that even the smallest English parish council had such a power, and of course, under the plans, ultimate sovereignty rested with the United Kingdom.

Although George Robertson would have preferred to have been notified in advance about the timing of the announcement on the referendum, he believes that, had John Smith been alive, he too would have come round to the idea of a referendum because he too had been scarred by the experience of 1978 (when the Labour Party hierarchy had driven the devolution proposals, but they had ultimately lacked popular support).[154] Once the Scottish two-question referendum in September 1997 had been endorsed by a margin of three to one, and the tax-varying powers by two-and-a-half to one, these Blairite adjustments to the devolution plan were viewed as a huge success: they had the effect of entrenching and legitimising the Scottish Parliament, more so than if no referendums had been held at all.

It is not possible to say definitively whether a two-question referendum would have been arrived at under John Smith's leadership. It is worth recalling that Smith had been in favour of a tax-raising power late in the day in 1978, but had been overruled by senior ministers (see chapter 6). That fact, however, is a far cry for arguing that he would have seen the need for a separate referendum question on the matter. Nor is it likely that potential opposition from northern English Labour MPs would have overly concerned Smith, as his pal Donald MacCormick discovered during an interview shortly before John died: 'The eyes widened to an intense owlish stare behind the glasses. "They will just be told", he grated, "that's how it is".'[155]

Perhaps it is fitting that two of John's closest friends from university, Donald Dewar, then Secretary of State for Scotland, and Derry Irvine, the Lord Chancellor, ensured that Smith's 'unfinished business' was completed. Their legacy to Scotland is the great speed with which they turned the White Paper[156] into an Act of Parliament. One can argue about the extent to which the Act was watered down from the White Paper, but by holding a successful pre-legislative referendum the government could argue that they had an agreed White Paper backed by the Scottish people, which boxed in the opponents of the Bill, including the House of Lords and parts of Whitehall.

Whatever the arguments over the Scottish devolution referendum, it is not stretching the imagination too far to suggest that Smith would have implemented constitutional reform in a more welcoming, wholehearted and relaxed way than Tony Blair. On the day he'd been elected leader, Smith had commented: 'Nothing would give me greater pleasure than to hand over responsibility from Westminster and Whitehall.'[157] Smith would not have emulated Blair's inept handling of Labour's selection process for the Labour leader in Wales and the mayoral elections in London. For all Blair's preaching over pure OMOV in 1993 (see chapter 22), as Prime Minister he abandoned the concept in favour old-fashioned trade union stitch-ups to exclude Rhodri Morgan as leader of the Welsh Labour Party, and Ken Livingstone as Labour's candidate in London. It is also a moot point whether Dennis Canavan would have been allowed to stand as a Labour candidate for the Scottish Parliament elections under John Smith's leadership.

*

John Smith's memory survives. In 1995, the John Smith Memorial Trust was established: Gordon Brown, Derry Irvine, Jack Cunningham, John McCluskey and Donald Dewar were its original trustees. A year later, the trust established the John Smith Fellowship Programme, which aims to nurture democratic awareness and to enhance the skills of future generations of politicians and professional people in the independent republics of the former Soviet Union. Each year, around 20 fellows are brought to Britain for an intensive six-week programme of study and first-hand insight into the workings of Britain's democratic institutions. Almost all of the day-to-day work of the trust is undertaken by Emma Maclennan, a former member of Smith's economic secretariat, in association with the British Council, who provide a range of support services, and the Lord Chancellor's Department, who provide some of the funding for the programme.[158]

Shortly after Smith's death, there was talk of acquiring Hale's House in Musselburgh as the base for a John Smith Think Tank, but it came to nothing. Instead, Gordon Brown and others helped to establish the John Smith Institute, a separate organisation from the John Smith Memorial Trust. The Institute is not a pressure group, but rather a forum where ministers, business-men and others can meet to research and debate the constantly changing relationship between government, society and the economy in its broadest terms, taking John Smith's belief in a strong economy and a fair society as their inspiration. The invited speakers are honoured to give the annual John Smith Institute Lecture. Past speakers have included Senator Edward Kennedy. In the spring of 2004, George Robertson, the former Defence Secretary and Secretary General of NATO, gave the lecture to mark the tenth anniversary of John Smith's death.

What of the tangible reminders of John Smith's life? Five bronze busts, sculpted by Professor Sir Eduardo Paolozzi, were cast: Elizabeth has one; another is displayed at the Scottish National Portrait Gallery in Queen Street, Edinburgh; there is one each at the Court of Session and the Glasgow University Union; and the fifth was unveiled in the House of Commons in January 1997, sadly the weekend that John's mother, Sarah, died aged 86.[159] However, the bespectacled likeness is not superlative. It is fitting that the extraordinary man with the commonest name should remain for posterity somehow inimitable.

Twenty-Six
CONCLUSION

I T SAYS MUCH that by the time John Smith died he was probably more secure in his post than any leader of an opposition since Harold Wilson, 1970–4. Donald Macintyre rightly concludes that Smith's consensual style of leadership 'left a party more unified and more respected than it had been since the 1960s'.[1] Writing shortly after his death, Clare Short sums up best how this had been achieved: 'John unified and therefore massively strengthened the Party by being completely unsectarian. Because he knew himself and was at ease with himself he treated everyone with respect.'[2]

That much can be agreed, but was Smith a moderniser? Seyd and Whiteley see the Smith period as 'an interregnum'[3] in the otherwise onward march of the Kinnock and Blair's periods of modernisation. Charles Clarke, probably Smith's biggest critic, agrees with this analysis: 'Tony Blair was the linear descendant of Neil Kinnock as a modernising Labour leader, John Smith was not.'[4] In fact, the argument at the time was not between modernisers and traditionalists, but about the *pace* of reform. Norman Hogg sums up best why Smith reformed OMOV, but rejected reform of Clause IV:

> John was a product of the Labour Party of Gaitskell, Wilson and Callaghan, and he had a deep commitment to preserving it, realising that certain things had to be done, like introducing OMOV in order to secure that kind of Party. In that sense, he was a moderniser, but it had to be done in a way that would not offend the traditional principles of the Party. He liked the way the Labour Party did things. New Labour felt that they couldn't make that old system work, and made significant changes – like Clause IV – wholesale reform of which John had rejected.[5]

Tudor Jones is very near the mark when he argues that John Smith's leadership left 'the Labour Party at last broadly united and with the cause of its modernisation cautiously sustained'.[6] That achievement was mainly due to the Labour leader's hard-fought, hugely significant victory over OMOV. Roy Hattersley approves of Smith's low-profile approach to Clause IV: 'I have learned, during the forty years since Clement Attlee was Prime Minister, that the Party does best when it is at peace with itself.'[7] But Derek Foster's honest appraisal is that under John Smith's leadership 'modernisation was going along at a pace that most of the Party felt comfortable with', but that in retrospect, the modernisers were probably right that modernisation needed to go a faster pace, because of the 'natural inertia of the Labour movement', and the fact that the electorate had moved on.[8] In part, this was due to the contraction of Labour's traditional working-class base, but mainly because Labour still needed to convince the voters that it could run the economy. It depends whether one believes, in every circumstance, that the needs of the Labour Party have to come before the perceived needs of the electorate.

Gordon Brown, more than anyone else, realised early on the importance of prudence, but he had first learned all about that from the 'Original Mr Prudence', John Smith. In order to make absolutely sure of Labour's victory, Brown went somewhat further than his mentor would have done, agreeing to stick to the Tory spending plans in the first two years of Labour's first term. Brown had to overdo the prudence because when he took the shadow Chancellor's job, he did not then have the standing with the electorate that John Smith had achieved. As a result of his successful stewardship of the British economy in the last eight years, Brown certainly possesses it now.

Because of the strong values instilled by his parents, Smith remained consistent to his principles throughout his life, but he had the savvy to succeed in the rough world of politics. He had left the parental home aged only fourteen. Smith blended principle with pragmatism, rejecting socialist utopian ideals. He was the politician who gave the Labour Party the combination of social justice on the one hand, and economic efficiency on the other: you had to create the wealth before you set about wealth redistribution. Listening to the views of business was at the core of Smith's thinking before Tony Blair and Gordon Brown ever appeared on the scene, but he also understood the value of involving the trade unions in a dialogue between both sides of industry. Chris Smith recalls: 'John gave the Party a feeling of what we were about. The best and only way of achieving Labour's values was through social justice. Social justice was what drove him, and he gave it back to the Labour Party.'[9]

Chris Smith believes that Smith was 'the best Prime Minister we never had'.[10] Smith's greatest plaudits have come from those on the left of the party. Michael Foot stresses Smith's 'good temperament' and 'mastery of the House of Commons', which would have made him 'a truly great Labour Prime Minister'.[11] Foot adds, 'he would have been a very great advantage for the Party. I think he had a better understanding of the Labour movement than others do.'[12] Tony Benn believes: 'Smith would have been a better leader than Tony Blair. It would have been a completely different party.'[13]

For figures on the right, like Denis Healey, Smith's early death was 'one of the greatest tragedies to beset the Labour Party . . . the country was robbed of a great Prime Minister'. Smith's strength was 'sturdy commonsense', but he lacked the charisma of Tony Blair and the appeal to the middle classes that 'now make up 80 per cent of the electorate'. In fact, 'he [Smith] didn't go in for charisma and didn't cultivate the press to the same extent'. For that reason, Healey feels that Smith would have made a better – indeed 'wonderful' – Prime Minister than a leader of the opposition.[14] Smith's skills and previous experience under Wilson and Callaghan ideally suited him for high ministerial office. Moreover, Smith had the ideal psychological balance essential to withstand the pressures of the job of Prime Minister. And yet, even if Smith would have made a better Prime Minister than a leader of the opposition, his 22 months as Labour leader were associated with a highly successful period of exploiting the Major government's disarray on issues such as the ERM, Maastricht, broken tax promises and standards in public life.

Chris Smith is right when he says that John gave the Labour Party 'courage' at perhaps its lowest point of all – its 1992 general election defeat. In more than one wake after the 1992 defeat, the collective Labour cry was: 'If not now, ever?'[15] John Smith restored Labour Party morale after the very important but bruising reforms of the Kinnock period. Tony Benn wrote in his diaries on the day after Smith's death that: 'He performed a completely different function from Neil Kinnock – he healed the wounds of the Party.'[16] Smith's political profile in the media suffered from the fact that he met so many unsung people in the Labour movement, but that was what was required at the time. Had he lived, the next phase would have been about projecting John Smith's values to the electorate in the run-up to the 1997 general election, but also facing up to the hard policy choices of a party on the verge of government.

Smith's enduring legacy is his own strength of character. In today's political world, it is hard to think of a British politician whose death would be received with as much genuine grief, public outpouring of affection, and media coverage as Smith received. Most political figures get one day's coverage and the media circus moves on. Roy Jenkins's recent death is a case in point. Queuing up on the way into the church at Smith's funeral, Roy Hattersley recalls overhearing Magnus Linklater discussing with one of the political editors why so many people had been moved to tears, and why there was so much sadness. The explanation was that no other previous leader of the Labour Party, not Kinnock, not Foot, not Callaghan, Wilson or Gaitskell, had the integrity of Smith.[17] Tony Benn agrees that Smith should be remembered primarily for his 'integrity and very strong character'.[18]

How many of our politicians today share more than a couple of John Smith's special qualities? He was completely unsnobbish, and had that common touch with ordinary people; he never sought to take the credit for policy ideas thought up by his subordinates; he helped out people even when there was no direct benefit to him; he wrote hundreds of handwritten thank you notes that rarely got the detail wrong, valuing every human being, and respecting their desire for recognition. He was a politician (yes, a politician!) with no burning desire to write down his achievements for posterity or to be on the front page of the newspapers every day. He was a political figure who hated an entourage and always just wanted to be himself; he was a leader of a political party who never sought to use the power of his position to gain personal advantage, whether it was waiting his turn in a queue in the House of Commons canteen, or giving as many as possible people a lift in a car supposedly reserved for him;[19] and he was a man who had an ability to make friends and colleagues laugh until they were in agony. John Smith, in the words of his friend, the writer Dirk Robertson, was 'extraordinary at being ordinary'.[20] He was a normal member of the human race.

At the end of Blair's second administration, New Labour still doesn't have a clear idea of what it stands for. Initially, Blair borrowed his ideas from the Third Way in America, but then stole shamelessly from the Conservatives' clothes at a time when the electorate had lost faith in the Conservatives' ability to run the economy. New Labour vacated its predecessor's position on the left of centre of British politics, and occupied a political vacuum on the right of centre vacated involuntarily by the Conservatives. But in terms of ideas, it didn't fill that vacuum with any defining ideology. For all the criticism from the modernisers that Smith lacked a defining idea, what is Blair's vision, apart from a ruthless ability to win elections by pandering to the concerns of middle-income, *Daily Mail* reading voters?

Blair's ability to unsettle and unnerve the Conservative Party for a decade is his greatest achievement. In the decade between 1994 and 2004, the Conservatives were simply rendered irrelevant. But New Labour is beginning to discover one of the longer-term lessons of politics: that parties are not merely vote-winning machines; they also have souls: elastic bands can only be stretched so far before they ping back or snap. Blair seems set upon an entirely different course, determined to push ahead with yet more modernisation that apes the philosophy of Margaret Thatcher.

There are two ways of running the Labour Party. Smith, like Harold Wilson and James Callaghan, believed in keeping as many people on board as possible, including the left and the trade union movement in the interests of party unity. All three Labour leaders were Labour Party men, ruling from the centre ground. Hugh Gaitskell, Neil Kinnock and Tony Blair, by contrast, took a more blunderbuss approach because they believed that that was the only way the Labour Party could modernise itself. That approach has achieved great leaps forward, adapting Labour to a constantly changing world, but the question, however, in the present circumstances is whether the continual head-banging leadership, characteristic of the Blair period, is always the best way of running of things, or whether a more inclusive approach, involving all of the party, including the left and the unions (remember them?), is required.

Finally, if you don't constantly argue the case for democratic socialism in the modern globalised world, then forces far more powerful will smother it. Smith was not a philosopher, but his advice to the Labour Party in 1993 in his famous *Reclaiming the Ground* lecture stands just as true twelve years later:

> We ought, therefore, in the battle of ideas which is at the centre of the political struggle, to be confident in the strength of our intellectual case. But I believe we must also argue for our cause on the basis of its moral foundation. It is a sense of revulsion at injustice and poverty and denied opportunity, whether at home or abroad, which impels people to work for a better world, to become, as in our case, democratic socialists.[21]

NOTES

Prologue

1 Labour had made a net gain of 88 seats nationally, despite having done well in the 1990 elections against the backdrop of anti-poll tax protests. The party won 45 per cent of the vote, way ahead of the Liberal Democrats on 27.5 per cent, with the Conservatives languishing in third on 27 per cent.

2 The poll was conducted from 6–7 May 1994, and sampled 1,438 people.

3 Colin Rallings, David M. Farrell, David Denver and David Broughton (eds), *British Elections and Parties Yearbook 1995* (Frank Cass: London), p. 198. The data presented here was derived from the 'Gallup 9,000', as presented in *Gallup Political and Economic Index*.

4 *The Nine o'Clock News* (specially extended), BBC1, Thursday, 12 May 1994 (transcript).

5 More accurately, the European Communities (Amendment) Bill.

6 James Naughtie, *The Rivals. The Intimate Story of a Political Marriage* (Fourth Estate: London, 2001), p. 52.

7 Tony Benn, *Free at Last! Diaries 1991–2001*, edited by Ruth Winstone (Hutchinson: London, 2002), p. 217 (Wednesday, 12 January 1994).

8 Interview with Lord Gordon of Strathblane CBE, 12 March 2003.

9 Alastair Campbell, 'Here's one Labour supporter who's not so happy', *The Spectator*, 30 April 1994. Also quoted in Jon Sopel, *Tony Blair: The Moderniser* (Michael Joseph: London, 1995), pp. 170–1.

10 Martin Westlake (with Ian St John), *Kinnock. The Biography* (Little, Brown and Company: London, 2001), p. 629.

11 HC Debs, 12 May 1994, c. 431.

12 Christian Wolmar, 'Jollity and wit at gala dinner', *The Independent*, 13 May 1994.

13 Interview with Ann Barrett, 21 June 2003.

14 Rt Hon. John Smith QC MP, Speech at European Gala Dinner, London, 11 May 1994 (transcript).

15 HC Debs, 12 May 1994, c. 431.

16 Interview with Lord Whitty, 12 March 2003.

17 Alastair Campbell, 'John Smith's Great Journey', *Today*, 13 May 1994.

18 Larry Whitty had indicated to Smith that the latter post had control of the purse strings, so he pressed successfully on behalf Pauline Green, the leader of the European Parliamentary Labour Party. She sat downstairs, while Rocard and Smith sat upstairs discussing her future. Interview with Lord Whitty, 12 May 2003; interview with David Ward, 7 June 2003.

19 Interview with Rt Hon. Chris Smith MP, 11 February 2003.

Chapter 1

1 What follows is largely based on research into the Smith family tree conducted by John Smith of Tarbert, a cousin of John Smith, and supplemented by evidence drawn from gravestones in Tarbert cemetery by Andy McSmith, who wrote a fine biography of the Labour leader, entitled *Playing the Long Game* (Verso: London, 1993), published ten months before Smith's death. However, the greater part of my own biography refers to a later edition: Andy McSmith, *John Smith. A Life. 1938–1994* (Mandarin Paperback, revised and updated edn: London, 1994).

2 Interview with Professor Sir Neil MacCormick, 3 October 2003.

3 McSmith, *John Smith*, p. 8.

4 For instance, Brian Wilson, Labour MP for Cunninghame North since 1987 and, like Smith, a pupil at Dunoon Grammar School, was also born on the mainland, rather than on Islay.

5 Telephone interview with Mary McCulloch, 26 November 2003.

6 Ibid.

7   Ibid.
8   The following four paragraphs draw, to some extent, on a beautifully written article about Ardrishaig by Peter Millar, originally compiled for *The Sunday Times Magazine* to mark Smith's election as leader of the opposition, but reproduced two years later on Smith's death. See Peter Millar, 'John Smith's schooldays', Four-page special, *The Sunday Times* (Scottish edn), 15 May 1994.
9   Ibid.
10 Telephone interview with Mary McCulloch, 26 November 2003.
11 *BBC Reporting Scotland*, Thursday, 12 May 1994 (transcript).
12 Peter Millar, op. cit.; Barry Wigmore, 'The son of "Hairy" Smith with a wicked grin like Just William', *Today*, 13 May 1994.
13 Telephone interview with Mary McCulloch, 26 November 2003.
14 Ibid.
15 Isabel Hilton, 'John Smith from Ardrishaig: will go far', *The Independent*, 16 July 1992.
16 Peter Millar, op. cit.
17 In 1991, MacKay became a life peer and, as Lord MacKay of Ardbrecknish, served as Minister of State for Social Security in John Major's second government from 1994–7, before being made Chairman of Committees in the House of Lords in November 2000. A keen fisherman, he died in February 2001 at the age of only 62.
18 Michie was subsequently elevated to the peerage as Baroness Michie of Gallanach.
19 Telephone interview with Mary McCulloch, 26 November 2003.
20 Isabel Hilton, op. cit.
21 Telephone interview with Mary McCulloch, 26 November 2003.
22 Jane Franchi, 'Commentary', *The Funeral of the Rt Hon. John Smith QC MP*, BBC 1, Friday, 20 May 1994 (transcript).
23 Telephone interview with Mary McCulloch, 26 November 2003.
24 Archie usually taught a split class of primary 6 and 7, owing to the small size of the school. Telephone interview with Mary McCulloch, 26 November 2003.
25 McSmith, *John Smith*, p. 9.
26 Telephone interview with Mary McCulloch, 26 November 2003.
27 Ibid.
28 Helen Puttick, Karen Rice and Tom

Curtis, 'Frank Sinatra and a man who always did it his way', *Edinburgh Evening News*, 12 October 2000.
29 Lynda Lee-Potter, 'Luck that saved John Smith's life', *Daily Mail*, 26 January 1989.
30 Telephone interview with Mary McCulloch, 26 November 2003.
31 *Airdrie and Coatbridge Advertiser*, 16 October 1992.
32 Donald Dewar, 'Tribute', in Gordon Brown and James Naughtie, *Life and Soul of the Party* (Mainstream: Edinburgh, 1994), p. 20.
33 James Gordon, 'Tribute', in Brown and Naughtie, *Life and Soul of the Party*, p. 58.
34 Interview with Donald Robertson QC, 11 November 2003.
35 'A Day in the Life of . . . John Smith', *The Sunday Times Magazine*, 7 January 1990.
36 *Desert Island Discs*, BBC Radio Four, (transmitted, 28 May 1991), in Brown and Naughtie, *Life and Soul of the Party*, p. 158 (transcript).
37 Isabel Hilton, op. cit.
38 Peter Millar, op. cit.
39 Interview with Donald Robertson QC.
40 Isabel Hilton, op. cit.
41 John Smith, transcript of speech to Dunoon Grammar School, 350th Dinner, 8 November 1991 (first draft). Michael Crick files.
42 McSmith, *John Smith*, p. 15.
43 Telephone interview with Rt Hon. Lord Robertson of Port Ellen, 7 July 2003.
44 Bob McLaughlan, 'Dear John', *The Herald*, 13 May 1994.
45 Ibid.
46 Ibid.
47 Telephone interview with Mary McCulloch.
48 *Glasgow University Guardian*, 8 December 1961.
49 Lesley Duncan, 'Former *Herald* journalist dies at the age of 64, after a varied career', *The Herald*, 22 July 1999; Arnold Kemp and Donald Dewar, 'Robert McLaughlan', *The Herald*, 24 July 1999.
50 Telephone interview with Rt Hon. Lord Robertson of Port Ellen.
51 Alison Duncan, interview with John Smith, Reception, Dunoon 350th Dinner, 8 November 1991 (transcript). Michael Crick files. BBC's *Reporting Scotland* also ran a piece about Dunoon Grammar's 350th Anniversary, which included Shelley

Jofre interviews with John Smith and Brian Wilson.

52 Telephone interview with Mary McCulloch, 21 October 2004.

53 Alison Duncan, interview with John Smith, op. cit.

54 Telephone interview with Rt Hon. Lord Robertson of Port Ellen.

55 John Smith, transcript of speech to Dunoon Grammar School, 350th Dinner, op. cit.

56 Maclean died of a heart attack in May 1962, only a year after his retirement from Dunoon Grammar. 'Obituary: Neil Maclean', *Glasgow Herald*, 5 May 1962.

57 Interview with Baroness Smith of Gilmorehill DL, 4 December 2002.

58 *Desert Island Discs*, Brown and Naughtie, *Life and Soul of the Party*, pp. 152–3. (transcript); Lynda Lee-Potter, op. cit.

59 Telephone interview with Mary McCulloch, 26 November 2003.

60 John Smith, transcript of speech to Dunoon Grammar School, 350th Dinner, op. cit.

61 Telephone interview with Rt Hon. Lord Robertson of Port Ellen; Brian Wilson agrees, describing John's speech as 'perfectly judged . . . full of humour, nostalgia and appreciation of the educational grounding which had sent him on his way'. Brian Wilson, 'Giving people a chance', *The Herald*, 13 May 1994. See also, Brian Wilson, 'A Scot who kept faith with his roots', *Independent on Sunday*, 15 May 1994.

62 Fiona Millar, interview with John Smith, *She Magazine* (February, 1993), final proofs, 10 November 1992. Murray Elder papers, Box 2.

63 Interview with Lord Gordon of Strathblane CBE, 12 March 2003.

64 Interview with Kenneth Munro, 29 September 2003.

65 HC Debs, 11 November 1970, c. 502.

66 John Smith, transcript of speech to Dunoon Grammar School, 350th Dinner, op. cit.

67 Interview with Ruth Wishart, 15 January 2004.

68 Interview with Professor Sir Neil MacCormick, 3 October 2003.

69 *Desert Island Discs*, Brown and Naughtie, *Life and Soul of the Party*, p. 150 (transcript).

70 'A Day in the Life of . . . John Smith', op. cit.

71 *The Guardian*, 13 May 1994.

72 Naughtie, *The Rivals*, p. 42.

73 'Shoreditch', *New Statesman & Society*, 2 October 1992.

74 *Mirror*, 12 May 1994. Quoted in Naughtie, *The Rivals*, p. 59.

75 Gordon Brown, *James Maxton* (Mainstream: Edinburgh, 1986).

78 Telephone interview with Kenneth Munro, 6 November 2004.

79 Interview with Lord Gordon of Strathblane CBE.

Chapter 2

1 Paul Anderson and Nyta Mann, *Safety First. The Making of New Labour* (Granta Books: London, 1997), p. 273.

2 Andrew Roth and Byron Criddle, *Parliamentary Profiles, A–D, 1997–2002* (Parliamentary Profiles: London, 1998), p. 618.

3 Wright was elected as the Conservative member for Glasgow Pollok at the 1967 by-election, but he lost the seat at the 1970 general election. After a distinguished academic career at Glasgow and the University of London, Wright died in August 2003, aged 87.

4 Interview with Professor Sir Neil MacCormick, 3 October 2003.

5 In December 1930, the then Rector of Glasgow University, Stanley Baldwin opened the New Union Building, which replaced Stenhouse's Corner at the foot of University Avenue.

6 Gerald Warner, *Conquering By Degrees. Glasgow University Union. A Centenary History, 1885–1985* (Glasgow University Union: Glasgow, 1985), pp. 202–5.

6 Generally, there were six debates per year in the Glasgow Union, and three major debates in the Queen Margaret, the Women's Union. The Labour and Tory Parties also had a separate debate against each other every year.

8 The afternoon session was uncommon in other Scottish University Unions, but provided Glasgow Union with an invaluable training ground for future debaters. New undergraduates were encouraged to participate by means of a Maiden Speaker's Prize.

9   Interview with Dr J. Dickson Mabon, 15 May 2003.
10 Glasgow University Archive Services, GB248 DC198/1/55 *Glasgow University Magazine*, Vol. 68, November 1956. Hereafter *GUM*.
11 Marcus [John Smith], 'Debates', *GUM*, March 1960.
12 For a pleasing account of Peel's inaugural address, see Norman Gash, *Sir Robert Peel. The Life of Sir Robert Peel after 1830* (Longman: London, 1972), pp. 151–7.
13 This section is largely drawn from an article by Peter W. Richmond, Conservative Club Treasurer, 1958–9, and President of the Union, 1960–1, who wrote a six-part series on all the political clubs in *GUM* during the 1961–2 academic year. Peter Richmond, 'Politics in the University. 1. The Tory Club', *GUM*, November 1961.
14 Venator, 'Fifth Union Debate', *GUM*, March 1958. Taylor later served as Conservative and Unionist MP for Glasgow Cathcart from 1964–79. After losing his Glasgow seat, just as Mrs Thatcher formed a government, Taylor quickly re-entered Parliament at the Southend East by-election and has served in the area ever since. Since 1997, Taylor's redrawn constituency has been known as Rochford and Southend East.
15 McCurley has since defected to the Liberal Democrats, and stood unsuccessfully for the Scottish Parliament in 1999 in Eastwood.
16 Peter Richmond, 'Politics at the University. 3. The Liberals', *GUM*, January 1962.
17 Interview with Rt Hon. Sir Menzies Campbell CBE QC MP, 17 January 2004. Somewhat surprisingly, given his high public profile, Menzies Campbell declined to stand for the Liberal Democrat leadership in the summer of 1999, instead playing a 'godfather' role to the eventual winner, Charles Kennedy, himself a former President of the Glasgow Union (1980–1), and winner of the coveted *Observer* Mace in 1981. Mark Stuart, 'Constituency and Regional Profiles', in Charlotte Adams (ed), *Dod's Scottish Parliament Companion 2002. First Edition* (Vacher Dod Publishing: London, 2002), p. 205.

18 Interview with Rt Hon. Sir Menzies Campbell CBE QC MP.
19 'Black Dog', *Daily Express,* 13 May 1994.
20 McSmith, *John Smith*, pp. 17–18
21 Interview with Professor Sir Neil MacCormick.
22 The Scottish Nationalist Association had a considerable record of success in Rectorial elections, with R. B. Cunninghame Graham being narrowly beaten by Stanley Baldwin in 1928, followed by successes with Compton Mackenzie (1931), John MacCormick (1950), Tom Honeyman (1953) and (perhaps surprisingly) Lord Reith in 1965. Peter Richmond, 'Politics at the University. 5. The Scottish Nationalists', *GUM*, April 1962; written correspondence with Professor Sir Neil MacCormick, 4 October 2004.
23 Warner, *Conquering by Degrees*, p. 151.
24 Interview with Professor Sir Neil MacCormick.
25 Peter Richmond, 'Politics at the University. 4. The Labour Club', *GUM*, February 1962.
26 Deny-All [Neil MacCormick], 'Debates. Sixth Union Debate Report', *GUM*, March 1962.
27 Ibid.
28 Interview with Dr J. Dickson Mabon.
29 Peter Richmond, 'Politics in the University. 6. The Far Left', *GUM*, May 1962.
30 Interview with Lord Gordon of Strathblane CBE, 12 March 2003. The minutes of the Distributist Club for Sunday, 4 November 1956 show that it was adjourned so that members could watch the news headlines on Suez and Hungary. Glasgow University Archive Services, GB248 DC372/1/1 Minutes of the Distributist Club. Minutes of Committee meeting held in Queen Margaret Union on Sunday, 4th November at 3.30 pm. (Between 1954–67, the minutes of the Distributist Club were kept in an old Avondale half-bound account book). Two days earlier, the Union had debated an Emergency Resolution on Suez, voting by 130 votes to 75 at quarter to one in the morning (an impressive tally of people participating at that hour) in favour of calling for the immediate withdrawal of Britain's armed forces from Egypt. *GUM*, November 1956.

31 Interview with Professor J. Ross Harper CBE, 18 February 2003.

32 Interview with Lord Gordon of Strathblane CBE.

33 Peter Richmond, 'Politics in the University. 2. The Distribs.', *GUM*, December 1961.

34 Venator, 'The First Debate', *GUM*, November 1959.

35 J.H.M. [James H. McMeekin (Conservative)], 'Debates: Secretary's Debate', *GUM*, December 1959.

36 Ibid.

37 Interview with Rt Hon. Sir Menzies Campbell CBE QC MP, 20 January 2004.

38 J.H.M. [James H. McMeekin (Conservative)], op. cit.

39 G.H. [Gordon Hunter], 'Looks at . . . The Debaters', *GUM*, December 1959.

40 Ben Trovato [R. Edward Davidson], 'Inter-'Varsities Debate', *GUM*, December 1960.

41 Written correspondence with Lord Gordon of Strathblane CBE, 2 November 2004.

42 Interview with Professor Sir Neil MacCormick.

43 'The Fleeting Hour', *GUM*, December 1959.

44 Tory Club President, 1959–60.

45 J.H.M. [James H. McMeekin (Conservative)], 'Inter-'Varsities', *GUM*, December 1959.

46 *GUM*, February 1960.

47 From 1954 until 1959, there had been two Scottish rounds of the *Observer* tournament, until the Scottish Union of Students, in an act of stupidity, cut Scotland's representation in half.

48 A solicitor and company director, who later stood unsuccessfully for the SDP/Liberal Alliance against Gordon Brown in Dunfermline East at the 1983 general election. *The Times Guide to the House of Commons*, June 1983 (Times Books: Revised edn, London 1984), p. 100.

49 James McMeekin, 'Debates: The Scottish Round of the *Observer* Tournament', *GUM*, December 1960.

50 Ben Trovato [R. Edward Davidson], 'Debates: *Scotsman* Trophy', *GUM*, February 1961.

51 *The Scotsman*, 11 February 1962. The other judges were Dr G. Hamilton, past President of Aberdeen Debaters and Dr R.

Illesley, Treasurer of Aberdeen Debaters.

52 Interview with Lord Gordon of Strathblane CBE.

53 Interview with Professor J. Ross Harper CBE.

54 'Black Dog', *Daily Express*, op. cit.

55 Interview with Dr J. Dickson Mabon.

56 Interview with Rt Hon. Sir Menzies Campbell CBE QC MP.

57 Interview with Kenneth Munro, 29 September 2003.

58 MacKay was a Liberal in his student days, standing unsuccessfully as the Liberal candidate for Argyll in 1964 and 1966. Eventually, he switched to the Conservatives, and won Argyll at the second time of asking in 1979.

59 The Slasher [John Mackay], 'Debates', *GUM*, March 1961.

60 'Ben Trovato [R. Edward Davidson] takes stock', *GUM*, March 1961.

61 A similar debate had been held 25 years before to mark Sir Hector's arrival at the University. *GUM*, April 1961.

62 Ben Trovato [R. Edward Davidson], 'The End of an Era: Sir Hector's Farewell', *GUM*, May 1961.

63 Donald MacCormick, 'A diligent and brilliant believer in all that was best', *The Sunday Times*, 15 May 1994.

64 In the West of Scotland, a 'left-footer' is a derogatory term for a Catholic.

65 Haymarket [James McMeekin], 'Westerland Wizards! Big Board Blitz dumps Damp Debaters', *GUM*, April 1961.

66 Telephone interview with Mary McCulloch, 26 November 2003.

67 Interview with Kenneth Munro.

68 The Glasgow Union second team of Malcolm Mackenzie (Conservative) and David Miller (Liberal) had the difficult task of opening the debate, and lost out to Edinburgh for second place.

69 'The Fleeting Hour', *GUM*, December 1961.

70 Oxford had won the inaugural contest in 1954, but Glasgow had not entered the competition that year. Thereafter, Glasgow won the Mace in its second, third and fourth year, Dickson Mabon and Andrew Kennedy triumphing in 1955, Roger J. McCormick and Scott Birnie in 1956, with Jimmy Gordon and Ronnie Anderson completing the hat-trick in 1957.

71 Interview with Lord Gordon of

Strathblane CBE.

72   Interview with Dr J. Dickson Mabon.

73   Ossington [Ian O. Bayne (Distributist)], 'Debates. Fifth Debate', *GUM*, February 1962.

74   Interview with Kenneth Munro.

75   Marcus [John Smith], 'Debates', *GUM*, March 1960.

76   James McMeekin and Gordon Hunter, 'Letter to the Editor', *GUM*, April 1960.

77   John Smith, 'Letter to the Editor', *GUM*, April 1960.

78   Rt Hon. Lord Irvine of Lairg PC QC, 'Tribute', in Brown and Naughtie, *Life and Soul of the Party*, p. 106; Malcolm Rifkind, *Question Time Special*, BBC 1, Thursday, 12 May 1994 (transcript).

Chapter 3

1   After Labour's general election defeat in 1959, the Labour League of Youth was renamed the Young Socialists in a fresh attempt to attract younger members. Subsequently, the organisation became known as the Labour Party Young Socialists to distinguish itself from a myriad of left-wing organisations.

2   Peter Richmond, 'Politics at the University. 4. The Labour Club', *GUM*, February 1962.

3   Interview with Lord Gordon of Strathblane CBE, 12 March 2003.

4   Following the death on 8 January 1958 of Walter Elliot, former Secretary of State for Scotland from October 1936 until May 1940. Michael Stenton & Stephen Lees, *Who's Who of British Members of Parliament*, Volume IV, 1945–1979. A Biographical Dictionary of the House of Commons (The Harvester Press Ltd: Brighton, 1981), p.107.

5   Private information.

6   Chris Cook & John Ramsden, *By-elections in British Politics* (Macmillan: London, 1973), p. 195. Dr Maurice Miller then won the seat for Labour at the 1964 general election.

7   Jim Gilchrist, 'Obituary: Donald Dewar', *The Scotsman*, 12 October 2000.

8   *Glasgow University Guardian*, 13 October 1961.

9   At the 1959 general election, Sir James Henderson-Stewart had polled 26,585 as against J. Nicol, the Labour candidate,

who trailed back on 11,421. *The Times House of Commons, October 1959* (The Times Office: London, 1959), p. 209.

10   Sir John Gilmour, 1876–1940, Secretary of State for Scotland from July 1926 to June 1929; Michael Stenton & Stephen Lees, *Who's Who of British Members of Parliament*, Vol. III, 1919–1945. A Biographical Dictionary of the House of Commons (The Harvester Press Ltd: Brighton, 1979), p. 128.

11   'Unionists hope for "Something Similar". Liberals in Good Heart', *Glasgow Herald*, 1 November 1961.

12   More precisely, from 1886 to December 1918, when he was defeated. Stenton & Lees, *Who's Who of British Members of Parliament*, Vol. III, 1919–1945, p. 11.

13   Interview with Dr J. Dickson Mabon, 15 May 2003.

14   Interview with Rt Hon. Lord Healey of Riddlesden CH MBE, 12 February 2003. The following March, Healey was the guest speaker at the Labour Club's Union Dinner. *GUM*, February 1962.

15   'Liberal Vote Holds Key to Result', *Glasgow Herald*, 3 November 1961.

16   Telephone interview with Mary McCulloch, 26 November 2003.

17   'Inglorious Fifth in East Fife', *Glasgow Herald*, 6 November 1961.

18   Telephone interview with Mary McCulloch.

19   Interview with Kenneth Munro, 29 September 2003.

20   Third behind Perth and East Perthshire and Kinross and West Perthshire.

21   Leach, aged 30, had contested Edinburgh West in 1959, finishing in third place.

22   'Labour "becoming Second Tory Party"', *The Scotsman*, 2 November 1961.

23   The same night, John S. Maclay, Secretary of State for Scotland, spoke in support of Sir John Gilmour. 'Need for unity stressed. Support Government says Maclay', *The Scotsman*, 4 November 1961.

24   'Liberal hopes rise after canvas', *The Scotsman*, 6 November 1961; 'Liberals under attack. "Using circus type methods – Unionist"', *The Scotsman*, 7 November 1961.

25   'Inglorious Fifth in East Fife', *Glasgow Herald*, 6 November 1961.

26   'Unionists hope for "Something Similar." Liberals in Good Heart', *Glasgow Herald*, 1

November 1961.
27 'Three candidates are confident of victory. Unionists a strong favourite', *The Scotsman*, 8 November 1961.
28 Robert Kemp, 'Half an Hour of Routine Brightness', *Glasgow Herald*, 7 November 1961.
29 'Tory win likely in East Fife Today', *The Scotsman*, 8 November 1961.
30 The official results were as follows: Sir John Gilmour (Unionist) 15,948 (47.4%); John Smith (Labour) 8,882 (26.4%), Donald Leach (Liberal) 8,786 (26.1%). Conservative majority 7,066. Turnout 67.3%. F. W. S. Craig (ed), *British Parliamentary Election Results, 1950–1970* (Political Reference Publications: Chichester, 1971), p. 645.
31 'Conservatives hold East Fife', *The Scotsman*, 9 November 1961.
32 Interview with Lord Gordon of Strathblane CBE, 12 March 2003.
33 McSmith, *John Smith*, p. 30.
34 MacKenzie won the Glasgow Rutherglen by-election held on 14 May 1964, and later went on to serve as Minister of State for Industry, 1975–6, and Minister of State at the Scottish Office, 1976–9.
35 Interview with Lord Hogg of Cumbernauld, 4 November 2003.
36 In 1978, Labour's Willie Small announced his retirement from Glasgow Garscadden, then died provoking a by-election in March of that year, in which Dewar comfortably beat off the challenge of the SNP.
37 Interview with Rt Hon. Lord Irvine of Lairg PC QC, 30 April 2003.
38 Former Secretary of State for Commonwealth Relations from October 1947 to February 1950, and then Labour's front bench spokesman on the United Nations and disarmament.
39 *Glasgow University Guardian*, 8 December 1961.
40 Ossington [Ian O. Bayne], 'Debates', *GUM*, February 1962.
41 There seems to be some doubt as to the spelling of Luthuli's name. Nearly all contemporary references at Glasgow (including all the campaign literature) refer to 'Lutuli', and yet almost every subsequent written account includes the 'h' in Luthuli's name.
42 The role of Rector, who is elected by

students every three years to represent their interests, is unique to Scottish universities.
43 Donald Dewar, 'Tribute', in Brown and Naughtie, *Life and Soul of the Party*, p. 20.
44 *GUM*, October 1959.
45 Interview with Professor Sir Neil MacCormick, 3 October 2003.
46 *GUM*, November 1959.
47 'Our man in East Fife', *Glasgow University Guardian*, 10 November 1961.
48 Written correspondence with Lord Gordon of Strathblane CBE, 2 November 2004.
49 Interview with Kenneth Munro.
50 Interview with Baroness Ramsay of Cartvale, 24 June 2003.
51 In 1956, Labour had put up Earl Attlee, the former Prime Minister, finishing second.
52 In 1955, Labour had 34 seats, the Conservatives and their allies, 36 MPs, while the Liberals had just one. *The Times House of Commons, October 1959*, p. 249.
53 *GUM*, November 1959.
54 *GUM*, March 1958.
55 Interview with Dr J. Dickson Mabon.
56 In March 1960, 67 Africans were shot dead and 186 wounded after protesting about the Verwoerd government's introduction of the pass laws.
57 Interview with Kenneth Munro.
58 Overwhelmingly endorsing Luthuli's candidature on Sunday, 14 October 1962. 'Vote Lutuli', Albert Lutuli Rectorial Campaign Committee Pamphlet (Printed by Geo. C. Fairservice Ltd: Glasgow, 1962).
59 It was fairly typical for the names of various candidates to be touted, and then for it all to come to nothing. In April 1962, for instance, John M. Bannerman, chairman of the Scottish Liberal Party, was rumoured to be standing on a joint Liberal-GUSNA ticket for the Rectorial election in October, and around the same time Michael Foot was mentioned as a possible candidate for the Labour Club, but neither candidate stood. *Glasgow University Guardian*, 30 April 1962.
60 Interview with Kenneth Munro.
61 'The Case for Luthuli', *GUM*, October 1962.
62 Interview with Kenneth Munro.
63 Interview with Rt Hon. Sir Menzies Campbell CBE QC MP, 20 January 2004.
64 The Albert Lutuli Rectorial Campaign,

standard letter asking for donations, c. August 1962.

65 Lutuli Campaign – Donations and Messages of Support, August–October 1962. Reproduced by kind permission of Rt Hon. Sir Menzies Campbell CBE QC MP.

66 Lutuli Campaign – Donations and Messages of Support, August–October 1962.

67 Interview with Rt Hon. Sir Menzies Campbell CBE QC MP.

68 Lutuli Campaign – Donations and Messages of Support.

69 Ibid.

70 Written correspondence with Cliff Michelmore CBE, 2 November 2004.

71 Lutuli Campaign – Donations and Messages of Support.

72 Ibid. Ironically, Lord Reith went on to serve as Lord Rector of Glasgow from 1965–8.

73 Lutuli Campaign – Donations and Messages of Support.

74 Interview with Rt Hon. Sir Menzies Campbell CBE QC MP.

75 Rosebery had served as Liberal MP for Midlothian from 1906–10, and briefly held the post of Secretary of State for Scotland at the end of World War Two in a caretaker capacity.

76 Glaswegian term meaning the police.

77 'Muck heap. How low will they get?', Glasgow University Guardian, 15 October 1962.

78 'Vote Lutuli', Albert Lutuli Rectorial Campaign Committee Pamphlet.

79 Private information.

80 A one-room house in a tenement, what in today's estate agent speak would be called 'a studio apartment'.

81 Interview with Kenneth Munro.

82 Private information.

83 A Glaswegian term meaning to be led away, usually against one's will.

84 'Lutuli is Chief – Battle Royal', Glasgow University Guardian, 27 October 1962; Six out of the 32 were found guilty. 'Six out of Thirty-two', Glasgow University Guardian, 23 November 1962.

85 Interview with Rt Hon. Sir Menzies Campbell CBE QC MP.

86 'What has happened to our Rector?', Glasgow Union Guardian, 8 February 1963.

87 'Empty Gesture?', Glasgow University Guardian, 10 May 1963.

88 Peter Richmond, 'Politics at the University. 4. The Labour Club', GUM, February 1962.

89 Interview with Dr J. Dickson Mabon.

90 Interview with Rt Hon. Lord Rodgers of Quarry Bank, 20 January 2004.

91 Peter Richmond, op. cit.; 'Ear to the ground', Glasgow University Guardian, 13 October 1961.

92 Donald MacCormick, 'A diligent and brilliant believer in all that was best', The Sunday Times, 15 May 1994.

93 Glasgow University Guardian, 27 October 1961.

94 Peter Richmond, op. cit.

95 Our debates correspondent, 'Shabby Chicanery at Labour Club AGM', Glasgow University Guardian, 30 April 1962.

96 Gaitskell intended to respond to the National Coal Board's pit closure programme by blaming the government, not the NCB's chairman, Lord Robens. 'May Day Arrests in Glasgow', Glasgow Herald, 7 May 1962.

97 Kenneth Munro also wrote a letter of congratulation to Gaitskell, but the Labour Club censored it. Interview with Kenneth Munro.

98 Problem [Donald Dewar], 'Eye Witness at Queen's Park', GUM, May 1962. Alan Alexander, Whip Secretary of the Labour Club, also attacked the left-wingers' behaviour at the May Day parade. See Alan Alexander, 'Labour and CND', Glasgow University Guardian, 11 May 1962.

99 McSmith, John Smith, pp. 21–3.

100 Andy McSmith claims that that night, Gaitskell spoke at a Glasgow University dinner held to celebrate the election of Albert Luthuli as the university's new Rector, but that could not have been the reason because Luthuli was not elected until October 1962. McSmith, John Smith, p. 22.

101 Hugh MacPherson, 'Upright Rabelaisian', Tribune, 24 May 1994.

102 McSmith, John Smith, p. 22.

103 Interview with Rt Hon. Thomas Clarke JP MP, 20 January 2004.

104 Tom Clarke, 'And all that mighty heart is lying still', Airdrie and Coatbridge Advertiser, 20 May 1994.

105 Brian Brivati, Hugh Gaitskell (Richard Cohen Books: London, 1996), pp. 440–1.

106 Interview with Professor Sir Neil MacCormick.

107 What follows is largely based on Andy McSmith's thoroughly researched account of the Woodside episode. See McSmith, *John Smith*, pp. 23–9.

108 Craig (ed), *British Parliamentary Election Results, 1950–1970*, p. 622.

109 McCrindle also stood unsuccessfully as the Labour candidate for Sheffield Hallam at the 1983 general election, finishing in third place.

110 Craig (ed), *British Parliamentary Election Results, 1950–1970*, p. 663.

111 E-mail correspondence with Paul Foot, 30 December 2003.

112 McSmith, *John Smith*, pp. 27–8.

113 Carmichael was selected to fight Glasgow Hillhead, but Roy Jenkins, the by-election victor in 1982, defeated Carmichael at the 1983 general election.

114 Paul Foot, 'London Diary', *New Statesman*, 8 December 1978. Many thanks are due to the late Paul Foot for helping me to track down this reference.

115 E-mail correspondence with Paul Foot.

116 Barry Wigmore, 'The son of "Hairy" Smith with a wicked grin like Just William', *Today*, 13 May 1994.

117 John Smith, 'My Scotland' (undated), in Brown and Naughtie, *Life and Soul of the Party*, p. 120; McSmith, *John Smith*, pp. 32–3; interview with Professor Sir Neil MacCormick.

118 Hugh MacPherson, 'Upright Rabelaisian', *Tribune*, 20 May 1994.

119 James Gordon, 'Tribute', in Brown and Naughtie, *Life and Soul of the Party*, p. 58.

120 John Smith, 'My Scotland' (undated), in Brown and Naughtie, *Life and Soul of the Party*, p. 120.

121 Sarah Smith, 'Our Father' (August 1994) in Brown and Naughtie, *Life and Soul of the Party*, pp. 114–5.

122 John Smith, 'I Love Islands' (undated), in Brown and Naughtie, *Life and Soul of the Party*, p. 123.

123 John Smith, 'My Scotland' (undated), in Brown and Naughtie, *Life and Soul of the Party*, p. 120.

124 Minister Emeritus of Bishopton and a former warden of the Iona Community House.

125 Douglas Alexander, 'Coming home', *Christian Socialist Magazine*, Commemorative Issue (No. 187), Spring 2004, p. 8.

126 *Scotland In Trust*, (The National Trust for Scotland Magazine), 2004; www.nts.org.uk

127 Interview with Lord Gordon of Strathblane CBE. Neil MacCormick and Derry Irvine agree. Interview with Professor Sir Neil MacCormick; interview with Rt Hon. Lord Irvine of Lairg PC QC.

128 Interview with Baroness Smith of Gilmorehill DL, 4 December 2002.

129 Elizabeth Smith, 'Introduction', in Brown and Naughtie, *Life and Soul of the Party*, p. 11.

130 Private information.

131 Written correspondence with Lord Gordon of Strathblane CBE.

132 Interview with Baroness Smith of Gilmorehill DL, 16 March 2004.

133 Ibid.

134 More accurately, in 1928, the National Party of Scotland was formed, followed in 1933 by the Scottish Party. These two organisations merged in 1934 to form the Scottish National Party (SNP). James G. Kellas, *The Scottish Political System* (Cambridge University Press: Cambridge, Second edition, 1973), p. 128.

135 McSmith, *John Smith*, pp. 36–37.

136 Having achieved that feat on 16 June 1963.

137 Interview with Baroness Smith of Gilmorehill DL.

138 Sir Fitzroy Maclean also served as Under-Secretary and Financial Secretary to the War Office from October 1954 to January 1957; Conservative MP for the Lancaster division of Lancashire from October 1941–59; Bute and North Ayrshire from 1959 until his retirement in February 1974.

139 Elizabeth Smith, 'Introduction', in Brown and Naughtie, *Life and Soul of the Party*, p. 12.

140 Lewis Chester, 'The Scorning Scotsman', *Independent on Sunday*, 26 May 1991.

141 Interview with Baroness Smith of Gilmorehill DL.

142 Sir William Kerr-Fraser, was then Principal of Glasgow University. He had formerly served as Permanent Under-Secretary of State at the Scottish Office from 1978–88, and later became a near neighbour of the Smiths in Edinburgh. *The Herald*, 13 May 1994; Tam Dalyell, 'Obituary: John Smith', *The Independent*,

15 May 1994.

143 John Smith's name is simply denoted as 'Smith', while Adam Smith's name has now been written out in full to distinguish between the two Smiths.

Chapter 4

1 Interview with Rt Hon. Lord Irvine of Lairg PC QC, 30 April 2003; interview with Lord McCluskey, 13 May 2003.

2 Interview with Donald Robertson QC, 11 November 2003. The names have been changed to preserve client confidentiality.

3 Interview with Rt Hon. Sir Menzies Campbell CBE QC MP, 20 January 2004.

4 Ibid.

5 Interview with Professor J. Ross Harper CBE, 18 February 2003.

6 Interview with Rt Hon. Sir Menzies Campbell CBE QC MP.

7 Interview with Rt Hon. Lord Gill, 11 November 2003.

8 Written correspondence with Professor David Walker CBE QC, 30 December 2003.

9 Interview with Rt Hon. Sir Menzies Campbell CBE QC MP.

10 Interview with Rt Hon. Lord Gill.

11 Interview with Rt Hon. Sir Menzies Campbell CBE QC MP.

12 The term 'devilling' means a junior barrister working without payment to gain experience. It can also mean to perform another person's drudgery; to do very menial work.

13 Interview with Lord McCluskey.

14 Alan Rusbridger, 'Why Labour has been betting on Smith', *The Guardian*, 14 February 1986.

15 Isabel Hilton, 'John Smith from Ardrishaig: will go far', *The Independent*, 16 July 1992.

16 McSmith, *John Smith*, p. 34.

17 Interview with Lord Gordon of Strathblane CBE, 12 March 2003.

18 Interview with Rt Hon. Sir Menzies Campbell CBE QC MP.

19 Interview with Lord McCluskey.

20 Labour MP for West Fife from 1950–74, and for Fife Central from 1974–87.

21 Interview with Rt Hon. Sir Menzies Campbell CBE QC MP.

22 Interview with Lord Kirkwood, 21 October 2003.

23 Interview with Professor J. Ross Harper CBE.

24 Smith had some assistance in drafting writs from consulting general styles, dummy cases, and a large body of previous pleadings in *Reported Cases*.

25 Interview with Lord Kirkwood.

26 Interview with Lord McCluskey.

27 Interview with Lord Kirkwood.

28 Interview with Lord McCluskey.

29 Interview with Rt Hon. Lord Gill.

30 Kirkwood stood unsuccessfully in Dunfermline in 1964, 1966 and 1970.

31 Interview with Lord Kirkwood.

32 Interview with Rt Hon. Sir Menzies Campbell CBE QC MP.

33 Judges tended not to go to Bar dinners, limiting themselves to Faculty balls. Nor were female advocates ever invited, despite the fact that women had been admitted to the Bar since 1924.

34 Interview with Lord McCluskey.

35 Telephone interview with Mary McCulloch, 26 November 2003.

36 Interview with Lord McCluskey.

37 One exception is where the advocate has a 'retaining fee'. In Smith's day, only big organisations such as the Edinburgh Corporation or the *Daily Record* would pay counsel an annual retaining fee, a modest sum, giving an organisation or an individual the power, should they wish to exercise it, to instruct an advocate, via a clerk of the court, that they do not wish their client to act against the interests of their organisation.

38 Interview with Rt Hon. Lord [Ranald] MacLean, 18 November 2003.

39 In the 1970s, centralisation led to the establishment of Faculty Services Ltd, and any clerks who wanted to carry on in the profession became employees of the company. This change was soon followed by the centralised collection of fees, a welcome development for struggling advocates.

40 Private information.

41 Interview with Rt Hon. Sir Menzies Campbell CBE QC MP.

42 Interview with Lord Kirkwood.

43 Interview with Rt Hon. Lord [Ranald] MacLean.

44 Interview with Lord McCluskey.

45 Interview with Donald Robertson QC, 11 November 2003.

46 Private information.

47 Malcolm Rifkind was a near neighbour, but although they worked in the same profession, Malcolm and John were not that close socially, and of course, their politics were entirely different. Telephone interview with Rt Hon. Sir Malcolm Rifkind KCMG QC, 7 January 2004.

48 Interview with Lord Gordon of Strathblane CBE.

49 Paul Wilnenius, 'Banker's looks hid the joker', *Today*, 13 May 1994.

50 Interview with Kenneth Munro, 29 September 2003.

51 Simon Hoggart, 'Sharp wit with an inner fire', *The Guardian 2*, 13 May 1994. A fellow advocate recalls the last sentence as, 'So sit in the corner, you wee c***, shut your cakehole, and listen to what he says.' Private information.

52 Interview with Lord Gordon of Strathblane CBE.

53 Interview with Kenneth Munro.

54 Interview with Lord Gordon of Strathblane CBE.

55 Interview with Kenneth Munro.

56 Interview with Rt Hon. Lord Irvine of Lairg PC QC.

57 Naughtie, *The Rivals*, p. 25.

58 Interview with Rt Hon. Lord Irvine of Lairg PC QC.

59 Ruth Wishart, 'Those sad, surreal 10 days', *The Herald*, 7 May 2004.

60 Naughtie, *The Rivals*, p. 176.

61 Interview with Rt Hon. Lord Irvine of Lairg PC QC.

62 Ibid.

Chapter 5

1 E. E. Schattschneider, *Party Government* (Rinehart & Company: New York, 1942). For a more critical analysis of the impact of gatekeeper attitudes on the British Parliament, see Pippa Norris and Joni Lovenduski, *Political Recruitment* (Cambridge University Press: Cambridge, 1995).

2 Isabel Hilton, 'John Smith from Ardrishaig: will go far', *The Independent*, 16 July 1992.

3 Interview with Lord Gordon of Strathblane CBE, 12 March 2003.

4 Interview with Lord McCluskey, 13 May 2003.

5 McSmith, *John Smith*, p. 42.

6 Harthill is located on the M8 between Glasgow and Edinburgh, and is mainly known for its service station.

7 Clarke went on to become Labour MP for Coatbridge and Airdrie at the June 1982 by-election. Smith promoted him to Scottish spokesperson in 1992, but he was replaced by George Robertson in 1993. He recovered from illness to briefly serve as shadow spokesperson for Development and Co-operation. In 1994, he became Labour's spokesperson on Disabled Peoples' Rights, but when the Blair government was formed he was shifted to become Minister of State at the Department of National Heritage (later known as Culture, Media and Sport) in charge of Films and Tourism. In July 1998, he was sacked from the government, and resumed his long-running campaign to improve the rights of disabled people.

8 The Labour Party minutes incorrectly record Smith as having won by one vote at the North Lanarkshire Selection Conference. Minutes of the meeting of the Parliamentary Labour Party held on Wednesday, 18 May 1994 at 11.30 am in Committee Room 14.

9 Interview with Rt Hon. Thomas Clarke JP MP, 20 January 2004.

10 McSmith, *John Smith*, p. 43.

11 Interview with Professor J. Ross Harper CBE, 18 February 2003.

12 John Smith, 'Reforming our Democracy', Inaugural Richard Stewart Memorial Lecture, Glasgow University, 23 October 1992.

13 Smith's margin of victory was only 5,019, compared with Herbison's majority of 8,303 in 1966. Craig (ed), *British Parliamentary Election Results 1950–1970*, p. 655.

14 McSmith, *John Smith*, p. 44.

15 Martin Dempsey, *Question Time Special*, BBC 1, Thursday, 12 May 1994 (transcript).

16 HC Debs, 10 November 1970, c. 244.

17 HC Debs, 10 November 1970, c. 245.

18 Teddy Taylor had been educated at the High School of Glasgow, then a non-fee-paying grammar school.

19 HC Debs, 11 November 1970, c. 502.

20 HC Debs, 11 November 1970, c. 503.

21 HC Debs, 11 November 1970, c. 505.

22 HC Debs, 28 October 1971, cc. 2211–2218.

Philip Norton, *Dissension in the House of Commons, 1945–74* (Macmillan: London, 1975), pp. 395–8.

23 *The United Kingdom and the European Communities* (Cmnd. 4715).

24 HC Debs, 26 July 1971, c. 130.

25 Interview with Dr J. Dickson Mabon, 15 May 2003.

26 Telephone interview with Rt Hon. Bruce Millan, 22 January 2004.

27 Including Betty Boothroyd, who won the West Bromwich West by-election in May 1973.

28 Interview with Rt Hon. Lord Rodgers of Quarry Bank, 20 January 2004.

29 Interview with Rt Hon. Lord Irvine of Lairg PC QC, 30 April 2003.

30 HC Debs, 18 October 1972, c. 346.

31 HC Debs, 20 November 1973, c. 1264.

32 HC Debs, 20 November 1973, c. 1267.

33 Interview with Rt Hon. Lord Rodgers of Quarry Bank.

34 Interview with Baroness Smith of Gilmorehill DL, 16 March 2004.

35 The Criminal Justice (Scotland) Act 1980 markedly tightened the law on criminal evidence, considerably lengthening the duration of criminal cases.

36 Interview with Professor J. Ross Harper CBE.

37 Lynda Lee-Potter, 'Luck that saved John Smith's life', *Daily Mail*, 26 January 1989.

38 Written correspondence with Kenneth Munro, 14 November 2004.

39 Interview with Lord McCluskey.

40 Interview with Lord Kirkwood, 21 October 2003.

41 Colin Hughes, 'Labour's chief prosecutor returns', *The Independent*, 15 March 1989.

42 Interview with Rt Hon. Lord [Ranald] MacLean, 18 November 2003.

43 Grant died in a road accident on 19 November 1972. Stenton & Lees, *Who's Who of British Members of Parliament, Volume IV, 1945–1979*, p. 139.

44 For details of the campaign to release Meehan, see Ludovic Kennedy, *On My Way to the Club* (Fontana Paperback edition: Glasgow, 1990), pp. 312–5.

45 McSmith, *John Smith*, p. 40.

46 Ibid.

47 Ludovic Kennedy, *A Presumption of Innocence. The Amazing Case of Patrick Meehan* (Victor Gollancz: London, 1976), pp. 16–17.

48 *Question Time Special*, BBC 1, Thursday, 12 May 1994 (transcript).

49 Written correspondence with Sir Ludovic Kennedy FRSL, 13 January 2004.

50 Written correspondence with Sir Ludovic Kennedy FRSL, 5 November 2004.

51 Interview with Lord McCluskey.

52 MacPherson, a science student, and former President of the International Club, became Secretary of the Labour Club and Secretary of the Union in 1962.

53 Hugh MacPherson, 'Upright Rabelaisian', *Tribune*, 20 May 1994.

54 Donald MacCormick, 'A diligent and brilliant believer in all that was best', *The Sunday Times*, 15 May 1994.

55 Interview with Lord McCluskey.

56 Interview with Kenneth Munro, 29 September 2003.

57 Bob McLaughlan, 'Dear John', *The Herald*, 13 May 1994.

58 Alan Rusbridger, 'Why Labour has been betting on Smith', *The Guardian*, 14 February 1986.

59 Interview with Lord McCluskey.

60 John Wheatley served as Solicitor-General for Scotland from March until October 1947, before being made Lord Advocate, serving from October 1947 until October 1951. He sat as the Labour member for Edinburgh East from November 1947 until January 1954, and later chaired a famous Commission on Local Government. *Royal Commission on Local Government in Scotland 1966–69*, Cmnd. 4150 (Wheatley Commission). John Wheatley was also the nephew of John Wheatley, the Labour MP for Shettleston from November 1922 until his death in May 1930, who served as Health Minister in the first Labour government, from January until November 1924.

61 In recent memory, only Peter Fraser, now Lord Fraser of Carmyllie, has proved the exception to the rule. Fraser served as Solicitor-General for Scotland from 1982–9, rising to become Minister of State at the Scottish Office, from 1992–5, and then Minister of State at the Department of Trade and Industry from 1995–7. *Dod's Parliamentary Companion, 2002* (Vacher Dod Publishing: London, New Parliament edition, 2001), p. 567.

62 Interview with Rt Hon. Lord Irvine of Lairg PC QC.

63 Telephone interview with Rt Hon. Bruce Millan.

64 Hattersley had just joined the government as Minister of State for Foreign and Commonwealth Affairs.

65 Interview with Rt Hon. Lord Hattersley, 20 February 2003.

66 Interview with Rt Hon. Lord Irvine of Lairg PC QC.

67 Lewis Chester, 'The Scorning Scotsman', *Independent on Sunday*, 26 May 1991.

68 Interview with Rt Hon. Lord Healey of Riddlesden CH MBE, 12 February 2003.

69 Telephone interview with Rt Hon. Bruce Millan, 22 January 2004. See for example the Second Reading debate of the Offshore Petroleum Development (Scotland) Bill, 19 November 1974, cc. 1108–1240.

70 Interview with Rt Hon. Tony Benn, 6 March 2003.

71 Interview with Rt Hon. Lord Irvine of Lairg PC QC.

72 Tony Benn, *Against the Tide. Diaries 1973–76* (Arrow Books: London, 1990), p. 481 (Tuesday, 16 December 1975); p. 528 (Tuesday, 9 March 1976).

73 Interview with Rt Hon. Tony Benn.

74 According to Philip Ziegler, Hugh Dalton is said to have come up with the nicknames for Kaldor and Balogh. Philip Ziegler, *Wilson. The Authorised Life of Lord Wilson of Rievaulx* (Weidenfeld & Nicolson: London, 1993), p.93.

75 Interview with Rt Hon. Tony Benn.

76 McSmith, *John Smith*, p. 63.

77 McSmith, *John Smith*, p. 66; p. 335.

78 Tony Benn, *Against the Tide. Diaries 1973–76*, p. 467 (Tuesday, 25 November 1975).

79 McSmith, *John Smith*, pp. 68–9.

80 Interview with Rt Hon. Tony Benn; for more details on the tensions between Benn and Ingham, see Robert Harris, *Good and Faithful Servant. The Unauthorised Biography of Bernard Ingham* (Faber & Faber: London, 1990), pp. 60–9.

81 Michael Hatfield, 'Lawyer pilots the devolution proposals', *The Times*, 3 March 1978.

82 Margaret van Hattem, 'The behind-the-scenes fixer moves to centre stage', *Financial Times*, 12 February 1986.

83 Interview with Rt Hon. Tony Benn, 6 March 2003.

84 Ibid.

85 HC Debs, 30 April 1975, c. 597.

86 Benn, *Free at Last!*, p. 161 (Monday, 8 February 1993).

87 *Observer Profile*, John Smith, 2 November 1986, in Robert Low (ed.), *The Observer Book of Profiles* (Virgin Books: London, 1991), p. 240.

88 John Smith, 'Parliamentary Report', in *Conference Report. Ninety-second Annual Conference of the Labour Party* (Labour Party: London, 1993), p. 95.

89 See for example, Rt Hon. John Smith QC MP, Press Notice, extract from speech to the Annual Delegate Conference of the Banking Insurance and Finance Union, Norbeck Castle Hotel, Blackpool, 13 May 1991. Kinnock Collection, Box 429.

90 Jeff Lovitt, interview with John Smith, 'Safe in Labour's hands', *Tribune*, 7 September 1990.

Chapter 6

1 Interview with Stuart Scott Whyte, 20 September 2003.

2 Ziegler, *Wilson*, p. 453.

3 *Royal Commission on the Constitution: Report* (HMSO: London, 1973), Cmnd. 5460 (Kilbrandon Commission). Two members of the Commission, Crowther-Hunt and Peacock, disagreed with the report's findings, and issued a *Memorandum of Dissent*.

4 Private information.

5 There were two ministerial committees on devolution, dealing with different levels of the issue. Harold Wilson chaired the senior one.

6 Quinlan later served as Permanent Under-Secretary at the Department of Employment from 1983–8, and then as Permanent Secretary at the Ministry of Defence from 1988–92.

7 Scott Whyte had worked as an Assistant Secretary in the Cabinet Office under George Thomson who had been given responsibility for local government reform. He subsequently served as resident Under-Secretary at Dover House from 1969–74 under Gordon Campbell and Willie Ross.

8 Scott Whyte also helped to produce a Green Paper in December 1976 on the possibilities of devolution to regional governments in England – *Devolution: the*

English Dimension: a consultative document (Office of the Lord President of the Council) – but it was largely ignored. Interview with Stuart Scott Whyte. Bruce Millan points out that the idea came from Peter Shore, who was an English nationalist, but a supporter of Scottish devolution. Millan agrees with Scott Whyte that nobody paid attention to the Green Paper. Telephone interview with Rt Hon. Bruce Millan, 22 January 2004.

9 Members of the Unit also worked closely with officials in the Welsh Office, the Scottish Office and other affected government departments.

10 Quoted in Christopher Harvie, Scotland and Nationalism. Scottish Society and Politics, 1707–1977 (George Allen & Unwin: London, 1977), p. 263.

11 Andrew Marr, The Battle for Scotland (Penguin Books: Harmondsworth, 1992), pp. 140–1.

12 David Scott, 'Scots rap Labour NEC for "jumping the gun"', The Scotsman, 19 August 1974.

13 Ibid.

14 Democracy and Devolution: proposals for Scotland and Wales (Cmnd. 5732).

15 HC Debs, 10 May 1976, c. 24.

16 Interview with Sir Michael Quinlan, 28 May 2003.

17 Interview with Stuart Scott Whyte.

18 Devolution Within the United Kingdom: Some Alternatives for Discussion, p. 20, paragraph e.

19 Interview with Sir Michael Quinlan, 28 May 2003.

20 Telephone interview with Sir John Garlick, 2 September 2003. At the time, Garlick chaired a committee of permanent secretaries which met only half a dozen times in total, but which charted the main timetable and strategy for devolution across Whitehall.

21 Interview with Sir Michael Quinlan.

22 Interview with Rt Hon. Lord Healey of Riddlesden CH MBE, 12 February 2003.

23 Telephone interview with Rt Hon. Bruce Millan.

24 Private information.

25 Interview with Sir Michael Quinlan.

26 Our Changing Democracy (Cmnd. 6348).

27 In March 1975, the Scottish Labour Party conference voted against giving a future Scottish Assembly much in the way of

economic powers.

28 Quoted in Harvie, Scotland and Nationalism, pp. 265–6.

29 Labour MP for South Ayrshire, 1970–6.

30 John Robertson, MP for Paisley since 1961.

31 McSmith, John Smith, p. 74.

32 David Butler and Gareth Butler, British Political Facts 1990–1994 (Macmillan: 7th edn, Basingstoke, 1994), p. 136.

33 Interview with Rt Hon. Michael Foot, 20 February 2003.

34 Interview with Rt Hon. Tony Benn, 6 March 2003.

35 Written correspondence with Rt Hon. Lord Callaghan of Cardiff KG, 1 April 2003; Mervyn Jones, Michael Foot's biographer, agrees: 'His [Smith's] exceptional head for complex details, his legal training and his Scottish background made him ideal for the job.' Mervyn Jones, Michael Foot (Victor Gollancz: Paperback edn, London, 1995), p. 399.

36 Simon Hoggart and David Leigh, Michael Foot. A Portrait (Hodder & Stoughton: London, 1981), p. 194.

37 Written correspondence with Rt Hon. Lord Callaghan of Cardiff KG.

38 Telephone interview with Rt Hon. Bruce Millan.

39 Interview with Murray Elder, 30 April 2003.

40 Maureen Cleave, 'Smiling John Smith', Daily Telegraph Magazine, 3 March 1990.

41 Written correspondence with Elizabeth Thomas, 30 May 2003.

42 Interview with Rt Hon. Michael Foot.

43 Ibid.

44 Written correspondence with Rt Hon. Lord Callaghan of Cardiff KG.

45 Interview with Professor Sir Neil MacCormick, 3 October 2003.

46 John Smith, 'A matter of debate: the Kilbrandon Report', The Scotsman, 7 November 1973. Also quoted in McSmith, John Smith, pp. 76–7.

47 John Smith, 'A matter of debate: the Kilbrandon Report', op. cit.

48 John Smith, 'The political scene: cards on the table for home rule', Daily Record, 31 May 1974. Also quoted in McSmith, John Smith, p. 76.

49 David Scott, op. cit. Also quoted in David Steel, A House Divided. The Lib-Lab Pact and the Future of British Politics (Weidenfeld & Nicolson: London, 1980),

pp. 99–100.

50 David Scott, op. cit.

51 Interview with Dr J. Dickson Mabon, 15 May 2003.

52 Interview with Professor Sir Neil MacCormick.

53 *Committee on Financial Aid to Political Parties* (Cmnd. 6601) (Houghton Committee).

54 Interview with Professor Sir Neil MacCormick.

55 The Romans suppressed and absorbed almost all of the Etruscan culture.

56 Interview with Professor Sir Neil MacCormick.

57 Interview with Lord Hogg of Cumbernauld, 4 November 2003.

58 Interview with Lord Mackay of Drumadoon, 11 November 2003.

59 For years, the proposed home for the Scottish Parliament in Edinburgh.

60 Menzies Campbell, 'A Prelude to Warfare', *The Sunday Times Scotland*, 15 May 1994.

61 Interview with Rt Hon. Sir Menzies Campbell CBE QC MP, 20 January 2004.

62 Interview with Sir Michael Quinlan.

63 HC Debs, 16 December 1976, c. 1741.

64 Private information.

65 Interview with Sir Michael Quinlan.

66 Telephone interview with Sir John Garlick, 2 September 2003.

67 Interview with Stuart Scott Whyte.

68 Non-government amendments normally obtain briefing from officials on the lines of 'accept', 'reject', or 'promise to consider', always accompanied with paragraphs of reasoning. When dealing with such paperwork, Smith required very little additional help. Nor did Smith require much note-passing from officials in the civil servants' box in Parliament. Interview with Stuart Scott Whyte.

69 Telephone interview with Rt Hon. Bruce Millan.

70 Interview with Lord McCluskey, 13 May 2003.

71 *Devolution to Scotland and Wales: Supplementary Statement* (Cmnd. 6585).

72 Telephone interview with Rt Hon. Bruce Millan, 22 January 2004.

73 Cmnd. 6890.

74 Interview with Stuart Scott Whyte.

75 Ibid.

76 Interview with Sir Michael Quinlan.

77 Telephone interview with Mary McCulloch, 26 November 2003.

78 Three other Scottish Conservatives – John Corrie, Hector Monro and George Younger – also offered their resignations, but these were refused. Philip Norton, *Dissension in the House of Commons, 1974–1979* (Clarendon Press: Oxford, 1980), p. 212. Following the resignation of Buchanan-Smith, Mrs Thatcher appointed Teddy Taylor, Conservative MP for Glasgow Cathcart since 1964, as shadow Secretary of State for Scotland.

79 Leo Abse, Labour MP for Pontypool from 1968–87, later wrote a bizarre attack on the psyche of Tony Blair, entitled, *Tony Blair. The Man Behind the Smile* (Robson Books: revised paperback edn, London, 2001).

80 It is worth noting here that, whereas in 1979, Labour held post-legislative referendums in Scotland and Wales, in 1997 the Scots and the Welsh voted in pre-legislative referendums. In other words, the broad principle of devolution was put before the people, and then Parliament deliberated upon the detail, producing the Scotland Act and the Wales Act.

81 Westlake, *Kinnock*, p. 128.

82 Jones, *Michael Foot*, pp. 412–3.

83 Abse, *Tony Blair: The Man Behind the Smile*, p. 3.

84 Harvie, *Scotland and Nationalism*, p. 268. Curiously, Harvie puts the date for the Second Reading vote as 17 December 1976, when it in fact occurred a day earlier.

85 Including Reg Prentice, Labour MP for Newham North-East and then a member of the Cabinet as Minister for Overseas Development, who survived initially, but then resigned of his own volition later that month. Norton, *Dissension, 1974–1979*, pp. 211–22.

86 A guillotine is simply a parliamentary device deployed by the government to limit the time available to debate any stage or stages of a Bill. It used to be deployed when determined opponents of Bills sought to hold up a Bill's passage. Now, most government bills have automatic programme motions, formally limiting the time for debating each stage of a bill.

87 Interview with Sir Michael Quinlan; telephone interview with Rt Hon. Bruce Millan.

88 For more on Mackintosh's life, see Greg

Rosen, 'Reputations. John P. Mackintosh: His Achievements and Legacy', *Political Quarterly*, Vol. 70, No. 2, April-June 1999, pp. 210–8.

89 By 244 votes to 62. Norton, *Dissension, 1974–1979*, pp. 223–4; Steel, *A House Divided*, p. 94; HC Debs, 25 January 1977, cc. 1447–1450.

90 James Mitchell, *Strategies for Self-Government. The Campaigns for a Scottish Parliament* (Polygon: Edinburgh, 1996) p. 319.

91 Interview with Sir Michael Quinlan.

92 Norton, *Dissension, 1974–1979*, pp. 239–40; Hoggart and Leigh inaccurately claim that 43 Labour MPs abstained, when they mean that 22 voted against and 21 abstained from voting. Hoggart and Leigh, *Michael Foot*, p. 194.

93 Margaret Vaughan, 'Labour's rising star with talent for pulverising the Tories', *Glasgow Herald*, 19 May 1986.

94 Interview with Rt Hon. Michael Foot.

95 HC Debs, 24 February 1977, c. 1691.

96 Interview with Rt Hon. Michael Foot.

97 In May 1977, the SNP performed extremely well in the Scottish district council elections, polling 27 per cent of the vote.

98 HC Debs, 14 November 1977, cc. 721–726. Only 11 Labour MPs voted against the principle of the Bill. Norton, *Dissension, 1974–1979*, pp. 274–5.

99 Bruce Millan recalls that the devolution ministers were strongly against inserting the declaratory provision in the Bill because such a provision was against UK legislative practice and had no substantive effect, but, they believed, would give opponents of the Bill another chance to delay the passage of the Bill. However, the provision was inserted in the Bill at the insistence of a number of Cabinet ministers who were 'at best lukewarm if not hostile to devolution'. Written correspondence with Rt Hon. Bruce Millan, 22 October 2004.

100 During the course of this chapter, I occasionally refer to 'Smith believed', or 'Smith's line' on devolution. The demands of writing a biography entice the author into giving more of a starring role to the central character than is perhaps strictly historically accurate. 'Smith's line', emerged, of course, from the collective decision-making process in the Steering Committee of Ministers, which in turn operated within the constraints of what the Cabinet was prepared to accept.

101 HC Debs, 22 November 1977, cc. 1392–1393.

102 HC Debs, 22 November 1977, cc. 1402–1404.

103 Norton, *Dissension, 1974–1979*, pp. 281–2.

104 HC Debs, 23 November 1977, cc. 1577–1588.

105 Ayes 107, Noes 290. HC Debs, 23 November 1977, cc. 1587–1590; Steel, *A House Divided*, p. 94.

106 Steel, *A House Divided*, p. 101.

107 HC Debs, 17 July 1978, cc. 111–115; cc. 150–152.

108 Ayes 61, Noes 306. HC Debs, 10 January 1978, cc. 1607–1608. Apparently, the Conservatives were given a free vote. Norton, *Dissension, 1974–1979*, pp. 301–2.

109 Private information.

110 HC Debs, 11 January 1978, cc. 1725–1738; Norton, *Dissension, 1974–1979*, pp. 303–4.

111 Ayes 35, Noes 133. HC Debs, 11 January 1978, cc. 1763–1764. The Conservatives abstained.

112 More accurately, a Conservative amendment attempting to exclude family planning and abortion failed. The Conservatives were given a free vote on the issue. Norton, *Dissension, 1974–1979*, pp. 305–6.

113 HC Debs, 17 January 1978, cc. 289–292.

114 HC Debs, 25 January 1978, cc. 1452–1456.

115 Ayes 122, Noes 184. HC Debs, 25 January 1978, cc. 1457–1460.

116 HC Debs, 3 June 1997, cc. 275–278. However, the Conservative amendment moved by Bill Cash took place during the passage of the Referendums (Scotland and Wales) Bill, the Bill that prepared the way for the pre-legislative referendums in September 1997, not during the Scotland Bill, which came after the referendums had passed.

117 Cook had represented Edinburgh Central since February 1974.

118 HC Debs, 9 May 1978, c. 1079; quoted in Jones, *Michael Foot*, p. 411.

119 Paul Routledge, *Gordon Brown. The Biography* (Simon & Schuster: London, 1998), p. 79.

120 Telephone interview with Rt Hon. Bruce Millan.

121 Interview with Rt Hon. Michael Foot.

122 Interview with Dr J. Dickson Mabon.

123 HC Debs, 25 January 1978, cc. 1537–1538.

124 In actual fact, the Cunningham amendment was an amendment to an amendment. The original amendment, put down by the Labour MP Bruce Douglas-Mann had favoured only a 30 per cent rule. Cunningham's amendment to Douglas-Mann's amendment was carried by 166 votes to 151, a majority against the government of fifteen, with 35 Labour MPs supporting it. The House then voted on the main amendment (Douglas-Mann's amendment) as amended by Cunningham, and it was this vote that the government lost by 168 votes to 142! Norton, *Dissension, 1974–1979*, pp. 311–12; HC Debs, 25 January 1978, cc. 1541–1548.

125 HC Debs, 25 January 1978, cc. 1510–1517.

126 Hamish Watt, an SNP whip, and Douglas Henderson, the MP for Aberdeenshire South.

127 Telephone interview with Rt Hon. Bruce Millan.

128 Fred Emery, 'Mr Foot gives apology to Commons over voting delay', *The Times*, 27 January 1978; HC Debs, 26 January 1978, cc. 1596–1601. The Speaker, George Thomas, even published a report of the Serjeant at Arms into the unseemly affair.

129 Vernon Bogdanor, 'The 40 per cent rule', *Parliamentary Affairs*, Vol. 33, No. 3 (1980), p. 249.

130 John Bochel, David Denver and Allan Macartney (eds), *The Referendum Experience. Scotland 1979* (Aberdeen University Press: Aberdeen, 1981), pp. 7–9.

131 HC Debs, 25 January 1978, cc. 1547–1552; Norton, *Dissension, 1974–1979*, p. 313.

132 HC Debs, 14 February 1978, cc. 252–257.

133 HC Debs, 14 February 1978, cc. 257–264.

134 HC Debs, 14 February 1978, cc. 297–302; Norton, *Dissension, 1974–1979*, pp. 326–7.

135 HC Debs, 15 February 1978, cc. 573–579.

136 HC Debs, 15 February 1978, cc. 597–602.

137 HC Debs, 15 February 1978, cc. 601–606. This time, 38 Labour members voted against the Government line. Norton, *Dissension, 1974–1979*, pp. 327–9.

138 On a three-line whip the government won by a comfortable margin of 297 votes to 257, with only seven Labour MPs voting against their party. HC Debs, 22 February 1978, cc. 1599–1606. Although, according to Norton, as many as 20 Labour MPs may

also have abstained. Norton, *Dissension, 1974–1979*, p. 333.

139 Gerry Hassan and Peter Lynch, *The Almanac of Scottish Politics* (Politico's: London, 2001), p. 342.

140 Mitchell, *Strategies for Self Government*, p. 322.

141 Telephone interview with Rt Hon. Lord Robertson of Port Ellen, 7 July 2003.

142 The female protester was later found to be the daughter of the Prime Minister of Malta.

143 This amusing if smelly tale draws largely from an account in *The Times*, 7 July 1978.

144 Maureen Cleave, 'Smiling John Smith', *Daily Telegraph Magazine*, 3 March 1990; McSmith, *John Smith*, pp. 87–8.

145 HL Debs, 4 April 1978, cc. 103–106.

146 HC Debs, 16 July 1978, cc. 678–679.

147 Steel, *A House Divided*, p. 95; Norton, *Dissension, 1974–1979*, pp. 358–9; HC Debs, 6 July 1978, cc. 733–738.

148 HL Debs, 16 May 1978, cc. 205–208.

149 HL Debs, 4 April 1978, cc. 158–160.

150 HL Debs, 4 May 1978, cc. 415–418.

151 HL Debs, 4 May 1978, cc. 493–496.

152 HL Debs, 9 May 1978, cc. 889–892.

153 HL Debs, 3 May 1978, cc. 249–252.

154 HL Debs, 9 May 1978, cc. 845–848.

155 HL Debs, 9 May 1978, cc. 915–918.

156 HL Debs, 9 May 1978, c. 916.

157 HL Debs, 8 June 1978, cc. 1539–1540.

158 HL Debs, 13 June 1978, cc. 275–278.

159 HC Debs, 17 July 1978, cc. 163–173.

160 HC Debs, 17 July 1978, cc. 197–202; Norton, *Dissension, 1974–1979*, pp. 363–4.

161 Ayes 286, Noes 286. HC Debs, 17 July 1978, cc. 201–206. Norton, *Dissension, 1974–1979*, pp. 364–5.

162 HC Debs, 26 July 1978, cc. 1642.

163 Ayes 276, Noes 275. HC Debs, 26 July 1978, cc. 1659–1666.

164 Ayes 266, Noes 286. HC Debs, 26 July 1978, cc. 1665–1670; Norton, *Dissension, 1974–1979*, pp. 373–5.

165 HC Debs, 18 July 1978, cc. 471–474.

166 HL Debs, 27 July 1978, cc. 951–968.

167 Abse, *Tony Blair. The Man Behind the Smile*, pp. 4–5.

168 On a referendum held the same day, the Welsh voted by a margin of four to one against the government's devolution proposals.

169 Interview with Lord Mackay of Drumadoon.

170 Interview with Rt Hon. Sir Menzies Campbell CBE QC MP.
171 Steel, *A House Divided*, p. 101; quoted in Peter Riddell, 'Profile: John Smith', *The Listener*, 2 October 1986.
172 Allan Massie, 'The right man at the wrong time', *Daily Telegraph*, 14 April 1992.
173 David Steel acknowledges that Smith 'earned his place in Cabinet for his patient and skilful handling of the issue'. Steel, *A House Divided*, p. 101.

Chapter 7

1 *The Guardian*, 31 August 1978.
2 See Kenneth O. Morgan, *Callaghan. A Life* (Oxford University Press: Oxford, 1997), p. 642.
3 Interview with Lord McCluskey, 13 May 2003.
4 Michael Hatfield, 'Lawyer pilots the devolution proposals', *The Times*, 3 March 1978.
5 Interview with Rt Hon. Michael Foot, 20 February 2003.
6 Written correspondence with Rt Hon. Lord Callaghan of Cardiff KG, 1 April 2003.
7 Edmund Dell, 1921–99, Labour MP for Birkenhead from 1964–79. Dell also voted in favour of European entry on 28 October 1971, resigning from the front bench as opposition spokesman on Trade, and later became a founding member of the SDP.
8 Telephone interview with Sir Thomas Harris, 22 September 2003.
9 Elizabeth Smith, 'Introduction', in Brown and Naughtie, *Life and Soul of the Party*, p. 13.
10 Written correspondence between Elizabeth Smith and Elizabeth Thomas, 22 November 1978. Reproduced by kind permission of Elizabeth Thomas.
11 Maureen Cleave, 'Smiling John Smith', *Weekend Telegraph Magazine*, 17 March 1990.
12 Sarah Smith, 'Our Father' in Brown and Naughtie, *Life and Soul of the Party*, p. 114.
13 Fiona Millar, interview with John Smith, *She Magazine* (February, 1993), Final proofs, 10 November 1992. Murray Elder papers, Box 2.
14 Sarah Smith, op. cit.
15 Fiona Millar, op. cit.
16 Roy Hattersley, 'Radical, rational and

right', *The Guardian*, 13 May 1994.
17 John Smith, 'On Being a Father', in Brown and Naughtie, *Life and Soul of the Party*, p. 117.
18 Telephone interview with Mary McCulloch, 26 November 2003.
19 Interview with Lord Mackay of Drumadoon, 11 November 2003.
20 Interview with Lord Gordon of Strathblane CBE, 12 March 2003.
21 John Sergeant, *Give Me Ten Seconds* (Pan Books: London, 2002), pp. 185–6.
22 Telephone interview with Sir Thomas Harris.
23 John Smith, transcript of speech to Dunoon Grammar School, 350th Dinner, 8 November 1991 (first draft). Michael Crick files.
24 Private information.
25 Patrick Wintour, 'Leviathan at Westminster: How Jim Callaghan built a government in his own image', *New Statesman*, 23 March 1979.
26 Telephone interview with Sir Thomas Harris.
27 See Jones, *Michael Foot*, pp. 409–10.
28 Interview with Murray Elder, 30 April 2003.
29 HC Debs, 10 November 1978, cc. 1453–1454.
30 HC Debs, 22 March 1979, c. 1760.
31 Telephone interview with Sir Thomas Harris.
32 Ibid.
33 Interview with Kenneth Munro, 29 September 2003.
34 Telephone interview with Sir Thomas Harris.
35 Labour MP for Coventry South West from February 1974 to May 1979, and for Preston from 1987 until her death on 2 September 2000.
36 Private information.
37 Telephone interview with Sir Thomas Harris.
38 Private information.
39 Telephone interview with Sir Thomas Harris.
40 McSmith, *John Smith*, p. 94.
41 The government was acting on the findings of the Bullock Committee Report, first published in 1977. *Committee of Inquiry on Industrial Democracy* (Cmnd. 6706).
42 Elinor Goodman, 'Dell's successor likely

to take harder line on worker directors', *Financial Times*, 13 November 1978.

43 The Companies Bill hoped to implement EEC directives on disclosure and auditing, and to give effect to the Labour Government's White Paper, *The Conduct of Company Directors* (Cmnd. 7073), first published in November 1977.

44 Such illegal practices had been highlighted by the famous Boesky case on Wall Street.

45 HC Debs, 20 November 1978, c. 941.

46 HC Debs, 20 November 1978, c. 938.

47 McSmith, *John Smith*, pp. 93–4.

48 The Bill, which had cross-party support, received its Royal Assent in April 1979. HC Debs, 4 April 1979, c. 1394.

49 Particularly, the Intergovernmental Maritime Consultative Organisation's (IMCO) Protocol to the International Convention for the Safety of Life at Sea, 1974. HC Debs, 30 November 1978, c. 780.

50 Telephone interview with Kenneth Munro, 6 November 2004.

51 For Smith's Second Reading speech on the Merchant Shipping Bill, see HC Debs, 30 November 1978, cc. 778–789.

52 Cmnd. 7233.

53 HC Debs, 15 February 1979, cc. 647–658w.

54 HC Debs, 15 February 1979, cc. 657–658w.

55 HC Debs, 27 June 1980, cc. 1019–1020.

56 HC Debs, 27 June 1980, c. 1030.

57 Interview with Murray Elder, 16 November 2004.

58 Written correspondence with Robin Gray CB, 23 March 2003.

59 Private information.

60 Hugh MacPherson, 'Upright Rabalasian', *Tribune*, 20 May 1994.

61 Written correspondence with Robin Gray CB.

62 HC Debs, 28 March 1979, cc. 583–588.

63 McSmith, *John Smith*, pp. 95–6.

64 Interview with Lord McCluskey; interview with Lord Gordon of Strathblane CBE.

65 Thomas Harris, diary, May 1979.

66 Vincent Cable later became a convert to the SDP and has served as the Liberal Democrat MP for Twickenham since 1997.

67 Thomas Harris, diary, May 1979.

68 Telephone interview with Sir Thomas Harris.

69 Thomas Harris, diary, May 1979.

70 Alastair Campbell, 'John Smith's Great Journey', *Today*, 13 May 1994.

71 Mike Goldwater, 'Why he's no longer just plain old John Smith', *Woman's Own*, 27 September 1986.

72 Telephone interview with Rt Hon. Bruce Millan, 22 January 2004.

73 Interview with Baroness Smith of Gilmorehill DL, 4 December 2002.

74 Thomas Harris, diary, May 1979; HC Debs, 20 July 1979, cc. 2183–2197.

75 HC Debs, 20 July 1979, c. 2184.

76 A parliamentary term, meaning the use of stalling tactics to delay proceedings.

77 Thomas Harris, diary, July 1979.

78 HC Debs, 23 July 1979, cc. 110–113.

89 HC Debs, 23 July 1979, c. 113.

80 HC Debs, 23 October 1979, cc. 220–236. On this occasion, Nott managed to speak for 50 minutes.

81 Thomas Harris, diary, July 1979.

Chapter 8

1 Elizabeth Smith, 'Introduction', in Brown and Naughtie, *Life and Soul of the Party*, p. 13.

2 Interview with Lord Mackay of Drumadoon, 11 November 2003; interview with Rt Hon. Lord [Ranald] MacLean, 18 November 2003.

3 Interview with Rt Hon. Lord [Ranald] MacLean.

4 Interview with Lord Mackay of Drumadoon.

5 Interview with Baroness Smith of Gilmorehill DL, 4 December 2002.

6 Interview with Rt Hon. Paul Boateng MP, 6 September 2004.

7 Interview with Professor J. Ross Harper CBE, 18 February 2003.

8 Interview with Lord Gordon of Strathblane CBE, 12 March 2003.

9 Interview with Lord Hogg of Cumbernauld, 4 November 2003.

10 From 1985–94, Smith was vice-chairman of the Britain-Russia Centre (formerly the GB-USSR Association). Tam Dalyell, 'Obituary: John Smith', *The Independent*, 13 May 1994.

11 'Black Dog', *Daily Express*, 13 May 1994.

12 Interview with Lord Hogg of Cumbernauld.

13 Interview with Lord Mackay of Drumadoon.

14 Simon Hoggart, 'Sharp wit with an inner fire', *The Guardian 2*, 13 May 1994.

15 'RAF pilot tells of celebration after crash',

Glasgow Herald, 11 January 1983.

16   Arnot McWhinnie, 'Big Two Take on RAF', *Daily Record*, 31 December 1982; Iain Gray, 'RAF officers on trial over loss of jet', *Glasgow Herald*, 10 January 1983.

17   Interview with Professor J. Ross Harper CBE, 18 February 2003.

18   Interview with Rt Hon. Sir Menzies Campbell CBE QC MP, 20 January 2004.

19   John England, 'Missile Jet's Vital Flaw', *Daily Record*, 11 January 1983; 'Jet missile safety device was faulty, court martial told', *Glasgow Herald*, 12 January 1983; John England, 'Faulty System in RAF plane', *Daily Record*, 12 January 1983.

20   'Jet crew found guilty over shot-down plane', *Glasgow Herald*, 15 January 1983.

21   Interview with Professor J. Ross Harper CBE.

22   'Guilty of £7m Blast', *Daily Record*, 15 January 1983.

23   'Phantom crew can fly again', *Glasgow Herald*, 17 January 1983. The verdicts and sentences were confirmed six weeks later.

24   Interview with Professor J. Ross Harper CBE.

25   Interview with Lord Mackay of Drumadoon.

26   Ibid.

27   Interview with Rt Hon. Paul Boateng MP.

28   McSmith, *John Smith*, p. 102.

29   *The Times*, 7 September 1984.

30   *The Times*, 6 September 1984.

31   *The Times*, 4 September 1984.

32   Senator of the College of Justice in Scotland from 1972–87. Michael Bruce QC, then an Advocate Depute acted on behalf of the Crown. Bruce later became a Senator of the College of Justice in Scotland, taking the title, Rt Hon. Lord Marnoch.

33   *Glasgow Herald*, 27 September 1984.

34   *Glasgow Herald*, 19 July 1984.

35   *Glasgow Herald*, 27 September 1984.

36   *The Times*, 27 September 1984.

37   *Glasgow Herald*, 27 September 1984.

38   Ibid.

39   Gary Moore was released when the murder charge was dropped against him, and Thomas Gray was also cleared of murder, but still faced a charge of attempted murder.

40   Stephen McGregor, 'One accused cleared of Doyle murder charge', *Glasgow Herald*, 5 October 1984; *Glasgow Herald*, 6 October

1984; *The Times*, 6 October 1984; 9 October 1984.

41   Allan Laing, 'Two get life for mass murder of Doyle family', *Glasgow Herald*, 11 October 1984; *The Times*, 11 October 1984.

42   However, Thomas Gray's appeal against his fourteen-year murder conviction was upheld.

43   *The Herald*, 18 March 2004; *Sunday Mail*, 21 March 2004.

Chapter 9

1   Peter Riddell, 'Profile: John Smith', *The Listener*, 2 October 1986; Kinnock failed to get elected onto the shadow Cabinet because there were only twelve places available. In 1981, the number of places was increased to fifteen. Butler and Butler, *British Political Facts 1990–1994*, p. 142.

2   Lewis Chester, 'The Scorning Scotsman', *Independent on Sunday*, 26 May 1991.

3   Butler and Butler, *British Political Facts, 1990–1994*, p. 136.

4   Christopher Brocklebank-Fowler, MP for Norfolk North-West.

5   Ivor Crewe and Anthony King, *SDP. The Birth, Life and Death of the Social Democratic Party* (Oxford University Press: Oxford, 1997), p. 105.

6   Interview with Rt Hon. Michael Foot, 20 February 2003.

7   Crewe and King, *SDP*, p. 105.

8   Crewe and King, *SDP*, pp. 106–7.

9   Andy McSmith, *Faces of Labour. The Inside Story* (Verso: London, 1996), p. 34.

10   Interview with Rt Hon. Lord Hattersley, 20 February 2003.

11   Elizabeth Smith, 'Introduction', in Brown and Naughtie, *Life and Soul of the Party*, p. 13.

12   Simon Hattenstone, 'The Monday interview: Saint Michael', *The Guardian*, 4 November 2002.

13   Interview with Lord Gordon of Strathblane CBE, 12 March 2003.

14   Interview with Rt Hon. Sir Menzies Campbell, CBE QC MP, 20 January 2004.

15   Interestingly, Crewe and King list Roy Hattersley, Roy Mason, Merlyn Rees and Eric Varley in this loyalist category, but not John Smith. Crewe and King, *SDP*, p. 107.

16   Crewe and King, *SDP*, p. 108.

17   Naughtie, *The Rivals*, p. 47.

18 Crewe and King, *SDP*, pp. 113–14.

19 Labour MP for Caithness and Sutherland from 1966 to March 1981, and then for the SDP, and later, the Liberal Democrats until 1997; Liberal Democrat MP for Caithness, Sutherland and Easter Ross from 1997–2001. Raised to the peerage as Baron Maclennan of Rogart in Sutherland in 2001.

20 Lewis Chester, op. cit.

21 Interview with Rt Hon. Lord Rodgers of Quarry Bank, 20 January 2004.

22 Crewe and King, *SDP*, p. 304.

23 Mike Goldwater, 'Why he's no longer just plain old John Smith', *Woman's Own*, 27 September 1986.

24 Interview with Ann Barrett, 21 June 2003.

25 Private information.

26 *Newsnight*, 24 March 1986.

27 Simon Hughes spoke in favour of an amendment which proposed that any British contribution to collective European defence should be non-nuclear. The Assembly backed the amendment, and it was widely seen as a disaster for the Alliance. David Owen closed down his office for the day, refusing to answer any telephone calls, and the newspapers ran with headlines such as 'Alliance Shattered', 'Steel humiliated', and 'Doctor in Distress'. See David Owen, *Time to Declare* (Michael Joseph: London, 1991), p. 665; Roy Jenkins, *A Life at the Centre* (Macmillan: London, 1991), pp. 591–2; David Steel, *Against Goliath. David Steel's Story* (Weidenfeld & Nicolson: London, 1989), pp. 271–4.

28 Interview with Rt Hon. Sir Menzies Campbell CBE QC MP.

29 Tudor Jones, *Remaking the Labour Party. From Gaitskell to Blair* (Routledge: London, 1996), p. 112.

30 McSmith, *John Smith*, p. 118.

31 Ibid.

32 Telephone Interview with Rt Hon. Bruce Millan, 22 January 2004.

33 Interview with Rt Hon. Lord Hattersley.

34 Interview with Baroness Goudie, 21 January 2004.

35 Ibid.

36 McSmith, *John Smith*, p. 99.

37 Rentoul, *Tony Blair*, p. 83.

38 John Sweeney, 'Macbuddha: the Tories' bogeyman', *Evening Standard*, 12 September 1988.

39 Interview with Ruth Wishart, 15 January 2004.

40 *Tribune*, 10 October 1982.

41 *Report of the Annual Conference of the Labour Party*, 1983 (Brighton, 1983), p. 100; *Tribune*, 7 October 1983. Jon Sopel is therefore correct to suggest that Smith had never served on the NEC until he became leader, but wrong to say that he had never sought to serve on the NEC. Sopel, *Tony Blair*, p. 150.

42 Naughtie, *The Rivals*, p. 29.

43 Interview with Kenneth Munro, 29 September 2003.

44 Mark Wickham-Jones, *Economic Strategy and the Labour Party. Politics and Policy-making, 1970–83* (Macmillan Press Ltd: Basingstoke, 1996), p. 205.

45 Interview with Rt Hon. Lord Healey of Riddlesden CH MBE, 12 February 2003.

46 David Dimbleby interview with John Smith, *Labour Party Conference Live* (Bournemouth), BBC 1, 3 October 1985.

47 McSmith, *Faces of Labour*, p. 303.

48 David Kogan and Maurice Kogan, *The Battle for the Labour Party* (Kogan Page Ltd: London, 2nd edn, 1983), p. 197.

49 For the best account of this episode, see Michael Crick, *Militant* (Faber and Faber: London, 1984), p. 191.

50 Irvine and Blair based their legal advice on the Pembroke judgment of 1968. Desmond Donnelly, a right-wing Labour MP, had been expelled from the NEC, but sections of his Pembroke Constituency Party stood by him, and disaffiliated from the Labour party. The NEC established a new CLP in Pembroke, repossessing the assets of the old one, resulting in the case being brought before the courts. Mr Justice Megarry ruled that the NEC was bound by the principles of natural justice to give the dissidents a fair hearing.

51 Crick, *Militant*, p. 191.

52 Interview with Rt Hon. Lord Irvine of Lairg PC QC, 30 April 2003.

53 *The Times Law Reports*, 16 December 1982. This account is largely drawn from Eric Shaw, *Discipline and Discord in the Labour Party. The politics of managerial control in the Labour Party, 1951–87* (Manchester University Press: Manchester, 1988), pp. 238–40; see also Sopel, *Tony Blair*, pp. 52–4.

54 Interview with Rt Hon. Lord Irvine of

Lairg PC QC.

55 Sopel, *Tony Blair*, p. 55.

56 Peter Mandelson and Roger Liddle, *The Blair Revolution: Can New Labour Deliver?* (Faber and Faber: London, 1996), p. 37. Denis Healey has no recollection of his drinks cupboard being raided. Interview with Rt Hon. Lord Healey of Riddlesden CH MBE.

57 Interview with Murray Elder, 16 November 2004.

58 On the first anniversary of John Smith's death, Blair wrote an article for the *Daily Mirror*, paying tribute to the former Labour leader, and recalling their uproarious time in China. Tony Blair, 'Debt I owe to a great man', *Daily Mirror*, 12 May 1995; Sopel, *Tony Blair*, p. 99.

59 Interview with Rt Hon. Lord Irvine of Lairg PC QC.

60 Sopel, *Tony Blair*, p. 148.

61 David Butler and Dennis Kavanagh, *The British General Election of 1983* (Macmillan: Basingstoke, 1984), p. 153.

62 *The Times Guide to the House of Commons, June 1983*, p.22; p.167.

63 Interview with Rt Hon. Lord Hattersley.

64 Westlake, *Kinnock*, p. 237.

65 Jim Innes, 'Labour's big campaign is a battle of the Scots', *Glasgow Herald*, 26 August 1983.

66 Interview with Rt Hon. Lord Hattersley.

67 Denzil Davies and Gwyneth Dunwoody each polled miniscule totals for the deputy leadership. Butler and Butler, *British Political Facts, 1900–1994*, p. 136.

68 Varley's departure led to the Chesterfield by-election in March 1984, which resulted in Tony Benn's return to the House of Commons.

69 Minutes of a meeting of the Parliamentary Labour Party Held on Wednesday 18 May 1994 at 11.30 am in Committee Room 14.

70 David Simpson: 'Mammon: John Smith – The New Face of Labour', *The Observer*, 17 May 1987; Norman Tebbit, *Upwardly Mobile* (Weidenfeld & Nicolson: London, 1988), p. 232.

71 Standing Committee F had 37 sittings, and ran from 22 November 1983 to 1 March 1984. Official Report, Standing Committee F.

72 Naughtie, *The Rivals*, pp. 43–4.

73 Interview with Lord Hogg of Cumbernauld, 4 November 2003.

74 Naughtie, *The Rivals*, p. 33.

75 Although Brown became chief opposition spokesperson on Trade and Industry in November 1989, serving until 1992, he worked very closely with Smith on Labour's policy review. See chapters 12–14. And of course, Smith worked closely with Brown in the period from 1992–4, though tensions between the two over the extent to which Labour should modernise itself started to emerge. For more details, see chapter 21.

76 John Rentoul, *Tony Blair* (Little, Brown and Company: London, 1995), pp. 174–5.

77 Naughtie, *The Rivals*, p. 43.

78 *Newsnight*, BBC 2, 30 November 1983.

79 *BBC News*, 28 March 1983.

80 *Question Time*, BBC 1, 21 June 1984.

81 Steven Condie, *The Miners' Strike*, BBC 2, 27 January 2004.

82 Ibid.

83 Smith's predecessor, Peter Shore, had slid from third to sixth place in the shadow Cabinet elections, while Smith had gone down from fourth to fifth place.

84 John Kampfner, *Robin Cook* (Phoenix Paperback edn: London, 1999), p. 60. Cook really had nothing to complain about since he had slumped from tenth to fifteenth place in the shadow Cabinet elections. Butler and Butler, *British Political Facts, 1900–1994*, p. 142.

85 Selina Scott interview with John Smith, *Breakfast Time*, BBC 1, 21 November 1984.

86 NEC, *A Future That Works* (Labour Party: London, 1984).

87 NEC, *Social Ownership* (Labour Party: London, 1986).

88 *Britain Will Win* (Labour Party: London, 1987).

89 Eric Shaw, *The Labour Party Since 1979. Crisis and Transformation* (Routledge: London, 1994), pp. 47–9; p. 229.

90 David Simpson, 'Mammon: John Smith – The new face of Labour', *The Observer*, 17 May 1986.

91 Robert Kuttner, *The Economic Illusion: False Choices Between Prosperity and Social Justice* (University of Pennsylvania Press: Philadelphia, 1987).

92 Rt Hon. John Smith QC MP, *The Eighth John Mackintosh Memorial Lecture*, May Day 1987, reproduced in Brian Brivati (ed), *Guiding Light. The Collected Speeches of John Smith* (Politico's: London, 2000),

pp. 53–77.

93 Brivati (ed), *Guiding Light*, pp. 54–55.

94 Brivati (ed), *Guiding Light*, p. 75.

95 Interview with Lord Haskel, 20 October 2003.

96 Nicholas Faith, 'Obituary: Lord Montague of Oxford', *The Independent*, 8 November 1999.

97 Ibid.

98 Ibid.

99 Interview with Lord Haskel.

100 'Obituary: Michael Montague', *The Times*, 8 November 1999.

101 Interview with Lord Haskel.

102 Donald MacCormick, 'A diligent and brilliant believer in all that was best', *The Sunday Times*, 15 May 1994.

103 Jobs and Industry Campaign. Kinnock Collection, Box 455.

104 Tony Manwaring, 'Jobs and Industry – Campaign Video', RD: 3245/December 1984. Jobs and Industry Campaign. Kinnock Collection, Box 455.

105 Colin Brown, *Fighting Talk. The Biography of John Prescott* (Simon & Schuster: London, 1997), p. 143.

106 Wickham-Jones, *Economic Strategy and the Labour Party*, pp. 215–16.

107 Ibid.

108 Matthew Coady, 'Mirror Profile: The tortoise and the hares', *Daily Mirror*, 1 October 1984.

109 Simon Hoggart, 'Sharp wit with an inner fire', *The Guardian 2*, 13 May 1994.

110 HC Debs, 15 February 1980, cc. 1977–1982.

111 In February 1985, a similar fate befell Enoch Powell's Unborn Children (Protection) Bill that would have rendered it unlawful for a human embryo created by in vitro fertilisation to be used for any other purpose except to enable a woman to bear a child.

112 Susan Millns and Sally Sheldon, 'Abortion', in Philip Cowley (ed), *Conscience and Parliament* (Frank Cass: London, 1998), p.14. On the Bill's Second Reading, Smith again found himself voting with the minority of Labour back benchers, with 36 voting for the principle of the Bill, and 173 voting in the no lobby. HC Debs, 21 January 1988, cc. 1293–1298.

113 Millns and Sheldon, 'Abortion', in Cowley (ed), *Conscience and Parliament*, pp. 14–6.

114 HC Debs, 24 April 1990, cc. 273–294.

115 Interview with Murray Elder.

116 Sean French, 'Diary', *New Statesman & Society*, 24 July 1992.

117 Steve Platt, 'Letters', *New Statesman & Society*, 31 July 1992.

118 It is worth noting here the disastrous consequences of a party leader not allowing a free vote on an issue where his or her party is split. Iain Duncan Smith's decision to impose a three-line whip on the issue of unmarried couples (either of the same sex or of different sexes) being allowed to adopt provoked uproar in his party. See the debate on the Adoption and Children Bill. HC Debs, 4 November 2002, cc. 24–100; Philip Cowley, Letter to the Editor, 'Opposition should not crack the whip', *Daily Telegraph*, 6 November 2002. Note, however, that the Liberal Democrats also imposed a whipped vote, although Labour allowed a free vote.

119 HC Debs, 22 January 1971, c. 1480.

120 Private information.

121 Lewis Chester, op. cit.

122 Interview with Murray Elder.

123 The House of Commons opposed Currie's amendment by 307 votes to 280, but voted in favour of reducing the age of consent from 21 to eighteen by a margin by 427 votes to 162. Melvyn D. Read and David Marsh, 'Homosexuality' in Cowley (ed), *Conscience and Parliament*, p. 35. The Labour Party split 212–39 on sixteen, and 227 to 13 on eighteen. HC Debs, 21 February 1994, cc. 115–123.

124 Editorial, 'A question of conscience', *New Statesman & Society*, 25 February 1994.

Chapter 10

1 See Magnus Linklater and David Leigh, *Not With Honour* (Sphere Books Ltd: London, 1986); Hugo Young, *One of Us. A Biography of Margaret Thatcher* (Pan Books: final edition, London, 1993), pp. 431–59.

2 Alan Rusbridger, 'Why Labour has been betting on Smith', *The Guardian*, 14 February 1986

3 HC Debs, 13 January 1986, cc. 779–780.

4 HC Debs, 13 January 1986, c. 781.

5 The British Government had a stake in the Airbus project, to the tune of £250 million in launch aid, 80 per cent of which would not be recoverable if the sales of the aircraft did not go ahead. HC Debs, 13

January 1986, cc. 781–782.

6 HC Debs, 13 January 1986, c. 782.

7 HC Debs, 13 January 1986, c. 787–788; c. 790.

8 Linklater and Leigh, *Not With Honour*, p. 157.

9 HC Debs, 13 January 1986, c. 872.

10 HC Debs, 13 January 1986, c. 873.

11 Ibid.

12 HC Debs, 13 January 1986, cc. 874–875.

13 HC Debs, 13 January 1986, c. 875.

14 HC Debs, 13 January 1986, cc. 875–876.

15 Edward Pearce, 'Labour's school debaters line up for larynx duty', *New Statesman & Society*, 5 June 1992.

16 HC Debs, 15 January 1986, c. 1089.

17 At the time, Mayhew was also acting Attorney-General, because Sir Michael Havers, the holder of that post, was ill.

18 HC Debs, 15 January 1986, c. 1157.

19 *Newsnight*, BBC 2, 15 January 1986.

20 *This Week, Next Week*, BBC 1, 19 January 1986.

21 *Newsnight*, BBC 2, 22 January 1986.

22 HC Debs, 23 January 1986, c. 450; Hugo Young, *One of Us*, p. 252.

23 HC Debs, 23 January 1986, c. 453.

24 *Newsnight*, BBC 2, 24 January 1986.

25 Ibid.

26 Mark Stuart, *Douglas Hurd. The Public Servant* (Mainstream Publishing: Edinburgh, 1998), p. 174.

27 HC Debs, 27 January 1986, cc. 646–647.

28 HC Debs, 27 January 1986, c. 649.

29 HC Debs, 27 January 1986, cc. 651–658.

30 HC Debs, 27 January 1986, cc. 661–662.

31 However, as Sir Peter Tapsell, the Conservative Member for East Lindsey, immediately pointed out in an intervention: 'The point about Sir Winston Churchill is that he did re-rat.' HC Debs, 27 January 1986, c. 663.

32 Mike Goldwater, 'Why he's no longer just plain old John Smith', *Woman's Own*, 27 September 1986.

33 HC Debs, 23 January 1986, c. 455. Tam Dalyell had raised the matter in a question to the Prime Minister earlier in the emergency debate. HC Debs, 27 January 1986, c. 656.

34 HC Debs, 27 January 1986, c. 682.

35 Ibid.

36 Ibid.

37 Mike Goldwater, op. cit.

38 HC Debs, 27 January 1986, c. 683.

39 HC Debs, 27 January 1986, c. 683.

40 Widely reported at the time, and Mrs Thatcher later confirmed she had made the remark in a *TVam* interview with David Frost during the 1987 general election campaign. Young, *One of Us*, p. 454; p. 635.

41 For a similar view, see Westlake, *Kinnock*, p. 391.

42 *Newsnight*, BBC 2, 5 February 1986.

43 Margaret Vaughan, 'Labour's rising star with talent for pulverising the Tories', *Glasgow Herald*, 19 May 1986.

44 HC Debs, 5 February 1986, cc. 310–316.

45 *This Week, Next Week*, BBC 1, 6 February 1986.

46 Edward Pearce, 'The rise of Mr Smith', *Sunday Telegraph*, 6 April 1986.

47 Juliet Gordon & Neil Wenborn, *The History Today Companion to British History* (Collins & Brown: London, 1995), p. 344.

48 See for example, Margaret van Hattem, 'The behind-the-scenes fixer moves to centre stage', *Financial Times*, 12 February 1986; Alan Rusbridger, 'Why Labour has been betting on Smith', *The Guardian*, 14 February 1986; Edward Pearce, 'The rise of Mr Smith', *Sunday Telegraph*, 6 April 1986; Margaret Vaughan, 'Labour's rising star with talent for pulverising the Tories', *Glasgow Herald*, 19 May 1986.

49 Peter Riddell, 'Profile: John Smith', *The Listener*, 2 October 1986.

50 John Sweeney, 'Macbuddha: the Tories' bogeyman', *Evening Standard*, 12 September 1988.

51 Mike Goldwater, op. cit.

52 *Daily Telegraph*, 6 February 1986.

53 *Observer Profile*, John Smith, 2 November 1986, in Low (ed.), *The Observer Book of Profiles*, p. 238.

54 Moore's fellow judges in 1986 were: Ferdinand Mount of *The Spectator*, James Naughtie of *The Guardian*, Colin Welch of the *Daily Mail*, Alan Watkins of *The Observer*, Peter Jenkins of *The Sunday Times*, Peter Riddell of the *Financial Times*.

55 *The Spectator*, 22 November 1986.

56 Frank Johnson, 'Plain John Smith takes the honours', *The Times*, 20 November 1986.

57 A Scottish drinking vessel.

58 Interview with Rt Hon. Lord Hattersley, 3

March 2003.

59 *Observer Profile*, John Smith, 2 November 1986, in Low (ed), *The Observer Book of Profiles*, p. 238.

60 Interview with Ann Barrett, 21 June 2003.

61 *Newsnight*, BBC 2, 27 May 1987.

62 BBC News coverage, 1 June 1987.

63 Butler and Kavanagh get the date wrong for the *Election Call* programme, placing it on 22 May, five days earlier. David Butler and Dennis Kavanagh, *The British General Election of 1987* (Macmillan: Basingstoke, 1988), pp. 122–123. Curiously, Andy McSmith's biography of Smith has nothing to say on this episode.

64 McSmith, *John Smith*, pp. 110–11.

65 Interview with Dr J. Dickson Mabon, 15 May 2003.

66 Labour Party election broadcast, 21 May 1987.

67 Labour Party election broadcast, 8 June 1987.

68 BBC election night coverage, 11 June 1987.

69 Ruth Wishart, 'Fit to shadow the Chancellor', *The Scotsman*, 23 January 1989.

70 'Profile: John Smith – Serious about power', *The Independent*, 12 March 1988.

Chapter 11

1 In 1987, the shadow Cabinet comprised 22 members of whom fifteen were elected. Another seven, including the leader, Neil Kinnock, and his deputy, Roy Hattersley, were ex-officio members, together with the Chief Whip and the PLP chairman.

2 Richardson was rewarded with a new post – shadow Minister for Women's Rights. Henry Pelling and Alastair J. Reid, *A Short History of the Labour Party* (Macmillan Press Ltd: 11th edn, Basingstoke, 1996) p. 179. Henry Pelling, an academic at both Oxford and Cambridge, died in October 1997.

3 Caroline Rees, 'shadow Cabinet now has Tribune Group majority', *Tribune*, 10 July 1987.

4 Interview with Baroness Goudie, 21 January 2004.

5 In his biography of Neil Kinnock, Martin Westlake inaccurately lists John Smith as shadow Home Secretary, a post he never held. Westlake, *Kinnock*, p. 424.

6 Donald Macintyre, *Mandelson. The Biography* (HarperCollins Publishers: London, 1999), p. 140.

7 Roy Hattersley, *Who Goes Home? Scenes from a Political Life* (Warner Books: London, 1996), p. 283.

8 Bryan. Gould, *Goodbye to All That* (Macmillan: Basingstoke, 1995), pp. 195–6.

9 Gould, *Goodbye to All That*, p. 197; Macintyre, *Mandelson*, p. 155.

10 Hattersley, *Who Goes Home?*, pp. 288–9.

11 Gould, *Goodbye to All That*, p. 196.

12 Kinnock initially offered Prescott Transport, but Prescott refused. Prescott then asked for the Defence portfolio, but had to settle for Energy. Brown, *Fighting Talk*, pp. 172–3.

13 Anderson and Mann, *Safety First*, p. 67.

14 Elizabeth Smith, 'Introduction', in Brown and Naughtie, *Life and Soul of the Party*, p. 13.

15 Interview with Lord McCluskey, 13 May 2003.

16 A large shipment of whisky was transported to the Middle East. John Smith's clients were the 'liner agents' for the sellers (the 'principals'). The 'purchasers' of the whisky contracted with the agents to buy it for X dinars per case. The exchange rate was approximately 0.65 dinars to the pound. The agents invoiced the goods to the purchasers in sterling. Having done so, they should have sought payment for the sterling equivalent of X dinars, which is £X *divided* by 0.65, which yields approximately one-and-a-half times £X. Instead, they invoiced for £X *multiplied* by 0.65, which yielded about two-thirds of £X. The purchasers happily paid up on the – surprisingly low – invoices. But when the principals asked their agents for the money, the agents discovered that they had sought and received only about 40 per cent of the full price from the purchasers. The purchasers, not surprisingly, refused to pay any more than the invoiced price; and the balance was not recoverable from them. The legal point in dispute became, which of the other parties involved – the agent or the principals – should bear the loss. The answer, after somewhat complicated proceedings, was that the agents should bear the loss because ultimately it was they who had made the mistake. *Trans Barwil Agencies (UK) Ltd v*

John S. Braid & Co Ltd (No. 2), reported in *Scots Law Times*, 1990, p.182.

17 Interview with Lord McCluskey.

18 Interview with Rt Hon. Lord Healey of Riddlesden CH MBE, 12 February 2003.

19 Fiona Millar, interview with John Smith, *She Magazine*, final proofs, 10 November 1992. Murray Elder papers, Box 2.

20 Interview with Ann Barrett, 21 June 2003.

21 From 1981–5, Ward had worked with the World Development Movement, a Non-Governmental Organisation (NGO), dealing with development issues.

22 Rt Hon. John Smith QC MP, speech to Overseas Development Council, Washington DC, 14 October 1987. David Ward papers.

23 Interview with David Ward, 28 April 2003.

24 Interview with Rt Hon. Lord Hattersley, 3 March 2003.

25 Interview with Murray Elder, 26 November 2002; interview with David Ward.

26 Interview with Rt Hon. Chris Smith MP, 11 February 2003.

27 Ibid.

28 Interview with David Ward, 7 June 2003; McSmith, *John Smith*, p. 182.

29 See Macintyre, *Mandelson*, pp. 156–159. Martin Westlake mistakenly records this meeting as occurring in August 1988, a year later. Westlake, *Kinnock*, p. 460.

30 Macintyre, *Mandelson*, p. 156.

31 Macintyre, *Mandelson*, p. 157.

32 Interview with Rt Hon. Lord Hattersley.

33 Interview with Baroness Smith of Gilmorehill DL, 26 November 2002.

34 Interview with Rt Hon. Chris Smith MP.

35 Interview with Rt Hon. Lord Hattersley.

36 Interview with David Ward.

37 Private information.

38 See for example, 'Must Kinnock go?' *The Economist*, 18 June 1988; Edward Pearce, 'A leader too far', *New Statesman & Society*, 22 July 1988; R. W. Johnson, 'Loss leader', *New Statesman & Society*, 28 July 1989.

39 Westlake, *Kinnock*, p. 461.

40 Interview with David Ward.

41 Interview with Rt Hon. Lord Hattersley.

42 Hattersley, *Who Goes Home?*, p. 291.

43 In 1988, Ron Todd's union held around one fifth of the union block votes at Labour Party conferences within the electoral college.

44 Officially, the EETPU was expelled from the TUC for refusing to abide by the 'Bridlington principles' of 1939 that forbade unions from poaching each other's members. Unofficially, the union was expelled for entering into single-union, no-strike deals with large companies.

45 'The Labour Leadership Debate', *Newsnight Special*, BBC 2, 2 October 1988.

46 Brown, *Fighting Talk*, p. 184.

47 McSmith, *John Smith*, p. 164; Robert Gilson, 'How party wrangles took their toll on Labour's top star', *Daily Express*, 11 October 1988.

48 Lewis Chester, 'The Scorning Scotsman', *Independent on Sunday*, 26 May 1991.

49 Elizabeth Smith, 'Introduction', in Brown and Naughtie, *Life and Soul of the Party*, p. 14. Unfortunately, in this account, Elizabeth recalls the date of her husband's first attack as October 1989 when in fact it occurred a year earlier.

50 *Desert Island Discs*, BBC Radio Four (transmitted, 28 May 1991), in Brown and Naughtie, *Life and Soul of the Party*, p. 156 (transcript).

51 Interview with Ruth Wishart, 15 January 2004.

52 Kate Muir, 'Red Rose of Taxes', *The Times* (Saturday Review), 14 March 1992.

53 Interview with Ruth Wishart.

54 Lynda Lee-Potter, 'Luck that saved John Smith's life', *Daily Mail*, 26 January 1989.

55 Interview with Rt Hon. Lord Irvine of Lairg PC QC, 30 April 2003.

56 Interview with Kenneth Munro, 29 September 2003.

57 'A Day in the Life of . . . John Smith', *The Sunday Times Magazine*, 7 January 1990.

58 Telephone interview with Rt Hon. Sir Malcolm Rifkind KCMG QC, 7 January 2004.

59 E-mail correspondence with Rt Hon. Lord Fraser of Carmyllie QC, 16 February 2004.

60 Interview with Lord McCluskey.

61 Interview with Rt Hon. Lord [Ranald] MacLean, 18 November 2003.

62 E-mail correspondence with Rt Hon. Lord Fraser of Carmyllie QC.

63 Interview with Baroness Smith of Gilmorehill DL, 4 December 2002.

64 Written correspondence between Rt Hon. John Smith QC MP and Elizabeth Thomas, 31 October 1988. Reproduced by kind permission of Elizabeth Thomas.

65 Ruth Wishart, 'Tribute', *The Scotsman*, 13 May 1994.

66 John Smith, 'Diary: Casting the first, and second, stone', *The Guardian*, 7 January 1989.

67 Interview with Ruth Wishart.

68 Interview with Lord Gordon of Strathblane CBE, 12 March 2003.

69 John Smith, 'Diary: Casting the first, and second, stone', op. cit.

70 Donald Macintyre, 'A man to put heart into the economy', *Sunday Correspondent*, 30 September 1990.

71 Kate Muir, 'Red Rose of Taxes', *The Times* (Saturday Review), 14 March 1992.

72 *Kilroy*, BBC 1, 11 April 1989.

73 Interview with Professor Sir Neil MacCormick, 3 October 2003.

74 Adam Nicolson, 'Iona: Smith's inspiration becomes his resting place', *Sunday Telegraph*, 22 May 1994.

75 *Desert Island Discs*, BBC Radio Four (transmitted, 28 May 1991), in Brown and Naughtie, *Life and Soul of the Party*, p. 156 (transcript).

76 Interview with Ruth Wishart.

77 *Desert Island Discs*, Brown and Naughtie, *Life and Soul of the Party*, p. 152; pp. 155–6 (transcript).

78 Interview with Ruth Wishart.

79 Lord McCluskey, *Question Time Special*, BBC 1, Thursday, 12 May 1994 (transcript).

80 Interview with Lord McCluskey.

81 Principal Private Secretary to Rt Hon. Gordon Campbell MC, and Rt Hon. William Ross MBE from 1973–5.

82 Written correspondence with Professor Sir Neil MacCormick, 4 October 2004.

83 The Lairig Ghru presents a reasonable challenge for an inexperienced walker. At the height of the Pass – which 'Lairig' means in Gaelic – it reaches 3,000 feet. Interview with Rt Hon. Lord [Ranald] MacLean.

84 Ibid.

85 Ibid.

86 Interview with Rt Hon. Sir Menzies Campbell CBE QC MP, 20 January 2004.

87 Interview with Sir Gavin Laird CBE, 21 January 2004.

88 Interview with Rt Hon. Lord [Ranald] MacLean.

89 Interview with Sir Gavin Laird CBE; interview with Rt Hon. Lord [Ranald] MacLean.

90 Interview with Alan Haworth, 15 December 2003.

91 Interview with Lord Mackay of Drumadoon, 11 November 2003; interview with Rt Hon. Lord [Ranald] MacLean.

92 Sir Hugo Munro tabulated all the Munros in the late Victorian period, but he died with just one Munro left to climb.

93 Interview with Alan Haworth.

94 Ibid.

95 Interview with Rt Hon. Chris Smith.

96 Henderson entered Parliament as the Labour MP for Newcastle upon Tyne North in 1987, and subsequently became Minister of State at the Foreign and Commonwealth on the election of New Labour in 1997. A year, later he was shifted sideways to Minister of State for the Armed Forces at the Ministry of Defence, before being sacked from the government in July 1999.

97 Moonie had become Labour MP for Kirkcaldy in 1987, and in 2000 entered the Blair government as Parliamentary Under-Secretary of State at the Ministry of Defence. Since June 2003, he has been on the Labour back benches.

98 John Smith, 'Munro Diary', Diary reading with Alan Haworth, 15 December 2003. Haworth reckons that Smith probably fell 800 feet, but still a long way.

99 Ibid.

100 Interview with Alan Haworth.

101 On a second attempt at Bynack More, John was foiled by fog, but he finally bagged it on his third attempt on 14 August 1993, his 105th Munro. Interview with Alan Haworth.

102 Murray Elder, 'The Munros' in Brown and Naughtie, *Life and Soul of the Party*, p. 127.

103 Interview with Alan Haworth.

104 HC Debs, 25 October 1988, cc. 173–181.

105 Ruth Wishart, 'Fit to shadow the Chancellor', *The Scotsman*, 23 January 1989.

106 Butler and Butler, *British Political Facts, 1900–1994*, p. 142.

107 McSmith, *John Smith*, p. 169.

108 Interview with Rt Hon. Thomas Clarke JP MP, 20 January 2004.

109 Galbraith is a consultant neurosurgeon by profession, and served as the Labour MP for Strathkelvin and Bearsden from 1987–2001. From 1999, Galbraith was an MSP in the Scottish Parliament, serving in

the Scottish Executive as Education Minister (under Donald Dewar), and subsequently at Environment (under Henry McLeish), until ill health forced him to resign in March 2001. He stood down at the May 2003 Scottish parliamentary elections, at which point Strathkelvin and Bearsden was won by Dr Jean Turner, an Independent.

110 Ruth Wishart, 'Fit to shadow the Chancellor', *The Scotsman*, 23 January 1989.

111 Interview with Ann Barrett.

112 *The Government's expenditure plans 1989–90 to 1991–92*, Chapter 8, Department of Transport (Cm. 608), Chart 8.20, p. 17.

113 HC Debs, 9 February 1989, c. 1159.

114 See for example, John Smith, 'Diary: Casting the first, and second, stone', *The Guardian*, 7 January 1989; Maureen Cleave interview with John Smith, 'Smiling John Smith', *Telegraph Weekend Magazine*, 17 March 1990.

115 *Wogan*, BBC1, 25 May 1988; 1 February 1989; 20 January 1992.

116 Bryan Gould polled 9 per cent and John Prescott 4 per cent. Patrick Seyd and Paul Whiteley, *Labour's Grass Roots. The Politics of Party Membership* (Clarendon Press: Oxford, 1992), p. 159.

117 Seyd and Whiteley, *Labour's Grass Roots*, pp. 49–50.

118 Seyd and Whiteley, *Labour's Grass Roots*, p. 154.

119 Bruce Anderson, 'Could Mr Smith go to Downing Street?', *Sunday Telegraph*, 8 October 1989.

120 McSmith, *John Smith*, p. 187.

121 Maureen Cleave, 'Smiling John Smith', *Daily Telegraph Magazine*, 3 March 1990.

122 Lawson also suggested to Mrs Thatcher at the time that the Bank of England should be made independent, as another means of controlling inflation, but the Prime Minister rejected the idea.

123 Thatcher had famously said that 'you can't buck the market', while Walters believed the idea of Britain entering the ERM was 'half-baked'. See Nigel Lawson, *The View from No. 11. Memoirs of a Tory Radical* (Corgi Books: paperback edn, London, 1993), pp. 505–8; Young, *One of Us*, p. 551.

124 HC Debs, 7 June 1989, c. 248.

125 HC Debs, 7 June 1989, c. 248.

126 Brian Griffiths, Special Adviser to Mrs Thatcher and Head of the Prime Minister's Policy Unit, 1985–1990.

127 HC Debs, 7 June 1989, c. 249.

128 HC Debs, 7 June 1989, c. 249.

129 Interview with Baroness Smith of Gilmorehill DL, 26 November 2002.

130 Interview with David Ward; interview with Ann Barrett.

131 Interview with Baroness Smith of Gilmorehill DL.

132 Interview with Rt Hon. Michael Foot, 20 February 2003.

133 John Smith, 'Lawson all at sea in a Barber boom', *The Sunday Times*, 14 August 1988. Mentioned in John Sweeney, 'MacBuddha: the Tory's bogeyman', *Evening Standard*, 12 September 1988.

134 Interview with Baroness Smith of Gilemorehill DL.

135 HC Debs, 24 October 1989, c. 688.

136 HC Debs, 24 October 1989, c. 689.

137 HC Debs, 24 October 1989, c. 689.

138 Philip Stephens, *Politics and the Pound. The Conservatives' Struggle with Sterling* (Macmillan: Basingstoke, 1996), p. 134.

139 *Question Time*, BBC 1, 21 June 1990.

140 Simon Heffer, 'Out of the shadows', *Daily Telegraph*, 2 November 1989; Michael Cassell and Peter Norman, 'Man in the News – John Smith: Advocate of a social democratic economy for Britain', *Financial Times*, 4 November 1989.

141 Peter Jenkins, 'Labour's most precious asset', *The Independent*, 31 October 1989.

142 Michael Cassell and Peter Norman, op. cit.

143 HC Debs, 31 October 1989, cc. 191–200.

144 HC Debs, 31 October 1989, cc. 200–201.

145 The other judges in 1989 were: Noel Malcolm of *The Spectator*, Alan Watkins of *The Observer*, Colin Welch of the *Daily Mail*, Ian Aitken of *The Guardian* and Simon Heffer of the *Daily Telegraph*.

146 *The Spectator*, 25 November 1989.

147 In the shadow Cabinet poll, Robin Cook finished third, Blair fourth and Kaufman fifth. Pelling and Reid, *A Short History of the Labour Party*, p. 181.

148 For a good example of a boring Smith speech in this period, see Brivati (ed.), *Guiding Light*, pp. 117–32; HC Debs, 23 January 1990, cc. 758–768.

149 Anthony Seldon, *Major. A Political Life* (Weidenfeld & Nicolson: London, 1997), p. 104.

150 Interview with Rt Hon. Chris Smith MP.

151 HC Debs, 21 March 1990, cc. 1125–1134.
152 Interview with David Ward, 7 June 2003.
153 E-mail correspondence with Rt Hon. Neil Kinnock, 22 October 2004.
154 *Newsnight*, BBC 2, 28 September 1990.
155 Bagehot, 'June's budget, in March', *The Economist*, 23 March 1991.
156 Interview with Rt Hon. Chris Smith MP.

Chapter 12

1 Each of Labour's policy review groups was co-chaired by two convenors, one a member of the NEC, and the other the party's shadow Cabinet spokesperson for the subject under review. The rest of a typical group comprised three front bench Labour MPs, three more members of the NEC, a secretary from the party's policy-development directorate, and a researcher. Although such joint NEC-PLP committees had first been established in early 1984, it was only by 1987 that they had become formalised in this way. Wickham-Jones, *Economic Strategy and the Labour Party*, p. 216.
2 Interview with Rt Hon. Chris Smith MP, 11 February 2003.
3 Private information.
4 Wickham-Jones, *Economic Strategy and the Labour Party*, p. 216.
5 Interview with Lord Eatwell, 24 November 2003.
6 Steven Fielding, *The Labour Party: Continuity and Change in the Making of New Labour* (Palgrave Macmillan: Basingstoke, 2002), p. 74.
7 HC Debs, 15 March 1988, c. 1017.
8 Lewis Chester, 'The Scorning Scotsman', *Independent on Sunday*, 26 May 1991.
9 Interview with Rt Hon. Chris Smith MP.
10 Tony Benn, *The End of An Era, Diaries 1980–1990*, edited by Ruth Winstone (Arrow Books Ltd: London, 1994), p. 544. (Wednesday, 25 May 1988).
11 Labour Party, *Meet the Challenge, Make the Change: A New Agenda for Britain* (Labour Party: London, 1989).
12 Anderson and Mann, *Safety First*, p. 70; Bryan Gould, *A Future for Socialism* (Jonathan Cape: London, 1989), pp. 137–49.
13 Interview with David Ward, 7 June 2003.
14 For examples of very dull interviews, see Jonathan Dimbleby, interview with John Smith, *On the Record*, transcript, 1 October 1989; BBC Press Service, from the editor, David Dimbleby interviews Rt Hon. John Smith QC MP, Tuesday, 3 October 1989; TV-am, *Frost on Sunday*, interview with John Smith, (transcript), 20 October 1991 and 12 January 1992. David Ward papers.
15 Interview with David Ward.
16 Gavyn Davies, 'Economic Strategy for the Next Labour Government' undated, 1990 (pre-ERM entry, probably February 1990). Kinnock Collection, Box 163.
17 In Germany, a certain level of banks' reserves, known as a minimum reserve ratio, were deposited at the Bundesbank. Jeff Lovitt, interview with John Smith, 'Safe in Labour's hands?', *Tribune*, 7 September 1990.
18 *The Economist*, 17 February 1990.
19 Peter Rodgers, 'Smith on a loser with credit control', *The Independent*, 23 August 1990.
20 Interview with Sir Gavin Laird CBE, 21 January 2004.
21 Letter from Rt Hon. John Smith QC MP to Eric Hammond OBE, general secretary, EEPTU, 24 July 1989. David Ward papers.
22 Labour Party, *Opportunity Britain* (Labour Party: London, April 1991), p. 37. Minimum Wage Policies, 1991. Kinnock Collection, Box 422.
23 *Channel Four News*, 5 June 1991.
24 *Daily Telegraph*, 17 June 1991.
25 *Newsnight*, BBC2, 26 April 1991.
26 *The One o'Clock News*, BBC1, 4 July 1991.
27 Michael White and Will Hutton, 'Lad o'parts a man for all seasons', *The Guardian*, 9 March 1992.
28 Interview with Sir Gavin Laird CBE.
29 Interview with David Ward.
30 Blair had finished an impressive fifth in the shadow Cabinet elections.
31 Gould, *Goodbye to All That*, p. 221.
32 Wickham-Jones, *Economic Strategy and the Labour Party*, p. 216.
33 Interview with Rt Hon. Chris Smith MP, 11 February 2003.
34 E-mail correspondence with Andrew Graham, 8 November 2004.
35 Interview with Lord Desai, 10 June 2003.
36 In 1996 Currie was raised to the peerage as Lord Currie of Marylebone.
37 Anderson and Mann, *Safety First*, p. 399; interview with Lord Eatwell.
38 Letter from Chris Smith to Neil Kinnock

(undated, c. 1990). Economic and Monetary Union, Kinnock Collection, Box 117.

39 Jones, *Remaking the Labour Party*, p. 126; Shaw, *The Labour Party Since 1979*, pp. 94–5; Anderson and Mann, *Safety First*, p. 73; Fielding, *The Labour Party*, p. 73.

40 Jeff Lovitt, op. cit.

41 Ibid.

42 Interview with Lord Desai.

43 Jones, *Remaking the Labour Party*, p. 126.

44 Rt Hon. John Smith QC MP, speech to the German Chamber of Commerce, 19 June 1991. David Ward papers. See also *Financial Times*, 20 June 1991; Bagehot, 'Sozial partnerschaft', *The Economist*, 16 November 1991.

45 Interview with Kenneth Munro, 18 November 2003.

46 Between May and December 1991, the secretariat and other researchers produced 28 briefing papers on economic policy. Economic Brief, 1991 and 1992. Kinnock Collection, Box 429.

47 Interview with David Ward and Emma Maclennan, 7 June 2003.

48 Dan Corry and Cathy Ashley, 'Budget Brief 1989', prepared by the shadow Cabinet Economic Secretariat, 8 March 1989. Kinnock Collection, Box 425.

49 Interview with David Ward.

50 Interview with Emma Maclennan, 8 June 2003.

51 *The Economist*, 14 April 1990.

52 Interview with Rt Hon. Margaret Beckett MP, 19 November 2003.

53 Interview with David Ward.

54 Kampfner, *Robin Cook*, p. 85.

55 McSmith, *Faces of Labour*, p. 325.

56 The 'economic foursome' later appeared in a party political broadcast with Neil Kinnock in April 1991. It is also worth pointing out here that although Robin Cook held the Health and Social Security portfolio, along with the 'economic foursome', he rapidly proved himself to be an incisive debater in the House of Commons and a good performer on television and radio.

57 Shaw, *The Labour Party Since 1979*, p. 132.

58 Dan Corry, 'Economic Policy After the Review' Draft, shadow Cabinet Economic Secretariat, 22 June 1989. Minutes of the Economic Sub-Committee. Kinnock Collection, Box 429.

59 Dan Corry, 'Public Spending: Some Issues' (Economic Policy Sub-Committee, February 1990). Kinnock Collection, Box 163.

60 E-mail correspondence with Dan Corry, 11 November 2004.

61 Interview with David Ward, 28 April 2003.

62 Notes to NK [Neil Kinnock] from Gordon Brown, undated. c. 1990. shadow Cabinet briefings. Kinnock Collection, Box 83.

63 Margaret Beckett, 13 February 1990. Quoted in John Eatwell, 'Public Spending: Some Issues', (Economic Policy Committee, February 1990). Kinnock Collection, Box 163; minutes of the Third Meeting of the Economic Policy Sub-Committee held on 26 February 1990, W1, House of Commons. Kinnock Collection, Box 163.

64 Interview with David Ward.

65 Interview with Rt Hon. Margaret Beckett MP.

66 Labour Party, *Looking to the Future* (Labour Party: London, 1990).

67 By 1992, Labour's general election manifesto, *It's Time to Get Britain Working Again* (Labour Party: London, 1992), had earmarked water for public control, rather than public ownership. Anderson and Mann, *Safety First*, p. 72.

68 Anderson and Mann, *Safety First*, p. 212.

69 Indeed, Gordon Brown has abolished both the married couples allowance and mortgage interest rate relief at all income levels.

70 Another problem for Smith lay in the unfairness for middle-income earners inherent in the British tax system. In 1992, the moment employees earned more than £20,280, they paid a marginal rate of tax of 34 per cent (25 per cent in income tax; 9 per cent in national insurance); but if they earned one pound less than that, then their marginal rate of tax was just 25 per cent. Voters earning incomes of around £20,000 and upwards (and £20,000 was not much above the average incomes of £17,000) were therefore acutely sensitive to the idea of higher taxes.

71 Kenneth Baker, *The Turbulent Years. My Life in Politics* (Faber and Faber: London, 1993), pp. 344–8.

72 A note from the policy director to the Policy Review Group Convenors, 'Preparing for Government. Future Work

on Policy Development', November 1989 (PD: 2334). Kinnock Collection, Box 163.

73 A note from the policy director, 'Home Policy / International / Local Government Committees: Work of the Policy Review Groups', PD 2360, January 1990. Kinnock Collection, Box 163. (Larry Whitty's note, referring to the NEC's agreement in December 1989 of the 'next phase' of the policy review is also mentioned in this document.)

74 Minutes of the First Meeting of the Economic Policy Sub-Committee held on 29 January 1990, W4, House of Commons. Kinnock Collection, Box 163.

75 Andrew Graham, Smith's main economic adviser, also attended the Economic Policy Sub-Committee, as well as sitting in on several of the meetings of the shadow Cabinet. E-mail correspondence with Andrew Graham, 8 November 2004.

76 Interview with Rt Hon. Margaret Beckett MP.

77 Minutes of the first meeting of the Economic Policy Sub-Committee held on 29 January 1990, op. cit. Such items were actually agreed at the sub-committee's meeting on 14 November 1989.

78 John Eatwell [unsigned], briefing meeting of Economic Sub-Committee, 16 January 1990, 5 pm in shadow Cabinet Room, Minutes of Economic Policy Sub-Committee, 1989. Kinnock Collection, Box 429.

79 Minutes of the second meeting of the Economic Policy Sub-Committee held on 12 February 1990, W4, House of Commons. Kinnock Collection, Box 163.

80 Minutes of the third meeting of the Economic Policy Sub-Committee held on 26 February 1990, W1, House of Commons. Kinnock Collection, Box 163.

81 Minutes of the fifth meeting of the Economic Policy Sub-Committee held on 26 March 1990, W4, House of Commons. Kinnock Collection, Box 163.

82 Interview with David Ward, 7 June 2003.

83 Cunningham finished eighteenth in the shadow Cabinet elections in 1989, and became Labour's campaign co-ordinator and shadow leader of the House of Commons, positions he held until 1992.

84 Before entering Parliament, Blunkett had been leader of Sheffield City Council from 1980–7.

85 *Local Services, Local Choices, Local Taxes. Labour's Approach to the Poll Tax, the National Business Tax and the Reform of Local Government Finance* (Labour Party: London, 1990).

86 Gould, *Goodbye to All That*, p. 230.

87 Gould, *Goodbye to All That*, p. 229.

88 Interview with Lord Eatwell.

89 Interview with Rt Hon. Margaret Beckett MP.

90 John Eatwell, briefing paper to Neil Kinnock, re Economic Sub-Committee, 30 January 1990 – 'Meeting devoted to Bryan Gould's alternative to poll tax', Minutes of Economic Sub-Committee, Kinnock Collection, Box 429.

91 John Eatwell to Neil Kinnock, 'Note for Meeting with Bryan Gould', 21 May 1990. Poll Tax. Kinnock Collection, Box 524.

92 Ibid.

93 Nicholas Timmins, 'Profile: John Smith: Confidently waiting in the wings', *The Independent*, 22 March 1990.

94 Interview with Rt Hon. Margaret Beckett MP.

Chapter 13

1 Interview with David Ward, 7 June 2003.

2 Baker feared a collapse of the dollar. For more details, see Lawson, *The View from No. 11*, pp. 535–40.

3 Rt Hon. John Smith QC MP, 'Interdependence, Exchange Rates and the International Economy', speech to the American Chamber of Commerce (UK) lunch, Intercontinental Hotel, London, Wednesday, 22 March 1989. David Ward papers.

4 Again, see Lawson, *The View from No. 11*, pp. 552–7.

5 The G7 emerged when the five largest capitalist economies – Britain, France, the United States, Germany and Japan – admitted Italy and Canada. The heads of government met annually, but the finance ministers had more regular meetings. Lawson, *The View from No. 11*, p. 556–7.

6 Rt Hon. John Smith QC MP, 'Interdependence, Exchange Rates and the International Economy', speech to the American Chamber of Commerce (UK) lunch, Intercontinental Hotel, London, Wednesday, 22 March 1989; Smith's speech was subsequently turned into an

article for *Atlantic*, the journal of the American Chamber of Commerce (UK) in May 1989. David Ward papers.

7   At this point in time, Labour opposed an independent Bank of England because they believed it would be run by unelected bankers, and would not be subject to democratic control by politicians. For the same reason, they also opposed the idea of a European Central Bank put forward at the time by the Delors Committee on Monetary Union, chaired by the European Commission President, Jacques Delors.

8   Stephens, *Politics and the Pound*, pp. 106–7.

9   Gould, *Goodbye to All That*, pp. 216–7.

10 Gould, *A Future for Socialism*, p. 83.

11 Report of the Parliamentary Committee meeting, Wednesday, 28 June 1989. David Ward papers; Eric Shaw, *The Labour Party Since 1979*, p. 97. Neil Kinnock stresses that it was important to keep Gould 'on board', and obviously Gould was more tied in than ever when 'his' condition had been accepted. E-mail correspondence with Rt Hon. Neil Kinnock, 22 October 2004.

12 Cathy Ashley, minutes of the Economic Sub-Committee meeting, 27 June 1989. (6 July 1989). Minutes of Economic Sub-Committee, 1989. Kinnock Collection, Box 429; Report of the Parliamentary Committee Meeting held on Wednesday, 28 June 1989. David Ward papers.

13 These were known as the 'Madrid' conditions, agreed at the Madrid Summit in May 1989. Principally, the United Kingdom agreed to take further measures to reduce its inflation rate, make progress against inflation, while the European Community would make progress on the completion of the single market, including the abolition of exchange controls. However, the adoption of a single currency would, according to Mrs Thatcher, not be acceptable to the House of Commons. Geoffrey Howe, *Conflict of Loyalty* (Macmillan: London, 1994), p. 582; Young, *One of Us*, pp. 556–9.

14 John Major, *The Autobiography* (HarperCollins*Publishers*: London, 1999), p. 151. Paul Richards from Samuel Montagu and Sir Michael Butler, a former Foreign Office official, came up with the hard ecu idea.

15 Jeremy Paxman, interview with John

Smith, *Newsnight*, BBC2, 21 June 1990.

16 HC Debs, 23 October 1990, cc. 269–277.

17 Interview with David Ward.

18 David Gow and Will Hutton, 'Pohl dents hopes for ERM entry', *The Guardian*, 20 September 1990.

19 Interview with Rt Hon. Frank Dobson, MP, 24 April 2003.

20 *Financial Times*, 2 October 1989.

21 David Buchan, 'Labour "willing to look at EMU"', *Financial Times*, 19 October 1989.

22 Rt Hon. John Smith QC MP, statement to the Socialist Group of the European Parliament, Brussels, Wednesday, 18 October 1989. David Ward papers; *The Independent*, 19 October 1989.

23 Interview with David Ward.

24 See Martin Kettle, 'Red carpet for the envoy with a red rose', *The Guardian*, 20 October 1989.

25 David Ward, extract from note of meeting between John Smith and Michel Rocard, Paris, October 1989. David Ward papers.

26 E-mail correspondence with David Ward, 7 November 2004.

27 David Ward, extract from note of meeting between John Smith and Karl Otto Pohl, Bundesbank, Frankfurt, October 1989. David Ward papers.

28 Michael Jones, 'It's all change for the role reversal express', *The Sunday Times*, 22 October 1989.

29 Martin Kettle, 'Red carpet for the envoy with a red rose', *The Guardian*, 20 October 1989.

30 Maureen Cleave, 'Smiling John Smith', *Weekend Telegraph Magazine*, 17 March 1990. From 1986 onwards, Labour held six-monthly Joint Economic Policy Committees meeting with the West German SPD (September 1989), and after the fall of the Berlin Wall, Konrad Elmer from the SPD in the old East Germany joined Wolfgang Roth, leader of the old West German SPD, at these joint gatherings. John Smith, opening statement to the Labour Party/SPD Commission on European Affairs, London, 2 April 1990, New Release. David Ward papers.

31 Quoted in Peter Shore, *Leading the Left* (Weidenfeld & Nicolson: London, 1993), p. 183.

32 In July 1986, Andrew Graham had edited a Labour Economic Policy Group (LEPG)

Report, which was sent to Neil Kinnock. E-mail correspondence with Andrew Graham, 8 November 2004.

33 Fax from Chris Allsopp (New College, Oxford) to John Eatwell, 'The case of the UK: credibility', 25 February 1990. Kinnock Collection, Box 163.

34 Gavyn Davies, 'Economic Strategy for the Next Labour Government' undated, 1990 (pre-ERM entry, probably February 1990). Kinnock Collection, Box 163.

35 Labour did not have a credible incomes policy in place for the 1992 general election, despite being warned about this weakness. Ken Coutts and Wynne Godley, 'Macro-economic strategy in 1991–1992' (undated, probably February 1990). Kinnock Collection, Box 163. Coutts and Godley also warned about high unemployment inside the ERM. Again, many of these issues had been first aired by Andrew Graham in his July 1986 LEPG report. E-mail correspondence with Andrew Graham, 8 November 2004.

36 Gavyn Davies, 'Economic Strategy for the Next Labour Government', op. cit.

37 Andrew Graham, 'Updating the Policy Review. Macro-economic Policy', 20 February 1990. Kinnock Collection, Box 163.

38 Speech by Rt Hon. John Smith MP to the EPLP Business Conference, 'What Future for the North East?', Newcastle, Monday, 16 September 1991. Kinnock Collection, Box 116.

39 David Ward, 'Economic and Monetary Union', Economic Policy Sub-Committee, 12 February 1990. David Ward papers.

40 Neil Kinnock's notes, shadow Cabinet discussion, 7 November 1990. Economic and Monetary Union, Kinnock Collection, Box 117.

41 Frank Dobson, 'Ways of Formulating and Executing Monetary Policy', November 1990. Economic and Monetary Union, Kinnock Collection, Box 117; Frank Dobson, 'European Central Bank: Summary of Points for Discussion' re. meeting of the Economic Sub-Committee, 30 August 1991, Carlton Highland Hotel, Edinburgh, Kinnock Collection, Box 116.

42 Interview with Rt Hon. Frank Dobson MP.

43 The Intergovernmental Conference on Economic and Monetary Union: A Position Paper (prepared following shadow Cabinet discussion on 7th Nov [1990]). Economic and Monetary Union, Kinnock Collection, Box 117.

44 NEC, 'Labour's Approach to the Intergovernmental Conference on Economic and Monetary Union and subsequent developments in the European Community', Wednesday, 28 November 1990. European Community, 1991. Kinnock Collection, Box 460; NEC press release, 'The Intergovernmental Conference on Economic and Monetary Union', 28 November 1990. Kinnock Collection, Box 116.

45 Anderson and Mann, Safety First, p. 136.

46 Nigel Spearing, Labour Common Market Safeguards Committee, 'Euro-Money, Fool's Gold and Labour', undated. c. November/December 1990. Kinnock Collection, Box 96.

47 Speech by the Rt Hon. John Smith QC MP, shadow Chancellor of the Exchequer, to the Royal Institute of International Affairs, Chatham House, on Tuesday 29 January 1991 – 'The Future of the European Community'. Kinnock Collection, Box 116.

48 Note from John Eatwell to Neil Kinnock, re: draft statement for NEC meeting on Monday, 8 July 1991. Kinnock Collection, Box 116.

49 The NEC meeting was being convened to discuss the talks at the Confederation of Socialist Parties of the European Community (CONFED) that had taken place in Luxembourg in early June 1991, the Luxembourg EC Summit, and progress in the Intergovernmental Conference on Economic and Monetary Union.

50 Note from John Eatwell to Neil Kinnock, op. cit.

51 Westlake, Kinnock, p. 508. Westlake draws on evidence here from the Kinnock archive in Churchill College, Cambridge, Box 116.

52 'Private and confidential', To: John Eatwell (copy to The Rt Hon. Neil Kinnock MP) From: John Smith, 1 July 1991, 'Europe Paper'. Kinnock Collection, Box 116.

53 Interview with Rt Hon. Frank Dobson MP.

54 'Private and confidential', To: John Eatwell, op. cit.
55 Stuart, *Douglas Hurd*, p. 285.
56 Interview with Lord Eatwell, 24 November 2003; *The Nine o'Clock News*, BBC 1, 30 August 1991; Lord Davies of Oldman, secretary of the PLP and the shadow Cabinet from 1979–92, recalls that the Economic Sub-Committee did indeed meet in Edinburgh. Many thanks are due to Alan Haworth for eliciting this information from Lord Davies.
57 Rt Hon. John Smith QC MP, speech to Deutsche Bank Seminar, Berlin, Thursday, 12 September 1991. David Ward papers.
58 George Robertson MP, 'The EC Intergovernmental Conferences – A Labour Strategy', undated, c. autumn 1991 (post Labour Party conference, but before 24 October 1991 – meeting of CONFED). European Community, 1991. Kinnock Collection, Box 460.
59 Interview with Rt Hon. Chris Smith MP, 11 February 2003.
60 Interview with David Ward, 28 April 2003.
61 Article 107 of the Maastricht Treaty clearly stated that there would be no accountability.
62 Rt Hon. John Smith QC MP, speech to the Association for the Monetary Union of Europe and the Institut Français des Relations Internationales, Paris, Wednesday, 5 February 1992.
63 Westlake, *Kinnock*, p. 508.

Chapter 14

1 HC Debs, 19 February 1992, c. 363.
2 Interview with Rt Hon. Chris Smith MP, 11 February 2003.
3 Interview with Rt Hon. Paul Boateng MP, 6 September 2004.
4 Julia Langdon, *Mo Mowlam. The Biography* (Little, Brown and Company: London, 2000), p. 182.
5 Interview with Rt Hon. Chris Smith MP.
6 Interview with Rt Hon. Paul Boateng MP.
7 Michael Cassell and Peter Norman, 'Man in the News – John Smith: Advocate of a social democratic economy for Britain', *Financial Times*, 4 November 1989.
8 Editorial, 'The day of decision', *Financial Times*, 9 April 1992.
9 Michael Cassell and Peter Norman, op. cit.
10 Interview with David Ward, 7 June 2003.
11 Interview with Lord Haskel, 20 October 2003.
12 Some 55 per cent of lecturers believed that Labour's policies would be good for the economy, while 36 per cent thought they would be bad. City economists, on the other hand, split 39 per cent to 43 per cent. *The Economist*, 14 April 1990.
13 *The Economist*, 14 April 1990.
14 *Sunday Correspondent*, 29 April 1990.
15 Interview with David Ward.
16 Alex Brummer, 'Notebook: Labour's envoy to Washington finds his face now fits', *The Guardian*, 20 April 1990; see also Andrew Stephen's America, 'Labour registers under the name of Mr Smith', *The Observer*, 22 April 1990.
17 John Pienaar, 'Smith steps up drive to sell Labour policy as "market-friendly"', *The Independent*, 17 April 1990; Alan Travis, 'Smith pledges prudence', *The Guardian*, 16 April 1990; Martin Walker, 'No dash for growth by Labour, Smith tells US', *The Guardian*, 17 April 1990.
18 Editorial, 'Showman Smith', *The Guardian*, 18 April 1990.
19 Editorial, 'Leave it to Smith', *The Scotsman*, 17 April 1990 (echoing P.G. Wodehouse).
20 Stewart Dickson, 'Yankee Bosses are Voting for Labour', *Daily Mirror*, 17 April 1990.
21 David Hughes, 'Inside Politics: Labour's Mr Smith goes to Washington', *The Sunday Times*, 14 April 1990.
22 Editorial, 'Labour's foreign friends', *The Independent*, 18 April 1990.
23 George Gordon, 'Mr Smith goes to Washington (And Nobody Really Notices)', *Daily Mail*, 19 April 1990.
24 Interview with David Ward.
25 Interview with Lord Haskel.
26 Labour Party, 'shadow Chancellor Begins Week of Talks in Tokyo', Press notice, April 1991. David Ward papers.
27 Interview with David Ward.
28 Ibid.
29 Ibid.
30 Rt Hon. John Smith QC MP, speech to Keidanren Japan-EC Committee, Tokyo, Thursday, 11 April 1991. Six weeks before, Smith had delivered a similar pro-European message to another largely Japanese audience, this time to representatives of Mitsubishi Bank. Rt

Hon. John Smith QC MP, speech to Mitsubishi Bank, London 27 February 1991. David Ward papers.

31 *Breakfast News*, BBC1, 12 April 1991.

32 Economic Secretariat, 'Economic brief: Recent Analysis of Labour's Policies', 17 June 1991. Economic Brief, 1992. Kinnock Collection, Box 429.

33 *On the Record*, BBC1, 3 November 1991.

34 *The Times*, 11 November 1991.

35 Briefing Note: Labour Economic Team European Tour, 31 January 1992. David Ward papers.

36 Interview with Rt Hon. Margaret Beckett MP, 19 November 2003.

37 Briefing Note: Labour Economic Team European Tour, 31 January 1992. David Ward papers.

38 Interview with David Ward.

39 Beregovoy served as Minister for Financial Affairs in the socialist governments of Fabius, Rocard and Cresson, before becoming the French Prime Minister in April 1992. However, after the French legislative elections, in which the socialists lost 200 seats, Beregovoy shot himself on May Day 1993.

40 Interview with David Ward.

41 Interview with Lord Desai, 10 June 2003.

42 Interview with Rt Hon. Paul Boateng MP.

43 See Shore, *Leading the Left*, pp. 172–3.

44 Gould, *Goodbye to All That*, pp. 224–5.

45 See for example, Sarah Baxter, 'Political Column: Timid at heart', *New Statesman & Society*, 7 September 1990; Austin Mitchell, 'Politics: Valium party', *New Statesman & Society*, 5 April 1991.

46 Shaw, *The Labour Party Since 1979*, Chapter 4, pp. 81–107.

47 Shaw, *The Labour Party Since 1979*, p. 137.

Chapter 15

1 Interview with David Ward, 28 April 2003.

2 Interview with Rt Hon. Margaret Beckett MP, 19 November 2003.

3 David Hill, 'The Labour Party's strategy', in Ivor Crewe and Brian Gosschalk (eds), *Political Communications: The General Election Campaign of 1992* (Cambridge University Press: Cambridge, 1995), p. 37.

4 Interview with David Ward, 28 April 2003.

5 Interview with David Ward, 7 June 2003.

6 Notes of shadow Cabinet meeting, undated, c.1990. shadow Cabinet

briefings, 1990. Kinnock Collection, Box 83.

7 Interview with Lord Eatwell, 24 November 2003.

8 Philip Gould, *The Unfinished Revolution. How the Modernisers Saved the Labour Party* (Little, Brown and Company: London, 1998), p. 122.

9 Gould, *The Unfinished Revolution*, pp. 120–1.

10 Quoted in Gould, *The Unfinished Revolution*, p.121.

11 Westlake, *Kinnock*, pp. 542–3.

12 Interview with David Ward, 28 April 2003.

13 Interview with Rt Hon. Margaret Beckett MP.

14 Gould, *The Unfinished Revolution*, p. 121.

15 Interview with Rt Hon. Lord Hattersley, 3 March 2003.

16 Interview with Rt Hon. Chris Smith MP.

17 Interview with Rt Hon. Margaret Beckett MP.

18 Andy McSmith, 'John Smith, 1992–94', in Kevin Jeffreys (ed), *Leading Labour. From Keir Hardie to Tony Blair* (I.B. Tauris: London, 1999), p. 200.

19 Interview with Rt Hon. Hilary Armstrong MP, 11 February 2003.

20 Interview with Rt Hon. Chris Smith MP. Mark Wickham-Jones agrees. Wickham-Jones, *Economic Strategy and the Labour Party*, p. 222.

21 Interview with Rt Hon. Lord Hattersley.

22 Interview with Lord Whitty, 12 March 2003.

23 Interview with Rt Hon. Paul Boateng MP, 6 September 2004.

24 Written correspondence with Lord Desai, 29 October 2004.

25 Shaun Woodward, 'The Conservative Party's Strategy', in Crewe and Gosschalk (eds), *Political Communications*, p. 30.

26 *The Nine o'Clock News*, BBC 1, 5 May 1991.

27 Shaun Woodward, 'The Conservative Party's Strategy', in Crewe and Gosschalk (eds), *Political Communications*, p. 30.

28 Gould, *The Unfinished Revolution*, p. 124. Curiously, Gould's record of what Smith supposedly said was not noted down until 24 April 1992, after the general election. Gould, *The Unfinished Revolution*, p. 408.

29 Gould, *The Unfinished Revolution*, p. 123.

30 Quoted in Gould, *The Unfinished Revolution*, p. 124.

31 Gould, *The Unfinished Revolution*, pp.

125–6.

32 Gould, *The Unfinished Revolution*, p. 128.
33 Gould, *The Unfinished Revolution*, pp. 125–6.
34 Westlake, *Kinnock*, p. 546.
35 Philip Gould, in particular, believed that 'The shadow Chancellor has high credibility in the economic area and this should be maximised.' Gould, *The Unfinished Revolution*, p. 123.
36 Gould, *The Unfinished Revolution*, p. 127.
37 Interview with Rt Hon. Chris Smith MP.
38 Philip Gould, 'Labour's Tax Nightmare', *New Statesman*, 30 October 1998.
39 'People-metering' is a controversial method of measuring voters' responses to political messages, mainly on television. A sample of voters turn a dial to register positive or negative reactions to politicians, producing a graph that changes second-by-second.
40 John Rentoul, Nick Robinson and Simon Braunholtz, 'People-metering: scientific research or clapometer?', in Crewe and Gosschalk (eds), *Political Communications*, pp. 108–9; p. 117.
41 Macintyre, *Mandelson*, p. 225; Westlake, *Kinnock*, p. 545.
42 Interview with David Ward. Bob Hawke then defeated Malcolm Fraser, leader of the Liberal-National Party government in the general election, serving as Prime Minister of Australia from 1983–91. *Keesing's Contemporary Archives* 1983, pp. 32126–8.
43 Westlake, *Kinnock*, p. 545.
44 Interview with David Ward, 28 April 2003.
45 Interview with Rt Hon. Lord Hattersley.
46 Interview with Rt Hon. Frank Dobson MP, 3 March 2003.
47 Maureen Cleave, 'Smiling John Smith', *Daily Telegraph Magazine*, 3 March 1990.
48 Interview with David Ward.
49 See David Butler and Dennis Kavanagh, *The British General Election of 1992* (Macmillan: Basingstoke, 1992) pp. 77–99.
50 Interview with Lord Eatwell.
51 Edwina Currie, *Diaries 1987–1992* (Little, Brown and Company: London 2002), p. 301.
52 Interview with Rt Hon. Chris Smith MP.
53 Dan Corry and Nick Pecorelli, Economic Secretariat, 'Economic Brief: An Economy Stuck in a Damaging Recession', 23 January 1992; Jon Cruddas, Economic

Secretariat, 'Economic Brief: Unemployment – The Costs and the Solutions', 13 February 1992; Dan Corry and Nick Pecorelli, 'Economic Brief: The UK Recession and the World Economic Situation', 13 February 1992; Dan Corry and Nick Pecorelli, 'The Economic Picture', 14 February 1992. Economic Brief, 1992. Kinnock Collection, Box 429.
54 Dan Corry and Nick Pecorelli, 'Economic Brief: VAT and the Tories', 30 January 1992. Economic Brief 1992. Kinnock Collection, Box 429.
55 Economic Secretariat, 'Economic Brief', 12 February 1992. Kinnock Collection, Box 423.
56 *Financial Times*, 28 January 1992.
57 Butler and Kavanagh, *Election of 1992*, p. 97.
58 General Secretary, 'Report to NEC: The general election', 21 June 1992. (GS: 21/6/92). Kinnock Collection, Box 180.
59 Westlake, *Kinnock*, pp. 512–5.
60 Interview with David Ward, 7 June 2003; Michael Cassell, 'Labour "to impose top tax rate" from £40,000 level', *Financial Times*, 14 April 1989.
61 Hypothecation is the idea, still much loved by the Liberal Democrats, of allocating a defined percentage of tax revenues for spending in a specific area, such as the NHS. The aim is to convince the voters that their money will go directly to pay for services that they wish to see improved.
62 Interview with Rt Hon. Chris Smith MP.
63 Westlake, *Kinnock*, p. 528.
64 Westlake incorrectly records the date of the Luigi's episode as 15 January 1992 on page 529 of his biography of Kinnock, but by page 550, he correctly cites the date as 14 January 1992.
65 The six journalists were Andy McSmith of the *Daily Mirror*, Jill Sherman of *The Times*, Jon Sopel from the BBC, Alison Smith of the *Financial Times*, Alan Travis of *The Guardian*, and Mark Webster of ITN. McSmith, *John Smith*, p. 343.
66 Private information.
67 Letter from Rt Hon. Neil Kinnock MP to Rt Hon. John Smith QC MP, 14 January 1992. David Ward papers.
68 *Meet the Challenge, Make the Change*, p. 33; *Looking to the Future*, p. 9.
69 *Opportunity Britain*, p.14.
70 John Eatwell [unsigned], briefing meeting

of Economic Sub-Committee, 16 January 1990, 5 pm in shadow Cabinet Room, minutes of Economic Policy Sub-Committee, 1990. Kinnock Collection, Box 429.

71 John Eatwell, 'A Sceptical Look at the Economic Policy Parts of the Policy Review' (Economic Policy Sub-Committee, February 1990). Kinnock Collection, Box 163.

72 Interview with Lord Eatwell.

73 Letter from Rt Hon. Neil Kinnock MP to Rt Hon. John Smith QC MP, op. cit.

74 Ibid.

75 Andrew Dilnot, 'Personal View. Tax reforms – from the absurd to the ridiculous', *Financial Times*, 8 January 1992.

76 Interview with Lord Eatwell.

77 Interview with David Ward, 7 June 2003.

78 Interview with Lord Eatwell.

79 Westlake, *Kinnock*, p. 545.

80 Interview with David Ward.

81 Martin Westlake incorrectly claims that the *Financial Times* article was held back until 17 January, when in fact it was published on 16 January that week. Westlake, *Kinnock*, p. 529; Alison Smith and Philip Stephens, 'Labour may scale back National Insurance plans', *Financial Times*, 16 January 1992.

82 The ICM, conducted for *The Guardian*, showed the Conservatives on 42 per cent with Labour just behind on 41 per cent.

83 Interview with David Ward.

84 McSmith, *John Smith*, pp. 240–1.

85 Robin Oakley and Jill Sheerman, 'Labour hesitates over speedy tax changes', *The Times*, 16 January 1992; Alison Smith and Philip Stephens, 'Labour may scale back National Insurance plans', *Financial Times*, 16 January 1992.

86 Collins was subsequently elected to Parliament as the Conservative Member for Westmorland and Lonsdale in May 1997.

87 HC Debs, 16 January 1992, c. 1095.

88 McSmith, *John Smith*, pp. 242–3.

89 Interview with Rt Hon. Chris Smith MP.

90 Interview with David Ward.

91 Interview with Rt Hon. Lord Hattersley, 3 March 2003.

92 E-mail correspondence with David Ward, 7 November 2004.

93 Interview with Rt Hon. Lord Hattersley.

94 Macintyre, *Mandelson*, pp. 225–6.

95 Interview with Lord Whitty.

96 McSmith, *John Smith*, pp. 243–4.

97 See also, Benn, *Free at Last!*, p. 78. (Wednesday, 19 February 1992).

98 Michael Portillo, *The Economics of John Smith* (Conservative Political Centre: July 1992), p. 14.

99 Ken Livingstone, Letter to Labour MPs, 23 April 1992. Papers on Labour Party leadership elections, 1992, Kinnock Collection, Box 19; See also, Ken Livingstone, 'Uniting Europe means rejecting its economic policies', *New Statesman & Society*, 1 May 1992.

100 Interview with Rt Hon. Margaret Beckett MP.

101 Hattersley, *Who Goes Home?*, p. 312.

102 Gould, *The Unfinished Revolution*, p. 128.

Chapter 16

1 Norman Lamont, *In Office* (Little, Brown and Company: London, 1999), p. 172.

2 Lamont, *In Office*, p. 174.

3 Interview with Rt Hon. Chris Smith MP, 11 February 2003.

4 Gould, *The Unfinished Revolution*, p. 118. Quoted from Gould's diary.

5 Interview with Lord Eatwell, 24 November 2003.

6 HC Debs, 10 March 1992, cc. 762–768.

7 Interview with Lord Eatwell.

8 Interview with Rt Hon. Margaret Beckett MP, 19 November 2003.

9 Interview with David Ward, 7 June 2003.

10 Beckett adds: 'We had a shrewd idea the Tories were misrepresenting the size of the gap by, say, £8 billion. No one guessed how much worse things actually were – hence my caution.' Interview with Rt Hon. Margaret Beckett MP.

11 HC Debs, 11 March 1992, c. 859.

12 For example, if Smith reversed the 20 pence band and cut national insurance by 1 per cent, higher earners would benefit, but those earning between £3,000–£10,000 would be worse off.

13 Interview with Baroness Smith of Gilmorehill DL, 4 December 2002.

14 Interview with Lord Gordon of Strathblane CBE, 12 March 2003.

15 Gould, *The Unfinished Revolution*, p. 128. Again, curiously Gould quotes from his own diary dated 20 April 1992, apparently

written *after* the general election, p. 408.

16 Labour Party News Release, shadow Budget, Institute of Civil Engineers, 16 March 1992. David Ward papers; interview with Rt Hon. Chris Smith MP.

17 David Hare, Notes on 1992 general election campaign, Monday, March 16 1992, A15. Kinnock Collection, Box 616.

18 Interview with Lord Desai, 10 June 2003.

19 Benn, *Free at Last!*, p. 86. (Monday, 16 March 1992). However, four years later, Benn agreed with Margaret Beckett that Smith's shadow Budget was a mistake, at least, in the sense that 'it came too late'. Benn, *Free at Last!*, p. 350 (Thursday, 11 January 1996).

20 Interview with Lord Eatwell.

21 Steven Webb, Graham Stark and Chris Giles at the Institute for Fiscal Studies produced a report entitled 'The Distributional Effects of Labour's shadow Budget', which backed Smith's view that four out of five families would benefit from Labour's tax plans, while only 9 per cent (those earning more than £30,000) would lose. Kenneth Newton, 'Caring and Competence: The Long, Long Campaign', in Anthony King et al, *Britain at the Polls 1992* (Chatham House Publishers Inc: New Jersey, 1992), p. 145.

22 'Letter to the Editor from Lord Hollick and others', *The Times*, 18 March 1992.

23 'Letter to the Editor from Sir Allen Sheppard and others', *The Times*, 17 March 1992.

24 The Liberal Democrats' manifesto was entitled *Changing Britain for Good*.

25 Martin Harrison, 'Politics on the Air', in Butler and Kavanagh, *Election of 1992*, p. 170.

26 Lamont, *In Office*, p. 180.

27 Shaun Woodward, 'The Conservative Party's strategy', in Crewe and Gosschalk (eds), *Political Communications*, p. 33.

28 Lamont, *In Office*, pp. 180–181.

29 That same week, there was also a larger than expected trade deficit, although on 21 March the rate of inflation remained unchanged at 4.1 per cent.

30 Bagehot, 'When it all seemed to slide', *The Economist*, 4 April 1992; quoted in Butler and Kavanagh, *Election of 1992*, p. 124.

31 Interview with Rt Hon. Michael Foot, 20 February 2003.

32 Martin Harrison, 'Politics on the Air', in Butler and Kavanagh, *Election of 1992*, p. 186.

33 This paragraph is largely drawn from Martin Harrop and Margaret Scammell, 'A Tabloid War', in Butler and Kavanagh, *Election of 1992*, pp. 198–9.

34 Edward Whitley, 'No Place Like Home', *The Spectator*, 21 March 1992.

35 Interview with Rt Hon. Margaret Beckett MP.

36 David Sanders, 'Why the Conservatives won again', in King et al, *Britain at the Polls*, p. 181.

37 The *Times*, 20 March 1992.

38 Roy Hattersley, *Fifty Years On. A Prejudiced History of Britain Since the War* (Little, Brown and Company: London, 1997), p. 371.

39 Interview with Lord Whitty, 12 March 2003.

40 'Smearwatch', *New Statesman*, 20 March 1992.

41 For the worst offender, see Anatole Kaletsky, 'Labour plants a tax time-bomb under would-be middle class', *The Times*, 16 March 1992; Anatole Kaletsky, 'Smith turns the tables on Thatcher's children', *The Times*, 17 March 1992; Anatole Kaletsky, 'Where pips will squeak', *The Times*, 18 March 1992.

42 Karen Gardiner, 'Points we want to Address', March 1992. David Ward papers.

43 Andrew Graham, re: Kaletsky's Article in *The Times*, Tuesday, 17 March 1992. David Ward papers.

44 Yvette Cooper, 'Middle Incomes', March 1992. David Ward papers.

45 Emma Maclennan, Economic Secretariat, 'Economic Brief: You're Better off with Labour; You're Worse off with the Tories', undated, c. February 1992; Dan Corry and Nick Pecorelli, 'Comparing the 1970s and the 1980s: Destroying the Tory Myths', undated, 1992. Economic Brief, 1992. Kinnock Collection, Box 429.

46 Interview with Emma Maclennan, 7 June 2003.

47 Interview with Lord Eatwell.

48 David Hare, notes on 1992 general election campaign. Tuesday, March 24 1992, A21. Kinnock Collection, Box 616.

49 Interview with Murray Elder, 4 December 2002.

50 Bagehot, 'A study in Brown', *The Economist*, 11 January 1992.

51 Interview with Rt Hon. Helen Liddell MP, 19 November 2003.
52 Ibid.
53 Ibid.
54 Ibid.
55 Helen Liddell, 'He was witty, he was bright and could spot fools at ten paces!', *Daily Record*, 13 May 1994.
56 Interview with Ann Barrett, 21 June 2003.
57 Interview with Rt Hon. Helen Liddell MP.
58 McSmith, *John Smith*, pp. 257–258.
59 Interview with Rt Hon. Helen Liddell MP.
60 Paul Wilnenius, 'Banker's looks hid the joker', *Today*, 13 May 1994.
61 Interview with David Ward, 7 June 2003.
62 Interview with David Ward; interview with Lord Eatwell.
63 Fax from David Ward to John Smith, Election Night Statements, April 1992. David Ward papers.
64 Westlake, *Kinnock*, p. 592.
65 Interview with Lord Eatwell.
66 Interview with Lord Desai.
67 Anderson and Mann, *Safety First*, p. 87; Meghnad Desai, *Tribune*, 13 November 1992.
68 Telephone interview with Lord Desai, 29 October 2004.
69 Interview with David Ward, 28 April 2003.
70 Written correspondence with Rt Hon. Neil Kinnock, 8 January 2004.
71 Interview with Rt Hon. Helen Liddell MP.
72 James Naughtie, 'A Political Life Observed', in Brown and Naughtie, *Life and Soul of the Party*, p. 54.
73 Naughtie, *The Rivals*, p. 43; interview with Rt Hon. Helen Liddell MP.
74 Interview with Rt Hon. Helen Liddell MP.
75 Martin Dempsey, *Question Time Special*, BBC1, Thursday, 12 May 1994 (transcript).
76 David Hill, 'General Election Campaign – Some Observations' NEC, 24 June 1992 (CCD 1/92/93). Kinnock Collection, Box 180.
77 David Hill, 'General Election Campaign – Some Observations' NEC, 24 June 1992 (CCD 1/92/93); Philip Gould, 'Polling Presentation', Special NEC, Thursday, 18 June 1992. Kinnock Collection, Box 180.
78 David Hare, Notes on the 1992 general election Campaign, Thursday, March 12 1992, A11. Kinnock Collection, Box 616.
79 General Secretary, 'Report to NEC: The General Election', 21 June 1992. (GS: 21/6/92). Kinnock Collection, Box 180.
80 Kampfner, *Robin Cook*, p. 87.
81 Naughtie, *The Rivals*, p. 49.
82 Donald MacCormick, 'A diligent and brilliant believer in all that was best', *The Sunday Times*, 15 May 1994.
83 Private information.
84 Westlake, *Kinnock*, p. 541.
85 For a recent example, see 'Advantage Brown', Editorial, *The Sunday Times*, 21 March 2004.
86 Interview with Rt Hon. Lord Hattersley, 3 March 2003.
87 Interview with Rt Hon. Chris Smith MP.
88 Brian Wilson, 'Giving people a chance', *The Herald*, 13 May 1994; see also, Brian Wilson, 'A Scot who kept faith with his roots', *Independent on Sunday*, 15 May 1994.
89 Interview with Rt Hon. Helen Liddell MP.
90 Nicholas Timmins, 'Party looks for victory from a mirror image', *The Independent*, 18 July 1992.
91 Clive Soley, 'Discussion of General Election', minutes of a special party meeting held on Wednesday 1 July 1992 at 11 am in Committee Room 14.
92 Butler and Kavanagh, *Election of 1992*, p. 147.
93 Anthony Heath, Roger Jowell and John Curtice, *The Rise of New Labour. Party Policies and Voter Choices* (Oxford University Press: Oxford, 2001), p. 44.
94 Heath, Jowell and Curtice, *The Rise of New Labour*, p. 44.
95 Ivor Crewe and Anthony King, 'Did Major win? Did Kinnock lose? leadership Effects in the 1992 election', in Anthony Heath, Roger Jowell and John Curtice with Bridget Taylor (eds), *Labour's Last Chance? The 1992 Election and Beyond* (Dartmouth: Aldershot, 1994), pp. 125–48.
96 Every month the pollsters Gallup ask the voters who would make the best Prime Minister. John Major enjoyed a lead over Neil Kinnock of around 20 per cent

throughout 1991. By January 1992, this lead had increased to 22 per cent. However, from January onwards, Kinnock narrowed the gap, so that by the week of the election, while 39 per cent of the electorate favoured Major, 28 per cent preferred Kinnock. Nevertheless, Kinnock remained significantly less popular than Major. Gallup Political and Economic Index, Reports 377 and 380, January and April 1992.

97 See John Curtice and Holli Semetko, 'Does it matter what the papers say?', in Heath et al (eds), *Labour's Last Chance?*, pp. 43–64.

98 *The Times*, 1 April 1992.

99 Robert Waller, 'The polls and the 1992 General Election', in Crewe and Gosschalk (eds), *Political Communications*, p. 190.

100 Private information.

101 Private information.

102 General Secretary, 'Report to NEC: The General Election', 21 June 1992. (GS: 21/6/92). Kinnock Collection, Box 180.

103 Crewe and King, 'Did Major win? Did Kinnock lose?', in Heath et al (eds), *Labour's Last Chance?*, pp. 134–5; David Sanders, 'Why the Conservative Party Won – Again', in Butler and Kavanagh (eds), *General Election of 1992*, pp. 171–222.

104 David Hill, 'General Election Campaign – Some Observations' NEC, 24 June 1992 (CCD 1/92/93). Kinnock Collection, Box 180.

105 David Hare, Notes on 1992 general election Campaign, Friday, April 3 1992, Labour Strategy Meeting, A63. Kinnock Collection, Box 616.

106 Philip Gould, 'Polling Presentation', Special NEC, Thursday, 18 June 1992. Kinnock Collection, Box 180.

107 David Hare, Notes after the 1992 general election, chatting with Philip Gould, c. May 1992, A96. Kinnock Collection, Box 616.

108 Interview with Lord Eatwell.

109 Peter Riddell and Philip Webster, 'Interview with Margaret Beckett', *The Times*, 21 June 1994.

110 Interview with Rt Hon. Chris Smith MP.

111 Interview with Lord Whitty. For supporting evidence, see General Secretary, 'Report to NEC: The General Election', 21 June 1992. (GS: 21/6/92); David Hill, 'General Election Campaign –

Some Observations' NEC, 24 June 1992 (CCD 1/92/93). Kinnock Collection, Box 180.

112 Hattersley, *Fifty Years On*, p. 372.

113 Interview with Lord Whitty.

114 David Hill, 'General Election Campaign – Some Observations' NEC, 24 June 1992 (CCD 1/92/93). Kinnock Collection, Box 180.

Chapter 17

1 David Hare, Notes post-1992 general election Campaign, chatting with Neil Kinnock, c. May 1992, A87. Kinnock Collection, Box 616.

2 David Hare, Notes post-1992 general election Campaign, chatting with Philip Gould, c. May 1992, A97. Kinnock Collection, Box 616.

3 John Smith and Margaret Beckett had agreed that they would meet, win or lose, to thank the members of the Treasury team. Written correspondence with Rt Hon. Margaret Beckett MP, 20 October 2004.

4 Interview with Yvette Cooper, 16 March 2004.

5 Hattersley, *Who Goes Home?*, p. 312.

6 *On the Record*, BBC 1, Sunday, 12 April 1992 (transcript).

7 Interview with Lord Whitty, 12 March 2003.

8 *Tribune*, 1 May 1992.

9 As the *New Statesman & Society* pointed out at the time, a 'shoe-in' or 'shoo-in' is American slang for a horse that wins a race by prearrangement. The animal, not needing to run to win, can merely be shooed over the winning line. Therefore, the person or candidate standing for election can receive a 'shoe-in' if he or she secures the backing of all the key people, obviating the need for a contest. 'Shoreditch', *New Statesman & Society*, 24 April 1992.

10 Interview with Lord Whitty.

11 Interview with Rt Hon. Margaret Beckett MP, 19 November 2003.

12 Interview with David Ward, 7 June 2003.

13 Rentoul, *Tony Blair*, pp. 254–6.

14 For two of the worst culprits, see Rentoul, *Tony Blair*, pp. 260–1; Gould, *The Unfinished Revolution*, p. 187.

15 Interview with Rt Hon. Lord Hattersley, 3

16 Macintyre, *Mandelson*, p. 232.

17 Sixty-four per cent of the 138 Labour MPs surveyed in a *Sunday Times* poll selected Smith, while only 16 per cent preferred Brown, though he was clearly in second place. Macintyre, *Mandelson*, p. 232.

18 Macintyre, *Mandelson*, pp. 233–4; Naughtie, *The Rivals*, p. 44.

19 Routledge, *Gordon Brown*, pp. 163–4.

20 Macintyre, *Mandelson*, p. 234.

21 Macintyre, *Mandelson*, p. 235.

22 Interview with Rt Hon. Margaret Beckett MP; Mark Seddon, 'The Tribune interview: Margaret Beckett, Going Places', *Tribune*, 22 May 1992; Rentoul, *Tony Blair*, p. 258.

23 Interview with Rt Hon. Margaret Beckett MP.

24 Rentoul, *Tony Blair*, p. 259.

25 Shore, *Leading the Left*, p. 175.

26 Brown, *Fighting Talk*, p. 209.

27 Clare Short, 'If Smith wins, Gould must be deputy', *Tribune*, 24 April 1992.

28 The PLP was not due to meet until 27 April. R. K. Alderman and Neil Carter, 'The Labour Party leadership and Deputy leadership elections of 1992', *Parliamentary Affairs*, 46, No. 1 (1993), p. 50; p. 55.

29 Interview with Lord Whitty.

30 Colin Byrne, 'A leadership fix that would betray Labour's reforms', Letters to the Editor, *The Guardian*, 13 April 1992.

31 Gould, *The Unfinished Revolution*, p. 112.

32 Brown, *Fighting Talk*, p. 209.

33 Paul Routledge, *Mandy. The Unauthorised Biography of Peter Mandelson* (Simon & Schuster: London, 1999), p. 137.

34 Rentoul, *Tony Blair*, p. 257.

35 Edward Pearce's Sketch, 'Some people really should put a sock in it', *New Statesman & Society*, 24 April 1992.

36 Interview with Lord Whitty.

37 Leonard P. Stark, *Choosing a Leader. Party Leadership Contests in Britain from Macmillan to Blair* (Macmillan: London, 1996), p. 156. Stark interviewed Kinnock, Hattersley and Beckett in the first half of 1993.

38 Interview with Rt Hon. Margaret Beckett MP.

39 Kinnock's basic plan was to truncate the timetable to just nine weeks from nomination to election, and then to ask the party conference in October retrospectively to endorse the decision.

40 Briefing note, Charles Clarke to Neil Kinnock, re: NEC, Tuesday, 14 April 1992. Kinnock Collection, Box 303.

41 Neil Kinnock's notes, NEC, Tuesday, 24 April 1992. Kinnock Collection, Box 303.

42 Ibid.

43 Blunkett originally wanted a longer delay until October. Interview with Lord Whitty. The closing date for nominations was set for Tuesday, 28 April. Alderman and Carter, 'Labour Party Leadership', *Parliamentary Affairs*, 46, p. 51.

44 David Hare, Notes on 1992 general election Campaign, Tuesday, March 10 1992, Budget Day, A11. Kinnock Collection, Box 616.

45 Gould, *Goodbye to All That*, p. 253.

46 Gould, *Goodbye to All That*, p. 258.

47 Gould, *Goodbye to All That*, p. 255.

48 Alderman and Carter, 'Labour Party Leadership', *Parliamentary Affairs*, 46, p. 54.

49 Caroline Rees, 'The *Tribune* interview, John Prescott, The Tough Guy', *Tribune*, 5 June 1992.

50 Brown, *Fighting Talk*, p. 215.

51 Naughtie, *The Rivals*, p. 42.

52 Kampfner, *Robin Cook*, p. 89.

53 Statement by the Rt Hon. John Smith QC MP, Tuesday, 14 April 1992. David Ward papers.

54 Interview with David Ward.

55 Kampfner, *Robin Cook*, p. 90; Sopel, *Tony Blair*, p. 134.

56 Macintyre, *Mandelson*, pp. 236–237.

57 Letter from Robin Cook to Labour MPs. Quoted in Alderman and Carter, 'Labour Party Leadership', *Parliamentary Affairs*, 46, pp. 54–5.

58 Interview with Rt Hon. Frank Dobson, MP, 24 April 2003.

59 *The Times*, 6 February 1992.

60 Clive Soley, 'Why I am backing Bryan Gould', *Tribune*, 1 May 1992.

61 Clare Short, 'If Smith wins, Gould must be deputy', *Tribune*, 24 April 1992.

62 See for example, Peter Hain, 'Euro-bank is a danger', *Tribune*, 26 February 1993.

63 In the wake of the 1988 Labour leadership and deputy leadership contest, the party had raised from 5 per cent to 20 per cent the threshold both for the leadership and the deputy leadership contests to stop

damaging annual challenges from left-wingers like Tony Benn.

64 McSmith, *Faces of Labour*, p. 64.

65 *Tribune*, 1 May 1992.

66 Raised to the peerage as Baroness Gould of Potternewton in 1993.

67 *The Times*, 28 April 1992. Quoted in Stark, *Choosing a Leader*, p. 216.

68 *Tribune*, 1 May 1992.

69 Written correspondence with Lord Whitty, 26 October 2004.

70 Alderman and Carter, 'Labour Party Leadership', *Parliamentary Affairs*, 46, p. 56; Joyce Gould, Facsimile to Labour MPs, 27 April 1992, 10.32 am. Papers on Labour Party leadership elections, 1992, Kinnock Collection, Box 19; minutes of special meeting of the PLP held on Monday 27 April 1992 at 12 noon in Committee Room 10.

71 *Tribune*, 1 May 1992. Alderman and Carter argue quite rightly that no one seriously expected Clwyd to gain the required number of signatures. Alderman and Carter, 'Labour Party Leadership', *Parliamentary Affairs*, 46, p. 53.

72 Alderman and Carter, 'Labour Party Leadership', *Parliamentary Affairs*, 46, pp. 56–7.

73 Benn's backing for Smith was justified on the grounds that his Chesterfield CLP had voted to support Smith. Benn, *Free at Last!*, p. 103. (Sunday, 12 April 1992). A day later, Bryan Gould rang Benn seeking his backing, but Benn refused. Benn, *Free at Last!*, p. 103 (Monday, 13 April 1992).

74 At an earlier meeting of the PLP on 13 May 1992, Alan Williams successfully moved an amendment that ensured two separate meetings of the PLP, one for the leadership contenders, and one for the candidates for the deputy leadership, rather than the original proposal for just one single hustings meeting. Minutes of the party meeting held on Wednesday 13 May 1992 at 11.30 am in Committee Room 10.

75 Interview with Alan Haworth, 16 December 2003.

76 Benn, *Free at Last!*, p. 112 (Wednesday, 3 June).

77 Female voters in 1992 were generally less likely to vote Labour than male voters.

78 John Smith, leadership election Leaflet. Papers on Labour Party leadership elections, 1992. Kinnock Collection, Box 19.

79 John Smith, *New Paths to Victory. A Leadership Election Address*, April 1992, Papers on Labour Party Leadership elections, 1992. Kinnock Collection, Box 19.

80 Sopel claims the document was 6,000 words long, Macintyre that it stretched to 8,000 words. Sopel, *Tony Blair*, p. 134; Macintyre, *Mandelson*, p. 236. Sopel wins the prize for being closest – it was around 6,650 words long.

81 Interview with David Ward.

82 Ibid.

83 Patricia Hewitt, draft statement by John Smith, April 1992. David Ward papers.

84 Gould, *The Unfinished Revolution*, p. 161.

85 Smith, *New Paths to Victory*, p. 4.

86 In the 1992 shadow Budget, Smith had supported the idea of an annual statement for the environmental impact of government policies.

87 A cross-party pressure group, advocating wholesale constitutional reform. Charter 88 marked the tercentenary of the Glorious Revolution of 1688 calling for a new constitution for Britain, and launched a petition in pursuit of its aims.

88 Smith, *New Paths to Victory*, pp. 5–7.

89 Smith, *New Paths to Victory*, pp. 8–9.

90 Rentoul, *Tony Blair*, p. 262.

91 *The Times*, 18 July 1992. Quoted in Stark, *Choosing a Leader*, p. 115.

92 Martin Kettle, interview with Bryan Gould, *The Guardian*, 16 April 1992.

93 'Bryan Gould for ideas, and a forward-looking agenda'. Papers on Labour Party leadership elections, 1992. Kinnock Collection, Box 19.

94 Robin Oakley and Philip Webster, 'Gould enters contest with tax challenge', *The Times*, 15 April 1992.

95 Paul Anderson, 'The *Tribune* Interview: Bryan Gould. The ideas man', *Tribune*, 8 May 1992.

96 Gould, *Goodbye to All That*, p. 247.

97 Bryan Gould, Letter to Labour MPs, 4 June 1992. Papers on Labour Party Leadership elections, 1992. Kinnock Collection, Box 19.

98 *On the Record*, BBC1, 5 July 1992 (transcript).

99 Brown, *Fighting Talk*, p. 228.

100 Gould held Southampton Test from

October 1974 until his defeat in 1979.

101 Rt Hon. John Smith QC MP, Opening Statement at the Fabian Society Debate, Central Hall, Westminster, Wednesday, 20 May 1992 (press notice). David Ward papers.

102 Patrick Wintour, 'Mr Smith: Labour's new moralist', *The Guardian*, 18 July 1992.

103 *Tribune*, 24 April 1992.

104 Caroline Rees, 'Gould only contender with something to say', *Tribune*, 3 July 1992.

105 In fact, the 'dream ticket' was a media term. According to Neil Kinnock, he and Hattersley ran separate campaigns, but with periodic precautionary checks to ensure that they did not contradict each other. They produced just one short joint statement. E-mail correspondence with Rt Hon. Neil Kinnock, 22 October 2004.

106 Interview with Rt Hon. Margaret Beckett MP.

107 Margaret Beckett, *Modernisation Manifesto*, Papers on Labour Party Leadership elections, 1992. Kinnock Collection, Box 19; Mark Seddon, 'The Tribune interview. Margaret Beckett, Going Places', *Tribune*, 22 May 1992.

108 Margaret Beckett, *Modernisation Manifesto*, Papers on Labour Party Leadership elections, 1992. Kinnock Collection, Box 19.

109 Mark Seddon, 'The *Tribune* interview. Margaret Beckett, Going Places', *Tribune*, 22 May 1992.

110 Alan Watkins, *The Road to No. 10. From Bonar Law to Tony Blair* (Duckworth: London, 1998), p. 168.

111 Gould, *Goodbye to All That*, p. 263.

112 Alderman and Carter, 'Labour Party Leadership', *Parliamentary Affairs*, 46, p. 61.

113 Gould gained a respectable 68 votes in the PLP (7 per cent of the total electoral college votes) to Smith's 23 per cent (out of a possible 30 per cent), but Smith trounced Gould in the trade union section. Its 40 per cent share of the electoral college split 38.5 per cent to Smith, with just 1.5 per cent going to Gould. Only the votes of the construction workers – 160,000 – ended up with Gould. The Dagenham MP was unlucky that even when he polled respectably in union ballots (which were themselves fairly

rare), the result was on a winner-takes-all basis, so he took 30,000 votes from Smith's own union (GMB), but Smith pocketed his 110,200 votes plus Gould's 30,000. Similarly, the shopworkers split 76,000 to 10,000 in Smith's favour, and yet Smith pocketed all the votes. Gould could only gain about one per cent in the CLP sections of the electoral college, while Smith managed 29 per cent of the 30 per cent available. Shore, *Leading the Left*, p. 176; Sopel, *Tony Blair*, p. 136; Watkins, *The Road to No. 10*, p. 169.

114 The union-CLP-PLP electoral college ratios in the deputy leadership contest were as follows: Beckett 25:19:13; Prescott 12:7:9; and Gould 1:1:7. Watkins, *The Road to No. 10*, p. 169.

115 McSmith, 'John Smith. 1992–94', in Jeffreys (ed.), *Leading Labour*, p. 202.

116 *The Nine o' Clock News* (specially extended), BBC 1, Thursday, 12 May 1994 (transcript).

117 Interview with Ruth Wishart, 15 January 2004.

118 'Shoreditch', *New Statesman & Society*, 24 July 1992.

119 See, for example, *Daily Express*, 17 July 1992; *Mail on Sunday*, 19 July 1992.

120 Quoted from 'Fourth Estate: A regular monitor of the tabloid press', *New Statesman & Society*, 24 July 1992; see also Anthony Bevins, 'Ministers unleash political mugging on eve of election', *The Independent*, 18 July 1992.

121 Interview with Ruth Wishart.

Chapter 18

1 Interview with Ann Barrett, 21 June 2003.

2 Until 2003 an Assembly Member for Mid and West Wales, and Deputy Minister for the Environment, Rural Affairs, Culture and the Welsh language.

3 Interview with Murray Elder, 17 September 2003.

4 Interview with Baroness Ramsay of Cartvale, 24 June 2003.

5 Interview with Ann Barrett.

6 Interview with Murray Elder, 26 November 2002.

7 McSmith, *Faces of Labour*, p. 36.

8 Elder had a weakened heart, following rheumatic fever as a boy, and the muscle finally gave in, necessitating the heart

transplant operation.

9   Kennedy was then an SDP MP.

10   Interview with Murray Elder, 26 November 2002.

11   Ward dealt with Treasury, DTI, Foreign Policy and Overseas Aid (with Meta Ramsay helping out in these two areas), Defence and green issues; Pat McFadden's portfolio covered Health, Social Security, Employment, Local Government and Housing, Transport, Northern Ireland and Scotland; and Delyth Evans dealt mainly with Home Office issues, Education, the Citizen's Charter, Women, Arts/Heritage, Agriculture and Wales. leader's Office, Policy Unit: division of portfolios [undated]. Murray Elder papers, Box 1.

12   Interview with Mike Elrick, 10 June 2003.

13   Interview with Ann Barrett.

14   Ibid.

15   Ibid.

16   Ibid.

17   Interview with Mike Elrick.

18   Interview with Lord Whitty, 12 March 2003.

19   Interview with Murray Elder, 30 April 2003.

20   Labour's director of organisation from 1985–93.

21   Interview with Lord Whitty, 12 March 2003. David Butler and Martin Westlake, British Politics and European Elections, 1994 (St Martin's Press: New York, 1995) pp. 118–19; Benn, Free at Last!, p. 174. (Wednesday, 5 May 1993).

22   Interview with Rt Hon. Hilary Armstrong MP, 11 February 2003.

23   Interview with Murray Elder, 12 February 2003.

24   Interview with Ruth Wishart, 15 January 2004.

25   Interview with Murray Elder, 12 February 2003.

26   Interview with Rt Hon. Hilary Armstrong MP.

27   Ibid.

28   Interview with Rt Hon. Margaret Beckett MP, 19 November 2003.

29   Ibid.

30   Interview with Baroness Ramsay of Cartvale.

31   Graham was then Vice-Master of Balliol, and for much of the autumn term of 1992 was 'Vicegerent', as the Master was on

leave. In the first half of 1993, Graham lost the Mastership election, but subsequently became Master of Balliol after Smith's death. Largely because of these internal college events, Graham played far less of a role in Smith's first year-and-a-half as leader than had been the case from 1988–92. E-mail correspondence with Andrew Graham, 9 November 2004.

32   Interview with Lord Haskel, 20 October 2003.

33   Interview with Sir Gavin Laird CBE, 21 January 2004.

34   Interview with Rt Hon. Michael Foot, 20 February 2003.

35   Interview with Rt Hon. Derek Foster MP, 24 June 2003.

36   Interview with Rt Hon. Hilary Armstrong MP.

37   Interview with Rt Hon. Frank Dobson MP, 3 March 2003.

38   Simon Hoggart, 'Sharp wit with an inner fire', The Guardian 2, 13 May 1994.

39   Interview with Rt Hon. Frank Dobson MP.

40   Simon Hoggart, op. cit.

41   Andy McSmith, 'Life and Soul of the Party', The Guardian 2, 13 May 1994; Ben Pimlott, 'Not a Gaitskell, but perhaps an Attlee', Independent on Sunday, 15 May 1994.

42   Kate Muir, 'Red Rose of Taxes', The Times, 14 March 1992.

43   Interview with Leo Beckett, 19 November 2003.

44   Interview with Rt Hon. Margaret Beckett MP.

45   Interview with Rt Hon. Derek Foster MP.

46   Interview with Alan Haworth, 15 December 2003.

47   Interview with Mike Elrick.

48   Interview with Ann Barrett.

49   David Hare, Notes on 1992 general election Campaign, Thursday, March 26 1992, A32. Kinnock Collection, Box 616.

50   David Hare, Notes after 1992 general election Campaign, chatting to Neil Stewart, c. May 1992, A83. Kinnock Collection, Box 616.

51   E-mail correspondence with Rt Hon. Neil Kinnock, 22 October 2004.

52   Interview with Rt Hon. Frank Dobson MP.

53   Interview with Lord Whitty.

54   'Maintaining Contacts', Letter from Larry

Whitty to Murray Elder, 10 September 1992. Murray Elder papers, Box 1.

55   Ibid. Neil Kinnock claims that his diary will show that he had roughly twice-yearly meetings with part or all of the PLP in the House of Lords. E-mail correspondence with Rt Hon. Neil Kinnock.

56   Ibid.

57   Interview with Dr Lynne Jones MP, Politico's, London, 18 June 2002.

58   Sarah Baxter, 'Kinnock's new look at old socialism', *New Statesman & Society*, 4 February 1994.

59   Benn, *Free at Last!*, p. 178. (Wednesday, 19 May 1993).

60   McSmith, *Faces of Labour*, p. 25.

61   E-mail communication with Paul Foot, 30 December 2003.

62   Interview with Rt Hon. Michael Foot.

63   Interview with Murray Elder, 12 February 2003.

64   Interview with David Ward, 8 June 2003.

65   Skinner also greatly appreciated the public expenditure increases secured under Blair and Brown, something he still gets quite excited about, having lived through the cuts of the 1970s.

66   Interview with Murray Elder, 26 November 2004.

67   Interview with Rt Hon. Hilary Armstrong MP.

68   Interview with Rt Hon. Derek Foster.

69   Private information.

70   Interview with Lord Whitty.

71   Interview with Rt Hon. Margaret Beckett MP.

72   HC Debs, 17 January 1994, cc. 624–628. Galloway's name is absent from the printed division list.

73   Minutes of the party meeting held on Thursday 20 January 1994 at 6 pm in Committee Room 10.

74   Interview with Rt Hon. Derek Foster MP.

75   Ibid.

76   Interview with Rt Hon. Frank Dobson MP, 24 April 2003.

77   Interview with Rt Hon. Frank Dobson MP, 3 March 2003.

78   Interview with Rt Hon. Hilary Armstrong MP.

79   Interview with Ann Barrett.

80   Interview with Leo Beckett.

81   Sopel, *Tony Blair*, p. 150.

82   Jones, *Remaking the Labour Party*, pp. 131–2.

83   Interview with Rt Hon. Derek Foster MP.

84   Ibid.

85   E-mail correspondence with Murray Elder, 29 November 2004.

86   Interview with Lord Whitty.

87   Ibid.

88   Benn, *Free at Last!*, p. 124. (Thursday, 23 July 1992).

89   The 1990 Labour Party conference had endorsed in principle the establishment of a new Joint Policy Committee, comprising equal numbers of members from the NEC and the shadow Cabinet, one representative each from the European Parliament and from local government, and the chairperson of the National Policy Forum, the 80-member body established by Neil Kinnock the previous year. *Democracy and Policy Making in the 1990s*. See Larry Whitty, 'Democracy & Future Policy making. Consultative Document to All Constituency Labour Parties & All Affiliated Organisations', 11 April 1991. Kinnock Collection, Box 199.

90   More accurately, Neil Kinnock had borrowed the idea substantially from the Swedish Social Democratic Workers' Party 'Policy Board', and adapted it to suit Labour Party and UK needs. E-mail correspondence with Rt Hon. Neil Kinnock, 22 October 2004.

91   Shore, *Leading the Left*, p. 180.

92   Wickham-Jones, *Economic Strategy and the Labour Party*, p. 213.

93   Fielding, *The Labour Party*, p. 128.

94   Interview with Lord Whitty.

95   Meghnad Desai, 'No easy way out of trouble', *Tribune*, 7 May 1993.

96   Interview with Lord Desai, 10 June 2003.

97   Ibid.

98   HC Debs, 6 May 1993, cc. 270–271.

99   Interview with Lord Desai.

100 HC Debs, 6 May 1993, c. 281.

101 Ibid.

102 Interview with Lord Desai.

103 *Tribune*, 14 May 1993.

104 Interview with Lord Desai.

105 Meghnad Desai, 'Financing Full Employment', *Tribune*, 21 January 1994. For more free-thinking ideas in this period, see Meghnad Desai, 'A basic income is essential', *Tribune*, 1 April 1994.

106 Gould, *Goodbye to All That*, p. 263.

107 Interview with Murray Elder, 11 February 2003.

108 E-mail correspondence with Murray Elder, 29 November 2004.
109 Interview with Lord Hogg of Cumbernauld, 4 November 2003.
110 Langdon, *Mo Mowlam*, p. 222.
111 Mowlam finished joint sixth on 135 votes with Chris Smith and Harriet Harman, but Mowlam and Harman benefited from a rule-change in the shadow Cabinet elections in 1989 – members of the PLP were obliged to cast at least three votes for women candidates to validate their ballot papers. Langdon, *Mo Mowlam*, p. 224.
112 The UN Conference on the Environment and Development (UNCED) had organised an 'Earth Summit' in Rio de Janeiro in June 1992, which had raised global awareness of environmental issues.
113 Interview with Rt Hon. Chris Smith MP, 11 February 2003.
114 Interview with Rt Hon. Hilary Armstrong MP.
115 Interview with Rt Hon. Tony Benn, 6 March 2003.
116 Interview with Rt Hon. Margaret Beckett MP.
117 Interview with Rt Hon. Chris Smith MP.
118 Interview with Rt Hon. Hilary Armstrong MP.
119 Interview with Murray Elder, 12 February 2003.
120 Brown, *Fighting Talk*, p. 232.
121 Interview with Murray Elder, 12 February 2003.
122 Neil Kinnock's notes of a shadow Cabinet meeting, undated, c. 1990. shadow Cabinet Briefings, 1990. Kinnock Collection, Box 83.
123 Letter from John Prescott MP to Murray Elder, 23 April 1993. Murray Elder papers, Box 1.
124 Kampfner, *Robin Cook*, p. 91; p. 96.
125 Brown, *Fighting Talk*, p. 233; Kampfner, *Robin Cook*, p. 96.
126 Interview with Murray Elder, 12 February 2003.
127 Interview with Rt Hon. Frank Dobson MP, 3 March 2003.
128 Cledwyn Hughes stood down and Ivor Richard took over as leader of the Labour peers.
129 Interview with Mike Elrick.

Chapter 19

1 Benn, *Free at Last!*, p. 132 (Tuesday, 15 September 1992).
2 Interview with Rt Hon. Tony Benn, 6 March 2003.
3 Joe Rogaly, 'Reliable Scot resists hammer horror tactics', *Financial Times*, 17 July 1992.
4 As early as June 1991, Gavyn Davies, Chief UK Economist at Goldman Sachs and professor of economics at the LSE, had argued that 'the only acceptable realignment' would be 'revaluation of the D-mark versus the pound, leaving sterling's value against other currencies unchanged'. *Financial Times*, 5 June 1991. And we've already seen how Neil Kinnock, John Eatwell and Charles Clarke conspired – without Smith knowing – to plan an immediate realignment of the pound had Labour been elected in April 1992 (see chapter 16).
5 Rt Hon. John Smith QC MP, speech to European Parliamentary Party, Strasbourg, 9 June 1992. Press notice. David Ward papers; see also Ivo Dawnay, 'Labour exploits Tory split by changing Maastricht tactics' *The Times*, 10 June 1992.
6 McSmith, *Playing the Long Game*, p. 210.
7 Paul Anderson, interview with John Smith, 'Easy Does it?', *Tribune*, 19 June 1992.
8 HC Debs, 2 July 1992, c. 1050.
9 Neil Kinnock, 'Letter to the Editor', *Financial Times*, 16 July 1992.
10 David Ward, 'Why should we argue for an ERM realignment?' Undated, c. July 1992. David Ward papers.
11 Interview with Lord Eatwell, 24 November 2003.
12 Andrew Graham, Some Key Points on Economic Policy: Yesterday's Discussion and some reactions to your notes (copy to John Smith), 24 July 1992. David Ward papers.
13 Fax from David Ward to John Smith, In Confidence, 5 September 1992. David Ward papers.
14 Ibid.
15 Ibid.
16 Fax from David Ward to John Smith, In Confidence, 7 September 1992. David Ward papers.
17 Philip Webster, 'Labour draws up jobs and homes package', *The Times*, 2 September

18 Patricia Tehan and Nicholas Wood, 'Union leaders put pressure on Smith over devaluation', *The Times*, 9 September 1992; David Goodhart and Alison Smith, 'Pressure on Labour over Maastricht', *Financial Times*, 9 September 1992.

19 Nicholas Wood, 'Smith told to quash rebellion over the pound', *The Times*, 10 September 1992; Alison Smith, 'Labour confusion on ERM deepens', *The Times*, 10 September 1992.

20 McSmith, *Playing the Long Game*, p. 231. Although, there are no PLP minutes for 10 September 1992.

21 Routledge, *Gordon Brown*, pp. 168-9.

22 Rentoul, *Tony Blair*, p. 267.

23 Anderson and Mann, *Safety First*, p. 86; Kampfner, *Robin Cook*, p. 92; Naughtie lists Jack Straw, Robin Cook and David Blunkett as having doubts about Smith's European policy around this time. Naughtie, *The Rivals*, p. 48.

24 At the Bath Summit on 5 September, the Chancellor of the Exchequer had made a disastrous attempt to browbeat the Bundesbank into cutting interest rates immediately. See Stephens, *Politics and the Pound*, pp. 228-33.

25 Andrew Graham, Note to Gordon Brown and John Smith, 'Exchange Rates: A Bungled Opportunity', 14 September 1992. David Ward papers.

26 A smaller group of core countries established a Deutschmark bloc, which eventually became the single currency. Andrew Graham, 'Thoughts on the currency crisis', 17 September 1992, cc. Margaret Beckett, Gordon Brown, Tony Blair, Robin Cook, Harriet Harman, Murray Elder, Meta Ramsay, David Hill, Hilary Coffman. David Ward papers.

27 National Executive Committee Statement, *Europe: Our Economic Future*, 23 September 1992. Kinnock Collection, Box 623.

28 Benn, *Free at Last!*, p. 133 (Wednesday, 23 September 1992).

29 Sadly, on 19 January 1993, Judith Chaplin died aged only 53. On 6 May that year, the government then lost the Newbury by-election to the Liberal Democrats on a swing of 28.4 per cent.

30 HC Debs, 24 September 1992, c. 17.

31 Interview with David Ward, 7 June 2003.

32 Seldon, *Major*, p. 461.

33 HC Debs, 24 September 1992, c. 22. Curiously, Brian Brivati's *Guiding Light* omits this truly memorable performance from his otherwise excellent selection of Smith speeches.

34 Major, *Autobiography*, p. 339.

35 *Daily Mail*, 25 September 1992.

36 Peter Riddell, 'Tripped up at the worst time', *The Times*, 25 September 1992.

37 Editorial, 'Mellor and Major', *The Times*, 25 September 1992.

38 Matthew Symonds, 'The jury's still out on Smith's charges', *The Independent*, 25 September 1992.

39 Interview with David Ward, 7 June 2003.

40 Interview with David Ward, 28 April 2003.

41 On 27 May 1993, John Major reshuffled his Cabinet, offering Lamont the post of Environment Secretary, but Lamont refused and resigned from the government. Seldon, *Major*, p. 376.

42 *Hansard* incorrectly recorded the show as *Some Mothers Do 'Ave Them*.

43 HC Debs, 9 June 1993, c. 292. In April 1993, the start of the Grand National was completely botched after several jockeys failed to take notice of a false start. On 3-4 June 1993, the Holbeck Hall Hotel near Scarborough fell into the sea when the cliff it was standing on crumbled away.

44 Interview with David Ward, 28 April 2003.

45 Interview with David Ward, 7 June 2003.

46 HC Debs, 12 May 1994, c. 438.

47 Interview with Rt Hon. Hilary Armstrong MP, 11 February 2003.

48 Interview with Rt Hon. Michael Foot, 20 February 2003.

49 Interview with Rt Hon. Frank Dobson MP, 3 March 2003.

50 Clare Short, 'John Smith's qualities and quality', *Tribune*, 27 May 1994.

51 Interview with Rt Hon. Hilary Armstrong MP.

52 Interview with Murray Elder, 30 April 2003.

53 Interview with Murray Elder, 4 December 2002.

54 Anthony Howard, 'John Smith the lost leader', *The Times*, 13 May 1994.

55 *Ninety-first Annual Conference Report of the Labour Party*, 1992, p. 101.

56 *Ninety-first Annual Conference Report of the Labour Party*, 1992, p. 104.

57 Ruth Wishart, 'Tribute', *The Scotsman*, 13

May 1994.

58 Benn, *Free at Last!*, p. 135 (Friday, 2 October). On the Wednesday, Benn spoke with Smith and told him 'what a pleasure it was that he didn't hector', presumably like Kinnock, p. 135 (Wednesday, 30 September).

59 Interview with Ann Barrett, 21 June 2003.

60 Interview with Leo Beckett, 19 November 2003.

61 Interview with Ann Barrett.

62 Gould, *Goodbye to All That*, p. 268.

63 Interview with Mike Elrick, 10 June 2003.

64 Bruce Anderson, 'Could Mr Smith go to Downing Street?', *Sunday Telegraph*, 8 October 1989.

65 The by-election for Gould's Dagenham constituency was held on 9 June 1994, the same day as the European elections. Judith Church, Labour's candidate, comfortably held onto the seat with a majority of 13,344.

66 Shaw, *The Labour Party Since 1979*, p. 225.

67 HC Debs, 12 May 1994, c. 430.

68 Interview with Murray Elder, 4 December 2002.

69 Simon Hoggart, 'Sharp wit with an inner fire', *The Guardian 2*, 13 May 1994.

70 Correspondence between Rt Hon. John Major MP and Rt Hon. John Smith MP, December 1992–January 1993. Murray Elder papers, Box 1.

71 Interview with Rt Hon. Hilary Armstrong MP.

72 Interview with Murray Elder, 4 December 2002.

73 Ibid.

74 Benn, *Free at Last!*, p. 130 (Wednesday, 2 September 1992).

75 Major, *Autobiography*, p. 432.

76 *The Times*, 19 December 1992.

77 Interview with Rt Hon. Hilary Armstrong MP.

78 Ministerial powers to exclude suspected terrorists living in Northern Ireland from visiting the mainland, or vice versa. Such powers had been used against Gerry Adams.

79 Letter from Rt Hon. Tony Blair MP to Rt Hon. John Smith MP, 15 February 1994. Murray Elder papers, Box 1.

80 Letter from Rt Hon. John Major MP to Rt Hon. John Smith QC MP, 10 March 1994. Murray Elder papers, Box 1.

81 Quoted in letter from Rt Hon. John Major

MP to Rt Hon. John Smith QC MP, 10 March 1994. Murray Elder papers, Box 1.

82 Ibid.

83 Ibid.

84 Letter from Rt Hon. John Smith QC MP to Rt Hon. John Major MP, 10 March 1994. Murray Elder papers, Box 1.

85 Ibid.

86 Ibid.

87 Prime Minister's Questions used to involve two 20-minute sessions on Tuesday and Thursday afternoons. In May 1997, Tony Blair, without consulting the House of Commons, switched PMQs to just one session on a Wednesday at 3 pm lasting 30 minutes. Then in January 2003, in an effort to make PMQs more media-friendly, and to fit them into the new morning sittings, PMQs was shifted again, this time to 12 noon on Wednesdays.

88 Interview with Rt Hon. Hilary Armstrong MP; interview with Murray Elder, 26 November 2002.

89 Interview with David Ward, 7 June 2003.

90 Interview with Murray Elder, 11 February 2003.

91 Interview with Rt Hon. Hilary Armstrong MP.

92 Simon Hoggart, 'Sharp wit with an inner fire', *Guardian 2*, 13 May 1994.

93 Seldon, *Major*, p. 461.

94 Robert Hardman, 'Labour leader's star quality lacks wattage', *Daily Telegraph*, 11 May 1994; see HC Debs, 10 May 1994, c. 150.

95 Interview with Rt Hon. Hilary Armstrong MP.

96 See for example, Stuart, *Douglas Hurd*, p. 271; p. 282; Douglas Hurd, *Memoirs* (Little, Brown: London, 2003), pp. 414-15.

97 Seldon, *Major*, p. 461.

98 Major, *Autobiography*, p. 566.

99 Letter from Rt Hon. John Major MP to Rt Hon. John Smith QC MP, 24 March 1994. Murray Elder papers, Box 1. See HC Debs, 15 March 1994, cc. 740-41.

100 Benn, *Free at Last!*, p. 217. (Wednesday, 12 January 1994).

101 Hugh MacPherson, 'Upright Rabelaisian', *Tribune*, 20 May 1994.

102 For more details on the QMV row, see Stuart, 'The Sapping of Authority' in *Douglas Hurd*, pp. 370-81.

103 HC Debs, 22 March 1994, c. 134.

104 Andrew Grice and Jonathan Todd, 'Smith

in 24-hour U-turn on 35 hours', *The Sunday Times*, 2 November 1993.

105 HC Debs, 10 February 1994, c. 443.

106 Major, *Autobiography*, p. 590.

107 Seldon, *Major*, pp. 450-1.

108 Interview with Rt Hon. Lord Hurd of Westwell CH CBE, Westwell, 13 June 1997.

109 HC Debs, 29 March 1994, c. 798.

Chapter 20

1 David Baker, Andrew Gamble and Steve Ludlam, 'The Parliamentary Siege of Maastricht 1993: Conservative Divisions and British Ratification', *Parliamentary Affairs*, 47 (1994), p. 56.

2 Philip Cowley and Philip Norton with Mark Stuart and Matthew Bailey, *Blair's Bastards: discontent within the Parliamentary Labour Party*. Research Paper in Legislative Studies 1/96 (Hull: University of Hull Centre for Legislative Studies, 1996); Philip Cowley and Philip Norton, *Are Conservative MPs Revolting? Dissension by Government MPs in the British House of Commons 1979-96*. Research Papers in Legislative Studies 2/96 (Hull: University of Hull Centre for Legislative Studies, 1996).

3 Interview with Rt Hon. Tony Benn, 6 March 2003.

4 HC Debs, 22 April 1993, cc. 483-486; Philip Webster and Robert Morgan, 'Rebels lose referendum battle', *The Times*, 22 April 1993.

5 In any case, the government had a majority over Labour of 65, and Kaufman knew that a number of pro-European Labour MPs would have refused to vote against the Bill.

6 The Labour Party's 1992 manifesto had promised that a future Labour government would end the Conservative opt-out from the Social Chapter. *It's Time to Get Britain Working Again*, p. 13.

7 Minutes of the party meeting held on Wednesday 13 May 1992 at 11.30 am in Committee Room 10.

8 Ibid.

9 Three Labour MPs, Tony Banks, Tam Dalyell and Andrew Faulds, voted for the government. HC Debs, 21 May 1992, cc. 597-600; '22 Tories rebel on Maastricht', *The Times*, 22 May 1992.

10 Eighty-four Conservatives eventually

signed EDM 174 – 'Future Development of the EEC' (3 June 1992) – which became known as the 'Fresh-Start' motion, calling for the abandonment of the Treaty. See David Baker, Andrew Gamble, Steve Ludlam, 'Whips or Scorpions? The Maastricht Vote and the Conservative Party', *Parliamentary Affairs*, 46 (1993), pp. 151-66.

11 On seeing a copy of Benn's motion sent by Alan Haworth, Acting Secretary of the PLP, Neil Kinnock noted in the margins: 'No such amendments are being put or will be put.' Kinnock Collection, Box 623.

12 The motion was signed by Peter Hain, Richard Burden, Roger Berry, Clare Short, Bridget Prentice, Clive Betts and John Denham.

13 Nicholas Timmins, 'Labour disarray as Benn presses referendum call', *The Independent*, 11 June 1992. Patrick Wintour called it 'a heated, and sometimes shambolic meeting'. Patrick Wintour, 'Labour keeps a lid on dissent', *The Guardian*, 11 June 1992.

14 Minutes of the party meeting held on Wednesday 10 June 1992 at 11.30 am in Committee Room 14.

15 Ibid.

16 Naughtie, 'A Political Life Observed', in Brown and Naughtie, *Life and Soul of the Party*, p. 51.

17 TUC General Council, 'The Maastricht Treaty and Trade Union Goals', 22 July 1992. David Ward papers.

18 Benn, *Free at Last!*, p. 134 (Monday, 28 September 1992).

19 Composite 69, moved by Tom Burlison (GMB) and seconded by Gavin Laird (AEEU), was carried. Composite 70, urging the PLP to oppose the ratification of Maastricht, and calling for a renegotiated Treaty to be put to a referendum, was defeated. Both Tony Benn and George Robertson spoke in the debate. *Record of Decisions, Ninety-First Annual Conference of the Labour Party* (Blackpool, 1992), p. 5. Kinnock Collection, Box 623; Shore, *Leading the Left*, p. 179.

20 Larry Whitty to John Smith, Annual Conference 1993, Strictly Private and Confidential, 23 March 1993. Murray Elder papers, Box 2.

21 Minutes of the party meeting held on

Wednesday 21 October 1992 at 11.30 am in Committee Room 14.

22 On 21 October 1992, the opposition Motion was defeated by 322 votes to 309, with six Conservatives voting for the Labour motion, and at least a further five abstaining. HC Debs, 21 October 1992, cc. 526-530.

23 HC Debs, 25 March 1993, c. 1233; HC Debs, 29 June 1993, c. 820.

24 Minutes of the party meeting held on Thursday 25 March 1993 at 6 pm in Committee Room 10.

25 For the Second Reading of the Coal Bill, see HC Debs, 18 January 1994, cc. 711-800. Only one Conservative, Elizabeth Peacock, voted against the government during the entire passage of the Bill.

26 HC Debs, 2 June 1992, c. 715.

27 One Labour MP, Dennis Skinner, voted with the Conservatives against the Liberal Democrat motion. The Labour front bench line was to abstain. HC Debs, 16 November 1992, cc. 72-113.

28 Minutes of the party meeting held on Wednesday 18 November 1992 at 11.30 am in Committee Room 14.

29 HC Debs, 18 March 2003, c. 798.

30 Minutes of the party meeting held on Wednesday 21 April 1993 at 11.30am in Committee Room 14.

31 HC Debs, 19 April 1993, cc. 23-25.

32 Minutes of the party meeting held on Wednesday 21 April 1993, op. cit.

33 HC Debs, 7 December 1994, cc. 313-314. See Stuart, *Douglas Hurd*, p. 326.

34 Interview with Rt Hon. Derek Foster MP, 24 June 2003.

35 Charles Kennedy, *The Future of Politics* (HarperCollins Publishers: London, 2000), p. 8.

36 Telephone interview with Rt Hon. Lord Robertson of Port Ellen, 7 July 2003.

37 Ibid.

38 Interview with Rt Hon. Derek Foster MP.

39 Interview with Baroness Goudie, 21 January 2004.

40 Letter from Rt Hon. John Smith, QC, MP to Rt Hon. John Major MP, 6 October 1992. Murray Elder papers, Box 2.

41 Telephone interview with Rt Hon. Lord Robertson of Port Ellen.

42 Telephone interview with Rt Hon. Bruce Millan, 22 January 2004.

43 Written correspondence with Rt Hon.

44 Telephone Interview with Rt Hon. Bruce Millan.

45 Ibid.

46 Written correspondence with Rt Hon. Neil Kinnock, 8 January 2004.

47 Telephone interview with Rt Hon. Lord Robertson of Port Ellen.

48 Written correspondence with Rt Hon. Neil Kinnock.

49 Telephone Interview with Rt Hon. Lord Robertson of Port Ellen.

50 Written correspondence with Rt Hon. Neil Kinnock.

51 Telephone interview with Rt Hon. Bruce Millan; written correspondence with Rt Hon. Neil Kinnock.

52 Interview with Rt Hon. Derek Foster MP.

53 Minutes of the party meeting held on Thursday 29 October 1992 at 6 pm in Committee Room 10.

54 HC Debs, 4 November 1992, cc. 377-381.

55 Twenty-three Conservatives voted against the government. HC Debs, 4 November 1992, cc. 381-385.

56 Interview with Rt Hon. Derek Foster MP.

57 Minutes of the party meeting held on Thursday 18 February 1993 at 6pm in Committee Room 11.

58 Minutes of the party meeting held on Thursday 14 January 1993 at 6pm in Committee Room 11; minutes of the party meeting held on Thursday 21 January 1993 at 6pm in Committee Room 12; minutes of the party meeting held on Thursday 28 January 1993 in Committee Room 11; minutes of the party meeting held on Thursday 18 February 1993 at 6 pm in Committee Room 11.

59 Minutes of the party meeting held on Wednesday 14 April 1993 at 11.30 am in Committee Room 14.

60 Interview with Rt Hon. Derek Foster MP. See for example, 'Debate on Treaty is cut short', *The Times*, 2 February 1993; Philip Webster and Nicholas Wood, 'Ministers back down from late sitting on Treaty', *The Times*, 12 March 1993.

61 Minutes of the party meeting held on Thursday 18 February 1993 at 6 pm in Committee Room 11.

62 The opposition operated a three-line whip throughout, but Jack Cunningham later agreed to a weekly briefing meeting for all Labour back benchers for the duration of

the Bill's passage. Minutes of the party meeting held on Wednesday 2 December 1992 at 11.30 am in Committee Room 14.

63 Minutes of the party meeting held on Thursday 26 November 1992 at 6 pm in Committee Room 9.

64 Ibid.

65 Minutes of the party meeting held on Wednesday 20 January 1993 at 11.30 am in Committee Room 14.

66 For details of the Edinburgh Summit, see Stuart, *Douglas Hurd*, pp. 308–11.

67 On 20 September 1992, the French referendum on Maastricht had been carried by 50.95 per cent to 49.05 per cent. Charles Bremner and Robin Oakley, 'Knife-edge French "yes" brings problems for Major', *The Times*, 21 September 1992.

68 Interview with David Ward, 7 June 2003.

69 Telephone interview with Rt Hon. Lord Robertson of Port Ellen, 8 September 2003.

70 Peter Riddell, 'Opaque Smith clouds EC issue', *The Times*, 19 January 1993.

71 Minutes of the party meeting held on Wednesday 20 January 1993 at 11.30 am in Committee Room 14.

72 Telephone interview with Rt Hon. Lord Robertson of Port Ellen, 7 July 2003.

73 Interview with Rt Hon. Derek Foster MP.

74 HC Debs, 21 April 1993, c. 410.

75 HC Debs, 4 May 1993, c. 140.

76 The leadership amendment also stated that economic policymaking in the EC should be made more democratically accountable by ensuring that ECOFIN became 'the effective political counterpart to European Central Bank'. By putting down an amendment, the leadership ensured that Smith would have the opportunity of speaking last, winding up the debate. Interview with Alan Haworth, 15 December 2003.

77 Minutes of the party meeting held on Wednesday 17 February 1993 at 11.30 am in Committee Room 14.

78 Ibid.

79 Ibid.

80 A substantive motion was then put, and 'carried by a large majority'. Minutes of the party meeting held on Wednesday 17 February 1993 at 11.30 am in Committee Room 14.

81 David Alton was the only Liberal Democrat to vote with the government.

HC Debs, 8 March 1993, cc. 715-19.

82 Article 104c and the attached Protocol on Excessive Budget deficits.

83 Minutes of the party meeting held on Wednesday 10 March 1993 at 11.30 am in Committee Room 14.

84 The amendment claimed that matters related to the budget deficit required 'political judgement', and stated that 'The PLP strongly believes that levels of growth, investment and employment' had to be included in member state's medium term budgetary position, and recognised that 'real economic convergence is the necessary pre-condition of any move towards economic and monetary union'.

85 Minutes of the party meeting held on Wednesday 10 March 1993 at 11.30 am in Committee Room 14.

86 A substantive motion was then put, and carried by 'a large majority'. Ibid.

87 Interview with Alan Haworth

88 Interview with David Ward.

89 Bill Cash's amendment deleting the Protocol on the Transition to the Third Stage of EMU attracted 39 Labour rebels. HC Debs, 19 April 1993, cc. 104-107; while his amendment opposing Article 12.1 of the Protocol on the European System of Central Banks and of the ECB attracted 47 Labour rebels. HC Debs, 19 April 1993, cc. 107-110.

90 Minutes of the party meeting held on Thursday 13 May 1993 at 6pm in Committee Room 10.

91 Ibid.

92 The demand for a referendum on the Treaty continued to rumble on both the Labour and Conservative back benches. On 21 April 1993, the House voted decisively by 363 to 124 against a referendum. Some 38 Conservatives, and 65 Labour back benchers rebelled against front bench advice. HC Debs, 20 May 1993, cc. 468-471; 'Maastricht bill clears Commons despite big revolt', *The Times*, 21 May 1993.

93 *Tribune*, 28 May 1993. *Tribune* gives the number of Labour rebels voting against the party line as 66, but excludes the two tellers, Nigel Spearing and Ron Leighton. The five Labour MPs who voted in favour of Third Reading were Andrew Faulds, John Home Robertson, Calum MacDonald, Giles Radice and Brian

Sedgemore.

94   Telephone interview with Rt Hon. Lord Robertson of Port Ellen.

95   '"Timebomb" clause poses new threat to Maastricht', *The Times*, 31 March 1993.

96   Minutes of the party meeting held on Wednesday 14 April 1993 at 11.30 am in Committee Room 14.

97   Minutes of the party meeting held on Thursday 29 April 1993 at 6 pm in Committee Room 10.

98   This paragraph is largely drawn from Stuart, 'Game, Set and Match: The Parliamentary Ratification of the Maastricht Treaty, April 1992-July 1993', in Stuart, *Douglas Hurd*, p. 313.

99   HC Debs, 22 July 1993, cc. 499-504.

100   HC Debs, 22 July 1993, cc. 519-528.

101   HC Debs, 22 July 1993, cc. 529-541. Oddly, Brian Brivati includes Smith's 22 July 1993 speech in his anthology of Smith's best speeches. Brivati, *Guiding Light*, p. 225–39.

102   The vote was subsequently found to have been 317 to 316 in favour of the government due to a counting error by a Conservative whip. The Speaker's casting vote was therefore not necessary.

103   HC Debs, 22 July 1993, cc. 604-612.

104   George Robertson, 'Maastricht madness', *Tribune*, 30 July 1993.

105   Telephone interview with Rt Hon. Lord Robertson of Port Ellen.

106   Seldon, *Major*, p. 388.

107   Major, *Autobiography*, p. 384. Tony Benn agrees that 'Smith was very good – he made fun of Major quite successfully.' Benn, *Free at Last!*, p. 193 (Friday, 22 July 1993).

108   Telephone interview with Rt Hon. Lord Robertson of Port Ellen.

109   Interview with Rt Hon. Derek Foster MP.

110   Minutes of the party meeting held on 18 February 1993 at 6 pm in Committee Room 11.

111   Telephone interview with Rt Hon. Lord Robertson of Port Ellen.

112   Rt Hon. John Smith QC, press release, 9 December 2003.

113   Minutes of the party meeting held on Thursday 9 December 1993 at 6 pm in Committee Room 10.

114   Minutes of the party meeting held on Thursday 13 January 1994 at 6 pm in Committee Room 10.

115   Ibid.

116   Interview with Rt Hon. Derek Foster MP.

117   Minutes of the party meeting held on Thursday 13 January 1994 at 6 pm in Committee Room 10.

118   Interview with Rt Hon. Derek Foster MP.

119   Minutes of the party meeting held on Thursday 28 April 1994 at 6 pm in Committee Room 10. The following Wednesday, Foster presented the PLP with a fuller report, outlining these supposedly significant concessions. The government pledged: not to table all stages of a Bill in one day without the prior agreement of the opposition; maximum advance notice would be given of guillotines on the Annunciator; statements would be available no later than 3pm and would not be given out to the press before delivery; and no government statements would be made on Opposition Days. In return, Labour would recommence negotiations on the Jopling Report, *Report from the Select Committee on Sittings of the House* (Session 1991-92) (House of Commons Papers 20 I, 20 II). Minutes of the party meeting held on Wednesday 4 May 1994 at 11.30am in Committee Room 14.

120   Interview with Rt Hon. Derek Foster MP.

Chapter 21

1   Quoted in Macintyre, *Mandelson*, pp. 244–5.

2   See, for example, Philip Stephens, 'Labour's leader-in-waiting', *Financial Times*, 16 July 1992; Sarah Baxter, 'Winning Labour a moral majority', *New Statesman & Society*, 10 December 1993; Benn, *Free at Last!*, p. 148. (Saturday, 14 November 1992); Routledge, 'Backbench Novice' in *Mandy*, Chapter Nine, pp. 136–53.

3   Sopel, *Tony Blair*, p. 137.

4   Ivo Dawnay, 'Scottish sword-play', *Financial Times*, 15 July 1992.

5   Benn, *Free at Last!*, p. 124 (Thursday, 23 July 1992). See also, Brown, *Fighting Talk*, p. 234.

6   Memo from Philip Gould to Murray Elder, Assessment of Current Position, 20 May 1993. Murray Elder papers, Box 2.

7   Tony Blair, 'A battle we must win', *Fabian Review*, Vol. 105, No. 5, September/October 1993, p.1.

8   Gould, *The Unfinished Revolution*, p. 179.

9   Quoted in Sopel, *Tony Blair*, p. 124.

10 David Hare claims that the story was told to him by Neil Kinnock. E-mail correspondence with Sir David Hare, 2 November 2004.

11 Hattersley, *Who Goes Home?*, p. 312.

12 Nick Raynsford, 'Sleepwalking into Oblivion?', *Fabian Review*, Vol. 104, No. 6, November 1992, p. 1, p.3.

13 Stuart Hall, 'Post Mortem: No new vision, no new votes', *New Statesman & Society*, 17 April 1992.

14 Brown, *Fighting Talk*, p. 234.

15 Shore, *Leading the Left*, p. 187.

16 Naughtie, *The Rivals*, p. 51.

17 Interview with Rt Hon. Lord Hattersley, 3 March 2003.

18 Ibid.

19 Alastair Campbell, 'John Smith's Great Journey', *Today*, 13 May 1994.

20 Jeff Lovitt, interview with John Smith, 'Safe in Labour's hands?', *Tribune*, 7 September 1990.

21 Peter Riddell, 'That Missing Spark', *The Times*, 1 July 1993.

22 See also, Roger Berry, 'Who's afraid of public spending?', *Tribune*, 9 July 1993.

23 Janet Anderson, PPS to Margaret Beckett, took over as Tribune Group secretary.

24 Robert Shrimsley, 'Hain loses Tribune job in loyalist "reprisal"', *Daily Telegraph*. Hain lost by 37 votes to 34.

25 Bryan Gould, 'A radical recipe for Labour', *New Statesman & Society*, 19 February 1993; 'Time to abandon super-caution', *New Statesman & Society*, 16 July 1993. Gould also attacked Labour's stance towards the Maastricht Treaty: Bryan Gould, 'Treaty trickery', *Tribune*, 18 December 1992; and for similar views, Peter Hain, 'Euro-back is a danger', *Tribune*, 26 February 1993.

26 *Tribune*, 9 July 1993.

27 Both Margaret Beckett and Murray Elder agree on this point. Interview with Rt Hon. Margaret Beckett MP, 19 November 1993; interview with Murray Elder, 26 November 2002.

28 Interview with Ruth Wishart, 15 January 2004.

29 News Release, statement by Gordon Brown MP, shadow Chancellor, Wednesday, 15 September 1993. Murray Elder papers, Box 1.

30 Summary Plan: Economic Campaigning 1993 [undated]. Murray Elder papers, Box 1.

31 Peter Riddell and Philip Webster, 'Interview with Margaret Beckett', *The Times*, 21 June 1994.

32 Extract from Speech by Rt Hon. John Smith QC MP, to the General Council Dinner at the Scottish Trades Union Congress, Thursday, 23 April 1992. David Ward papers.

33 *Tribune*, 5 March 1993.

34 Labour Party, *Report of the Working Party on Electoral Systems* (Labour Party: London, March 1993) (Plant Report). Plant recommended a modified first-past-the-post system, a version of the Alternative Vote (AV), although he personally had favoured the Additional Member System (AMS). Under AV, the old single-member constituencies would remain, but each voter would be asked to list their second preference. If no candidate received more than half of the votes cast, then the second preference votes of those backing all but the top two candidates would be reallocated amongst the two front-runners until one attained 50 per cent of the vote.

35 McSmith, *John Smith*, p. 326.

36 Paddy Ashdown, *The Ashdown Diaries* (Allen Lane. The Penguin Press: Harmondsworth, 2000), p. 42 (11 May 1989).

37 *Tribune*, 26 June 1992. Quoted in Rentoul, *Tony Blair*, p. 451.

38 Interview with Murray Elder, 12 February 2003.

39 Paul Anderson, interview with John Smith, 'Easy Does it?', *Tribune*, 19 June 1992.

40 Now Lord Rooker, Minister of State at various government departments since 1997.

41 Ivo Dawnay, 'Smith to seek overhaul of "creaking constitution"', *Financial Times*, 30 November 1992.

42 'Constitutional Issues', Letter from Jeff Rooker MP to Rt Hon. John Smith MP, 3 December 1992. Murray Elder papers, Box 1.

43 'Constitutional Issues', Letter from the office of the leader of the opposition to Jeff Rooker MP, 15 December 1992. Murray Elder papers, Box 1.

44 Note from Jeff Rooker MP to Rt Hon. John Smith MP, undated [December 1992]. Murray Elder papers, Box 1.

45 Roth and Criddle, *Parliamentary Profiles, L-R, 1997–2002*, p. 1855.

46 Letter from Rt Hon. John Patten MP to Rt Hon. John Smith QC MP, 19 March 1993. Murray Elder papers, Box 1.

47 Minutes of the party meeting held on Wednesday 12 May 1993 at 11.30 am in Committee Room 14.

48 Labour MP for Leeds Central from 1983 until his death in May 1999, after having served as Minister of State at the Foreign and Commonwealth Office.

49 The pugnacious Member for Birmingham Northfield from October 1982 to June 1983, and Warley West from 1992–7, and for the redrawn seat of Warley since 1997. A defence minister in Blair's first administration, rising to Minister of State level, then shifting to Transport, Local Government and the Regions in 2001, and then to Northern Ireland in the June 2003 reshuffle.

50 Labour MP for Lichfield and Tamworth, from October 1974 until his defeat in 1979. Subsequently elected as Labour MP for The Wrekin, serving from 1987–97, and then for Telford, 1997–2001. Served as PPS to Tony Blair, as leader of the opposition, from 1994–7, and again from 1997–2001, before being elevated to the House of Lords.

51 Minutes of the party meeting held on Wednesday 12 May 1993 at 11.30 am in Committee Room 14.

52 Benn, *Free at last!*, p. 178 (Wednesday, 19 May 1993).

53 The NEC had met on Wednesday, 28 April 1993 to consider the Plant Report, but had deferred making any decision on the report until 19 May, pending a consultation exercise.

54 *Tribune*, 21 May 1993.

55 Interview with Murray Elder, 12 February 2003.

56 Peter Riddell and Philip Webster, 'Interview with Margaret Beckett', *The Times*, 21 June 1994.

57 David Broughton, 'Chronology of Events', in David Broughton, David M. Farrell, David Denver and Colin Rallings (eds), *British Elections and Parties Yearbook 1994* (Frank Cass: London, 1995), p. 234.

58 Derek Fatchett's first-past-the-post group had attracted the support of 86 Labour MPs, and on the other side of the debate, 62 back benchers, including Peter Mandelson, supported Jeff Rooker, chairman of the Labour Campaign for Electoral Reform.

59 Interview with Murray Elder, 12 February 2003.

60 Under AMS, voters would have two votes, one for their constituency and one for the regional top-up, allowing parties (especially the Conservatives and the SNP) to gain top-up seats, even though they struggled to beat Labour in the first-past-the-post seats. It should be noted, however, that the numbers outlined here were proposed during the George Robertson/Jack McConnell period, not the earlier Donald Dewar/Murray Elder period.

61 McSmith, *Faces of Labour*, p. 329.

62 Quoted in Anderson and Mann, *Safety First*, p. 213.

63 Kirsty Milne, 'Fair Dealing: Interview with Sir Gordon Borrie', *New Statesman & Society*, 5 February 1993.

64 Interview with Lord Borrie QC, 2 June 2003.

65 Kirsty Milne, 'Fair Dealing: Interview with Sir Gordon Borrie', op. cit.

66 Interview with Lord Borrie QC.

67 The fourteen were: Tony Atkinson, professor of political economy at Cambridge and John Gennard, professor of industrial relations at the University of Strathclyde; David Marquand, former Labour MP for Ashfield from 1966–7, an SDP-splitter and Steve Webb, a programme director at the Institute for Fiscal Studies, and later Liberal Democrat MP for Northavon from 1997; Christopher (later Lord) Haskins, chairman of Northern Foods; Margaret Wheeler, an officer of the Confederation of Health Service Employees; the Very Rev. John Gladwin, Provost of Sheffield, and architect of the Archbishop of Canterbury's 'Faith in the City' initiative; Anita Bhalla, a Birmingham journalist; Bernard Williams, a philosopher from Oxford, and formerly married to Shirley Williams; Ethne McLaughlin, a social administration academic from Queen's University, Belfast and Penelope Leach, a

child psychologist; Emma Maclennan, a former junior member of Smith's shadow Treasury team as a Labour employee, who had gone on to become vice-chair of the Low Pay Unit and whose partner was David Ward, Smith's director of Policy Operations; Bert Massie, director of the Royal Association for Disability and Rehabilitation and Ruth Lister, a former director of the Child Poverty Action Group. Quoted from Anderson and Mann, *Safety First*, pp. 420–1. See also Stephen Overell, 'A Who's Who of Labour's Commission on Social Justice: Great and good?', *Tribune*, 22 January 1993.

68 Interview with Lord Borrie QC.

69 The Commission went to a great deal of effort to define 'social justice', coming up with something incorporating a hierarchy of four ideas: that all citizens were of equal value to society; that citizens were entitled to have their basic needs met; that each person should have the right to develop their life chances to the fullest of their abilities; and that society should attempt to reduce and, if possible, eradicate unjust inequalities. Commission on Social Justice, *Social Justice: Strategies for National Renewal* (Vintage: London, 1994), pp. 17–18 (Hereafter, *Strategies for National Renewal*).

70 Commission on Social Justice, *Strategies for National Renewal*, pp. 61–90.

71 Interview with Lord Borrie QC.

72 Ibid.

73 Ibid.

74 Interview with David Ward, 7 June 2003.

75 During its deliberations, Brown sent a copy of a biography of William Beveridge – Jose Harris's *William Beveridge* (Clarendon Press: Oxford, 1977) – to the Commission, indicating more than a passing interest in its deliberations. Interview with Lord Borrie QC.

76 Independent Commission on International Development Issues, *North-South: a programme for survival* (Pan: London, 1981) (Brandt Report).

77 E-mail correspondence with Murray Elder, 29 November 2004.

78 Interview with David Ward, 7 June 2003.

79 John Smith, 'Reinventing the United Nations', The Robert F. Kennedy Memorial Lecture, 4 November 1993 in Brivati (ed.), *Guiding Light*, pp. 240–52.

80 Interview with David Ward, 28 April 2003.

81 In some respects, the Treasury team before 1992 had already examined the issue of green taxation, so the boat had been pushed out already.

82 Interview with Rt Hon. Chris Smith MP, 11 February 2003.

83 *Tribune*, 11 June 1993.

84 Anderson and Mann, *Safety First*, p. 46.

85 E-mail correspondence with Andrew Graham, 9 November 2004.

86 Anderson and Mann, *Safety First*, p. 46.

87 Benn, *Free at Last!*, pp. 194–5 (Wednesday, 28 July 1993).

88 Joint Policy Committee, Minutes of the Seventh Meeting of the Joint Policy Committee, House of Commons 20 September 1993 (Policy Directorate: JPC Minutes (8)/September 1993), Murray Elder papers, Box 1. Colin McCaig also mentions a private Labour Party briefing memoranda from John Smith's leader's office when examining the development of Labour's education policy under Kinnock, Smith and Blair. Colin McCaig, 'New Labour and Education, Education, Education', in Steve Ludlam and Martin J. Smith (eds), *New Labour in Government* (Macmillan Press Ltd: Basingstoke, 2001), p. 190; p. 288.

89 McSmith, *Faces of Labour*, p. 326.

90 Interview with Rt Hon. Hilary Armstrong MP, 11 February 2003.

91 Interview with Murray Elder, 12 February 2003.

92 Interview with Rt Hon. Hilary Armstrong MP.

93 Interview with Murray Elder.

94 Routledge, *Gordon Brown*, p. 168.

95 Paul Anderson, interview with John Smith, 'Easy Does it?', *Tribune*, 19 June 1992.

96 Interview with Rt Hon. Lord Hattersley.

97 Interview with Lord Desai, 10 June 2003.

98 Ibid.

99 For a classic example, witness the way Peter Hain was forced to change his speech calling for a 'grown up and honest debate on tax'. Michael White, Sarah Hall and Larry Elliott, 'Hain forced to retreat on rich tax', *The Guardian*, 21 June 2003.

100 Interview with David Ward, 28 April 2003.

101 Minutes of a special party meeting held on Tuesday 23 November 1993 at 11.30am in

Committee Room 14.

102 Routledge, *Gordon Brown*, pp. 173–4.

103 Quoted in Routledge, *Gordon Brown*, p.185.

104 Macintyre, *Mandelson*, p. 255.

105 Brown finished fourth behind Robin Cook, Frank Dobson and John Prescott, though still ahead of Blair. McSmith, *Faces of Labour*, p. 329.

106 Routledge, *Gordon Brown*, p. 174.

107 Interview with Rt Hon. Chris Smith MP.

108 Interview with Rt Hon. Lord Hattersley.

109 Desai was never as concerned as Smith about political accountability, but rather about the need for fiscal and monetary co-ordination between European finance ministers. Interview with Lord Desai.

110 The three Scottish Labour MPs were Malcolm Chisholm, Jimmy Hood and Jimmy Wray.

111 Benn, *Free at Last!*, p. 165 (Thursday, 4 March 1993).

112 Editorial, 'Empty Mr Smith goes to Bournemouth', *Tribune*, 12 February 1993.

113 Routledge, *Gordon Brown*, p. 186.

114 Anderson and Mann, *Safety First*, p. 45.

115 For the definitive work on the beliefs and economic strategy of Gordon Brown, see William Keegan, *The Prudence of Mr Gordon Brown* (John Wiley & Sons Ltd: Chichester, paperback edn, 2004).

116 Seyd and Whiteley, *New Labour's Grassroots*, pp. 7–8.

117 E-mail correspondence with Murray Elder, 29 November 2004.

118 (Heinemann: London, 1966–1988), 8 vols.

119 Ben Pimlott, 'The Legacy of a Valued Leader', *New Century*, Issue 4: July-August 1994; see also, Ben Pimlott, 'Not a Gaitskell, but perhaps an Attlee', *Independent on Sunday*, 15 May 1994.

120 Bryant, a former Church of England priest, wrote biographies of Stafford Cripps and Glenda Jackson and was elected Labour MP for Rhondda in June 2001.

121 Chris Bryant (ed.), *Reclaiming the Ground* (London: Spire, 1993). This book contained a foreword by Tony Blair. A year later, a completely separate book, *John Smith. An Appreciation* (Hodder & Stoughton: London, 1994), did not contain Smith's lecture or the foreword by Tony Blair. Nevertheless, due to a printing error, Tony Blair's name is listed on the

contents page of *An Appreciation* as the author of the foreword, and yet, Bryant (or 'Brayant' as his name is mis-spelt) supplies the introduction instead. E-mail correspondence with Chris Bryant MP, 7 November 2003.

122 Gordon Brown, 'John Smith's Socialism: His Writings and Speeches', in Brown and Naughtie, *Life and Soul of the Party*, pp. 61–103.

123 Interview with Lord McCluskey, 13 May 2003.

124 Interview with Murray Elder, 29 October 2002.

125 Elizabeth Smith, 'Introduction', in Brown and Naughtie, *Life and Soul of the Party*, p. 13.

126 Interview with Rt Hon. Lord Irvine of Lairg PC QC, 30 April 2003.

127 Ibid.; interview with Lord Gordon of Strathblane CBE, 10 March 2003.

128 Interview with Lord Hogg of Cumbernauld, 4 November 2003; interview with Lord Gordon of Strathblane CBE.

129 Interview with Rt Hon. Lord Irvine of Lairg PC QC.

130 Interview with Baroness Smith of Gilmorehill DL, 4 December 2002; interview with John Battle MP, 13 July 2004.

131 Interview with Lord Hogg of Cumbernauld; interview with David Ward, 7 June 2003.

132 Interview with Lord Hogg of Cumbernauld.

133 William Temple, *Christianity and Social Order* (Penguin: Harmondsworth, 1942).

134 John Smith, 'Reclaiming the Ground', reproduced in *Christian Socialist* (John Smith Commemorative Issue), Issue 187, Spring 2004, p. 10.

135 Smith, 'Reclaiming the Ground', *Christian Socialist*, p. 11.

136 John Smith's great friend, Bob McLaughlan, may have encouraged him to look at the philosophy of Adam Smith, notwith-standing the fact that in later life McLaughlan became very right-wing, and was a great admirer of Margaret Thatcher.

137 Ivo Dawnay, 'Scottish sword-play', *Financial Times*, 15 July 1992.

138 Interview with John Battle MP.

139 Interview with Rt Hon. Paul Boateng MP, 6 September 2004.

140 Interview with Murray Elder, 12 February 2003; see also Paul Anderson, interview with Gordon Brown, 'New Economics', *Tribune*, 1 January 1993.

141 Jones, *Remaking the Labour Party*, p. 132.

142 Ben Clift, 'New Labour's Third Way and European Social Democracy', in Ludlam and Smith (eds), *New Labour in Government*, p. 57.

143 Interview with Rt Hon. Frank Dobson MP, 3 March 2003.

144 Interview with Murray Elder, 12 February 2003.

145 See Robert B. Reich, *The Work of Nations: Preparing Ourselves for 21st-century Capitalism* (Simon & Schuster: London, 1991).

146 Interview with Rt Hon. Frank Dobson MP.

147 Interview with Murray Elder, 12 February 2003.

148 Ibid.

149 Interview with Rt Hon. Frank Dobson MP.

150 Gould, *The Unfinished Revolution*, p. 177.

151 Routledge, *Gordon Brown*, pp. 175–6; Rentoul, *Tony Blair*, p. 273.

152 Philip Gould and Patricia Hewitt, 'Lessons from America', *Renewal*, January 1993.

153 Gould, *The Unfinished Revolution*, p. 176.

154 Benn, *Free at Last!*, pp. 159–60. (Wednesday, 27 January 1993). Around half of this quotation is taken from Benn's unedited diaries. Interview with Rt Hon. Tony Benn, 6 March 2003.

155 Interview with Rt Hon. Tony Benn.

156 Quoted in Rentoul, *Tony Blair*, p. 274.

157 Quoted in Macintyre, *Mandelson*, p. 241.

158 Macintyre, *Mandelson*, p. 241.

159 Naughtie, *The Rivals*, p. 212.

160 Paul Anderson, interview with Tony Blair, 'Boy Wonder', *Tribune*, 29 January 1993.

161 Hugh MacPherson, 'Smith's lessons in sticking to principles', *Tribune*, 8 May 1992.

162 Interview with Ann Barrett, 21 June 2003.

163 Kampfner, *Robin Cook*, p. 91.

164 Gould, *The Unfinished Revolution*, p. 179.

165 Interview with Rt Hon. Margaret Beckett MP, 19 November 2003.

166 Minutes of the party meeting held on Thursday 25 February 1993 at 6pm in Committee Room 10.

167 Tim Mills, The Labour Party. Background Qualitative Research, September/October 1993. Murray Elder papers, Box 2.

168 Sally Morgan and Rex Osborne [Political Strategy Officer], Outline Polling Group Structure (undated, c. end 1993). Murray Elder papers, Box 2.

169 Interview with Rt Hon. Margaret Beckett MP.

170 Interview with Mike Elrick, 10 June 2003.

171 'Background Information: Vocabulary That Worked Well; Vocabulary That Didn't Work Well', undated, (c. 1993). Murray Elder papers, Box 1.

172 Interview with Rt Hon. Margaret Beckett MP.

173 Ibid.

174 Interview with Murray Elder, 12 February 2003.

175 Minutes of the party meeting held on Wednesday 8 December 1993 at 11.30 am in Committee Room 14.

176 Telephone interview with Rt Hon. Lord Robertson of Port Ellen, 7 July 2003.

177 David Ward, 'Note to John Smith: Some thoughts after the first six months' (undated, c. January 1993), David Ward papers.

178 Memorandum from Delyth Evans to John Smith [Copies to Murray Elder and David Ward], 2 June 1993. Murray Elder papers, Box 2.

179 Interview with Baroness Ramsay of Cartvale, 10 September 2003.

180 David, Delyth and Andrew, 'Themes for the 21st Century'. A note for John Smith. David Ward papers.

181 Interview with Murray Elder, 17 September 2003.

182 Ibid.

183 Briefing for Use of the Selected Polling Data, October/November 1993; Memo from Philip Gould to Murray Elder, Assessment of Current Position, 20 May 1993; Murray Elder papers, Box 2. Opinion leader Research, Debrief of Two Group Discussions Carried out for the Labour Party on 8 June 1993, 14 June 1993 (Confidential). Murray Elder papers, Box 2.

184 Opinion leader Research, Debrief of Two Group Discussions Carried out for the Labour Party on 8 June 1993, 14 June 1993 (Confidential); Briefing for Use of the Selected Polling Data, October/November 1993. Murray Elder papers, Box 2.

185 Briefing for Use of the Selected Polling

Data, October/November 1993. Murray Elder papers, Box 2. After chairing (or 'moderating') four focus groups in September 1993, Tim Mills of NOP also concluded that their views made 'grim reading' for Labour. Tim Mills, The Labour Party. Background Qualitative Research, September/October 1993. Murray Elder papers, Box 2.

186 Philip Gould, Fighting the Fear Factor, 28 October 1993. Murray Elder papers, Box 2. Steven Fielding agrees, adding that such feelings were especially prevalent among people who had 'done well out of the 1980s, [but] were also vulnerable to economic instability'. Fielding, The Labour Party, p. 97.

187 Briefing for Use of the Selected Polling Data, October/November 1993. Murray Elder papers, Box 2.

188 David Hill, 'What the Electorate Think of Us' (undated, c. late autumn 1993). Murray Elder papers, Box 2.

189 Interview with Ann Barrett.

190 David Ward, 'Note to John Smith: Some thoughts after the first six months' (undated, c. January 1993). David Ward papers. Coverage of the JPC launch was indeed low key, and largely reserved for the inside pages of the broadsheets. See for example, Philip Webster, 'Smith's aims to regain Labour initiative on economic policy', The Times, 19 December 1992.

191 David Ward, 'Note to John Smith: Some thoughts after the first six months', op. cit.

192 Memorandum from Delyth Evans to John Smith [Copies to Murray Elder and David Ward], 2 June 1993. Murray Elder papers, Box 2.

193 Ibid.

194 Ibid.

195 Andrew Marr, 'Don't read too much Tolstoy, Mr Smith', The Independent, 20 January 1994.

196 Anthony Heath, Roger Jowell and John Curtice, How Britain Votes (Permagon Press: Oxford, 1985).

197 Letter from Rt Hon. the Lord Rodgers of Quarry Bank to Rt Hon. John Smith QC MP, 16 April 1993. Murray Elder papers, Box 1.

198 Interview with Rt Hon. Lord Rodgers of Quarry Bank, 20 January 2004.

199 Interview with Baroness Ramsay of Cartvale.

200 Sopel, Tony Blair, p. 152.

201 Alastair Campbell, 'John Smith's Great Journey', Today, 13 May 1994.

202 Interview with Ann Barrett.

203 E-mail correspondence with Sir David Hare, 2 November 2004.

204 Interview with David Ward, 7 June 2003.

205 Quoted in Macintyre, Mandelson, p. 241.

206 Woman's Own, 21 June 1993.

207 Telephone conversation with Baroness Smith of Gilmorehill DL, 12 November 2002.

208 Ibid.

209 Interview with Ann Barrett.

210 Peter Kosminsky, The Project, Episode 1, BBC1, 10 November 2002 (transcript).

211 Michael Brunson, A Ringside Seat. An Autobiography (Hodder & Stoughton: London, 2000), pp. 314–7.

212 Rentoul, Tony Blair, p. 5.

213 Gould, The Unfinished Revolution, p. 178; Sopel, Tony Blair, pp. 158–60; Rentoul, Tony Blair, pp. 283–307; Routledge, Gordon Brown, pp. 168–9; pp. 186–7.

214 Routledge, Gordon Brown, p. 182. Routledge uses the notion of 'two sturdy oxen' for his chapter title outlining the growing influence of Brown and Blair during the leadership of John Smith, pp. 161–88.

215 Brown, Fighting Talk, p. 228.

216 John Smith, interview with ITN, 4 December 1992 (transcript).

217 Hattersley, Fifty Years On, p. 374.

Chapter 22

1 Macintyre, Mandelson, p. 242.

2 Neil Kinnock, 'Discussion of General Election', Minutes of a special party meeting held on Wednesday 1 July 1992 at 11 am in Committee Room 14.

3 Charles Clarke, Briefing Note: John Edmonds, 15.30, undated, c. 1991. Kinnock Collection, Box 199.

4 Neil Kinnock, covering letter, Memorandum of Selection and Reselection, 20 May 1992, OMOV. Kinnock Collection, Box 180.

5 Ibid.

6 A similar sense of frustration is revealed in another briefing paper, A Settlement with the Trade Unions and the Labour Party, written shortly before Neil Kinnock's last NEC as Labour leader (24 June 1992),

written either by Neil Kinnock or Charles Clarke. The top of the document is headed: 'My Ideas Only, Neil'. Charles Clarke/Neil Kinnock, *A Settlement with the Trade Unions and the Labour Party*, undated (June, 1992), OMOV. Kinnock Collection, Box 180.

7 NEC Minutes, 27 May 1992 (Wed), 10 am, OMOV. Kinnock Collection, Box 180.

8 Ibid.

9 Written correspondence with Larry Whitty, 26 October 2004.

10 Charles Clarke, Briefing Note to Neil Kinnock, prior to meeting with Bill Morris, 'your room', 16.30 pm, undated, c. early June 1992, OMOV. Kinnock Collection, Box 180.

11 Written correspondence with Lord Whitty, 25 April 2003.

12 Neil Kinnock's notes, NEC, Tuesday, 24 April 1992. Kinnock Collection, Box 303.

13 In a note prepared for the NEC meeting on 24 June, Whitty had suggested establishing 'an authoritative Review Group to look at all aspects of the relationship and make recommendations for any rule changes to the 1992 and 1993 Annual Conferences'. Labour Party/Trade Union Relations (GS: 22/6/92) [Draft note by the general secretary] (sent to all members of the NEC, 22 June 1992 in advance of 24 June 1992 NEC). Kinnock Collection, Box 180.

14 Charles Clarke, Briefing Note to Neil Kinnock, prior to meeting with Robin Cook, 'your room', 10 am, undated (June, 1992), OMOV. Kinnock Collection, Box 180.

15 Sopel, *Tony Blair*, p. 149.

16 Westlake, *Kinnock*, p. 613. Kinnock still believes that the GMB '*would* have backed down', adding: 'Does anyone seriously believe that Edmonds and his Executive would have screwed John Smith, their most prized member?' E-mail correspondence with Rt Hon. Neil Kinnock, 22 October 2004. Conversely, it may well be that the GMB underestimated Smith, and thought he would back down because they were convinced he was headed for defeat.

17 Rentoul, *Tony Blair*, pp. 316–7.

18 Interview with Murray Elder, 26 November 2002.

19 Interview with Rt Hon. Derek Foster MP,

24 June 2003.

20 Interview with Murray Elder, 26 November 2002.

21 Charles Clarke, Briefing Note to Neil Kinnock, prior to meeting with Robin Cook, 'your room', 10 am, undated (June, 1992), OMOV. Kinnock Collection, Box 180.

22 Ibid.

23 Interview with Murray Elder, 26 November 2002. David Ward agrees with Murray Elder that Smith made 'a justifiable decision to delay OMOV', citing almost identical reasons to Elder. Interview with David Ward, 7 June 2003.

24 Interview with Lord Whitty, 12 March 2003.

25 Interview with Rt Hon. Derek Foster MP.

26 Interview with Rt Hon. Frank Dobson MP, 3 March 2003.

27 Interview with David Ward, 7 June 2003.

28 Composite 9, Card Vote 8: For: 3,193,000; Against 2,118,000. Record of Decisions, *Ninety-first Annual Conference of the Labour Party* (Blackpool, 1992), p. 18. Kinnock Collection, Box 623.

29 Nigel Harris, from the engineering union (AEEU), Margaret Prosser (TGWU), Tom Burlison (GMB), Diana Jeuda (USDAW), Richard Rosser (TSSA), Tom Sawyer (NUPE), Gordon Colling (chair of the Party and GPMU) and Tony Clarke (UCW).

30 Anderson and Mann, *Safety First*, p. 432.

31 Larry Whitty's initial list did not include John Evans, but it included John Edmonds and Bill Morris, neither of whom served on the Review Group. Labour Party/Trade Union Relations (GS: 22/6/92) [Draft note by the general secretary] (sent to all members of the NEC, 22 June 1992 in advance of 24 June 1992 NEC). Kinnock Collection, Box 180. The reason is that John Evans should have been included in both lists ex officio as chair of the Organisation Committee. Originally, the committee was devised, with John Smith's agreement, as a joint party/affiliated union body. It was hoped that Bill Morris and John Edmonds would have been invited onto it. This proposition was put to them both informally, but Bill Morris in particular was adamant that he did not wish to serve, and that the working group should be a *party* initiative to which the

unions could react. Hence it reverted by the time it was announced to being an NEC working group. Written correspondence with Lord Whitty, 26 October 2004.

32 Interview with Lord Whitty.

33 Written correspondence with Whitty, 26 October 2004.

34 Rentoul, *Tony Blair*, p. 320.

35 Interview with Lord Whitty.

36 Quoted in Sopel, *Tony Blair*, p.161.

37 Although these ballots were introduced only nine months after Blair became leader when the party members voted on the new Clause IV. Rentoul, *Tony Blair*, p. 344.

38 Rentoul, *Tony Blair*, p. 324.

39 For this version of events, see Sopel, *Tony Blair*, pp. 160–2; Rentoul, *Tony Blair*, pp. 324–5.

40 Fraser Nelson and Jason Beattie, interview with Hilary Armstrong, 'Ten years on – Labour's lost leader', *The Scotsman*, 19 July 2002.

41 Interview with Rt Hon. Hilary Armstrong MP, 11 February 2003.

42 Fraser Nelson and Jason Beattie, interview with Hilary Armstrong, op. cit.

43 This definition is taken from Larry Whitty [to John Smith], Trade Union Links with the Party. Possible Consensus Position, 6 July 1993. Strictly Private and Confidential. Murray Elder papers, Box 2.

44 Rentoul, *Tony Blair*, pp. 322–3.

45 McSmith, *Faces of Labour*, p. 333.

46 Anderson and Mann, *Safety First*, p. 320.

47 Rentoul, *Tony Blair*, p. 325.

48 Naughtie, *The Rivals*, p. 45.

49 Rentoul, *Tony Blair*, p. 309.

50 Paul Anderson, interview with Tony Blair, 'Boy Wonder', *Tribune*, 29 January 1993.

51 Switching to a one third system for each of the PLP, the CLPs and the unions; a one third system, but with only those trade unionists who were also full Labour Party members being allowed to vote; and the scrapping of the union element in the electoral college, leaving a 50–50 system between the PLP and the CLP. *Labour Party – Trade Union Links: Interim Report of the Working Group and Questionnaire* (February 1993), p. 15.

52 Interview with Lord Whitty.

53 Larry Whitty to John Smith, Annual Conference 1993, 23 March 1993. Strictly Private and Confidential. Murray Elder papers, Box 2.

54 Ibid.

55 Rentoul, *Tony Blair*, p. 326; interview with Lord Whitty.

56 See Tom Sawyer, 'Levy-payers link-up', *Tribune*, 7 June 1993.

57 McSmith, *Faces of Labour*, p. 180.

58 See also, Tom Sawyer, 'Don't ditch the union link', *Tribune*, 1 May 1992.

59 Watkins, *The Road to No. 10*, p. 171.

60 See John Prescott, 'Levy-plus is the answer', *Tribune*, 11 June 1993.

61 Brown, *Fighting Talk*, pp. 228–9.

62 Rentoul, *Tony Blair*, pp. 329–31.

63 Dave Osler, 'Leader accused of by-passing discussion', *Tribune*, 28 May 1993.

64 Rentoul, *Tony Blair*, p. 328.

65 *Tribune*, 28 May 1993.

66 In April 1993, Ben Lucas, the LCC chair, turned down Spellar's offer of a joint campaign on OMOV. *Tribune*, 23 April 1993.

67 *Tribune*, 2 July 1993.

68 *Tribune*, 16 July 1993.

69 Interview with Lord Whitty. He also feared that the Labour Party would face very substantial financial losses if it introduced too low a reduced fee for trade union levy-payers, and not enough union members signed up to the scheme. Dave Osler, 'Levy-plus membership at £3 could herald "bankruptcy" for Labour', *Tribune*, 30 July 1993.

70 Letter from Larry Whitty to John Smith, Trade Union Links, 6 July 1993. Strictly Private and Confidential. Murray Elder papers, Box 2.

71 Paul Routledge and Andy McSmith, 'Godfather and his MacMafia', *The Observer*, 18 July 1993.

72 Quoted in Bill Hagerty, 'The Right Route', *Tribune*, 23 July 1993.

73 Peter Riddell, 'That Missing Spark', *The Times*, 1 July 1993.

74 The seven opponents of the compromise were Tony Benn (the only MP to oppose Smith), Tom Burlison, Gordon Colling, Bill Connor, Dan Duffy, Diana Jeuda and Charlie Kelly.

75 Dave Osler, 'Smith scores tactical victory on OMOV', *Tribune*, 23 July 1993.

76 Robin Cook, OMOV Campaign. A Position Paper, 6 May 1993. Murray Elder papers, Box 2.

77 Interview with Murray Elder, 17 September 2003.

78 Rentoul, *Tony Blair*, p. 326.

79 In April 1993, the Union of Shop, Distributive and Allied Workers' conference expressed a preference for the Registered Supporters' Scheme; Smith attended and spoke at the Fire Brigades' Union conference in Bridlington on 14 May, but the vote on OMOV went against the leadership line; a similar fate befell Smith at the Union of Communication Workers at the end of May; at the GMB's Portsmouth conference in June, a union source was quoted as saying: 'We have moved far enough. Any other changes will be down to the party leadership.' The union's conference then backed the Registered Supporters' Scheme. At the TGWU conference in Bournemouth, Bill Morris told delegates on the Monday (5 July): 'If I was asked to advise Mr Smith, I would just say "talk to us".' On the Wednesday (7 July), Smith addressed the conference, calling on trade unions to become individual Labour Party members 'in thousands, indeed hundreds of thousands', but the following day (8 July), once again he lost the vote. *Tribune*, 7 June 1993; 9 July 1993.

80 John Smith, 'Speech to FBU Conference', Bridlington, 14 May 1993. Murray Elder papers, Box 2. See also John Smith, 'Speech to MSF Conference', Blackpool, Fax Copy, 24 May 1993. Murray Elder papers, Box 1.

81 Dave Osler, 'Smith charms OMOV doubters', *Tribune*, 10 September 1993.

82 John Smith, Address to TUC, 7 September 1993. In Gordon Brown's otherwise excellent summary of Smith's speeches, 'John Smith's Socialism', Brown omits the words 'the exchange rates' when quoting from Smith's TUC speech. Brown and Naughtie, *John Smith: Life and Soul of the Party*, p. 70.

83 Interview with Rt Hon. Frank Dobson MP.

84 Brown, *Fighting Talk*, p. 233.

85 'A new deal for the trade unions from Labour', *Tribune*, 10 September 1993.

86 Benn, *Free at Last!*, p. 197 (Tuesday, 7 September 1993).

87 Interview with Rt Hon. Tony Benn, 6 March 2003.

88 Sopel, *Tony Blair*, p. 163; for a similar view, though one slightly less harsh on Smith, see Rentoul, *Tony Blair*, pp. 333–4; Naughtie, *The Rivals*, p. 48.

89 Interview with Rt Hon. Frank Dobson MP.

90 Gordon Brown, *How We Can Conquer Unemployment* (Labour Finance and Industry Group, September 1993). The title of the pamphlet echoed Lloyd George's famous Keynesian pamphlet, *Can We Conquer Unemployment?* Anderson and Mann, *Safety First*, p. 92.

91 See Robert Taylor, 'Employment Relations Policy', in Anthony Seldon (ed.), *The Blair Effect. The Blair Government 1997–2001* (Little, Brown and Company: London, 2001), p. 247.

92 Interview with Rt Hon. Hilary Armstrong MP.

93 Dave Osler, 'The rebellion that wasn't', *Tribune*, 10 September 1993.

94 John Edmonds, 'Opinion has swung in favour of unions', *Tribune*, 17 September 1993. There was however, one practical result from Smith's speech: Garfield Davies, General Secretary of the Union of Shop, Distributive and Allied Workers (USDAW), announced that his union would ditch its original conference decision and support OMOV, after he apparently deployed old-fashioned brutal tactics to get his executive to change its mind. Dave Osler, 'Smith charms OMOV doubters', *Tribune*, 10 September 1993.

95 Interview with Rt Hon. Hilary Armstrong MP.

96 Interview with Murray Elder, 12 February 2003.

97 Sopel, *Tony Blair*, pp. 163–4.

98 Interview with Murray Elder, 12 February 2003.

99 Interview with Lord Whitty.

100 Denis Healey also recalls Edmonds as taking 'a centrist view' in the 1970s. Interview with Rt Hon. Lord Healey of Riddlesden CH MBE, 12 February 2003.

101 Interview with Murray Elder, 12 February 2003.

102 John Edmonds, Labour Party Trade Union Links, 27 May 1993 (Fax copy from Pat McFadden to Murray Elder). Murray Elder papers, Box 2.

103 Written correspondence between Rt Hon. John Smith QC MP and Elizabeth

Thomas, 11 September 1993. Reproduced by kind permission of Elizabeth Thomas.

104 Interview with Murray Elder, 26 November 2002.

105 Macintyre, *Mandelson*, p. 242.

106 Interview with Murray Elder, 26 November 2002.

107 Sopel, *Tony Blair*, pp. 229–30. Irvine confirms that he had indicated to Smith that he should make the OMOV issue a vote of confidence. Interview with Rt Hon. Lord Irvine of Lairg PC QC, 30 April 2003.

108 Letter from Larry Whitty to John Smith, Voting Estimates on Parliamentary Selections, 9 August 1993 (Strictly Private and Confidential). Murray Elder papers, Box 2.

109 Larry Whitty, Assessment of Conference Vote. Parliamentary Selections, 9 August 1993 (Strictly Private and Confidential). Murray Elder papers, Box 2.

110 Interview with Murray Elder, 29 October 2002.

111 Interview with Baroness Smith of Gilmorehill DL, 26 November 2002.

112 Interview with Rt Hon. Hilary Armstrong MP.

113 E-mail correspondence with David Gardner, 29 November 2004.

114 Interview with Lord Whitty, 12 March 2003.

115 Raised to the peerage as Baroness Gibson of Market Rasen in the County of Lincolnshire, 2000.

116 Interview with Rt Hon. Hilary Armstrong MP.

117 Smith had given his leader's address on the previous day (Tuesday, 28 September).

118 *Ninety-second Annual Conference Report of the Labour Party* (Brighton, 1993), p. 134.

119 Ibid.

120 To judge for yourself, see *Ninety-second Annual Conference Report of the Labour Party*, 1993, pp. 136–7.

121 *Ninety-second Annual Conference Report of the Labour Party*, 1993, p. 137.

122 *Ninety-second Annual Conference Report of the Labour Party*, 1993, pp. 138–9.

123 McSmith, *Faces of Labour*, p. 334.

124 Interview with Rt Hon. Hilary Armstrong MP.

125 Interview with Lord Whitty.

126 Interview with Murray Elder, 26 November 2003.

127 Interview with Rt Hon. Margaret Beckett MP, 19 November 2003.

128 Ibid.

129 Quoted in Rentoul, *Tony Blair*, p. 341.

130 Brown, *Fighting Talk*, p. 222.

131 Quoted in Rentoul, *Tony Blair*, p. 341.

132 Interview with Rt Hon. Margaret Beckett MP.

133 Brown, *Fighting Talk*, p. 222.

134 Interview with Rt Hon. Hilary Armstrong MP.

135 Interview with Dr Lynne Jones, Politico's, London, 18 June 2002.

136 Interview with Rt Hon. Hilary Armstrong MP. Sopel incorrectly claims that MSF 'switched sides'. In fact, they only abstained. Sopel, *Tony Blair*, p. 164.

137 Brown, *Fighting Talk*, p. 225.

138 Interview with Rt Hon. Hilary Armstrong MP.

139 Brown, *Fighting Talk*, p. 222.

140 Leader's Office, 'CLP OMOV Voting Spreadsheet', Undated (c. late September 1993). Murray Elder papers, Box 1.

141 Interview with Rt Hon. Hilary Armstrong MP.

142 Ibid.

143 Philip M. Williams, *Hugh Gaitskell* (Oxford University Press, revised paperback edn., Oxford, 1982), pp. 357–60.

144 Written correspondence with Lord Whitty, 25 April 2003.

145 Interview with Lord Whitty.

146 Written correspondence with Lord Whitty, 25 April 2003.

147 Brown, *Fighting Talk*, p. 224.

148 *Ninety-second Annual Conference Report of the Labour Party*, 1993, p. 162.

149 *Ninety-second Annual Conference Report of the Labour Party*, 1993, p. 164.

150 Bill Hagerty, 'Smith scrapes though in key vote on OMOV', *Tribune*, 1 October 1993.

151 Brown, *Fighting Talk*, p. 226.

152 Macintyre, *Mandelson*, p. 243.

153 Interview with Rt Hon. Lord Healey of Riddlesden CH MBE.

154 Naughtie, *The Rivals*, p. 48.

155 Rentoul, *Tony Blair*, pp. 341–2.

156 Interview with Baroness Smith of Gilmorehill DL, 4 December 2002.

157 Sarah Smith, 'Our Father', in Brown and Naughtie, *Life and Soul of the Party*, p. 113.

158 *Desert Island Discs*, BBC Radio Four (transmitted, 28 May 1991), in Brown and Naughtie, *Life and Soul of the Party*, p.159 (transcript).

159 Interview with Ann Barrett, 21 June 2003; interview with David Ward, 7 June 2003.

160 Interview with Rt Hon. Hilary Armstrong MP.

161 Interview with Mike Elrick, 10 June 2003.

162 Ibid.

163 Letter from Larry Whitty to Murray Elder, Trade Union Funding of the Party, 1 December 1993 (Strictly Private and Confidential). Murray Elder papers, Box 2.

164 BBC News, 5 September 1990.

165 Interview with Sir Gavin Laird CBE, 21 January 2004.

166 Letter from Rt Hon. John Smith QC MP to Gavin Laird, 15 October 1993; reproduced with the kind permission of Sir Gavin Laird CBE.

167 See also, Rentoul, *Tony Blair*, p. 347.

168 Interview with David Ward, 30 April 2003.

169 Interview with Rt Hon. Lord Irvine of Lairg PC QC.

170 Smith's primary aim, that trade unionists should vote as individuals in compulsory ballots in the selection of parliamentary candidates, was achieved. In return, the old 40:30:30 (unions: membership: MPs) electoral college system that had been in place, with one or two revisions, since 1981 for leadership elections, shifted to a one-third system split between the unions, the members and a combination of MPs and MEPs. Blair's preferred option had been to split leadership elections exclusively between party members and MPs. Of course, Blair was later elected under the system of OMOV agreed in September 1993. But the block vote remained at party conference: it was formally cut from 90 per cent to 70 per cent in 1993 (as a result of reforms first agreed under Neil Kinnock), and then, when the Labour membership reached 300,000, it was subsequently cut to 49 per cent.

171 Interview with Rt Hon. Lord Healey of Riddlesden CH MBE.

172 Hattersley, *Fifty Years On*, p. 373.

173 For this view, see Sopel, *Tony Blair*, p. 165; and Rentoul, *Tony Blair*, p. 342; pp. 346–7; Naughtie, *The Rivals*, p. 48.

174 Interview with Rt Hon. Hilary Armstrong MP.

175 Williams, *Gaitskell*, p. 319.

176 Jack Straw, *Policy and Ideology* (Blackburn Labour Party: Blackburn, 1993).

177 Neil Kinnock, *Tomorrow's Socialism* BBC2, 5 February 1994.

178 Interview with Rt Hon. Hilary Armstrong MP.

179 Jack Straw, general election 1992. Section 4: Policy and Ideology (draft), 12 September 1992. Murray Elder papers, Box 2.

180 Straw, *Policy and Ideology*, p. 10.

181 Written correspondence with Rt Hon. Jack Straw MP, 15 January 2004.

182 'Preface', *Policy and Ideology*.

183 Written correspondence with Rt Hon. Jack Straw MP.

184 Ibid.

185 Ibid.

186 Ibid.

187 Ibid.

188 Jack Straw, 'John Smith the colleague', *The Times*, 13 May 1994.

189 Interview with Rt Hon. Lord Hattersley, 3 March 2003; David Ward also recalls that Smith was furious with Jack Straw for writing the pamphlet. Interview with David Ward, 7 June 2003.

190 Written correspondence with Rt Hon. Jack Straw MP.

191 Written correspondence with Kenneth Munro, 14 November 2004.

192 *Today*, BBC Radio Four, 24 February 1994.

193 Jones, *Remaking the Labour Party*, p. 134; Rentoul, *Tony Blair*, p. 413.

194 Interview with Rt Hon. Frank Dobson MP, 24 April 2003.

195 Interview with David Ward, 7 June 2003.

196 Interview with Murray Elder, 16 November 2004.

197 See Brivati (ed.), *Guiding Light*, pp. 212–25.

198 Smith's plan to rework Clause IV was revealed by Ward to John Rentoul in his biography of Tony Blair, published in September 1995. Rentoul, *Tony Blair*, pp. 413–4; Brown, *Fighting Talk*, p. 259; Philip Webster, 'Author reveals John Smith's Clause 4 plan', *The Times*, 20 September 1995.

199 The NEC accepted Gaitskell's statement of aims on 16 March 1960. Williams, *Gaitskell*, pp. 330–2.

200 By 50.9 per cent to 49.1 per cent, on Thursday, 6 October 1994, after Blair had made a speech on the Tuesday, indicating he wished to scrap Clause IV. Philip Webster, 'Blair stuns left with proposal to scrap Clause Four', *The Times*, 5 October

1994; Philip Webster, 'Blair scorns defeat on Clause IV', *The Times*, 7 October 1994.

201 Anderson and Mann, *Safety First*, p. 33.

202 Heath, Jowell and Curtice, *The Rise of New Labour*, p. 107; p. 118.

203 Interview with Murray Elder, 2 July 2003.

Chapter 23

1 Interview with Rt Hon. Hilary Armstrong MP, 11 February 2003.

2 Interview with Lord Gordon of Strathblane CBE, 12 March 2003.

3 Interview with Rt Hon. Frank Dobson MP, 3 March 2003.

4 Interview with Mike Elrick, 10 June 2003.

5 Interview with Ann Barrett, 21 June 2003.

6 Ibid.

7 Interview with Mike Elrick.

8 Interview with Alan Haworth, 15 December 2003.

9 Interview with Rt Hon. Lord [Ranald] MacLean, 18 November 2003.

10 John Smith 'Munro Diary', diary readings with Alan Haworth, 15 December 2003.

11 Interview with Alan Haworth.

12 Ibid.

13 Ibid.

14 Alan Haworth, 'Obituary: John Smith', PLP Minutes, 18 May 1994.

15 Quoted from John Smith, 'The Munros', in Brown and Naughtie, *Life and Soul of the Party*, p. 129; itself an edited extract from the foreword of Peter Drummond and Ian Mitchell, *First Munroist. The Rev. A. E. Robertson: his life, Munros and photographs* (Ernest Press: Glasgow, 1993).

16 Although Laird's birthday fell in March, the walk was arranged for May. Interview with Sir Gavin Laird CBE, 21 January 2004.

17 Gormley died of cancer on Thursday, 27 May 1993. *The Times*, 28 May 1993.

18 *The Times*, 28 May 1993.

19 Interview with Sir Gavin Laird CBE.

20 Interview with Rt Hon. Lord [Ranald] MacLean; interview with Mike Elrick.

21 In early 1993, the Indian High Commissioner and Mr Hinduja (the senior member of the wealthy and powerful Hinduja family) invited Jack Cunningham and Swraj Paul to India in early 1993, but Cunningham indicated he did not want to go. Jack Cunningham, Undated note, c. early 1993. Murray Elder papers, Box 2. Early in 1994, Smith also

received an invitation to visit Korea. Thomas Harris, Smith's former Principal Private Secretary at the Department of Trade and, by this stage, British Ambassador in Korea (1994–7), always regretted that Smith never made it across to see him, and indeed was doubly unlucky; when Elizabeth Smith visited Korea in 1997, Harris had moved on to become Director-General of Export Promotion at the Department of Trade and Industry the month before. Telephone interview with Sir Thomas Harris, 20 September 2003.

22 Interview with Baroness Ramsay of Cartvale, 24 June 2003.

23 Interview with Mike Elrick.

24 Interview with Rt Hon. Helen Liddell MP, 19 November 2003.

25 Telephone interview with Rt Hon. Lord Robertson of Port Ellen, 8 September 2003.

26 Of MDC's 20 councillors, seventeen were Catholic and Labour, and three were SNP and Protestant.

27 Wendy Scott, 'Straight Talking: Interview with Tom Clarke MP', *Airdrie and Coatbridge Advertiser*, 9 September 1994.

28 If 1989–92 figures are used, then excluding strategic projects, Coatbridge received £2.207 million, while Airdrie received £2.159 million, and the surrounding villages were allocated £809,000. William Clark, 'Liddell Admission on spending in Monklands', *The Herald*, 22 June 1994. If 1989–94 figures are used, then excluding strategic projects, £3.346 million was spent on Coatbridge, £3.578 million on Airdrie, with £889,000 allocated to the other areas. However, both sets of figures exclude capital projects, which accounted for 77 per cent of the general services budget in the period 1989–94. David Willis, 'Now it's official', *Airdrie and Coatbridge Advertiser*, Wednesday, 2 August–Tuesday 8 August 1995.

29 Eileen McAuley, 'Secret Forms Shock', *Airdrie and Coatbridge Advertiser*, 7 August 1992.

30 At the end of August 1992, Tommy Morgan, Peter Sullivan and Brian Brady had their appeals against suspension rejected, but their suspensions were cut by one month: Morgan and Sullivan's suspension was reduced to three months,

while Brady served a two-month ban. Jim Logue was later banned for four months at a special joint meeting of the District Labour Party (DLP) and the council's ruling Labour group. *Airdrie and Coatbridge Advertiser*, 28 August 1992; 18 September 1992.

31 In actual fact, there were three different coloured forms: applicants for manual work tended to be given green forms, people applying via job centres applied using pink forms, and office workers applied on white forms. John Hutchison and David Willis, 'About turn', *Airdrie and Coatbridge Advertiser*, Wednesday 15 November – Tuesday, 21 November 1995.

32 'Provost' is the Scottish term for a mayor.

33 Eileen McAuley, 'They would say that wouldn't they? Provost dismisses "jobs for the boys claims" as bunkum', *Airdrie and Coatbridge Advertiser*, 14 August 1992.

34 'Group leader Brooks raps "pop star" rebels', *Airdrie and Coatbridge Advertiser*, 28 August 1992.

35 Eileen McAuley, 'One Big Happy Family'; 'Relatives on Council Payroll', *Airdrie and Coatbridge Advertiser*, 21 August 1992; 28 August 1992.

36 Peter Millar, 'Have-nots cry foul on John Smith's doorstep', *The Sunday Times*, 15 November 1992; Joan McAlpine, 'Trouble in John Smith's back yard', *New Statesman & Society*, 27 August 1993.

37 Eileen McAuley, 'Labour Chiefs Order Mafia Probe', *Airdrie and Coatbridge Advertiser*, 6 November 1992.

38 See Anne Smith and Ninian Dunnett, 'Labour at war in John Smith's backyard', *The Sunday Times*, 1 November 1992; see also Euan Ferguson, 'Red Barons work up a jobs racket', *Scotland on Sunday*, 1 November 1992.

39 Telephone interview with Rt Hon. Lord Robertson of Port Ellen; Mike Elrick agrees. Interview with Mike Elrick.

40 Interview with Mike Elrick.

41 *Airdrie and Coatbridge Advertiser*, 4 September 1992.

42 *Airdrie and Coatbridge Advertiser*, 25 September 1992.

43 Labour MP for Stirling since 1997. Parliamentary Private Secretary to Donald Dewar from 1997–8, Assistant Government Whip from 1999–2001, and Government Whip, from 2001 to June 2003, when she became Parliamentary Under-Secretary of State at the Department for Constitutional Affairs.

44 The other inquiry members were vice-chairman Johann Lamont, Scottish Labour treasurer, Esther Quinn and Scottish organiser, Gerry O'Brien.

45 Ken Smith, 'Auditors examine Monklands' books', *The Herald*, 23 December 1992.

46 Lang was replying to a question from Sir Anthony Durant, the English Conservative MP for Reading West. HC Debs, 18 November 1992, c. 285.

47 HC Debs, 16 December 1992, cc. 416–417.

48 HC Debs, 16 December 1992, c. 417.

49 Ibid.

50 HC Debs, 16 December 1992, c. 444–445.

51 Including EDMs 856, 991, 992 and 1040.

52 Eileen McAuley, 'Dear John', *Airdrie and Coatbridge Advertiser*, 27 November 1992; 11 December 1992.

53 Eileen McAuley, 'Dover MP may return to dig more dirt in Monklands', *Airdrie and Coatbridge Advertiser*, 8 January 1993.

54 Eileen McAuley, 'Over to you John: Pressure mounts on Labour leader to investigate', *Airdrie and Coatbridge Advertiser*, 8 January 1993.

55 Ibid.

56 'Tom Clarke defends scandal-hit council', *Airdrie and Coatbridge Advertiser*, 29 January 1993.

57 Eric Wright, 'Tom vows to bounce back in January', *Airdrie and Coatbridge Advertiser*, 27 November 1992. Henry McLeish, then Labour's Scottish Local Government spokesperson deputised in Clarke's absence.

58 Interview with Rt Hon. Thomas Clarke JP MP, 20 January 2004.

59 Eileen McAuley, 'New Horizons', *Airdrie and Coatbridge Advertiser*, 29 October 1993.

60 Interview with Rt Hon. Thomas Clarke MP.

61 For instance, provosts and council convenors would serve no more than two terms of office, there would be a more equitable distribution of committee posts among Labour group members, and councillors could only be involved in the appointment of senior officials. William Clark and Kirsty Scott, 'Demands for new Monklands inquiry', *The Herald*, 5 March

1993.

62 *Daily Record*, 5 March 1993.

63 *Evening Times*, 5 March 1993.

64 *The Sunday Times*, 7 March 1993.

65 *Daily Record*, 5 March 1993.

66 Eileen McAuley, 'Labour Supremo to meet Airdrie Rebels', *Airdrie and Coatbridge Advertiser*, 27 November 1992. In May 1993, an independent consultancy firm, Ashdown Millan, examined MDC's recruitment procedures separately from the Labour inquiry. Its report called for councillors to cease involvement in staff selection below chief official grade, suggested the redesign of job application forms to ensure equal opportunities, and advised that the Employment Service should play a greater role in identifying suitable candidates. *Review of Personnel Procedures For Monklands District Council*, Ashdown Millan Planning & Projects Consultancy, May 1993. Michael Crick files; 'Council told to overhaul jobs system', *Airdrie and Coatbridge Advertiser*, 21 May 1993.

67 Eileen McAuley, 'Labour leader under siege!', *Airdrie and Coatbridge Advertiser*, 9 April 1993.

68 Erlend Clouston, 'Monklands mourns a steadfast MP', *The Guardian*, 13 May 1994.

69 Eileen McAuley, 'Labour leader under siege!', *Airdrie and Coatbridge Advertiser*, 9 April 1993.

70 Eileen McAuley, 'Scottish minister blasts Smith's "Mafia" silence', *Airdrie and Coatbridge Advertiser*, 21 May 1993.

71 The Dover MP tried three times without success to intervene during the leader of the opposition's speech on the government's economic and social policy. HC Debs, 9 June 1993, cc. 292–296; see also HC Debs, 22 June 1993, c. 243.

72 HC Debs, 13 January 1994, cc. 330–331.

73 Eileen McAuley, 'Fowler attacks silence', *Airdrie and Coatbridge Advertiser*, 4 February 1994.

74 Eileen McAuley, 'Inquiry Tip-Off', *Airdrie and Coatbridge Advertiser*, 11 February 1994.

75 HC Debs, 7 February 1994, cc. 28–71.

76 Minutes of the party meeting held on Thursday 3 February 1994 in Committee Room 12.

77 HC Debs, 7 February 1994, cc. 50–51.

78 Eileen McAuley, ' "Mafia" Routed',

Airdrie and Coatbridge Advertiser, 2 July 1993; Eileen McAuley, 'Smith sees change of the "Old Guard"', *Airdrie and Coatbridge Advertiser*, 2 July 1993.

79 Eileen McAuley, 'Landslide Win', *Airdrie and Coatbridge Advertiser*, 4 March 1993; Denis Campbell and Jackie Kemp, 'All change at Monklands as old guard walk out', *Scotland on Sunday*, 6 March 1994.

80 Jim Logue, Peter Sullivan and Brian Brady. Eileen McAuley, 'Verdict is "Guilty"', *Airdrie and Coatbridge Advertiser*, 8 April 1994; Ken Symon, 'Resign calls to council leaders', *Evening Times*, 1 April 1994.

81 Letter from Brian Brady to Martin [surname not provided] (submitted in support of Tom McFarlane), 14 April 1993. Michael Crick files.

82 Notes of taped meeting between Councillor Brady and Mr J. Dempsey, Director of Leisure and Recreation, undated. Michael Crick files. See Eileen McAuley, 'Tape Shock', *Airdrie and Coatbridge Advertiser*, 21 January 1994; Eileen McAuley, 'Secret Tape Row', *Airdrie and Coatbridge Advertiser*, 18 February 1994.

83 Letter from Tom McFarlane (undated), c. March/April 1993. Michael Crick files.

84 Letter from Peter Sullivan (submitted in support of Tom McFarlane, 14 March 1993. (Stamped by Transport and General Workers Union, 2 April 1993). Michael Crick files.

85 Letter from Tom McFarlane (undated), c. March/April 1993. Michael Crick files.

86 Letter from Peter Sullivan (submitted in support of Tom McFarlane), 14 March 1993. (Stamped by Transport and General Workers Union, 2 April 1993); letter from Jim Logue (submitted in support of Tom McFarlane), 11 April 1993. Michael Crick files.

87 Eileen McAuley, 'Corridors of Power', *Airdrie and Coatbridge Advertiser*, 18 February 1994.

88 *The Industrial Tribunals Scotland*, Case No: S/4393/92, 30 March 1994. Michael Crick files.

89 Interview with Michael Crick, 24 November 2003.

90 Interview with Mike Elrick.

91 Interview with Michael Crick.

92 Michael Crick, Diary, 2 April 1994.

93 Ibid.

94 E-mail correspondence with Mike Elrick, 10 November 2004.

95 Michael Crick, diary, 2 April 1994.

96 Transcript of *Newsnight* piece, April 1994. Michael Crick files.

97 Transcript of interview between Michael Crick and Tom McFarlane, April 1994. Michael Crick files.

98 Interview with Mike Elrick.

99 Having studied the rise and fall of the Militant Tendency in the past, Michael Crick could not help but draw comparisons between Monklands in the early 1990s and Liverpool in the early 1980s. Transcript of *Newsnight* piece, April 1994. Michael Crick files. See Crick, *Militant*.

100 Alex Salmond, 'How the mighty totter', *The Herald*, 23 June 1994.

101 John Hutchison and David Willis, 'Family firm', *Airdrie and Coatbridge Advertiser*, Wednesday, 22 November–Tuesday, 28 November 1995. Eddie Cairns and Tom Clarke agreed with this analysis. 'Ex-provost denies nepotism', *Airdrie and Coatbridge Advertiser*, Wednesday, 29 November–Tuesday, 5 December 1995; Tom Clarke, 'Campaign Targets', *Airdrie and Coatbridge Advertiser*, Wednesday, 22 November–Tuesday, 28 November 1995.

102 Indeed, in April 1993, not only was McAuley named 'Journalist of the Year' at the Annual Bank of Scotland Press Awards, but also by this stage the Press Commission had rejected all the complaints that had been previously made by MDC. *Airdrie and Coatbridge Advertiser*, 30 April 1993.

103 'Newspaper didn't play "sectarian card"', *Airdrie and Coatbridge Advertiser*, Wednesday, 29 November – Tuesday, 5 December 1995.

104 Interview with Michael Crick.

105 John Rentoul incorrectly records the date as Sunday, 10 April. Rentoul, *Tony Blair*, p. 347.

106 Donald MacCormick, 'A diligent and brilliant believer in all that was best', *The Sunday Times*, 15 May 1994.

107 Interview with Mike Elrick.

108 Interview with Elizabeth Munro, 29 September 2003.

109 Labour MP for Barking from 1979–94.

110 Michael Foot, 'A man who rose above the lies', *The Observer*, 15 May 1994.

111 John Smith, 'Munro Diary', diary readings with Alan Haworth, 15 December 2003.

112 Interview with Kenneth Munro, 29 September 2003.

113 Interview with Mike Elrick.

114 Interview with Lord Hogg of Cumbernauld, 4 November 2003.

115 Brunson, *A Ringside Seat*, pp. 212–3.

116 Alastair Campbell, 'John Smith's Great Journey', *Today*, Friday, 13 May 1994.

117 Interview with Rt Hon. Lord Irvine of Lairg PC QC, 30 April 2003; David Blunkett with Alex MacCormick, *On A Clear Day. An Autobiography* (Michael O'Mara Books Ltd: London, 1995), p. 176.

118 HC Debs, 29 April 1994, c. 555. For the Second Reading debate on Berry's Bill, see HC Debs, 11 March 1994, cc. 524–585.

119 Minutes of the party meeting held on Thursday 21 April 1994 at 6pm in Committee Room 10.

120 HC Debs, 10 May 1994, c. 155.

121 Minutes of the party meeting held on Thursday 21 April 1994 at 6pm in Committee Room 10; minutes of the party meeting held on Thursday 28 April 1994 at 6pm in Committee Room 10.

122 Minutes of the party meeting held on Thursday 28 April 1994 at 6pm in Committee Room 10.

123 Interview with Mike Elrick.

124 Alastair Campbell, 'John Smith's Great Journey', *Today*, 13 May 1994.

125 Simon Hoggart, 'Sharp wit with an inner fire', *The Guardian 2*, 13 May 1994.

126 From 1979–99.

127 Peter Hetherington, 'The punishing lifestyle of a workaholic', *The Guardian*, 13 May 1994.

128 Telephone interview with Rt Hon. Lord Robertson of Port Ellen, 7 July 2003.

129 John Smith's itinerary, Monday 9 May–Sunday 15 May. David Ward papers. HC Debs, 9 May 1994, cc. 95–99. Smith did not vote during a division on another EC Document later that evening, on equal pay. HC Debs, 9 May 1994, cc. 122–126.

130 The by-election was caused by the death of James Boyce. Labour won with a majority of 6,954, with the Liberal Democrats in second, and the Conservatives trailing a distant third. Tim Austin (ed.), *The Times Guide to the House of Commons, 1997* (Times Books: London, 1997), p. 277.

131 Paul Wilnenius, 'Banker's looks hid the

joker', *Today*, 13 May 1994.
132 HC Debs, 10 May 1994, c. 150.
133 Major, *The Autobiography*, p. 688.
134 The commission controversially proposed splitting the town of Airdrie, and merging Smith's Monklands East constituency into a redrawn Cumbernauld and Airdrie North. Not only would the proposal have split Airdrie in half, it would have turned Smith's redrawn seat into an SNP-Labour marginal, including the predominantly SNP area of Hilltop-Abronhill. 'Safe Seat Row', *Airdrie and Coatbridge Advertiser*, 26 November 1993.
135 Interview with Lord Hogg of Cumbernauld.
136 Tom Clarke, 'And all that mighty heart is lying still', *Airdrie and Coatbridge Advertiser*, 20 May 1994.
137 Interview with Rt Hon. Thomas Clarke JP MP.
138 The redrawn constituency moved southwards to the old mining village of Shotts, at the expense of John Reid in Motherwell North, who lost Motherwell Fortissat, as Reid's seat was renamed Hamilton North and Belshill. Meanwhile, Tom Clarke's new Coatbridge and Chryston gained back the whole of Coatbridge and the Campsies. Interview with Rt Hon. Thomas Clarke JP MP; Eileen McAuley, 'John wins final fight', *Airdrie and Coatbridge Advertiser*, 5 August 1994.
139 *The Nine o'Clock News* (specially extended), BBC1, Thursday, 12 May 1994 (transcript).
140 Interview with Ann Barrett.
141 *Question Time Special*, BBC1, Thursday, 12 May 1994 (transcript).

Chapter 24

1 By this stage, two other Labour MPs had learned about what had happened to John. Barry Sheerman, who lived in the Barbican, saw the commotion, and was therefore one of the first to know about John. Meanwhile, Ian McCartney, not actually on the scene, was with the London Ambulance Service, in his capacity as Labours' junior health spokesman, and heard over the radio with horror what was happening. Minutes of the meeting of the Parliamentary Labour Party held on Wednesday 18 May 1994 at 11.30 am in Committee Room 14.
2 Interview with Rt Hon. Hilary Armstrong MP, 11 February 2003.
3 Interview with Lord Gordon of Strathblane CBE, 12 March 2003.
4 Interview with Rt Hon. Lord Irvine of Lairg PC QC, 30 April 2003.
5 Telephone interview with Rt Hon. Lord Robertson of Port Ellen, 8 September 2003.
6 Interview with Mike Elrick, 10 June 2003.
7 Simon Hoggart, 'Sharp wit with an inner fire', *The Guardian 2*, 13 May 1994.
8 Interview with Mike Elrick.
9 Interview with Baroness Ramsay of Cartvale, 10 September 2003.
10 Ibid.
11 Ibid.
12 Ibid.
13 Interview with Kenneth and Elizabeth Munro, 29 September 2003.
14 Interview with Baroness Ramsay of Cartvale.
15 Interview with Rt Hon. Helen Liddell MP, 19 November 2003. Liddell's brief statement read: 'The family are very grateful for the outpouring of compassion and concern they have received. Understandably, everyone is very upset, and while they welcome the sympathy they don't wish to make any other statement.' *Today*, 13 May 1994.
16 Interview with Baroness Ramsay of Cartvale.
17 Interview with Mike Elrick; interview with Baroness Ramsay of Cartvale.
18 Interview with Rt Hon. Helen Liddell MP.
19 Interview with Ruth Wishart, 15 January 2004.
20 Brunson, *A Ringside Seat*, pp. 211–3; p. 215.
21 *Question Time Special*, BBC 1, Thursday, 12 May 1994 (transcript). Videotape kindly supplied by Kenneth and Elizabeth Munro.
22 Seldon, *Major*, p. 460.
23 Major, *Autobiography*, p. 590.
24 Seldon, *Major*, p. 460.
25 Interview with Murray Elder, 12 February 2003.
26 A West of Scotland phrase referring to the giving of small presents, designed to show that you care.
27 Iain Wilson, 'shadow over area so proud of its MP', *The Herald*, 13 May 1994.

28 *Airdrie and Coatbridge Advertiser*, 20 May 1994.

29 *The Nine o'Clock News* (specially extended), BBC1, Thursday, 12 May 1994 (transcript).

30 *BBC Reporting Scotland*, Thursday, 12 May 1994 (transcript); William Clark, 'The note that brought the Tory conference to a halt', *The Herald*, 13 May 1994.

31 HC Debs, 12 May 1994, c. 431.

32 HC Debs, 12 May 1994, c. 432.

33 HC Debs, 12 May 1994, c. 436.

34 HC Debs, 12 May 1994, c. 433.

35 HC Debs, 12 May 1994, c. 436.

36 HC Debs, 12 May 1994, c. 434.

37 HC Debs, 12 May 1994, c. 437.

38 HC Debs, 12 May 1994, c. 438.

39 Interview with Rt Hon. Chris Smith MP, 11 February 2003.

40 Interview with Rt Hon. Margaret Beckett MP, 19 November 2003.

41 Minutes of the party meeting held on Thursday 12 May 1994 at 6 pm in Committee Room 10.

42 Interview with Lord Whitty, 12 March 2003.

43 John Passmore, 'Flowers flood the "condolence room"', *Evening Standard*, 13 May 1994; Steve Boggan, 'Party HQ gathers messages of grief', *The Independent*, 13 May 1994.

44 *The Nine o'Clock News* (specially extended), BBC1, Thursday, 12 May 1994 (transcript).

45 *The Herald*, 13 May 1994.

46 'Un renovateur prudent', *Le Monde*, mai 14, 1994.

47 International Press Review, 'A death to prompt French regrets', *Financial Times*, 16 May 1994.

48 *The Herald*, 13 May 1994.

49 *Today*, 13 May 1994.

50 *Daily Mirror*, 13 May 1994.

51 Editorial, 'Man of honour in cynical times', *The Independent*, 13 May 1994.

52 Hugo Young, 'Never Did a More Decent Man Rise to the Top of British Politics', *The Guardian*, 13 May 1994. Also quoted in Jones, *Remaking the Labour Party*, p. 131.

53 *The Observer*, 13 May 1994. Quoted in Jones, *Remaking the Labour Party*, p. 131.

54 Interview with Baroness Ramsay of Cartvale.

55 John's mother, Sarah Smith, by now well into her late eighties, lived near Annie

Kelly in a nursing home in Aberdour, but was too frail to attend the funeral.

56 Advocate since 1971; barrister since 1990; former Lothian Regional councillor, from 1973–84, and unsuccessful Labour candidate in Edinburgh West in February and October 1974.

57 Interview with Baroness Ramsay of Cartvale; interview with Elizabeth Munro; interview with Ruth Wishart.

58 Interview with Elizabeth Munro.

59 Interview with Ruth Wishart.

60 Interview with Kenneth Munro.

61 Interview with Baroness Ramsay of Cartvale.

62 Interview with Ruth Wishart.

63 Interview with Baroness Smith of Gilmorehill DL, 4 December 2002.

64 Interview with Baroness Ramsay of Cartvale.

65 Written correspondence between Elizabeth Smith and Elizabeth Thomas, 12 November 1994. Reproduced by kind permission of Elizabeth Thomas.

66 Letter from Shirley Sheppard to Ann Barrett, 13 May 1994. Ann Barrett papers.

67 Letter from Tony Blair MP to Ann Barrett, 16 May 1994. Ann Barrett papers.

68 Alan Haworth, 'Obituary – John Smith', 18 May 1994.

69 Robert Burns, 'Epitaph on my own friend, and my father's friend, Wm Muir in Tarbolton Mill', Verse Two. The poem was written in 1784–5 when Burns was only 25–26. I am indebted to Professor David Denver of Lancaster University for supplying this information.

70 In October 1993, Smith had shown his progressive credentials by increasing from three to four the number of women MPs who had to be elected on to the shadow Cabinet, as a result of a PLP review committee report in June of that year. 'Elections in the PLP', Second Report of the PLP Review Committee, June 1993. Smith achieved these reforms, despite a huge rearguard action from traditionalists within the PLP. See Sarah Baxter, 'A boy's own story', *New Statesman & Society*, 29 October 1993.

71 Minutes of a meeting of the Parliamentary Labour Party held on Wednesday 18 May 1994 at 11.30 am in Committee Room 14.

72 Interview with Murray Elder, 17 September 2003.

73 Embarrassingly, Paul Routledge gives the date of Smith's funeral as Friday, 27 May, a week later. See Routledge, *Gordon Brown*, p. 199. The tribute book to Smith, *Life and Soul of the Party*, also gives the wrong date, this time as 19 May. Brown and Naughtie, *Life and Soul of the Party*, p. 19.

74 Jane Franchi, 'Commentary', *The Funeral of the Rt Hon. John Smith QC MP*, BBC1, Friday, 20 May 1994 (transcript).

75 Anne Simpson, 'Farewell to an uncommon John Smith', *The Herald*, 21 May 1994.

76 *The Funeral of the Rt Hon. John Smith QC MP*, BBC1, Friday, 20 May 1994 (transcript).

77 James Gordon, 'Tribute', in Brown and Naughtie, *Life and Soul of the Party*, pp. 57–60.

78 Rt Hon. Lord Irvine of Lairg PC QC, 'Tribute', in Brown and Naughtie, *Life and Soul of the Party*, pp. 105–106.

79 Telephone interview with Mary McCulloch, 26 November 2003.

80 Jane Franchi, 'Commentary', *The Funeral of the Rt Hon. John Smith QC MP*, op. cit.

81 Interview with Baroness Ramsay of Cartvale.

82 Interview with Elizabeth Munro.

83 Donald Dewar, 'Tribute', in Brown and Naughtie, *Life and Soul of the Party*, pp. 19–20. Curiously, in what must be a typing error, having watched a videotape of the full service, Dewar supposedly refers to his 'post Presbyterian moments', when he actually said 'most Presbyterian moments'.

84 A Scots word, meaning 'stubborn'.

85 Donald Dewar, 'Tribute', in Brown and Naughtie, *Life and Soul of the Party*, pp. 19–20.

86 Legend has it that in Reilig Odhrain, the ancient burial ground by the abbey, rest the remains of 48 Scottish, four Irish and eight Norwegian kings.

87 A Scots word, meaning 'setting aside the fact'.

88 Jane Franchi, 'Commentary', *The Funeral of the Rt Hon. John Smith QC MP*, op. cit.

89 The Signet Library, built between 1810–2, stands in Parliament Square West, off the Royal Mile. The exterior of the three-storey building is of classical construction, designed by Robert Reid, and the interior by William Stark. It belongs to the Society of Writers to Her Majesty's Signet, the oldest body of lawyers in Scotland. The Signet was the private seal of the early Stuart kings. I am indebted to Edinburgh City Council for this information.

90 Benn, *Free at Last! Diaries, 1991–2001*, pp. 241–4 (Friday, 20 May 1994).

91 *Daily Express*, 21 May 1994.

92 Interview with Lord Gordon of Strathblane CBE.

93 Adam Nicolson, 'Iona: Smith's inspiration becomes his resting place', *Sunday Telegraph*, 22 May 1994.

94 Written correspondence with Rev. Norman J. Shanks, 11 January 2005.

95 Interview with Murray Elder, 17 September 2003.

96 Written correspondence with Rev. Norman J. Shanks.

97 Interview with Lord Gordon of Strathblane CBE.

98 Interview with Ruth Wishart.

99 Interview with Baroness Ramsay of Cartvale.

100 Interview with Professor Sir Neil MacCormick, 3 October 2003.

101 Interview with Ruth Wishart; Ruth Wishart, 'Those sad, surreal 10 days', *The Herald*, 7 May 2004.

102 Interview with Rt Hon. Lord Irvine of Lairg PC QC; interview with Lord Gordon of Strathblane CBE; interview with Lord McCluskey, 13 May 2003.

103 Interview with Ruth Wishart.

104 Interview with Baroness Ramsay of Cartvale.

105 Written correspondence with Lord Gordon of Strathblane CBE, 2 November 2004.

106 Ruth Wishart, 'Those sad, surreal 10 days', *The Herald*, 7 May 2004.

107 The funeral party that lowered John's coffin into the ground was augmented by two other men – Donald MacCormick and Kenneth Munro. Thus, John was laid to rest by a party which included his three immediate successors as chairman of the Labour Club at Glasgow University – Donald MacCormick (1960–1), Donald Dewar (1961–2), and Kenneth Munro (1962–3). Written correspondence with Kenneth Munro, 14 November 2004.

108 Kenny Farquharson, 'A commoner among kings', *Scotland on Sunday*, 22 May 1994.

109 Interview with Ruth Wishart.

110 Ibid.

111 Written correspondence with Professor Sir Neil MacCormick, 4 October 2004.

112 Interview with Baroness Ramsay of Cartvale; telephone interview with Mary McCulloch.

113 For example, on Sunday, 22 May, in Leicester of all places, St Gabriel's church held a 'Celebration of the life of John Smith QC, MP', attended by local Labour MPs, Jim Marshall and Keith Vaz. After the service, a commemorative tree was planted in the grounds of the Leicester church. Leicester newspaper cuttings. Ann Barrett papers.

114 Eileen McAuley, 'A fighter to the end', *Airdrie and Coatbridge Advertiser*, 3 June 1994.

115 Memorial Service for Rt Hon. John Smith QC MP, Sir John Wilson Town Hall, Airdrie, 27 May 1994, Order of Service. Ann Barrett papers.

116 Memorial Service for Rt Hon. John Smith QC MP, Westminster Abbey, 14 July 1994, Order of Service. Ann Barrett papers.

117 Ibid.

118 *The Guardian*, 15 July 1994.

Chapter 25

1 Lewis Carroll, *Alice's Adventures in Wonderland and Through the Looking-Glass* (Everyman: London, 1993; first published in 1865; and by Everyman in 1929), p. 99.

2 Jenkins, *A Life at the Centre*, p. 618. At the time, Jenkins was mainly referring to the problem that, with autobiography, it is not possible, by definition, to end the subject's life by putting oneself in the grave!

3 Williams, *Gaitskell*, p. 424.

4 Williams, *Gaitskell*, p. 428.

5 Richard Crossman, *The Guardian*, 11 January 1963. Quoted in Williams, *Gaitskell*, p. 425.

6 Tony Benn, *Out of the Wilderness. Diaries 1963–67* (Arrow Books: London, 1991), p. 1 (Friday, 18 January 1963).

7 Joe Haines, 'Gaitskell and Smith . . . tragic echoes of history', *Today*, 13 May 1994. See also Geoffrey Goodman, 'Another tragedy, but without successors', *The Independent*, 13 May 1994; Ben Pimlott, 'Not a Gaitskell, but perhaps an Attlee', *Independent on Sunday*, 15 May 1994; Alan

Watkins, 'In the midst of death, we are in electoral arithmetic', *Independent on Sunday*, 15 May 1994.

8 Quoted from Brivati, *Hugh Gaitskell*, p. 414.

9 Williams, *Gaitskell*, p. 415.

10 Williams, *Gaitskell*, p. 315.

11 Hugh MacPherson, 'Upright Rabelaisian', *Tribune*, 20 May 1994.

12 Peter Sinclair, 'Echoes of a national tragedy six years ago', *Daily Record*, 12 October 2000.

13 See Gordon Brown, 'A lifetime built on a passion for social justice', *The Herald*, 12 October 2000; Donald Dewar, 'Our Donald: direct, accessible and utterly honest', *The Scotsman*, 12 October 2000.

14 James Buxton, 'An architect of Scottish home rule', *Financial Times*, 12 October 2000.

15 Nick Britten, 'Death of a political gentleman', *Daily Telegraph*, 12 October 2000; Kirsty Scott and Gerard Seenan, 'The Death of a Decent Man', *The Guardian*, 12 October 2000.

16 See Meta Ramsay, 'Dry wit and a taste for mischief'; Ross Harper, 'A Diplomat and a real charmer'; Kenneth Munro, 'He was truly unique'; Menzies Campbell, 'Loyal to the party and his friends'; Roy Hattersley, 'Memories of a man of integrity', *Sunday Herald*, 15 October 2000. Many thanks to Kenneth and Elizabeth Munro for supplying the press cuttings on the death of both John Smith and Donald Dewar.

17 Mark Stuart, 'What if John Smith had lived?', in Duncan Brack and Iain Dale, *Prime Minister Portillo and other things that never happened. A collection of political counterfactuals* (Politico's: London, 2003), pp. 313–31.

18 For academic support for this assertion, see Seyd and Whiteley, *New Labour's Grassroots*, p. 7

19 See, for example, Steve Richards, 'Britain in the euro, taxes up: now PM Smith faces a gloomy outlook', *The Independent*, 8 May 2004; Robin Cook, 'If John Smith were alive, imagine how different this Labour government would be', *The Independent*, 7 May 2004; Roy Hattersley, 'The abiding myth about John Smith', *The Guardian*, 10 May 1994.

20 Williams, *Gaitskell*, pp. 447–52; pp. 453–5 (page numbers are drawn from the 1982

revised edition).

21 See Alastair Campbell, 'Living the Legacy', *Labour Today*, Spring 2004, pp. 26–7; The same article was published in *The Herald* on 13 March 2004, under the title, 'How one man's death changed our political landscape'.

22 Seldon, *Major*, pp. 460–1.

23 Quoted in Simon Heffer, 'Normal disservice will be resumed as soon as possible', *The Spectator*, 21 May 1994.

24 *Monklands: Not in My Backyard* (Conservative Research Department: London, 11 April 1994). Michael Crick files.

25 Joy Copley and Peter Jones, 'Major vows to finish the task', *The Scotsman*, 14 May 1994.

26 Labour polled 44.2 per cent of the vote, winning 62 of the 87 British seats, making them the largest socialist group in the European Parliament. The Conservatives lost fourteen seats, but polled 28 per cent, 1 per cent more than they had attained at the local elections a month before. In fourteen of the eighteen seats where the Conservatives held on, they would have lost on a further swing of only 2 per cent. Butler and Westlake, *British Politics and European Elections 1994*, p. 256; p. 263.

27 Butler and Westlake, *British Politics and European Elections 1994*, p. 263.

28 See, for example, Colin Brown, 'Tragedy gives respite to Major leadership', *The Independent*, 13 May 1994.

29 Peter Oborne, 'Smith gave me new hope by Heseltine', *Evening Standard*, 12 May 1994.

30 See, for example, Colin Brown, 'Heseltine declares himself 100% healthy', *The Independent*, 14 May 1994.

31 See, for example, Joe Haines, 'Gaitskell and Smith . . . tragic echoes of history', *Today*, 13 May 1994.

32 Under Smith's OMOV reforms, if the leader became 'unavailable' when the Labour Party was in opposition, the deputy leader would automatically become leader temporarily, or *pro tem*. The NEC would then decide either to hold a ballot as soon as possible, or to wait until the Labour Party conference.

33 However, Jack Straw kindly agreed to chair campaign meetings and press conferences during the Euro-elections. Interview with Rt Hon. Margaret Beckett

MP, 19 November 2003.

34 For a start, the leader's office needed financing during the three-month leadership contest, an issue that was mainly dealt with by Murray Elder. The problem was partly resolved in August 1994 when both the TGWU and the GMB each provided a £15,000 interest-free loan, repayable within three months to meet the salaries of people still working in the leader's office. Murray Elder papers, Box 2.

35 Interview with David Ward, 7 June 2003.

36 Interview with Rt Hon. Margaret Beckett MP.

37 She also had precedent on her side: Neil Kinnock and Roy Hattersley had both stood for the leadership and the deputy leadership in 1983. Ibid.

38 Ibid.

39 Peter Riddell and Philip Webster, 'Interview with Margaret Beckett', *The Times*, 21 June 1994.

40 Routledge, *Gordon Brown*, p. 202.

41 Interview with Leo Beckett, 19 November 2003.

42 Although Prescott stood for both positions, he never seriously thought that he could win the leadership, whereas Beckett genuinely stood to win it.

43 The only other name mentioned in the local Airdrie media as being in the frame was Anne McGuire, the chair of the Labour Party in Scotland. Eileen McAuley, 'Labour set for by-election', *Airdrie and Coatbridge Advertiser*, 27 May 1994.

44 Interview with Rt Hon. Helen Liddell MP, 19 November 2003.

45 Private information.

46 Interview with Rt Hon. Helen Liddell MP.

47 'Battle for Monklands Contest will be bloody and bruising', *Airdrie and Coatbridge Advertiser*, 10 June 1994. The two other candidates were Ian Smart, a Cumbernauld lawyer, and Tom McCabe, leader of Hamilton's Labour-run council.

48 Private information.

49 Eileen McAuley, 'Labour's "better deal" for Monklands East', *Airdrie and Coatbridge Advertiser*, 1 July 1994; William Clark, 'Tales to tell in vicious campaign', *The Herald*, 24 June 1994.

50 William Clark, 'Liddell Admission on spending in Monklands', *The Herald*, 22 June 1994; On Thursday, 23 June, Liddell

declared at Airdrie's West Parish Church during an open meeting organised by the Movement for Christian Democracy: 'I hear the concerns of local people and I am absolutely determined to get to the bottom of these allegations once and for all.' 'Liddell votes to "get to the bottom" of figure dispute', *Airdrie and Coatbridge Advertiser*, 24 June 1994. The rowdy meeting, involving all the main candidates, descended into naked sectarianism, and was later described by Brian Wilson as 'one of the most unedifying public meetings which modern Scottish politics can have produced'. Brian Wilson, 'Politics and prejudice', *The Herald*, 29 June 1994.

51 William Tinning, 'SNP raises stake on bias claims', *The Herald*, 28 June 1994.

52 Interview with Rt Hon. Thomas Clarke JP MP, 20 January 2004.

53 Eileen McAuley, 'Poll Axed', *Airdrie and Coatbridge Advertiser*, 1 July 1994.

54 William Clark and Duncan Black, 'Labour split by Monklands "bias"', *The Herald*, 28 June 1994.

55 Ibid.

56 Interview with Rt Hon. Thomas Clarke JP MP.

57 Eileen McAuley, 'Poll Axed', *Airdrie and Coatbridge Advertiser*, 1 July 1994.

58 Labour MP for Glasgow Provan from 1979–97, and for the redrawn constituency of Glasgow Baillieston from 1997 onwards.

59 'Labour's Monklands gaffe', *The Herald*, 30 June 1994.

60 In 1997, the constituency was redrawn as Coventry South.

61 Interview with Rt Hon. Thomas Clarke JP MP.

62 William Clark, 'Reward for the winner of a poisoned prize', *The Herald*, 2 July 1994. Monklands East was renamed Airdrie and Shotts as a result of the revised 1995 Boundary Commission changes. By the 1997 general election, Liddell's majority stood at 15,412.

63 Interview with Rt Hon. Thomas Clarke JP MP.

64 Nicholas Wood, 'Labour beats SNP to hang on to John Smith's seat', *The Times*, 1 July 1994.

65 Ken Smith, 'Salmond rejects Liddell's claim of sectarian campaigning', *The Herald*, 2 July 1994; Alex Salmond,

'Scottish card the only trump . . . for everyone', *The Herald*, 2 July 1994.

66 William Clark, 'Labour holds Smith's seat', *The Herald*, 1 July 1994.

67 *Airdrie and Coatbridge Advertiser*, 8 July 1994.

68 Interview with Rt Hon. Helen Liddell MP.

69 Eileen McAuley, 'In from the Cold', *Airdrie and Coatbridge Advertiser*, 9 September 1994.

70 On Thursday, 6 October 1994, MDC voted seventeen to three to go ahead with the inquiry, after debating a resolution moved by Eddie Cairns, and seconded by Councillor Brooks. Alex Dowdalls, 'Public Inquiry "Is no cop-out"', *Airdrie and Coatbridge Advertiser*, 14 October 1994.

71 Maurice Hart, chief executive of MDC, Denis Ward, Legal Services director, and Archie Strange, finance director. Alex Dowdalls, 'Don't Do it!', *Airdrie and Coatbridge Advertiser*, 7 October 1994.

72 Eric Wright, 'We told you so', *Airdrie and Coatbridge Advertiser*, Wednesday, 21 June-Tuesday, 27 June 1995.

73 In late October 1995, Labour called in NEC chair, Joanna Jaude, and vice-chair, Tom Burlison, to help out Penn, and held a two-day hearing in November 1995. 'Labour to beef up MDC inquiry team', *Airdrie and Coatbridge Advertiser*, Wednesday, 25 October–Tuesday, 31 October 1995.

74 Interview with Rt Hon. Thomas Clarke JP MP.

75 In January 1995, in the subsequent election for provost, Eric Burns defeated Hugh Lucas on the toss of a coin after an eight – eight tie. Eddie Cairns was ill, and did not vote.

76 Under section 7 of the Local Government and Housing Act 1989.

77 On closer inspection, Nimmo Smith discovered that 48 relatives of councillors, not 66, were employed by MDC, and that Black had spent £26,518 less than he had been allocated to conduct the inquiry. William A Nimmo Smith, *The Report of the Monklands Inquiry* (Edinburgh: 15 December 1995), p. 32; p.61; 'On the cheap', *Airdrie and Coatbridge Advertiser*, Wednesday, 22 November–Tuesday, 28 November 1995.

78 Nimmo Smith, *Report*, p. 83.

79 Nimmo Smith, *Report*, p. 40.

80 Nimmo Smith, *Report*, p. 41. 'Council cleared', *Airdrie and Coatbridge Advertiser*, Wednesday, 27 December 1995–Tuesday, 2 January 1996.

81 'Local MPs welcome Inquiry conclusions', *Airdrie and Coatbridge Advertiser*, Wednesday, 27 December 1995–Tuesday, 2 January 1996.

82 Quoted in Routledge, *Gordon Brown*, p. 203.

83 Rentoul, *Tony Blair*, p. 348. Mike Elrick recalls the anecdote about the bet, but has no clear recollection of precisely when the conversation took place. Interview with Mike Elrick, 10 June 2003.

84 Francis Elliot and Colin Brown, 'Blair knew that Smith named him, not Brown, as successor', *Sunday Telegraph*, 1 December 2002.

85 Interview with David Ward, 7 June 2003.

86 Quoted in Rentoul, *Tony Blair*, p. 348.

87 Macintyre, *Mandelson*, p. 254.

88 Interview with Rt Hon. Lord Irvine of Lairg PC QC, 30 April 2003.

89 Naughtie, *The Rivals*, p. 52.

90 Interview with Rt Hon. Lord Hattersley, 3 March 2003.

91 Naughtie, *The Rivals*, p. 52.

92 Interview with Rt Hon. Lord Hattersley.

93 Interview with Rt Hon. Lord Irvine of Lairg PC QC.

94 Interview with Mike Elrick.

95 Interview with Rt Hon. Derek Foster MP, 24 June 2003.

96 Naughtie, *The Rivals*, p. 54.

97 Interview with Rt Hon. Derek Foster MP.

98 A Northern word meaning 'wading'.

99 Interview with Rt Hon. Derek Foster MP.

100 Interview with David Ward, 7 June 2003.

101 Interview with Mike Elrick.

102 Naughtie, *The Rivals*, p. 58.

103 Sopel, *Tony Blair*, p. 133.

104 Quoted in Macintyre, *Mandelson*, p. 256.

105 McSmith, *Faces of Labour*, p. 335; see for example, Sarah Baxter, 'Why I think Tony Blair should be the next leader', *Evening Standard*, 13 May 1994.

106 Naughtie, *The Rivals*, p. 59.

107 Routledge, *Gordon Brown*, p. 194; see for example, Gordon Brown, 'So Modest John', *Daily Record*, 13 May 1994; Gordon Brown, 'John kept faith with people', *The Independent*, 13 May 1994.

108 *The Nine o' Clock News* (specially extended), BBC1, Thursday, 12 May 1994 (transcript).

109 Macintyre, *Mandelson*, p. 255.

110 Ibid.

111 Rentoul, *Tony Blair*, p. 361.

112 Quoted in Routledge, *Mandy*, p. 156.

113 Macintyre, *Mandelson*, p. 257.

114 Routledge, *Gordon Brown*, p. 197; for a full text of the letter, see Macintyre, *Mandelson*, pp. 258–9; Routledge, *Mandy*, pp. 156–8.

115 Macintyre, *Mandelson*, p. 261.

116 Macintyre, *Mandelson*, p. 266; for an alternative view, see Routledge, 'The Blair Plot', *Mandy*, Chapter Ten, esp. pp. 154–9.

117 Quoted in Naughtie, *The Rivals*, p. 63.

118 Macintyre, *Mandelson*, p. 262.

119 Routledge, *Mandy*, p. 272.

120 Arguably, Brown could have drummed up a good deal of trade union support, but he would have faced opposition on the left from Robin Cook and John Prescott, and he risked splitting the modernisers' vote and the party. Macintyre, *Mandelson*, p. 260. James Naughtie also points that Nick Brown and Andrew Smith were drumming up support on behalf of Brown, and that when a member of the Brown camp asked John Edmonds of the GMB if Blair might win, Edmonds is said to have replied, 'Over my dead body.' Naughtie, *The Rivals*, p. 63. It is just possible that Brown could have run on an anti-modernising ticket, but in doing so he would have gone against everything he had previously said and done.

121 Naughtie, *The Rivals*, p. 59.

122 Minutes of the party meeting held on Thursday 16 June 1994 at 6 pm in Committee Room 10.

123 Minutes of the Party meeting held on Wednesday 6 July 1994 at 11.30 am in Committee Room 14.

124 Nicholas Wood, 'How Labour voters made their choice', *The Times*, 22 July 1994.

125 Rentoul, *Tony Blair*, p. 5.

126 Minutes of the party meeting held on Wednesday 19 October 1994 at 11.30 am in Committee Room 14.

127 'Editorial', *The Sunday Times*, 15 May 1994.

128 Gould, *The Unfinished Revolution*, p. 182.

129 McSmith, *Faces of Labour*, p. 335.

130 Blair quickly gained a leadership satisfaction rating of 58 per cent, some nine points higher than Smith had

achieved in the final poll taken before his death. Stark, *Choosing the Leader*, p. 159. After only one year, a Gallup poll showed that Blair was the most popular opposition leader since records began, with 68 per cent of respondents claiming he was doing a good job, compared with Smith's peak of 53 per cent. *Daily Telegraph*, 9 June 1995.

131 Interview with Rt Hon. Tony Benn, 6 March 2003.

132 Ibid.

133 Seyd and Whiteley, *New Labour's Grassroots*, p. 6

134 For similar arguments, see Shaw, *The Labour Party Since 1979*, pp. 222–3.

135 Gould, *The Unfinished Revolution*, p. 195.

136 Ludlam and Smith (eds), *New Labour in Government*, pp. 256–7.

137 Andrew Gamble and Gavin Kelly, 'Labour's New Economics', in Ludlam and Smith (eds), *New Labour in Government*, pp. 181–3.

138 Ludlam and Smith (eds), *New Labour in Government*, pp. 256–7.

139 Mandelson and Liddle, *The Blair Revolution*, pp. 2–3.

140 Peter Mandelson, 'To Govern is to choose', *Fabian Review*, Vol. 109, No. 2, Summer–Autumn 1997, pp. 1–2.

141 Interview with Lord Whitty, 12 March 2003.

142 Interview with Lord Gordon of Strathblane CBE, 12 March 2003.

143 Seldon (ed.), *The Blair Effect*.

144 Written correspondence with Lord Whitty, 25 April 2003.

145 Steve Broggan, 'Blair invokes memory of John Smith', *The Independent*, 30 April 1997.

146 Robert M. Worcester and Roger Mortimore, *Explaining Labour's Landslide* (Politico's: London, 1999), p. 141.

147 Nicholas Timmins, 'Blair promises to undo "quango state"', *The Independent*, 16 July 1994; Kevin Brown, 'Blair targets Lords in pledge on reforms', *Financial Times*, 16 July/17 July 1994.

148 Anthony Seldon, *Blair* (The Free Press: London, 2004).

149 Telephone interview with Rt Hon. Lord Robertson of Port Ellen, 2 November 2004.

150 Ibid.

151 Ibid.

152 Ibid.

153 *The Scotsman*, 4 April 1997.

154 Telephone interview with Rt Hon. Lord Robertson of Port Ellen.

155 Donald MacCormick, 'A diligent and brilliant believer in all that was best', *The Sunday Times*, 15 May 1994.

156 *Scotland's Parliament* (Cm. 3658).

157 Nicholas Timmins, 'Party looks for victory from mirror image', *The Independent*, 18 July 1992.

158 www.johnsmithmemorialtrust.org

159 Telephone interview with Mary McCulloch, 26 November 2003.

Chapter 26

1 Macintyre, *Mandelson*, p. 252.

2 Clare Short, 'John Smith's qualities and quality', *Tribune*, 27 May 1994.

3 Seyd and Whiteley, *New Labour's Grassroots*, pp. 6–8.

4 Gould, *The Unfinished Revolution*, p. 178.

5 Interview with Lord Hogg of Cumbernauld, 4 November 2003.

6 Jones, *Remaking the Labour Party*, p. 134.

7 *The Observer*, 15 January 1995. Quoted in Rentoul, *Tony Blair*, p. 416.

8 Interview with Rt Hon. Derek Foster MP, 24 June 2003.

9 Interview with Rt Hon. Chris Smith MP, 11 February 2003.

10 Ibid.

11 Interview with Rt Hon. Michael Foot, 20 February 2003.

12 Simon Hattenstone, 'The Monday interview: Saint Michael', *The Guardian*, 4 November 2002.

13 Telephone conversation with Rt Hon. Tony Benn, 1 March 2003.

14 Interview with Rt Hon. Lord Healey of Riddlesden CH MBE, 12 February 2003.

15 Interview with Rt Hon. Chris Smith MP.

16 Benn, *Free at Last!*, p. 239. (Thursday, 12 May 1994).

17 Interview with Rt Hon. Lord Hattersley, 3 March 2003.

18 Telephone conversation with Rt Hon. Tony Benn.

19 Interview with Leo Beckett, 19 November 2003.

20 Telephone interview with Dirk Robertson, 6 January 2004.

21 Smith, 'Reclaiming the Ground', *Christian Socialist*, p. 11.

INDEX

Exchange Rate Mechanism (ERM), 255,
257
five economic tests, 284
hillwalking, 153, 154, 155-156
and JS, 16, 123, 194, 394, 397-398, 409
leadership contest
1992,
Colin Byrne letter, 226
decides not to run as deputy leader,
224-225
Margaret Beckett's campaign
manager, 228
1994, 301-302, 389, 394-399
and pact with Tony Blair, 398, 399
New Democrats' influence, 306, 307,
308
reputation for fiscal prudence, 173, 194,
409
rise to prominence, 156, 157, 161
Shadow Chancellor,
differences with JS on realignment of
pound, 258
economic policy as, 292, 300-303
full employment issue, 331
windfall tax, 395
Shadow Trade and Industry portfolio,
168, 172, 193, 200
member of JS's economic team, 172,
175
Brown, Nick, 197, 225
Brunson, Michael, 372
Bryant, Christopher, 303
Buchan, Janey, 45, 46
Buchan, Norman, 45, 88
Buchanan-Smith, Alick, 84
Burlison, Tom, 324, 325
Burns, Andrew, 350
Burns, Robert, 378, 384
Burns, Terry, 214, 215, 216
Bush, George (Senior), 190-191
Butler, Rab, 36-37
Butlin, Billy, 35
Butterfield, Day, Devito, Hockey, 308
Byers, Stephen, 285
Byrne, Colin, 201, 226

Cable, Vince, 105
Caborn, Richard, 108, 228
Cairns, Eddie, 353, 359, 360, 391, 393
Caledonian Club, 108
Caledonian MacBrayne Ferries (CalMac),
382
Callaghan, James, 73, 95, 243, 253, 276,
379
on devolution, 78-79
on JS, 79, 95
JS learns from his political style, 161,
243
leadership contest 1976, 78
Cameron, Alastair, 152
Campaign for Democratic Socialism
(CDS), 41
Campaign for Nuclear Disarmament
(CND), 12, 42, 43
Campaign For Recovery, 301, 302
Campaign Group, 143
Campaigns and Election Committee, 308
Campbell, Alastair, 2, 318, 397, 404
on JS, 2, 105, 316, 366
Campbell, Kenna, 380
Campbell, Menzies, 51,53-54, 66, 93, 117,
153, 372
background, 19
on Donald Dewar, 81
on JS, 26, 16, 52, 81, 110, 116, 117, 368,
374
Luthuli campaign, 37, 38
Campbell-Savours, Dale, 284, 358
Canada, 56, 83-84
Canavan, Dennis, 90, 374, 406
Carey, Archbishop George, 375, 384
Carman, George, 260
Carmichael, Neil, 45-46
Castle, Barbara, 38
Catto, Henry, 190-191
Chalmers, James, 6
Chalmers, John, 101
Channon, Paul, 136-137, 140
Chaplin, Judith, 212, 259
China, 121
Christian Socialists, 303, 305-306, 345

Gordon Brown decides to scrap, 300-301

spending pledges, 196-197

Shadow Cabinet elections,

1979, 115

1983, 122

1984, 124

1987, 143-144

1988, 156

1989, 161

1992, 252

1993, 356

Shadow Communications Agency (SCA), 196, 198

Shah, Eddie, 123

Shanks, Elizabeth, 49

Shanks, Norman, 382, 383

Shanks, Robert, 49

Shanks, William, 49

Shaw, David, 354-355, 357, 362, 393

Shaw, Eric, 173, 194

Sheerman, Barry, 146

Sheppard, Shirley, 378

Shore, Peter, 115, 143, 180, 250, 282-283, 284

on JS's Scottishness, 291

Short Clare, 226, 230, 246, 274, 289, 307, 308

on JS, 261, 408

OMOV, 321, 323, 328

Short, Ted, 75-76, 77, 78

Silkin, John, 115

Sillars, Jim, 78

Singapore, 101

single currency, 184-187

Skinner, Dennis, 246, 249, 259, 280, 287, 289

opposition to Maastricht Bill, 272

Westland Affair, 132, 133

Slovenia, 274

Smith, Adam, (economist) 305

Smith, Alison, 204-205

Smith, Annie, (sister of JS), 6, 7, 8, 12, 27, 56, 376, 384

Smith, Archibald Leitch, (father of JS), 5, 6, 7, 8, 11, 12, 14, 20, 32, 44, 46, 149

Smith, Catherine, (daughter of JS), 66, 96-97, 154, 370, 371

see also, Smith John, family life

Smith, Chris, 3, 145-146, 199, 222, 253, 306, 315, 374

Environmental Protection Spokesperson, 253, 299

hillwalking, 154, 155, 363

JS's Treasury Team, 161-162, 164, 170, 172, 187, 189, 197, 198-199, 200, 206, 218,

on JS's political style, 3, 253, 409

Smith, Elizabeth, (wife of JS), 13, 57, 65, 105, 107, 116, 150, 154, 209, 213, 317, 333, 339, 348, 365, 404

background, 48-50

children, 66, 96, 97

courtship and marriage to JS, 48, 49-50, 56

feelings when JS joins Cabinet, 96

on JS and Peter Mandelson, 147

JS's death, 369-372, 376-378

letters of condolence, 377-378

silver wedding anniversary, 237

peerage, 50

work for St Andrew's Foundation, 145

see also, Smith, John, family life

Smith, Jane, (daughter of JS), 96, 97, 154, 371

see also, Smith, John, family life

Smith, Jim, 360

Smith, John,

ancestry, 5-6

childhood, 6-7, 8-9, 10-12, 13

death, 369

family wake, 376-377

funeral, 379-384

memorial services, 384

public grief, 375

tributes, 373-376

education, 8-9, 10-12, 13

at Glasgow University,

art classes, 27

campaign for Rector, 34-41

canvasses for Labour Party, 30

debating, 17, 20-21, 22-23, 24-27,